INTERNATIONAL HUMAN RIGHTS

A Comprehensive Introduction

Michael Haas

Routledge
Taylor & Francis Group

LONDON AND NEW YORK

First published 2008
by Routledge
2 Park Square, Milton Park, Abingdon, Oxon, OX14 4RN

Simultaneously published in the USA and Canada
by Routledge
270 Madison Avenue, New York, NY 10016

Routledge is an imprint of the Taylor and Francis Group, an informa business

© 2008 Michael Haas

Typeset in Garamond by Keystroke, 28 High Street, Tettenhall, Wolverhampton
Printed and bound in Great Britain by TJ International Ltd, Padstow, Cornwall

British Library Cataloguing in Publication Data
A catalogue record for this book is available from the British Library

Library of Congress Cataloging in Publication Data
A catalog record for this book has been requested

Library of Congress Cataloging-in-Publication Data
Haas, Michael.
International human rights : a comprehensive introduction / Michael Haas.
p. cm.
Includes bibliographical references and index.
1. Human rights. I. Title.
K3240.H33 2008
341.4'8–dc22
2007021866

ISBN10: 0–415–77454–3 (hbk)
ISBN10: 0–415–77455–1 (pbk)
ISBN10: 0–203–93626–4 (ebk)

ISBN13: 978–0–415–77454–3 (hbk)
ISBN13: 978–0–415–77455–0 (pbk)
ISBN13: 978–0–203–93626–9 (ebk)

To the memory of Stanley Mark Castillo

INTER...

man rights:
ncreasingly
man rights,
ıman rights
ho they are

ime
ocial rights,

: and inter-

programs
imal rights,
environmental rights)

Richly illustrated throughout with case studies, controversies, court cases, think
points, historical examples, biographical statements, and suggestions for further
reading, *International Human Rights* is the ideal introduction for all students of
human rights. The book also will be useful for human rights activists to learn how
and where to file human rights complaints in order to bring violators to justice.

Michael Haas has devoted most of his career as a Professor of Political Science at the
University of Hawai'i to teaching, research, and public service centering on human
rights. He not only filed civil rights complaints that resulted in the adoption of
affirmative action in the Aloha State to benefit all races, including Caucasians,
Filipinos, and Native Hawai'ians, but he also played a role in stopping the secret
funding by Washington that reached the Khmer Rouge during the 1980s. He recently
conferred honorary doctorate degrees in his current role as Chair of the International
Academic Advisory Council at the University of Cambodia.

CONTENTS

TABLES

PREFACE

With the end of the Cold War, human rights concerns loom much larger on the world stage than ever before. But no comprehensive textbook on human rights has existed until now to provide a foundation for those seeking to become acquainted with the main parameters of the field of study.

I am most indebted for the inspiration of the book to Professor Seth Thompson of Loyola Marymount University, who proposed that I teach a course on international human rights in 1998, though I had not previously done so. Subsequently, I taught the course at California State University campuses at Fullerton and Los Angeles as well as at Occidental College. When I first I contemplated readings for students, and I began to outline lectures, I quickly realized that a comprehensive textbook was lacking but needed. The present volume is the result.

The book has a number of features. Since various examples are mentioned throughout, each chapter is punctuated with tabular details and boxed summaries of court cases and historic events to provide brief explanations that should stimulate readers to find more information, such as by writing term papers. Discussion topics are identified to enable readers to think more carefully about controversies; instructors may utilize the various topics for classroom discussions or as suggested class projects. The lifespans of prominent persons are provided in each chapter to identify the eras in which they lived. Chapter notes appear at the end with details on particular points, sometimes at length. References provide opportunities for further reading on many topics that cannot be covered in depth within an introductory textbook. A Glossary provides helpful definitions. Readers will also note my tendency to bullet key points throughout the text.

The present volume is a continuation of an earlier effort, *Improving Human Rights* (1994), in which I performed statistical operations on data regarding human rights observance. I return to that assignment in Chapter 8. As before, the main focus in the volume is on human rights activism, that is, the way in which individuals and organizations over time have heroically sought to advance human rights, whether through philosophical pleas, drafting of important legal documents, or by taking direct action.

Many casual observers often assume that the subject of human rights is peripheral to an understanding of contemporary world politics, yet the opposite is the case: one cannot understand world politics today without attention to human rights. Moreover, the present volume departs from other textbooks in delineating the vast extent to which individual countries and intergovernmental organizations are now bringing perpetrators of human rights horrors to account through concerted diplomatic, economic, legal, and even military action.

Human rights issues have been the main focus of my academic career and much of my personal life. As an adoptee and a gay person, I perhaps have a unique perspective. Throughout more than three decades of teaching at the University of Hawai'i, from 1964–1978, I enjoyed the experience of a Caucasian living in a land where Asians, Pacific Islanders, and persons of mixed ancestry constitute a numerical majority and have established a multicultural milieu that competes quite successfully with the American culture that for the most part nonintrospectively pervades the other forty-nine states.

Several persons have provided assistance in my efforts. I therefore want to acknowledge the following: Robert Benson, Loyola University School of Law; Alice Bouras, Registry of the European Court of Human Rights; Lori Galway, International Criminal Court; Barry K. Gills, University of Newcastle; Riham Hazboun, UNESCO; Kevin Johnson, University of California at Davis; Michael Kilburn, Endicott College; Oliver Liang, International Labor Organization; Michael J. Lightfoot, Ranjana Natarajan, and Ann Richardson, human rights attorneys in the Los Angeles area; David K. Malcolm, University of Notre Dame of Australia; filmmaker Giacomo Martelli; Begoña Martínez Alfonso, UN Geneva office; Sheena Neogi, Human Rights Committee (of the International Covenant on Civil and Political Rights); Philip Richards, American Embassy, Belgium; Geoffrey Robinson, UCLA; Judith Yontef, Van Nuys Law Library; S. Seetaram, Caribbean Community; Jan Malinowski, Council of Europe's Tatiana Tassoni, World Bank; and Auret van Heerden, President and CEO, Fair Labor Association.

In addition, I would like to thank some of my former students, who contributed many ideas while writing term papers in my courses over the years: Muneeza Ansari, Michael Cooper, Chris De Guía, Benjamin García-Ascue, Daisy M. Jones, S. Billie Kim, Jennifer Lane, Betsy Murphy, Priscilla Palmer, Carla Riedl-Stevens, Thanapoon Rimchala, Mark Robinson, Saeko Tew, and John Walker.

I have also benefited from criticisms of earlier drafts in the preparation of the manuscript. One comment, that the text appears to highlight shortcomings of the United States in regard to human rights, missed the point. The American approach to human rights is unique not only in having a federal system that complicates treaty ratification but also in providing a system of checks and balances in which courts and the Congress can in time limit the excesses of presidents. Human rights peculiarities of today are likely to be mitigated in later years, as the legal framework allows for continuing correction.

Although I once contemplated cutting sections on animal rights and environmental rights to shorten the manuscript length, I changed my mind on receiving the comment that the topics were not only much needed additions to a human rights textbook but were written in an especially readable manner. In any case, readers can judge for themselves whether sections on human responsibilities toward animals and the environment are integral to an understanding of important perspectives on traditional human rights concerns.

I am dedicating the book to the memory of Stanley Mark Castillo, a longtime companion of some twenty years whose untimely death occurred in 1998 while he was in the prime of his life. His indomitable spirit, even in the face of health adversity in his final years, remains a constant source of inspiration.

Michael Haas
Los Angeles

ABBREVIATIONS

ACC	Arab Cooperation Council
ACLU	American Civil Liberties Union
AFL	American Federation of Labor
AIDS	Acquired Immune Deficiency Syndrome
AIU	Amnesty International USA
ALF	Animal Liberation Front
AMIS	African Mission on the Sudan
ANCOM	Andean Community
APRM	African Peer Review Mechanism
ARU	American Railway Union
ASEAN	Association of South East Asian Nations
ATCA	Alien Tort Claims Act
ATO	alternative trade organization
AU	African Union
BSEC	Organization of the Black Sea Economic Cooperation
BTO	Brussels Treaty Organization
CACJ	Central American Court of Justice
CACM	Central American Common Market
CARICOM	Caribbean Community
CAT	Committee Against Torture
CBSS	Council of the Baltic Sea States
CEDAW	Committee on the Elimination of Discrimination Against Women
CEN–SAD	Community of Sahel–Saharan States
CERD	Committee on the Elimination of All Forms of Racial Discrimination
CESCR	Committee on Economic, Social and Cultural Rights
CFA	Committee on Freedom of Association (of the International Labor Organization)
CIA	Central Intelligence Agency (of the United States)
CITES	Convention for International Trade in Endangered Species of Wild Fauna and Flora
CMS	Convention on the Conservation of Migratory Species of Wild Animals
CMW	Committee on the Protection of the Rights of All Migrant Workers and Members of their Families
COE	Council of Europe

COMESA	Common Market for Eastern and Southern Africa
Comintern	Communist International
CRC	Committee on the Rights of the Child
CSCE	Conference on Security and Cooperation in Europe
CSocD	Commission for Social Development (of the United Nations)
CSSDCA	Conference on Security, Stability, Development and Cooperation in Africa
CSW	Commission on the Status of Women (of the United Nations)
DDT	dichloro-diphenyl-trichloroetha
DEA	U.S. Drug Enforcement Administration
DNA	deoxyribonucleic acid (the molecule containing genetic instructions used in the development and functioning of all living organisms)
EAC	East African Community
EAPC	Euro-Atlantic Partnership Council
EC	European Community
ECCAS	Economic Community of Central African States
ECHR	European Court of Human Rights
ECO	Economic Cooperation Organization
ECOMOG	ECOWAS Monitoring Group
ECOSOC	UN Economic and Social Council
ECOWAS	Economic Community of West African States
ECSC	European Commission for Steel and Coal
EEC	European Economic Community
EDSA	Epifanio de los Santos Avenue (in Manila)
EEA	European Economic Area
EFTA	European Free Trade Association
EU	European Union
EUFOR	European Military Force
EurAsEC	Eurasian Economic Community
Euratom	European Atomic Energy Agency
Europarl	European Parliament
Europol	European Law Enforcement Association
FAO	Food and Agricultural Organization of the United Nations
FBI	Federal Bureau of Investigation (of the United States)
FLA	Fair Labor Association
FLO	Fairtrade Labeling Organizations International
FTAA	Free Trade Area of the Americas (proposed)
GATT	General Agreement on Tariffs and Trade
GCC	Cooperation Council for the Arab States
GRI	Global Reporting Initiative
GSP	generalized system of preferences
HRC	Human Rights Committee
IACHR	Inter-American Court of Human Rights
IBE	International Bureau of Education
IBRD	International Bank for Reconstruction and Development
ICAO	International Civil Aviation Organization (of the United Nations)
ICC	International Criminal Court

ICJ	International Court of Justice
ICSID	International Finance Corporation (of the World Bank)
ICTR	International Criminal Tribunal for Rwanda
ICTY	International Criminal Tribunal for the Prosecution of Persons Responsible for Serious Violations of International Humanitarian Law Committed in the Territory of the Former Yugoslavia Since 1991
IDA	International Development Association (of the World Bank)
IDP	internally displaced person
IFAD	International Fund for Agricultural Development (of the United Nations)
IFAT	International Federation of Alternative Trade
IFAW	International Fund for Animal Welfare
IFC	International Finance Corporation (of the World Bank)
IFOR	Implementation Force (in Bosnia)
IIIC	International Institute of Intellectual Co-operation
ILO	International Labor Organization
IMCO	Intergovernmental Maritime Consultative Organization
IMF	International Monetary Fund
IMO	International Maritime Organization
INS	U.S. Immigration and Naturalization Service
Interpol	International Criminal Police Agency
ITLOS	International Tribunal for the Law of the Sea
IWW	International Workers of the World
KFOR	Kosovo Force
KLA	Kosovo Liberation Army
LAS	League of Arab States
LRA	Lord's Resistance Army (of Uganda)
MARPOL	International Convention for the Prevention of Pollution from Ships
MERCOSUR	Mercado Común del Sur
MFN	most-favored-nation (treaty provision)
MIGA	Multilateral Investment Guarantee Association (of the World Bank)
MSF	Médecins sans Frontières
NAACP	National Association for the Advancement of Colored People
NAFTA	North American Free Trade Area
NATO	North Atlantic Treaty Organization
NED	National Endowment for Democracy
NEPAD	New Partnership for Africa's Development
NGO	nongovernmental organization
NIEO	new international economic order
NPT	Non-Proliferation Treaty
NTB	nontariff trade barrier
NTR	normal trade relations
OAPEC	Organization of Arab Petroleum Exporting Countries
OAS	Organization of American States
OAU	Organization of African Unity
OCHA	Office for the Coordination of Humanitarian Affairs (of the United Nations)
OECD	Organization for Economic Co-operation and Development

OEEC	Organization for European Economic Cooperation
OHCHR	Office of the High Commissioner for Human Rights
OILPOL	International Convention for the Prevention of Pollution of the Sea by Oil
OPEC	Organization of Petroleum Exporting Countries
OSCE	Organization for Security and Cooperation in Europe
OSI	Office of Special Investigations (at the U.S. Department of Justice)
PACE	Parliamentary Assembly of the Council of Europe
PCA	Permanent Court of Arbitration
PCIJ	Permanent Court of International Justice
PETA	People for the Ethical Treatment of Animals
PIF	Pacific Islands Forum
PLO	Palestine Liberation Organization
POW	prisoner of war
PQLI	Physical Quality of Life Index
RA	Rainforest Alliance
RCD	Regional Cooperation for Development
SAARC	South Asian Association for Regional Cooperation
SADC	Southern African Development Community
SADCC	Southern African Development Co-ordination Conference
SACN	South American Community of Nations
SAN	Sustainable Agricultural Network
SCO	Shanghai Cooperation Organization
SFOR	Stabilization Force (in Bosnia)
SPCA	Society for the Prevention of Cruelty to Animals
TNC	transnational corporation
TVPA	Torture Victim Protection Act
UMA	Union du Maghreb Arabe
UN	United Nations
UNCHR	United Nations Commission on Human Rights
UNCTAD	United Nations Conference on Trade and Development
UNCTC	United Nations Center for Transnational Corporations
UNDP	United Nations Development Program
UNEP	United Nations Environmental Program
UNESCO	United Nations Educational, Scientific, and Cultural Organization
UNGASS	United Nations General Assembly
UNHCR	United Nations High Commissioner for Refugees
UNHRC	United Nations Human Rights Council
UNICEF	United Nations Children's Fund (originally United Nations Children's Emergency Fund)
UNIDO	United Nations Industrial Development Organization
UNIFEM	United Nations Development Fund for Women
Unocal	Union Oil Company of California
UNPFII	United Nations Permanent Forum on Indigenous Issues
UNRRA	United Nations Relief and Rehabilitation Administration
UNSC	United Nations Security Council
UNSG	United Nations Secretary-General

UNTC	United Nations Trusteeship Council
UPU	Universal Postal Union
USAID	U.S. Agency for International Development
WBCSC	World Business Council for Sustainable Development
WEU	Western European Union
WFP	United Nations World Food Program
WHO	World Health Organization
WTO	World Trade Organization

CHAPTER 1

Introduction

A most astonishing development in world history is occurring today. Concern over the observance of human rights clearly has become such a high priority that some current and former government leaders are being brought to justice for violations of international human rights within domestic and international tribunals. One might conclude that the world community has determined that the horrors of the twentieth century will not be repeated in the twenty-first century by calling into account contemporary human rights violators.

The world is also changing dramatically in the present age of rapid communication and continual movement of goods, ideas, messages, and persons across international borders. What happens to individuals in one country often has profound implications for other countries. For example, Third World sweatshops operating with hazardous working conditions or child labor in poorer countries may compete with businesses that respect workers' rights in industrial democracies. Human rights are not only at the forefront of concern today for prosecutors and criminal lawyers but also for businesses, trade unions, and workers in the global economy.

The present volume seeks to explain the philosophical traditions and historical forces that have brought human rights issues into the international arena as well as to identify the variety of human rights and the many concrete efforts to improve human rights observance around the world so that readers not only will appreciate that human rights have a solid intellectual and legal foundation but also will become aware of what is being done to improve human rights observance today. First, however, fundamental terms need to be clarified.

COURT CASE 1.1 THE TRIAL OF AUGUSTO PINOCHET (2000–2006)

In 1998, Augusto Pinochet (1915–2006) was arrested in London for extradition to Spain to be tried for crimes against humanity committed while he was president of Chile from 1973–1990. After considerable legal maneuvering as well as a return to Chile, Pinochet was indicted by a Chilean court in 2000 for several crimes, including kidnapping, murder, torture, and illegal burial. His trial was ongoing at the time of his death.

COURT CASE 1.2 THE TRIAL OF SLOBODAN MILOŠEVIĆ (2001–2006)

In 2001, Slobodan Milošević (1941–2006) was flown from Belgrade to The Hague to be tried by the International Criminal Tribunal for the Former Yugoslavia. He was charged with 66 counts, including crimes against humanity, genocide, and war crimes, especially for orchestrating the "ethnic cleansing" of Muslims in Bosnia and Croats in Croatia during the 1990s while he was president of Yugoslavia. Milošević died while in detention during 2006 before a ruling was issued on his case.

COURT CASE 1.3 *HAMDAN V RUMSFELD* (2006)

In 2006, the Supreme Court of the United States ruled in a case brought by the New York-based Center for Constitutional Rights, *Hamdan v Rumsfeld* (548US05–184), that Donald Rumsfeld (1932–) while Secretary of Defense violated Article 3 of the four Geneva Conventions of 1949 by refusing to allow a prisoner under the custody of the U.S. military, to be tried in a regularly constituted court. In so doing, the justices by implication identified George W. Bush (1946–), the author of the executive order that established the court, as a potential war criminal who might be sued. Although some cases have been filed already, heads of state can only be put on trial after they leave office.

BASIC DEFINITIONS

The term *international* is an easily defined adjective, referring to a relationship that involves or transcends two or more individual states. Indeed, the world today consists of states with porous borders that relate to one another economically and in many other ways. Sometimes the term "international" is contrasted with "regional," the latter referring to a smaller, contiguous geographic area of the globe.

Human refers to *homo sapiens*, those who in some accounts descended from Adam and Eve, rather than to animals, minerals, and vegetables.

The term *rights* has several meanings. One meaning is "the power or privilege to which one is justly entitled," with such examples as property rights, mineral rights, stockholder rights, and film rights. But none of the four examples appears central to what is meant by human rights, and the phrases "power or privilege" and "justly entitled" suggest that a right is acquired by special means rather than possessed from birth by all persons regardless of race, color, creed, gender, and the like.

Although there is no consensus on the precise meaning of the term "human rights," nearly everyone agrees that human rights involve the ability to demand and enjoy a minimally restrictive yet optimal quality of life with liberty, equal justice before law, and an opportunity to fulfill basic cultural, economic, and social needs. At the same time, the identification of specific rights has changed over time; new rights have emerged as humans have redefined their perspectives about what is desirable and intolerable as civilized beings.

Rights also presuppose *responsibilities*. Humans must be moderate in their pursuits, respecting the rights of others. Institutions of governments are responsible both for protecting against abuse and injustice and for ensuring and facilitating human development. If humans and governments act otherwise, the human rights project will end.

A fuller understanding of the term "international human rights" requires a discussion about the different ways in which alternative conceptions have been formulated. One may find greater enlightenment by examining the presumed sources of rights, rights as legal relations, the practical effects of assuming the existence of rights, and by contrasting types of rights through an analysis of subcategories.

SOURCES OF RIGHTS

Philosophically, the term "rights" has at least two types of meanings:

- **Moral rights.** A "right" can be viewed as an ethical justification for setting up, maintaining, and respecting protections of individuals. In other words, "rights" owe their origins to such basic values as autonomy, dignity, or equality; the logical inference is that certain values should be upheld institutionally. But how can one know what is a moral right? Presumably, moral rights are established by argumentation, by appeals to something called "justice," or by the principle that humans should possess "freedom." The moral rights approach is a *rationalist* understanding of rights, in which rights are considered to be self-evidently imprescriptible.
- **Legal rights.** Alternatively, a "right" can be defined as a type of institutional arrangement in which interests are guaranteed legal protection, choices are guaranteed legal effect, or goods and opportunities are provided to individuals on a guaranteed basis. How do we know what is a "right"? The answer is to read a law book. A focus on legal rights is a *positivist* understanding of rights in which humans gain or lose rights depending upon the current state of the law. In short, a "right" can exist only when laws or judicial opinions say so specifically.

The American Declaration of Independence states moralistically that the rights of life, liberty, and the pursuit of happiness are inalienable and self-evident, but the meaning is vague. In contrast, specific legal rights are contained in the American Bill of Rights. However, the Ninth Amendment provides for the possibility of an expansion in the number of identifiable rights. For example, there is no mention of a right to marry either in the Constitution or in the various amendments to the Constitution. Nevertheless, the Supreme Court asserted that there is a right to marry in 1967 while ruling in *Loving v Virginia* (388US1) that no state had the power to deny a marriage license to a man and a woman.

"RIGHTS" AS LEGAL RELATIONS

Nevertheless, conceptual clarity remains elusive, even for legal rights. Following the formulation of Wesley Hohfeld (1879–1918), four different types of legal relations are often called "rights."

- **Powers** are the capabilities of a particular person to uniquely do something because of power status. For example, individuals have a right to will possessions to anyone. However, almost everyone has the power to harm another, so powers must be limited or there would be no rights.
- **Immunities** are actions that persons with higher power status cannot do to ordinary persons. For example, if someone owns property, and oil is found on the property, a rights-respecting state will not have the power to take that property away without providing reasonable compensation.
- **Liberties**, sometimes called privileges, are actions that can be taken without the approval of anyone or any institution. However, there is a limit to the exercise of liberties – when the liberties of others are infringed. The term **civil liberties**, as used in the United States, refers to prohibitions on what government can do to individuals, as specified in the Bill of Rights, where everyone is assured of such liberties as freedom of the press. Civil liberties can also be called civil rights.[1]
- **Claim-rights** are obligations of others to us; they are the other side of the same coin as liberties. To claim a right to privacy, for example, is to tell others that they should not intrude into our personal space. The term *civil liberties*, as used in the United States, refers to the obligation of government not to infringe on various freedoms; the guarantees of civil liberties are found in the American Bill of Rights, as adopted in the late eighteenth century. **Minority rights**, on the other hand, are primarily based on three amendments (thirteenth, fourteenth and fifteenth) that were passed shortly after the Civil War (1861–1865) to prohibit discrimination against former slaves, though later constitutional amendments and laws have expanded coverage to other classes of persons, notably other minorities, women, the elderly, and the disabled. Minority rights protections recognize that only governments have the ultimate power to stop discrimination against persons who belong to nonmainstream groups, whereas civil liberties refer to what government is not supposed to do to all persons.

Liberties and claim-rights are together understood around the world to mean human rights. But rights are also formulated in terms of immunities and liberties to assure individuals that they have many residual powers outside the sphere both of government and of other powerful institutions. Readers should be aware that a debate is ongoing among scholars about the formal definition of "human rights" because lawyers, political scientists, sociologists, and others approach the subject with differing perspectives.

EFFECTS OF HUMAN RIGHTS

Isaiah Berlin (1909–1997) distinguishes between two types of liberty. **Negative liberty** exists when there are limits on adverse human behavior, whereas **positive liberty** is the power to act autonomously. Similarly, the concept of human rights has two basic effects with regard to human actions:

- Rights place *limits* on actions of others by offering a measure of protection to individuals and to specific groups. In short, certain actions are banned.
- Rights also offer individuals and specific groups the *power* to seek redress and to give them a way to impose limits on those who would violate their rights. In other words, rights are trump cards, to use the analogy of Ronald Dworkin (1931–), with which to annul adverse actions that might be taken by powerful groups, institutions, and persons.

DISCUSSION TOPIC 1.1 DEFINING "HUMAN RIGHTS"

There are several ways of defining or approaching the subject of human rights but no consensus. Which conception is the most useful? What are the practical consequences of defining "human rights" in different ways? Can rights exist without responsibilities?

CLASSIFICATIONS OF HUMAN RIGHTS

Another way to understand human rights is in terms of generations of rights. Karl Vasak's *The International Dimensions of Human Rights* (1982) suggests three generations based on the French trichotomy between liberty, equality, and fraternity: (1) Civil and political rights constitute the first generation, which focus on issues of liberty. (2) Economic, social, and cultural rights are the second generation, with a concern on equality. (3) The third generation, he argues, is concerned with a wide range of issues, including the rights to development, a healthy environment, group self-determination, and peace.

A chronological approach finds more complexity than a generational classification (Table 1.1). The significance of the signing of the Magna Carta in 1215 was to limit the absolute authority of rulers by writing down limits to the powers of government in the form of a contract. Eventually, *constitutions* emerged as contracts between people and governments that state the boundaries of what government can and cannot do. The modern quest to protect *civil liberties* in constitutions and through legislation first emerged in the eighteenth century, when American, British, and French citizens sought to protect personal freedoms, particularly freedom of conscience, in Bills of Rights.

The extension of *political rights* made headway in the nineteenth century, as requirements for those eligible to vote were reduced; instead of allowing only wealthy males to exercise the franchise, the movement toward universal suffrage gained acceptance. *Minority rights* advanced as slavery was abolished worldwide. During the mid-nineteenth century, the earliest Geneva Conventions called attention to rights of civilians and soldiers in time of war; what were then identified as **war crimes** evolved into an additional concern for **crimes against humanity** and **crimes against peace** during the twentieth century. With the establishment of socialism in Russia during the early twentieth century, there was a focus on new issues, namely, **economic, social, and cultural rights**. The peace settlement immediately following World War I established the principle of the *self-determination of peoples*, thus extending rights from individuals to ethnic groups. The **right to peace**, implicit in the establishment of both the League of Nations and the United Nations, was explicitly stated within a treaty adopted in 1984, though the agreement has not gone into force because of insufficient ratifications. A new frontier, the extension of rights to *gays, lesbians, bisexuals, and the transgendered*, awaits a consensus as the twenty-first century begins.

Some scholars have argued that there is a *right to democracy*, by which they usually mean the free exercise of such political rights as the right to vote. However, dictatorships have elections, and many newly democratizing countries give citizens political rights but do not respect their civil rights. A country that admits political rights but not civil rights is known as an **illiberal democracy**.

TABLE 1.1 HUMAN RIGHTS GENERATIONS

Type of rights	*First recognized*
Constitutional rights	13th–18th century
Civil liberties	18th century
Political rights	19th century
Minority rights	19th century
Rights of persons in wartime	19th century
Economic, social, and cultural rights	20th century
Right of self-determination; group rights	20th century
Right to peace	20th century
Gay rights	20th century

TABLE 1.2 **ALTERNATIVE CATEGORIZATIONS OF HUMAN RIGHTS**

Categorizer	*Categories of human rights*
Constant (1815)	Liberty of the ancients
	Liberty of the moderns
Muskie (1980: 8) and	Freedom of violations of the human person
Vance (1977[1979]: 310)	Rights of fulfillment of economic needs
	Civil and political rights
Shue (1980)	Liberty
	Security rights
	Subsistence rights
Donnelly and Howard (1988)	Survival rights
	Membership rights
	Empowerment rights
	Other rights
United Nations Development	Equality of opportunity
Program (1992: 31)	Freedom of expression
	Personal security rights
	Rights of political participation
	Rule of law

Yet another way to define "human rights" is to delineate analytical subtypes (Table 1.2). Analytical categorizations can serve to focus attention on different problem areas. Swiss philosopher Benjamin Constant (1767–1839) contrasted the *liberty of the ancients* (freedom from government coercion) from the *liberty of the moderns* (freedom to participate in government), that is, civil rights as distinct from political rights. A few of the categories in Table 1.2 have been reviewed above, but there are some innovations as well. Edmund Muskie (1914–1996) and Cyrus Vance (1917–2002), former U.S. Secretaries of State, identified **freedom of violations of the human persons** as the right to be personally secure, which is otherwise identified under the term "security rights." "Survival rights" and "subsistence rights" refer to the **right to life**, in particular to have food, clothing, and shelter. In some clever category schemes, **civil rights** are referred to as "membership rights" and "freedom of expression rights," whereas **political rights** have been referred to as "empowerment rights" or "political participation rights."

GLOBALISM VERSUS STATISM

The chapter began by citing breakthrough events in the development of international human rights, that is, instances when rulers of various states have been called into account for misdeeds perceived by governments, by an international organization, and even by a nongovernmental organization formed of private individuals. The concept of "international human rights" is relatively recent. Throughout most of human history, states were either isolated from one another or governed by an imperial center. When the Roman Empire fell, national states gradually emerged in Europe that were jealous of their power and unwilling to be criticized for misconduct. Although the Catholic Church sought to impose a moral order, using the threat of excommunication, the rise of Protestantism contested the Vatican's claim to universal jurisdiction. Wars over religious preferences then convulsed Europe from the time of Martin Luther (1483–1546) until the Westphalia peace agreement of 1648, which established the principle that governments have **sovereignty**, that is, not only have unlimited power within the borders of their countries but also have no right to act in response to what other governments do inside their borders (unless the lives of their own citizens are in danger). The concept of human rights, thus, initially arose inside countries because of a **statist** concept of the world polity, namely, that the only legitimate units of international politics are national states.

The nation-state system, hence, was a European idea. Membership in the system was conferred by a reciprocal exchange of diplomatic representatives. A primary role of the diplomat abroad was to look out for a country's commercial interests. Trade agreements were formalized into legal contracts, that is, interstate treaties. As the number of commercial and noncommercial treaties increased, so did the scope of international law, but the Westphalian principle of nonintervention in the domestic affairs of other countries applied only to members of the state system so that colonialism and imperialism could proceed unabated.

The contemporary world now lives in a post-Westphalian era. Most countries are members of the state system, and colonialism is mostly limited to control of a few isolated islands with small populations, but state sovereignty is no longer sacrosanct. The **globalist** perspective is that actions inside the borders of one country impact other countries, international organizations, or nongovernmental organizations because there is a single world economy and polity. Rules written for the planet can now brand domestic actions of individual states not only as illegal but also can lead to a determination that noncompliant governments are international outlaws that must be brought to justice through enforcement actions by members of the world community. The sources of such interventionist rules, as found in the corpus of **international law**, are treaties and international customs that confer on states the power to intervene in the domestic affairs of other countries in order to enforce global norms of proper state behavior. A state's sovereignty, in other words, is now secure only when a government behaves according to norms generally respected by the world community or rules encoded in declarations and treaties adopted at international conferences on a wide range of issues, including human rights.

Human rights concerns are part of the globalization that has been taking place in the last two decades since the end of the Cold War. The **economic globalization** that has developed with the collapse of the barter-based socialist system headed by the Soviet Union is one of worldwide capitalism. Meanwhile, new competitive economic forces in the world have prompted observers to apply a **communitarian globalization** in which common norms and values must necessarily be the underpinning for a stable economic and political order. A third trend is **informational globalization**, as individuals tune in to global media that often provide compelling images of human rights. Some alarmists claim that globalization is leading to world government, but there is no such future prospect; governments still cling to their sovereignty, even as global forces continue to undermine the scope of their power. In any case, one response to globalization is that the demand for greater respect toward human rights is emerging all over the globe.

DESIGN OF THE VOLUME

A book on international human rights would have been very short indeed before the formation of the United Nations in 1945. Today, a textbook on the subject can only provide a foundation or introduction to a vast realm of contemporary reality.

The present volume, accordingly, seeks to identify the basic parameters of international human rights. The discussion includes how the concept of international human rights has developed over time (Chapters 2–4), the variety of types of human rights (Chapters 5–7), empirical findings from statistical research on human rights (Chapter 8), institutional efforts to promote human rights in the United States, Europe, and the Third World (Chapters 9–13), and concludes with a discussion of some of the newest dimensions in the field of human rights as well as a discussion of problems with the rights-based approach (Chapter 14). The aim is to provide a comprehensive picture of the content of international human rights law, why international human rights have increasingly risen to the world prominence, what is being done about violations of human rights, and what might be done to further promote the cause of international human rights so that everyone may one day have their rights respected regardless of who they are or where they live.

CHAPTER 2

The philosophical basis for human rights

Scholars examine the philosophical basis of human rights for several reasons. One is to demonstrate that respect for human rights has grown over time and has a solid foundation. A second reason is to note that there are contradictions within and across various human rights traditions, both religious and secular. The present chapter provides both contexts for understanding how human rights are perceived today.

RELIGIOUS ORIGINS OF HUMAN RIGHTS

Many major religions have stressed various elements of human rights (Table 2.1). Because millions around the world are so fervently loyal to religious tenets, a review of the major faiths is an important window into understanding the varieties of perspectives about human conduct, not only across the various religions but also within competing sects. Although the religious traditions tend to focus on individual duties, prohibitions, and responsibilities, they have been reinterpreted in modern times to have laid a foundation for the development of human rights.

Hinduism, perhaps the oldest surviving religion, originated about 4,500 years ago and is so named because of its emergence along the Indus River. Its sacred texts, codified some 1,500 years ago, address the importance of duty and good conduct toward others. All human life is to be loved and respected without distinction as to friend or foe. The first and foremost ethical principle of Hinduism is noninjury to others; no pain should be inflicted on another. As a corollary, one must practice charity and compassion to the hungry, the sick, the homeless, and the unfortunate.

TABLE 2.1   HUMAN RIGHTS ADVOCATES IN MAJOR RELIGIONS

Religions	Thinkers	Lifespan	Principal messages
Hinduism	Krisha Chaitanya	1478–1533	Legal equality
	Mahatma Gandhi	1869–1948	Self-determination
			Nonviolence
			Equality
Buddhism	Siddhattha Gotama	c. 404–484 BCE	Free speech
			Religious freedom
			Right to die
	Dalai Lama XIV	1935–	Self-determination
			Nonviolence
Confucianism	Confucius	c. 551–479 BCE	Right to humane governance
	Mencius	371–289 BCE	Right to rebel
	Hsun-Tzu	300–230 BCE	Right to education
Judaism	Moses	c. 1304–1237 BCE	Self-determination
			Proportional punishment
	Isaiah	fl. 8th century BCE	Right to food, shelter
	Moses Maimonides	1135–1204	Freedom from captivity
			Right to non-poverty
Christianity	Jesus of Nazareth	c. 4 BCE–33 CE	Freedom of thought
			Opposition to lynching
			Duty to aid the needy
	St. Paul of Tarsus	3–67	Nondiscrimination
	Thomas Aquinas	1227–1274	Natural rights
	Bartolomé de las Casas	1484–1566	Indigenous peoples' rights
			Against exploitation and slavery
	Martin Luther	1483–1546	Freedom of conscience
Islam	Mohammed	571–632	Racial equality
			Religious freedom
			Nonexploitation
	Al-Farabi	c. 870–950	Self-determination
			Equality
	Mawlana Abu'l A'la Mawduli	1903–1979	Many rights

Through good deeds, an individual can accumulate merit and advance toward freedom from earthly impediments. In addition, humans have no priority over the world of nature. The basic Hindu texts contain few political prescriptions, implicitly advocating governance that does not injure individuals. However, some Hindu scholars originally upheld the traditional pre-Hindu caste system, believing that those in highest caste (the Brahmins) have derived more merit from previous incarnations and that the caste system delineates a natural order between those who do manual as opposed to mental labor. Some contemporary Hindus in India still oppose compulsory education and do not frown on child labor, believing that primary schools train children for mental labor, which is only for the brightest children, whose families can afford to keep them off the labor market in their youth.

Nevertheless, in the sixteenth century, Hindu philosopher *Krisha Chaitanya* (1478–1533) espoused the principle of equality before the law, and in the twentieth century the teachings of *Mahatma Gandhi* (1869–1948) brought a fresh interpretation to Hinduism, focusing on the right of self-determination of peoples, the duty of nonviolence, and the principle of equality. However, Gandhi was assassinated by a disciple of the Hindu nationalist ideologue Vinayak Damodar Savarkar (1910–1949), also a nontraditional Hindu. In 2001, a Charter on Hindu International Human Rights was published on the website of the Hindu Human Rights Group.

Buddhism, which is some 2,500 years old, has the rituals of a religion regarding the afterlife but does not recognize a supreme being. Arising within the heartland of Hinduism, Siddhattha Gotama (*c.* 404–484 BCE), renamed *Buddha*, responded to the rise of urban societies in which materialism and the exploitative division of labor emerged to supersede the simpler life of self-sufficient agriculture. Born in the warrior caste, he rejected all its privileges, which he felt were illusions depriving him of the possibility of liberation from earthly suffering. After an ascetic life for six years, he divined that self-transcendence can best be achieved by altruistic service to others. To assert his philosophy in the context of a Hindu orthodoxy, Buddha was implicitly claiming the rights of free speech and freedom of religion. Buddhism is a philosophy that stresses respect for all persons, compassion for and healing of those in pain, and opposition to the caste system; one must overcome one's selfish cravings by practicing charity and love to those in need, not only spiritually but also intellectually and materially. Accordingly, Buddhist monasticism, open to both men and women, encourages learning in order to discover new ways to relieve suffering. There is an implicit balance in Buddhism between individualism and Hindu collectivist notions. Outside India, Buddhism developed somewhat more freely, notably in Sri Lanka, Southeast Asia, and East Asia. The foremost contemporary Buddhist, the *Fourteenth Dalai Lama* (1935–), argues that if we understand the fundamental humanity that unites us all, we can solve problems through kindness, love, and respect for others. Explicitly, he has argued for the right of self-determination of the Tibetan people.

Confucianism, though not a religion in the usual sense, was founded before Buddhism by a scholar named Kong Fuzi (*c.* 551–479 BCE), now known as *Confucius*, who was born in an era in which civil authority was precarious due to aggression between various feudal states inside what was later called China. Confucianism eschews attempts to find a basis for knowledge or philosophy in otherworldly speculation, preferring to focus on empirical and practical wisdom. Confucians venerate ancestors rather than a deity. They believe that harmony and cooperation will exist when all persons honor their duties toward others, overcoming their own self-interest and egotism. Confucianism recognizes the existence of social hierarchies, so moral individuals will reciprocally follow the responsibilities of their positions in life; thus, women are supposed to be subordinate to men, the younger are to respect their elders, and all are to obey the will of just rulers. One notable quote is "Do not impose on others what you yourself do not desire." But another is "Women are worthless." Confucius emphasized the rectitude of the rulers, not the institutions or processes of governance, so there is no opposition between the individual and the state unless the ruler is unjust or the individual fails to carry out reciprocal obligations.

Rulers and ruled, similar to members of families, coexist interdependently. The people have obligations within the context of the family and the state, not apart from the family and the state.

Two later thinkers further developed Confucianism during the period of the warring states (480–221 BCE) that ultimately ended feudalism. *Mencius* (371–289 BCE) coined the term "mandate of heaven," which is not based on a notion of an afterlife but instead on the imperative of rulers to govern humanely and to advance the material well-being of the ruled, including the opportunity for education. If a ruler does nothing to rectify a decline in material conditions causing suffering among the masses, the mandate of heaven is said to have ended, conferring an obligation on the people to overthrow the ruler in order to reestablish humane rule and, thereby, social harmony. For Mencius, governmental repression through cruel punishment results in a breakdown of the mutual trust required by a peaceful society. More broadly, when a superordinate person fails to carry out the duties prescribed in social hierarchies, the subordinate person has a right to leave the relationship; thus, individuals can be liberated from unjust rulers as well as from cruel family members. As a corollary, Confucians oppose most wars as squanderings of domestic resources.

Whereas Confucius and Mencius believed that humans are naturally good, *Hsun-Tzu* (300–230 BCE) had the opposite belief. He placed his faith in the power of education to eradicate evil tendencies. Hsun-Tzu wrote: "In order to relieve anxiety and eradicate strife, nothing is an effective as the institution of corporate life based on a clear recognition of individual rights." Hsun-Tzu, thus, has the distinction of being the first to articulate the concept of human rights.

Judaism of the Ten Commandments of *Moses* (c. 1304–1237 BCE) is based on the principle that humans have obligations to God as well as to one another. The form of the principles is law, prescribed divinely. Observance of legal precepts is supposed to result in justice. Moses, of course, liberated the Hebrews from Egypt, an action that retrospectively may be said to have been based on the principle of self-determination, and he did not argue for the broader position on the abolition of slavery for non-Hebrews. Unlike the religions of Asia, the Hebrews developed much of their political culture in Egypt with the painful knowledge that the people often have different interests from the state. The purpose of the biblical story of Cain and Abel is to point out that all humans are indeed the keepers of our brothers and sisters. The story of the Great Flood contains the moral that God is willing to punish wickedness. Since humans are created in the image of a just God, they have the obligation to behave justly and the power to punish wickedness; the "eye for an eye" maxim suggests that there should be proportionality in punishing crime.

The moral about Sodom's destruction is that the residents were wicked, but the only evidence of their sins was extreme inhospitality to the angels sent to save the only just family in town, thus implying that what was wrong was that the townspeople did not observe the principle of just treatment of all persons.[1] However, God is said to have given certain land to the Hebrews, who thus are chosen people with special rights, committed by their historical experience and mandated by God to establish a just and wise social order second to none among the peoples of the world. After the Hebrews settled in Israel, thereby becoming Israelites, the explanation for the later loss of sovereignty over the Holy Land was wickedness, that is, failure to develop a just society.

While in exile from Israel during the eighth century BCE, the prophet *Isaiah* (740–781 BCE) further described Judaic morality in a more proactive manner – allowing the oppressed to be free, sharing food with the hungry, and giving shelter to the homeless, implying the right of non-poverty. Judaism, as later expounded by the Aristotelian-influenced physician-philosopher Rabbi Moses ben Maimon (1135–1204), known as *Moses Maimonides*, is a religion that pursues moral excellence because all humans are born with free will. Based on the principle of beneficence, he prescribed a transformative generosity to the poor based on equality and partnership rather than dependence. Maimonides, having fled his hometown, Córdoba, when non-Muslims were being persecuted, wrote in support of the use of force to stop violence, thus presenting a moral argument for what has evolved from the concept of the just war to the principle of humanitarian intervention. Today, Israel's control of Occupied Territories populated by Arabic-speaking Palestinians is sometimes criticized as at variance with Judaic human rights principles.

Some thinkers, notably Karl Jaspers (1883–1969), have argued that an important shift toward espousing human rights took place in what he calls the "axial age" from 900–200 BCE. During those years, Buddha, Confucius, Isaiah, and Socrates redefined ethics in terms of compassion, not dogma. Repulsed by violent means, all four sought peaceful methods of conflict resolution. According to Jaspers, they established the foundations of modern philosophy.

Jesus of Nazareth lived at a time when Romans oppressed Jews. His message that all should be good Samaritans, caring for those in need (Luke 10:29–37), was that the Romans should not be dislodged by terrorism or superior force but rather by converting them to a new way of thinking in which all are treated with compassion and equality. Jesus, similarly, criticized the pursuit of wealth and was able to convince a lynch mob not to stone to death a woman accused of adultery (John 8:7). Christian theology developed in part from Jesus's attack on Jewish religious authorities for doctrinal intolerance and indifference to human suffering; he thereby demanded the right to articulate unapproved views.

HISTORIC EVENT 2.1   THE LAST DAYS IN THE LIFE OF JESUS OF NAZARETH (33 ce)

Having criticized temple priests and scholars by calling them hypocrites, Jesus of Nazareth (c. 4 BCE–33 CE) was arrested one night by religious authorities, detained by a religious tribunal without a charge, flogged and humiliated until morning, interrogated about his opinions without benefit of an attorney to the point of self-incrimination, and finally forwarded to secular authorities on the charges of forbidding payment of taxes to Rome and stirring up rebellion. Although secular authorities determined that he broke no law, he was sentenced to death by a king who responded to a demand from public opinion. En route to the place of execution, he was further tortured. When he arrived, he was crucified and tortured in the final hours of his life.

The circumstances surrounding Jesus's arrest, interrogation, and death indicate clearly that he was a prisoner of conscience, a man whose freedom of speech was not protected. Accordingly, his mistreatment constitutes a paradigm case for the denial of human rights. However, many ordinary Christians today do not comprehend the human rights implications of his experience and his message, believing instead that what happened was "God's will."

After Jesus's crucifixion, *St. Paul of Tarsus* (3–67) began to codify such Christian principles as, "There is neither Greek nor Jew, nor slave nor free, nor man nor women, but we are all one in Christ" (Galatians 3:27–28), which can be interpreted as promoting equality among believers. However, intolerance is suggested by a statement that salvation in the afterlife comes only to those who believe in what Jesus professed (John 3:16). In short, some Christians consider Christianity to be an exclusivist religion unlike the more syncretic Buddhist and Hindu faiths that accept a commonality to all religions.

There are several contradictions between reports about Jesus's teachings and St. Paul's advice to the early Christians. For example, Paul accepted slavery (Ephesians 6:19). Jesus associated with an apparent prostitute (Luke 7:39), whereas Paul urged Christians to have nothing to do with such people (1 Corinthians 5:9–13). Jesus suggested that his followers should grudgingly pay taxes to Rome (Mark 12:17), and Paul went considerably beyond in arguing that rulers are legitimate and should be obeyed because their authority comes from God (Romans 13:1–3). Nevertheless, some disciples refused to obey Roman law that conflicted with God's law (Acts 5:29). Some early believers, moreover, followed the principle "From each according to his ability, to each according to his needs" (Acts 2:44–47), a quotation cited by Karl Marx many centuries later in an effort to persuade Christians to accept his vision of a just society.

Thomas Aquinas (1227–1274), influenced by Aristotle (384–322 BCE), developed the notion that human law is legitimate to the extent that it conforms to natural law, which in turn is to be derived from divine law through the exercise of human reason. In short, he transformed the notion that God's law is superior to human law into a theory of natural rights. In choosing between God's law and human law, a Christian would have to look to the church for guidance. In 1277, however, Pope John XXI (1215–1277) condemned some of Aquinas's references to Aristotle as anti-Christian.

In 1512, *Bartolomé de las Casas* (1484–1566) became the first bishop ordained in the "New World." Objecting that the Spanish were committing atrocities on the native peoples of the Americas, he eventually resigned his position, returned to Spain, and began to develop a concept of the rights of indigenous peoples, including the right to live without exploitation.

In 1517, when *Martin Luther* (1483–1546) nailed ninety-five theses to the Wittenberg Church, he was primarily seeking to reform Christianity by stopping excesses and resolving contradictions. The excesses referred to such practices as requiring payments to the church in order to assure salvation in an afterlife. The contradictions applied to Catholic theology. After Pope Leo X (1475–1521) responded by excommunicating him in 1520, Luther asserted that all believers have freedom of conscience. The Protestant Reformation was underway when Luther's followers began to follow a different theology in which, for example, salvation was regarded entirely as a decision of God, independent of the clergy.

Conflicts within Christian teachings, however, had the consequence that secular philosophies developed the concept of human rights more broadly within Christian countries. Although a concern for human rights is now central to Catholic doctrine, liberation theology has not been accepted by Rome because of supposed Marxist influences, and recent Popes have condemned certain sexual practices as well as the right of persons of the same sex to carry on a love relationship despite recognition of same-sex partners being blessed in early church records.[2]

Islam or *Mohammedism* started approximately 1,500 years ago. Muslims believe that Mohammed received revelations from God over the years 610–632, as revealed by the Angel Gabriel; in short that Mohammed was the messenger of Allah. The Qu'ran, the sacred text of Islam, was completed in 651. According to Muslim belief, God revealed to Mohammed that he was the final prophet in a long line which began with Jewish patriarchs and prophets and most recently included Jesus, the second most important prophet in Islam. The five pillars of Islam, according to Mohammed, are the profession of faith, prayer, paying an alms tax, fasting during Ramadan and pilgrimage to Mecca. Muslims believe that one's possessions belong to God, so the more affluent should share with the poor. The Qu'ran explicitly states that there should be religions toleration. Although Mohammed initially sought to expel Jews from Arabia, he relented when some of his Arab allies proposed that Jews should instead pay tribute to remain in lands controlled by Muslims.

The Qu'ran also deals with non-religious matters, teaching for example that there should be equality among the races and the sexes, though in some communities they may be separated. In some Muslim communities, men may marry up to four women, provided the first wife agrees. The Qu'ranic principle that the witness of two women is equal to that of one man doubtless assumed that women were illiterate and could not write down their testimony; in the modern world, when Islamic women are literate, some Qu'ranic scholars advocate updating that principle. In economic matters, Mohammed preached against flaunting wealth, the tyranny of vested interests, and usury. The obligation of the religious tax reminds everyone that they should help the poor, and the most affluent are encouraged to make voluntary contributions beyond the minimum tax. At the same time, Mohammed held slaves; although he accepted the practice of manumission, especially for those converting to Islam, he also directed slave-owners to be kind to slaves.

An apparent paradox within the Islamic world is that Indonesia, the world's largest country in numbers of Muslims, demonstrates far more respect for human rights today than countries nearer to Saudi Arabia, the home of the holy city of Mecca. One answer is that Islamic law (*shari'ah*), which developed over three centuries after Mohammed died, codifies social practices and etiquette that were accepted in countries nearest Arabia but not necessarily required by Mohammed. Unusual practices found in some Islamic countries (cutting off hands, posses organized against infidels, harems, veils etc.) have little to do with the teachings of Mohammed.

Following the natural rights idea of the Aristotelian-influenced Islamic philosopher *Al-Farabi* (*c.* 870–950), the contemporary scholar *Mawlana Abu'l A'la Mawdudi* (1903–1979) has made a case that Mohammed actually launched the human rights movement. Among the principles contained in the Qu'ran, he argues, are the rights to life, property, inheritance, education, security, privacy, association, marriage or nonmarriage, free expression, religion, legal equality, political participation, and protest against tyranny, as well as freedom from arbitrary imprisonment, dishonor, and infanticide.[3]

PHILOSOPHICAL ORIGINS OF HUMAN RIGHTS

The world's major religions are riddled with sects, each privileging different and often competing principles. Indeed, the major faith-based disagreements about the scope of human rights are taking place *within* the major religious traditions rather than across those divides. Accordingly, the need to bridge the diversity by finding a universal logic to support universal principles has led many important thinkers to turn to analytical and ethical philosophy (Table 2.2).

Common to the major religions is a belief that humans have duties and responsibilities as well as prohibitions ("Thou shalt not . . ."). The desirable states of affairs, thus, require humans to behave a certain way in order to please a deity or to follow an important conception of how societies should be organized, as recorded in a written text. Secular philosophies, however, tend to see an opposition between humans and governments, such that humans have rights that governments must respect. According to most secular philosophies, governments either are prohibited from acting in certain ways toward humans or are expected to provide a framework for individuals to achieve a better life. Governments, in other words, have ethical responsibilities to individuals because of human characteristics and potentials.

Within philosophical speculation, the concept of natural rights provided the initial basis for the development of the notion of human rights. *Aristotle* (384–322 BCE) believed that individuals should flourish, that is, develop intellectually and morally as much as possible. He concluded from his analysis of the polities of his day that the best governments acted to protect liberty by preventing encroachments upon the conditions under which humans can reach a fulfillment of their capabilities.

When Rome achieved supremacy, economic activity assured riches to many citizens, who demanded a voice in government. Accordingly, the Senate was formed as a check on executive power. Perhaps the most famous senator was *Marcus Tullius Cicero* (140–1443 BCE), who formulated a theory of natural law, a law superior to human laws that can be derived by rational thought and to which the executive authority should be subject. A century later, Christians who refused to obey Roman law that conflicted with God's law were therefore articulating an idea that had already gained some currency in the Mediterranean world.

The concept of natural law developed later into a theory of natural rights in which rulers should respect the rights of citizens. Indeed, Aristotle's impact on Al-Farabi, Aquinas, and Moses Maimonides was to promote the idea of natural rights, but there were limits to the scope of Aristotle's conceptions. Aristotle's influence on Aquinas may have resulted in the papal doctrine that good works are the key to salvation, but Luther disputed the notion that salvation could be purchased by good deeds. However, Aquinas was sufficiently influenced by Aristotle's concept of natural rights to assert the principle of freedom of conscience. De las Casas, similarly, sought to turn upside down Aristotle's argument that some people are naturally born to be rulers or slaves so that he could persuade the Spanish conquistadors to stop exploiting and slaughtering the native population of the Americas.

TABLE 2.2   SECULAR HUMAN RIGHTS ADVOCATES

Thinkers	Lifespan	Principal contributions
Aristotle	384–322 BCE	Liberty
Marcus Tullius Cicero	140–43 BCE	Natural law
Jean Bodin	1529–1596	Right to property, Freedom of religion
Hugo Grotius	1583–1645	International law, Right to security, Right to justice
Thomas Hobbes	1588–1679	Social contract for security
John Locke	1632–1704	Right to life, liberty, health, property
Voltaire	1694–1778	Right to free press, speech, fair trial, Against slavery
Baron de Montesquieu	1689–1755	Constitutional checks and balances, Against slavery
Jean-Jacques Rousseau	1712–1778	Popular sovereignty, Against slavery
Immanuel Kant	1724–1804	Self-determination
Edmund Burke	1729–1797	Rights conferred only through politics, Property rights
Marquis de Condorcet	1743–1794	Women's rights, Equality of political rights, Against slavery
Thomas Jefferson	1743–1826	Right to pursue happiness, Religious toleration
Jeremy Bentham	1748–1842	Civil and political liberties
James Madison	1751–1849	Democratic checks and balances
Johann G. Fichte	1762–1814	Self-determination, Freedom of the press, speech, Right to education, Right to work
Georg W. F. Hegel	1770–1831	Freedom of association and thought, Right to education, Property rights
James Mill	1773–1836	Freedom of speech, press, religion, Economic freedom
John Austin	1790–1859	Law as the only source of rights
Auguste Comte	1798–1857	Altruism as a basic principle
John Stuart Mill	1806–1873	Free speech, Government to prevent harm to individuals
Karl Marx	1818–1883	Workers' rights
Friedrich Engels	1820–1895	Workers' rights

HISTORIC EVENT 2.2   KING JOHN SIGNS THE MAGNA CARTA (1215)

As the younger brother of King Richard I (1157–1199), King John (1166–1216) was crowned king upon Richard's death at a time when there was no fixed rule on succession to the monarchy. His claim to legitimacy was disputed by Richard's nephew, who had a claim to some British-held territory in France. To secure his title to the throne, John killed his rival, but lost the territory in a war with France. As a result, he had fewer barons to tax. When taxes increased on the English barons to make up the difference, they objected. Next, John refused to accept the Pope's nominee for Archbishop of Canterbury, whereupon Pope Innocent III excommunicated him. To regain papal approval, John ceded England and Ireland to the Pope and offered to pay rent to the Pope, again angering the barons, who mobilized troops to take London by force. To regain his throne, John was then required at Runnymede meadow to sign the Magna Carta, which set up a committee of barons who could meet at any time to overrule his actions.

Although the English nobles coerced King John into signing the Magna Carta in 1215, few rulers elsewhere were forced to limit their power for several centuries. Neither Aquinas nor de las Casas challenged the legitimacy of the kings of Europe. Following St. Paul's view of the proper role of citizens, monarchs insisted that they ruled by divine right, thereby excluding the possibility that individuals might assert their rights against the state. However, if a ruler were judged to be a heretic, divine right no longer applied. Lutherans and the Popes, of course, differed on which rulers were heretics, and the result was warfare between Catholic and Protestant states in the sixteenth and seventeenth centuries.

During the wars of religion, French philosopher *Jean Bodin* (1529–1596) began to question the sources of sovereignty, that is, who had the power to make enforceable law. While some rulers were being declared illegitimate on religious grounds, Bodin argued that governments should respect "the laws of God, and natural liberty and the natural right to property." In 1572, Bodin argued that individuals are sovereign with respect to their own property, just as states hold sovereignty over tangible real estate within certain borders. He believed that rulers and states must respect private property and have no right to enslave a free person. Based on his view of natural law, Bodin said that rulers should be subject to the same laws as the ruled; otherwise, they are tyrants. He did not believe that subjects had a right to disobey laws or to overthrow tyrants. He also pleaded for religious toleration as a way to quell internal strife within countries. Bodin's arguments regarding sovereignty were directed in part at the Holy Roman Emperor and the Pope, who were claiming that they could confer legitimacy on a state. For Bodin, neither authority had the right to intrude into state sovereignty.

One sector of the interstate conflict in the sixteenth century was between Catholic Spain and Protestant Holland, the latter a trading country that established a republic and thus had no king claiming a divine right to rule. Pondering the international chaos, Dutch scholar *Hugo Grotius* (1583–1645) went beyond Bodin's theory of sovereignty to assert that laws of governments should neither transgress natural law nor violate natural rights. Two natural rights are the rights to justice and security; rulers should provide both, and the ruled should not place security in jeopardy by disobeying just laws or by rebelling. Regarding the instability produced by European religious wars, Grotius advocated international law, that is, a set of principles on which governments might agree so that a stable world order could replace the frequent resort to force in order to solve interstate disputes. What he meant was that the customary ways in which states coexist peacefully should be codified into principles of international law. Grotius also adapted Bodin's theory of sovereignty to say that states were the sovereign authorities whose domestic laws should not be questioned by those in other states. He felt that governments could reciprocally accept the principle, obviously drawn from Christian theology, that they should not treat other states in a manner that they would not want to be treated. Instead of having might make right, governments should accept one another's legitimacy and move on to the task of providing the good life for citizens.

▍ HISTORIC EVENT 2.3 THE THIRTY YEARS' WAR (1618–1648)

The Western Roman Empire ended in 476, when the invading Ostrogoths forced the last emperor, Romulus Augustus, to abdicate. In 800, Pope Leo III (?–816) decided to intrude into state affairs by crowning Charlemagne (c. 742–814) as Imperator Augustus in order to reward his help in putting down a rebellion in Rome. The Pope hoped to encourage Charlemagne, king of what is now known as France and whose conquests added Germany and Italy to his realm, to reestablish the Roman Empire as the protector of the papacy, and *vice versa*. Although Charlemagne was not particularly interested in the Pope's scheme, later popes supported the establishment of what they called the Holy Roman Empire after Charlemagne's successors split up his domain. Otto the Great (912–973), ruler of the one of the domains, is usually considered to have founded the Holy Roman Empire in 962. The emperor, understood to be a Catholic, was chosen in an election mostly by several German-speaking kings of the Christian realm. The Thirty Years' War began in 1618, when Holy Roman Emperor Matthias (1557–1619) sought to impose Catholic Ferdinand II (1578–1637) onto Protestant Bohemia. The Bohemians revolted, and soon many European countries took sides in a complex series of wars that lasted until 1648. A major issue was whether Catholic kings could impose their religion upon Protestant subjects, but an even larger issue was which state might establish geopolitical hegemony in Europe. Eventually, Catholic France sided with Protestant states to prevent the alliance between Austria and Spain from achieving a dominant position in Europe.

Although Grotius was concerned that a state might violate principles of natural law in dealing with its own people, preserving a peaceful international order was a more important goal than fighting to determine whether Catholicism or Protestantism should prevail, since the prosperity resulting from trade in a world at peace would benefit all. However, Europeans could then close ranks against the rest of the world in order to give licenses to businesses for profitable colonial exploitation in parts of the nonwhite world where international law did not apply.

Grotian principles were endorsed after his death in the Peace of Westphalia of 1648, which settled the Thirty Years' War through two treaties that established the principle of state sovereignty. That is, rather than resorting to war in order to determine the state religion of a country, that matter was left to the ruler of each state. The Westphalian world of sovereign states, which has existed ever since, came with a price. Rulers were free to commit unspeakable acts toward their own citizens without fear that other states would intervene to stop atrocities. French Protestants, known as Huguenots, who had been persecuted before Westphalia, soon realized that their fate hung in the balance, and they left Catholic France for many other countries, including a large-scale migration to South Africa in 1688–1689. (Carrying the logic of the Wesfalian nonintervention principle to an extreme, Adolf Hitler (1889–1945) developed a plan to exterminate Jews in the belief that he was not violating the very foundation of international law.)

While the European continent was embroiled in the Thirty Years' War, yet another armed conflict was being fought in England. From 1642–1649, a civil war pitted royal power against nobles who sought supremacy for parliament. The civil war ended with the restoration of the monarchy, and the crowning of Charles II (1660–1684) as king. In 1651, *Thomas Hobbes* (1588–1679) published *The Leviathan* that developed the concept of a social contract under which humans surrendered their "state of nature" rights to governmental authority in order to benefit from stable rule. Hobbes's innovation, colored by the experience of the Magna Carta as well as the civil war, was to argue that individuals existed before governments and only accepted rule by superordinate governments to the extent that the rulers would guarantee their right to security. Hobbes, however, did not entertain a broader concept of human rights in which individuals had rights that government should not abridge.

Later in the seventeenth century, Charles II was succeeded by James II (1685–1688), a Catholic. Protestant nobles, who objected to Catholic rule, then conspired to invite Prince William of Orange (1650–1702) and his wife, Mary (1662–1694), King James's Protestant daughter, to sail from Holland with an army to overthrow James II. Known as the Glorious Revolution, Parliament celebrated the event by adopting a Bill of Rights.

After *John Locke* (1632–1704) authored an essay on the toleration of religious differences in 1667, he was asked to write a constitution by one of the proprietors of the Carolina colony just as he was formulating his political philosophy in broader terms. Although his constitution was not immediately accepted, in 1691 he published a remarkable thesis that differs fundamentally from the Hobbesian social contract. In contrast with Hobbes, who posited the surrender of individual rights to the state in order to obtain security, Locke believed that government was set up not only to protect the natural rights of individuals against arbitrary rule by government but also to stop private citizens from jeopardizing the rights of others. Specifically, he argued that individuals instituted government to protect the rights to life, liberty, health, and property. When governments fail to do so, they violate the social contract, whereupon the people have the right to dissolve such governments and to institute new ones.

Locke's social contract theory in turn inspired *Thomas Jefferson* (1743–1826) to formulate reasons for thirteen British colonies in North America to declare themselves independent in 1776. Similar to Locke, Jefferson espoused a theory of inalienable rights endowed by a Creator, with governments deriving their powers from the consent of the governed. However, he added a new right when he replaced Locke's rights to life, liberty, and property with the rights to "life, liberty, and the pursuit of happiness." Jefferson justified American independence as the consequence of "a history of repeated abuses and usurpations, all having in direct object the establishment of an absolute tyranny . . .," as he stated in the Declaration of Independence. Jefferson objected to slavery in his first draft of the Declaration, though he retained slaves on his Virginia plantation, but delegates from other Southern states insisted on removing that passage.

Jefferson was not only influenced by Locke but also by the French-speaking philosophers of the eighteenth century, among whom perhaps the four most notable are Voltaire, the nom de plume of François Marie Arouet; Charles-Louis de Secondat, the Baron de Montesquieu; Jean-Jacques Rousseau; and Jean-Antoine-Nicolas de Caritat, the Marquis de Condorcet. All four thinkers believed in the basic principle of the Enlightenment that science and human progress depend upon truth and are retarded by the suppression of free thought, whether by governmental or non-governmental organizations. The project of the Enlightenment was to create a safe space for intellectuals and scientists to exchange ideas, which would ultimately benefit humanity. They opposed dogma, censorship, and intolerance of diverse beliefs in a search for universally valid principles that harmoniously govern nature, humanity, and society, believing that human reason will ultimately triumph over obscuritanism and superstition.

Voltaire (1694–1778) dared to be more explicit about natural rights while exiled in England during the late 1720s. Whereas social harmony within the sovereign states of Europe was generally thought to require religious homogeneity, Voltaire learned in London that the English had social order despite diverse religious preferences, even though non-Anglicans suffered from legal restrictions and social prejudice. Why? Because economic freedom diverted their attention from religious matters. Moreover, he said, "If there were only one religion in England, there would be danger of tyranny; if there were two, they would cut each other's throats; but there are thirty, and they live happily together in peace." Often jailed for his views, Voltaire's epigram about freedom of speech, religion, and of the press, "I detest what you write, but I would give my life to make it possible for you to continue to write," was later paraphrased as "I disapprove of what you say, but I will defend to the death your right to say it." Complaining bitterly that the laws of France were written in slavish response to dogmatic papal decrees without regard to natural rights, he advocated a strict separation of church and state. His public fame resulted from writing in defense of several persons accused of nothing more than attending a Protestant church service, giving shelter to a Protestant overnight, and failing to take off a cap to a member of the clergy on the street. Incensed that hearsay was accepted as definitive evidence in court, his conception of a fair trial was that it "is better to risk saving a guilty person than to condemn an innocent one." Although he considered Africans to be genetically inferior, Voltaire also opposed slavery as contrary to natural rights,.

Montesquieu (1689–1755), another exponent of natural rights, further developed the concept of the separation of powers into the three branches of government by proposing that they should check and balance one another. His goal was to deter the abuse of power by government so that individuals could exercise their natural rights. Montesquieu also endorsed the concept of international law for resolving interstate conflict, believing that all persons were citizens of the universe and that states foolishly trying to add territory by waging war would inevitably have to defend their borders with war. Although in principle he opposed slavery along the lines of de las Casas's arguments, he excused the practice insofar as the conquerors of the Americas needed labor to establish their supremacy.

The eloquence of Voltaire and the logic of Montesquieu are in stark contrast with the ambiguity of *Rousseau* (1712–1778), who lived for a time in a part of Switzerland only three miles across the border from Voltaire's estate in France. Residing in a small Protestant country without a monarch, Rousseau in 1752 sought to redefine the concept of the social contract in terms of popular sovereignty. Since all humans are born free (but are everywhere in chains), he argued, governments are set up to implement the general will of the people, who seek to preserve their freedom but must live together in communities. How can the general will of the people be determined? Scholars of Rousseau provide varying interpretations on critical passages in his writings; some stress majoritarianism, others argue that he favors a unanimous consensus. In either case, Rousseau argued that only small countries could achieve true democracies through a deliberative process in which all have a voice. Rousseau was fundamentally opposed to slavery. When the French Revolution began, Rousseau (as well as Montesquieu and Voltaire) was dead and could not comment on what ensued. Nevertheless, Rousseau's writings were evidently consulted to justify the Jacobin reign of terror.

HISTORIC EVENT 2.3 THE FRENCH REVOLUTION (1789–1799)

When the spendthrift monarch Louis XVI (1754–1793) ran out of funds, he attempted to impose a land tax. The king hoped to get approval for his tax by convening in 1789 a meeting of the Estates General, a legislative body of the clergy, nobles, and middle class that had not met since 1614. Instead, the ideas of Montesquieu, Rousseau, and Voltaire inspired several leaders to convene a legislative assembly out of some delegates from all three classes with the aim of proposing a constitution. The National Constituent Assembly then adopted several reforms, including the abolition of feudalism and of special privileges for the clergy, issued

continued

the Declaration of the Rights of Man and Citizen in 1789, and promulgated a constitution in 1791. One faction within the National Constituent Assembly, the Jacobins, sponsored political clubs that grew in strength to the point where they controlled the government, guillotined the king and queen in 1793, and in the Reign of Terror (1793–1794) executed many perceived opponents of the revolution, including some of the early supporters of the revolution. In 1794, the Jacobins were ousted by the moderate Girondist faction, who in turn banned the Jacobin clubs, executed several Jacobin leaders, and adopted a new constitution in 1795. Napoléon Bonaparte (1769–1821), which had been fighting wars elsewhere in Europe from 1795, ended the revolution in 1799 by means of a coup d'état.

The principal author of the American constitution, *James Madison* (1751–1849), took issue with Rousseau's claim that democracy would only be possible in tiny states. In the *Federalist Paper #10*, published anonymously in 1788, he argued that a democracy would work in a larger country if the government were limited by institutional as well as regional checks and balances. Constitutions, following Montesquieu, should embody a qualified majority rule principle so that the majority would be less likely to tyrannize over the minority. However, Madison was a slave-owner, and his constitution legitimated slavery; otherwise, Southerners would not ratify the constitution. To appease Northern opponents of slavery, the constitution banned American participation in the slave trade from 1808.

The salons of Paris, where those of a philosophical bent could converse, were often run by women. In 1787, *Condorcet* (1743–1794), first articulated the notion that women are entitled to equal rights. He argued that women were rational beings and therefore could be educated at the same level as men. Similarly, he felt that natural rights should be conferred on believers of all religions, and that slavery should be abolished.

Another Enlightenment thinker was the Protestant Prussian *Immanuel Kant* (1724–1804), who rejected the notion that conferring sovereignty on enlightened despots or the people would be sufficient to ensure that justice would prevail. Instead, he wrote in 1785 that laws should be based on a universal principle, known as the categorical imperative: "act only on that maxim through which you can at the same time will that it should become a universal law." Political authorities should treat humans as ends, not means. Starting from the assumption that all humans are rational, Kant derived the principles of human dignity, individual autonomy, and political equality. Kant then argued for the superiority of representative governments whose political power is restricted by a constitution that prevents either monarchical or democratic despotism. In 1795, while French armies commanded by Napoléon Bonaparte were liberating European countries from absolute monarchies, Kant extended his theory to prescribe how peace could be achieved in international relations – when states respect one another just as humans must respect other humans. He favored the principle of self-determination of peoples, the abolition of standing armies, noninterference by one state in the internal affairs of another state, and a world entirely composed of a federation of constitutional, representative governments.

Johann Gottlieb Fichte (1762–1814), enormously impressed with Kant, visited the latter in 1792 and published his first major work in 1796. An initial admirer of the French revolution, he accepted the right of revolution to establish representative democracy. However, in response to the unwelcome occupation of Berlin by Napoleonic armies in 1806, he advanced the principle of national self-determination and even died as a volunteer in the war against France. Fichte derived the concept of human rights from the premise that all humans are rational. Concerned that individuals must be free yet restricted in some way so that order can be maintained, he echoed Jefferson in his concept of the political contract (not the social contract) as an agreement between citizens and the state wherein government is instituted to protect individual rights, particularly freedom of speech and of the press, so that philosophical and scientific inquiry would not be impeded. He also advanced the principle of the right to education and advocated state regulation of the economy to ensure the right of gainful employment. Rather than conceiving of morality as the source for law, Fichte saw that the rational basis for laws resided in the necessity for states to maintain order and to protect individual rights. Thus, for Fichte punishment for a crime is dictated by the need to maintain order rather than to enforce morality.

Meanwhile, the reaction in England to the French revolution was to recast the pursuit of human rights into an evolutionary political context. *Edmund Burke* (1729–1797) was among those shocked by the violence against legitimate political institutions. Writing first in 1790, he conceived of states as organic entities that grow in accordance with their own national needs. He eschewed the toppling of monarchs or redrafting of constitutions based on the latest philosophical speculations pretending to claim universal validity. The English people had liberties, particularly those relating to property rights, because political bargains over the years conferred those rights. Burke, hence, came close to endorsing what is now called the positivistic conception of rights, namely, that rights only exist to the extent they are written down on paper as the outcome of a political process operating in a particular country. From 1793, during the Jacobin phase of the revolution, Burke condemned the purge of those who were perceived to be in disagreement with the new democratic order, including some who originally supported the revolution. He was primarily seeking a way to legitimate the English aristocracy, which feared a similar revolution in England and was therefore opposed to considering humans as having equal rights.

Shortly before Burke wrote, *Jeremy Bentham* (1748–1842) in 1789 had tried to reformulate the logic of governance so that the rising middle class could gain power over the economically declining aristocracy. Bentham first debunked the concept of natural rights, referring to "rights" as "nonsense," and "natural rights" as "nonsense upon stilts." Previously, God was assumed to be the source of natural law and thus natural rights, but Bentham was an atheist. Instead, he grounded his ethics on the principle of "the greatest good for the greatest number." When legislators deliberate alternatives, he would have them adopt policies that benefit more rather than fewer persons. His "felicific calculus" was designed to legitimate laws adopted by the majority party in parliament, and he condemned legislation favoring special (aristocratic) interests. He agreed in principle with Burke's anticipation of the positivist approach to human rights by saying that "from real laws come real rights." Bentham's ethics is called "utilitarianism" because he stressed the concept of "utility" as a property that brings "benefit, advantage, pleasure, good, or happiness." In practical terms, he was arguing for parliamentary supremacy and the extension of voting rights to the middle class as well as for civil and political liberties, notably freedom of speech, press, and religion.

In 1820, *James Mill* (1773–1836), Bentham's tenant and intellectual best friend, cautioned that freedom of the press does not include a license to libel. A utilitarian, Mill was also an advocate of laissez-faire economics, arguing for deregulation of the economy by the government. Although he opposed the caste system in India, he also excused continued British imperialism in India as a means to bring the population greater happiness through the diffusion of European culture.

Often known as the originator of sociology, *Auguste Comte* (1798–1857) in 1822 developed a three-phase theory of history. The theological phase consisted of the era in which religion dominated human thought. He equated the Enlightenment with the metaphysical phase, when the concept of individual rights was held to be at a higher plane than religious dogma. In the positivist or scientific phase, human problems would be conceived empirically rather than theologically or theoretically, so the principles of the Enlightenment would be encoded into law if they were workable. In coining the word "altruism," he turned utilitarianism upside down, arguing that individuals should place the good of all above majoritarian self-interest.

In 1832, *John Austin* (1790–1859) formulated the positivist thesis as a view that law is what has been posited (decided). In postmodernist discourse, he was saying that law is necessarily a political construction. Similar to Bentham, he argued that rights emerge from political deliberation and decisionmaking, not from abstract theorizing. Human rights, in other words, are not universal; they are specific to particular countries. To distinguish Comte from Austin, the latter's theory is sometimes called "legal positivism."

James Mill's son, *John Stuart Mill* (1806–1873), felt that majoritarianism might lead to Jacobin restrictions on the minority's ability to speak freely. Writing in 1859, he argued that the need for a free society takes precedence over majority preferences, that a multiplicity of opinions is necessary so that truth can be determined in a marketplace of ideas. The main purpose of government, according to Mill, is to "prevent harm to others." Whereas Bentham would not allow the theistic concept of natural rights into the front door of the house of utilitarianism, John Stuart Mill admitted the concept of human rights into the back door. He reasoned that the freedom of speech was more important than the prerogatives of the majority because error can only be corrected if the right to free expression is guaranteed

In addition to Fichte and Kant, the French revolution had a profound affect on two other major German philosophers – Hegel and Marx. Whereas Comte sought to trichotomize history into a unilinear progression from superstition to science, *Georg Wilhelm Friedrich Hegel* (1770–1831) in 1820 conceptualized human development as a zigzag dialectical contest of ideas in which the prevailing worldview (thesis) is challenged by an alternative worldview (antithesis), thus causing tension between the two currents that provokes a synthesis to develop in order to resolve the contradiction. Whereas John Stuart Mill viewed intellectual debates among alternative policies as a marketplace with more than two possible views resulting in a convergence on what is considered truth, Hegel believed that a single accepted worldview played a much more basic role in shaping the spirit of the times within three historical eras. In the earliest era, human are savages with freedom to think, feel, and act. In the second era, the savage accepts the tyranny of civilization and law. In the third stage, the civilized individual under the law achieves liberty. Unlike Mill's pluralistic marketplace, Hegel (as well as Burke and Rousseau) argued that in politics there must be a fundamental consensus on the principles governing the relationship between individuals and government. Hegel anticipated a gradual increase in human freedom, provided that a balance could be maintained between individualistic tendencies and the needs of the community for order. Thus, the thesis of the individual's quest for self-actualization meets the antithesis of government's need to provide order, resulting in a synthesis wherein government will respect basic human rights, notably the rights to association, education, property, religion, and speech. Whereas Locke insisted on the right to property in terms of possession, enjoyment, and distribution, Hegel focused on the way in which property can be used so that individuals will achieve their maximum potential as human beings.

Karl Marx (1818–1883) then turned Hegel on his head, claiming that what underlies history is a dialectical process that is economic and material rather than abstract and intellectual, with each later economic system prevailing over the earlier. For Marx, there was a dialectical contest between feudalism and primitive communism, with capitalism as the later antithesis of the feudal thesis. In both cases, there was no synthesis; instead, the antithesis displaced the thesis because each new method of capital accumulation provided the resources for a newly emergent class to gain the political power to enforce its will. Since capitalists always strive to outcompete their rivals, monopolies will emerge under capitalism when the most efficient corporation is left standing, having vanquished all competitors. Then a monopolistic business in one sector will seek to control other sectors, leading perhaps ultimately to a single corporation in control of international business and world trade. Since capitalists only survive if they can accumulate capital by exploiting workers, paying them less than the value of the goods that they produce, monopoly corporations will seek to control governments in order to suppress workers. Then the workers, whose labor is fundamental to the economic order, will become conscious that they can withhold their labor, thereby forcing the barons of industry to surrender political power. When workers take over the state, they will establish socialism by having the state take over hitherto dominant corporations. Communism will emerge when the state is itself abolished because the governmental function of providing order will no longer be required when all accept the legitimacy of an equalitarian, interdependent economic system. Before socialism, in short, the quest for "rights" is illusory, since bourgeois-dominated governments suppressed workers. Indeed Marx favored the abolition of property rights.

In a sense, Marx was the last great philosopher on the subject of human rights. When Marx and his collaborator *Friedrich Engels* (1820–1895) wrote the *Manifesto of the Communist Party* in 1848, revolts arose all over Europe as the people demanded democratic rights. Even though most uprisings were suppressed, the people continued to believe that they were entitled to have governments respect their rights. Accordingly, a modest victory was achieved by the mid-nineteenth century in the long philosophical quest to raise the consciousness of humans to claim their rights. The multitude who believed in human rights was no longer interested in arcane philosophical arguments; they were increasingly determined to struggle for their rights. The resulting social movements on behalf of human rights are described in the following chapter.

METAPHILOSOPHICAL JUSTIFICATIONS FOR HUMAN RIGHTS

Throughout the history of philosophy, several generic types of justifications for human rights have been articulated. As new rights are proposed, such as the right of gays and lesbians to be accorded certificates of marriage from governments, the philosophical arguments return in public policy debates. A summary of various metaphilosophical arguments may help to clarify the disparate strands, which still vie for acceptance whenever new claims are made (Table 2.3).

Natural law. Natural law theorists argue that there are certain self-evident principles regarding rulers and the ruled, as established either by God or by nature. Thus, rights under natural law are viewed as protections against having the state limit human freedom. For many natural law theorists, there is a private sphere where

TABLE 2.3   HUMAN RIGHTS JUSTIFICATIONS

Theories	*Exponents*	*Principal arguments*
Natural law	Cicero, Aquinas, Bodin, Grotius, Voltaire, Finnis, Montesquieu, Condorcet	Life should be in conformity with God or nature.
Social contract theory	Hobbes, Locke, Jefferson, Rousseau	Individuals contract with governments to provide rights in order to get a stable social order.
Communitarianism	Confucius, Aristotle, Aquinas, Etzioni	There should be a balance between individualism and the need for social order.
Rationalism	Kant, Fichte	Individuals should treat one another as ends, not means.
Utilitarianism	Bentham, Mill	The greatest good for the greatest number; free trade must be fair.
Liberal democratic theory	Madison, Lincoln	The majority rules so long as minority rights are respected.
Stages-of-growth theory	Comte, Hegel	Progress is a step-by-step process.
Marxism	Marx, Engels	From each according to his ability, to each according to needs.
Social democratic theory	Lenski, Myrdal	Welfare states respect economic and social rights as well as civil and political rights.
Legal positivism	Austin	Rights are legally enacted, thus exist only when granted by governments.

government must not intrude. Today, there has been a revival of natural law as a wellspring for political speculation, involving such theorists as *John Finnis* (1940–). There are Natural Law parties in Britain, Israel, and the United States.

Social contract theory. Hobbes argued that in a state of nature individuals live an unstable existence, so they contract with government to provide order. Locke and most other social contract theories have assumed that individuals have rights before entering society, so the social contract is an agreement in which states respect individual rights. The concept of the social contract, of course, starts from the premise that all humans are rational, that is, can exercise free will autonomously, responsibly, and sensibly. Although Madison's constitution, thus, was understood as a contract between government and those who demanded limits to the powers entrusted to various branches of government, the constitution was nearly silent about human rights. After the constitution was ratified, the Bill of Rights was adopted as the first ten amendments to the constitution.

Communitarianism. Communitarians advocate a balance between individual rights and the needs of society, since life has no meaning apart from the communities in which humans live. Most of the various religious traditions stress a need to maintain a healthy coexistence between communities and individuals. Confucianism is especially explicit about the need for a balance between humans and government. Except for Hobbes and Rousseau, social contract theorists have often been accused of fostering extreme individualism, with little regard for the needs of the society as a whole. Aquinas's understanding of Aristotelian ethics is clearly communitarian. Communitarians argue that humans have both rights and responsibilities, and one of the responsibilities is to ensure that others are well cared for. Communitarians point out that humans are collectively responsible for the satisfaction of the basic human needs of all people, so majorities should not press their claims at the expense of those whose basic needs are unmet; no one should go to bed hungry. Communitarianism is the official philosophy of the Roman Catholic Church, which has spurned the liberation theology of de las Casas and Gustavo Gutiérrez (1928–) as too Marxist. Liberation theology exponents, who identify the need to combat injustice and poverty, nevertheless do so in communitarian terms. Among the secular communitarians, the most prominent is sociologist *Amitai Etzioni* (1929–), who believes that there should be a balance between rights and responsibilities.

Rationalism. Rationalists believe that humans act rationally, that is, behave in accordance with self-interest. Kant's main ethical principle, the categorical imperative, asks humans to apply a test in order to determine whether a particular behavior is ethical. The test is to assess whether one's behavior, if carried out by everyone else, would lead to moral outcomes. Kant believed that his principle went beyond the Golden Rule in Christian theology, arguing that ethics are derived neither from notions about nature or contracts, but instead are obvious to any rational or reasonable person. Fichte followed in his tradition. Rights, thus, are only respected because they are in the interests of individuals as well as the societies in which they live.

Utilitarianism. Bentham argued that what is socially desirable is that which provides the greatest good (or self-interest) for the greatest number of persons. Utilitarians generally deny that humans have any right to legal guarantees which cannot otherwise be supported by specific calculations about what is useful to large numbers of individuals in society. Of course, some economic rights might indeed emerge from such calculations, such as the protection against insider trading in the stock market and against anti-trust violations that restrain free commerce. John Stuart Mill later revised Bentham's utilitarianism to make a careful argument for protection of individual rights, but the philosophical basis remained primarily in terms of self-interest, not religious morality. At the international level, a chaotic world can only frustrate world trade, which requires an orderly, peaceful environment. Modern-day utilitarians, sometimes called economic liberals or neoliberals, argue that free trade must also be fair, that is, involve both an exchange of goods across international boundaries without artificial trade barriers and production by workers who are employed under humane occupational conditions.

Liberal democratic theory. Whereas the literal definition of "democracy" is rule by the people, the concept was redefined by *James Madison* to mean that government should be limited by separating power into independent branches of government that can check and balance one another. *Abraham Lincoln* (1809–1865) reformulated democracy as "government of the people, by the people, and for the people." The American Bill of Rights, as derived from social contract theory, did not protect minorities until amendments to the constitution were adopted after the Civil War (1861–1865) that guaranteed equal rights with particular reference to former slaves. Although "democracy" then became a Lincolnesque "majority rule with minority rights," the mainstream groups in power have the option of choosing which minority rights to protect and which to reject. During major periods of American history, the rights of ethnic minorities were not protected – the era of slavery, the abandonment of efforts to promote equality for African Americans after 1876, and today, when the civil rights struggle is not very high on the public policy agenda.[4] The rights of women, the handicapped, gays and lesbians, prisoners, and many other groups were certainly not respected when the American Bill of Rights was adopted, and they struggle today to gain respect for their rights within many of the most advanced democracies. Minorities must be vigilant and appeal to the better judgment and good sense of the majority in order to enjoy rights, so liberal democratic theory stresses prohibitions on government action in the form of federalism, separation of powers, and civil and political rights.

HISTORIC EVENT 2.4 THE MASSACRE NEAR TIANANMEN SQUARE (1989)

From 1978, the economic reforms embraced by Communist Party leader Deng Xaioping (1904–1997) brought China increasing prosperity, but two groups were dissatisfied. The intellectuals and their students wanted democratic reforms, and the industrial workers did not enjoy increased wages during the inflation associated with rapid economic growth; both resented the fact that Party leaders were pocketing some of the prosperity. In 1986–1987, student protests demanded democracy but died down. Because he expressed some sympathy with the students, Hu Yaobang (–1989) was forced to resign as Communist Party General Secretary in 1987, so his mysterious death in 1989 provided an occasion for the students to memorialize his passing. They went to Tiananmen Square, camped out, were visited by Communist Party Secretary Zhao Ziyang (1919–2005), and asked to meet Hu's chief rival, Premier Li Peng (1928–), to request the Party to honor his legacy. In response, Li turned down the request and Deng accused the students of fomenting political unrest, whereupon some 50,000 students went to Tiananmen to support the student leaders. When the Communist press condemned the students, they began to agitate for freedom of the press. Soon, workers joined the students, finding common interest in the student protest regarding a lack of political transparency and their bitterness over rampant corruption. Soon, the population of the Square reached about 100,000. When students and workers demanded to negotiate with the Party leaders, and student strikes spread in other cities of China, the Party leaders felt that power might slip from their hands, so they declared martial law, and the military dispatched tanks and troops toward Tiananmen Square. In the ensuing massacre, an estimated 2,000 died in the streets leading up the square, which was finally cleared by fixed bayonets. Zhao was stripped of his role as Deng's successor and placed under house arrest.

Stages-of-Growth Theory, according to Hegel, depicts history as an endless serious of challenges to the existing order, resulting in progress; Comte finds an endstate in the process. *John Locke* and *Adam Smith* (1623–1790) envision the advancement of economic rights as prior to all other rights, whether in political or social development. China is perhaps the major country where the denial of human rights has been portrayed so prominently on television, as the scene of a lone protestor trying to stop a tank, which ultimately gunned down students and their supporters near Tiananmen Square during 1989. When asked to justify the slaughter of nearly two thousand persons on June 4, the government at first referred to the inherent right to keep order. But when sanctions were imposed by many Western countries, the government responded with a series of annual White Papers, articulating the view that economic rights are prior to civil and political rights. A similar view, of course, was long stressed by leaders of the Soviet Union. Chinese Communist leaders claimed that the need to end poverty and raise living standards trumps the right to protest. In 2007, Premier Wen Jiabao (1942–), who had visited the Tiananmen demonstrators with Zhao Ziyang (1919–2005) in 1989, argued that China's weak legal system must be strengthened before democratic reforms can be enacted. Writing after the collapse of the Soviet Union, Francis Fukuyama (1952–) has even predicted that the liberal democratic imperative had come closer to an end to the Hegelian dialectic, that is, the "end of history." Stages-of-growth theory, in other words, sees progress as inexorable.

Marxism. The various left-wing ideologies inspired by Marxism point out that human rights have little meaning so long as there is a rigid class structure in society.

Social equality, therefore, must come before legal equality. Many lack the funds to assert their rights in courts, and even the concept of an independent judiciary is an illusion so long as elites appoint judges. Marx thought that the abolition of feudal and bourgeois classes was necessary to produce social equality among the remaining class, the proletariat, thus finding a different endstate in the stages-of-growth approach of Comte and others. Although most countries that adopted Marxian socialism failed to fulfill the promise of a good life, and indeed failed to respect the rights of owners of private property, Marx nevertheless was shrewd in grasping the principle that differences between groups generate conflict and competition among groups, such that topdogs always enjoy more privileges than underdogs.

Social democratic theory. Contemporary **social democracies** in Scandinavia and Western Europe, however, have provided welfare state benefits for the unfortunate, thus mitigating the need for a class struggle. Social democratic theory, as developed by *Gerhard Lenski* (1924–) and *Gunnar Myrdal* (1898–1987), stresses the need for government to provide not only a liberal democratic political framework but also rights for workers, welfare benefits for those not in the workforce, full employment, universal health care, and extensive educational opportunities as guarantees of stability. The wealthiest segment of the population must support a welfare state, if only to ensure social stability.

Legal positivism. A "right" is only what a government says is a "right," so rights are governmentally constructed, not claims with a philosophical basis. Legal positivists, thus, accept rights in particular countries during specific times and places, but they deny that rights are universal.

There are differences of opinion within each of the metaphilosophical approaches. Accordingly, *John Rawls* (1921–2002), heroically tried to synthesize several theories. Although he has also been classified as a neo-Kantian, his principle, "greatest good of the greatest number of people" is clearly in the vocabulary of utilitarianism. According to his "original position," the Lockean state of nature, which ends when humans agree to limited government to protect life, liberty, and property, is an inadequate formulation. Instead, he argues that individuals agree to a government that not only guarantees civil liberties but also provides equality of opportunity and the greatest benefit to the least fortunate members of society.

DISCUSSION TOPIC 2.1 PHILOSOPHICAL OR RELIGIOUS BASIS FOR HUMAN RIGHTS?

Several religious traditions and alternative secular philosophies support human rights to a greater or lesser extent. Which tradition is most and least responsible for the development of human rights? Which tradition provides the best promise today for the advancement of human rights?

METAPHILOSOPHICAL OPPONENTS OF HUMAN RIGHTS

Not all philosophers accept the concept of human rights. A summary of meta-philosophical arguments against the idea of human rights may prove useful in understanding resistance to the extension of human rights around the world today (Table 2.4).

Traditionalism. Religious fundamentalism is one of the major barriers to human rights in the world today. When the tenets of a religion are ossified, limited to a specific set of beliefs formulated in the past, with no possibility of adaptation to new circumstances, human rights are unlikely to advance. One example of traditionalism is Wahhabism, an Islamic sect dominant in Saudi Arabia that follows the precepts of *Muhammad ibn Abd-al-Wahhab* (1703–1792), who believed that Islam should be practiced exactly as originally required by Mohammed. Wahhabists brand as heretics any Muslim who listens to music, watches television, takes or views photographs of humans, wears charms, and otherwise adopts any new Islamic practices. Fundamentalists in other religions, similarly, find models of morality in an ideal past.

Elitism. Burke, though arguing in favor of tradition, subscribed to a different theory – elitism. Although he believed in natural law, Burke denied that human rights could be derived from natural law. He noted that humans are unequal, so his version of natural law leaves inequality intact. He referred to the excesses of the French Revolution as motivated by the "monstrous fiction" of human equality. Likewise, dictators from time immemorial have constituted themselves as the elite of society and hence have denied human rights to the masses. Instead of a democratic order, Burke favored leaving political decisions to the aristocracy, similar to the concept of the philosopher king developed by *Plato* (428–328 BCE).

Relativism. Although some traditionalists tend to conflate current cultural practices with narrow readings of religious doctrine, secular traditionalist opponents of civil and political human rights often justify their opposition in terms of relativism, that is, their cultural context. For example, *Friedrich Karl von Savigny* (1779–1861)

TABLE 2.4   HUMAN RIGHTS OPPONENTS

Theories	*Opponents*	*Principal arguments*
Traditionalism	Wahhab	The wisdom of the ages should be respected, not violated.
Elitism	Plato, Burke	Humans are born unequal.
Relativism	von Savigny, Maine, Lee Kuan Yew	Human rights are culture-bound.
Scepticism	Hume	"Rights" have no empirical basis.
Frustration-aggression theory	Freud	Industrialization requires repression, which leads to savagery.
Social darwinism	Spencer, Sumner, Morgenthau	The strong rule the weak.
Social constructionism	Foucault	Elites establish orthodox views to justify denying human rights.

and *Henry Maine* (1822–1888) asserted that the likelihood that human rights will be respected is a function of cultural and environmental factors unique to particular communities and thus are culture-bound, unlikely to develop within certain cultures. Accordingly, *Lee Kuan Yew* (1923–), Singapore's longtime prime minister, has asserted the concept of "Asian values" to justify denial of civil and political human rights, even though many Asians disagree with Lee's view that the community is more important than the individual. Whereas the West tries to protect individuals from the oppressive state, according to Lee, the East wants to protect the state from misbehaving individuals. His view that East and West have distinct cultures, however, ignores their mutual interpenetration and cultural learning over the centuries as well as the fact that the Universal Declaration of Human Rights was coauthored by delegates from China, Europe, Lebanon, and the United States. Although Lee's concept of "Asian values" has served as a rhetorical justification to violate the civil and political rights of his democratic opponents in Singapore, after his retirement he predicted that pictures of the cruel treatment of individuals by governments appearing on television around the world would ultimately bring greater convergence between East and West on global human rights standards.

A more positive statement of the need to multiculturalize the human rights agenda, which clearly began in the West, has been presented by African scholar Makau Mutua (1958–). His aim is to reconcile the apparent contradiction between respect for diversity and the universalistic claims of human rights advocates.

Scepticism. According to sceptics, primacy in human thought should be given to what is real, and what is real must be observable. *David Hume* (1711–1776) and the positivists believe that rights have no empirical basis; they cannot be seen or touched, so they are arbitrary mental constructs. When Bentham declared that natural rights were "nonsense upon stilts," he was endorsing Hume's anti-dogma insight; however, he and John Stuart Mill went beyond Hume to find a utilitarian basis for human rights.

Frustration-Aggression Theory. The pessimistic writings of *Sigmund Freud* (1856–1939) suggest the futility of pursuing the goal of human rights. For Freud, the advance of civilization requires suppression of individual personality; that is, the division of labor associated with industrialization transforms workers into undifferentiated cogs within an economic system that has little place for the respect of individuals. Accordingly, Freud argued, humans develop frustrations in their daily lives, and from time to time the consequence is savage aggression toward scapegoats. Although Freud personally did not oppose the idea of human rights, his theory predicts that human rights campaigns will inevitably fail, since politics is a matter of groups endlessly struggling for larger and larger pieces of the pie. Since might makes right, such ideas as human rights are illusions; underlying needs for dominance are more basic. Since power is the mother tongue of politics, as Freud argued, "rights" can easily be abolished. Although Freud's psychological theories have been largely discredited, his philosophical views in *Civilization and Its Discontents* (1930) serve as yet another explanation for the difficulty of gaining wider acceptance of a rights-based approach to world problems.

Social darwinism. After biologist *Charles Darwin* (1809–1882) found evidence to support the theory of biological evolution, he applied his insight to humans. In both cases, he derived the scientific law that the fit survive, and the weak die out. Sociologists *Herbert Spencer* (1820–1903) and *William Graham Sumner* (1840–1910) developed the Darwinian law into a social principle, namely, that there is an ongoing struggle for existence, such that the strong must dominate the weak for the human race to survive. Human rights for the weak, thus, are counter to the biological imperative. Although their extrapolation from Darwin's writings is clearly pseudo-scientific, social darwinism even today guides much opposition to human rights. A similar theory in the academic study of international relations is known as *realism*, the chief exponents of which are political scientist *Hans Morgenthau* (1904–1980) and former Secretary of State *Henry Kissinger* (1923–). According to the realists (or neorealists, as some latter-day advocates prefer), states seek survival, so they maximize their interests, giving much priority to military power. States that fail to pursue their self-interests tend to lose out to those that do. Realists infer that human rights concerns will always be secondary and must yield to the primary aim of state self-preservation in an international system that is inherently chaotic, lacking a superordinate authority. Indeed, some realists believe that human rights issues are raised by powerful countries only to intimidate other countries; they discount the notion that human rights concerns are an independent force in world politics, especially since the most powerful countries often violate human rights with impunity.

Social constructionism. Austin and the legal positivists believe that "rights" have no philosophical basis and are only identified when governments wish to do so; governments may extend or cancel so-called rights at their whim. Burke agreed. Social constructionism takes a somewhat similar view, namely, that "truth" is socially constructed, and elites who control institutions of government and the media are able to control what nonelites believe to be true. In other words, "rights" are conferred or denied by elites whenever they choose to do so; their aim is to stay in power. For example, Americans do not entirely comprehend the concept of "social class," since those in power have tried to maintain the promise of upward social mobility as a part of the "American dream." Although such social constructionists as *Michel Foucault* (1926–1984) are primarily interested in deconstructing repressive ortho-doxies of elites, their support for human rights is implicit, but their expectations are pessimistic. Social constructionists believe that ideas about social reality (social constructs) are often taken for granted as common sense; but in fact ideas about politics and society are invented within particular cultures and polities to serve the purposes of those in power.

DISCUSSION TOPIC 2.2 PHILOSOPHICAL CRITIQUES OF HUMAN RIGHTS

Is the quest for human rights realistic or unrealistic? Who has won the philosophical debate – proponents or opponents? Do the opponents provide a healthy critique that proponents must answer? What is their likely reply?

HUMAN RIGHTS ADVOCACY MOVEMENTS

An insightful analysis has been presented by Makau Mutua, who is disturbed that the principal human rights action paradigm is of "savages–victims–saviors." That is, he views the West as perceiving itself imperialistically as the savior of powerless non-Western victims of human rights who are being treated savagely by their own kind. Communitarian African preindustrial societies, he argues, perceive local governments as dispensers of justice rather than as enemies of individualism.

Mutual contrasts four human rights advocacy movements. The **constitutionalists** are the academic scholars and international lawyers who seek to build components of a world constitution that can limit unchecked economic and governmental power. The **conventional doctrinalists** are members of the nongovernmental organizations that identify those who abuse human rights and then call upon governments and international organizations to intervene. The **political strategists** are found within leaders of the most powerful governments, the World Bank, and the World Trade Organization; they often give lip service to human rights, he claims, while they pursue a hidden agenda of advancing economic and political power for the rich. He considers himself a **cultural pluralist** who wants to reconcile the universalistic pretensions of human rights with equally valid claims that all peoples have a right to have their diverse cultures respected. Accordingly, he favors a reexamination and modification of basic human rights

A fifth category should be added for the **humanitarianists**, that is, for those who contribute funds to private aid organizations and those who labor on behalf of the impoverished to offer food, medicine, and shelter. Although the quality and quantity of their aid is sometimes criticized, humanitarian workers should not be forgotten, since they perhaps do more to advance human rights attainments than those who pursue macroeconomic and macropolitical agendas.

CONCLUSION

For centuries, the level, of concern about human rights was limited to philosophical speculation, and most philosophers gave higher priority to other issues. Today, human rights issues fill the front pages of newspapers because there is widespread concern about violations. Philosophical speculation succeeded in inspiring action, especially the revolutions of Britain, France, and the United States, which resulted in Bills of Rights. In a sense, the positivist approach won, since the only human rights that are backed by the weight of authority around the world are those which been encoded into laws and treaties. The following chapter traces the development of human rights by delineating historical movements, as inspired by the various theories of human rights, which produced important documents that now serve as the foundation for international law regarding human rights.

CHAPTER 3

The historical basis for human rights

Thanks to philosophical speculation, as reviewed in the previous chapter, the view increasingly grew that individuals should determine their own destinies without governmental interference. As fundamental rights were codified into law, citizens were accorded basic rights. The historical development of human rights can be traced through certain documents that emerged over time (Tables 3.1–3.4). However, early rulers who attempted to guarantee rights were not always followed by successors with similar commitments. Rights become more irreversible when obtained in struggles by social movements, as the chapter below indicates.

BASIC DOCUMENTS OF HUMAN RIGHTS

The preamble to the constitution of Iraq, as adopted in 2005, notes that "on our land, the first law put in place by mankind was written; in our nation, the most noble era of justice in the politics of nations was laid down." The drafters of the constitution were referring to the written body of laws known as *Code of Hammurabi*, issued by King Hammurabi (1810–1750 BCE) of ancient Babylon in 1780 BCE. The code was a systematic compilation of earlier judgments, many of which dealt with enforcement of contracts, including the marriage contract. On matters of criminal justice, those accused must be caught in the act, and unfair judges were to be fined and removed from their positions. However, some provisions among the 283 entries were harsh, for example setting the death penalty for false testimony by a witness or by a house-builder whose home collapses on a dweller.

TABLE 3.1 EARLY DOCUMENTS OF HUMAN RIGHTS

Document	Adopted
Code of Hammurabi	1780 BCE
Torah	1280–500 BCE
Charter of Cyrus	539 BCE
Asoka's edicts	c. 280 BCE
Christian Gospel	50–125
Constitution of Medina	622
Charter of Liberties	1100
Magna Carta	1215
Provisions of Oxford	1258
Provisions of Westminster	1259

The *Torah*, as first revealed by Moses (*c.* 1304–1237 BCE), contains a legal code of 613 commandments, in which the prohibition on bearing false witness is a human rights element, as is the commandment to help the destitute and needy. However, the Torah's recognition of slavery is at variance with contemporary human rights principles, and the "eye for an eye" acceptance of capital punishment is widely opposed in Europe today.

In 539 BCE, Cyrus the Great (580–530 BCE) entered Babylon and proclaimed what is now known as the *Charter of Cyrus*, which has been claimed as the first human rights document because the word "rights" specifically appears therein. The text proclaims few rights, but the most notable are religious freedom and cultural toleration. In addition, land could be taken over only with just compensation to the owner, forced labor was banned, and slavery was abolished.

The democracy that flourished in Athens during the fifth century BCE was unprecedented in allowing male citizens to vote, participate in a legislature, and serve in executive positions, though a pragmatic aim was to provide a forum in order to enlist support from the people to pay taxes for war. The only documentary legacies are historical accounts. Plato (428–3428 BCE) clearly was unhappier with Athenian democracy than Aristotle (384–322 BCE), but neither based their evaluations on principles of human rights.

The *Edicts* of the Indian emperor Asoka (304–232 BCE), carved on stone pillars, provide a clue to an advocacy of human rights that focused on relief from suffering. Among the principles stated are humane treatment of prisoners, religious toleration, and impartial justice. Other edicts opposed capital punishment and torture of humans as well as animals.

The *Christian Gospel*s of Matthew, Mark, Luke, and John, as recorded after the death of Jesus of Nazareth (*c.* 4 BCE–33 CE), contains clear statements about the obligation to attend to the needs of the poor, a hint about opposition to capital punishment for adultery, but no condemnation of the human rights injustices associated with the arrest and interrogation of Jesus. The denial of freedom of speech, indignities after his arrest, and the crucifixion were accepted as predestined.

Perhaps the first written constitution is the *Constitution of Medina*, in which the prophet Mohammed (570–632) regulated the government of the Medina city-state, when Christians, Jews, Muslims, and pagans lived together equally and peacefully. No person is allowed to be left in poverty, but murder is to be avenged with murder.

The Romans were prolific in legal matters but did not recognize human rights. From the *Law of the Twelve Tables* (450 BCE) to the *Corpus Juris Civilis* (533 CE) of the Emperor Justinian I (483–565), Roman law mostly codified property rights, with more rights to persons of higher status.

In 930, the world's first parliament opened in Iceland among the Viking settlers, who founded an independent state. However, in 1262 Iceland became a colony of Norway, which in turn was ruled by Denmark from 1380. There is no record of a human rights element other than the implicit Icelandic separation of power between executive and legislative branches of government.

In 1066, a conquering army from Normandy took control of England and placed a French-speaking army of occupation over an English-speaking kingdom. To ease some of the tension, King William (1028–1087) sought the advice of a council of Saxon nobles and church officials before making laws. In 1100, King Henry I (1068–1135) issued the *Charter of Liberties*, which granted certain freedoms to church officials (prohibitions of the purchase of church positions and of the confiscation of church property) and to the nobles (freedom from overtaxation, right of inheritance). However, the grant was revocable, in no way implying that there were limitations on the absolute authority of the monarchy.

The technology of warfare advanced during the Middle Ages, so monarchs needed funds to pay workers to manufacture armaments. Although Spanish monarchs formed the Cortes as an advisory body of nobles in the eighth century, during the twelfth century they expanded the Cortes to include members of the urban middle class in order to solicit money for the war to drive the Moors from Spain. When they obtained the wealth of the New World from the fifteenth century, they reduced the power of the Cortes, which was not revived until 1874.

On June 10, 1215, King John under duress signed the *Magna Carta*, which acknowledged that monarchs no longer had absolute power. The Magna Carta reiterated the Charter of Liberties, placed the king on an equal footing with the nobility, and made the powers of the monarch subject to the law. One extraordinary provision was that a council of twenty-five barons could meet at any time to overrule any action by the king; they were entitled to seize the king's castles and possessions to enforce any disagreement. In addition to a separation of power between the institutions of the monarchy and the nobility, the Magna Carta provided that the executive authority could arrest nobles, but they had a right to defend themselves in judicial proceedings conducted in accordance with the law, including a trial with a jury consisting of fellow nobles, some ninety years later known as the right of *habeas corpus*. The king could not levy taxes without the approval of the barons. The barons then took an oath to respect the king, who in turn swore to respect baronial power.

When John later disavowed the Magna Carta, civil war broke out. After John died during the war in 1216, regents of his successor, Henry III (1207–1272), ended the war by agreeing to accept the Magna Carta, which was reissued that year but without the provision for the council of twenty-five. However, the Magna Carta was reissued in various watered-down forms over the years until the English barons forced Henry III to accept the *Provisions of Oxford* of 1258 (superseded in 1259 by the *Provisions of Westminster*), which established a parliament to monitor the performance of a council of fifteen members that was entrusted with the responsibility to supervise ministerial appointments, local administration, and the custody of royal castles. When Henry III obtained papal approval in 1261 to disavow what he had signed under pressure, another civil war erupted. In 1265, the Earl of Leicester (1218–1265) declared that elections would be held for the council, which was to become the parliament; those eligible to vote were freeholders. In 1295, Henry III's successor Edward I (1239–1307) finally accepted the parliament as legitimate. In 1305, he accepted the principle of *habeas corpus*, which had been implicit in the Magna Carta. During the reign of Edward III (1312–1377) parliament became bicameral, with nobles and higher clergy sitting in the upper house, knights and burgesses in the lower house; laws and taxes required approval of both houses as well as the assent of the monarch.

In 1302, Philip the Fair (1268–1314) of France convened the Estates-General, a tricameral arrangement to ask for the approval of the First Estate (clergy), the Second Estate (nobility), and the Third Estate (commoners) to levy taxes. Priests elected clergy in the First Estate, the king decided which nobles would serve in the Second Estate, and there was a limited election of Third Estate delegates from cities favored by the king. However, the Estates-General were seldom summoned. Parliaments also arose in Central Europe and Scandinavia during the Middle Ages, but with few powers exercised by the common people. Sweden's Rikstag, which can be traced to 1435, lacked significant power until 1809.

The English monarchs often sought to marginalize their parliaments by asserting executive authority. Charles I (1625–1649), for example, took out loans, quartered troops in houses of commoners, and imprisoned those who opposed his policies. Discontent with the monarchy, which led Edward Coke (1552–1634) to have parliament issue the *Petition of Right* of 1628 (Table 3.2), which extended certain principles to commoners that had earlier been granted to the nobles, namely, that taxes can only be levied with parliament's consent, no person could be imprisoned without showing just cause, no soldiers could be quartered upon the citizenry, and martial law could not be used in peacetime. Although Charles I accepted the Petition in principle, he ignored the provisions in practice.

In 1649, Charles I was deposed and executed due to the revolution of Oliver Cromwell (1599–1658), who sought to make parliament supreme over the crown. Once in office, however, Cromwell proved to be just as dictatorial, provoking a successful counterrevolution, and parliament restored the monarchy in 1660. The new king, Charles II (1660–1685), was a Protestant, but he contemplated a possible conversion to Catholicism. His son, the future James II (1633–1701 (ruled 1685–1688)), became a Catholic in 1671; when he succeeded to the throne, he was not welcomed by the Protestant nobles, so he tried to arrest his opponents, which led parliament to pass the *Habeas Corpus Act* of 1679. To stay on the throne, he appeased the Protestants by issuing the *Declaration for Liberty of Conscience* in 1687, which established the principle of freedom of religion, thereby rescinding some forms of discrimination against those who did not belong to the Church of England. Still

TABLE 3.2 **HISTORICAL DOCUMENTS OF HUMAN RIGHTS IN THE SEVENTEENTH AND EIGHTEENTH CENTURIES**

Document	Adopted
Petition of Right (England)	1628
Peace of Westphalia	1648
Habeas Corpus Act (England)	1679
Declaration for Liberty of Conscience (England)	1687
English Bill of Rights	1689
Act of Settlement (England)	1701
American Declaration of Rights and Grievances	1774
Virginia Declaration of Rights	1776
Declaration of Independence	1776
Catholic Relief Act (England)	1778
American Constitution	1787
Declaration of the Rights of Man and Citizen	1789
Declaration of the Rights of Women and Citizen	1790
American (Federal) Bill of Rights	1791

dissatisfied, the Protestant nobles conspired to bring over his son-in-law, Prince William of Orange (1650–1702), who sailed from Holland to England with troops in 1688, overthrew James II, and was crowned king. As a condition of occupying the throne, the new monarch agreed to sign the *English Bill of Rights* in 1689, one provision of which was that no Catholic could henceforth become king. Otherwise, parliament was to be supreme in lawmaking, especially regarding taxation and the maintenance of a standing army; parliamentary speech would be immune from prosecution, and elections would be free and fair. Other provisions in the Bill of Rights were the freedom to petition the king, the right of Protestants to bear arms, freedom from cruel and unusual punishment, freedom from excessive bail, and freedom from fines and forfeitures without trial. Then the *Act of Settlement* of 1701 provided that monarchs could not determine their successors; only parliament could do so.

HISTORIC EVENT 3.1 THE PEACE OF WESTPHALIA (1648)

The Peace of Westphalia consisted of two nearly identically worded treaties – one signed by four Catholic countries at Münster, the other by two Protestant countries at Osnabrück. The practical effect was for European countries, particularly the Holy Roman Empire, to recognize the principle that leaders of countries could determine

continued

the state religion without outside interference. Those espousing a minority religion were guaranteed freedom to worship. Boundaries of several states were redrawn, especially in German-speaking Europe, which consisted of hundreds of city-states and principalities. But the German states were still subordinate to the Holy Roman Empire, which could depose princes. France and Sweden also reserved the right to intervene if terms of the treaty were violated. Subsequently, France upset the balance of power, seeking hegemony in the European state system, first under Louis XIV (1638–1715) and later under Napoléon Bonaparte (1769–1821).

Although developments in England established some principles of human rights, they did not contribute to the body of international law. In 1648, the Thirty Years' War ended with the *Peace of Westphalia*, which established the current system of nation-states and advanced international law as the new basis for proper relations among governments. Three principles were established: (1) The **equality of states** was recognized as a basic component of international law, though states differed considerably in power. (2) Perhaps the most fundamental concept was the recognition of **state sovereignty**, that is, that governments should treat one another as supreme in domestic matters and no longer depended upon papal approval to have their legitimacy respected. After 1648, rulers were free to determine their own state religion, and they pledged to tolerate other religions among their subjects. (3) The treaty established the **principle of noninterference** in the domestic affairs of other countries. Under the Westphalian system, rulers respected one another's religious convictions, thus making religious toleration a principle of international affairs. However, governments could complain about the mistreatment of their own citizens abroad and had the right to rescue them from harm.

DISCUSSION TOPIC 3.1   DOES THE WESTPHALIAN STATE SYSTEM PROMOTE HUMAN RIGHTS?

How does the Westphalian state system serve to advance human rights? Did Westphalian principles provide any protection for those massacred near Tiananmen Square in 1989? Did the Westphalian nation-state system bring about an environment consistent with Grotius's expectations that international law would bring peace? Currently, most nation-states compete for power with international organizations, global corporations, and the dominant superpower, the United States, so are the principles of the Westphalian state system a fiction today?

After Westphalia, several international mass movements gradually emerged to establish an irreversible momentum toward the worldwide recognition of human rights. The first is the movement to establish democracy.

THE DEMOCRATIC MOVEMENT

Theories about democratic forms of rule leapt off the pages of philosophers' treatises onto the soil of North America when the American colonies decided to revolt against Britain. In 1774, Granville Sharp (1735–1813), grandson of the Archbishop of York, published *A Declaration of the People's Natural Rights to a Share in the Legislature*. He gave a copy to Benjamin Franklin (1706–1790), who in turn had the tract republished in the colonies. Sharp's thesis inspired the formation later that year of the Continental Congress, a deliberative body composed of delegates from the thirteen colonies. Many colonists were British citizens, but they were not allowed to elect members to the parliament in London. Accordingly, the Continental Congress decided not to submit legislation to the English parliament for approval. One of the first acts of the Continental Congress was to adopt a *Declaration of Rights and Grievances*, which primarily claimed that the colonists had the same rights as British citizens, including the right to be represented in a legislative body, trial by jury, and the right to assemble. The Declaration objected to the maintenance of a standing army by England in the colonies and the quartering of troops in private homes; the colonists were taxed to pay for the troops, so they objected to taxation without representation in the English parliament.

In 1776, a *Declaration of Rights* was incorporated into the constitution of Virginia, one of several constitutions that the colonies in rebellion adopted to replace the colonial charters under which they had been governed. One month later, delegates from the colonies drafted the *Declaration of Independence*, in which Thomas Jefferson substituted the right to "pursue happiness" for the right to property that had been identified by one of his favorite philosophers, John Locke (1632–1704).

In 1777, the Continental Congress adopted the *Articles of Confederation and Perpetual Union*, which were fully ratified by 1781 as a treaty among thirteen states with a unicameral Congress that elected a President but with no power to tax or to regulate trade. When Britain recognized American independence in 1783 under the terms of the Treaty of Paris, the newly independent country continued to hobble along under the Articles of Confederation, which many perceived to be unsatisfactory. For example, each state could erect tariffs against the rest, so there was no guarantee that a national economy would ever develop.

In 1787, a new constitution was drawn up, establishing a stronger central government that could prevent states from impeding interstate commerce, with such protections as a prohibition against *ex post facto* legislation (declaring a past action to be a crime) and bills of attainder (a law making someone a criminal without a trial). But a significant human rights flaw in the constitution was the recognition of slavery as legal throughout the country, even in states where the practice was formerly prohibited. However, many leaders wanted more civil liberties protections and argued against ratification of the constitution. The framers then promised on their honor

TABLE 3.3   PROVISIONS OF THE AMERICAN BILL OF RIGHTS

Article	Human rights provision
1	Freedom of religion, press, assembly, petition
2	Right to bear arms
3	Soldiers cannot be forced to live in the homes of civilians.
4	Right not to be unreasonably searched; no warrants without probable cause
5	No arrest for capital or infamous crime without indictment; no double jeopardy; no self-incrimination; no loss of life, liberty, property without due process of law; no government seizure of private property for public use without just compensation
6	Right to speedy trial by impartial jury where criminal defendant is informed of the accusation, confronted by accusers, and has an attorney in defense who can subpoena witnesses
7	Right of trial by jury for civil lawsuits, using common law
8	No excessive bail or fines; no cruel or unusual punishments
9	Rights not mentioned are retained by the people.
10	Powers not delegated to government are reserved by the people and the states.

to amend the constitution accordingly after the document was ratified by the required number of nine states.

The *Bill of Rights*, ratified in 1791, consisted of the first ten amendments to the Constitution (Table 3.3).[1] However, the Bill of Rights originally applied to the federal government, mainly Washington, DC, residents; states were not covered, and the Eleventh Amendment of 1795 stripped federal courts from jurisdiction over non-consenting state governments.

Inspired in part by the American Revolution, the leaders of the French Revolution issued the *Declaration of the Rights of Man and Citizen* of 1789 and the *Declaration of the Rights of Women and Citizen* of 1790. Unlike the American Declaration of Independence, which proclaimed the right of thirteen colonies to self-government, the French Declarations were intended to apply universally, not just to France. The rights identified in both documents went beyond those stated in the American Bill of Rights to include the right to security and the right of resistance to oppression. The Declaration regarding rights of males, but not females, was encoded into France's first constitution in 1791.

Having declared that peoples everyone should enjoy fundamental rights, France under Napoleon Bonaparte conscripted citizens to overthrow the monarchs of Europe. By the early nineteenth century, semidemocratic Britain eventually joined the despotisms of Austria, Prussia, and Russia to stop Napoléon in order to restore the balance of power in Europe. The Congress of Vienna in 1814–1815 then redrew the map of Europe to undo changes effected by the French armies. Leaders of the four major powers, joined by France in 1818, established a Concert of Europe (congress system) as an arrangement to consult together in order to suppress democratic uprisings. However, the arrangement quickly fell apart; Britain soon stopped supporting the reactionary aims, and democratizing France did so in 1830.[2]

As of 1815, only Britain, France, and the United States formally recognized a wide range of individual rights, though Spain granted men the right to vote in 1812. All four countries granted the right to vote only to property owners, however, so only about 1 percent of the population was eligible to vote.

In 1832, Britain's Reform Act extended the right to vote to middle class males, but the common people, men and women, were still disfranchised. Accordingly, in 1838 William Lovett (1800–1877) issued the *People's Charter*, which began a campaign of parliamentary reform known as the Chartist Movement that made the following demands: (1) universal suffrage, (2) equal electoral districts, (3) abolition of the requirement that members of parliament must own property, (4) payment for members of parliament, (5) annual general elections, and (6) the secret ballot. Although the suffrage proposal originally envisaged female suffrage, the movement later dropped interest in females and demanded only universal male suffrage. Thomas Carlyle (1795–1881) further publicized the People's Charter movement in his tract *Chartism* (1839). Although the tenor of the Chartist movement was radical, all the demands but the annual election eventually became law, the earliest by 1858, the latest by 1911.

The realization that states could become democratic and prosper spread to the masses throughout Europe from the early part of the nineteenth century. In 1848, there were uprisings all over Europe as the disfranchised rose in revolt against undemocratic rulers. Britain and France no longer supported the antidemocratic mood of the Congress of Vienna, and the crude suppression of the revolts by undemocratic governments in 1848 only encouraged pro-democratic forces to pressure governments even more to gain the right to vote. After 1848, male suffrage was extended by several countries in Europe, including France, though property or tax requirements for voting were still imposed. In 1853, Britain granted voting rights to all adult males residing in their New Zealand colony.

By the turn of the twentieth century, revolutionary ferment grew stronger inside the Austro-Hungarian and Ottoman empires, where the democratic quest morphed into nationalist movements. In 1914, a Serbian nationalist assassinated Austrian Archduke Franz Ferdinand (1863–1914), and within a few months World War I broke out. When the war was over, the Austro-Hungarian, German, and Ottoman (Turk) empires were dissolved. Nascent democratic states (Czechoslovakia, Hungary, and Poland) soon appeared in their place. The democratic imperative had been established on a worldwide basis, though the perfection of democratic principles remains a challenge today.

ANTISLAVERY MOVEMENT[3]

Although slaves revolted for centuries, and such philosophers as Montesquieu condemned the practice, only in 1569 did an English court declare that slavery was illegal. However, the discovery of the New World opened up vast lands for Europeans to clear for agriculture. Slaves were imported to the colonies in the Americas for that purpose, but in time the demeaning treatment of Africans provoked opposition. In 1700, Boston judge Samuel Sewall (1652–1730) wrote *The Selling of Joseph* in which he developed a thesis against slavery out of his experience with a slave named Adam, who sought his freedom.

To mushroom, the antislavery movement needed a leader with a large following. When John Wesley (1703–1791) published *Thoughts Upon Slavery* (1744), he had a mass base for antislavery opposition as the founder of Methodism. Unitarians and members of the Religious Society of Friends, the Quakers, also opposed slavery on moral grounds, though for centuries the biblical "curse of Canaan" was understood by Christians, Jews, and Muslims to be a divine statement that Africans were destined to be slaves.

Granville Sharp, champion of democratic reform, also decried the practice of slavery. First, he espoused the cause of a slave who had been beaten almost to death by his master and abandoned. His tract, *The Injustice and Dangerous Tendency of Tolerating Slavery in England* (1769), so shamed the master that the slave become a free man. When a slave from Virginia who managed to escape to England filed a writ of habeas corpus in 1772 to end his slave status, Sharp supported his petition, which was successful in *Somersett v Knowles*.

Meanwhile, leaders in the Northern states in rebellion against England opposed slavery. The first draft of the Declaration of Independence expressed disapproval over slavery, but the South would not compromise, so the final draft dropped the provision. As a compromise in the Constitution of 1787, slavery was legalized, but the importation of slaves was to end by 1808. Nevertheless, Abigail Adams (1744–1818), spouse of the second American President John Adams (1735–1826), was among those who opposed slavery and was unhappy with the compromise that appeased Southern states so that they would ratify the Constitution.

In 1787, Sharp and his friend Thomas Clarkson (1760–1846) formed the Society for the Abolition of the Slave Trade, which was later supported by Wesley and William Wilberforce (1759–1833), the latter an Evangelical member of parliament who was in a position to obtain support for the abolitionist cause at the highest levels of government. Formation of the Society marked the first time in history when large numbers of people in one country were mobilized to protest the plight of people of another color in another part of the world. At a time when half the slaves were being transported from Africa to America on British ships, the movement threatened profits of British companies, so the appeal had to be based on morality. Clarkson was assigned to collect data about the slave trade, so he interviewed some 20,000 sailors, secured physical evidence in the form of handcuffs, leg-shackles, thumb screws, instruments for forcing open slaves' jaws, and branding irons, and then published *A Summary View of the Slave Trade and of the Probable Consequences of Its Abolition* (1787).

After attending meetings of the British Society, Jacques-Pierre Brissot (1754–1793) formed a parallel Société des Amis des Noirs in France during 1788. His society attracted membership from the Marquis de Condorcet (1743–1794), the Marquis de Lafayette (1757–1834) who supported the American Revolution, and National Constituent Assembly President, the Comte de Mirabeau (1749–1791). In 1794, the

Assembly decreed an end to slavery in the French colonies. In 1788, the British parliament was so inundated by petitions to end the slave trade that a law was passed to regulate conditions on slave ships, and in 1792 some 300,000 Britons boycotted West Indian sugar, produced by slaves. The success of the Haitian independence movement provided further impetus to the movement. By 1807, the last year when the U.S. Constitution allowed the slave trade, the British parliament passed the *Abolition of the Slave Trade Act* (Table 3.4). The Society for the Abolition of the Slave Trade was renamed the Society for the Mitigation and Eventual Abolition of Slavery in 1807 and the British and Foreign Anti-Slavery Society in 1823, but only men were admitted. Meanwhile, women's antislavery groups formed in seventy English towns in response to the campaign of Quaker Elizabeth Heyrick (1769–1831), who forged a network of female antislavery societies that gained momentum after publication of her *Immediate, Not Gradual Abolition* (1825). The women differed from the gradualist approach advocated by the men. In 1830, after Heyrick became treasurer of the Anti-Slavery Society, she insisted that the Society should call for immediate abolition. In 1833, following major slave revolts in Jamaica during the previous two years, parliament passed the *Slavery Abolition Act*. However, such legislation was meaningless because the slave trade largely occurred in international waters, and no country had yet decided to enforce the legislation.

HISTORIC EVENT 3.2 THE HAITIAN INDEPENDENCE STRUGGLE (1790–1803)

In 1697, Spain ceded the western part of Hispaniola to France, which established coffee and sugar plantations and imported slaves from Africa to work under such harsh working conditions that in 1751–1758 they put down a revolt by runaway slaves. By 1778, there were some 500,000 slaves, 60,000 French, and 25,000 nonslave mulattos. After the French Revolution began, the National Constituent Assembly requested the colonial legislature to enfranchise the mulattos. After the colonists refused, the mulattos revolted in 1790 under the leadership of Vincent Ogé (1755–1791) by destroying towns, burning plantations, and executing the French, but they did not mobilize the slaves. In 1791, former slave François Dominique Touissaint l'Ouverture (1743–1803), assumed leadership of the revolt after Ogé was executed. In 1794, when slavery was abolished by the Paris government, l'Ouverture persuaded the French to accept him as the territory's governor while the colony remained under French sovereignty. In 1795, Napoléon seized power in France. In 1802, he sent a large force to depose l'Ouverture, who made peace with the French and retired. General Jean-Jacques Dessalines (1758–1806), l'Ouverture's military commander, agreed to the peace until word spread that Napoleon intended to reestablish slavery. Dessalines then resumed the struggle. Many French soldiers had died of yellow fever, and at the end of 1803 the French surrendered to rebel forces. Dessalines declared independence on behalf of an independent country named Haiti on January 1, 1804.

The adversaries of the War of 1812 (Britain and the United States) promised to stop the slave trade under the terms of the *Treaty of Ghent* of 1814, which ended the war. But once again no action was taken to implement the pledge.

In 1814–1815, foreign ministers of the victorious powers (Austria, England, Prussia, Russia) over the armies of Napoléon Bonaparte met at Vienna along with a delegate from the restored Bourbon monarchy in France. Responding to the antislavery movement, they declared in the *Final Act of the Congress of Vienna* of 1815 that the slave trade was morally repugnant. Although the Final Act recognized the rights of the Polish minorities in Austria, Prussia, and Russia, the principal aims were to legitimize all five monarchial countries and to establish a five-power consultative process.

Revolutions against Spain in the Americas abolished slavery in the 1820s. In 1831, Nat Turner (1800–1831) led a slave revolt in which fifty-five whites were massacred in Virginia. As a result, there was a crackdown on slaves throughout the South, denying them for example the opportunity to receive an education. Thereafter, the American Colonization Society arose as a movement to encourage slaves to return to Africa; the Maryland legislature, for example, provided $200,000 for that purpose in 1833.

Then in 1840, national abolitionist movements joined together to form the Anti-Slavery International for the Protection of Human Rights, which convened the first World Anti-Slavery Conference to focus attention on the issue. By placing the issue of slavery in the larger context of human rights, the movement signaled the arrival of a wider agenda than abolition of slavery.

Within the United States, Harriet Beecher Stowe (1811–1896), her brother Henry Ward Beecher (1813–1887), William Lloyd Garrison (1805–1879), and others formed various organizations, held meetings, conducted studies, published books, and utilized the press to dramatize the slavery as immoral. While Garrison printed current news events about slave conditions in his publication *The Liberator* (1831–1865), Stowe's novel about the horrors of slavery, *Uncle Tom's Cabin* (1852), was much more widely read. From the beginning of the United States, Southern states controlled Congress by virtue of the rule that representation in the House of Representatives was constitutionally based on the number of residents in each state, with slaves counted as three-fifths of a person. As new states were admitted, the South wanted to expand slavery, but the North was adamantly opposed.

In *Dred Scott v Sanford* (1857), the Supreme Court (60US393) ruled that a slave named Dred Scott was not automatically freed when he moved with his master to a state where slavery was outlawed, further outraging antislavery advocates into realizing that Northern farmers could import the cheap labor of slaves. The emergence of the Republican Party, and particularly the candidacy of antislavery advocate Abraham Lincoln (1809–1865), meant that the North and the South were on a collision course. The train wreck occurred in 1861, even before President Lincoln took office, when a Southern militia fired on the federal arsenal of weaponry at Fort Sumter in the harbor of Charleston, South Carolina.

By 1862, while the United States was engaged in the Civil War, ten European countries had adopted legislation to stop ships on the high seas suspected of transporting slaves. President Abraham Lincoln issued the *Emancipation Proclamation* in 1862, to go into effect on January 1, 1863, but he only declared an end to slavery

TABLE 3.4   HISTORICAL DOCUMENTS OF HUMAN RIGHTS IN THE NINETEENTH AND EARLY TWENTIETH CENTURIES

Document	Adopted
Abolition of the Slave Trade Act (Britain)	1807
Treaty of Ghent	1814
Final Act of the Congress of Vienna	1815
Catholic Emancipation Act (Britain)	1829
Slavery Abolition Act (Britain)	1833
People's Charter (Britain)	1838
Declaration of Sentiments (United States)	1848
Declaration of Paris	1856
Emancipation Proclamation	1862
Lieber Code	1863
Convention for the Amelioration of the Condition of the Wounded on the Field of Battle	1864
Thirteenth, Fourteenth, and Fifteenth Amendments (United States)	1866, 1868, 1870
Declaration of the Rights of Women in the United States	1876
Final Act of the Congress of Berlin	1885
Project of an International Declaration Concerning the Laws and Customs of War	1874
Declaration of the Rights of Women in the United States	1876
Manual of the Laws and Customs of War	1880
Final Act of the Congress of Berlin	1885
Erfurt Program	1891
Rerum Novarum	1891
General Act for the Repression of the African Slave Trade	1890
treaties adopted at the First and Second Hague Conferences	1899 and 1907
Bern Conventions	1905 and 1906
Balfour Declaration	1917
Wilson's Fourteen Points	1918
Treaty of Versailles (including the Covenant of the League of Nations)	1919
Constitution of the International Labor Organization	1919
Statute of the Permanent Court of International Justice	1920
Nineteenth (Susan B. Anthony) Amendment	1920
General Act for the Pacific Settlement of International Disputes	1924
Locarno Peace Pact	1925
Slavery, Servitude, Forced Labor and Similar Institutions and Practices Convention	1926
General Treaty for the Renunciation of War	1928

in the states that seceded, not in Delaware, Kentucky, Maryland, and Missouri, which had slaves but did not secede. In 1866, after the Civil War, slavery was abolished in the United States by the *Thirteenth Amendment* to the Constitution; in the next fifteen years, more than fifty countries on all continents followed suit.

The *Fourteenth Amendment* applied the Bill of Rights to the states so that former slaves would receive due process and equal justice before the law in order to undo the badges of slavery. However, provisions of the Bill of Rights were not forced upon the states until specific Supreme Court rulings during the twentieth century.[4] The *Fifteenth Amendment* forbade the states to deny the right to vote on the basis of race, although African Americans were subsequently discouraged from exercising the franchise by means subtle and not so subtle until public opinion demanded passage of the Voting Rights Act of 1965.

In 1885, the *Final Act of the Congress of Berlin* declared an end to the slave trade, and in 1890 the *General Act for the Repression of the African Slave Trade* was adopted at a conference in Brussels. Brazil continued to allow slavery until 1899.

HISTORIC EVENT 3.3 THE CONGRESS OF BERLIN (1878–1885)

German Chancellor Otto von Bismarck (1815–1898) perceived the Treaty of San Stefano after Russia's victory in the Russo-Turkish War of 1877–1878 as upsetting the balance of power among the major countries in Europe. In particular, he feared that Slavic-speaking minorities would revolt, undermining the stability of the Austro-Hungarian empire. In addition, the defeat of the Ottoman Turks implied that Russian power would be extended to the Mediterranean Sea, where Britain and France hoped to control Palestine and Egypt. Accordingly, Bismarck convened a meeting at Berlin to draw up a new treaty with input from Austria-Hungary, Britain, Italy, Russia, and Turkey. Delegates from Greece, Montenegro, Romania, and Serbia were consulted during the congress but were not admitted as full partners to the deliberations. The meeting was the largest multicountry conference thus far held in Europe. The Russians, who had proclaimed the independence of Montenegro, Romania, and Serbia, as well as an autonomous Bulgaria under nominal Ottoman rule, conceded little. They agreed to independence for a smaller Bulgaria, returning the rest (including Macedonia) to Turkish control, and allowed Austria to administer Bosnia-Herzegovina. Turkey agreed to respect the rights of non-Muslims in their lands. Failure to agree on a border between Greece and Turkey fueled a war during 1897.

Thanks to the work of the Temporary Slavery Commission of the League of Nations, a treaty was adopted in 1926. The *Slavery, Servitude, Forced Labor and Similar Institutions and Practices Convention*, also known as the Slavery Convention of 1926, which made prohibition of slavery a matter of international law, entered into force in 1927.

The antislavery movement was the first worldwide mass-based movement for human rights. However, forced labor is still a problem in the world today, affecting millions of unfortunate people.

SUFFRAGETTE MOVEMENTS

In 1776, New Jersey allowed women to vote on an equal basis with men if they owned property. During the American Revolution Abigail Adams complained that women were not given the same rights as men. Educated at home because women were not admitted to school, she successfully campaigned for the right of girls to receive a formal education.

In 1792, Mary Wollstonecraft (1759–1797) of England set forth the first feminist critique of male tyranny over females in *A Vindication of the Rights of Woman*. Her most constructive proposal was for the right to education by females. In 1807, however, New Jersey rescinded female suffrage, setting back what might have developed into a trend. Nevertheless, in 1838 Britain allowed women to vote in its Pitcairn Islands colony.

In 1840, Elizabeth Cady Stanton (1815–1902), a staunch American abolitionist and Quaker, sought to attend the World Antislavery Convention in London with her spouse, only to learn that women were not admitted. Outraged, she returned to the United States to organize the first Women's Rights Convention at Seneca Falls, New York, in 1848, when she persuaded the delegates to adopt the *Declaration of Sentiments*. In 1850, the first of several national women's rights conventions was held, advocating not only the right to vote but also liberalization of divorce laws.

In 1851, Anne Knight (1786–1862) formed the Sheffield Female Political Association, the first women's suffrage organization in Britain. Later, similar groups emerged throughout the country. In 1866, the parliament of the Isle of Man became the first in the world to grant equal voting rights for men and women. In 1867, when John Stuart Mill (1806–1873) unsuccessfully presented a petition for the female franchise to parliament, the London National Society for Women's Suffrage was founded.

After the victory of the North in the Civil War, progressive women in the United States focused their attention on suffrage. In 1866, Stanton and fellow Quaker Susan B. Anthony (1820–1906) founded the American Equal Rights Association to lobby for such reforms as the Fourteenth and Fifteenth Amendments. In 1868, they launched the newspaper *The Revolution* in Rochester, with the masthead "Men their rights, and nothing more; women, their rights, and nothing less." However, Anthony and Stanton were bitterly disappointed when the Fourteenth and Fifteenth Amendments failed to establish the principle of women's equality. From 1869, Anthony appeared before Congress each year until her death in 1906 to lobby for female suffrage.

In 1869, the women's movement in the United States split. Anthony and Stanton formed the National Woman Suffrage Association, which opposed the Fifteenth Amendment because women were excluded. After the Fifteenth Amendment was ratified in 1870, the group favored a constitutional amendment to grant equality to women. A rival American Woman Suffrage Association was also founded in 1869, electing antislavery leader Henry Ward Beecher as the first president. The latter's strategy of getting female suffrage on a state-by-state basis bore fruit when the Territory of Wyoming granted the right to vote to women in 1869 and the Utah Territory in 1870. However, Congress revoked Utah's female suffrage in 1887.

In 1870, forty-four women voted in Massachusetts, though their ballots were not counted. In 1872, Anthony and a dozen others tried to vote, were arrested, found guilty and fined for violating the voting laws in a 1873 court proceeding where they were denied the right of trial by jury, and fined. Suffragette demonstrations were then held at the centennial anniversaries of the Boston Tea Party in 1873, the Battle of Lexington in 1874, and the Declaration of Independence in Philadelphia in 1876, where Anthony read the *Declaration of the Rights of Women in the United States*.

In *Minor v Happersett* (1874), the Supreme Court (88US162) ruled that women, though citizens, had no constitutional right to vote. However, in 1878 a constitutional amendment prohibiting the states from denying women the right to vote was first introduced in Congress.

COURT CASE 3.1 *MINOR V HAPPERSETT* (1874)

In 1869, Francis (1820–1892) and Virginia Minor (1824–1894) wrote a book claiming that the right of women to vote was established by the Fourteenth Amendment. An officer of the National Woman Suffrage Association, Virginia attempted to register to vote in St. Louis, Missouri, in 1872; she wanted to vote in the presidential election that year. Voting registrar, Reese Happersett, however, informed her that only men could do so. Minor then sued, retaining her husband as her attorney. After losing her case in the Missouri courts, he took her case the U.S. Supreme Court, which ruled in 1874 that women were indeed citizens according to the constitution and subsequent laws, but that eligibility of women to vote was not a privilege of citizenship created by the Fourteenth Amendment.

In 1887, the two rival American suffragette organizations merged, forming the National American Woman Suffrage Association. Meanwhile, Socialist parties came out for the right of women to vote throughout Europe, and in 1893 New Zealand became the first country to grant the franchise to females. The state of South Australia followed suit in 1894. In 1900, the Labour Party in England was founded, with female suffrage an original plank in its platform. In 1906, Finland became the first European country to allow women's suffrage.

In 1905, the first militant suffragette action took place when Christabel Pankhurst (1880–1958) was arrested for disrupting a speech of Foreign Minister Sir Edward Grey (1862–1933). She was fined but refused to pay, resulting in a sentence of seven days imprisonment.

In 1907, some three thousand women marched from Hyde Park to the Strand, demanding the vote and the American suffragettes began to adopt the tactics of their English counterparts – parades, street speakers, and pickets. In 1908, a suffragette rally in London attracted 250,000 in Hyde Park, and in 1909 women smashed the windows of government offices and department stores. A suffragette riot in 1910 resulted in 120 arrests after police attacks on women protesters at parliament.

In 1913, the year when women received the vote in Norway, suffragette violence escalated in England. Mary Richardson (1889–1961) slashed the Rokeby Venus in the National Gallery, and other suffragettes vandalized paintings in Manchester and Birmingham. An arson campaign was launched at racecourses, churches, and unoccupied homes of politicians. And Emily Wilding Davison (1872–1913) threw herself under the king's horse at the Epsom Derby and died.

During World War I, the suffragette movement was suspended. Women gained considerable recognition for working in factories while men were at war. Public opinion was more favorable to the movement after the war, and women received the franchise in 1918–1920 within Austria, Britain, Czechoslovakia, Germany, Hungary, Poland, and the United States. Nevertheless, equality between the sexes remains to be achieved throughout the world.

THE TRADE UNION MOVEMENT

By 1150, workers throughout most of Western Europe had formed craft guilds, but they declined with the arrival of industrialization and were abolished during the French Revolution, by the British parliament in 1814 and 1835, and throughout the German states. Craft guilds, however, reappeared as the industrial revolution progressed within burgeoning cities among journeymen shipwrights, printers, tailors, stonecutters, carpenters, and others. By the 1830s, workers met in public squares to demand higher wages and better working conditions, but employers often called troops to quell demonstrations and riots, deeming trade unions to be illegal.

Factory and living conditions were deplorable, as the novels of Charles Dickens (1812–1870) and others described. Welsh industrialist Robert Owen (1771–1858), who reminisced that pre-industrial society had Poor Laws and a *noblesse oblige* belief that the more fortunate should take care of the less fortunate, was upset that unregulated factories were bringing about social chaos. His *A New View of Society* (1813) advocated a utopian socialism of small industrial villages run cooperatively by worker-residents. He owned and ran such a village in Britain from 1805–1815, and in 1824 moved to New Harmony, Indiana, to set up the first of sixteen model industrial villages. When the experiment failed, he returned to England in 1828 to lobby for laws to protect workers from rampant exploitation. Although Owen's enterprises turned a profit, other industrialists believed that pandering to workers would place them at a competitive disadvantage, both nationally and internationally.

Due to the objectionable practice of recruiting children for work, the English parliament slowly began to protect child labor. The Cotton Factories Regulation Act of 1819 set the minimum working age at nine and maximum working hours at twelve. The Regulation of Child Labor Law of 1833 required clean conditions of work. In 1847, the Ten Hours Bill limited working hours to ten for children and women; the law was extended in 1867 to small factories and workshops. Collectively known as the Factory Acts, they sought to provide safety and sanitation in all workshops and regulated the hours of labor for women and children.

During the 1830s and 1840s, humanitarian industrialist Daniel Le Grand (1783–1859) in France and parliamentarian Charles Hindley (1850–1924) in England proposed an international treaty to regulate conditions of labor so that no country that provided humane conditions for workers would suffer a competitive disadvantage in the increasingly global economy. In 1843, Belgian Edouard Ducpétiaux (1804–1868) was the earliest to advocate an international labor organization, and he convened the first international conference on labor issues at Brussels in 1856.

The Chartist movement, which began in 1838, was the first grassroots worker's movement, though the focus was on electoral reform. Impressed by the Chartist movement and further encouraged by the political discontent that was spilling over into mass uprisings in 1848, Karl Marx (1818–1883) and Friedrich Engels (1820–1895) issued the *Manifesto of the Communist Party* (1848). They interpreted the widespread unrest throughout European cities as a significant advance in a class struggle that began when capitalist elites vanquished feudal authorities, creating a bourgeois class of owners and a proletarian class of workers. Indeed, the industrial revolution emerged when business owners organized workers into factories to mass produce goods for sale in an international market, thus bringing laborers in close touch with one another. Efforts to organize workers within industrial countries stimulated Marx and Engels to imagine a worldwide labor movement. In 1864, Marx assumed a key position in the newly formed International Workingmen's Association, later called the First International, and tried to build a socialist worker's movement out of a diverse collection of representatives of left-wing political parties.

HISTORIC EVENT 3.4 THE REVOLUTIONS OF 1848–1849

Economic conditions in Europe deteriorated in the 1840s, including serious crop failures. Rural residents moved to the cities in search of a better life in the new factories, where working conditions were harsh, only to find that there were few jobs due to the economic downturn. The middle class was also adversely affected by the increased cost of food. In 1848, King Louis-Philippe (1773–1850) attempted to ban fundraising banquets on behalf of French workers, whereupon the people attacked the police, the king abdicated, and the new Second Republic proclaimed the right to work and universal male suffrage. Events in Paris stimulated revolutionaries elsewhere. Provisional governments arose in Austrian-held Milan and Venice with the intention of merging into a united Italy. A Hungarian government demanded independence of Austria. The Polish in Posen (Poznań) fought occupying German troops, and a Polish committee declared that Austria should cede Galicia to Poland. Czech nationalists agitated for independence from Austria. Revolts also broke out in the independent states of Bavaria and Saxony. At first, some of the rulers offered democratic concessions. Later, they used troops to quell the demonstrations and rescinded democratic reforms almost everywhere. France, meanwhile, remained in turmoil. Louis Bonaparte (1808–1873), nephew of Napoléon Bonaparte, was elected President of the Second Republic, but he staged a coup in 1851 and held a referendum in 1852 that served to replace the Second Republic with the Second Empire. Calling himself Napoleon III, he continued in power until 1870.

When skilled workers increasingly demanded more pay, employers broke down the work into a set of simple tasks that could be performed by unskilled workers on an assembly line, thus splitting the workforce into an upper and lower proletariat, according to the analysis of Vladimir Lenin (1870–1924). Next, the invention of machines began to replace unskilled workers. Unions tried to organize, but most were suppressed.

In 1868, Susan B. Anthony advocated an eight-hour day and equal pay for equal work. Although women were excluded from most trade unions, she encouraged women in the garment and printing trades to form workingwomen's associations. In 1869, she was elected president of the Workingwomen's Central Association, but the National Labor Union Congress resisted her efforts when she urged women to replace jobs of men on strike as typesetters.

In 1869, Uriah Stephens (1821–1882), aware that union organizers and members were often shot dead, founded the Holy and Noble Order of the Knights of Labor in Philadelphia as a secret society. In 1882, the Knights went public, declaring that they opposed strikes; membership expanded as they encouraged employers to establish recreation and welfare programs. Another union with similar goals, the Brotherhood of Locomotive Firemen, was formed in 1876 by Eugene V. Debs (1855–1926).

Formation of the Paris Commune in 1871, however, frightened governments and industrialists throughout Europe. British trade unions sought to dissociate themselves from the "red terrorists of Paris." The leaders of the Paris Commune were ultimately exiled and disunited. More moderate union leaders tried to unseat Marx, who transferred the headquarters of his organization from London to New York, where his followers were predominant. However, Marx remained in England, so the leaderless movement waned and collapsed in 1876.

HISTORIC EVENT 3.5 THE PARIS COMMUNE (1871)

In 1870, Prussia attacked France. By 1871, Prussian troops had defeated the French and attempted to occupy Paris, but Parisians peacefully refused to cooperate and restricted them to a few city blocks. When a quisling French authority then tried to enter Paris to collect arms, the population resisted. Instead, the people organized the first successful workers' revolution and held an election with universal suffrage for an independent municipal government, known as the Paris Commune. The reforms of the new worker's government included separation of church and state, and the guillotine was abolished. Factories abandoned by industrialists were reopened and run by workers as cooperatives, and night work was abolished for bakers. Three months after the election, a collaborationist French army returned with sufficient weapons to put down the Paris Commune. Some 30,000 unarmed workers then were massacred, thousands were arrested, and about 7,000 were exiled.

After two preliminary meetings of socialist parties, the International Socialist Congress met in Paris during 1889. Attended by delegates from twenty countries, including Engels, the conference launched the Socialist International, formally adopted the principles of the International Workingmen's Association of 1864, and advocated a gradualist approach. The meeting, known as the founding of the Second (Socialist) International, declared May Day as an international working-class holiday. Nine subsequent meetings were held, adopting resolutions on various subjects, including opposition to colonialism. Lenin, who attended the early conferences, broke with the organization in 1903, as he preferred a revolutionary approach.

In 1886, a strike at the McCormick Harvester factory in Chicago for an eight-hour day led to a mass rally of strikers in Haymarket Square. After the English-speaking rally concluded, the German-speaking workers remained to hear speeches in their language, whereupon police ordered the crowd to disperse. A bomb was then lobbed toward the police officers, who in turn opened fire. At least ten died, fifty were wounded, eight were convicted of murder. Public sympathy for the Knights of Labor then evaporated.

Workers disappointed with the Knights of Labor had already formed the Federation of Organized Trades and Labor Unions in the United States during 1881 as an umbrella organization for craft unions. After the Haymarket Massacre, the Federation was reorganized in 1886 as the American Federation of Labor (AFL), which was dedicated to worker solidarity. Rather than opposing capitalism, AFL's founder Samuel Gompers (1850–1924) felt that workers should avoid harsh rhetoric and seek negotiations with management to improve the lot of workers; boycotts and strikes should be used only as a last resort. He refused to ally with the Socialist Party and instead sought to support friends and oppose enemies in the Democratic and Republican parties. His first priority was union recognition; the second priority was higher wages and better working conditions. The AFL represented mostly white workers of the upper working class and opposed membership by African Americans as well as immigrants from Asia and Europe. The AFL sought to outlaw "yellow dog" contracts (requiring workers to pledge not to join a union), to limit the courts' power to stop strikes through injunctions, and to obtain exemption from anti-trust laws that were being used to criminalize labor's use of picketing, boycotts, and strikes to support workers' demands. In 1890, Congress responded to one of the AFL's lesser concerns by including in the Trade Act a provision banning the import of goods produced abroad by prison labor.

From 1883 to 1889, Germany became the first country to adopt legislation establishing obligatory accident, disability, health, and old-age insurance programs. The aim was to wean workers away from their support of a more radical socialist agenda. Although only the top segments of the working class were covered, the reforms whetted the appetite of workers around the world to establish what later became known as the welfare state.

Perhaps the boldest assertion of the rights of workers came in 1891 from two different sources. In May, Pope Leo XIII (1810–1903) issued the encyclical *Rerum Novarum* (captioned *Rights and Duties of Capital and Labor*), which asserted, "since wage workers are numbered among the great mass of the needy, the State must include them under its special care and foresight." While firmly opposing socialism, the encyclical endorsed the right of workers to a living wage, safe and sanitary working conditions, humane work duties, reasonable hours of work, holidays and Sundays off from work, rest periods, and the right to join peaceful trade unions; the Pope also opposed child labor and work too strenuous for women.

Later in 1891, the German Social Democratic Party, which was committed to socialism, issued at its convention in Erfurt a document known as the *Erfurt Program*, proclaiming opposition to "not only the exploitation and oppression of wage earners, but every kind of exploitation and oppression, whether directed against a class, a party, a sex, or a race." The Erfurt Program not only demanded rights for workers but also a broad range of civil and political rights.

In 1893, Debs formed the first industrial union, the American Railway Union (ARU), to represent railway workers more forcefully than the AFL. The following year he organized a successful strike against the Great Northern Railway for higher wages. Some three thousand workers at the Pullman Company, which made railroad cars in Chicago, then asked for ARU support to go on strike for higher pay. Debs agreed. However, when the company secured a court injunction to stop the strike, workers refused to go back to work, and some 12,000 Army troops were called to the scene. Thirteen strikers were killed, fifty-seven were wounded, Debs was imprisoned, and the ARU disbanded.

In 1897, the International Association for the Legal Protection of Workers was formed at Basel, Switzerland, followed by a congress in Brussels later that year. In 1901, the International Association for Labor Legislation was established, also at Basel, to provide support for branches established within various countries to alleviate adverse working conditions through laws to protect safety and health on the job, to provide unemployment compensation, and pensions for workers no longer able to work. Within each branch, study groups investigated labor conditions, legislatures were lobbied, and pending bills were critiqued. In 1900, Spain became the first country to adopt a worker's compensation law, and four European countries followed in 1901.

In 1905 and 1906, conferences were held at Bern, where the world's first international labor standards conventions were adopted. Known as the **Bern Conventions**, they banned night work for women and the manufacture of matches with white phosphorus.

In 1905, the International Workers of the World (IWW) was founded in Chicago at a convention of two hundred anarchists, socialists, and radical trade unionists from all over the United States. The most famous IWW leader, Debs, had become a socialist after reading the writings of Karl Marx for the first time while in prison, and he ran as the Socialist Party's candidate for president four times from 1904 to 1920. Whereas Debs provided a democratic socialist agenda, the IWW was accused of wanting to overthrow capitalism. Successful in organizing the largely foreign-born women workers of the woolen industry in Lawrence, Massachusetts, and agricultural, longshore, and lumber workers elsewhere, the IWW became a target for government prosecution and vigilantism after the success of the Communist revolution in Russia in 1917.

In 1918, Lenin organized the Third International, also known as the Communist International (Comintern), which died with the collapse of the Soviet Union in 1991. The Socialist International, nevertheless, currently continues to bring together socialist parties, which now lobby for worker protection within the global political economy rather than the former goal of world socialism.

In 1919, Gompers was a delegate within the American delegation at the Versailles Peace Conference. Together with trade union representatives from other countries, he forged the Constitution of the International Labor Organization (ILO). The rights of workers have increasingly been respected, thanks to the ILO and welfare states within industrial democracies.

HUMANE WARFARE MOVEMENT

Another movement to recognize the universality of human rights principles emerged from the barbarity of warfare. Women took the initiative. During the Crimean War (1853–1856), the Grand Duchess Elena Pavlovna (1784–1803) organized the Sisters of Mercy to help the wounded on the Russian side, and the British nurse Florence Nightingale (1820–1910) served on the British side. On arriving home, Nightingale campaigned about the need to save lives on the battlefield.

In addition to the Treaty of Paris, which ended the Crimean War, the countries involved issued the *Declaration of Paris*, which adopted principles of maritime warfare. Privateering was abolished, neutral ships were to be respected, and blockades were to be honored only if supported with sufficient force.

HISTORIC EVENT 3.6 THE CRIMEAN WAR (1854–1856)

In 1852, Napoléon III persuaded the Ottoman Turks to sign treaties that recognized French sovereignty over the Holy Land, infuriating Russia. In 1853, the Turks attacked the Russian army on the Danube (Moldavia and Wallachia), but the Russians destroyed the Turkish fleet on the Black Sea. Concerned that Russian power was expanding into the Mediterranean, France and Britain issued an ultimatum, demanding that Russia relinquish control over the two Danubian principalities, allow all nations free access to the Danube, give up the right to intervene in the Ottoman Empire on behalf of Orthodox Christians, and revise a treaty dealing with the straits between the Black Sea and the Mediterranean (the Dardanelles). When Russia refused most of the terms, British and French fleets came to Turkey's defense, arriving at the Crimean peninsula to lay siege to the fortress at Sebastopol and penetrating as far as the Don River in Russia to cut off supplies to the fortress. Meanwhile, Britain and France attacked Russia in the Baltic Sea, which one member of the British parliament criticized for causing the deaths of innocent civilians. In 1856, the conflict concluded with the Treaty of Paris, which ended Russia's special privileges along the Danube, demilitarized the Black Sea, and the major powers agreed to respect the territorial integrity of the Ottoman Empire from Turkey to the Middle East. Those wounded during the war were left for dead, without the attention of nurses until Elena Pavlovna (1784–1803) and Florence Nightingale (1820–1910) arrived at the end of 1854. In all, 130,000 persons died in combat, from disease, and because their wounds were left unattended.

In 1859, Jean-Henri Dunant (1828–1910), the Swiss citizen who founded the European counterpart of the Young Men's Christian Association, went to the Battle of Solferino (where Italy secured French troops to detach Italian-speaking territories from Austria) to see for himself whether Florence Nightingale was exaggerating. At the end of the fifteen-hour battle, there were 40,000 wounded soldiers lying on the ground without medical attention, presumably left to die. After spending three days organizing local townspeople to attend to as many of the wounded as they could, he went to Paris to persuade Napoléon III to issue the following order: "Doctors and surgeons attached to the Austrian armies and captured while attending to the wounded shall be unconditionally released; those who have been attending to men wounded at the Battle of Solferino and lying in the hospital at Castiglione shall, at their request, be permitted to return to Austria."

When Dunant returned to Geneva, he published *A Memory of Solferino* (1862), which proposed a society within each nation to aid the wounded and in case of conflict of arms and to help the military medical services. He sent his book to the president of Geneva's Society of Public Welfare, Gustave Moynier (1826–1910), who then invited Dunant to a meeting of the Society. Those present agreed to found the Permanent International Committee of the Relief of the Wounded.

An organizing committee then formed to host the Geneva International Conference in 1863, which was attended by delegates from sixteen countries. The conference created the International Committee of the Red Cross, which in 1864 was first called to action in the Danish-Prussian War. (By 1874, there were twenty-two national Red Cross societies in European countries, and soon the Red Cross movement spread to other continents. In 1876, the Ottoman Turks founded the Red Crescent Society, a counterpart of the Red Cross within Muslim countries.)

Meanwhile, international laws of warfare were codified in 1863 during the Civil War of the United States in a document known as the Lieber Code. In 1864, Dunant, Moynier, and others persuaded the Swiss government to convene a diplomatic conference at Geneva. Attended by representatives from seventeen countries, the meeting adopted the *Convention for the Amelioration of the Condition of the Wounded on the Field of Battle*. Until then, war was generally thought to be beyond the bounds of international law. The Geneva Convention, as the treaty became known, detailed the rights of medical personnel and wounded soldiers. The Geneva Convention was amended in 1906 and 1929, and four more Geneva Conventions were adopted after World War II.

HISTORIC EVENT 3.7 ISSUANCE OF THE LIEBER CODE (1863)

President Abraham Lincoln (1809–1865) asked Columbia University professor Francis Lieber (1800–1872) in 1862 to summarize principles of the international law of warfare. In 1863, Lincoln released *General Orders No. 100, Instructions for the Government of Armies of the United States in the Field*, known as the Lieber Code. The instructions, the first official comprehensive codification of laws of warfare, were welcomed in Europe.

Because Russia stopped the advance of Napoléon Bonaparte in 1812, and Russia played an important role at the Congress of Vienna in 1814–1815, the Russian army was subsequently known as the "army of Europe," ready to restore the balance of power when needed. Accordingly, Russian rulers and foreign ministers considered themselves to be important architects of the peace that lasted without general war during the nineteenth century.

In 1874, Tsar Alexander II (1818–1881), with the concurrence of Leopold II of Belgium (1835–1909), invited fifteen countries to attend a conference at Brussels to examine comprehensive Russian proposals to extend the law of war beyond the 1864 Geneva Convention, which covered only the sick and wounded in time of war. Although the delegates at Brussels subscribed to a detailed statement, *Project of an International Declaration Concerning the Laws and Customs of War*, a proposed agreement in the form of a Convention on the Laws and Customs of War was never ratified. Later in 1874, the Institute of International Law set up a committee to study the Brussels Declaration with a view to codifying the laws of warfare. As a result, a *Manual of the Laws and Customs of War* was drawn up by the Institute in a meeting at Oxford in 1880.

At the end of the nineteenth century, a naval arms race was being waged between Britain and Germany; there appeared to be no end in sight, as larger and larger warships were built. A military showdown was thought to be the inevitable consequence of the arms race. In 1898, Russian Foreign Minister, Count Mikhail Muraviev (1845–1900), circulated a letter regarding the possibility of a disarmament conference to ambassadors in St. Petersburg for transmittal to their home governments. In 1899, when the response was favorable, Queen Wilhelmina of the Netherlands (1880–1962) and Tsar Nicholas II of Russia (1868–1918) invited twenty-six countries to The Hague to attend what was called the First International Peace Conference in order to consider disarmament, revision of existing principles governing naval and land warfare, and a procedure for peaceful settlement of international disputes.

The ten-week conference, also known as the First Hague Conference, had several positive results, though disarmament was not achieved. The most important outcome was the *Convention for the Pacific Settlement of International Disputes*, in which the countries agreed that before launching war they should submit disputes with other countries to the good offices or mediation of one or more friendly powers. A crowning achievement at the conference was the establishment of the Permanent Court of Arbitration (PCA) to sit at The Hague in order to handle disputes on an *ad hoc* basis, that is, not necessarily bound by international legal precedents. Subsequently, arbitration treaties were negotiated by many countries around the world.

The rest of the accomplishments at The Hague dealt with humane warfare. The *Convention With Respect to the Laws and Customs of War on Land* in effect adopted the Brussels Declaration and the Oxford Manual. The *Convention for the Adaptation to Maritime Warfare of the Principles of the Geneva Convention of the 22nd August, 1864* dealt with hospital ships and similar issues. Three separate declarations prohibited launching explosive and projectiles from balloons, using poison gas, and using hollow-point bullets.

In addition, the Final Act of the conference expressed a desire for the 1864 Geneva Convention to be revised in accordance with the achievements at the conference. The countries also agreed to reconvene in order to draw up additional laws of humane warfare. In 1906, the Geneva Convention was then revised at a conference called by the Swiss government.

Meanwhile, the American Peace Society in Boston successfully pressured the Massachusetts legislature in 1903 to urge President Theodore Roosevelt (1858–1919) to establish a regular conference on international affairs. In 1904, the Interparliamentary Union, an organization of legislators from around the world, urged a second Hague conference to complete the unfinished business of the first. Roosevelt then called for the Second International Peace Conference, which was held at The Hague in 1907. Nicholas II formally opened the meeting, and the United States pressed for disarmament, limitations on the use of force to collect foreign debts, and a permanent court that would develop international law through interstate disputes. The International Council of Women presented a petition signed by two million women in twenty countries, urging the conference to bring about world peace.

After four months of work, the Second Hague Conference added more details to the treaties adopted in 1899. The most important innovation was the assertion that war is only legal after previous and explicit warning, such as a declaration of war or ultimatum in which war is an option.

However, the 1907 treaties lacked ratifications from seventeen states which had ratified the treaties signed in 1899, and the prize court never was set up as a result. To the chagrin of the American delegation, the proposal for a world court was turned down. Nevertheless, American delegate Joseph Choate (1832–1917) secured a resolution for a third conference to be held by 1915 or 1916. The outbreak of World War I, the cataclysm that all the countries were trying to prevent, meant that there was no Third Hague Conference.

After World War I, more treaties were adopted to set limits and conditions on the conduct of war. The most notable was the *General Treaty for the Renunciation of War* of 1928, which placed a total ban on the use of force in international affairs; all countries agreed to settle their disputes peacefully as a matter of international law. However, the optimism of the 1920s was trampled upon during the 1930s, as Germany, Italy, and Japan took unilateral actions in defiance of the agreements. World War II then devastated Asia and Europe and brought war to the shores of colonial possessions in the Pacific. Although the United Nations and four Geneva Conventions emerged after the carnage that claimed sixty-two million lives, the barbarity of war continues.

RELIGIOUS FREEDOM MOVEMENT

From the thirteenth century, peace treaties between Christian rulers and the Ottoman Empire had provisions respecting the religious practices of conquered peoples. After the Reformation, some treaties drawn up by Christian monarchs contained guarantees for religious minorities. The Peace of Westphalia of 1648 allowed the ruler in each country designate the state religion; however, an unfortunate result was that religious minorities suffered discrimination.

Many early settlers in the thirteen colonies that later became the United States were freethinkers of various kinds, that is, individuals who refused to belong to the Church of England and were therefore ineligible to serve in the British parliament. To ensure a separation of church and state, the American *Constitution* prohibited any religious test for public office, and the *Bill of Rights'* First Amendment guaranteed freedom of religion.

In the *Final Act of the Congress of Vienna*, guarantees of religious equality were pledged to multiethnic Belgium and Switzerland. The delegates even made specific reference to the plight of Jews in Germany and the rights of the Polish within the states that absorbed pieces of Polish territory (Austria, Prussia, and Russia). Although Britain, France, and Russia intervened on behalf of Greeks under Ottoman rule in 1827, which led to the independence of Greece in 1829, Britain and France only offered verbal protests when Russia brutally cracked down on Polish independence movements in 1831 and 1863.

Most of Ireland consisted of Catholics, who were ineligible from the reign of Henry VIII (1491–1547) to own land or to be elected to the British parliament. In 1778, the *Catholic Relief Act* permitted landownership, which meant that many Catholics in Ireland and elsewhere in the British Isles were eligible to vote but still not to sit in parliament. In 1823, Daniel O'Donnell (1775–1847) formed the Catholic Association to lobby for religious equality; he ran for election in 1838, won the most votes, but was not allowed to take his seat in parliament. As a result of his agitation, in 1829 Britain adopted the *Catholic Emancipation Act*, which allowed the wealthiest Catholics to stand for election, though full voting rights for Catholics as well as less affluent Protestants awaited the Reform Acts of 1832, 1867, and 1884. Further restrictions on Catholics were repealed over the years, but one still remains: No Catholic can become the reigning monarch of the United Kingdom of Great Britain and Northern Ireland.

In the Ottoman Empire, responding to an outcry regarding the persecution and even massacres of non-Muslims, the Sultans issued decrees guaranteeing religious liberty in 1839 and 1856. Nevertheless, mistreatment continued. In 1878, Russia was victorious in the Russo-Turkish War and forced the Ottoman Empire to sign the Treaty of San Stefano, which recognized the independence of three Orthodox Catholic countries (Montenegro, Romania, and Serbia) as well as the autonomy of Bulgaria from Ottoman rule. One feature of the *Final Act of the Congress of Berlin* in 1885 was to require the four new governments to respect the rights of Jewish minorities as a condition of their diplomatic recognition, though enforcement was left to the four states themselves.

Journalist Theodor Herzl (1860–1904) was so shaken by the outpouring of anti-Semitism in France, where he covered the Dreyfus treason trial in 1894, as well as in his native Austria in 1895, that he wrote *A Jewish State* (1896). He thereby launched the Zionist movement, that is, a proposal for an independent Jewish state. In 1897, the first Jewish Congress was convened in Basel. Later, Chaim Weizmann (1874–1952) spearheaded the movement. Other Jewish leaders preferred a more generic campaign to recognize minority rights. In 1898, the International League of Human Rights formed in response to the Dreyfus affair to bring world attention to the cause of human rights; among the supporters was Albert Einstein (1879–1955).

COURT CASE 3.2 THE DREYFUS TRIALS (1894 AND 1899)

In 1894, Captain Alfred Dreyfus (1859–1935) was accused of passing military secrets to Germany and convicted of treason. The evidence against him was a handwritten note found in a wastebasket of a Germany military attaché by a cleaning woman who worked for French intelligence. The right-wing anti-Jewish press publicized his alleged role before the prosecutor's office determined that the handwriting was not that of Dreyfus. The French High Command, however, went ahead with the prosecution rather than risk looking incompetent, a revelation that might have caused senior military officers to be fired and the government to be voted out of office. In fact, the note was revealed to have been planted by counterintelligence officer Major Ferdinand Esterhazy (1847–1923) to confuse the Germans. Because the French were afraid of admitting the ruse, Esterhazy was acquitted of charges. In 1899, potentially exonerating evidence surfaced, thanks to another intelligence officer, and Dreyfus was retried. However, he was again convicted. In 1904, French President Émile Loubet (1838–1929) pardoned him, and the court reversed his second conviction. Right-wing and left-wing politicians held strong opinions. Novelist Émile Zola (1840–1902) authored a strong "open letter" in the left-wing press, accusing the government of anti-Semitism and of violating Dreyfus's right to a fair trial. Zola, in turn, was convicted of libel and sought exile in England rather than serving time in prison for his statement.

Atrocities committed by the Ottomans against Armenian Christians in 1894–1896 and especially in 1915 resulted in international disfavor toward the Ottomans, who were allied with the defeated Axis Powers (Austria-Hungary and Germany) in World War I. After the Ottomans were defeated by an invasion of British troops in 1917, Weizmann's efforts bore fruit when Britain issued the *Balfour Declaration*, which invited Jews to resettle in British-controlled Palestine. The idea that states should consist of single nations rather than having multinational populations was vigorously espoused by Woodrow Wilson (1856–1924), who made the concept a centerpiece of his *Fourteen Points* in 1918, a declaration containing basic principles that shaped the Treaty of Versailles, which ended the war with Germany.

HISTORIC EVENT 3.8 THE PARIS PEACE CONFERENCE (1919–1920)

The Treaty of Versailles, which formally ended the war with Germany, was one of several treaties drawn up from 1919–1920, sometimes known collectively as the

continued

Peace of Paris, which redrew the maps of Europe and the Middle East after World War I. Separate treaties were also drawn up for Austria (Treaty of Saint-Germain, 1919), Bulgaria (Treaty of Neuilly, 1919), Hungary (Treaty of Trianon, 1920), and the Ottoman Empire (Treaty of Sèvres, 1920). The Treaty of Saint-Germain established the new states of Czechoslovakia, Romania, and Yugoslavia (then known as the Kingdom of Croats, Serbs, and Slovenes). A seventh treaty, the Treaty of Lausanne of 1923, revised the Treaty of Sèvres. One aim in carving the various "successor states" out of the former Austro-Hungarian empire was to provide a buffer of independent states, eager to guard their sovereignty, which would thereby deter Germany from territorial expansion. Except for Armenia and the Hejaz (now part of Saudi Arabia), most states in the Middle East that were dismembered from Turkey became League of Nations Mandates.

Enforcement of rights under the treaties negotiated at Paris and elsewhere, however, focused on ethnicity more than religion. Accordingly, the League of Nations took no action when Iraqis massacred Syrians in 1933. The principle of freedom of religion was more firmly accepted after horrific evidence about the Nazi slaughter of Jews at deathcamps came to light immediately after World War II. Even so, religious persecution continues in the world today.

DISCUSSION TOPIC 3.2 WHICH HUMAN RIGHTS MOVEMENTS HAVE BEEN MOST SUCCESSFUL?

Why did the nineteenth century spawn so many human rights movements? Which have been more successful – and why? Which movements led most directly to the formation of the League of Nations?

INTERNATIONAL ORGANIZATION MOVEMENT

The final historical movement on behalf of human rights is the effort to establish an intergovernmental organization where diplomats can be in constant touch to prevent war. Philosophers from Pierre Dubois (1250–1312) to Immanuel Kant (1724–1804) had long urged the establishment of such a body.

During the nineteenth century, the Concert of Europe was formed at the Congress of Vienna as a consultative body so that the major powers (Austria, Britain, Prussia, Russia, and later France) could meet in case a nationalist movement threatened to undo the balance of power, and the early result was intervention in relatively minor uprisings. As the century progressed, England and France became more democratic and less interested in suppressing the will of the people. A gathering of seven states (adding Italy and the Ottoman Turks) occurred in the Congress of Berlin of 1878–1885, again demonstrating the feasibility of involving major powers to manage European affairs on a continuing basis. In 1874, the first intergovernmental organization of global scope was formed; known as the Universal Postal Union (UPU), the aim was to standardize mail traffic around the world. UPU proved that intergovernmental cooperation among disparate countries was feasible.

Proposals for an organization of all the independent governments of the world were put forward during World War I from several quarters. The Fourteenth Point of Woodrow Wilson was as follows: "A general association of nations must be formed under specific covenants for the purpose of affording mutual guarantees of political independence and territorial integrity to great and small states alike." Pressure from nongovernmental organizations to establish an intergovernmental body resulted in the formation of the League of Nations, which institutionalized cooperation among sovereign states.

Although the leaders of some countries at the Versailles Conference were skeptical of Wilson's proposal, his arguments prevailed, and the League was born, with a headquarters in Geneva, Switzerland, a country that had been neutral throughout the war and had a long peace-loving tradition. Two other intergovernmental organizations relevant to human rights were also formed, namely, the International Labor Organization (ILO) and the Permanent Court of International Justice (PCIJ); the ILO was ratified in 1920, PCIJ in 1921. The United States never joined the League of Nations because Wilson would not allow the Senate to attach reservations to the treaty, though Washington joined both the ILO and the PCIJ. Senators feared that membership in the League might result in sending American troops abroad again, but ILO and PCIJ were viewed as consistent with the American tradition of advancing international law.

The *Covenant of the League of Nations*, as adopted in Article I of the Treaty of Versailles, committed members to "promote international co-operation and to achieve international peace and security," according to the preamble, which went on to commit the governments "not to resort to war" and to "the maintenance of justice." The words "human rights" do not appear. Nevertheless, within the provisions of the covenant, the following principles were stated or implied:

- women may work for the League;
- the right of self-determination;
- "freedom of conscience and religion, subject only to the maintenance of public order and morals;"
- "the prohibition of abuses such as the slave trade, the arms traffic and the liquor traffic;"
- "fair and humane conditions of labor for men, women, and children;"
- supervision of treaties to suppress "traffic in women and children, and the traffic in opium and other dangerous drugs;"
- "improvement of health, the prevention of disease and the mitigation of suffering."

However, the framers of the Treaty of Versailles rejected a pledge, sponsored by Japan, for racial equality, primarily because Americans and Europeans wanted to keep their colonial possessions.

The Covenant set up an Assembly, composed of all member states, and a Council, a smaller body consisting of the Principal Allied and Associated Powers (Britain, France, Italy, Japan, United States) plus four countries first designated in the text and subsequently to be elected by the Council. Decisions of both bodies required unanimity, thereby limiting effectiveness. The United States, which did not join the League, never sat on the Council.

The *Constitution of the International Labor Organization* was drafted by the Versailles peace conference's Labor Commission, chaired by Samuel Gompers. Article 13 of the Versailles Treaty contains the ILO's constitution, which begins with the following statement:

> Whereas the League of Nations has for its object the establishment of universal peace, . . . such a peace can be established only if it is based upon social justice [because] such injustice, hardship, and privation to large numbers of people . . . produce unrest so great that the peace and harmony of the world are imperiled . . .

ILO's constitution, which was adopted as an independent treaty, then set the following agenda regarding "humane conditions of labor" for the organization:

- "regulation of the hours of work, including the establishment of a maximum working day and week;"
- "regulation of the labor supply;"
- "prevention of unemployment;"
- "provision of an adequate living wage;"
- "protection of the worker against sickness, disease and injury arising out of his employment;"
- protection of children and women;
- "provision for old age and injury;"
- protection of migrant workers;
- "recognition of the principle of freedom of association" and
- "organization of vocational and technical education and other measures . . ."

The ILO, headquartered in Geneva, was far more committed to improving rights for individuals than was the League. The ILO's founding document has been the basis for more than 170 international agreements over the years, such as the Convention Concerning Forced or Compulsory Labor of 1932. In 1946, the ILO became a Specialized Agency of the United Nations after amending its constitution in 1944 to reflect the new status.

Article 14 of the Covenant asked the League to draw up a separate agreement for a world court. In 1920, the Council asked ten eminent jurists to draft such an agreement. Their proposed *Statute of the Permanent Court of International Justice*, in turn, was submitted to and approved by the Assembly later that year. The only specific human rights provision was for five PCIJ judges to convene in cases of labor rights unless a party to the dispute wanted a hearing by the entire fifteen-member court. Subsequently, decisions were rendered in sixty-six cases, many of which were about nationality issues. The PCIJ was superseded in 1946 by the International Court of Justice within the United Nations system.

Perhaps the most important PCIJ judgment was an Advisory Opinion in the *Danzig Railway Officials* or *Jurisdiction of the Courts of Danzig* case. For the first time, international law was declared by a world court to apply not just to governments but also to individuals, provided of course that states wrote human rights provisions about individuals into treaties. Based on the ruling in the Danzig case, the PCIJ ruled in the *Rights of Minorities in Upper Silesia* case of 1928 that parents had a right to determine the language of instruction for their children in government-operated schools.

COURT CASE 3.3 THE DANZIG RAILWAY OFFICIALS CASE (1928)

The Convention of Paris, a 1920 treaty between Poland and the Free City of Danzig, contained provisions authorizing the regulation of conditions of employment of former employees of the Danzig railways, some of whom had been kept on the job by the successor agency, the Polish Railways Administration. In 1921, an implementing agreement was adopted by both parties. In 1925, some former Danzig employees sought to sue Polish authorities in a Danzig court, based on the agreement, to receive compensation for unpaid pensions and salaries. The Polish government, however, refused to accept the jurisdiction of Danzig courts, and the League's High Commissioner for Danzig agreed in 1927 that the employees had no standing to sue in Danzig courts. Accordingly, the League of Nations Council asked the Permanent Court of International Justice for an Advisory Opinion on the matter. In 1928, the court held that the treaty contained "rules creating individual rights . . . [that are] enforceable by the national courts," consistent with the doctrine of *direct effect*, which had been recognized by the Central American Court of Justice in *Diaz v. Guatemala* (1909). Instead of making a judgment about the claims, the court's Advisory Opinion informed the claimants that they could present their case before a Danzig court, contrary to the ruling of the High Commissioner and over the objections of the Polish government, which in turn was directed to accept whatever the court might rule. The full name of the case is the *Jurisdiction of the Courts of Danzig (Pecuniary Claims of Danzig Railway Officials Who Have Passed into the Polish Service, Against the Polish Railways Administration)*.

Besides the ILO and PCIJ, the League of Nations made progress regarding human rights in several additional ways: (1) implementing the basic pledges in the seven peace treaties of the Peace of Paris after World War I, (2) setting up a Health Organization, (3) establishing an Organization to assist refugees and stateless persons, and (4) sponsoring new international agreements. Previous international movements (for democracy, the abolition of slavery, women's rights, workers' rights, humane warfare, minority rights) became incorporated into the institutional framework of the League of Nations.

The seven treaties of the Paris peace conference addressed problems resulting from arbitrary boundaries drawn around the new states, such that religious and ethno-linguistic minorities would have been left at the mercy of the dominant nationality group in each country. In part due to pressure from Jewish advocates of minority protections at Versailles, the treaties contained six innovations:

- One provision authorized **mixed arbitral tribunals** to settle property claims. However, when properties of minorities were adversely affected by later agrarian reforms, the tribunals ruled that they had no jurisdiction because the reforms were domestic laws outside the terms of the peace treaties. Subsequently, the German-Polish Convention of 1922 set up a three-member Arbitral Tribunal and a five-member Upper Silesian Mixed Commission consisting of equal membership of Germany and Poland; the remaining member was chosen by the League Council.

- The new states were required to have **minority treaties** to protect minority populations. The aim was to assure that ethnic identities would be protected so that minorities would be loyal members of the new states. The various minority treaties, such as the Treaty Between the Allied and Associated Powers and the Kingdom of the Serbs, Croats and Slovenes on the Protection of Minorities of 1919, left enforcement to the League of Nations Council, which set up a Minorities Question Section in the League Secretariat to hear petitions. Few petitions ever resulted in corrective action because their resolution depended on cooperation with the very states that were accused of misconduct.

- **Plebiscites**, once used by Napoléon Bonaparte to legitimize French rule over conquered territories, were authorized to determine by an election under which government among adjacent governments a minority population preferred to live. In 1921, for example, a plebiscite was held in Upper Silesia to determine whether residents wanted to be ruled by Germany or Poland.

- An **exchange of population** was specified in the Convention Concerning the Exchange of Greek and Turkish Populations of 1923. Orthodox Christians in Anatolia were then exchanged for Muslims in Greece. However, following that example, the Soviet Union forcibly resettled millions of Muslims in Central Asia to Russian provinces and vice versa during World War II. The practice has rarely been used ever since.

- The League also created the **Permanent Mandates Commission**, since the peace settlement transferred sixteen colonial possessions of the defeated countries to six of the victorious countries with the stipulation that the rights of the subject populations must be protected. In general, the mandate powers agreed to consider the "well-being and development of such peoples [to] form a sacred trust of civilization . . . until such time as they are able to stand alone." There were three classes of mandates. "A" mandates were close to independence. "B" mandates were to be prepared for eventual independence. "C" mandates were considered incapable of self-government for an extended period of time. Mandate countries were to ensure freedom of conscience and religion and an end to the slave trade. Palestine, one of the "A" Mandates, was assigned to Britain in 1922. The mandate countries, in turn, reported to the Mandate Commission, but no provision was made to monitor progress toward independence of the mandated territories. In addition, the commission directly administered two territories – Saarland (until 1935, when the residents in a plebiscite agreed to return to German sovereignty),[5] and Danzig (until the army of Nazi Germany seized control in 1939). Except for South Africa's mandate over South West Africa (Namibia), all the League mandates were either granted independence after World War II or transferred into the UN trusteeship system.[6]

• A **petition system** was established. Members of minority groups could contact the mixed arbitral tribunals or the League with complaints about mistreatment, as did ethnic Germans living in Poland in the Upper Silesia case mentioned above. Authorized to assess violators in order to compensate victims of mistreatment, the tribunals and the League accepted the petitions as informational only and pursued the complaints on behalf of the affected class, that is, beyond the immediate problems of the individuals lodging the complaints.

The redrawing of the European map left German minorities in several countries. Adolf Hitler (1889–1945) exploited the self-determination principle to justify the unilateral reoccupation of the Rhineland in 1936,[7] the annexation of Austria in 1936, the occupation of the Sudetenland in Czechoslovakia in 1938, and the annexation of Danzig in 1939. After securing approval at the Munich Conference of 1938 to take possession of Sudetenland, Nazi troops marched in to take control of all Czechoslovakia without a shot being fired. At Munich, Britain and France had drawn a line for Hitler's irredentism at the Polish border. When Germany attacked Poland in 1939, therefore, World War II had begun.

The League advanced international cooperation in other ways. In 1907, the International Office of Public Health began at Rome to promote the implementation of treaties dealing with sanitation, though later the body undertook studies of epidemics. The League of Nations Health Organization, established in 1920 at Geneva, was charged with the task of combating disease around the globe; primary foci were leprosy, malaria, and typhus. Both are forerunners of the current World Health Organization, a Specialized Agency of the United Nations.

The League of Nations also set up a Commission for Refugees in 1921, headed by Fridtjof Nansen (1861–1930). After he died, the Commission was renamed in 1931 as the Nansen International Office for Refugees and supplemented from 1933–1938 by the High Commission for Refugees Coming from Germany. The first major task was to provide financial, legal, and material assistance to 400,000 prisoners of war and refugees from Russia, but the scope expanded in 1922 to Armenian refugees from Turkey, refugees from Nazi Germany after 1933, Saar refugees in 1935, Austrian refugees in 1938, and Sudetenland refugees in 1938. Especially notable accomplishments were (1) the establishment of an international passport for stateless refugees, (2) adoption of the Refugee Convention of 1933, (3) settlement of Saar refugees in Paraguay, (4) construction of villages to house upwards of 40,000 Armenian refugees in Syria and Lebanon, and (5) the resettlement of another 10,000 refugees in Soviet Armenia. In 1938, the League located in London an office under the name High Commissioner for Refugees Under the Protection of the League, but the number of refugees was overwhelming, especially after World War II began.

The League also set up a Temporary Slavery Commission in 1922, at first to draft a treaty on the subject. After the Slavery Convention was adopted in 1926, the body continued as the Slavery Commission to implement the convention's goal of ending slavery, human trafficking in prostitutes ("white slavery"), and the drug trade. The Commission was charged with the responsibility of compiling records on all three issues. As a result, some 200,000 slaves were emancipated in Sierra Leone during 1927, raids in Africa stopped slave traders, and the deathrate of Tanganyikan workers was lowered from about 50 percent to 4 percent.

In addition, the League sponsored several treaties. The most famous is the *General Act for the Pacific Settlement of International Disputes* (1924), known as the Geneva Protocol, which mandated the compulsory arbitration of international disputes, thus enabling an aggressor to be identified as a country refusing to do so. Other treaties on the law of war are discussed in Chapter 7.

Although the 1924 Geneva Protocol and the 1925 Locarno agreements were designed to prevent the outbreak of a new world war, the United States was not involved. Accordingly, Secretary of State Frank Kellogg (1856–1937) contacted Foreign Minister Aristide Briand (1862–1932), urging a wider agreement. What resulted is the *General Treaty for the Renunciation of War*, known popularly as the Pact of Paris or as the Kellogg–Briand Pact of 1928. The treaty renounced war as an instrument of national policy and pledged signatories to use only peaceful means for settling disputes except in case of self-defense against states fulfilling responsibilities under the league.

HISTORIC EVENT 3.9 THE LOCARNO PEACE PACT (1925)

Outside the League, five separate peace agreements, known as the *Locarno Peace Pact* of 1925, provided firmer guarantees than the 1924 Geneva Protocol, since Germany signed voluntarily and thus was reinvited into the family of nations on an equal basis. Most important was a Treaty of Mutual Guarantee that guaranteed existing frontiers between Belgium, France, and Germany, as well as the demilitarization of the Rhineland. The countries also agreed not to declare war on one another unless the terms of the agreement were flagrantly violated or unless the League authorized action against an aggressor. In addition, there were four arbitration treaties between Germany on the one hand and, on the other hand, Belgium, Czechoslovakia, France, and Poland, all of whom pledged to settle disputes peacefully. If one of the countries failed to observe the terms of the pact, the others were pledged to help the aggrieved country. The idea for the pact came from German Prime Minister Gustav Stresemann (1878–1929), who persuaded French Foreign Minister Aristide Briand (1862–1932).

At the same time, the covenant advanced a new alternative to war – **economic sanctions**. Although an oil embargo was discussed against Japan for its military occupation of Manchuria in 1931 and against Italy for its invasion of Abyssinia (Ethiopia) in 1935, support was insufficient. However, the embargo on oil exports to Japan by the United States (outside the League) on August 1, 1941, provided Tokyo with a pretext for the bombing of Pearl Harbor on December 7 to achieve a quick victory in the Pacific.

CONCLUSION

The American and French revolutions opened the eyes of the people about their rights. The industrial revolution so enlarged the number of city dwellers and exploited workers that they became politically conscious. But consciousness raising would have been impossible without the broadening of educational opportunities to provide a qualified workforce for the industrial revolution. As literacy increased, the idea spread that everyone is entitled to be treated equally, thereby whetting the appetite of the people for a better life. Nevertheless, struggles for human rights lagged behind human suffering, awaiting leaders to take bold steps.

The various social movements that accelerated progress in human rights provide an important lesson, namely, that progress in human rights has required a struggle by courageous leaders with the support of mass-based organizations. Each movement has left a legacy in the form of nongovernmental organizations that are active today. With the establishment of permanent intergovernmental organizations, institutional watchdogs attended to some immediate problems while documenting the need for even more human rights protections.

While the attention of the League was directed to war prevention and the fulfillment of economic and social rights, the League of Nations failed in its main mission to prevent World War II. But that very failure planted seeds for a more concerted effort to attend to human rights problems, as discussed in the following chapter.

CHAPTER 4

The contemporary basis for human rights

Whereas previous eras developed international human rights incrementally, albeit in fits and starts, a new urgency emerged after World War II. Human rights were so massively violated during the war, notably by the mistreatment of civilians, that stern measures after the war seemed imperative. Otherwise, to paraphrase Supreme Court Justice Robert Jackson (1892–1954) in his opening statement at the Nuremberg War Crimes Trials, civilization itself would not survive.

The first postwar task was to set up a new structure of international institutions that might stop future international calamities. In time, more efforts were required to keep human rights issues at center stage. The current chapter focuses on how various actions taken by prominent individuals resulted in new agreements (Table 4.1), new concepts, and new institutions that have served to establish human rights concerns as fundamental to contemporary international relations. Most of the agreements were treaties that came into force when ratified by a substantial number of states; the rest were declarations of policy commitments.

In addition to the progress in forging the United Nations, the following developments have been responsible for advancing the cause of human rights since the end of World War II despite the Cold War obsession with *realpolitik*: war crimes trials, Africa's quest to end colonialism and racist regimes, people power revolutions, President Jimmy Carter's initiatives, activist nongovernmental organizations, and the development of international law.

TABLE 4.1 **SOME BASIC DOCUMENTS OF CONTEMPORARY INTERNATIONAL HUMAN RIGHTS**

Adopted	Name of instrument	In force
1941	Atlantic Charter	
1942	Resolution on German War Crimes by Representatives of Nine Occupied Countries	
1943	Declaration Concerning Atrocities	
1945	Potsdam Declaration	
1945	Charter of the United Nations	1945
1945	Agreement for the Prosecution and Punishment of the Major War Criminals of the European Axis	1945
1945	Charter of the International Military Tribunal	1945
1948	Universal Declaration of Human Rights	
1948	American Declaration of the Rights and Duties of Man	
1948	International Convention on the Prevention and Punishment of the Crime of Genocide	1951
1949	Geneva Conventions	1950
1950	European Convention for the Protection of Human Rights and Fundamental Freedoms	1953
1954	*Brown et al. v Board of Education of Topeka et al.*	1954
1960	Declaration on the Granting of Independence to Colonial Countries and Peoples	
1961	European Social Charter	1965
1967	International Covenant on Civil and Political Rights	1976
1967	International Covenant on Economic, Social, and Cultural Rights	1976
1969	Vienna Convention on the Law of Treaties	1980
1975	Final Act of the Helsinki Conference	
1981	African Charter on Human and Peoples' Rights	1981
1990	Charter of Paris for a New Europe	

THE UNITED NATIONS SYSTEM

When World War II broke out, the verdict on the effectiveness of the League of Nations was in: the League had failed. A new organization was needed to prevent war. In 1941, one of the eight points in the *Atlantic Charter* adopted by Winston Churchill (1874–1965) and Franklin Roosevelt (1882–1945) was to establish a new association of nations. One month later, representatives of ten additional countries agreed to the provisions. Two of the other provisions were to prohibit the use of force in international relations except in self-defense or when authorized by that new association and to respect the "inherent dignity" and "equal and inalienable rights" of all peoples.

In 1942, accordingly, diplomats from twenty-six countries met in Washington to adopt the *Declaration by United Nations*, a pledge that they would together defeat Germany, Italy, and Japan and would not make a separate peace. Although no postwar organization was identified, the name "United Nations" thereby gained currency.

At the Moscow Conference in 1943, the foreign ministers of Britain, China, the Soviet Union, and the United States proposed a "general international organization, based on the principle of the sovereign equality of all peace-loving states . . ." Later in 1943, Churchill, Roosevelt, and Josef Stalin (1878–1953) endorsed the idea at the Tehran Conference.

Meanwhile, several organizations were founded during 1943–1944 to be part of the proposed United Nations system – the Food and Agricultural Organization (FAO), the United Nations Relief and Rehabilitation Administration (UNRRA), the United Nations Educational, Scientific, and Cultural Organization (UNESCO). In 1944, the International Monetary Fund (IMF) and the International Bank for Reconstruction and Development (IBRD), the latter known as the World Bank, was established in a conference at Bretton Woods, New Hampshire. Next, American, Chinese, British, and Soviet delegates met at Dumbarton Oaks in Washington in August and September 1944 to draft a charter for the new United Nations organization.

The *Charter of the United Nations*, as adopted in 1945, was the first treaty of the postwar era to put human rights in the forefront. As adopted two months later, the Preamble of the Charter contains the following words:

> We the peoples of the United Nations, determined to save succeeding generations from the scourge of war; which twice in our lifetime has brought untold sorrow to mankind, and
>
> to reaffirm faith in fundamental human rights, in the dignity and worth of the human person, in the equal rights of men and women of nations large and small, and
>
> to establish conditions under which justice and respect for the obligations arising from treaties and other sources of international law can be maintained, and to promote social progress and better standards of life in larger freedom . . .

HISTORIC EVENT 4.1 THE UNITED NATIONS CONFERENCE ON INTERNATIONAL ORGANIZATION (1945)

After Allied troops crossed the English Channel to begin the drive to defeat Nazi Germany, plans were afoot to set up the United Nations. Invitations were issued to all the Allied powers to attend a meeting in April 1945 at San Francisco to work on a draft for an organization that had been conceived at Dumbarton Oaks a half year earlier. The Soviet Union insisted that seats be reserved for Byelorussia and the Ukraine but opposed Argentina, which was accused of being an ally of the Axis powers (Germany, Italy, and Japan), whereas Latin American countries insisted on Argentine participation. The United States then backed all three countries as a compromise. Although invited, the composition of the delegation from Poland, which had an unofficial government-in-exile in London, was disputed among the Allied governments, so the Polish seat was left vacant. Representatives of several nongovernmental organizations also assisted. With the addition of more countries than the Dumbarton Oaks four, several changes were made in the draft: (1) a recognition of regional organizations, (2) the creation of the Economic and Social Council and the Trusteeship Council, both with rotating memberships, (3) human rights, economic and technological issues were given more emphasis, (4) the World Court was to be set up independently, (5) a veto on the Security Council was limited to the five permanent members on substantive (nonprocedural) matters, (6) otherwise, the Security Council could issue binding decisions. In June, the draft was finalized as the Charter of the United Nations and signed by 50 of the 51 original member countries; Poland signed later. Ratification awaited approval of the five "founding members," namely, Britain, China, France, the United States, and the Soviet Union, as well as a majority of the other signatures. On October 24, 1945, the necessary number of ratifications had been received in London, the temporary seat of the UN. October 24 thenceforth has been celebrated as United Nations Day.

Hence, the first priority of the United Nations Charter is **peace,** and the second priority is **human rights**, though of course the concern for peace is articulated in terms of human rights.

Article 1 of the Charter lists one of the purposes as "promoting and encouraging" respect for human rights "without distinction as to race, sex, language, or religion." In Article 62, the newly created Economic and Social Council is urged to make recommendations "for the purpose of promoting respect and observance of human rights and fundamental freedoms for all."

However, Article 2 prohibits the United Nations from intervening "in matters which are essentially within the domestic jurisdiction" of any state. Thus, the goal of promoting human rights is limited by the Westphalian proscription on intervening in sovereign states. The UN, in other words, began as the most important contemporary institution for advancing international human rights, but the founders knew that the organization had to move cautiously. Although the League required a unanimous vote before authorizing action, the UN gave a veto only to the five major powers (Britain, China, France, the Soviet Union, and the United States) within the Security Council. The Charter states that obligations identified therein are to supersede all other treaty obligations.

The new UN had an implicit division of labor: the UN General Assembly and Security Council would handle civil and political rights issues; FAO, IBRD, IMF, UNRRA, and UNESCO would deal with economic and social problems. The adoption of a major declaration on human rights, meanwhile, was greatly influenced by a redefinition of the scope of human rights in regard to war crimes.

DISCUSSION TOPIC 4.1   IS THE UNITED NATIONS CHARTER CONTRADICTORY ABOUT HUMAN RIGHTS?

When the UN Charter was drafted in 1945, delegates to the San Francisco Peace Conference knew about the Nazi slaughter of millions of innocent civilians. The world also knew that the Soviet Union had also done so during the 1930s. Was there a contradiction by placing human rights in Article I and then barring the world community from intervening in states to stop human rights violations?

WAR CRIMES TRIALS

German and Japanese aggression during World War II clearly was contrary to international law. In 1942, leaders of governments in exile in London adopted a *Resolution on German War Crimes by Representatives of Nine Occupied Countries*, calling for the perpetrators of "imprisonments, mass expulsions, the execution of hostages and massacres" to be brought to justice after the war. In 1943, the *Declaration Concerning Atrocities* at the Moscow Conference by Churchill, Roosevelt, and Stalin called for postwar trials of major Nazi war criminals for their "atrocities, massacres and cold-blooded mass executions." The *Potsdam Declaration* of 1945 reiterated the desire to try war criminals.

Information about the mass deportations and slaughter of millions of persons was known to many leaders of Allied countries, but perhaps no person had greater knowledge than Raphael Lemkin (1900–1959), a Polish lawyer who in 1944 coined the word **genocide** to refer to what Nazi Germany was doing during the war in bringing a "Final Solution" to the "Jewish problem." In any case, after the war there was a need to address the brutal treatment in the concentration camps and elsewhere that had resulted in an extermination of six million Jewish people as well as millions of others deemed expendable by Nazis who believed Germans to constitute the "master race."

Not only were brutal crimes committed in the conduct of war but also atrocities against civilians that went beyond anything previously imagined. Previously, the international community had allowed sovereign states to treat their own people however they wished, but the magnitude of slaughter could not be ignored. The international community was now beginning to hold states accountable for actions inside their borders.

The Allied Powers considered various options in dealing with Nazi German officials who had violated the laws of warfare. Winston Churchill (1874–1965) favored summary execution, Josef Stalin (1878–1953) was keen on a show trial, but Franklin Roosevelt (1882–1945) demurred. In 1945, on becoming president, Harry Truman (1884–1972) strongly supported a proposal from Secretary of War Henry Stimson (1867–1950) to have a formal trial of Nazi officials in the best tradition of Anglo-European justice, and he secured agreement from Britain and the Soviet Union.

When Allied forces liberated the various concentration camps to see the horrific condition of the survivors, they agreed that major war criminals must be prosecuted. However, Allied leaders recalled that Kaiser Wilhelm (1859–1941) of Germany was to have been prosecuted for culpability in launching World War I, according to the Treaty of Versailles, yet he fled to the Netherlands, which refused to surrender him for trial. In part to avoid a similar situation, postwar Germany was divided into four occupied zones – one each governed by the victorious Allied powers (Britain, France, the Soviet Union, and the United States). Suspected war criminals were then brought under custody for trial.

HISTORIC EVENT 4.2 THE HOLOCAUST (1938–1945)

Adolf Hitler (1889–1945) became Chancellor of Germany in 1933. Soon, political dissidents and racial minorities, especially Jews, were rounded up and sent to concentration camps. In 1938, Hitler authorized a program known as *Aktion T-4* to liquidate nearly 200,000 persons with mental and physical disabilities, first children and later adults, for being biologically "unfit" as the first step in the Nazi program of "racial hygiene." The program was resisted by bureaucrats and members of the clergy, however, and was cancelled in 1941, but the precedent of exterminating undesirables had been established. When World War II started, Jews were first confined in ghettoes, and *Einsatzgruppen* (intervention forces) death squads were ordered to slaughter Poles, Communists, and Jews in the Soviet Union, resulting in about 1.6 million deaths. After extermination camps were constructed and opened at the end of 1941, some 3 million Jews and other "undesirables" were sent to the camps to be executed by Nazi officials and their collaborators in other countries. In 1945, the Nazis organized death marches, in which another 100,000 Jews died. In all, the death toll included at least 6 million Jews and 5 million non-Jews. The Holocaust is usually identified with the extermination of Jews.

In 1945, thirty articles were drawn up in the *Agreement for the Prosecution and Punishment of the Major War Criminals of the European Axis* and the *Charter of the International Military Tribunal* for trials at Nuremberg, the town in Germany where Adolf Hitler held many well-publicized rallies. The major offenses included the customary *war crimes*, based on the Geneva and Hague conventions, and two new crimes – *crimes against humanity* and *crimes against peace*. Although the words "genocide" and "holocaust" did not gain currency until later,[1] the postwar war crimes trials established significant precedents by defining the two new types of international crimes, placing individuals on trial with considerable publicity, and having international panels of jurists pass sentences that were regarded as fair and measured.

On December 28, 1945, the Allied Control Council issued Control Law 10, which authorized the occupying powers to prosecute "war criminals and similar offenders." Some 91,000 Germans accused of war crimes were then tried in German courts under the framework of the postwar military occupation of Germany; some 8,000 were convicted and received punishment. But the actions of top Nazi officials had been authorized by German law, so they could not be tried in German courts. A special international tribunal was needed instead. Accordingly, there were eleven special trials of major war criminals (Table 4.2).

The eleventh and most famous *Nuremberg War Crimes Trial* prosecution, the Ministries Case, involved Reich Ministers and other Nazi Party leaders, who of course did not commit specific acts on the battlefield. Instead, they were charged primarily with conspiracy to wage aggressive war in defiance of international treaties. As prosecutor, Robert Jackson presented five legal grounds for their indictments:[2]

- The Hague Conventions of 1899 and 1907
- Treaty of Versailles of 1919 (for violating the independence of Austria, Danzig, and Czechoslovakia as well as Germany's rearmament)
- Locarno Peace Pact of 1925 (wherein Germany had pledged to respect the territorial *status quo* of Belgium, France, Great Britain, and Italy)
- General Treaty for the Renunciation of War (the Kellogg–Briand Pact) of 1928
- United Nations Charter of 1945.

TABLE 4.2   **NUREMBERG WAR CRIMES TRIALS, 1946-1949**

Case name	Defendants	Charges	Verdict
Doctors case	23 Nazi physicians	Inhuman experiments	16 guilty, 7 acquitted
Einsatzgruppen case	24 in mobile killing units	Mistreatment of POWs and civilians; property destruction	24 guilty
Farben case	24 industrialists	Plunder and spoliation of private property	13 guilty, 11 acquitted
Flick case	6 industrialists	Slave labor; POW labor; confiscation of Jewish property	3 guilty, 3 acquitted
Hostage case	12 army officers	War crimes	8 guilty, 2 acquitted, 2 suicides
Judges case	16 judges	Crimes against humanity, war crimes	10 guilty, 4 acquitted, 1 died, 1 mistrial
Krupp case	12 industrialists	Slave labor and war crimes	11 guilty, 1 acquitted
Milch case	Field Marshall Erhard Milch	Murder; cruel treatment of POWs; inhuman experiments	guilty
Ministries case	21 Nazi leaders	Crimes against humanity and peace, war crimes	19 guilty, 2 acquitted
Pohl case	18 members of the Economic and Administrative Office	War crimes against POWs	15 guilty, 3 acquitted
Resettlement case	14 officials	Crimes against humanity	13 guilty 1 acquitted

When the Ministries Case concluded, twelve were sentenced to be executed (though one committed suicide), three were given life sentences, four were sentenced to fixed terms (from ten to twenty years), and two were acquitted. German courts, based on German law, later convicted the two who were acquitted. Judges in the Ministries Case consisted of a panel of jurists from the four occupying powers, thus constituting the first international criminal tribunal in world history. American officials carried out proceedings in the other ten cases. In addition, less prominent war criminals were tried by Britain, Canada, France, Norway, Poland, and the United States in various venues.

Japanese aggression was responsible for perhaps as many deaths as the Nazis, including twenty-three million Chinese, and the survival rate of prisoners of war (POWs) confined by the Japanese was considerably lower than in the German POW camps. In 1943, Britain, China, and the United States, pledged to "stop and punish Japanese aggression" during a conference in Cairo. One article of the *Potsdam Declaration* of 1945, which was targeted at both Germany and Japan, stated that "justice shall be meted out to all war criminals including those who have visited cruelties upon our prisoners."

The *International Military Tribunal for the Far East*, also known as the Tokyo War Crimes Tribunal, began deliberations in 1946, the year following Japan's surrender. Of eighty persons originally deemed complicit in the same three offenses defined at Nuremberg, twenty-eight high-level Japanese leaders were put on trial. Although the United States was the sole occupying power of Japan, jurists came from eleven countries (Australia, Britain, Canada, China, France, India, New Zealand, the Netherlands, the Philippines, the Soviet Union, and the United States). Joseph Keenan (1888–1954), the sole prosecutor, was an official of the U.S. Department of Justice who had distinguished himself in prosecuting organized crime. Seven officials were condemned to death, sixteen were sentenced to life imprisonment, two received prison terms, two died during the trial, and one was found not guilty by reason of insanity and set free.

Whereas Hitler died before the Nuremberg trials, Emperor Hirohito (1901–1989) was not put on trial as a condition of Japan's surrender. The Emperor's support legitimized the new constitution and the postwar government.

The Tokyo trials dragged on until 1948, longer than the Ministries Case at Nuremberg. In 1948, forty-two Japanese who had been considered for possible trial were released, including future Prime Minister Nobusuke Kishi (1896–1987). By then, Washington's highest priority was to normalize conditions in Japan in order to fight the Cold War in Asia, where Communist forces in China were approaching victory.

Subsequently, other countries in Asia put thousands of Japanese on trial for war crimes. In 1948, for example, the Netherlands convened a military tribunal concerning the sexual abuse of women. Held in Jakarta, several Japanese military officers were convicted of forcing thirty-five Dutch women to serve as involuntary prostitutes in "comfort stations." Other countries in Asia put some 5,600 Japanese on trial for war crimes in their own courts, resulting in 4,400 convictions. One of the most notable, conducted in Dutch-ruled Indonesia by Australian authorities in 1946, tried 93 Japanese for the Laha Massacre of 1942, when some 300 Australian and Dutch prisoners of war were selected at random and shot.

Although Bulgaria, France, Hungary, Romania, and Slovakia collaborated with Nazi Germany in rounding up Jews for the death camps, only France has prosecuted their own citizens as war criminals. Among the prosecutions, which began in 1979, the most famous was the trial and conviction of Klaus Barbie (1913–1991), known as the "Butcher of Lyon," who was tried in 1984 and sentenced to life in prison, where he died in 1991.

There was some controversy associated with the war crimes trials. Rather than being held accountable for the deaths of millions of civilians before and during World War II, the Soviet Union was one of the four powers sitting in judgment at Nuremberg. The February 1945 Anglo-America bombing of Dresden, including largely civilian targets, was not prosecuted as a war crime, and indeed the Soviets later vilified the Dresden overkill by the West in an effort to gain support in the East German zone that they occupied after the war. And the United States was never held accountable for massive bombing of Tokyo from 1942–1945 and dropping two atomic bombs on Japan in 1945, actions that produced considerable suffering among civilians despite their limited strategic value. A major reason is that the Geneva Convention did not yet apply to aerial warfare. Only in 1977 did an Additional Protocol to the Geneva Conventions prohibit indiscriminate bombing.

Although the trials certainly represented a form of "victor's justice," the important precedent of accountability for war crimes was established by the war crimes trials. Afterward, Lemkin's concept of genocide gained acceptance, and the *Convention on the Prevention and Punishment of the Crime of Genocide* was adopted in 1948. When the treaty went into force in 1951, many of those supporting the treaty anticipated that an international criminal court would be established, but the focus on the Cold War was preeminent.

The Nuremberg and Tokyo proceedings brought to light many heinous offenses committed during the war. Accordingly, the Diplomatic Conference of Geneva of 1949 drafted four *Geneva Conventions*, which updated earlier agreements in order to respond to unprecedented barbarities. Details of all four treaties, which went into force in 1950 and are explained in Chapter 7, provide the major framework for contemporary assessments of the illegality of human rights practices in wartime as well as in postwar occupations.

UNIVERSAL DECLARATION OF HUMAN RIGHTS

Eleanor Roosevelt (1884–1962), one of the delegates at the San Francisco conference in 1945, argued strongly that a major task for the UN would be to draw up a declaration stating principles of human rights. The first session of the UN Economic and Social Council (ECOSOC) in 1946 then created the Commission on Human Rights (UNCHR), charging the Commission with the initial task of preparing the following statements: (1) a universal bill of rights; (2) international declarations or conventions on civil liberties, the status of women, freedom of information and similar matters; (3) arrangements for the protection of minorities; and (4) arrangements for the prevention of discrimination on grounds of race, sex, language, or religion.

Next, French UNCHR delegate René Cassin (1887–1976) drafted the text of the *Universal Declaration of Human Rights* in consultation with Mrs. Roosevelt, Charles Malik (1906–1987) of Lebanon, and Peng-Chun Chang (1892–1957) of China. The General Assembly approved the Declaration in 1948 as an international bill of rights. Although the British wanted a binding, enforceable treaty, Mrs Roosevelt knew that the Senate would refuse to ratify any such document. Accordingly, she insisted that the Declaration should contain general principles, with a treaty to be drafted later. The most basic principles are as follows:

- right to life, liberty, and security of the person;
- right to an education;
- right to employment, paid holidays, protection against unemployment, and social security;
- right to full participation in cultural life;
- freedom from torture or cruel, inhumane treatment or punishment;
- freedom of thought, conscience, and religion;
- freedom of expression and opinion.

So resounding were the principles that twenty-three of the thirty articles were adopted unanimously. However, some countries were dissatisfied. Saudi Arabia objected to the provision on marriage rights. South Africa opposed the principle of racial equality. The Soviet Union wanted more respect for state sovereignty and more details regarding economic and social rights. Some progressive Western countries objected that the Declaration was not a binding treaty and instead consisted of mere words with no enforcement machinery.

Nevertheless, the impact of the Declaration was profound. Subsequently, eighty-nine countries modeled human rights provisions in their constitutions on the Declaration. Some scholars argue that the declaration remains important because the principles are stated in more fundamental terms than in the specifics of a treaty.

In 1948, the Declaration directly inspired the Western hemisphere to adopt the *American Declaration of the Rights and Duties of Man*. The Geneva Conventions of 1949 specifically pledged to achieve the principles of the Declaration. In 1950, the *European Convention for the Protection of Human Rights and Fundamental Freedoms* was adopted. The *African Charter on Human and Peoples' Rights* emerged in 1981. UNCHR drew up statements on various priorities over the years, as described in Chapters 5 and 6, to further specify the rights stated in the Declaration and then authorized work on treaties to define the principles in more concrete terms.

DELAY IN ADOPTING HUMAN RIGHTS TREATIES

After the Declaration was adopted, ECOSOC asked UNCHR to put the provisions of the Universal Declaration of Human Rights into the language of a single treaty. From 1949 to 1951, the Commission indeed worked on a single draft convention containing both civil and political and economic and social rights, but there was little progress while governments wrangled over how much attention to give to civil and political rights versus economic, social, and cultural rights.

In 1951, under pressure from Western governments, the General Assembly authorized the drafting of two separate covenants. Western countries argued that civil and political rights were **legal rights,** immediately enforceable and absolute, but economic, social and cultural rights were **program rights** that would take more time to implement. That is, civil and political rights were regarded as rights *against* the state, whereas economic and social rights required action *from* the state. Within the UN system, civil and political rights could be enforced through complaints and conciliation, whereas economic and social rights would have to be monitored by annual progress reports from governments.

In 1967, the resulting two human rights treaties were finally adopted by the General Assembly – the *International Covenant on Civil and Political Rights* and the *International Covenant on Economic, Social, and Cultural Rights.* The treaties were then submitted to governments for formal ratification, usually a process of approval by a legislative body in each country. However, neither treaty had sufficient ratifications to go into effect until 1976.

A major issue was how far such a treaty would authorize investigations into the internal affairs of nations. South Africa and the Soviet Union complained that the UN might intrude into internal affairs, an objection raised as well in the United States by such nongovernmental organizations as the American Bar Association. Should the treaty leave implementation and enforcement to nations themselves or should there be an international body to do so?

Under the Constitution of the United States, treaties upon ratification become the "law of the land" and thus may either conflict with or supersede federal, state, or local laws. For example, some Southern legislators feared that African Americans, using such a treaty as the legal basis for a lawsuit, could sue to end segregation. So great was the fear of the power of the UN that Senator John Bricker (1893–1986), a Republican who ran for Vice President in 1948 along with unsuccessful presidential candidate Thomas Dewey (1902–1971), introduced a resolution into the Senate demanding that the United States withdraw from all conventions, covenants, and treaties emerging from the UN that had anything to do with human rights. His reasoning was that the Declaration was foreign to the American tradition of constitutional rights and that under the Declaration the United States would be forced to surrender its sovereignty to "UN tyranny" on such matters as immigration. The subtext of Bricker's rhetoric was to depict candidates of the opposing Democratic Party, who supported the Declaration, as anti-American and guilty of treason.

The Cold War stopped progress toward adoption of a treaty. Many in the United States feared that the UN was proceeding too quickly to dismantle colonial empires that were providing stability to head off Communist revolutions. The Soviet Union was displeased with the failure of the UN to seat the newly consolidated People's Republic of China in 1949 as well as UN action that supported South Korea in the war with Communist North Korea from 1950–1953. The Soviet Union opposed any mechanism that would send investigators into countries under its control to report on the status of human rights. The Soviets even attacked civil and political rights as "bourgeois values."

The UN Commission on Human Rights was beset with contradictory pressures and lacked consensus. Some states wanted to water down provisions in the Declaration, while others wanted to add new rights. Britain and the United States insisted on moving forward only on civil and political rights, whereas the Soviet bloc wanted priority given to economic and social rights. There was no mood for compromise.

Disagreements existed even within the Western bloc. Eleanor Roosevelt, the United States delegate on the Commission, wanted no restrictions on freedom of speech. European countries that had been victimized by Nazi propaganda believed that the proposed treaty should prohibit any deliberate advocacy of war. European countries also wanted to ban racism, but many in the United States were opposed. In 1953, Dwight Eisenhower (1890–1961), upon becoming president, removed Eleanor Roosevelt from the Commission, and his Secretary of State John Foster Dulles (1888–1959) announced to the world that the United States would never become a party to any human rights treaty approved by the UN. The Soviet Union then condemned the United States for the action, saying that Washington had forfeited the right to lecture the world on human rights.

HUMAN RIGHTS BREAKTHROUGH: OUT OF AFRICA

In the 1950s, the human rights movement might have come to a halt except that some of the poorer countries found a clever way to advance human rights in a different way. What they stressed was the desire for prompt decolonization, a goal shared by the Soviet Union and the United States. Accordingly, Belgium, Britain, and France were on the defensive to grant independence to their colonies, especially in Africa, though they argued that many countries were not yet ready for self-government. In 1956, France responded by granting independence to Morocco and Tunisia, and Britain did so in the Sudan. In 1957, Britain granted independence to the Gold Coast, which was renamed Ghana. In 1958, after Charles de Gaulle (1890–1970) gained power, France granted independence to Guinea and promised independence by 1960 to the Central African Republic, Congo (Brazzaville), Dahomey, Gabon, Guinea, Ivory Coast, Madagascar, Mali, Mauritania, and Sénégal. In 1960, Belgium granted independence to the Congo (Kinshasa), though the country soon became embroiled in civil war.

By the mid-1960s, most African states had become independent, perhaps the greatest collective extension of human rights (by implementing the principle of self-determination of peoples) in the world's history. Membership in the UN swelled sufficiently to assure ratification of human rights treaties by the required number of states. The *International Covenant on Civil and Political Rights* and the *International Covenant on Economic, Social, and Culture Rights* were both ratified in 1967.

African states also brought to the General Assembly a fresh concern about self-determination, racial discrimination, and especially an opposition to white minority rule in Southern Africa. One of the first African initiatives was the UN's adoption in 1960 of the *Declaration on the Granting of Independence to Colonial Countries and Peoples*, which proclaimed that alien subjugation, domination, and exploitation constitute a denial of fundamental human rights and demanded that immediate steps be taken to grant independence to trusteeships and other non-self-governing territories in accordance with the wishes of the people.

African countries also agitated to end racism in Rhodesia and South Africa as well as South Africa's control of South West Africa (now Namibia). What followed were decades of diplomatic pressure and the first two cases of UN economic sanctions.

Britain treated Southern Rhodesia as a self-governing colony from 1923 and appeared to promise independence as soon as World War II ended. However, in 1954 London merged the territory into a federation with North Rhodesia and Nyasaland, whereupon leaders among the white British citizens embarked on negotiations for full independence. London disagreed. The federation was dissolved in 1963, and independence was conferred on Malawi (the former Nyasaland) and Zambia (the former Northern Rhodesia). In 1965, the remaining colony, Rhodesia, declared independence of Britain under a constitution that had no intention of turning power over to the majority African population. Accordingly, Britain referred the matter to the Security Council, which in 1966 voted an economic boycott of the country, urging countries to cease all trade and other commercial interactions with the county. Since Rhodesia relied heavily on trade with Britain, many businesses in London did not want to lose business, so they evaded participation in the boycott by dealing with intermediaries. Eventually, the British government cracked down, and in 1979 the Rhodesian government yielded to a new, democratic constitution for Zimbabwe, which then joined the UN in 1980. Thirteen years of sanctions had finally paid off.

Black residents of South Africa could not wait for the UN to act. After several of them protested in 1960, the government's massacre of unarmed demonstrators in what is known as the Sharpeville Massacre was quite a strategic blunder, as the event galvanized support among the new African states to bring the matter of *apartheid* (racial segregation) to the attention of the UN General Assembly. The UN responded by setting up the Special Committee on the Policies of Apartheid, called upon member states to boycott South African goods, and in 1963 adopted the *Declaration on the Elimination of All Forms of Racial Discrimination*. In 1965, the Declaration was placed on a treaty basis in the *International Convention on the Elimination of All Forms of Racial Discrimination*, which was adopted in 1965. Progress in dealing with *apartheid* was slow, however (Table 4.3).

HISTORIC EVENT 4.3 THE SHARPEVILLE MASSACRE (1960)

After *apartheid* began in South Africa in 1948, Blacks were required to show identification papers at checkpoints in order to leave their segregated townships to work in the cities. In 1960, some three hundred demonstrators peacefully began to protest the restrictive laws in Sharpeville township. Upon arriving at the scene, the police opened fire, and sixty-nine demonstrators were slaughtered. Four more demonstrators were shot in two other towns. The incident is collectively known as the Sharpeville Massacre.

TABLE 4.3   THE UNITED NATIONS' ROLE IN ENDING SOUTH AFRICAN
APARTHEID

Year	Organ	Action
1960	Security Council	Resolution demands an end to *apartheid* and racial discrimination.
1962	General Assembly	Resolution calls for a boycott of South Africa, sets up a Special Committee on the Policies of *Apartheid* of the Republic of South Africa to monitor and report on developments.
1963	Security Council	Resolution condemns *apartheid* and calls for a voluntary arms embargo.
1963	General Assembly	Resolution calls for an arms embargo.
1966	General Assembly	Resolution condemns *apartheid* as a "crime against humanity."
1967	Economic and Social Council	Resolution authorizing the Commission on Human Rights to study and report on human rights violations.
1968	General Assembly	Resolution calls for sports embargo.
1970	General Assembly	Resolution describes *apartheid* as "a crime against the conscience and dignity of mankind."
1970	General Assembly	Refuses to seat the South African delegation.
1972	Security Council	Resolution condemns *apartheid*.
1973	General Assembly	Adopts International Convention on the Suppression and Punishment of the Crime of Apartheid (in force 1976).
1977	Security Council	Resolution calls for a mandatory arms embargo and for South Africa to grant Namibia independence.
1983	General Assembly	Resolution calls for a boycott of any corporation trading with South Africa.
1984	Security Council	Resolution declares South Africa's new constitution "null and void."
1985	Security Council	Resolution recommends voluntary economic sanctions.
1994	Security Council	Resolution lifts all sanctions.

In 1963, the General Assembly called for a boycott, but Britain, France, and the United States continued to trade with the regime. In other words, UN resolutions were ineffective, but they kept the moral pressure on the Pretoria government. In 1967, the UN Economic and Social Council authorized the UN Commission on Human Rights to prepare a systematic report on South Africa's human rights violations. Then in 1976, ten thousand black schoolchildren in Soweto protesting the new requirement to learn Afrikaans were shot without warning, and at least 152 died, and in 1977 the death of anti-*apartheid* leader Steve Biko (1946–1977) while in custody made clear that the South African government was defying the UN. Accordingly, the Security Council decided to get tough with South Africa, ordering limited economic sanctions in 1977, though the United States vetoed resolutions to strengthen the boycott from 1979–1986.

By 1984, when the South African government drew up a new constitution establishing a tricameral legislative chamber for three races (white, Indians, coloreds), but none for blacks, the Security Council lambasted the effort. Economic sanctions finally began to work, as large corporations pulled out of the country. The first sign of a weakening in policy came in 1988, when Pretoria agreed to a UN peace plan to end South African rule over Namibia, which achieved independence two year later. Also in 1990, Nelson Mandela (1918–) was released from prison, *apartheid* laws began to be repealed, and the economic boycott ended. Mandela was elected President in 1994, and a new constitution was adopted in 1996.

Clearly, the UN must assume some credit for relentlessly authorizing economic sanctions to bring pressure on countries for unacceptable human rights conditions. For the first time, the world community had acted together to end nefarious human rights abuses inside sovereign states.

PEOPLE POWER

For centuries, mass protests of the common people have demanded action from governments to attend to their needs. The French Revolution began in part when the streets of Paris were filled by people who could not afford to buy food. In France and elsewhere, democratic reforms have provided elections so that the people can choose their leaders peacefully. Elections, accordingly, have replaced demonstrations and riots as methods for forcing leaders to step down. But when phony elections are held or minorities are ignored, the people have often arisen in mass demonstrations to promote human rights.

In 1918, Mohandas Gandhi (1869–1948) urged the residents of Bihar and Gujarat to engage in nonviolent civil disobedience in light of the British insistence on taxing them despite a famine. His fame arose from the experience, and he later protested British rule over India, organizing perhaps the largest mass protests and boycotts of British goods ever held. Indian independence was granted in 1947. However, mass protests in East Germany and Poland against Soviet rule were suppressed in 1953, so the technique of civil disobedience does not always work.

In 1954, the Supreme Court of the United States ruled that pupil assignment on the basis of race was illegal in *Brown et al. v Board of Education of Topeka et al.* (347US483). The decision applied nationwide. For many observers, the Supreme Court had taken the most sweeping action of the twentieth century to advance human rights. However, Topeka's Board of Education did nothing immediately to carry out the decision, so the Supreme Court was asked to rule on the matter again. In *Brown et al. v Board of Education of Topeka et al.* (349US294), the court responded in 1955 by saying that implementation should be with "all deliberate speed." Once again, most school boards refused to act, and Southern politicians were determined to continue racial segregation practices indefinitely.

HISTORIC EVENT 4.4 THE MONTGOMERY BUS BOYCOTT (1955–1956)

In 1955, Rosa Parks (1913–2005), a department store worker, boarded a bus in downtown Montgomery, Alabama, and sat in the fifth row, as the first four rows were traditionally reserved for whites. After white passengers filled up the first four rows, and more boarded, the bus driver asked those in the fifth and sixth rows to move, as was customary. Three African Americans moved, but Rosa refused. A volunteer for the National Association for the Advancement of Colored People (NAACP), which had filed the *Brown* case, she wanted to know what rights she had – and she wanted to know right then. Accordingly, she was arrested. Her arrest was then discussed by the NAACP, including African American pastors in town, who in turn asked a recent arrival in Montgomery, the Reverend Martin Luther King, Jr. (1929–1968), to lead a protest boycott of all buses by African Americans. After 384 days, the bus company gave in. In 1956, *Browder v. Gayle* (142FSupp707) affirmed that buses could no longer segregate passengers by race.

The Montgomery bus boycott of 1955–1956 was well publicized, revealing as it did that a mass movement could lead to human rights progress. King's leadership propelled him into world prominence. He was in demand to lead demonstrations in order to make the Supreme Court's rulings a reality and to advance the cause of human rights beyond education and transportation to voting and housing. His nonviolent approach, used by the American suffragettes as well as the followers of Gandhi, popularized the use of massive public protests to demand change when political systems were unwilling to act. Blacks and Whites joined together in various protests, including "Freedom Rides" into the South, in which they sat together on buses.

In 1965, President Lyndon Johnson (1908–1973) committed thousands of American troops to intervene in Vietnam's civil war (1954–1973), an episode known in the United States as the Vietnam War. Opponents soon began to hold rallies, both in the United States and in Europe, to persuade American leaders to withdraw. Later, mass demonstrations brought down undemocratic regimes in Thailand (1973), Iran (1979), and Nicaragua (1979).

The first use of the term "people power" was in connection with events in the Philippines during 1986, sometimes known as the "Edsa Revolution." Subsequently, Koreans took to the streets in Seoul during 1987 to end dictatorial rule; the Velvet Revolution brought democracy to Czechoslovakia during 1989, the Rose Revolution toppled the corrupt government of Georgia during 2003, the Orange Revolution protested election irregularities in the Ukraine during 2004–2005 to gain a new election; the Tulip Revolution overthrew the Kyrgystan government during 2005; and Lebanon's Cedar Revolution, which followed the assassination of popular prime minister Rafik Hariri (1944–2005), soon led to the withdrawal of Syrian troops from the country.

HISTORIC EVENT 4.5 "PEOPLE POWER" IN THE PHILIPPINES OUSTS FERDINAND MARCOS (1986)

In 1972, Ferdinand Marcos (1917–1989), who was ineligible for reelection for a third term as president of the Philippines, declared martial law on the pretext of coping with Communist insurgents. Although he lifted martial law in 1981, he continued in office on the basis of phony elections, arrest of opponents, control over the media, and transfer of assets from the economic elites to his political allies. The result was economic decline as foreign investment dried up due to increasing government mismanagement, terrorist incidents, and worker strikes. In 1983, when Marcos's health was noticeably deteriorating, his chief opponent, centrist Benigno Aquino, Jr. (1932–1983), returned to the country with the aim of persuading Marcos to reinstitute democracy before the terrorists made the country ungovernable. Aquino was shot dead on the tarmac of the airport in what appeared to be a crudely organized assassination. After a funeral procession involving two million persons, the centrist opposition gained strength, particularly when Cardinal Sin (1928–2005) urged the people to use peaceful means to bring back democracy. With Communist strength growing unabated, Marcos declared martial law again but yielded to American and domestic pressure to hold a snap election in 1986, one year ahead of schedule. Corazon Aquino (1933–), Benigno's widow, then ran for president, but Marcos declared that he was the winner. Because of allegations of election fraud, the Catholic bishops in the Philippines challenged Marcos's reelection, as did both the Minister of Defense, Juan Ponce Enrile (1924–) and Vice Chief of Staff of the Armed Forces, Lt. General Fidel Ramos (1928–), who barricaded themselves in military camps on opposite sides of the Epifanio de los Santos Avenue (EDSA), awaiting an attack from troops loyal to Marcos. Two hours later, Cardinal Sin, on the only independent radio, urged the people to express support by bringing food to soldiers in the camps. Soon, hundreds of thousands of people arrived, seemingly prepared to occupy the streets indefinitely. Members of the army began to defect, the government media was seized, rockets attacked the presidential palace, and Marcos refused to give the order to shoot the Edsa protesters. On an American helicopter, Marcos and his wife were flown to an American military base, where they boarded a military jet for exile in Honolulu. In all, the Edsa Revolution toppled Marcos from power in only four days.

Nevertheless, in 2001, an Edsa mass protest served to oust corrupt President Joseph Estrada (1937–), and Edsa III occurred later that year when he was arrested while his supporters demanded his reinstatement. In the latter case, President Gloria Macapagal-Arroyo (1947–) had the support of the army and was not opposed by the Catholic leadership, but the concept of human rights protests involving "people power" had been tarnished in the Philippines.

People power movements remain an important tool in the quest to advance human rights. However, large-scale demonstrations could support violations of human rights, as happened when Benito Mussolini (1880–1945) mobilized 20,000 Black Shirts to seize power in Italy during 1922, and Hitler's Brown Shirts attacked socialists in Germany during the 1920s. Similarly, after elections in Malaysia during 1969, Malays threw stones at Chinese snakedancers in Kuala Lumpur who were celebrating the defeat of the Malay political party; when the riot was quelled, some 200 Chinese had been massacred.

DISCUSSION TOPIC 4.1 WHEN IS "PEOPLE POWER" MOST LIKELY TO ADVANCE HUMAN RIGHTS?

From Mussolini's Black Shirts of 1922 to the Tulip Revolution of 2005, mass demonstrations have often produced political change. Comparing some of the "people power" examples, which are most likely to succeed? What conditions are most likely to guarantee that "people power" will advance human rights?

JIMMY CARTER'S REVOLUTIONS

In 1977, Jimmy Carter (1924–) took office as the twenty-eighth president of the United States. In his inaugural address, he stated, "Our commitment to human rights must be absolute, our laws fair, our natural beauty preserved; the powerful must not persecute the weak, and human dignity must be enhanced." Five months later, in a speech entitled, "Humane Purposes in Foreign Policy" he advocated a new Cold War strategy – the pursuit of the goals of "justice, equity, and human rights." Although not always consistently,[3] Carter made improvement in human rights a condition for receipt of foreign aid from the United States. Officers in American embassies around the world were assigned to keep track on human rights improvements, if any, and the State Department began to publish more comprehensive annual reports on the human rights record of almost every major country in the world (except for the United States).

The reorientation of American foreign policy from deterring an attack from Moscow to questioning the fundamental moral basis of the Soviet Union meant that Carter had to point out examples of what he meant in practice. In 1980, following the Soviet Union's invasion of Afghanistan, Carter announced that, in protest, no Americans would participate in the Olympic Games scheduled for Moscow. Other Western countries followed suit.

Carter is perhaps most remembered for his mediation that produced the Camp David Accords in 1978 between Israel's Menachem Begin (1913–1992) and Egypt's Anwar Sadat (1918–1981), thereby establishing a practice of presidential peace-making that most succeeding presidents have followed. The Accords involved Egypt's diplomatic recognition of Israel, which in turn returned the Sinai Peninsula to Egypt, and set the stage for recognition of an autonomous Palestinian Authority as a halfway house on the road to a sovereign Palestinian state.

The impact of Carter's human rights initiative was profound in raising worldwide consciousness about human rights. Scarcely covered by the press before, human rights issues were now catapulted into prominence and have never receded from world attention. Nevertheless, Carter's failure to address the human rights problems of the murderous Khmer Rouge in Cambodia as well as in Iran under the dictatorial Shah, residues of a Cold War strategy that began decades earlier, underscores the difficulty he experienced in reorienting American foreign policy from an almost exclusive concern on the Cold War imperative to contain the Soviet Union to a broad concern for human rights throughout the world.

HISTORIC EVENT 4.6 THE REIGN OF THE KHMER ROUGE (1975–1979)

In 1975, Cambodia was overwhelmed by the victorious Revolutionary Army of Kampuchea, led by Pol Pot (1925–1998) and other leaders of an ideologically left-wing group known as the Khmer Rouge. Within hours of victory, the population of the capital city of Phnom Penh was evacuated and reassigned to forced labor camps. Those who objected to the new order were killed, their bodies buried in what has been called the "killing fields." Lacking adequate food, medicine, and shelter, at least one million of those in the work camps died of disease, exhaustion, and starvation; thousands were killed because they were educated or otherwise were considered political enemies. In 1978, Vietnam's army entered Cambodia to drive the Khmer Rouge from power, and in 1979, a new Cambodian government was established.

When Carter left office in 1981, the world would not have been surprised if he were content to fade into obscurity along with other former presidents, some of whom had retired to a life of leisure. Carter, however, redefined the role of a former president in 1982 by setting up an organization that has had a major impact on world affairs – the Carter Center, located at Emory University in Atlanta. Although much of Carter Center activity in the early years consisted of conferences on such subjects as arms control, health policy, human rights, and sustainable development, the former president was later notable for his efforts to build homes, eradicate disease, mediate interstate conflicts, and participate in election observer missions. In 1998, he was the first recipient of the UN Human Rights Prize, and in 2002 he received the Nobel Peace Prize.

ENDING THE COLD WAR

During the Cold War, armies and nuclear weapons were poised for a possible World War III, so efforts to defuse tensions had a high priority on both sides of the so-called Iron Curtain that separated democratic Western Europe from communist Eastern

Europe. Although the Soviet Union floated the idea of a pan-European security conference in 1950, the Western powers were not interested because they believed that Moscow's real aim was to legitimate the Soviet-dominated government in East Germany and elsewhere in Eastern Europe, where puppet rulers and Soviet troops maintained dominance.

In 1962, nuclear war seemed imminent when President John Kennedy (1917–1963) was determined to rid Cuba of missiles that might be launched with nuclear warheads from Soviet bases. Diplomacy averted the crisis and then paved the way for a détente in East–West relations.

Building on the détente, the Soviet Union again proposed a European security organization. After preparatory talks in 1972, foreign ministers of Western and Eastern Europe met in 1973 to plan for a new organization. In 1975, thirty-three European states (all but Albania) joined Canada and the United States in signing the *Final Act of the Helsinki Conference*, which set up the Conference on Security and Cooperation in Europe (CSCE). The Soviet bloc signed to gain formal recognition of its European borders, increased trade, and a Western pledge not to oppose communism militarily and politically, while Western states wanted the Soviet bloc to accept human rights monitoring.

One of the guiding principles of CSCE in the 1975 declaration was "respect for human rights and fundamental freedoms, including the freedom of thought, conscience, religion or belief." CSCE then divided the focus into three security "baskets" – politico-military, economic-environmental, and human security.

The third basket involved efforts to promote democratic processes, the rule of law, and respect for human rights. Thus, CSCE members had the right to question infringements of minority rights. As a result, the Public Group to Assist the Implementation of the Helsinki Accords in the USSR, known as the Moscow Helsinki Group, formed to pressure the Soviet Union. Subsequently, the group prepared more than one hundred fifty reports on various issues.

Initially, greater human rights attainments inside the Iron Curtain seemed impossible. But continued discussion of human rights problems bore increasing fruit over time. Thanks to CSCE, humanitarian cases related to family contacts, family reunification, and binational marriage were positively solved.

Organizations similar to the Moscow Helsinki Group arose throughout various republics of the Soviet Union and Eastern European countries to monitor implementation of the Final Act and to take their leaders to task for falling short. Although such groups received reprisals inside the Iron Curtain, the content of the reports put Moscow on the defensive. The courage of members of the groups provoked citizens to defy authorities, leading to a widespread collapse of respect for dictatorial rule.

In 1984, Mikhail Gorbachëv (1931–) became General Secretary of the Communist Party of the Soviet Union. Because his country was economically bankrupt, he sought reforms to establish a Swedish-type welfare state with greater economic and political freedoms. He also permitted Eastern European countries to act independently of Moscow in liberalizing their economies, though East German leader Erich Honecker (1912–1994) refused. In 1989, after Hungary opened travel from the Communist East to the West in 1989, the Iron Curtain became porous, the Berlin Wall was breached, and the Communist experiment in Eastern Europe was over.

In 1991, Gorbachëv was ousted in a coup, and his successor, Boris Yeltsin (1931–2007), withdrew Russia from the Soviet Union, and the Soviet Union was no more. With the end of the largest monolithic opposition to civil and political human rights, democracies and free markets blossomed in Eastern Europe, though Communist governments remained in China, Indochina, North Korea, and Yugoslavia. In 1995, CSCE became the Organization for Security Cooperation in Europe (OSCE), to reflect a new interest in assisting transitions from dictatorships to democracies.

HISTORIC EVENT 4.7 THE DISMANTLING OF THE BERLIN WALL (1989–1991)

When the four-power military occupation of Germany ended in 1949, the Soviet zone was transformed into the German Democratic Republic, known as East Germany, whereas the zones of the Britain, France, and the United States were combined into the German Federal Republic, or West Germany. Berlin, which had been divided into four zones, was now entirely surrounded by East Germany, with an East Berlin and a West Berlin, the latter part of the West Germany. From 1949, some 2.5 million East Berliners moved to West Berlin to escape from Communist rule. In 1961, Communist authorities in East Germany erected a fence and later a concrete wall separating West Berlin from East Berlin, allowing movement only through military checkpoints. Successful illegal escapes numbered only about 300 per year, though East Germany could not block radio and television broadcasts from the West. For years thereafter, Communist Czechoslovakia, Hungary, and Poland also prevented East Germans from traveling to West Germany. Suddenly, in September 1989, Hungary opened the border with Austria. As a result, some 13,000 East German "tourists" began to exit through Austria to West Germany. Czechoslovakia, the conduit of travel from East Germany to Hungary, then negotiated an agreement with East Germany to allow safe direct passage of East Germans to West Germany. From early 1989, meanwhile, demonstrations demanding reforms had been held in Leipzig, East Germany, on Monday nights after services at the St. Nicholas Lutheran Church. By mid-October, despite several crackdowns on a few hundred demonstrators, the number of protesters swelled to 250,000 all over East Germany. Accordingly, the Communist Party replaced Party Secretary Erich Honecker (1912–1994), who had supervised the building of the Berlin Wall with Egon Krenz. Egon Krenz (1937–), then allowed East Germans free travel to West Germany which meant opening up the checkpoints along the Berlin Wall, whereupon East and West Berliners began to chip away at the Berlin Wall for souvenirs. In mid-1990, East German authorities began to dismantle the wall officially, a task that took slightly more than a year. The two parts of Germany formally reunited on October 3, 1990, while the demolition of the wall was ongoing.

With the world no longer divided between controlled and market economies, a global economy emerged. In 1994, the World Trade Organization (WTO) was established to police a world in which tariffs are being lowered to zero so that trade can flow more freely across international borders. However, human rights issues were not a part of the WTO agreement, and the lowering of trade barriers has meant that some First World corporations have increased their share of the world market by outsourcing goods to Third World countries where working conditions violate human rights standards established in treaties sponsored by the International Labor Organization. WTO, a global organization that would have been impossible during the Cold War, ironically began as a major world institution obstructing human rights progress, though the organization has more recently included human rights concerns in its programming.

NONGOVERNMENTAL ORGANIZATIONS (NGOS)

Nongovernmental international organizations were crucial in the development of the League of Nations and the United Nations as well as in the adoption of the Universal Declaration of Human Rights. They have mushroomed in number and scope in recent years. Of course, not all of the thousands of NGOs focus on human rights.

Whereas governments must attend primarily to the interests of their own citizens, many NGOs have a broader perspective. NGOs are particularly active not only in presenting information to intergovernmental human rights organizations but also in providing immediate publicity to serious problems, resulting in much speedier responses by the political arms of intergovernmental organizations as well as national governments. Many NGOs have Internet websites with up-to-date information on breaking news, solicit contributions, and accept memberships.

In 1977, the year when Carter was inaugurated, *Amnesty International*, a nongovernmental organization founded in 1961, won the Nobel Peace Prize. Amnesty International's struggle on behalf of "prisoners of conscience" initially focused on victims of free speech, torture by police and prison authorities, and similar violations of civil rights. Amnesty International is also famous for publishing annual reports on the status of human rights around the world. Based on their 1969 report that the Greek military junta (1967–1974) was systematically using torture against opponents, Amnesty International began to lobby for the International Convention Against Torture, which was finally adopted in 1984. Current campaigns go beyond the original focus on civil and political rights to encompass the arms trade, child soldiers, and rights violations by transnational corporations.

As an NGO, the *Nobel Committee*, had long focused attention on human rights by awarding the annual peace prizes. The last will and testament of dynamite inventor Alfred Nobel (1833–1896) set up an endowment for the Nobel Foundation to make awards – three for scientific advances, one for literature, and one for peace. (The prize in economics is conferred in his honor but is not paid from his endowment.) The Peace Prize is for the individual or organization that advances international brotherhood/sisterhood, suppresses or reduces standing armies, or establishes or furthers peace congresses. Prizes with specific attention to civil and political or economic, social, and culture rights have been awarded on many occasions.

An organization or person honored with a Nobel Prize can often become more effective than before. Membership of Amnesty International, for example, sky-rocketed after receipt of the Nobel Prize; the enhanced level of recognition served to attract contributions from individuals who previously did not know that the organization existed.

The oldest surviving international human rights NGO, founded in England during 1839 as the British and Foreign Anti-Slavery Society, is now known as *Anti-Slavery International*. Originally formed to abolish the slave trade, the organization now combats debt bondage and human trafficking.

The *International Committee of the Red Cross*, perhaps the most famous human rights NGO, was formed in 1864 to provide assistance to wounded soldiers on the battlefield. The organization also has the authority to inspect conditions of prisoners of war. In Muslim countries, the counterpart is the *Red Crescent*. In 1919, the two merged into an organization now known as the *International Federation of Red Cross and Red Crescent Societies*. Not all serious health problems are found on battlefields, so in 1971 the organization *Médecins sans Frontières* (MSF) was formed. Whereas the Red Cross provides emergency assistance, MSF has continuing field operations to assist in disasters, epidemics, and such humanitarian crises as the establishment of makeshift refugee camps. Both the Red Cross and MSF have received Nobel Peace Prizes.

Another important organization today is *Human Rights Watch*, which grew out of CSCE's monitoring arm, Helsinki Watch. Today, Human Rights Watch has suborganizations for each region, including Africa, the Americas, Asia, Europe and Central Asia, the Middle East and North Africa, and the United States. The organization identifies ongoing human rights problems, publicizes their existence, and pressures governments and international organizations to act. The focus is broad – on civil and political rights; economic, social, and cultural rights; and war crimes.

Many other human rights NGOs have emerged over the years. Their activities are described in detail on their websites, some as **advocacy** organizations goading governments in matters of civil and political rights, others as **operational** organizations working in the field where governments lack resources to meet goals of economic and social rights. NGOs, thus, mobilize individuals around the world to focus on human rights problems that governments might otherwise ignore. Some scholars refer to advocacy campaigns as the **mobilization of shame**, that is, the use of world public opinion to condemn violations and to demand redress for the aggrieved.

NGOs fill the void in two regions of the world where there are no intergovern-mental human rights bodies. In 1963, the *Arab Organization for Human Rights* was founded; operating in Cairo, the group receives complaints from individuals and groups, dispatches field missions to secure the release of political prisoners, and publishes reports. In 1998, the *Asian Human Rights Commission* was formed at a con-ference in Kwangju, Korea, where an Asian Human Rights Charter was first discussed. With headquarters in Hongkong, the latter organization is victim-oriented, seeking to build community-based organizations at the national level that work toward poverty eradication, gender equality, and rights of indigenous peoples and minorities.

With the rise of informational globalization, such media as CNN, feature films, and the Internet provide information about human rights issues, often with video images that galvanize action to redress injustice. One Hollywood-based NGO, the *Political Film Society*, has been giving annual awards to directors of films that raise consciousness about democracy, human rights, and peaceful methods for resolving conflicts.

NGOs constitute a major force driving the international human rights agenda in the world today. Many NGOs have consultative status with UN agencies and are represented at international conferences on human rights, pressing their agendas and often serving as transnational social movement organizations. The growth of human rights NGOs has skyrocketed over the past two decades, particularly in industrial democracies. Within less developed countries, citizens have increasingly joined human rights NGOs in recent years, especially in countries that ratify human rights agreements. Beleaguered groups have often attracted support from NGOs abroad to press claims on their behalf.

DISCUSSION TOPIC 4.2 WHICH NONGOVERNMENTAL ORGANIZATIONS ARE MOST EFFECTIVE?

Why are some NGOs more effective than others in dealing with human rights problems? Comparing more prominent with less prominent NGOs, what do their websites reveal about their levels of funding, and memberships as well as their scope of activities in terms of publicity and action in courts or in the field? Should Nobel Prizes be awarded to some NGOs that have not yet been recognized by the Nobel Committee?

THE DEVELOPMENT OF INTERNATIONAL LAW

Hugo Grotius (1583–1645), as noted in Chapter 2, hoped that relations between states could be regulated by law rather than continual armed hostility. His idea bore fruit with the adoption of treaties between governments. Treaties have been viewed as contracts between states, with each state bound to the contract as long as other parties abide by the terms of the agreement. In short, the glue holding together treaties is the good faith of the government officials who negotiate the terms, that is, under the principle *pacta sunt servanda* (Pacts must be respected). Nevertheless, circumstances can change. A treaty can be considered void when unanticipated fundamental conditions change, provided that the affected parties to the treaty agree; the governing principle is *clausula rebus sic stantibus* (things thus standing).

In practical terms, a country that violates a treaty can do so with impunity, since the world polity has no executive to enforce the terms. Although lawsuits for violations of treaties might be brought in national courts of countries adversely affected, the violating county could fail to appear in the legal proceeding and ignore the legal decision. Before World War II, countries could abide by or violate international law without fear of adverse consequences.

After World War II, the collective impact of the various forces of change has been to advance international law in significant ways. Before the war, international law was mainly concerned with issues of *state* sovereignty – immunities of states, their diplomatic representatives, and their property. What happened during and after the war was the recognition that the denial of fundamental human rights to individuals has a profound impact on relations between states. Thus, the role of the *individual* has played an increasing role within international law ever since the Nuremberg Trials.

What has happened is that the principle of *jus cogens* (compelling law) has emerged, thanks to efforts by the International Law Commission. Early scholars on international law said that a treaty would be void if contrary to morality or to basic principles of international law and could not override what was called natural law. When the theory of natural law lost favor, especially during the early years of the Cold War, *jus cogens* was forgotten. In 1969, the *Vienna Convention on the Law of Treaties* restated the concept, now based on the notion that certain principles constitute a higher law that has universal validity because recognized by the vast majority of states as having no exception, even in time of domestic disturbance or war. From 1980, when the Vienna Convention went into effect with sufficient ratifications, there appears to be some consensus based on international custom that at least nine principles have achieved the status of *jus cogens*:

- prohibition of the use of force to resolve international disputes (crimes against peace);
- prohibition of genocide, war crimes, and crimes against humanity;
- prohibition of piracy and terrorism;
- prohibition of slavery and the slave trade;
- prohibition of traffic in narcotic drugs;
- prohibition of traffic in persons for prostitution;
- self-determination of peoples;
- prohibition of racial discrimination, and
- prohibition of torture.

Additional candidates for the status of *jus cogens*, disappearances and prolonged arbitrary detention, are now being debated among scholars of international law.

The significance of *jus cogens* is that the nine or more principles can be cited to trump all domestic and international laws throughout the world, such that there is a hierarchy of principles. Treaties stating *jus cogens* principles, thus, cannot be repudiated. Countries that pass "universal jurisdiction" laws can proceed to try individuals outside their borders for offenses committed on their own citizens. The International Court of Justice may also assert a guilty finding for an international law infraction based on *jus cogens* if a factual basis can be established. Indeed, such a verdict was reached during 1986 in *Nicaragua v United States* regarding actions of the United States to support unprovoked military operations against a Nicaraguan harbor during 1983–1984, though Washington refused to accept the decision.

COURT CASE 4.1 *NICARAGUA V UNITED STATES* (1986)

In 1979, the Sandinista Party seized power in Nicaragua from dictator Anastasio Somoza Debayle (1925–1980) with the support of the people, elements of the Catholic Church, and other backers. The Sandinistas quickly established a universal literacy program and a sweeping land reform that stripped influential landowners of their property, who in turn left the country to organize a force in Honduras to overthrow the Sandinistas. One Sandinista leader boasted that the country was building socialism. Upon taking office in 1981, President Ronald Reagan (1911–2004) took exception to the socialist rhetoric and believed that Nicaragua was aiding Communist-supported rebels in El Salvador. Various opponents of the Sandinistas, under the umbrella term "Contras," gained clandestine financial support from the United States and other sources for a rebel army, which in turn not only destroyed bridges, crop fields, hospitals, power plants, and schools but also engaged in assassinations, kidnappings, rape, and torture. The Sandinistas remained in power, nevertheless, thanks to aid from Cuba and Eastern Bloc sources. In 1986, Nicaragua submitted a complaint to the International Court of Justice. Based on the testimony of five witnesses, the Court concluded that the United States illegally interfered in the internal affairs of Nicaragua during 1983–1984 by mining a major harbor as well as attacking a fuel supply facility, a naval base, a major port, and two towns. The Court ordered Washington to stop all military and paramilitary activities immediately and to pay reparations. Rather than deciding the case based on the UN Charter or the founding instrument of the Organization of American States, the Court ruled that the United States violated the *jus cogens* crime against peace as well as the trade treaty between Nicaragua and the United States of 1956. Washington rejected the decision and has not paid the $12 billion fine despite condemnation by the UN General Assembly for nonpayment. After the Sandinista government lost an election in 1990, Nicaragua dropped the complaint.

A distinction can be made between soft and hard international law. **Soft international law** exists where there are no penalties for violations. **Hard international law** involves penalties for violations. Since the end of World War II, the UN has been willing to send troops to stop aggression, national and international courts have placed defendants under arrest for international crimes pending the outcome of trials, and the World Trade Organization has authorized sanctions on recalcitrant countries, including the United States, so hard international law has clearly advanced.

Thus, as more treaties have been ratified, the international system has developed a more comprehensive constitutional-type framework. International law, in short, plays an increasingly important role in world politics. At the same time, the most powerful states have remained largely immune from the punitive enforcement of international legal requirements.

DISCUSSION TOPIC 4.3 DOES INTERNATIONAL LAW HAVE INDEPENDENT MORAL AUTHORITY?

International law was originally developed to serve as principles that would govern mutually beneficial relations between sovereign states. The sources are past international custom as well as treaties and other agreements between states. As long as states involved are satisfied that their interests are positively affected, international law is likely to be respected. When states mutually believe that conditions have changed, they can invoke the doctrine of *rebus sic stantibus* and formally denounce a treaty. Of course, states could also observe a treaty in the breach, that is, fail to carry out the terms without denouncing the treaty. The development of international human rights law was formally launched by the Westphalian treaties of 1648, and many agreements since that time have added to the law. To what extent are states now likely to observe human rights treaties that they have signed, even when the provisions are contrary to their interests?

THE STRUGGLE FOR HUMAN RIGHTS

Human rights provisions in various treaties, as promoted by international organizations, often have been ratified by countries only in principle, that is, as mere fine-sounding goals. Thus, observance of the provisions differs from country to country. Accordingly, there are three aspects of the struggle to promote international human rights – standard setting, information dissemination, and implementation:

- A major task of various international institutions is **standard setting**, which involves a more complete specification of the parameters of various rights. For example, many prisoners may be crowded into a single cell for days and consider their human rights to be violated thereby. What constitutes "overcrowding" is a matter for deliberation and negotiation in order to provide a standard criterion, based on a minimum square feet of space per person, on which to determine whether prisoners are being subjected to inhumane treatment in a particular prison. Chapters 5–7 identify some of the basic standards of contemporary human rights.
- A second element is **information dissemination**. The UN has declared December 10 each year as Human Rights Day. To heighten awareness, the UN has proclaimed "decades" for special activity. The third Decade to Combat Racism and Racial Discrimination ended in 2003, and in 2004 the Decade for Human Rights Education and the International Decade of the World's Indigenous Peoples came to a close. In addition, many publications have emerged from Amnesty International, the United Nations, and other sources on the subject of human rights. Yet another informational vehicle is the international conference on various aspects of human rights. However, the mass media are the major sources of information about international human rights today, including the Internet.

- **Implementation** of human rights standards is left primarily to governments, but the UN-organized economic boycotts of Rhodesia and South Africa prove that the world can act together to authorize action to enforce human rights standards by punishing unacceptable practices. Sanctions imposed outside the UN by some Western countries on China after the massacre near Tiananmen Square in 1989, though much less effective, provide another example of action to protest dissatisfaction.

The contemporary spread of human rights has come from two sources, namely, the **horizontal** trend, in which countries have been adopting constitutions with human rights provisions, and the **vertical** trend, in which international treaties have been establishing a new set of norms, institutions, and processes favorable to human rights observance. In an ideal world, there would be no international human rights problems; the first line of defense against human rights violations would be inside individual countries, which can prosecute violators at home, provided that there is a human rights infrastructure.

A country has an adequate **human rights infrastructure** if three elements are present: (1) legal norms establishing the parameters of human rights, (2) governmental institutions monitoring, publicizing, implementing, and enforcing human rights standards, and (3) nongovernmental groups pressuring governments to advance the cause of human rights.

CONCLUSION

The recognition of human rights lags behind human suffering, however, awaiting champions to come to the aid of the victims. In the period immediately after World War II, the victorious Western countries exercised leadership. During the height of the Cold War in the 1950s, however, the West backed away, eager to support any regime, democratic or dictatorial, which promised to fight Communism. In the 1960s, Third World countries concerned about decolonization and racism in South Africa put human rights issues back on the world political agenda at the UN. After South Africa became transformed into a democratic country, the landscape of Africa was still littered with repressive governments, and United Nations agencies began to exert leadership on behalf of human rights. When the UN became bogged down in disagreements, nongovernmental organizations emerged as the strongest force calling for international action on a variety of human rights issues. Today, many observers believe that the most effective stimuli for action on behalf of human rights are NGOs. According to one formulation, economic globalization is **globalization from above**, which can be tamed by the **globalization from below** that NGOs provide.

The impact of the historical and contemporary forces on behalf of human rights, nevertheless, is most concretely measured by an examination of provisions of major human rights treaties. Such a review appears in Chapters 5–7.

CHAPTER 5

Civil and political rights

BASIC CIVIL AND POLITICAL RIGHTS

The *International Covenant on Civil and Political Rights* was adopted in 1967 along with two Optional Protocols. *The First Optional Protocol* provides that an individual claiming to be a victim of a violation of civil or political rights may file a complaint against a state that signs the Protocol. The *Second Optional Protocol* contains a commitment to abolish the death penalty.[1]

The **optional protocols** allow the most enthusiastic countries to go beyond the high-sounding principles in the Covenant by agreeing to specific practices and procedures. The practice of optional protocols to human rights treaties, thus, allows for a compromise between countries that are satisfied with general commitments and those that want specific actions.

Not until 1976 were there sufficient formal ratifications for the treaty to go into effect. Many countries were happy to adopt a mere nonbinding Declaration, but the Covenant also authorized a procedure to monitor the human rights performance of any ratifying state. Because some countries took exception to some of the rights stated in the Covenant, their ratifications contained **reservations**, that is, they indicated that they did not approve of the Covenant in its entirety; instead, they would ignore or redefine a few provisions because of domestic political considerations. Most countries tolerated the reservations of other countries as a matter of courtesy, provided that they were not so numerous as to vitiate the spirit of the document.

Article 4 provides for special circumstances through the **right of derogation**, according to which specified rights may be abridged in case of public emergency.

Thus, some rights have priority over others, notably those dea[...]tion, civil liberties, and life itself. A state that invokes the right[...] supposed to inform the UN Secretary-General of the specific rights be[...] so that other countries can then notify their citizens about dangers in the[...] suspending certain civil and political rights abroad. However, certain provi[...] cannot be suspended even then (as asterisked in Table 5.1).

TABLE 5.1 INTERNATIONALLY RECOGNIZED CIVIL AND POLITICAL RIGHTS

Article	Rights conferred by the International Covenant on Civil and Political Rights
1	Right to self-determination of peoples
2* and 3*	Equality; nondiscrimination
2	Access to legal remedies for rights violations
6*	Right to life; death sentence only for serious crimes meted out by competent court
6*	Right of persons sentenced to death to seek commutations or pardons
6*	No death penalty for pregnant women or persons under 18
7*	No cruel and inhuman punishment
7*	No subjection to involuntary medical or scientific experimentation
8*	No slavery, slave trade, involuntary servitude, or (except for punishment, military service, or normal government service) forced or compulsory labor
9	Liberty and security of the person; no arbitrary arrest or detention
9	Those arrested must be informed why; right of habeas corpus (to be arraigned before a judge)
9	Right to a speedy arraignment and trial
9	Right of release from jail pending trial or sentence for most crimes
10	Segregation of convicted persons and minors in detention from unconvicted persons and adults
10	Right of prisoners to reformation and rehabilitation
11*	No imprisonment for nonpayment of debt
12	Right of movement and choice of residence inside one's country
12	Freedom to travel abroad and to reenter one's country
13	Right of aliens against arbitrary expulsion from a country
14	Right to a fair hearing by a competent, independent, impartial court
14	Presumption of innocence
14	Right to choose a defense attorney; right to adequate time to prepare a defense
14	Right to cross-examine witnesses
14	Protection against self-incrimination
14	Right to a language interpreter without charge
14	Right to appeal convictions and sentences
14	Right to compensation for false conviction
14	Protection against double jeopardy
15*	No ex post facto law (making past actions a crime); lighter sentence after penalties are reduced for a crime
16*	Right to be treated as a person before the law
17	Right to privacy

the International Covenant on Civil and Political Rights

efamation (public humiliation)

e, religion, and thought

ovide moral and religious education for their children

expression, ideas, and information

war allowed

iscrimination, hostility, or violence based on racial or religious hatred

21	assembly
22	Freedom... ciation
23	Protection of the family; right of adults to marry voluntarily and have children
23	Equal rights for spouses
23	Protection of children when marriage is dissolved
24	Right of children to have a name, have their birth registered, and other protections as minors
25	Right to political participation; right to have access to public service
27	Right of minorities to enjoy their own culture, language, and religion

*Rights that cannot be derogated.

Among the civil and political rights are enumerated in the International Covenant on Civil and Political Rights, the first to be mentioned is the right of self-determination. However, the very identification of a "minority" people within a state may be challenged by the dominant group. One of the most persistent demands for self-determination, which involves the peoples of Western Sahara, remains unfulfilled because Morocco insists that the "self" must include not only former Western Saharans living in Morocco but also Moroccans who moved to Western Sahara. The Kurds, who live inside the borders of Iraq, Iran, and Turkey, are the largest ethnic group in the world without a nation-state of their own.

HISTORIC EVENT 5.1 THE GENERAL ASSEMBLY FIRST REQUESTS A PLEBISCITE IN WESTERN SAHARA (1966)

South of Morocco along the Atlantic coastline lies the territory of Western Sahara, which became a Spanish protectorate in 1884 under the terms of the peace settlement reached at Congress of Berlin. In 1965, the UN General Assembly called upon Spain to decolonize Western Sahara, and from 1966–1973 the General Assembly kept asking Spain to hold a referendum on self-determination. In 1974, Spain agreed that a plebiscite would be held in early 1975, whereupon Morocco claimed sovereignty over the territory and asked the International Court of Justice to rule in its favor. One day after the Court ruled that Morocco had no legal claim to Western Sahara, some 350,000 unarmed Moroccan civilians entered Western Sahara as new residents. To date, the Moroccan government has refused to compromise regarding the determination of voters eligible to participate in a plebiscite.

AGREEMENTS DEALING WITH UNEQUAL TREATMENT

Most provisions in the International Covenant on Civil and Political Rights use terms that are left undefined, so subsequent agreements have been adopted to provide clarification. Most deal with issues of unequal treatment (Table 5.2).

Even before the International Covenant was adopted, the mistreatment of refugees was so critical that a *Convention Relating to the Status of Refugees* was adopted in 1954 and reformulated in 1960. Subsequent agreements have specified the rights of aliens, asylum seekers, disabled persons, indigenous peoples, migrant workers, minority groups, stateless persons, and women in order to mitigate discrimination against them.

In 1953 and 1956, the Slavery, Servitude, Forced Labor and Similar Institutions and Practices Convention of 1926 was revised. The latter revision, the *Convention on the Abolition of Slavery, the Slave Trade, and Institutions and Practices Similar to Slavery* was ratified in 1957. Today, some 27 million persons in the world have been bought for their labor and kept in slave conditions.[2] Since slavery is an unacceptable economic and social practice, the subject is discussed along with workers' rights in Chapter 6.

Another issue that came to a head was ***apartheid***, the form of extreme racial segregation practiced in South Africa. The *International Convention on the Elimination of All Forms of Racial Discrimination* of 1965, signed primarily due to pressure from African states, criminalized *apartheid* so that anyone responsible for racial separation in South Africa who traveled abroad could be arrested and tried in the court of any country ratifying the treaty. In 1978, the UN Educational, Scientific, and Cultural Organization (UNESCO) adopted the *Declaration on Race and Racial Prejudice* to put further pressure on South Africa.

Upon taking office as prime minister in 1990, transformational leader F. W. De Klerk (1936–) announced that he would ask parliament to rescind the various laws establishing racial separation and release Nelson Mandela (1918–), the major anti-*apartheid* leader, from prison after twenty-seven years of incarceration. The laws supporting *apartheid* were finally repealed in 1994. In 2001, the *Durban Declaration and Program of Action* at the World Conference Against Racism identified a post-*apartheid* agenda to combat discrimination against ethnic, linguistic, racial, and religious minorities.

Racial discrimination issues have stimulated agreements involving other classes of people. The *Convention on the Political Rights of Women* urged universal female participation in politics. Migrants are covered by the *International Convention on the Protection of the Rights of All Migrant Workers and Members of Their Families*, which is considered by the UN Office of the High Commissioner for Human Rights to be one of the "core international human rights instruments."[3]

AGREEMENTS DEALING WITH THE ADMINISTRATION OF JUSTICE

Many agreements are concerned with the administration of justice (Table 5.3). Perhaps the most prominent is the *International Convention Against Torture and Other Cruel,*

TABLE 5.2 **CIVIL AND POLITICAL RIGHTS TREATIES RELATING TO UNEQUAL TREATMENT**

Adopted	Agreements	In force
1951	Convention Relating to the Status of Refugees	1954
1966	• Protocol Relating to the Status of Refugees	1967
1952	Convention on the Political Rights of Women	1954
1953	Protocol Amending the Slavery Convention Signed at Geneva on 25 September 1925	1953
1954	Convention Relating to the Reduction of Statelessness	1975
1954	Convention Relating to the Status of Stateless Persons	1960
1956	Convention on the Abolition of Slavery, the Slave Trade, and Institutions and Practices Similar to Slavery	1957
1957	Convention Concerning the Protection and Integration of Indigenous and Other Tribal and Semi-Tribal Populations in Independent Countries	1959
1965	International Convention on the Elimination of All Forms of Racial Discrimination	1969
1973	International Convention on the Suppression and Punishment of the Crime of Apartheid	1976
1975	Declaration on the Rights of Disabled Persons	
1978	Declaration on Race and Racial Prejudice	
1981	Declaration on the Elimination of All Forms of Intolerance and of Discrimination Based on Religion or Belief	
1985	Declaration on the Human Rights of Individuals Who Are Not Nationals of the Country in Which They Live	
1990	International Convention on the Protection of the Rights of All Migrant Workers and Members of Their Families	2003
1992	Declaration on the Rights of Persons Belonging to National or Ethnic, Religious and Linguistic Minorities	
1993	Principles Relating to the Status of National Institutions (The Paris Principles)	
1993	Vienna Declaration and Program of Action	
1998	Declaration on the Right and Responsibility of Individuals, Groups, and Organs of Society to Promote and Protect Universally Recognized Human Rights and Fundamental Freedoms	
2001	Durban Declaration and Program of Action	
2006	Convention on the Rights of Persons with Disabilities	

Inhuman or Degrading Treatment or Punishment of 1984. After a General Assembly statement of principles on investigation of torture in 2000, the Convention's Optional Protocol of 2002 was drafted to authorize visits to places of detention in order to ensure that torture is not taking place.

Most agreements on the administration of justice are substantive. In addition, the UN General Assembly has established procedural guidelines and has encouraged member states to set up their own human rights agencies in the *Principles Relating to the Status of National Institutions* and in the *Declaration on the Right and*

TABLE 5.3 **CIVIL AND POLITICAL RIGHTS TREATIES ON THE ADMINISTRATION OF JUSTICE**

Adopted	Agreements	In force
1955	Standard Minimum Rules for the Treatment of Prisoners	
1975	Declaration on the Protection of All Persons from Being Subjected to Torture and Other Cruel, Inhuman or Degrading Treatment or Punishment	
1979	Code of Conduct for Law Enforcement Officials	
1982	Principles of Medical Ethics Relevant to the Role of Health Personnel, Particularly Physicians, in the Protection of Prisoners and Detainees Against Torture and Other Cruel, Inhuman or Degrading Punishment	
1984	International Convention Against Torture and Other Cruel, Inhuman or Degrading Treatment or Punishment	1987
2002	• Optional Protocol	
1984	Safeguards Guaranteeing Protection of the Rights of Those Facing the Death Penalty	
1985	Basic Principles on the Independence of the Judiciary	
1985	European Convention for the Prevention of Torture and Inhuman or Degrading Treatment or Punishment	1989
1985	Guidelines for Action on Children in the Criminal Justice System	
1985	Inter-American Convention to Prevent and Punish Torture	1987
1985	Standard Minimum Rules for the Administration of Juvenile Justice (Beijing Rules)	
1989	Principles on the Effective Prevention and Investigation of Extra-Legal, Arbitrary and Summary Executions	
1990	Basic Principles for the Treatment of Prisoners	
1990	Basic Principles on the Role of Lawyers	
1990	Basic Principles on the Use of Force and Firearms by Law Enforcement Officials	
1990	Guidelines for the Prevention of Juvenile Delinquency (Riyadh Rules)	
1990	Guidelines on the Role of Prosecutors	
1990	Rules for the Protection of Juveniles Deprived of Their Liberty	
1990	Standard Minimum Rules for Non-Custodial Measures (Tokyo Rules)	
1992	Declaration on the Protection of All Persons from Enforced Disappearances	
1997	Declaration of Basic Principles of Justice for Victims of Crime and Abuse of Power	
1998	Body of Principles for the Protection of All Persons Under Any Form of Detention or Imprisonment	
2000	Principles on the Effective Investigation and Documentation of Torture and Other Cruel, Inhuman or Degrading Treatment	

Responsibility of Individuals, Groups, and Organs of Society to Promote and Protect Universally Recognized Human Rights and Fundamental Freedoms. The former asks member states to set up human rights monitoring agencies; the latter encourages states to cooperate with civil society organizations that seek to advance human rights.

In addition, other agreements deal with crime victims, detainees, the disabled, extrajudicial punishment, juvenile justice, and the death penalty. Guidelines for the role of judges, lawyers, police, prison officials, and prosecutors have also been adopted.

EFFECTS OF THE TREATIES

Some observers claim that human rights treaties are worthless because many countries sign and later ratify without the slightest intention of implementing provisions. The symbolic gesture of becoming a party to a human rights treaty, in short, costs nothing and may give a false impression about widespread voluntary compliance. Indeed, some of the most heinous violators have ratified human rights treaties while continuing to violate human rights. Compliant countries are usually unwilling to embarrass noncompliant countries by filing complaints so that they will not jeopardize friendly economic relations.

Research on the before-after effects of ratifying human rights treaties, however, demonstrates that genuine progress occurs after ratifications. Countries that become parties to human rights treaties are more likely to adopt implementing legislation and to experience a reduction in violations. The effect, as may be expected, is least pronounced in dictatorships that suppress rising democratic aspirations. There is a modest increase in human rights performance among stable democracies, which have already reached an asymptote in human rights observance. The largest effects of human rights treaties are among those living in regimes intermediate between dictatorships, on the one hand, and democracies, on the other hand. Intermediate regimes often have two political forces, one of which is a strong supporter of human rights; once in power, the most progressive political party will seek to sign and to ratify the newest human rights treaties in order to lock in gains that otherwise might not be granted when the more conservative party takes office. In short, the adoption of human rights treaties has had a profound effect on voluntary compliance around the world.

TRANSITIONING FROM AN ERA OF HUMAN RIGHTS HORRORS

Some countries have endured horrendous eras of human rights violations by despicable regimes but have later turned the corner due to "people power" demonstrations, revolutions, transformational leaders, or other progressive political change. Victims of the former regime may justly feel that they should be compensated for their losses by those who perpetrated abuses, but the pursuit of justice may end up as an exercise in revenge that can delegitimize a new regime. For example, the guillotining of the royal family during the French Revolution morphed into a Reign of Terror that ultimately visited early proponents of the revolution. Similarly, Chinese and Russian revolutionary leaders proceeded to liquidate class enemies in order to eliminate opposition, but later some of the early supporters of the revolutions were also executed as rivals for political power.

HISTORIC EVENT 5.2 ARGENTINA'S "DIRTY WAR" (1976–1983)

Upon the death of Argentine President Juan Perón (1895–1974), his spouse María Estela (Isabelita) Martínez de Perón (1931–) took office. In 1976, she and the democratically elected government of Argentina were ousted by a military junta on the pretext of eliminating Communist influence in the country. Subsequently, from 10,000 to 30,000 left-leaning persons were arrested, detained in secret locations, tortured, and their ultimate whereabouts was unknown. Some were executed and buried at sea. Mothers of those who disappeared began in 1977 to gather after mass in the Plaza de Mayo outside the Buenos Aires cathedral to protest their disappearance by wearing white scarves. As one side of the square contains the presidential palace, the weekly Thursday protests were a direct challenge to the government. Soon, Amnesty International and the United Nations applied pressure on the government to account for those who had disappeared. In 1982, the government sought to annex the nearby British-held Falkland Islands, but Britain handed the government such a defeat that in 1983 the government granted a restoration of civil liberties, presidential elections were held, and the military leaders allowed Raúl Alfonsín (1927–) to take office as civilian president on condition that those in power from 1976–1983 would receive a blanket amnesty for any wrong-doing during their tenure in office. In 2005, however, the Argentine Supreme Court rescinded the amnesty. Those responsible for the "dirty war" are now being brought to justice.

When serious violations are occurring inside a country, the population may be so mortified that opponents remain passive. Alternatively, dissidents can attempt to secure attention from abroad so as to obtain verbal, judicial, economic, or military pressure on their governments. Several lessons have been learned from the experience in Argentina and other countries: First, victims must talk to one another and act in a subtle manner so that the repressive authorities will not be able to find a convenient way to repress the group that is protesting. Second, the loose aggregation of protesters should next form an organization to coordinate activities. Documenting individual cases is one of the most important activities for any such group, as in the case of *Nunca Más* in Argentina. Such documentation can be used as evidence in subsequent court actions. Third, the group should seek international recognition and even backing from such organizations as Amnesty International and Human Rights Watch. Fourth, using public statements, the objective should be to shame those in power with facts and to have pressure exerted from the outside, hoping that the rulers will be so mortified that they will agree to pass the baton of power, as when Nelson Mandela was released from prison in 1990.

How, then, should a new regime temper the desire for justice with the need to build legitimacy? There are several alternatives: (1) One strategy is to **do nothing**. After the American Revolution, prosecution of Americans who sided with the British was not on the political agenda; the healing of divisions was considered of paramount importance to unify the country. (2) There can be a *pro forma* **trial** of former leaders. After the Khmer Rouge regime ended in Cambodia in 1979, the new government put former leaders on trial *in absentia*, but the exercise was merely a formality because none of those accused of human rights violations was in custody, and there was no deliberation before a sentence was passed. (3) A **show trial** of a few top leaders may also be attempted to make an example of a violator; the televised proceedings of the trial of Saddam Hussein (1937–2006) for crimes against humanity in Iraq provide a recent instance. Show trials, however, can be shams, as former leaders are railroaded without due process, as in the Moscow Trials of 1936–1938 to eliminate opponents of Josef Stalin (1878–1953). (4) An **amnesty** may be granted; that is, those who committed human rights violations may be granted immunity from prosecution, as when the military regime in Argentina stepped down in 1983, allowing free elections to select a new government, provided that a blanket amnesty was granted to those who may have perpetrated human rights abuses and other crimes. (5) Of course, **prosecutions** may bring human rights violators to justice, either in courts or through complaints filed with **human rights commissions**. (6) A new approach is to organize a **truth commission**, in which evidence is compiled of the crimes of the former regime; those accused of crimes are sometimes asked to confess with or without an assurance of amnesty. The aim is to record an ugly period in the country's history as an example never to be repeated.

TRUTH COMMISSIONS

A **truth commission**, thus, seeks to compile an account of former wrongdoing on a case-by-case basis, whereas a **human rights commission** deals with individual complaints or ongoing patterns of misconduct to reach a specific remedy. Whereas permanent human rights commissions seek **retributive justice**, truth commissions are temporary bodies that have often sought **restorative justice** so that a new regime can go beyond on an earlier era of human rights violations by having violators, such as torturers, apologize to a victim and then have the apology accepted.

Thus, far, governments have sponsored twenty-nine truth commissions (Table 5.4). The El Salvador truth commission, the first to be set up with UN assistance, documented death squad assassinations, disappearances, extrajudicial executions, and peasant massacres during the 1980s, when a right-wing government sought to suppress what they perceived to be Marxists influenced by liberation theology. Thereafter, the UN sought to set up truth commissions in peace settlements after civil wars.[4]

Some of the bodies are called "truth and reconciliation" commissions. In the South African case, a Commission of Inquiry was set up before the Truth and Reconciliation Commission so that testimony about human rights violations under *apartheid* would deal with healing rather than fact finding. Conducted in a nonadversarial and sometimes nonpublic manner, truth and reconciliation commissions may encourage perpetrator and victim to meet each other again at a session where psychological wounds can heal on all sides. Truth commissions that have been victim-centered have

TABLE 5.4 **OFFICIAL TRUTH COMMISSIONS**

Country	Founded	Era covered	Report issued
Uganda	1974	1971–1974	1975
Bolivia	1982–1984	1967–1982	None (disbanded)
Argentina	1983–1984	1976–1983	1985
Uruguay	1985	1973–1982	1985
Zimbabwe	1985	1983	None
Uganda	1986–1995	1962–1986	None
Philippines	1986	1972–1986	None
Nepal	1990–1991	1961–1990	1994
Chile	1990–1991	1973–1990	1991
Chad	1991–1992	1982–1990	1992
Germany	1992–1994	1949–1989*	1994
El Salvador	1992–1993	1980–1991	1993
Rwanda	1992–1993	1990–1992	1993
Sri Lanka	1994–1997	1988–1994	1997
Haiti	1995–1996	1991–1994	1996
Burundi	1995–1996	1993–1995	1996
South Africa	1995–2000	1960–1994	1998; work ongoing
Ecuador	1996–1997	1979–1996	None (disbanded)
Guatemala	1997–1999	1962–1996	1999
Nigeria	1999-2001	1966–1999	Writing in progress
Peru	2000–2002	1980-2000	2003
Uruguay	2000–2001	1973–1985	Writing in progress
Panama	2001–2002	1968–1989	2002
Yugoslavia	2002	1991–2001	Work ongoing
East Timor	2002	1974–1999	2006
Sierra Leone	2002	1991–1999	Work ongoing
Ghana	2002	1966–2001	Work ongoing
Morocco	2004	2004–2005	2005
Indonesia	2005	1966–1998	None (disbanded)
Indonesia-East Timor	2005	1999	Work ongoing

*Concerning East Germany only.

Principal sources: Brahm (2004), based on (Hayner 1994; Bronkhorst 1995; Hayner 2001; www.ictj.org; www.usip.org/library/truth.html)

been the most successful in enabling the societies to transcend their past. Although amnesty is often a condition of setting up a commission, the South African body was empowered to grant amnesty as a reward for public testimony, whereas El Salvador passed an amnesty law after the commission's report became public.

HISTORIC EVENT 5.3 THE REIGN OF AUGUSTO PINOCHET (1973–1990)

In 1973, after Salvador Allende (1908–1973) was elected president of Chile, inflation skyrocketed and street fighting broke out. Allende then named Augusto Pinochet (1915–2006) as army commander in chief. But three weeks later, Pinochet's troops surrounded the presidential palace, declaring martial law, and Allende was reported dead. Subsequently, Pinochet sought to eliminate the leftist opposition, and he was responsible for the deaths or disappearances of some 3,000 persons and for the torture of approximately 30,000 detainees at Villa Grimaldi and other locations. Even though Chile's economy grew considerably while Pinochet was in power, the democratic opposition mushroomed to the point that Pinochet agreed in 1988 to hold a referendum on his continued rule. When he won only 43 percent of the votes in 1988, and a center-left coalition won parliamentary elections in 1990, Pinochet handed power to the new president on condition that he would continue as army commander, that the military-imposed constitution would remain in place, that there would be an amnesty for offenses committed by military officers during his rule, and that he would remain Senator for Life. Pinochet's abuses in power, nevertheless, were documented in the Rettig Commission report of 1991. After his arrest in 1998 in England, he returned to Chile in 2002, resigned as Senator, and was charged with tax evasion in 2005, but died before his trial. Michelle Bachelet (1951–), daughter of one of those who died while in custody at Villa Grimaldi, was elected president of Chile in 2006.

Truth commissions may also exist alongside tribunals that prosecute those who are named but have not come forward to confess their wrongdoing; examples are East Timor and Sierra Leone. Usually, however, the commissions make recommendations for subsequent action. Evidence from the Chilean commission, including the names of those who disappeared or were killed during 1973–1990, was introduced in the investigation of former President Augusto Pinochet (1915–2006), who stepped down as president on condition that he would be granted amnesty for any future prosecution of offenses committed during his reign. Pinochet pioneered the use of "disappearance" as a tool of repression.

Truth commissions also have been created by nongovernmental organizations. In one case, the government of Brazil turned down a proposal for a truth commission, whereupon Cardinal Paulo Evaristo (1921–) of São Paulo organized one instead. The Commission for Historical Clarification, which worked from 1996–1999 to document 626 massacres from 1962 to 1996 committed in Guatemala mostly by government forces against "internal enemies" (academics, Catholics, communists, Mayans, and other dissenters), was preceded by a report published in 1998 by the Catholic Archdiocese of Guatemala.[5]

Nongovernmental organizations have arisen from truth commissions. The New York-based International Center for Transitional Justice was founded in 2001 to provide consultants who can assist countries in establishing truth commissions. The Institute for Justice and Reconciliation arose in Cape Town, South Africa, during 2000 to focus on problems in Africa; the organization has assisted at the community level in Nigeria and Uganda. Both seek what they call **transitional justice.**

Although truth commissions seek the goals of deterrence, reconciliation, restorative justice, and social transformation, the jury is out on their ultimate benefits. Indeed, five commissions were disbanded or stopped because they were too controversial (Table 5.4). Others have been attacked because they are "victor's justice." The benign effects of the El Salvador case are in contrast with the South African Truth and Reconciliation Commission, which has been accused of harming race relations.

The two latest bodies were established after Indonesian courts acquitted several military personnel of human rights abuses under the era of former President Haji Mohammad Suharto (1921–). Members of the army killed an estimated 300,000–1,000,000 members of the Communist Party of Indonesia and their alleged sympathizers in 1965–1966 soon after bringing Suharto to power by a military coup. Later, there were bloody crackdowns of political dissidents, notably a massacre in 1984, when troops fired on several thousand Muslim protesters in Jakarta's Tanjuk Priok harbor who were demonstrating against restrictions on freedom of association. However, the commission was disbanded in 2007 due to lack of cooperation.

HISTORIC EVENT 5.4 EAST TIMOR ESTABLISHES A TRUTH COMMISSION (2002)

The island of Timor, colonized by Portugal in 1520, was formally divided between the Netherlands and Portugal in 1860. In 1949, the Dutch ceded their portion to Indonesia. In 1974, a war broke out in Portuguese-controlled East Timor between those favoring independence and those preferring integration into Indonesia. When Portugal withdrew in 1976, Indonesian troops moved into the vacuum, whereupon East Timorese appealed to world opinion, particularly after film footage of a massacre of 271 persons attending a funeral during 1991 appeared on television. In 1999, Indonesia accepted a UN plebiscite for the territory. Following a favorable vote for East Timor's independence, Indonesian military forces launched attacks on the residents, resulting in 1,400 deaths and displacing 250,000 from the homes. The UN then negotiated with Jakarta to end the violence and voted to authorize a military force in order to bring order to the territory. After the UN Transitional Administration for East Timor began operations in 1999 to prepare the territory for independence, further violence erupted in 2000 but subsided. East Timor became independent in 2002. One of the first acts of the new government was to establish the Commission for Reception, Truth and Reconciliation, which made a final report in 2006. Among the conclusions was to fix responsibility on the United States for greenlighting Indonesia to use violence to annex the territory from 1975–1999. In 2005, East Timor and Indonesia set up a joint Truth and Friendship Commission to investigate perpetrators of the violence in 1999. Prosecutions of offenders are expected to follow.

Some truth commissions have revealed more information than anticipated, resulting in pressure to prosecute those who assumed that they were being granted amnesty. In addition to the case of Pinochet, the amnesty granted in Argentina was struck down by its Supreme Court in 2005, opening the possibility that approximately 900 former officers and collaborators could be brought to trial. In 2006, former provincial deputy police commander Miguel Etchecolatz (1929–) was among the first to go on trial for his role in the Argentine "dirty war." He was accused of illegally arresting six persons, torturing two, and murdering four; however, one day after he was sentenced to life imprisonment, a key prosecution witness, Jorge Julio López (1928–), disappeared. Later that year, the first person involved in the "dirty war" was convicted. A twenty-five year sentence was handed down in the case of Julio Simón, a former police officer responsible for the torture and disappearance of a married couple in 1978 as well as the forcible reassignment of their eight-month-old daughter to a military officer's family. The suit had been brought by close relatives of the couple, José Poblete and Gertrudis Hlaczik. Whether such prosecutions will discourage future dictators from giving up power and allowing truth commissions to operate remains to be seen.

DISCUSSION TOPIC 5.1 WHEN ARE TRUTH COMMISSIONS USEFUL?

When massive human rights violations stop, where does justice begin? What happens to the perpetrators of violations of human rights in the former government when a new regime begins to respect human rights? What is the tradeoff between giving human rights abusers amnesty and bringing them into court? Can truth commissions play a role with terrorist groups? Among countries that have not accounted for systematic human rights violations in the past, which should organize truth commissions?

Truth commissions tend to occur in countries where governments are not equipped to handle investigative functions objectively, whether due to prejudice, tradition, or some other reason. Democratic countries have instead compiled reports rather than setting up commissions.[6] In addition, national and international courts are often too adversarial to handle the task of reconciliation. Most truth commissions arose in the democratic transitions of the 1990s, but they are unlikely to pursue nonstate terrorist groups, which are usually treated as international outlaws.

CIVIL AND POLITICAL RIGHTS AS "POSITIVE" RIGHTS

Often, the argument is made that political and civil rights are **negative rights**, that is, deal with what government should **not** do, thereby preserving individual freedom.

In contrast, economic, social, and cultural rights are often considered to be **positive rights** that can only advance when governments take innovative action to ensure a decent quality of life.

Within the United States, there is a similar distinction. **Civil liberties** are considered to be rights that governments cannot abridge, whereas **civil rights** are assured only when government acts aggressively to stop discrimination. Thus, civil liberties are considered to be negative rights, with civil rights as positive rights.

There is a further distinction. **Procedural rights** are steps required of governments before they can act; for example, a "fair trial" requires governments to provide the accused with an attorney and a hearing before an impartial tribunal. **Substantive rights** are about factual situations, such as the freedom to belong to a religion of one's choosing.

However, further analysis suggests that civil and political rights as well as civil liberties are not negative rights. They can only be attained when governments affirmatively carry out at least four tasks: (1) Governments must show respect for the goals of civil and political rights by making verbal statements that raise public consciousness to end prejudice and to stop violations. (2) Governments must create institutional machinery to enforce rights, such as by establishing human rights commissions. (3) Governments must deter violations and protect rights by setting up enforcement agencies that act, often dramatically, to stop and to redress violations. (4) Governments must spend money on goods and services to ensure rights, such as election safeguards, from tamper-proof voting machines to armed guards, to prevent fraud or voter intimidation.

Thus, civil and political rights impose both affirmative and negative obligations on governments. The affirmative obligation is to provide the infrastructure to guarantee that those who violate human rights will be held accountable in court. The negative obligation is for governments to refrain from interfering with the exercise of civil and political rights, such as the right of free speech.

CONCLUSION

Civil and political rights are often considered to be prior to all other rights. Without a free and fair public arena, individuals cannot seek redress for violations of economic, social, and cultural rights. However, protestors against violations of civil and political rights are most effective when individuals not only have the economic freedom and resources to hire lawyers on their behalf but also are seen as part of the mainstream rather than being treated as socially or culturally inferior. Thus, the two categories in practical terms deal with complementary rights, as stated in the *Vienna Declaration and Program of Action* that emerged from the World Conference on Human Rights in 1993. The next chapter, accordingly, reviews the parameters of economic, social, and cultural rights.

DISCUSSION TOPIC 5.2 WHAT ARE THE LIMITS OF CIVIL AND POLITICAL RIGHTS?

Do civil and political rights deal primarily with the freedom of individuals to live their lives without any government interference? How absolute are the claims against governments? What reasonable restrictions can governments impose on some individuals so that freedom of the many is maximized? Are civil and political rights luxuries primarily for affluent countries? How important are civil and political rights for poorer persons who barely have enough to eat and drink from day to day?

CHAPTER 6

Economic, social, and cultural rights

Although the world produces enough food to feed everyone, and transportation exists to get food to those who are hungry, millions are dying of malnutrition. The structure of the international food distribution system, which governments have the power to regulate, is clearly responsible. Similarly, homeless people sometimes camp outside vacant apartments and office buildings from London to Los Angeles despite the possibility that governments could rent unused housing units from property owners and allow the homeless to use them for shelter. In short, food and shelter are available for nearly everyone, but are not allocated on the basis of need. Sociologist Johan Galtung (1930–) refers to such cruel squandering of abundant resources as involving **structural violence**. What he means is that some people are dying from lack of adequate food and shelter, albeit slowly, due to political structures that ignore them.

The first systematic international recognition of economic and social rights appeared in 1919 within the Constitution of the International Labor Organization (ILO), which declared a desire to abolish the "injustice, hardship and privation" that workers have suffered and to guarantee "fair and humane conditions of labor." The text was a response in the West to the rise of Soviet Bolshevism, which threatened to advance throughout the rest of Europe. During the years between World Wars I and II, the ILO drafted treaties to promote the right to organize trade unions, a minimum working age, maximum hours of work, weekly rest periods, sickness protection, accident and old-age insurance, and freedom from discrimination in employment. During the Great Depression of the 1930s, the ILO also stressed the issue of unemployment insurance and the desirability of full employment.

When the Allied military campaign during World War II promised eventual victory, plans were afoot to organize the United Nations. Australia lobbied for a clause in the UN Charter pledging all countries to improve labor standards, provide for social security, and guarantee full employment by taking action through the General Assembly, the UN Economic and Social Council, and the ILO. The United States, however, opposed such a provision as intruding into the domestic affairs of states, so the pledge for international action was watered down to a mere principle to be implemented by individual states as they see fit. The Preamble of the UN Charter pledged governments to "promote social progress and better standards of life," but left the adoption of a bill of economic, social, and cultural rights to the future work of the UN.

In 1944, while efforts to organize the United Nations were underway, the American Law Institute set up a committee to draft an international bill of rights. In addition to listing the civil and political rights contained in the American Bill of Rights, the committee proposed the following economic and social rights: right to education, right to work, right to reasonable conditions of work, right to adequate food and housing, and the right to social security. The committee noted that economic and social rights had already been recognized in the constitutions of many countries – right to education (forty countries); right to work (nine countries); right to adequate housing (eleven countries), and right to social security (twenty-seven countries).

The proposed bill of economic, social, and cultural rights was supported for inclusion into the Universal Declaration of Human Rights in 1948 by Eleanor Roosevelt (1884–1962) on behalf the United States. Third World countries endorsed the proposal, but there was opposition from governments in Europe, which were undergoing postwar reconstruction, so a more modest statement rather than a binding treaty emerged.

After the UN was launched, its Commission on Human Rights was charged with the responsibility of translating the Declaration of Human Rights into the form of a single treaty. During the Cold War, however, the two sides in the debate between the primacy of civil and political rights versus economic and social rights were ideologically determined, as noted in the previous chapter. Western countries supported anti-Communist dictatorships that had no intention of supporting civil and political rights for their own people. The Soviet bloc, meanwhile, refused to support the Western bloc's text of the proposed treaty on economic and social rights, arguing that the language was insufficient.

By 1955, consensus had been reached about the main outlines of an agreement, but the Cold War and other considerations held up final approval. The European Social Charter of 1961 proved that a consensus on the subject was possible, at least among Western European states. Some of the formulations in the proposed treaty were modified from 1963 to 1966, and the final text of the *International Covenant on Economic, Social, and Cultural Rights*, as approved in 1966, entered into force in 1976.

BASIC ECONOMIC, SOCIAL, AND CULTURAL RIGHTS

The initial articles of the treaty deal mostly with substantive rights (Table 6.1). Later agreements have specified procedures to be followed in implementing the treaty, such as reporting requirements.

TABLE 6.1 INTERNATIONALLY RECOGNIZED ECONOMIC, SOCIAL, AND CULTURAL RIGHTS

Article	*Provisions of the International Covenant on Economic, Social, and Cultural Rights*
1(1)	Right to self-determination of peoples
1(2), 24	Freedom to dispose of natural wealth and resources
1(2)	Prohibition against deprivation of means of subsistence
1(3)	Obligation of trusteeship and colonial powers to promote self-government
2(1)	Obligation to use international assistance
2(1)	Obligation to pass laws to attain economic, social, and cultural rights
2(2)	Prohibition against discrimination based on race, color, sex, language, religion, political or other opinion, national or social origin, property, birth or other status
2(3)	Obligation to adopt legislative or other measures to attain economic, social, and cultural rights
2(4)	Obligation of developing countries to guarantee economic rights to the extent possible
3	Equal economic, social, and cultural rights for men and women
4	Rights may be democratically limited only if they promote the general welfare
5(1)	No reduction in attainment of basic rights to meet Covenant obligations
5(2)	No cancellation of rights previously granted by a government
6(1)	Right to work
6(1)	Right to choose occupation freely
6(2)	Obligation of governments to provide technical education
7a(i)	Right to fair wages and equal pay for equal work
7a(i)	Equal pay for equal work regardless of sex
7a(ii)	Right to a living wage
7b	Right to safe and healthy working conditions
7c	Equal opportunity for promotion (except for seniority and competence levels)
7d	Right to rest, leisure, limited working hours, paid periodic holidays
8(1a,2)	Right to form and join trade unions for all but armed forces, police, or government bureaucrats (subject to law and public order needs)
8(1b)	Right of trade unions to join together or to join international trade unions
8(1c)	Right of unions to function freely (subject to law and public order needs)
8(1d)	Right to strike (subject to law)
9	Right to social security, including social insurance
10(1)	Obligation to protect and assist families
10(1)	Right to choose marriage partners freely
10(2)	Right of mothers of newly born children to leave from work with pay or social security benefits and other special protection

TABLE 6.1 (CONTINUED)

Article	Provisions of the International Covenant on Economic, Social, and Cultural Rights
10(3)	Obligation to protect children from economic and social exploitation
10(3)	Prohibition of work of children harmful to morals or health
10(3)	Obligation to establish a minimum age for children to work
11(1)	Right to adequate and improving food, clothing, housing conditions freely chosen
11(2a)	Obligation of governments to improve and reform systems of production, conservation, distribution of food, and knowledge about nutritional principles
11(2b)	Obligation to ensure equitable distribution of world food for the needy
12(1)	Right to physical and mental health
12(2b)	Obligation to reduce stillbirths, infant mortality
12(2c)	Obligation to improve environmental and industrial hygiene
12(2c)	Obligation to prevent, treat, and control diseases, including work-related
12(2d)	Right to medical attention for sickness
13(1)	Right to education
13(1)	Obligation of education to promote the full development of personality, sense of dignity, respect for human rights and freedom; to empower democratic participation; to promote understanding, tolerance, friendship among all nations and racial, ethnic, or religious groups; further UN activities for peace
13(2a), 14	Obligation to provide free compulsory primary education either immediately or to design an implementation plan with a timetable
13(2b)	Obligation to provide secondary and technical education for all
13(2c)	Obligation to provide higher education for all who have the aptitude
13(2b,c)	Obligation to gradually provide free secondary, technical, higher education
13(2d)	Obligation to provide education for those not completing primary grades
13(2e)	Obligation to increase schools, provide fellowships, upgrade work conditions of teachers
13(3)	Right of parents to send children to nonpublic schools, if they meet minimum standards
13(3)	Right of parents to provide moral and religious education to children
13(4)	Right to establish schools that meet minimum standards
15(1a)	Right to take part in cultural life
15(1b)	Right to enjoy benefits of science and its applications
15(2)	Obligation to develop, conserve, diffuse science and culture
15(3)	Right of scientists to free inquiry
15(4)	International scientific and cultural cooperation and contacts are encouraged
23	Pledge to furnish technical assistance to meet obligations and rights

To clarify the meaning of provisions of the International Covenant on Economic, Social, and Cultural Rights, several agreements have been adopted, primarily by the UN General Assembly. According to the UN Office of the High Commissioner for Human Rights, three of the treaties are among the "core international human rights instruments" along with the International Covenant on Economic, Social and Cultural Rights (Table 6.2).

TABLE 6.2   CORE TREATIES ON ECONOMIC, SOCIAL, AND CULTURAL RIGHTS

Adopted	Treaties	In force
1966	International Covenant on Economic, Social, and Cultural Rights	1976
1979	Convention on the Elimination of All Forms of Discrimination Against Women	1981
1999	• Optional Protocol to the Convention on the Elimination of All Forms of Discrimination against Women	2000
1989	United Nations Convention on the Rights of the Child	1990
2000	• Optional Protocol to the Convention on the Rights of the Child on the Involvement of Children in Armed Combat	2002
2000	• Optional Protocol to the Convention on the Rights of the Child on the Sale of Children, Child Prostitution and Child Pornography	2002
1990	International Convention on the Protection of the Rights of All Migrant Workers and Members of Their Families	2003

While progress on the International Covenant on Economic, Social, and Cultural Rights was stymied due to Cold War antagonisms, the ILO nevertheless continued to sponsor treaties on issues of employment, classifying the most important as "fundamental" or "priority" treaties (Table 6.3). Treaties deal with child labor, collective bargaining, discrimination, equal pay, forced labor (peonage, serfdom, and slavery), the policy of full employment, and trade-union rights.

Although the concern over slavery has a long vintage, the reality is that at least 15 million persons, including many children, are estimated to be in debt bondage, mostly in India, Nepal, and Pakistan. Several treaties deal with the subject. In 1957, when the *Convention on the Abolition of Slavery, the Slave Trade, and Institutions and Practices Similar to Slavery* went into force, the ILO adopted the *Convention Concerning the Abolition of Forced Labor*, updating its 1930 on the subject.

The *Minimum Age Convention* allows work at fourteen, unless the year of compulsory education ends at fifteen. The *Worst Forms of Child Labor Convention* identifies unacceptable jobs for children, notably drug trafficking, prostitution, slavery, or anything harmful to health, hazardous, or contrary to moral values. Some observers note that many poor families in developing countries depend upon the income from their children, even in prostitution, so compliance may lag behind what government leaders may believe to be immoral.

ADDITIONAL AGREEMENTS

Meanwhile, other important declarations and treaties have been adopted (Table 6.4). Among the earliest is the *Convention for the Suppression of the Traffic in Persons and of the Exploitation of the Prostitution of Others* of 1949.

The UN Economic, Social, and Cultural Organization (UNESCO) sponsored the *Convention Against Discrimination in Education* (followed by a Protocol setting up a

TABLE 6.3 **BASIC TREATIES OF THE INTERNATIONAL LABOR ORGANIZATION**

Adopted	Treaty	Type	In force
1930	Convention Concerning Forced or Compulsory Labor	Fundamental	1932
1948	Freedom of Association and Protection of the Right to Organize Convention	Fundamental	1950
1949	Convention Concerning Freedom of Association and Protection of the Right to Organize	Fundamental	1951
1951	Convention Concerning Equal Remuneration for Men and Women Workers for Work of Equal Value	Fundamental	1953
1957	Convention Concerning the Abolition of Forced Labor	Fundamental	1959
1958	Convention Concerning Discrimination in Respect of Employment and Occupation	Fundamental	1960
1973	Convention Concerning Minimum Age for Admission to Employment	Fundamental	1976
1999	Convention Concerning the Prohibition and Immediate Action for the Elimination of the Worst Forms of Child Labor	Fundamental	2000
1947	Convention Concerning Labor Inspection in Industry and Commerce	Priority	1950
1964	Convention Concerning Employment Policy	Priority	1966
1969	Convention Concerning Labor Inspection in Agriculture	Priority	1972
1976	Convention Concerning Tripartite Consultations to Promote the Implementation of International Labor Standards	Priority	1978

commission to handle complaints), the *Convention Concerning the Protection of the World Cultural and Natural Heritage,* and the *Convention on the Means of Prohibiting and Preventing the Illicit Import, Export and Transfer of Ownership of Cultural Property.* The latter agreement stimulated lawsuits in 2005, when Greece and Italy sued the Getty Museum in Los Angeles for illegally removing art objects from their countries, and Perú asked Yale University to return some five thousand artifacts taken from Machu Picchu. Then in 2006, voluntary agreements by the Boston Museum and the Metropolitan Museum of Art in New York, respectively, returned thirteen and twenty-one artifacts to Italian ownership, which in turn considered them to be on loan. In 2007, the Getty and Yale followed suit.

The General Assembly has fostered several agreements with special protection for children, the disabled, older persons, mentally ill persons, and women. The *Convention on Consent to Marriage, Minimum Age for Marriage and Registration for Marriage,* adopted in 1962, was designed to liberate women by requiring states to pass laws on the subject. The agreement does not specify a minimum age, but in 1965 a General Assembly resolution recommended the age of fifteen as the minimum. According to English common law, the minimum marriage age for girls is twelve and fourteen for boys. Common-law marriages, wherein partners living together are regarded as legally married without obtaining a marriage certificate from a government agency, are

TABLE 6.4 OTHER AGREEMENTS ON SOCIAL, ECONOMIC, AND CULTURAL RIGHTS

Adopted	Agreements and treaties	In force
1949	Convention for the Suppression of the Traffic in Persons and of the Exploitation of the Prostitution of Others	1951
2000	• Protocol to Prevent, Suppress and Punish Trafficking in Persons, Especially Women and Children	
1957	Convention Concerning the Protection and Integration of Indigenous and Other Tribal and Semi-Tribal Populations in Independent Countries	1959
1960	Convention Against Discrimination in Education	1962
1962	• Protocol Instituting a Conciliation and Good Offices Commission to Be Responsible for Seeking a Settlement of Any Disputes Which May Arise Between States Parties to the Convention Against Discrimination in Education	1968
1961	European Social Charter	1965
1962	Convention on Consent to Marriage, Minimum Age for Marriage and Registration of Marriage	1964
1965	Recommendation on Consent to Marriage, Maximum Age for Marriage and Registration of Marriage	
1969	Declaration on Social Progress and Development	
1970	Convention on the Means of Prohibiting and Preventing the Illicit Import, Export and Transfer of Ownership of Cultural Property	1972
1971	Declaration on the Rights of Mentally Retarded Persons	
1972	Convention Concerning the Protection of the World Cultural and Natural Heritage	1975
1974	Charter of Economic Rights and Duties of States	
1974	Universal Declaration on the Eradication of Hunger and Malnutrition	
1975	Declaration on the Rights of Disabled Persons	
1975	Declaration on the Use of Scientific and Technological Progress in the Interests of Peace and the Benefit of Mankind	
1978	Declaration on Race and Racial Prejudice	
1981	Declaration of San José	
1986	Declaration on the Right to Development	
1989	Convention Concerning Indigenous and Tribal Peoples in Independent Countries	1991
1991	Principles for Older Persons	
1991	Principles for the Protection of Persons with Mental Illness and the Improvement of Mental Health	
1992	Agreement Establishing the Fund for the Development of the Indigenous Peoples of Latin America and the Caribbean	1993
1993	Declaration on the Elimination of Violence Against Women	
1993	Standard Rules on the Equalization of Opportunities for Persons with Disabilities	
1998	Universal Declaration on the Human Genome and Human Rights	
2000	Convention Against Transnational Organized Crime	2003

TABLE 6.4 (CONTINUED)

Adopted	Agreements and treaties	In force
2000	• Protocol Against the Smuggling of Migrants by Land, Sea and Air, Supplementing the United Nations Convention Against Transnational Organized Crime	2004
2000	• Protocol to Prevent, Suppress and Punish Trafficking in Persons, Especially Women and Children, Supplementing the United Nations Convention Against Transnational Organized Crime	2003
2000	United Nations Millennium Declaration	
2001	Declaration of Commitment on HIV/AIDS	
2001	Universal Declaration on Cultural Diversity	

recognized in Australia, Canada (except for Québec), New Zealand, the United Kingdom, and several states of the United States. Six countries allow twelve-year-olds to marry, and at least twenty-six countries have no minimum legal marriage age.

The *Declaration on Social Progress and Development* of 1969 specifies some of the major concerns of both International Covenants. With respect to social rights, the Declaration prioritizes protection of the family (including the welfare of children), education, equal opportunities, health, housing, poverty and illiteracy reduction, the right to freely chosen employment, scientific progress shared with the people, and welfare benefits for the poor. Later agreements provide more details on some of the priorities.

The *Convention Against Transnational Organized Crime* and associated Protocols of 2000 are the most recent treaties touching on economic and social rights, referring

DISCUSSION TOPIC 6.1 SHOULD MUSLIM WOMEN WEAR HEAD OR BODY COVERINGS?

Although veils are not required by the Islamic faith, the custom of headscarves, veils, and burkas (full body coverings) is being observed increasingly in Muslim and Western European countries, where there is some concern as well that ski masks and full-face motorcycle helmets can be used as disguises for persons engaging in criminal activity. Currently, France and Singapore ban headscarves in schools, and Denmark allows employers to impose a similar ban. Despite protests, Egypt prohibits headscarves on television, and Turkey also does so in public. Belgium, Britain, Germany, and the Netherlands are considering bans on the wearing of some or all of the coverings, but women in Russia won the right to use headscarves in identification photographs during 1997. Do partial or total bans on distinctive coverings in the name of promoting religious harmony and national security serve to infringe cultural rights? What are the limits to prohibitions and requirements regarding the wearing of certain clothing?

as they do to the smuggling of children, women, and slave laborers. Estimates vary, but at least 60,000 persons are trafficked each year, of whom 80 percent are females, and 70 percent end up in the commercial sex industry; the rest are in debt bondage, that is, are forced to work to pay off debts. In some cases, they are promised that they will hold a certain well-paying job, but on arrival in a country they are told that they must pay for the cost of their passage in a job that has insufficient remuneration to pay the debt for many years. Most of those going to developed countries work in the sex industry. Young women from South Asia are hired as domestic servant slaves in the Middle East. In Sri Lanka and Uganda, the largest category of slaves consists of child soldiers. Some eighty countries now have laws banning human trafficking; in 2005, however, only 4,700 were imprisoned for the offense.

In 2001, UNESCO sponsored the latest agreement, the *Universal Declaration on Cultural Diversity*, which recommends that governments should not only respect cultural rights (notably cultural education, media pluralism, multilingualism, and the protection of artists and authors as unique developers of culture) but also foster policies of integration that promote the interaction of diverse cultural groups. Although female genital circumcision exists in more than two dozen countries and is disapproved in other countries, the cultural practice has not been condemned universally.

INDIGENOUS PEOPLES' RIGHTS

International human rights developed from 1648, when the Peace of Westphalia recognized states, not peoples, as the basic units of world politics. According to the Paris Peace Conference that drew up the treaties with the defeated powers of World War I, empires were to be broken up into states in which each nationality group would enjoy their own homeland. The Austro-Hungarian Empire and the Ottoman Empire were then carved up into separate states, in order to correspond to the principle that no people should been governed by another. However, the "one nation, one state" concept was a fiction embodied in the Fourteen Points of Woodrow Wilson (1856–1924), which were the principles of the peace settlement that the United States represented at Versailles. Every government had minority populations, and many had indigenous peoples under their jurisdiction.

HISTORIC EVENT 6.1 THE SHOSHONE NATION AND THE UNITED STATES SIGN THE TREATY OF RUBY VALLEY (1863)

According to the terms of the Treaty of Ruby Valley, white settlers were allowed to cross Shoshone lands from Idaho's Snake River to the Great Salt Lake into Death Valley, California, from 1863. Subsequently, Washington interpreted the agreement to mean that the Shoshones had given up their land. After various unsuccessful efforts to enforce the treaty in court, Congress awarded the Shoshones $145 million in compensation for their land in the Western Shoshone Distribution Act of 2004.

Wilson did not apply the same principle to his own country, where indigenous peoples had been allowed to live on 55 million acres of reservations in thirty states, governed by tribal governments. Although a District Court in 1879 ruled in *United States ex rel. Standing Bear v George Crook* that native peoples living in the United States had the right to sue in American courts, many native peoples did not survive the onslaught of white settlers. Relations between the United States and fifteen of the indigenous peoples are based on treaties, which presupposes that both parties are sovereign, and indeed several tribal governments are now suing to regain fishing and other rights.

During the League of Nations era (1919–1946), the rights of indigenous peoples were not included on the agenda of human rights concerns. In 1922, for example, the Six Nations Iroquois Confederacy petitioned the League of Nations to prevent Canada from taking over Iroquois lands, but the petition was rebuffed. In 1945, a leader of the Iroquois nation sought to address the San Francisco conference that established the United Nations, but he was refused recognition.

During the early years of the UN, governments were eager to promote economic development, including encroachments on remote lands that had long been occupied by indigenous peoples who had preserved their way of without joining the world capitalist system. The very existence of distinct peoples was eventually threatened because the natural environments in which at least 350 million individuals, representing some 5,000 ethnolinguistic groups in 70 countries, were increasingly under attack. Complacently, the fate of indigenous peoples was thought to be protected by such treaties as the Convention on the Prevention and Punishment of the Crime of Genocide, the International Covenant on Civil and Political Rights, and the International Convention on the Elimination of All Forms of Racial Discrimination. The presumption was that native peoples had to assimilate (adopt the culture of the dominant group) in order to secure their rights. ILO's *Convention Concerning the Protection and Integration of Indigenous and Other Tribal and Semi-Tribal Populations in Independent Countries* of 1957 was also based on an assimilationist premise that clearly was not designed to handle the onslaught of corporations seeking to cut down rainforests and governments desiring to resettle their people from overcrowded cities to virgin lands.

In 1975, George Manual (1921–1989) invited thirty indigenous leaders from Canada, the United States, Australia, and New Zealand to a conference in Vancouver, Canada, where the World Council of Indigenous Peoples was formed. In 1981, the International Non-Governmental Organizations Conference on Indigenous Peoples and the Land, held at Geneva, advanced the concept of the **Fourth World** to refer to the world's indigenous peoples as contrasted with the **First World** (industrial democracies), **Second World** (nonmarket socialist economies), and **Third World** (developing countries). Both the Council and the Conference then pressured the UN to recognize their need to survive as distinct peoples.

In 1981 UNESCO's *Declaration of San José* responded by declaring **ethnocide** to be a form of cultural genocide that is an "extreme form of massive violation of human rights." "Ethnocide," the Declaration stated, exists when a people's "right to enjoy, develop and transmit its own culture and its own language, whether collectively or individually" is denied. The term had been coined by Raphael Lemkin (1900–1959), who also advanced the term "genocide." Nevertheless, ethnocide had been excluded from human rights protections under the Geneva Conventions.

In 1982, the UN Commission on Human Rights established the Working Group on Indigenous Populations, which asked five independent experts to make a comprehensive study of indigenous peoples and to make recommendations. The Working Group's report concluded that the distinctive characteristic of indigenous peoples is land-rootedness, so protection of their rights must involve an end to further encroachment on ancestral territories. In 1994, the Working Group adopted a draft Declaration on the Rights of Indigenous Peoples, but the forty-five articles were not accepted by governments represented on the Commission. The Working Group has continued to hold conferences, which have been attended in recent years by some 166 organizations of indigenous peoples.

In 1989, meanwhile, the ILO adopted the *Convention Concerning Indigenous and Tribal Peoples in Independent Countries* to replace the assimilationist treaty of 1971. Rejecting assimilationism, the new treaty prohibits "co-use, co-management, co-conservation, and non-removal or relocation without 'free and informed consent'," though indigenous peoples are not accorded a veto over the use of their ancestral lands.

Many of the most vocal groups represent the native peoples of the Americas. In 1992, the Second Summit Meeting of Ibero-American Heads of State adopted the *Agreement Establishing the Fund for the Development of the Indigenous Peoples of Latin America and the Caribbean* to provide financial resources for the many impoverished peoples whose environments had been severely damaged.

In 2002, one year after the Inter-American Court of Human Rights ruled in *Mayagna (Sumo) Community of Awas Tingni v Nicaragua* that native peoples have the right to maintain communal economic systems and to have sovereign control of their homelands, the UN Economic and Social Council set up the Permanent Forum on Indigenous Issues. The Forum has issued several declarations on such subjects as communication rights, elementary education, equality issues, and women's rights.

COURT CASE 6.1 *MAYAGNA (SUMO) COMMUNITY OF AWAS TINGNI V NICARAGUA (2001)*

In 1993 and 1995, a Nicaraguan government province granted logging concessions to private corporations from the Dominican Republic and South Korea, respectively. The concessions, which were on the lands of the Mayagna (Sumo) Community of Awas Tingni along the Atlantic coast, were granted without any attempt to obtain consent from the native people. With legal assistance from the World Wildlife Federation, the community complained to the Inter-American Commission on Human Rights in 1995 and to the Nicaraguan Supreme Court in 1997, both of which ruled in favor of the Awas Tingni people. After further negotiations with the Nicaraguan government, the Inter-American Commission on Human Rights in 1998 brought the case against the Nicaraguan government before the Inter-American

continued

Court of Human Rights, which ruled three years later that failure to obtain prior approval of the indigenous community was a violation of the American Convention on Human Rights, which requires governments to demarcate the boundaries of the territories where native peoples can exercise sovereign control and to accord them legal protection. The court awarded the indigenous community $30,000 for legal expenses and $50,000 for the community to spend for the benefit of its people.

In short, indigenous peoples are under threat around the world. Their rights have been gradually identified, but often too late for them to preserve their ways of life. Their priorities are land rights, self-determination, and social equality, but major international institutions, dominated as they are by states that suppress minority peoples, have failed to recognize their rights. The Universal Declaration on Cultural Diversity has yet to be placed on a treaty basis.

INTERNATIONAL AID TO REDUCE THE GAP BETWEEN RICH AND POOR NATIONS

While the International Covenant on Economic, Social, and Cultural Rights was being drafted, much American aid went to anti-Communist regimes, Soviet aid to pro-Soviet regimes, and World Bank aid to First World contractors to build infrastructure in the Third World so that giant corporations could profit by receiving lucrative construction and consulting contracts. Some observers also characterized the UN as staffed by bureaucrats who were so out of touch with the latest technological innovations that they were not dispensing useful technical assistance.

As more African countries joined the UN in the 1960s, the balance of power in the General Assembly shifted away from problems associated with the Cold War to a concern for poverty within the Third World. Although many First World leaders naïvely believed that Third World governments were solely at fault for failing to improve the quality of life of their peoples, the realization increasingly dawned in the Third World that their poverty was due to policies pursued in the economically dominant First World.

Accordingly, in 1964 the General Assembly convened the first UN Conference on Trade and Development (UNCTAD) to devise a coherent and effective strategy for Third World economic development. What UNCTAD first proposed was that developing countries should adopt **import substitution** strategies, that is, develop basic industries behind tariff walls so that poor countries could become more economically self-reliant. However, the private sector in developing countries lacked the capital required to develop heavy industry, so two patterns developed. In larger countries, tax revenues were used to establish government corporations, following a socialist model. In other countries, First World-based transnational corporations (TNCs) bought businesses in Third World countries to gain increasingly monopolistic control of national economies and later used their economic leverage to gain exemptions from regulations imposed on local businesses. While socialist Third World government enterprises foundered due to lack of competition, First World corporations in capitalist Third World countries used the import substitution strategy to exploit poorer countries but not to assist in developing their economies to the point of self-sufficiency. Even in the field of agriculture, TNCs within poor countries were sending food to rich countries, while local people were starving.

UNCTAD, a permanent UN body as of 1964, urged developed countries to allocate at least 0.7 percent of their gross national product for Third World aid. Half that amount was forthcoming, but with so many strings attached that Third World governments resented the aid conditions as constituting political interference on behalf of First World interests. In addition, the terms of trade declined for the Third World: they were paying increasingly more to import Western goods, while export revenues to the First World were declining. As First World corporations found new sources of primary products within developing countries, Third World earnings from natural resources fell due to increased world supply. By the end of the 1960s, there was a growing belief in UNCTAD that import substitution had failed to promote Third World prosperity.

When the 1970s began, the north–south split between the First and Third Worlds dominated the United Nations. Poorer countries of the south insisted that they had the right to receive considerably more aid for development, since they argued that countries in the north had become rich by exploiting them, first as colonies and later as economic neocolonies. The argument, in short, was articulated in terms of dollars and cents more than ideologies. However, First World leaders noted that Marxist theories from the Second World were increasingly being accepted as valid explanations for the dismal fate of the Third World, and some former colonial powers rejected the neocolonial thesis. Nevertheless, at least four significant developments shifted the initiative to the South.

First, member countries of the Organization of Petroleum Exporting Countries (OPEC) decided in 1970 that they would no longer allow Western oil corporations to determine the selling price for petroleum. They instead began to nationalize the oil industries and to set export prices, thereby showing that non-Western countries had more clout in the world economy than previously thought.

Next, French President Charles de Gaulle (1890–1970), who opposed the American involvement in the Vietnamese civil war, decided to undermine American financing of that conflict. He was aware that Americans were buying more wine and other goods from France than the French were buying from the United States, resulting in a trade surplus in favor of France. Since the meeting at Bretton Woods that set up the World Bank in 1944 also designated the U.S. dollar as the primary unit of international currency, which in turn was backed by gold deposits at Fort Knox, France in 1971 refused to accept dollars for American export purchases and instead demanded payment in gold. In response, President Richard Nixon (1913–1994) took the dollar off the gold standard, thereby forcing the price of the dollar to fluctuate in the world economy. The international economic order, which had been premised on the dollar backed by a fixed price of gold after World War II, was shattered. The world, therefore, lacked economic stability in a sea of shifting rates of exchange between national currencies.

In September 1973, the Summit Conference of Non-Aligned Nations, held in Algiers, called for a **new international economic order** (NIEO) that would replace the economic order that ended when the dollar was no longer backed by gold. The Third World wanted to end the exploitation and impoverishment inherent in the old order, which had consigned the Third World to ship minerals and other primary products at low prices to the First World and then to buy back goods made with the same products in Western countries at higher prices.

The *coup de grace* came in October 1973, after the Yom Kippur War broke out. While Israel responded to a surprise attack from Egypt and Syria, the Arab Organization of Petroleum Exporting Countries (OAPEC, not OPEC) limited shipments of oil to Israel's principal allies, notably the United States, Japan, and the Netherlands. To obtain sufficient petroleum, oil companies had to buy oil on the spot market, and the selling price quadrupled through 1974. Arab countries suddenly were awash with U.S. dollars, and a First World recession resulted as the increased cost of oil reverberated throughout their economies.

Accordingly, world economic instability prompted a call for action from the UN, where the Third World could outvote the First World. A Special Session of the General Assembly met in 1974 and adopted, without a formal vote, a manifesto entitled *Declaration and Program of Action of the New International Order*. Later that year, the General Assembly's regular session approved the *Charter of Economic Rights and Duties of States*. Among the specifics in the two documents and related NIEO proposals were the following:

- recognition of the concept of the right to development;
- national control of infrastructure on the basis of the principle of build–operate–transfer;
- relocation of First World industries to the Third World;
- joint ventures, so that First World corporations could only operate in the Third World in joint operations with local corporations;
- joint research so that patents could be filed in the Third World;
- concessional (long-term, low interest) loans with few strings attached for the Third World;
- technical assistance by First World consultants, not by permanent staff of UN organizations, including the development of marketing capabilities;
- a Third World emergency food supply program financed by food-importing countries;
- aid to increase agricultural productivity in the Third World;
- First World aid at 0.7 percent of their gross domestic product;
- reduction of First World tariffs;
- Third World debt cancelation or rescheduling;
- buffer stocks to stabilize commodity prices, that is, stockpiles of commodities that could be bought when prices were low and sold to ease spikes in prices when supplies were low;
- compensatory financing to stabilize Third World export earnings;
- indexing Third World export prices to First World exports;

- a code of conduct for First World corporations operating in Third World countries (as explained below);
- UN support for south–south technical assistance and other forms of cooperation, such as commodity cartels similar to OPEC.

In 1975, at another Special Session of the General Assembly, First World countries agreed to several concrete NIEO proposals. The resulting resolution endorsed many of the demands for New International Economic Order, representing a symbolic victory for the South, but the North attached reservations, and there were conflicting interpretations of the compromise. Some in the South wanted a complete restructuring of the world economy, with new institutions and new rules, but others were content with special programs and exemptions. In the end, implementation was largely left to the First World. For example, the demand for a code of conduct for corporations resulted in the formation of the UN Center for Transnational Corporations (UNCTC), but any implementation of such a code would have to be left to individual corporations, which initially resisted regulation.

In 2001, when President Ronald Reagan (1911–2004) took office, his government declared that NIEO was dead. Since America's experience with colonialism was primarily limited to the Philippines, he did not share the view that past colonialism required reparations. Instead, Reagan's supporters envisioned a world economy with free trade, a concept then called **economic liberalization**, with the following components:

- privatization, that is, the dismantling of government corporations in the Third World that had been set up during the era of import substitution;
- direct private sector loans and investment guarantees by the World Bank and related institutions to the Third World, thereby eliminating the middle man, that is, the former practice of making loans to governments which in turn made loans to private firms;
- deregulation, namely, phasing out governmental regulations of the economy so that market economics could operate more freely;
- export promotion, thereby replacing import substitution as the primary development strategy;
- free trade (tariff reduction) throughout the world, such that Western industrial goods would enjoy access to previously protectionist Third World countries, and First World corporations would increase their investment in the Third World to take advantage of the global reduction in tariffs.

However, subsidies on agricultural goods produced within the First World were left out of the new program of economic liberalization, which focused primarily on the manufacturing sector. The intellectual architects of Reagan's economic vision were followers of libertarian economist Milton Friedman (1902–2006).

In 1986, nevertheless, the General Assembly adopted the *Declaration on the Right to Development* in 1986. The resolution was only symbolic, a Third World reminder to the First World that more development aid was needed.

In 1989, the Berlin Wall fell, and the Second World soon disintegrated. Insofar as the Cold War pitted Second World advocates of the priority of economic and social rights over First World exponents of civil and political rights, the latter won. Economic and social rights were then backburnered by the First World at the behest of transnational corporations, which advocated a world economy driven by the law of supply and demand unfettered by governmental or international regulations. The dreams of a world of free trade as espoused by such economic philosophers as Adam Smith (1723–1790) and David Ricardo (1772–1823) seemed closer to reality than ever before in human history.

Even before capitalism triumphed over state socialism, market economies had been developing within China, Eastern Europe, the Soviet Union, and Vietnam. During the 1990s, democratic revolutions came along with the end of state socialism in Eastern Europe, whereas China and Vietnam adopted economic liberalization while continuing to crack down on democratic aspirations.

The term **globalization** then was increasingly used in the 1990s to describe several developments beyond economic liberalization:

- Former nonmarket economies entered the world capitalist system, producing a variety of low-cost consumer goods.
- Improvements in communications, especially through the Internet, made possible instantaneous shifts of capital across national boundaries, such that a country's economy could be devastated by large-scale sell-offs of its currency.
- Jet travel with relatively low-cost fuel facilitated the rapid movement of goods and people from one corner of the world to another.
- Transnational corporations bought out businesses in a wave of consolidations and mergers, such that they became global in geographic scope while many different kinds of businesses, from manufacturing to services, were vertically integrated inside the same corporate entity.
- The new demand for unskilled labor to produce goods for international markets led to internal migration of persons from the countryside to live in shantytowns within the Third World, away from their families.
- Jobs in the First World were increasingly outsourced to the Third World.

The power of global corporations began to be described as **corporate imperialism** insofar as profiteering businesses trampled on human rights, particularly workers' rights. Ironically, the elements of globalization had been identified by Karl Marx (1818–1893) as preconditions to the end of capitalism. For Marx, the contradictions of capitalism would not become obvious until the capitalist system spread to every nook and cranny of the globe, whereupon megamergers would lead to oligopolies and later to monopolies that exerted political control over workers beyond the boundaries of an increasingly irrelevant state system. When class-conscious workers realized that they could end their exploitation by collectively taking control of monopolistic businesses, according to Marx, socialism would emerge as a more attractive economic system of peace, prosperity, and human dignity.

But the collapse of the Berlin Wall ended the socialist experiment in Eastern Europe, so opponents of globalization have decried a neglect of human rights by transnational corporations and a failure of developed countries to support structural changes in the world economy that might provide more opportunities for poorer countries. Proponents, however, have pointed out that Third World countries have benefited considerably from globalization, since there has been considerable foreign investment and job creation in some of the poorest countries, thereby bringing more wealth that may be allocated by Third World governments to education and health. In short, globalization's supporters point to increases in the attainment of Third World economic and social rights, while opponents focus on deficiencies in regard to civil and political rights as well as to lagging economic and social rights attainments within the poorest countries in the world.

Adjusting to the globalization of the world economy in the 1990s, the World Bank Group concluded that loans to Third World countries had rarely achieved the objectives of economic development. Accordingly, there was a reorientation in some programming toward poverty reduction.

HISTORIC EVENT 6.2 THE SECOND WORLD CONFERENCE ON HUMAN RIGHTS (1993)

In 1989, the Second World of Communist countries collapsed, and economic assistance waned to the Third World, where East and West formerly competed to gain supporters. The Third World, feeling abandoned by the First World, began to complain for attention to their needs in terms of economic and social rights. In 1993, the Second World Conference on Human Rights convened in Vienna to resolve a growing dissensus over human rights priorities. In preparation for the conference, Asian countries met earlier in the year at Bangkok to endorse the proposition that economic and social rights should have priority over civil and political rights and that the major agreements on human rights should be rewritten to reflect the opinions of countries that were not consulted when they were written. They championed their views under the concept of "Asian values," that is, the importance of community and family needs over Western notions of individual rights. After considerable contention at the conference, the official position adopted by the delegates was a compromise – that the two sets of rights, civil-political and economic-social, are "universal, indivisible and interdependent and interrelated."

There was sharp disagreement at the Second World Conference of Human Rights at Vienna in 1993. At one extreme was the **developmentalist** view, advocated by some Third World countries, that economic and social rights are superior and prior to civil and political rights. At the other extreme was the **libertarian** view, advanced by some Anglo-American democracies, that economic and social rights are not rights at all and that treating them as rights serves to justify large-scale state intervention and provides an excuse for violating civil and political rights. European welfare state advocates of a middle position somewhere between developmentalism and libertarianism, sometimes known as **social market capitalism**, were not able to bridge the gap. The social safety net of social market capitalism, meanwhile, was in jeopardy within Europe, where the rising cost of welfare programs, especially for aging populations, was confronting a shrinking in government revenues due in part to mounting unemployment. As a result, the conference achieved little.

One year after the Vienna conference, the World Trade Organization (WTO) was formed. The pressure to consider trade in strictly economic terms resulted in pressure to reduce tariffs as well as nontariff trade barriers (NTBs). Laws adopted by governments to boycott goods produced by child labor, for example, were now subject to possible challenge as NTBs. Under WTO rules, any country with an unacceptable NTB is subject to a potential worldwide trade boycott. The specter emerged that the WTO could authorize trade sanctions against any country in order to roll back human rights advances that had taken decades to establish.

Although globalization has brought some prosperity to many poorer countries, which benefit from the resulting increase in investment, the labor force throughout the world has been subjected to three shocks: (1) First World unemployment has increased as factories relocate to Third World countries where the cost of labor is lower. (2) Third World workers often are often paid extremely low wages for long hours under conditions where occupational safety requirements are minimal. (3) When tariff-free goods from Third World factories are imported by the First World, corporations in the latter countries face such stiff competition that they have sought to keep wages low and to ask their governments not to enforce fair labor or occupational safety standards.

In short, WTO-led globalization has been viewed as condoning violations of economic and social rights on such a scale that protests have greeted meetings of various world economic summits, the most notable of which occurred at Seattle, which hosted the annual WTO meeting in 1999. Insofar as WTO rules continue to give priority to the free flow of trade over the rights of workers, the status of economic and social rights will be in disarray throughout much of the world. Pressure to reform WTO into a more socially conscious organization has led to some innovations in recent years, as described in Chapter 10.

DISCUSSION TOPIC 6.2 WHAT PRINCIPLES SHOULD GOVERN THE WORLD ECONOMY?

Proposals for a New International Economic Order (NIEO) were nixed by the economic liberalization of the 1980s and the economic globalization following the collapse of the Berlin Wall in 1989. The possible benefits of NIEO for the Third World, in short, were viewed as costs that the First World refused to bear. What are the costs and benefits of globalization? Who are the winners and losers in both the First World and the Third World today?

CODES OF CONDUCT

In 1971, the Reverend Leon Sullivan (1922–) joined the Board of Directors of General Motors; he was the first African American on the board of a major American corporation. Opposed to *apartheid* in South Africa, where General Motors was the largest employer of Black Africans, he formulated a set of principles to govern trade with the country that might serve to end the odious racist practice. Known as the **Sullivan Principles**, they were first employed in 1977 with the support of many corporations. The step-by-step approach to dismantle *apartheid* began with fair labor practices: (1) desegregation of employment facilities; (2) equal employment opportunity for all employees; (3) equal pay for equal work; (4) a minimum wage and salary structure; (5) increasing the number of Africans to managerial, supervisory, administrative, clerical, and technical jobs; (6) measures to improve the quality of employees' lives outside work; and (7) other practices, including allowing employees to form unions. Later, companies were urged to break the law openly, challenging the government to take legal action. Then came a demand to release Nelson Mandela (1918–) from prison, followed by the requirement that Blacks must be allowed to vote. Finally, *apartheid* itself was to be abolished or businesses would leave the country. Indeed, more than one hundred major corporations eventually departed, so weakening South Africa's economy that the desired political change, the end of *apartheid*, occurred in 1994.

In 1990, one year after the massacre in Beijing near Tiananmen Square, Reebok left China, objecting to martial law conditions and the presence of military personnel in its plants. In 1992, Sears, Roebuck decided to stop importing Chinese products produced by prisoners or by other forms of involuntary labor. In 1993, Levi Straus and Timberland ended operations and investment in China.

Meanwhile, consistent with the call for NIEO, the task of designing a global code of conduct was assigned by the General Assembly to the newly created UN Center for Transnational Corporations in 1973. But UNCTC failed to agree on a code of conduct during subsequent deliberations. In its last stand, the CTC attempted to gain acceptance for environmental and labor codes at the 1992 Earth Summit, but CTC's proposal was spurned in favor of a voluntary code of conduct proposed by the World Business Council for Sustainable Development (WBCSC), an organization of prominent transnational corporations in thirty-four countries formed in 1991. WBCSC advocates a policy of **free-market environmentalism**, that is, the development of environmental and labor standards by corporations that will be free from governmental or international regulation while not jeopardizing profits. Today, most Fortune 500 corporations and many others are members of WBCSD.

The increasing loss of First World jobs to textile mills in the Third World during the 1990s raised questions about substandard labor conditions. In some cases, child labor or prison labor has been used, working conditions have lacked occupational safety measures, and workers have been employed for more than forty hours per week, often at starvation wages. In 1995, pickets ringed Gap clothing stores and Starbucks coffeehouses, protesting violation of human rights standards by their suppliers; as a result, both signed codes of conduct. Also in 1995, U.S. immigration authorities uncovered a factory in El Monte, California, where seventy-one Thai nationals were locked up in an apartment complex for up to seventeen years to sew clothing for name brand manufacturers and retailers during eighteen-hour work days. In 1996, there was an outcry when news reporters found that the name of television actress Kathie Lee Gifford (1953–) was being attached to a line of clothing made by underage workers in Central America.

The events of 1995–1996 spurred U.S. Secretary of Labor Robert Reich (1946–) to launch a "No Sweat" campaign in 1996, bringing representatives from apparel industry corporations, environmental groups, labor unions, and human rights groups together into an Apparel Industry Partnership in order to draw up a code of conduct that would restrict imports of goods produced by children, forced labor, and workers required to labor more than sixty hours per week. The following year, the president's Council on Economic Priorities issued the *Workplace Code of Conduct and Principles of Monitoring*, promoting with the following conditions:

- a ban on the use of child and forced labor;
- prohibition of sexual harassment and worker abuse;
- a safe and healthy workplace;
- recognition of freedom of association and collective bargaining as basic rights;
- required payment of the local minimum wage or the prevailing industry wage, with overtime hours paid at the legal rate;
- use of independent external monitors to oversee implementation.

President Bill Clinton (1946–) endorsed the *Workplace Code* that year. Not all companies accepted the recommendations, however.

In 1997, Senator Edward Kennedy (1932–) unsuccessfully proposed a Congressional resolution to urge all American transnational corporations to adopt a code of conduct voluntarily, including a pledge to refrain from doing business in countries that violate human rights. Determining the content of codes of conduct has been problematic, though the ILO already has established many environmental and labor standards.

In 1999, the Fair Labor Association (FLA) was incorporated to serve as a forum for garment manufacturers that subscribe to the *Workplace Code of Conduct and Principles of Monitoring*.[1] The principles cover the issues of child labor, forced labor, nondiscrimination, fair labor standards regarding wages and hours of work, occupational health and safety, sexual harassment, and tradeunion rights. At least 250 American corporations have adopted codes of conduct, according to the nongovernmental organization Clean Clothes Campaign; Levi Strauss took the lead as early as 1991.

Today, several codes of conduct compete for acceptance today. **MacBride Principles**, developed in 1984 by the Irish National Caucus and eventually adopted by most corporations in Northern Ireland, were designed to address anti-Catholic employment discrimination by Protestants in Northern Ireland; they were endorsed by the U.S. Congress in 1998. The Coalition for Environmentally Responsible Economies, a coalition of business, labor, and public interest organizations, promote environmentally sound corporate practices that are known as the **Ceres Principles**; they were developed in 1989 following the environmentally devastating spill by the *Exxon Valdez* oil tanker in Prince William Sound, Alaska. **Caux Principles** were announced in 1994 by idealistic European and Japanese corporate leaders after deliberations at a roundtable discussion group that had met at Caux, Switzerland, from 1986; they focus on the goals of human dignity and the common good. In 1999, UN Secretary General Kofi Annan (1938–) launched the **Global Sullivan Principles for Corporate Responsibility**. In addition, a code of conduct was adopted by the UN Subcommission on the Protection and Promotion of Human Rights in 2001. In short, there is no consensus on the content of corporate codes of conduct.

In 2002, after five years of joint planning by the UN Environmental Program and the Coalition for Environmentally Responsible Economies, the Global Reporting Initiative (GRI) was launched, with a headquarters in Amsterdam. GRI accepts voluntary reports from more than 20,000 firms in 80 countries on their economic, social, and environmental practices based on fifty-seven core indicators in its Sustainability Reporting Framework.

In short, codes of conduct have arisen from five sources: (1) Corporations have initiated their own social audits. (2) Trade associations or industries have established standards. After the Bhopal tragedy, for example, the American Chemistry Council developed standards. (3) Nongovernmental organizations have launched efforts to encourage humane working conditions. (4) Governments have adopted fair labor standards legislation. (5) Intergovernmental organizations, especially the International Labor Organizations, have played important roles.

HISTORIC EVENT 6.3 THE BHOPAL INDUSTRIAL ACCIDENT (1984)

In 1984, the world's worst industrial accident occurred when forty tons of chemicals leaked from the Union Carbide pesticide plant in Bhopal, India, immediately resulting in some 7,000 deaths and 200,000 injuries. Two years later, an Indian court attempted to summon the head of the company for questioning, but he refused to appear; he became a fugitive. Thus far, he has eluded Interpol, and efforts to have Washington extradite him have failed. An investigation concluded by 1987 that Union Carbide was liable because alarm and safety systems had been scaled back to reduce costs. In 1989, the Indian government accepted a civil settlement of $470 million, though the government still has not disbursed $390 million to the victims. However, the company abandoned the plant without cleaning up the toxic chemicals, so the poisons remain to haunt the people, and one person per day dies from the exposure. In all, some 600,000 persons have been affected to date. In 1992, the head of Union Carbide and several Indian operators of the plant were charged with manslaughter in an Indian court. In 1999, Union Carbide was sued under the Alien Tort Claims Act in the United States, a case now on appeal. In 2001, Dow Chemical Company bought Union Carbide, which thereby hoped thereby to escape liability, but in 2005 the Indian court added Dow to the lawsuit and again asked the U.S. government to serve the former Union Carbide head with a subpoena. Meanwhile, charges brought against Dow in an American court to effect a cleanup were dismissed in 2003 because the Indian court was already handling the case.

FAIR TRADE

Codes of conduct are relevant to large corporations. The Fair Trade movement is concerned with the other side of the coin, namely, the conditions of work for small-scale primary agricultural producers. In 1860, the pseudonymously authored novel *Havelaar, or the Coffee Auctions of the Dutch Trading Company* attacked the evils of colonial exploitation of workers, in which former communal agricultural farmers were reduced to starvation levels by being dispossessed of their lands and forced to survive by working on Dutch coffee and tea plantations. Written by Eduard Douwes Dekker (1820–1887), the novel is often credited with inspiring anti-colonial movements around the world.

Soon after World War II, churches in Europe and North America decided to help millions of refugees and poverty-stricken communities by enabling them to sell handicrafts to through such organizations as the Mennonite Central Committee. In the 1960s, alternative trade organizations (ATOs) were formed to provide the middle men for trade between primary producers and such marketing firms as department stores.

In 1988, when the price of coffee nosedived, the Max Havelaar Foundation began to issue labels in the Netherlands for cans of coffee that met standards of Fair Trade, such as living wages for Third World workers. Then in 1989, the International Federation of Alternative Trade (IFAT) was formed as an alliance of ATOs with a headquarters in Oxon, England; currently, seventy ATOs from thirty countries are members.

In 1997, the Fairtrade Labeling Organizations International (FLO), a nongovernmental international organization, was formed in Bonn, Germany to develop fair trade principles and to certify products. Today, FLO has members in twenty countries from Europe to North America to Japan. In 1998, TransFair USA joined FLO, and the following year the organization began to certify Fair Trade Coffee, some of which has been available at Starbucks from the year 2000, as well as cocoa and tea. Other Fair Trade products include bananas, fresh fruits and juices, herbs, honey, rice, sugar, vanilla, sports balls, and one of Macy's latest products, beautiful handicraft baskets made by women in Rwanda who are seeking to bring wealth to their country.

The main criteria for certifying Fair Trade products, as developed by IFAT, FLO, and similar organizations, are as follows:

- **fair price** (farmer groups receive a minimum floor price, an additional premium for organic products, and are eligible for pre-harvest credit);
- **fair labor** (workers have freedom of association, safe working conditions, and a living wage);
- **direct trade** (products are purchased in bulk by fair trade ATOs, thereby eliminating the middle man);
- **democracy and transparency** (farmers and farm workers decide democratically how to invest profits);
- **community development** (profits are spent on upgrading the quality of products as well as on scholarships for members of the community);

- **gender equity** (equal pay for women and female involvement in community decisionmaking);
- **environmental sustainability** (harmful agrochemicals and genetically modified organisms are banned; farming is managed without adverse impacts on eco-systems).

The result is that 1.5 million primary producers in 50 countries are deriving at least $1 billion of additional income each year. Prices of Fair Trade products can be higher, but FLO encourages producer countries to process their products before shipment, such as by roasting and packaging coffee, so that they can undersell primary products that are processed in the First World.

MILLENNIUM DECLARATION

In the year 2000, the UN General Assembly convened a special session to consider goals to be achieved in the twenty-first century. The resulting United Nations Millennium Declaration of 2000 had much to say about economic, social, and cultural rights. In addition to urging First World countries to eliminate tariffs against the Third World and to cancel their official debts, the following goals and timetables were adopted by the UN General Assembly:

- To halve, by the year 2015, the proportion of the world's people whose income is less than one dollar a day and the proportion of people who suffer from hunger and, by the same date, to halve the proportion of people who are unable to reach or to afford safe drinking water.
- To ensure that, by the same date, children everywhere, boys and girls alike, will be able to complete a full course of primary schooling and that girls and boys will have equal access to all levels of education.
- By the same date, to have reduced maternal mortality by three quarters, and under-five child mortality by two-thirds, of their current rates.
- To have, by then, halted, and begun to reverse, the spread of HIV/AIDS, the scourge of malaria and other major diseases that afflict humanity.
- To provide special assistance to children orphaned by HIV/AIDS.
- By 2020, to have achieved a significant improvement in the lives of at least 100 million slum dwellers . . .

In addition to restating provisions of earlier UN Declarations, the Millennium Declaration raised new concerns. One is support for the concept of **sustainable development**, that is, structural changes in Third World countries that will enable them to grow economically in the global economy while respecting fundamental human rights and engaging in environmentally sound practices that enable future generations to satisfy basic human needs. The Millennium Declaration also includes a goal regarding foreign aid, which is to be provided by the most prosperous countries at 0.7 percent of national income.

In 2002, President George W. Bush (1946–) announced the Millennium Challenge Account as a substitute for the social and economic goals and timetables of the Declaration. The program stresses aid only to countries with

> "good governance," [that is, countries that] "root out corruption, respect human rights, . . . adhere to the rule of law[,] . . . invest in better health care, better schools and broader immunization . . . [and] have more open markets and sustainable budget policies, nations where people can start and operate a small business without running the gauntlets of bureaucracy and bribery."

Nevertheless, official American foreign aid is only 0.16 percent of national income.

Although some aid has indeed been squandered over the years, with little impact on economic growth in the poorest countries, there is a consensus today that aid for health care has been the most effective. The eradication of smallpox and considerable reduction in the incidence of guinea worms, leprosy, and river blindness has been due to carefully organized aid efforts. The Global AIDS Initiative, launched by President Bush in 2003, involves a promise to spend $15 billion over five years, though the incidence of HIV/AIDS has increased in part because condom distribution has been opposed by the United States.

PROBLEMS OF ACHIEVING ECONOMIC, SOCIAL, AND CULTURAL RIGHTS

Economic aid to developing countries is often justified as a way to encourage greater fulfillment of economic, social, and cultural rights – or even to provide preconditions for increased civil and political rights. The strategies of economic development reviewed above have changed because the results have not measured up. One reason is that on the world stage, economic, social, and cultural rights have simply been neglected in comparison with civil and political rights. There are several reasons:

- Treaties guaranteeing economic, social, and cultural rights concede that implementation depends upon the resources of a country. According to the International Covenant on Economic, Social and Cultural Rights, "Each State Party to the present Covenant undertakes to take steps, individually and through international assistance and cooperation, especially economic and technical, to the maximum of its available resources, with a view to achieving progressively the full realization of the rights recognized in the present Covenant . . ."
- Western countries have considerable economic and social attainments, whereas Third World countries have the poorest records. Leaders of some Third World countries say that they are too poor to improve the educational and health levels of their people, though such claims are often a smokescreen for elites and dictators.
- Many leading nongovernmental organizations, such as Amnesty International, have not focused on economic, social, and cultural rights. Other organizations, such as Médecins Sans Frontières (Doctors Without Borders), quietly work to improve conditions, but only during crises, that is, when problems have reached mammoth proportions.

- No innovative legal or concrete approaches to implementation have been developed or even proposed by countries that most strongly support economic, social, and cultural rights.
- Civil and political rights are stated in absolute terms, but economic, social, and cultural rights in the various treaties are phrased in softer terms, more as goals than as duties. States are only obligated to adopt incremental programs to achieve economic and social rights and to report to the UN on what the programs are and how much progress they are making. In others words, treaties guaranteeing civil and political rights say that government should absolutely not harm people, but the treaties dealing with economic and social rights do not insist on guarantees. People have rights and governments have duties in regard to civil and political rights; in contrast, people have economic, social, and cultural rights, but treaties do not insist that governments have strong obligations to fulfill their rights.
- Media can easily focus on guns pointed at protesters and similar dramas. Denials of economic, social, and cultural rights are more subtle and make headlines primarily when refugee camps provide visible evidence of desperate conditions.
- Monitoring by the Committee on Economic, Social and Cultural Rights (CESCR), which was established by the International Covenant on Economic, Social, and Cultural Rights, requires reports at five-year intervals and recommends action only in response to those reports. For example, in 1995 CESCR asked the Dominican Republic to provide homes to those living under bridges, on the sides of cliffs, in homes dangerously close to rivers, and to ravine dwellers, but the recommendation was by way of criticism that the government's response to Hurricane David, responsible for some 2,000 deaths in 1979, was inadequate.
- Boycotts of countries that deny civil and political rights often ignore the resulting adverse economic, social, and cultural consequences. When the international community adopts economic sanctions for a gross violator of civil and political rights, one consequence may be that masses are hit harder than elites. Accordingly, sanctions in place against Iraq after the Gulf War of 1991 so deprived children of food and medicine that the UN adopted an oil-for-food program.

CONCLUSION

Some critics, as noted in Chapter 5, argue that economic, social, and cultural rights are fundamentally different from civil and political rights. The counterargument, that the relationship is more complex, is supported by the following observations:

- The view that the cost of implementation is less for civil and political rights than for economic, social, and cultural rights lacks empirical support; nobody has yet calculated which is more expensive. Economists estimate that there is a considerable return on investment in primary education when considering such factors as reduced fertility, reduced infant mortality, lower population growth, improved family nutrition, and increased productivity. Running a dictatorship that suppresses civil and political rights is expensive, considering the cost of maintaining an army, a police force, and operating a system of surveillance on those capable of overthrowing the regime.

- The argument that guarantees of civil and political rights require less government action than guarantees of economic, social, and cultural rights is also wrong. Government must act to provide fair trials and to ensure free and fair elections, just as they must manage educational and health care systems.

- Civil and political rights are often claimed to be invariant, whereas economic, social, and cultural rights are claimed to be relative to the culture of each country. However, civil and political rights are quite variable. In Britain, officeholders can sue the press as well as stand-up comedians for libel, but in the United States officeholders take a lot of abuse because they are considered public figures; they must tolerate lies in the media.

- Another argument is that economic, social, and cultural rights can only be extended gradually, whereas civil and political rights are absolute and must be guaranteed immediately. But the right to vote was extended gradually in most Western countries, whereas the right to food requires immediate action on behalf of those who are starving.

- No democracy, as Amartya Sen (1933–) notes, has ever had a famine. Famines never kill the ruling class. In a country with free elections, opposing political parties, and a free press, crop failures will lead to collective action on behalf of those affected instead of stockpiling by elites while the masses starve.

- Little attention has been paid above on cultural rights, which most urgently affect persecuted minorities within states. One reason is that persecution, a violation of civil and political rights, gets more attention than the byproduct, cultural suppression. Although Article 5 of the Convention on the Elimination of All Forms of Racial Discrimination claims that the guarantee of equality before the law ensures the enjoyment of economic, social and cultural rights, in fact many ethnic and religious groups are treated unequally due to what mainstream groups may view as their quaint or unusual practices.

- Economic, social, and cultural rights affect more persons than civil and political rights. Children, who may be too young to participate in political life, have basic needs in regard to education, health, and other elements that are at the heart of the International Covenant on Economic, Social, and Cultural Rights.

- Arguments about whether civil and political rights are more important than economic, social, and cultural rights, or vice versa, can be easily deconstructed as cynical rhetoric used by governments to justify their deliberate neglect of certain basic rights.

Some observers claim that those who are poor, discriminated against, and deprived of human dignity are most likely to engage in armed insurrection against their own governments or in terrorist acts against foreign states. If so, there is a need to respect economic, social, and cultural rights in order to reduce domestic and international violence. The following chapter, which deals with rights of individuals when systematic violence erupts, may be seen as an extension of the principles of economic, social, and cultural rights, since wars and terrorist attacks can perhaps be measured in terms of economic, social, and cultural damage even more than in terms of violations of civil and political rights.

DISCUSSION TOPIC 6.3 WHAT CAN BE DONE TO PROMOTE ECONOMIC, SOCIAL, AND CULTURAL RIGHTS?

Deprivations of economic, social, and cultural rights are often neglected in comparison with denials of civil and political rights. What has been done to increase awareness of problems relating to economic, social, and cultural rights? What can be done? What kinds of action can best serve to improve economic, social, and cultural rights?

CHAPTER 7

Crimes against humanity, crimes against peace, and war crimes

Although the recognition of civil and political rights within countries may be traced to the Code of Hammurabi in 1780 BCE, the earliest systematic recognition of *international* human rights emerged from the doctrine of the **just war** of Saint Augustine (354–430). Subsequently, rules of warfare developed. But they were shattered during the world wars of the twentieth century. Currently, the focus has broadened to ban wars by governments against their own people, that is, crimes against humanity, as well as domestic and international terrorism.

DEFINING "WAR"

War must be distinguished definitionally from other violent or unfriendly acts. Otherwise, one country might perceive an unfriendly act as an act of war, mount a form of violent retaliation, and then the other side might respond, resulting in unintended war. Two forms of unfriendly behavior, accepted as not violating international law, are retorsion and reprisal. Neither are considered to be acts of war.

HISTORIC EVENT 7.1 AMERICAN DIPLOMATS ARE HELD HOSTAGE IN TEHRAN (1979–1981)

In 1979, some three hundred Iranians entered the U.S. embassy in Tehran and held sixty-three diplomats and three other American citizens hostage; three weeks later, thirteen were released. A request through diplomatic channels for the release of those held hostage was turned down. Iranian religious leader Ayatollah Ruhollah Khomeni (1902–1989), who earlier in the year inspired the revolution that toppled the regime of Shah Mohammad Reza Pahlavi (1919–1980), had accused America of being the "Great Satan." In response, Washington froze $8 billion in Iranian assets, blocked all Iranian oil imports to the United States, and the United States severed official diplomatic relations with Iran. In 1979, the International Court of Justice ruled in *United States v Iran* that Iran's action violated the Vienna Convention on Diplomatic Relations of 1961, but Tehran refused to comply with the court's order to release the hostages, to restore the embassy premises, and to pay reparations. In 1981, nine months after an abortive American rescue attempt, the hostages were released under an agreement mediated by Algeria in which the United States promised to unblock Iranian assets and resume trade. Washington, nevertheless, failed to honor the agreement after the hostages were released.

Retorsion is a peaceful response to an unfriendly act that does not violate a treaty but is unfriendly. Some examples of retorsion occurred after diplomats at the U.S. embassy in Iran were held hostage (Table 7.1). The first response was to freeze Iranian assets and to end trade relations with Iran. Even after the release of the hostages in 1981, the United States has refused to reestablish formal diplomatic relations, a second form of retorsion.

TABLE 7.1 RETORSIONS AND REPRISALS PERMITTED UNDER INTERNATIONAL LAW

Unfriendly act	Examples
Retorsion	Currency restrictions, denunciation of treaties, expulsion of diplomats or nationals of the other state, freezing or seizing assets from another state, jamming of radio broadcasts from abroad, military maneuvers and mobilizations on the border of another state, nonrecognition of one government and recognition of a rival government, increasing trade barriers, severance or withdrawal of diplomatic relations, verbal denunciations regarding another country
Reprisal	Attacks on commerce, blockades, boycotts and embargoes, landing of forces to rescue nationals abroad, limited military attacks and expeditions, including bombardments, seizure of vessels

A **reprisal**, in contrast, is an act of redress for a tangible injury. Reprisals may take the form of force under international law when the injured state gives notice of displeasure, requests compensation or cessation of harmful action, but the injuring state makes no response. As a self-help measure, a reprisal is acceptable under international law, provided that the reprisal is proportionate to the initial violation. The acceptance of reprisals under international law grew out of the medieval practice, now defunct, of *private reprisals* under which a person who suffered ill treatment from another community or its members might be authorized to seek redress by seizing property of a member of the errant community. The procedure was to have the government of an aggrieved person issue a "letter of marque and reprisal" to the victim, who was then authorized to take action. Today, such letters are not issued. Instead, governments directly take reprisals, though usually stronger governments do so against weaker countries. Accordingly, the abortive efforts to land helicopters in Iran during 1980 to rescue the American hostages could be considered a form of reprisal.

COURT CASE 7.1 THE NAULILAA ARBITRATION (1928)

In 1914, German civilian officials and soldiers crossed over the border of Portuguese Angola one day to discuss importing food into German Southwest Africa. Due to a mistranslation, a Portuguese officer seized a German official's bridle and struck him. The German then drew his pistol. Next, the Portuguese official ordered his men to fire, whereupon two German officers were killed, and the interpreter and another officer were interned. Shortly thereafter, German troops attacked and destroyed some forts and posts in Angola, though Germany and Portugal were not at war until 1916. After the war, Germany and Portugal agreed to submit the dispute, known as the Naulilaa Incident, to arbitration. In 1928, the arbitral tribunal ruled that Germany should pay for the damages because their disproportionate actions were not in response to a violation of international law by Portugal and thus were not lawful reprisals but rather resulted from a mere misunderstanding that led to imprudent behavior.

In contrast with retorsion and reprisal, **war** is usually defined as a state of armed hostility between sovereign nations or governments. However, war may technically exist if one state declares war against another without actually engaging in armed hostility. For example, Siam declared war on the United States during World War II to appease Japan, which used Siamese territory as a springboard for attacking British colonies in Southeast Asia, but Siam (now Thailand) and the United States never fought each other.

■ DEVELOPMENT OF THE LAW OF WARFARE

For centuries, wars were considered not to violate international law, though Greek and Roman law condemned the use of poison as an instrument of war. Such philosophers as Cicero (106–43 BCE), Augustine, and Thomas Aquinas (1225–1274) agreed that war could be justified, provided that the *aims* and the *means* were just. In other words, there has to be a good reason for going to war, and war must be fought humanely.

Over time, several principles developed in Christian theology about the concept of a **just war**. According to Augustine, "A just war is wont to be described as one that avenges wrongs, when a nation or state has to be punished, for refusing to make amends for the wrongs inflicted by its subjects, or to restore what it has seized unjustly."

For Aquinas and later theologians, the *principles* on which a just war could be waged are as follows: (1) **just authority** (Only rulers have the power to start a war, since they are required to maintain order; private warfare is outlawed.); (2) **just cause** or **rightful intention** (There is a right to stop gross evil and to promote good.); (3) **military necessity** (The use of force should be a response to an aggressor, whose actions are certain, grave, and lasting.); and (4) **last resort** (Efforts to resolve a conflict must exhaust all peaceful means before contemplating war.).

The *means* by which a war could be fought justly were as follows: (1) **humanity** (There should be no unnecessary violence and hence prisoners should be captured, not killed, and humanely treated.); (2) **chivalry** (The use of defensive force should not involve dishonorable means, expedients, or conduct: noncombatants should not be harmed, and no war should produce evils greater than those providing the pretext to war.); and (3) **proportionality** (Violence should be only enough to stop an evil and end in peace.).

Among the earliest legal principles (Table 7.2), the *Cáin Adomnáin* of 697, as agreed to by several Irish notables, authorized the death penalty for anyone killing a woman in time of war and penalties for slaying clerics, clerical students, and peasants on clerical land. In 989, six French bishops at the Synod of Charroux declared the *Pax Dei* (Peace of God), a law of warfare that was expanded and later spread throughout Europe. Among the provisions were immunity of children, clergy, merchants, peasants and women from attack in war. In 1027, the *Treuga Dei* (Truce of God) was promulgated, declaring that war could not take place on certain days of the year – initially Sundays, but later religious holidays, including the entire period of Lent, and Fridays. The clergy could threaten violators with excommunication, a limited sanction after the rise of Protestantism in the sixteenth century. In 1139, Pope Innocent II (who ruled from 1130–1143) urged a ban on the use of the crossbow as an overly cruel instrument of warfare in *Canon 29* issued by the Second Lateran Council in 1139.

Later, Dutch Protestant jurist Hugo Grotius (1583–1645) began to formulate a secular theory of the law of war, notably in his *The Freedom of the Seas* (1609), which argued that war should be banned in international waters. The Netherlands was trying to maintain a fleet to trade around the world, and interference by Britain and Spain was impeding the ambitions of his country.

TABLE 7.2   EARLY INTERNATIONAL AGREEMENTS DEVELOPING THE LAW OF WARFARE

Adopted	Document
697	*Cáin Adomnáin*
989	*Pax Dei*
1026	*Treuga Dei*
1139	Canon 29 (issued by the Second Lateran Council)
1675	Strasbourg Agreement
1815	Final Act of the Congress of Vienna
1856	Declaration of Paris
1864	Convention for the Amelioration of the Condition of the Wounded on the Field of Battle (Geneva Convention) (in force 1865)
1868	Additional Articles Relating to the Condition of the Wounded in War
1868	Declaration to the Effect of Prohibiting the Use of Certain Projectiles in Wartime (St. Petersburg Declaration)
1874	Project of an International Declaration Concerning the Laws and Customs of War (Brussels Declaration)

During the Thirty Years War (1618–1848), Grotius proposed that international law should govern relations between states. His advocacy of the development of a law of warfare in his 1625 volume *De jure belli ac pacis libri tres* (*Of Laws of War and Peace*) included a theory of just war in which natural law binds all states. His law of justifiable war (*jus ad bellum*) was that a country should only go to war to achieve the following *goals*:

- **defense:** Wars are just when they defend the national interest.
- **indemnity:** Wars are just if they recover damages inflicted by another state.
- **punishment:** War are just if they stop a gross ongoing injustice
- **last resort:** Wars are just only if peaceful methods fail to resolve an interstate conflict based on the preceding three pretexts.

In addition, Grotius's law of the conduct of war (*jus in bello*) required that the *means* used in warfare should be as follows:

- **discrimination:** Combat should not be directed at civilians.
- **humanity:** The sick and wounded should be cared for, and prisoners should be treated with respect.
- **proportionality:** The scope of the war should be minimal, calibrated only to the end sought.

Presumably, government leaders had to satisfy the requirements of *jus ad bellum*, whereas military personnel in the field would have to follow the principles of *jus in bello*. If a government authorized an army to violate the principles of *jus in bello*, then both would violate the law of warfare.

DISCUSSION TOPIC 7.1   WHEN WAS THE LAST TIME WHEN A "JUST WAR" WAS LAUNCHED AND FOUGHT?

Using the ethical and legal principles discussed above, which recent war could be characterized as just? The Iraq War of 2003? The Gulf War of 1991? Or some other recent war? Indicate why the war was just or unjust. If unjust, what could have been done differently to make the war just?

Consistent with Grotius's ideas, international law after the Peace of Westphalia of 1648 was recorded in the form of treaties between nation-states. Perhaps the first example of what developed as the treaty-based law concerning the conduct of warfare occurred in 1675, when France and the Holy Roman Empire signed the *Strasbourg Agreement* banning the use of poison or toxic bullets.

In 1815, the *Final Act of the Congress of Vienna* identified an unjust reason for aggression – war in breach of a treaty. A government must first denounce the treaty, thereby giving notice to the other party or parties to the treaty so that there might be an opportunity to negotiate a grievance short of war. The aim was to declare retroactively that France's Napoléon Bonaparte (1769–1821) had violated international law by launching aggressive war against Russia during 1812 in violation of a peace treaty, the Treaty of Tilsit of 1807.

The humane warfare movement that mushroomed after the Crimean War (1853–1856) resulted in the first international recognition of the law of warfare – the *Declaration of Paris* of 1856. The agreement, which concerned maritime warfare, banned privateering (hiring private shipowners to harass and seize enemy ships), insisted that blockades must be enforced to be respected, and clarified rules regarding goods carried by neutral countries.

In 1863, the United States issued the Lieber Code, which covered nearly all aspects of the conduct of the war, including how to treat the property and soldiers of the enemy. The main concept was the principle of **military necessity**, that is, that no more force should be employed than necessary in war. When the American Civil War (1861–1865) ended, however, only one soldier was punished for violating war crimes – Henry Wirz.[1]

COURT CASE 7.2   *United States v Wirz* (1865)

After the American Civil War (1861–1865), Confederate Captain Henry Wirz (1822–1865), who commanded the Andersonville Prison Camp, was tried and convicted before a military commission (AmStTrials657–874) for "conspiracy to

continued

destroy prisoners' lives in violation of the laws and customs of war" and "murder [of 12,921 persons] in violation of the laws and customs of war." He is first person ever charged, tried, and found guilty of being a war criminal. Other Confederate leaders and soldiers were pardoned, died, or left the country to avoid prosecution. As a matter of political expediency, Jefferson Davis (1808–1889), President of the Confederate States of America from 1861–1865, was never prosecuted; he retained popularity in the secessionist Southern states.

After the Battle of Solferino in the Austro-Italian War of 1859, pressure from Henri Dunant (1828–1910) and others resulted in the *Convention for the Amelioration of the Condition of the Wounded on the Field of Battle*, which was adopted in 1864, borrowing heavily from the Lieber Code. The Geneva Convention, as the 1864 treaty is commonly known, dealt with the treatment of the sick and wounded on battlefields: (1) The wounded have a right to receive medical treatment. (2) Prisoners of war are to be given food and clothing and protection under the law. (3) Those who carry white flags are inviolable. (4) Civilians must be protected from unlimited warfare. (5) The Red Cross has the right to treat wounded, to inform governments of the location of prisoners of war, to transmit mail and packets from families of prisoners, and to arrange repatriation of the seriously wounded. (6) Ambulances, hospitals, their personnel, patients, and medical evacuations are to be regarded as neutral. (7) Homes accommodating sick and wounded are exempt from quartering troops. (8) After wounds are healed, soldiers should go home, exempt from further combat. (9) Red crosses are to be used to signify medical facilities and personnel. In 1868, the Geneva Convention was supplemented by the *Additional Articles Relating to the Condition of the Wounded in War*, which (10) applies the same provisions to ships, and (11) belligerents that capture neutral medical personnel are to pay them and to allow them to work normally.

In 1868, an International Military Commission of major European powers met at St. Petersburg at the invitation of Tsar Alexander II (1818–1881). They agreed on the *Declaration to the Effect of Prohibiting the Use of Certain Projectiles in Wartime* known as the St. Petersburg Declaration. The main principle enunciated was that weapons of war should be limited to making an enemy force incapable of fighting. Thus, the principle that there should be no unnecessary suffering from collateral damage entered the laws of war. The specific ban in the Declaration was on explosive or flammable projectiles less than 400 grams.

The *Project of an International Declaration Concerning the Laws and Customs of War*, issued at a conference at Brussels during 1874, urged the following prohibitions: (1) poison or poisoned weapons, (2) arms, projectiles or material that would cause unnecessary suffering, (3) improper uses of white flags and red crosses, and (4) destruction of property unless militarily necessary. In addition, (5) surrendering soldiers were to be considered prisoners of war (POWs) and treated humanely. The Brussels Declaration was in the form of a proposed Convention on the Laws and Customs of War with fifty-six articles, but was so lengthy that adoption as a treaty required more time to consider each provision. The unfinished deliberations at the meeting encouraged Tsar Nicholas II (1868–1918) to convene a peace conference at The Hague in 1899.

THE HAGUE PEACE CONFERENCES

In 1899, when the International Peace Conference convened at The Hague, the principal item on the agenda was disarmament. Britain and Germany were locked into a naval arms race that presumably could only end in war. The main results of the conference, however, were in the development of the law of warfare; the disarmament goal was not achieved. The most significant advance was the *Convention for the Pacific Settlement of International Disputes*, which declared that all interstate disputes must be settled peacefully, that is, by good offices or mediation of a third party, by a neutral commission of inquiry, or by arbitration, and all countries should make themselves available as third parties. To help to resolve interstate disputes, a Permanent Court of Arbitration was formed at The Hague.

The remaining treaties and declarations at the Hague Conference amended and extended provisions of the 1864 Geneva Convention. Some new provisions, not obvious from the titles of the Declarations are as follows: (1) Superiors are responsible for acts of subordinates. (2) Soldiers cannot carry concealed weapons, engage in pillaging, or use bullets that expand or flatten inside the human body. (3) Treatment of POWs was clarified to involve the same clothing, food, and shelter as the capturing country's soldiers; payment for nonstrenuous, nonmilitary work; the establishment of an information bureau to disseminate information about POWs; postage-free mail; and the right to worship. (4) Neutral powers were to give safe passage to the sick and wounded and to confine captured belligerents away from the war theater, providing them with needed clothing, food, and medical attention. (5) In the event that a victorious country occupies a defeated country, the occupying power is required to provide (a) law and order, (b) to respect rights of the occupied in regard to their family, liberties, property, and religion, (c) to pay damages for the destruction of nonmilitary property, (d) impose taxes and require services only to defray the necessities of the occupation, (e) provide cash payments for requisitioned services, and (f) never engage in collective punishments.

TABLE 7.3   **AGREEMENTS DEVELOPING THE LAW OF WAR AT THE 1899 HAGUE CONFERENCE**

Document	In force
Convention for the Pacific Settlement of International Disputes	1900
Convention with Respect to the Laws and Customs of War on Land	1900
Convention for the Adaptation to Maritime Warfare of the Principles of the Geneva Convention of 1864	1900
Declaration Prohibiting Launching of Projectiles and Explosives from Balloons	1900
Declaration Concerning Asphyxiating Gases	1900
Declaration Concerning Expanding Bullets	1900

All six agreements were ratified and went into effect in 1900, though the treaty about weapons launched from balloons expired in 1905. The Final Act of the 1899 Hague Conference expressed a desire for another conference to deal with more questions, specifically the rights and duties of neutrals, limiting newly developed naval weapons, disarmament, inviolability of private property during naval warfare, and naval bombardments.

Four years later, the Convention for the Adaptation to Maritime Warfare was amended. The *Convention for the Exemption of Hospital Ships, in Time of War, from the Payment of All Duties and Taxes Imposed for the Benefit of the State* was signed by diplomats from twenty-five countries at The Hague in 1904 and entered into force in 1907.

In 1907, delegates to the Second Hague Conference expanded the laws of warfare (Table 7.4), in part because of the fear of a nasty war based on the newest technology, so one provision was a requirement to deactivate submarine mines and torpedoes when not in use. Most of the new provisions clarified the role of neutral countries. Officer POWs were declared to be exempt from work. Among The Final Act underscored the principle of the compulsory arbitration of international disputes as the most important result of the deliberations.

Following up the Final Act's recommendation, a conference on naval warfare was held at London in 1908–1909. The resulting *Declaration Concerning the Laws of Naval War* regarding blockades, contraband, prizes, transfer to a neutral flag, naval convoys, and searches never entered into force.

TABLE 7.4   AGREEMENTS DEVELOPING THE LAW OF WAR AT THE 1907 HAGUE CONFERENCE

Document	In force
Convention for the Pacific Settlement of International Disputes	1910
Convention Respecting the Limitation of the Employment of Force for the Recovery of Contract Debts	1910
Convention Relative to the Opening of Hostilities	1910
Convention Respecting the Laws and Customs of War on Land	1910
Convention Respecting the Rights and Duties of Neutral Powers and Persons in Case of War on Land	1910
Convention Relating to the Status of Enemy Merchant Ships at the Outbreak of Hostilities.	1910
Convention Relating to the Conversion of Merchant Ships into War-Ships	1910
Convention Relative to the Laying of Automatic Submarine Contact Mines	1910
Convention Concerning Bombardment by Naval Forces in Time of War	1910
Convention for the Adaptation to Maritime War of the Principles of the Geneva Convention	1910
Convention Relative to Certain Restrictions with Regard to the Exercise of the Right of Capture in Naval War	1910
Convention Concerning the Rights and Duties of Neutral Powers in Maritime War	1910
Declaration Prohibiting Launching of Projectiles and Explosives from Balloons	1909

World War I (1914–1918) shattered the expectations of the diplomats at the Hague conferences, who had planned to meet again in 1915 but were unable to do so when the war pitted so many European countries against one another. During the war, Germany used poison gas and fired on neutral ships in international waters, so preceding conference efforts appeared to have been in vain.

LEAGUE OF NATIONS ERA

The *League of Nations Covenant*, as contained within the Treaty of Versailles, called upon states collectively to prevent and stop wars by arbitration, diplomacy, submission to the League Council, or referral to the Permanent Court of International Justice. States were to delay going to war until three months after a decision by an international body about the validity of pretexts for war. If a state did not agree to such a procedure, other states could impose sanctions on those who went to war.

Article 227 of the Treaty of Versailles indicted Kaiser Wilhelm (1859–1941) for violating the laws of warfare. A special tribunal, with one judge to be appointed by each of the principal Allied and Associated Powers, was authorized to try him for a "supreme offense against international morality and the sanctity of treaties." However, he fled to the Netherlands, which refused to surrender him. Article 228 provided that Germany must hand over those who committed acts "in violation of the laws and customs of war" for trials before military tribunals.

In 1920, when a list of about 1,000 persons was drawn up, the new German democratic government feared that their trials would adversely stir up public opinion, so they instead proposed a trial before the highest court in Leipzig. The Allied Powers agreed, and twelve were tried. The most famous case involved two German naval commanders who were responsible for firing on survivors in lifeboats of a torpedoed British hospital ship. Of the twelve, only six were convicted, but given light sentences. Nevertheless, the precedent had been established that heads of state and military commanders could be tried for war crimes by a tribunal authorized by a multilateral agreement.

After the establishment of the League, the law of warfare expanded with the adoption of several new treaties (Table 7.5). The first two, adopted in 1922 and 1923, dealt with chemical warfare, warfare in the air and under sea, and the use of radio broadcasts to provide valuable intelligence information, but they never went into effect. Limits on bacteriological warfare were, however, established in an agreement adopted in 1925 and ratified by 1928.

In 1924, the *General Act for the Pacific Settlement of International Disputes*, also known as the Geneva Protocol, sought to define "aggression," a term left undefined in the League of Nations Covenant. The agreement, adopted by the League Assembly, simply said that an "aggressor" was a country that launched war without first submitting its dispute with another country to arbitration.

The most important treaty came in 1928, when war itself was outlawed in the *General Treaty for the Renunciation of War*, also known as the Pact of Paris or the Kellogg–Briand Pact. All interstate disputes were to be resolved peacefully thenceforth – with no exception whatsoever.

TABLE 7.5   AGREEMENTS DEVELOPING THE LAW OF WAR BETWEEN THE WORLD WARS

Adopted	Document	In force
1919	League of Nations Covenant	1920
1922	Treaty Relating to the Use of Submarines and Noxious Gases in Warfare (Treaty of Washington)	
1923	Rules Concerning the Control of Wireless Telegraphy in Time of War and Air Warfare	
1924	General Act for the Pacific Settlement of International Disputes (Geneva Protocol)	1928
1925	Protocol for the Prohibition of the Use of Asphyxiating, Poisonous or Other Gases, and of Bacteriological Methods of Warfare	1928
1928	General Treaty for the Renunciation of War	1929
1928	Convention on Duties and Rights of States in the Event of Civil Strife	1929
1928	Convention on Maritime Neutrality	1931
1929	Convention for the Amelioration of the Condition of the Wounded and Sick in Armies in the Field	1931
1929	Convention Relative to the Treatment of Prisoners of War	1931
1935	Treaty on the Protection of Artistic and Scientific Institutions and Historic Monuments (Roerich Pact)	1935
1937	The Nyon Agreement and Agreement Supplementary to the Nyon Agreement	1937

In 1928, two other treaties focused on civil wars and neutral ships in time of war. In 1929, two treaties amended and extended previous Geneva Conventions – the *Convention for the Amelioration of the Condition of the Wounded and Sick in Armies in the Field* and the *Convention Relative to the Treatment of Prisoners of War*. The latter has very detailed provisions regarding POWs. One important innovation was the right of monthly health inspections, which would ordinarily be handled by the Red Cross. Another is that POWs must be protected against insults, public curiosity, and violence.

The *Roerich Pact*, applicable only to the Americas, provided that historic monuments, museums, scientific, artistic, educational and cultural institutions and their personnel are neutral in war. The *Nyon Agreement* and its supplement provided that neutral merchant ships were permitted to defend themselves if attacked by a belligerent.

Of course, the various laws of warfare would be unnecessary if there were no wars, and the main hope of the League of Nations was that gradual disarmament would limit the ability to wage war. Some arms limitation conferences were held, and a few even resulted in agreements, but they later unraveled. After World War II broke out in 1939, many of the limitations on warfare were ignored. Due to the unprecedented use of massive aerial bombing, civilian populations suffered heavy losses as never before.

N THE NUREMBERG AND TOKYO WAR CRIMES TRIALS

In 1945, the *Agreement for the Prosecution and Punishment of the Major War Criminals of the European Axis*, and the *Charter of the International Military Tribunal* were drafted for the trials at Nuremberg. The defendants were charged with one or more of three major offenses, of which two were coined for the first time – crimes against peace and crimes against humanity. The term "genocide" had not yet come into currency and thus was not used. The exact text defining the three offenses is as follows:

> *Crimes against peace*: namely, planning, preparation, initiation or waging of a war of aggression, or a war in violation of international treaties, agreements or assurances, or participation in a common plan or conspiracy for the accomplishment of any of the foregoing.

> *War crimes*: namely, violations of the laws or customs of war. Such violations shall include, but not be limited to, murder, ill-treatment or deportation to slave labor or for any other purpose of civilian population of or in occupied territory, murder or ill-treatment of prisoners of war or persons on the seas, killing of hostages, plunder of public or private property, wanton destruction of cities, towns or villages, or devastation not justified by military necessity.

> *Crimes against humanity*: namely, murder, extermination, enslavement, deportation, and other inhumane acts committed against any civilian population, before or during the war, or persecutions on political, racial or religious grounds in execution of or in connection with any crime within the jurisdiction of the Tribunal, whether or not in violation of the domestic law of the country where perpetrated.

The Charter established the foundation for current international humanitarian law in two respects. First, a government's treatment of its own citizens is a matter of international concern, thus establishing a post-Westphalian international contract. Second, individuals are accountable for their acts. According to the Charter, the most important of the three offenses was the crime against peace.

Specific counts in the Nuremberg indictment charged Nazi leaders with a conspiracy to violate all three offenses and contained detailed descriptions of violations of international law. Many defendants sought exoneration on the ground that they were merely carrying out orders (the **headquarters doctrine**) or that they were unable to control what their subordinates did, but the court rejected both arguments, ruling that they had **command responsibility**. Interestingly, Nazi Germany treated most American, British, and other Allied prisoners of war according to the terms of the Geneva Convention; their reason was to ensure that Allied forces would treat German POWs in an equivalent manner. Meanwhile, Article 10 of the *Potsdam Declaration* of 1945, issued to demand Japan's surrender, suggested two types of war crimes:

- violation of international laws (such as the abuse of prisoners of war)
- obstructing democratic tendencies and civil liberties of the Japanese people.

One of the terms of Japan's surrender was the acceptance of the *Potsdam Declaration*.

In 1945, General Douglas MacArthur II (1880–1964), Supreme Commander of Allied Forces in the Southwest Pacific Area, decided not to wait for the terms of the Tokyo War Crimes Trial to be drawn up. Hastily, he arranged for an American military commission in Manila to try General Tomoyuki Yamashita, the Japanese commander of military operations in Southeast Asia. Yamashita was found guilty and was sentenced to death by hanging, but he appealed to the U.S. Supreme Court, which upheld the guilty verdict. He was the first general of a defeated enemy country ever tried for war crimes.

COURT CASE 7.3   *Application of Yamashita* (1946)

General Tomoyuki Yamashita (1888–1946), the Japanese commanding general in Malaya, the Philippines, and Singapore, was charged by an American military commission in Manila with two offenses – the Manila Massacre, a brutal attack on civilians, and with bayoneting hospital patients in Singapore. The tribunal, hastily organized in 1945 by General Douglas MacArthur II (1880–1964), handed down a guilty verdict despite evidence that one of the units in Manila disobeyed his order to retreat, other units acted without his specific orders, and he disciplined soldiers responsible for the bayoneting incident. After his conviction, he appealed to the U.S. Supreme Court, arguing that the documentary evidence was insufficient to link his commands with atrocities committed by his troops. In *Application of Yamashita* (327US1) the court in 1946 upheld the guilty verdict, based on the command responsibility doctrine.

The *Charter of the International Military Tribunal for the Far East*, which operated from 1946 to 1948, defined the same offenses as those used at Nuremberg. The counts in the Tokyo indictments were stated in the following terms:

- leading, organizing, instigating, or being accomplices in the formulation or execution of a common plan or conspiracy to wage wars of aggression;
- ordering, authorizing, and permitting inhumane treatment of prisoners of war and others;
- deliberately and recklessly disregarding the duty to take adequate steps to prevent atrocities (mass murder, rape, pillage, brigandage, torture and other barbaric cruelties upon the helpless civilian population;
- plundering public and private property);
- wantonly destroying cities, towns and villages beyond any justification of military necessity;
- waging aggressive and unprovoked war.

The high-profile Nuremberg Trials overshadowed the trials in the Far East, but they both established the principle that certain offenses applied everywhere in the world. Although the tribunals were criticized at the time to be a form of "victor's justice," Britain proposed that the Nuremberg court should be made permanent. Nevertheless, in 1946 the UN General Assembly accepted the principles and the judgments of the trials. Later, international criminal courts were established under the framework of the United Nations.

UNITED NATIONS ERA: EARLY ACCOMPLISHMENTS

A paramount objective of the *Charter of the United Nations* was to prevent future wars. In Article 2(4), unilateral *aggression* and the issuance of a *threat of war* are stated as violations of the basic principles of the UN Charter. Article 33 reiterates provisions of previous agreements about the requirement of parties to a dispute to "seek a solution by negotiation, enquiry, mediation, conciliation, arbitration, judicial settlement" and adds "resort to regional agencies or arrangements, or other peaceful means of their own choice." Articles 41–42 give the Security Council the power to authorize nonmilitary sanctions and, if necessary, to take military actions against recalcitrant states.

During the early years of the United Nations, there were many advances in the development of the law of war (Table 7.6). In 1946, with the aim of placing provisions of the postwar military tribunals at Nuremberg and Tokyo on a treaty basis, the *Convention on the Prevention and Punishment of the Crime of Genocide* was adopted, defining *genocide* as "acts committed with intent to destroy, in whole or in part, a national, ethnical, racial or religious group." Five prohibited acts are specified: (1) genocide, (2) conspiracy to commit genocide, (3) direct and public incitement to commit genocide, (4) attempt to commit genocide, and (5) complicity in genocide. More specifically, the treaty prohibits the following:

- killing members of the group;
- causing serious bodily or mental harm to members of the group;
- deliberately inflicting on the group conditions of life calculated to bring about its physical destruction in whole or in part;
- imposing measures intended to prevent births within the group;
- forcibly transferring children of one group to another group.

In 1968, the *Convention on the Non-Applicability of Statutory Limitations to War Crimes and Crimes Against Humanity* established two new principles – that there is no statute of limitations on crimes against humanity or war crimes and that states are obligated to extradite war criminals to countries which desire to place them on trial. Thus, war criminals cannot escape accountability under the principle of **universal jurisdiction**, that is, a person guilty of the offenses identified at Nuremberg and Tokyo can be captured and tried anywhere in the world. Former Nazi officials might change their names and conduct exemplary lives, but they were still subject to prosecution until their death. The *Principles of International Cooperation in the Detection, Arrest, Extradition and Punishment of Persons Guilty of War Crimes and Crimes Against Humanity*, adopted by the General Assembly in 1973, provides more details on how to extradite war criminals.

TABLE 7.6 **EARLY AGREEMENTS DEVELOPING THE LAW OF WAR IN THE UNITED NATIONS ERA**

Adopted	Document	In force
1945	Charter of the United Nations	1945
1946	Convention on the Prevention and Punishment of the Crime of Genocide	1951
1949	Convention for the Amelioration of the Condition of the Wounded and Sick in Armed Forces in the Field (First Geneva Convention)	1950
1949	Convention for the Amelioration of the Condition of Wounded, Sick and Shipwrecked Members of Armed Forces at Sea (Second Geneva Convention)	1950
1949	Geneva Convention Relative to the Treatment of Prisoners of War (Third Geneva Convention)	1950
1949	Convention Relative to the Protection of Civilian Persons in Time of War (Fourth Geneva Convention)	1950
1954	Convention for the Protection of Cultural Property in the Event of Armed Conflict	1956
1954	• Protocol for the Protection of Cultural Property in the Event of Armed Conflict	1956
1968	Convention on the Non-Applicability of Statutory Limitations to War Crimes and Crimes Against Humanity	1970
1973	Principles of International Cooperation in the Detection, Arrest, Extradition and Punishment of Persons Guilty of War Crimes and Crimes Against Humanity	
1974	Declaration on the Protection of Women and Children in Emergency and Armed Combat	
1977	Protocol Additional to the Geneva Conventions of 12 August 1949, and Relating to the Protection of Victims of Non-International Armed Conflicts	1978
1977	Protocol Additional to the Geneva Conventions of 12 August 1949, and Relating to the Protection of Victims of International Armed Conflicts	1979

The military excesses associated with World War II, from death camps to bombing raids, prompted efforts to expand previous Geneva Conventions, and in 1949 four Geneva Conventions were adopted. Mindful of the horrors of the Nazis, all four Conventions had three new major provisions: (1) Treatment of all detainees must be on an equal basis, that is, without regard to race, color, religion or faith, sex, birth or wealth. (2) All countries must hunt for those who violate the most serious offenses, namely, deliberate killing, torture, inhuman treatment, biological experimentation, and causing serious disease or injury, so that they can be brought to justice. (3) Anyone captured in wartime is entitled to a hearing before a "competent tribunal" to decide whether there is a reasonable basis for their detention. The purpose of insisting on a "competent tribunal" was to ensure that prisoners would not be processed by secret or unauthorized courts.

The *First Geneva Convention* extends previous coverage to civilians on land. One requirement of the treaty, to have honorable burials of enemy dead, was violated in 2005, when American military personnel burned bodies of two Taliban fighters rather than providing for their burial in accordance with Afghan custom. The *Second Geneva Convention* applies the same requirements to naval combat.

The *Third Geneva Convention* focuses on prisoners of war, including how to deal with those who commit criminal offenses or infractions of POW camp rules. The provision that POWs must be repatriated, even if they fear persecution after they return to their home country, complicated negotiations for an armistice to end the Korean War (1950–1953), so the UN General Assembly set up the Neutral Nations Repatriation Commission in 1953 to handle some 14,200 POWs who refused to return to China and North Korea. Despite efforts of the Commission to encourage repatriation, few changed their minds and were free to find refuge elsewhere, though twenty-three Americans reportedly refused to go home.

DISCUSSION TOPIC 7.2 HAS THE UNITED STATES VIOLATED GENEVA CONVENTIONS IN GUANTÁNAMO?

About 760 persons at the American naval base at Guantanámo, Cuba, were captured during the invasion of Afghanistan in November 2001. Most were rounded by Afghan and Pakistani bounty hunters, some simply because they had Casio watches, as that was the brand of watch reportedly worn by the hijackers on September 11, 2001. Ten were initially charged with war crimes for their roles in aiding Al-Qaida's attack on the United States on September 11, but they were initially denied access to attorneys and were to be tried in special courts set up without Congressional approval. Although the Supreme Court in *Hamdi v Rumsfeld* (547US507) and *Hamdan v Rumsfeld* (548US05–184) in 1994 and 1996, respectively, ruled that they have the right to lawyers and to be tried in legislatively authorized courts, the Military Commissions Act of 2006 in effect nullified the Supreme Court decisions. In 2004–2005, 558 were screened in special military administrative tribunals, as required by *Hamdi*, to determine whether they are "enemy combatants"; those so designated are to be tried in special courts. Of the initial 760, some 390 have been released as "no longer enemy combatants," some after being held for five years, and 54 have been deemed eligible for release but are still held because negotiations with their home countries for their repatriation have proved unsuccessful. As of early 2007, 385 detainees were held at Guantanamo, where they have the right to an annual hearing to review their status. Several have also complained of torture, and three have committed suicide. To what extent has the treatment of the detainees been a violation of international law?

One of the main considerations was to cover situations similar to the Nazi German takeover of Austria and Czechoslovakia, in which there was no formal declaration of war but instead armed forces of one country intruded into the territory of another country without resistance and remained as an occupying power. The *Fourth Geneva Convention*, accordingly, provides details about the administration of occupied territories. Among the most important requirements are the following:

- No "individual or mass forcible transfers, as well as deportations of protected persons from occupied territory to the territory of the occupying power or to that of any other countries . . ."
- Law and order is the responsibility of the occupying power.
- Prisoners of the occupying power who do not qualify for the full protection of POW status are entitled to "humane" treatment and to "the judicial guarantees which are recognized as indispensable by civilized peoples."

Provisions of the Fourth Geneva Convention were also applicable to the four-power occupation of Austria and Germany after World War II. Subsequent occupations that might be held to the same standard are Israel's occupation of the West Bank (1967–), the UN administrations of Cambodia (1991–1993) and Kosovo (1999–), and the American occupations of Iraq (2003–).

The Fourth Geneva Convention might conceivably be characterized as providing rules governing the **just peace**. Whenever a war concludes, even without an occupation, there is clearly a need for a standard to be applied to the way in which war is terminated. Although no such standard has been established, a consensus is developing with regard to four principles governing military occupations:

- The occupying power must restore and maintain order.
- The occupying power is responsible for economic reconstruction of damaged infrastructure and property.
- The occupying power should transfer sovereignty to the occupied people.
- Human rights violators should be tried and punished.

DISCUSSION TOPIC 7.3   IS ISRAEL'S OCCUPATION OF THE WEST BANK IN ACCORD WITH INTERNATIONAL LAW?

After World War I, Palestine was administered by Britain as a League of Nations Mandate. In 1948, while war erupted between Arab residents and Israeli independence forces, Jordan seized control of the territory west of the Jordan River, known as the West Bank, and Israel declared independence. In 1967, Israel captured the West Bank in the Six-Day War, though Jordan did not officially give up its claim until 1988. Meanwhile, the UN considered the West Bank to be occupied territories, and Israel put up signs accordingly. The Christian and Muslim Arabic-speaking residents of the West Bank have not been pleased with the arrangement, and Israel has allowed Jewish settlers to live in newly constructed small towns on the West Bank. Retaliatory attacks on Israeli civilians by Palestinian terrorists have resulted in some deaths. In response, Israel has often launched wholesale counterattacks, that is, collective punishments on entire villages, to root out the terrorists. Using a law authorizing indefinite detention, many Arabic-speaking persons have been arrested and held without trials for years, provoking terrorists to kidnap Israelis in order to arrange for exchanges. Despite nonratification of the Fourth Geneva Convention, is Israel violating international law? Should Israel ratify the Fourth Geneva Convention? Do the same considerations apply to the American occupation of Iraq, which began in 2003?

In 1977, two Additional Protocols to the Geneva Conventions were adopted. The *Protocol Relating to the Protection of Victims of International Armed Conflicts* prohibits the destruction of nonmilitary targets, so indiscriminate bombing is outlawed. Two possible examples, which occurred in 2006, are the Hezbollah's firing of rockets toward Israeli civilian targets and Israel's retaliation with cluster bombs. The Protocol extends Geneva Convention protections to those fighting colonial domination, alien occupation, and against racist regimes but specifically exempts mercenaries (paid soldiers) from Geneva Convention protections, thereby exempting Cuban volunteers in the Angolan civil war (1975–1991) from coverage. Protocol I also prohibits reprisals unless they are proportional. The *Protocol Relating to the Protection of Victims of Non-International Armed Conflicts*, known as Protocol II, applies Geneva Convention standards to parties engaged in civil wars.

Another Geneva Convention requirement is respect for the property of civilians and noncombatants, as many paintings had been stolen from Jewish persons and others by the Nazis. In 1951, a Conference on Jewish Material Claims Against Germany was held at The Hague. In attendance were the governments of Israel and West Germany as well as various Jewish nongovernmental organizations. Bonn agreed at the conference to pay $60 billion to Nazi victims in nineteen countries, the first time in history when victims of human rights violations were directly compensated. Then in 1954, the *Convention for the Protection of Cultural Property in the Event of Armed Conflict* and its associated *Protocol* were adopted, authorizing sanctions against those who would destroy, transfer, or find military uses for cultural property. The subject of cultural looting is further discussed in Chapter 9.

In 1974, the General Assembly adopted the *Declaration on the Protection of Women and Children in Emergency and Armed Combat*. A followup finally came in 2002, when the *Optional Protocol to the Convention on the Rights of the Child on the Involvement of Children in Armed Conflict* was adopted. The texts serve to supplement the Geneva Conventions.

UNITED NATIONS ERA: IMPACT OF THE COLD WAR

Although the Soviet Union was allied with Britain and the United States during World War II, the Soviet army's advance into Germany was accompanied by an effort to strengthen Communist Parties so that they could take control of countries in Eastern Europe. Western powers soon realized that the Soviet Union was spying on the United States, developing nuclear weapons independently, and was determined to expand influence into Asia and capitalist Western Europe. There was apprehension that the conflict might result in mutual annihilation, since both had nuclear weapons. The United States had already dropped atomic bombs in the war with Japan during 1945, so the Soviet Union sought to deter aggression from the United States. As long as the two countries avoided a war with each other, the conflict would continue but at a lower temperature, so a "cold war" was seen as preferable to a "hot war."

When civil war broke out between Soviet-backed North Korea and American ally South Korea during 1950, the conflict between the two economic systems was no longer hypothetical but real, with the use of nuclear weapons a feared possibility.[2] When the Security Council met to consider the Korean War, the Soviet Union was boycotting the body because Communist China was not yet accredited to the UN. The Security Council then authorized a UN Command, led by the United States, consisting of troops donated by several countries. The establishment of the UN Command in Korea, thus, became the first time when an international organization provided a collective armed response to international aggression. Angry, the Soviet Union returned to the Security Council, vowing to veto any future use of force by the body, thereby nullifying what many founders believed was the most important purpose for which the UN was established.

HISTORIC EVENT 7.2 THE UNITED NATIONS AUTHORIZES TROOPS TO DEFEND SOUTH KOREA (1950)

In 1949, the People's Army of Mao Zedong (1883–1976) was victorious in China, and a large number of Chinese under the leadership of the Chiang Kai-Shek (1887–1975) fled to Taiwan. However, the latter's Republic of China retained UN membership, as the United States and many other countries refused to recognize the legitimacy of the People's Republic of China. Moscow then protested by boycotting meetings of the Security Council. In 1950, civil war broke out in Korea. When the Security Council convened to respond, the Soviet Union, still maintaining its boycott, was absent and thus unable to veto a resolution to authorize a UN force to support the South Korean army, which was being pushed to the sea by Communist North Korea.

Accordingly, later in 1950 delegates in the UN General Assembly adopted Resolution 377, known as the *Uniting for Peace Resolution*, which declared that the

General Assembly could in the future authorize the use of force to stop aggression whenever the Security Council was deadlocked. Subsequently, Resolution 377 has been used sixteen times,[3] though in 1999 the American delegate to the UN argued that General Assembly authorization of force is "not legally binding."

The Cold War revived concerns about the use of unacceptable weapons, so some earlier treaties were expanded, and new treaties were drawn up (Table 7.7) including prohibitions on nuclear weapons as well as a ban on weapons in the oceans and in outer space. Earlier treaties concerning biological and chemical weapons were expanded to require the dismantling of all such instruments of warfare.

Possibly the most famous treaty reflecting Cold War concerns is the *Treaty on the Non-Proliferation of Nuclear Weapons* (NPT) of 1968, when the nuclear club consisted of Britain, France, the Soviet Union, and the United States. Fearing nuclear war by accident, the Soviet Union and the United States signed an *Agreement on Measures*

TABLE 7.7   AGREEMENTS DEVELOPING THE LAW OF WAR REFLECTING COLD WAR CONCERNS

Adopted	Document	In force
1950	UN Resolution 377 (Uniting for Peace Resolution)	
1967	Treaty on Principles Governing the Activities of States in the Exploration and Use of Outer Space, including the Moon and Other Celestial Bodies	1967
1968	Treaty on the Non-Proliferation of Nuclear Weapons	1970
1971	Agreement on Measures to Reduce the Risk of Outbreak of Nuclear War Between the United States of America and the Union of Soviet Socialist Republics	1971
1971	Treaty on the Prohibition of the Emplacement of Nuclear Weapons and Other Weapons of Mass Destruction on the Seabed and the Ocean Floor and in the Subsoil Thereof	1972
1972	Convention on the Prohibition of the Development, Production and Stockpiling of Bacteriological (Biological) and Toxin Weapons and on Their Destruction	1975
1976	Convention on the Prohibition of Military or Any Hostile Use of Environmental Modification Techniques	1978
1980	Convention on Prohibitions or Restrictions on the Use of Certain Conventional Weapons Which May be Deemed to be Excessively Injurious or to Have Indiscriminate Effects	1983
1980	• Protocol on Non-Detectable Fragments	1983
1980	• Protocol on Prohibitions or Restrictions on the Use of Mines, Booby-Traps and Other Devices	1983
1980	• Protocol on Prohibitions or Restrictions on the Use of Incendiary Weapons	1983
1980	• Protocol on Blinding Laser Weapons	1998
1984	Declaration on the Right of Peoples to Peace	

to Reduce the Risk of Outbreak of Nuclear War in 1971. Although the International Court of Justice ruled that the threat or use of nuclear weapons was illegal, by 2006 China, India, Israel, North Korea, and Pakistan had joined the club, and Iran appeared determine to gain admission. Nevertheless, regional treaties have sought to denuclearize various parts of the Third World, notably Africa, the Antarctic, the Caribbean, Central Asia, Latin America, Southeast Asia, and the South Pacific (Table 7.8).

COURT CASE 7.4 ADVISORY OPINION ON THE LEGALITY OF THE THREAT OR USE OF NUCLEAR WEAPONS (1996)

In 1994, the UN General Assembly, the World Health Organization, and six countries (Costa Rica, Egypt, Iran, Malaysia, New Zealand, and Nauru) decided to ask the International Court of Justice whether the threat or use of nuclear weapons was legal or illegal under international law, though several governments asked the court not to decide the matter (Britain, France, Germany, Italy, Russia, and the United States). Since opposing states did not agree to have the court determine a judgment, the justices issued an Advisory Opinion. In a short statement, the court noted that international law authorizes neither threats nor uses of nuclear weapons. Divided 7–7 in ruling whether such threats or uses might be acceptable in cases of extreme self-defense wherein the survival of a state is in jeopardy, the court nevertheless unanimously urged further progress on achieving nuclear disarmament.

From 1961–1971, the United States used the herbicide Agent Orange to defoliate the jungles of Vietnam in support of non-Communist South Vietnam in its civil war with the North. Several treaties were stimulated by the development of the new weapons technology. The *Convention on the Prohibition of Military or Any Hostile Use of Environmental Modification Techniques* bans nonpeaceful methods that have "widespread, long-lasting or severe effects" causing "destruction, damage or injury" to the planet. The *Convention on Prohibitions or Restrictions on the Use of Certain Conventional Weapons Which May Be Deemed to be Excessively Injurious or to Have Indiscriminate Effects* was designed as a shell agreement to ban as yet unidentified new weapons. Later Protocol agreements have proscribed weapons that engage in environmental modifications, have fragments not detectable by X-rays, and laser weapons.

Ronald Reagan (1911–2004), on becoming president in 1981, made clear that he would work to dismantle the "evil empire" of the Soviet Union. While he persuaded Congress to make large increases in military spending, his rhetoric seemed so bellicose that the General Assembly adopted the *Declaration on the Right of Peoples to Peace* in 1984.

In 1985, when Mikhail Gorbachëv (1931–) became the General Secretary of the Communist Party of the Soviet Union, Reagan found an interlocutor who was

TABLE 7.8   **REGIONAL TREATIES BANNING NUCLEAR WEAPONS**

Adopted	Name of document	In force
1959	Antarctic Treaty	1961
1967	Treaty for the Prohibition of Nuclear Weapons in Latin America and the Caribbean (Treaty of Tlatelolco)	1969
1967	• Protocols I, II	
1985	South Pacific Nuclear Free Zone Treaty (Treaty of Rarotonga)	1986
1986	• Protocols I, II, III	
1995	Treaty on the Southeast Asian Nuclear Weapon-Free Zone (Bangkok Treaty)	1997
1995	• Protocol	
1996	African Nuclear Weapon-Free Zone Treaty (Pelindaba Treaty)	
2002	Central Asian Nuclear-Weapon-Free Zone Treaty	

TABLE 7.9   **POST-COLD WAR TREATIES ON THE LAW OF WARFARE**

Adopted	Name of document	In force
1993	Convention on the Prohibition of Chemical Weapons	1997
1997	Convention on the Prohibition of the Use, Stockpiling, Production and Transfer of Anti-Personnel Mines and on Their Destruction	1998
1989	International Convention Against the Recruitment, Use, Financing and Training of Mercenaries	2001
1998	Statute of the International Criminal Court	2002
2000	Optional Protocol to the Convention on the Rights of the Child on the Involvement of Children in Armed Conflict	2002
2006	International Convention for the Protection of All Persons from Enforced Disappearance	

convinced that the nuclear arms race must end, as Moscow could not afford to continue the arms race. While the two negotiated arms reduction agreements, however, Gorbachëv adopted domestic reforms that ultimately led to the dismantling of the Berlin Wall, the reunification of Germany in 1989, and the collapse of the Soviet Union in 1991, and thereby the end of the Cold War.

UNITED NATIONS ERA: POST-COLD WAR ACCOMPLISHMENTS

The end of the Cold War has enabled more cooperation within the UN framework (Table 7.9). Among the advances to the law of war are prohibitions on chemical weapons, landmines, mercenaries, disappearances, and child soldiers. In the latter case, an estimated 300,000 children in at least forty countries have been recruited to fight, often after their fathers have died. The latest treaty, which deals with disappearances, was passed for several reasons; in addition to the "dirty wars" during Operation Condor, the American practice of secret "extraordinary renditions" after 9/11/2001, was outlawed. In 2006, aside from the American cases, in which suspected terrorists were flown to secret prisons in Poland, Romania, and elsewhere to be tortured, the UN reported that disappearances principally involved individuals in Colombia, Nepal, and the Russian Republic of Chechnya.

The most significant recent advance in the development of the law of warfare is the adoption of the *Statute of the International Criminal Court*, which reiterates the definition of **genocide** from the Genocide Convention, codifies provisions in the Geneva Conventions regarding **war crimes** (though adding some new provisions, such as a ban on conscripting those under fifteen), identifies (but leaves undefined until a later agreement) the **crime of aggression**, and clarifies the meaning of the remaining Nuremberg crime, **crime against humanity**. The latter' definition is expanded to mean any of the following as a part of a widespread or systematic attack directed against any civilian population:

- murder;
- extermination;
- enslavement;
- deportation or forcible transfer of population;
- imprisonment or other severe deprivation of physical liberty in violation of fundamental rules of international law;
- torture;
- rape, sexual slavery, enforced prostitution, forced pregnancy, enforced sterilization, or any other form of sexual violence of comparable gravity;
- persecution against any identifiable group or collectivity on political, racial, national, ethnic, cultural, religious, gender . . . , or other grounds that are universally recognized as impermissible under international law, . . . ;
- enforced disappearance of persons;
- *apartheid*;
- other inhumane acts of a similar character intentionally causing great suffering, or serious injury to the body or to mental or physical health.

DISCUSSION TOPIC 7.4 WHAT WARLIKE ACTS ARE LEGAL UNDER INTERNATIONAL LAW?

A country can go to war legally under international law, provided that the war is approved by the United Nations and is in self-defense. Go back to Table 7.1. Add a third row, labeled "War." Now fill in the row on the other side with examples of warlike acts that would be permissible under international law.

HUMANITARIAN MILITARY INTERVENTION

When the Cold War ended, competing interests of national groups within the Soviet Union and Yugoslavia came to the fore. Although the Soviet Union peacefully broke up into separate states, the disintegration of Yugoslavia into Croatia, Bosnia, Montenegro, Macedonia, Serbia, and Slovenia was much more difficult. "Ethnic cleansing," by means of expulsions, murders, and rapes, occurred as leaders of some ethnic groups sought to establish independent homelands within territories where other ethnic groups also had been living for centuries. While genocidal acts were ongoing, the international community looked on in horror, but with no standard operating procedure to justify action that would defend those being slaughtered.

Accordingly, the principle of **humanitarian military intervention** was advanced as a possible legitimate basis for states, individually or collectively, to dispatch military force across the borders of a country without invitation to prevent or to end grave and widespread violations of fundamental human rights. As clarified by the International Court of Justice, such humanitarian intervention must aim to prevent human suffering and "to protect life and health and to ensure the respect of persons" (*Nicaragua v United States*, 1986).

There are two types of humanitarian intervention. One type, **rescue of nationals**, was authorized by the Peace of Westphalia of 1648. Governments are allowed to undertake operations to rescue their own citizens who are at risk in another country, provided that three criteria are met: (1) imminent threat to life, (2) unwillingness of a country to protect citizens of another country, and (3) a limited operation. One example of a humanitarian rescue occurred at Entebbe airport in Uganda, when Israeli military rescued hijacked passengers. Similarly, Britain sent troops in 1999 to evacuate Britons from the civil war in Sierra Leone; they also secured the airport for incoming UN peacekeepers.

HISTORIC EVENT 7.3 THE ENTEBBE RAID (1976)

One day in 1976, an Air France flight bound from Paris to Athens en route to Israel was hijacked by seven Palestinians and flown to Uganda with at least 100 Israeli and Jewish passengers on board. Fearing that the hijackers were planning a massacre, some 200 Israeli commandos soon arrived at Entebbe airport, a battle ensued, Soviet-built airplanes were destroyed on the tarmac, and all the hijackers, three of the hostages, and twenty Ugandan soldiers died. Afterward, the Israeli soldiers departed, and the freed hostages were flown to safety.

The other type of humanitarian intervention, **rescue of populations from gross human rights violations**, is more controversial, unsettled under international law, and contrary to the Westphalian nonintervention principle. During the 1930s, three intervening countries claimed that they were acting in humanitarian terms – Japan's seizure of Manchuria (1931), Italy's conquest of Abyssinia (Ethiopia) (1935–1936), and Germany's entry into the Sudetenland in Czechoslovakia (1938). The world community, however, branded all three actions as aggression. Recalling that the colonization of what is now called the Third World was justified by European imperialists, including Rudyard Kipling (1865–1936) and John Stuart Mill (1806–1873), as a humanitarian crusade to bring Christian civilization to the non-Christian world, there is a danger that governments might use the principle of humanitarian intervention to commit war crimes.

Presumably, humanitarian military intervention should satisfy the principles of the just war. Indeed, some scholars have developed the concept of **just intervention** as an extension of the principle of the just war to the specific problem of ongoing genocide; in effect, they argue for mandatory intervention to stop severe human rights violations involving death on a massive scale.

If there is some acceptance of the need for humanitarian intervention, there is no universal agreement on the criteria to justify action. Setting the bar too high leads to inaction in the face of genocide; setting the bar too low enables states to claim the moral high ground as they engage in naked conquest under a humanitarian figleaf for the sake of geopolitical "regime change." Moreover, the right of self-determination and the principle of nonintervention are in conflict when a subnational group seeks to secede from a country, as international law recognizes no right of secession.

In 1999, UN Secretary-General Kofi Annan (1938–), noting at the Millennium Summit that the UN had failed to stop genocide in Bosnia (1992–1994), Rwanda (1994), and Kosovo (1996–1999), specified at least three conditions for legitimate humanitarian intervention: (1) genocidal acts, (2) UN authorization for action, and (3) multilateral participation. Nevertheless, the South Summit Declaration of the year 2000 passed a resolution firmly rejecting the concept of humanitarian intervention.

Accordingly, the Canadian Ministry of Foreign Affairs organized an International Commission on Intervention and State Sovereignty, consisting of twelve distinguished persons, to clarify the matter. Their report, issued in 2001, identified six threshold criteria to determine the legitimacy of humanitarian military intervention:

- just cause (large-scale loss of life ongoing or anticipated);
- right intention (to halt or avert human suffering);
- right authority (authorization by the UN or regional organizations);
- last resort (after nonmilitary measures have failed);
- proportional means (minimal scale, duration, intensity);
- reasonable prospects (success reasonably expected).

The latter condition would presumably include acceptance of the intervention by the people on whose behalf the intervention is launched. The Commission stressed that all governments are responsible for protecting their citizens from mass atrocities; but when they fail to do so, the world community has a responsibility to prevent serious situations before they get out of hand as well as to assist in post-intervention reconstruction. In 2005, the UN General Assembly's World Summit endorsed the "responsibility to protect" principle but stopped short of endorsing criteria to justify humanitarian intervention.

DISCUSSION TOPIC 7.5 WHEN IS HUMANITARIAN MILITARY INTERVENTION JUSTIFIED?

In which of the following cases was humanitarian military intervention justified?

- India's attack on Pakistan during 1971 as the latter made war on East Pakistan (now Bangladesh), resulting in ten million refugees pouring into India.
- Tanzania's invasion of Uganda in 1979 to end the regime of Idi Amin (1928–2003), who was responsible for liquidating approximately 300,000 political opponents, real and imagined, over the years of his rule (1971–1979).
- Vietnam's intervention in 1978–1989 to stop massive deaths in Cambodia that occurred during the reign of the Khmer Rouge from 1975.
- In the 1990s, the North Atlantic Treaty Organization military intervention in Bosnia and Kosovo, which were under attack from Serbian forces that seemed intent on imposing rule by Serb minorities in both regions of the former Yugoslavia.

In 1997, the bombing of Serbia by forces of the North Atlantic Treaty Organization to stop Serbia's ethnic cleansing in Kosovo produced so many civilian casualties that the practice of humanitarian intervention was called into question. Then Washington justified an attack on Iraq in 2003 in various terms without UN approval. Accordingly, some observers have soured on the concept of humanitarian military intervention as a form of neoimperialism. Thus, different opinions about humanitarian intervention will compete for acceptance until a treaty or UN declaration specifically deals with the concept.

LEGITIMATE SELF-DEFENSE

War, of course, is still permitted in self-defense; the UN Charter recognizes the "inherent right of individual or collective self-defense" (Article 51), a contemporary version of the doctrine of just war. Under current international law, there are two types legitimate self-defense – anticipatory and in reprisal.

The UN Charter prefers **reprisal self-defense** to be temporary. States that immediately defend themselves after being attacked are required to report their actions to the Security Council, which can then authorize their actions retroactively. However, the Security Council may vote against supporting a military response because of political considerations or due to a judgment that the action is not legitimate self-defense. To be legitimate, the following conditions must be present in the case of reprisal self-defense:

- **Second use of force:** There must be prior armed aggression (according to UN General Assembly, Resolution 3314 of 1974), which defines *aggression* as the use of armed force by one, and that are necessary for ending that aggression." For example, the victim of aggression must not occupy the aggressor state's territory unless strictly necessary.

- **Notification:** A state must give immediate advance warning to the UN Security Council.
- **Preclusion:** There is no alternative to a military response because the aggression is unabated rather than limited and the Security Council or a regional organization is not taking effective countermeasures. However, as soon as the Security Council acts, a country's right to armed self-defense ceases.
- **Proportionality:** According to the International Court of Justice in *Nicaragua v United States* (1986), the response must consist only of "measures proportional to the armed aggression that has occurred. Self-defense actions must be immediately reported to the UN Security Council.

Anticipatory self-defense is more problematic. The example of the *Caroline* incident (1837) has served to clarify criteria to justify anticipatory self-defense before an armed attack that has been followed ever since:

- **Imminent jeopardy:** A threat of armed attack will be carried out without delay on a state's territory, forces, or population.
- **Preclusion:** There is no alternative to self-defense because no other legitimate authority proposes to prevent or to stop the aggression.
- **Proportionality:** The self-defense is limited to stopping or preventing the aggression.
- **Notification:** Self-defense actions must be immediately reported to the UN Security Council.

HISTORIC EVENT 7.4 THE *CAROLINE* INCIDENT (1837)

In 1837, when the American steamer *Caroline* was being leased to run supplies to rebels seeking Canadian independence, British authorities went to the American side of the Niagara River to burn the vessel, in the process killing a watchman. Whereas the British claimed the right of self-defense, Americans were outraged at what they considered to be an act of piracy. Some Americans then organized unauthorized raids into Canada for the next four years, thus responding with piracy of their own. In 1842, Secretary of State Daniel Webster (1782–1852) disputed the British action of 1837 as self-defense. He argued that the right of anticipatory self-defense applies only when the threat is "instant, overwhelming, and leaving no choice of means, and no moment for deliberation," and the responsive measures are neither "unreasonable" nor "excessive." Although Lord Alexander Baring Ashburton (1774–1848) disputed Webster's conclusion that the British acted improperly, he admitted that his government erred because there was neither an announcement in advance nor an apology afterward about the action taken. Webster then closed the dispute on the basis of the British apology.

The concept of anticipatory self-defense has been stretched to the doctrine of **preemptive war** on the ground that a preventive first strike is preferable to a second strike after being devastated. Israel, for example sought in 1975 to justify a military assault on Palestinian villages in Lebanon because previous attacks on Israel had been launched from those villages. Subsequently, UN Security Council resolutions condemned Israel's attack, questioning the concept of preemptive self-defense where there had been no prior armed intervention. In 2004, however, a UN High Level Panel for Threats, Challenges and Change recommended reinterpreting the UN Charter in order to allow the right of preemptive military or police action in cases of non-imminent but urgent threats, provided that such action is approved by the UN Security Council. However, the principle of anticipatory self-defense can be interpreted in different ways by different persons, thus providing no clear guide for what is acceptable in international law.

DISCUSSION TOPIC 7.6 WAS THE SECOND GULF WAR JUSTIFIED AS LEGITIMATE SELF-DEFENSE?

In 2003, a coalition of countries led by the United States attacked Iraq and toppled President Saddam Hussein (1937–2006), claiming the right to remove weapons of mass destruction that might some day be used against them, even though the Security Council did not support the attack as legitimate self-defense. Was the action justified under international law?

INTERNATIONAL TERRORISM

The nexus between war crimes and criminal acts of international terrorist groups has yet to be fully developed. When the American constitution was written in 1787, pirates terrorized the high seas from the Caribbean to North Africa and beyond. Nine of the earliest treaties of the United States, the first signed with Morocco in 1786, were aimed at ensuring bilateral cooperation to stop the Berbers from piratical attacks emanating off the North African coastline, known as the Barbary Coast. Eventually, the American government tired of paying tribute to the Barbary States and instead authorized the Navy and Marines to root out the pirates in a series of military campaigns from 1801–1815. Pirates, the terrorists of the day, were among the earliest international criminals, and international criminal law authorized a ship's captain to hang a pirate from the mast of a ship in international waters, that is, beyond the borders of any country. In *U.S. v Smith* (18US53), the U.S. Supreme Court in 1820 allowed the prosecution of a pirate on the grounds that piracy on the high seas was a crime with **universal jurisdiction**. The Geneva Conventions expanded international criminal law to deal with war criminals as the functional equivalent of terrorists. The various treaties seeking to stop slavery also considered the slave trader as an international criminal. More recently, drug and human traffickers have come within the scope of international criminal law.

HISTORIC EVENT 7.5 TERRORISTS ATTACK THE WORLD TRADE CENTER AND THE PENTAGON (2001)

In September 11, 2001, four commercial airplanes were hijacked after they took off at Logan International Airport in Boston. After the hijackers, nineteen in all, seized control of the cockpits, they flew two of the airplanes toward New York City and crashed the airplanes into the twin towers of the World Trade Center in lower Manhattan. One airplane plunged into a portion of the Pentagon, the headquarters of the U.S. Department of Defense at Arlington, Virginia. A fourth hijacked airplane, with an unknown destination, crashed in an unpopulated field near Shanksville, Pennsylvania. The death toll includes 2,973 civilians, all nineteen hijackers, and twenty-four persons missing and presumed dead. The hijackers were among a group of twenty-seven members of Al-Qaida, an organization of Arabic-speaking individuals led by Osama Bin Laden (1957–), who had in 1996 and 1998 pronounced a "holy war" against what he considered the American occupation of the Arabian Peninsula, support for apostate Muslim governments, the devastation of the Iraqi people, humiliation of their Muslim neighbors, and Washington's support of Israel, in which he called upon members of his organization to engage in the killing of "Jews and the Americans."

Mary Robinson (1944–), while UN High Commissioner for Human Rights condemned the September 11, 2001, attacks on the United States as a crime against humanity under international law. Secretary General Annan, however, acknowledged in 2003 that provisions of the UN Charter were not articulated to the threat of global terrorism. Indeed, today the UN still bureaucratically assigns responsibility for dealing with problems of terrorism to its Office on Drugs and Crime, which also deals with human trafficking.

Before 9/11/2001, several treaties dealt with terrorist acts as criminal offenses (Table 7.10). Perhaps the most basic are the *Convention for the Suppression of Unlawful Seizure of Aircraft*, which bans hijackings, and the *Convention for the Suppression of Unlawful Acts Against the Safety of Civil Aviation*, known as the Montreal Convention, which applies to bombings aboard aircraft in flight. Several regional organizations have also adopted treaties on the subject.

Currently, two treaties are being negotiated on the subject. The Draft Comprehensive Convention on International Terrorism, which would obligate countries to cooperate in preventing and punishing terrorism acts, still needs to find consensus on a legal definition of "terrorism." One problem in securing a consensus definition is that the Organization of the Islamic Conference, an intergovernmental organization composed of fifty-seven states with large Muslim populations, seeks to exempt acts aimed at "liberation and self-determination." The second treaty, now called the Draft Convention for the Suppression of Acts of Nuclear Terrorism, would require countries to develop protection systems for nuclear and radioactive materials and devices, as well as for nuclear installations.

Some observers have argued that a Fifth Geneva Convention is needed to take into account the peculiar situation of international terrorism, applying the doctrine of anticipatory self-defense. In 2006, the Supreme Court of Israel, which ruled that assassinations against terrorists are permitted under international law when (1) there

TABLE 7.10 TREATIES OUTLAWING INTERNATIONAL TERRORISM

Adopted	Document	In force
1963	Convention on Offenses and Certain Other Acts Committed on Board Aircraft (Tokyo Convention)	1969
1970	Convention for the Suppression of Unlawful Seizure of Aircraft (Hijacking Convention)	1971
1971	Convention for the Suppression of Unlawful Acts Against the Safety of Civil Aviation (Montréal Convention)	1973
1988	• Protocol for the Suppression of Unlawful Acts of Violence at Airports Serving International Aviation	1989
1971	Convention to Prevent and Punish Acts of Terrorism Taking the Form of Crimes Against Persons and Related Extortion that Are of International Significance [by the Organization of American States]	1972
1973	Convention on the Prevention and Punishment of Crimes Against Internationally Protected Persons	1977
1977	European Convention on the Suppression of Terrorism	1978
1979	Convention Against the Taking of Hostages	1983
1979	Convention on the Physical Protection of Nuclear Material	1997
1987	SAARC Regional Convention on Suppression of Terrorism [by the South Asian Association for Regional Cooperation]	1988
2004	• Additional Protocol to the SAARC Regional Convention on Suppression of Terrorism	
1988	Convention for the Suppression of Unlawful Acts Against the Safety of Maritime Navigation	1992
1988	• Protocol for the Suppression of Unlawful Acts Against the Safety of Fixed Platforms Located on the Continental Shelf	1992
1991	Convention on the Marking of Plastic Explosives for the Purpose of Identification	1988
1997	Convention for the Suppression of Terrorist Bombings	2001
1998	Arab Convention for the Suppression of Terrorism	1999
1999	Convention of the Organization of the Islamic Conference on Combating International Terrorism	
1999	International Convention for the Suppression of the Financing of Terrorism	2002
2002	Inter-American Convention Against Terrorism	2003

is a well-based, strong and convincing information" that a targeted person is plotting a terrorist act, (2) less harmful means cannot stop a terrorist plotter, (3) and when "the expected harm to innocent civilians is not disproportional to the military advantage to be achieved by the attack." Not all international legal experts agree.

In 2005, UN Secretary General Annan formulated a fivefold UN strategy on terrorism with the following elements: (1) Dissuade alienated groups from using terrorism as a means to achieve their objectives. (2) Ensure that terrorists lack the means to commit violent acts. (3) Prevent countries from supporting terrorist groups. (4) Develop state capacity to prevent terrorism. (5) Support human rights. Unfortunately, his proposal requires funds that have not been forthcoming.

CONCLUSION

When the first Geneva Convention was adopted in 1864, only 10 percent of the casualties were civilian. Today, civil wars, ethnic cleansing, insurgency and counterinsurgency warfare, and indiscriminate bombing have become more common and deadly than interstate wars, and civilians account for the overwhelming percentage of casualties, so widespread agreement on the principles of warfare has not deterred decisionmakers from launching aggression.

The Geneva Conventions, which contain more than 400 articles regulating the conduct of nations involved in war, have been adopted or ratified by 186 nations. No other international treaties have been so widely accepted. The world community, therefore, implicitly recognizes that human rights issues involving international violence are more important than all others. Of course, the right to life is also accepted within treaties regarding civil, political, economic, social, and cultural rights.

Nations that ratify conventions and protocols dealing with the right to life and the right to peace are responsible for punishing violations committed by their own military officers as well as other individuals. When governments fail to do so, the international community may be called into action. Accordingly, Chapter 8 asks why some countries respect human rights more than others, and Chapters 9–13 identify how human rights violations are being handled in the world community today.

CHAPTER 8

Quantitative dimensions

Countries around the world differ substantially in their efforts to live up to human rights standards. Some countries are improving more rapidly than others. A quantitative study of worldwide human rights observance raises five questions. (1) Are there reliable and valid indicators of human rights performance? (2) Is the concept of human rights unidimensional or is the concept so broad that there are empirically identifiable subsets of human rights? (3) Do certain variables predict to varying degrees of human rights performance? (4) How can predictors of human rights attainments be explained theoretically? (5) What are the implications of the empirical evidence for policymakers? All five questions are answered below.

HUMAN RIGHTS DATA

Empirical analysis requires data. Such United Nations sources as the *Demographic Yearbook* (1948–) and the *Statistical Yearbook* (1948–) report quantitative figures on economic and social attainments, as supplied by most countries around the world. Other UN agencies have published their own statistical compendia.

In 1958, Phillips Cutright (1930–) constructed two measures of social security attainments from U.S. Social Security Administration data on countries around the world. His Social Insurance Program Experience index summed data for the years since a country adopted five types of social security programs (family allowance plans; old-age and survivor pensions; sickness and/or maternity programs; unemployment insurance; work-injury programs). Cutright's Social Insurance Program Completion index counted the number of new welfare programs adopted from the 1920s to the 1960s.

The Physical Quality of Life Index (PQLI), applied by Morris David Morris to data as far back as 1960, has also been used in several studies; the index is a composite of infant mortality, life expectancy, and literacy rates. Morris has discovered, for example, that PQLI has increased faster than measures of economic development.

In 1987, the Population Crisis Committee first began to issue annual reports, known as *The International Human Suffering Index*. The latter index rates 130 countries on eight measures of economic and social attainments (clean drinking water, daily calorie supply, GNP per capita, infant immunization, life expectancy, rate of inflation, secondary school enrollment, telephones per capita).

The most extensive compendium on economic and social indicators is published by the United Nations Development Program (UNDP), which from 1990 has issued an annual *Human Development Report* that provides data on a variety of socio-economic indicators, including a Human Development Index, based on attainments in life expectancy, literacy, purchasing power, and school enrollment sex equality among 174 countries.

For civil and political rights, however, the data have been qualitative, based on judgments, not precise statistical measures. Despite the difficulty, some institutions and scholars have pooled comparative judgments of different types of rights into scales, such as a three-point index from low to medium to high.

An early effort, a scale of democracy, appeared in a publication by Russell Fitzgibbon (1902–1979) in 1955. A plethora of democracy scales has appeared ever since, some focusing on specific aspects of democratic rule, such as freedom of the press or the fairness of judicial proceedings. The *International Human Suffering Index* also has ratings on civil rights and political freedom.

Although Amnesty International has published annual reports on many countries from 1960, the organization refuses to provide qualitative or quantitative measures based on the reports despite repeated claims that the United States is the "number one abuser of human rights."[1] Not to be outdone, Human Rights Watch has published its own annual report since 1992.

A pioneering effort to quantify judgments about human rights attainments was undertaken by Raymond Gastil (1931–) of Freedom House, which first issued a "Comparative Survey of Freedom" for 1972. With ratings claimed to be based on seventeen types of civil rights and nineteen political rights, Freedom House began to classify more than one hundred countries along seven-point scales for both concepts. Despite first claiming that the two scales are analytically distinct, Freedom House contradictorily issued a single composite rating of each country's "status of freedom." Subsequently, Freedom House added an index of "economic freedom" that placed market economies at the top and closed economies at the bottom and a "political torture scale" based on the extent of incarcerations for political opinions, use of brutality and torture, disappearances after police arrest, and political executions.

In 1975, the U.S. Department of State's annual *Country Reports on Human Rights Practices* began to provide judgments about human rights attainments across more than 150 countries, but excluding the United States. Although the reports began with a narrow scope, over time the categories of concern have risen to more than twenty distinct issues.[2] Several European countries have followed suit.

A more ambitious undertaking was the short-lived *World Human Rights Guide*, a compilation by a former Amnesty International employee whose pseudonym is Charles Humana. Basing his ratings on Amnesty International reports and more than two dozen other sources, his first compilation was for 1982, when he rated one hundred and eleven countries along four-point scales for forty civil and political rights. In addition, he reported on ten other aspects of human rights, using qualitative or quantitative measures, and he provided a composite rating expressed as a percentage. Humana's guidebook for 1986 expanded to include one hundred and twenty one countries, but with forty-five variables. His final effort, published in 1992, covered one hundred and four countries for forty variables. Still seeking a composite summary scale, he employed a weighting system that gave more importance to seven of his conceptual variables.

Political Terrorism scales, originally developed by Michael Stohl (1947–) in 1986, have also been used frequently in recent studies. Stohl's original scale measures the extent to which a population is subjected to disappearance, imprisonment, torture, or execution for political views.

In 1991, the UNDP publication accepted Humana's summary percentages as its Political Freedom Index, but dropped his judgments in light of later scholarly critiques. UNDP then came up with its own composite measures, including the Gender-Related Development Index, the Gender Empowerment Measure, and the Human Poverty Index. UNDP has also published reports for geographic regions.

Funds provided by the Millennium Challenge Account, as established by the United States in 2002, are allocated to countries on the basis of several screening criteria (Table 8.1), both civil-political and economic-social attainments. A major source of data is from the World Bank and related organizations.

One recent effort is the Gap Scale of Joe Foweraker and Todd Landman, which subtracts measures on a Rights-in-Practice Scale from a Rights-in-Principle Scale. A second, the award-winning CIRI Human Rights Data Set of David Cingranelli and David Richards, scales thirteen types of human rights for 195 countries for the years 1981–2004.

Despite the reliance on various data sources, many scholars have found inadequacies in the above compilations. Data on economic and social attainments were challenged at a conference of the International Association for Official Statistics in 2000 that was attended by seven hundred persons representing governments, intergovernmental and nongovernmental organizations, and scholars. Data on civil and political rights have been criticized even more often.

Although Freedom House ratings have been widely used by empirical scholars, the methodology is not transparent, ratings are subjective, and the scales appear to overlap conceptually. Freedom House, which no longer employs Gastil, has nevertheless sought to improve the validity of the scales.

The State Department reports were so criticized for biased judgments that a brief critique of the 1981 report was duplicated in soft cover by the Lawyers Committee for International Human Rights; recently renamed Human Rights First, the organization has continued to publish annual critiques, now in hard cover. During the

TABLE 8.1   PERFORMANCE CRITERIA FOR FUNDS FROM THE MILLENNIUM CHALLENGE ACCOUNT

Performance Criterion	Indicator	Source of data
Governing justly	Civil liberties	Freedom House
	Political rights	Freedom House
	Voice and accountability	World Bank Institute
	Government effectiveness	World Bank Institute
	Rule of law	World Bank Institute
	Control of corruption	World Bank Institute
Investing in people	Public primary education spending as percent of GDP	World Bank/national sources
	Primary education completion rate	World Bank/national sources
	Public expenditures on health as percent of GDP	World Bank/national sources
	Immunization rates: DPT and measles	World Bank/national sources
Promoting economic freedom	Country credit rating	*Institutional Investor*
	inflation	IMF
	3-year budget deficit	IMF/national sources
	Trade policy	Heritage Foundation
	Regulatory quality	World Bank Institute
	Days to start a business	World Bank

1990s, however, many scholars found the reports to be more objective and professional.

A more fundamental problem is methodological. The scales have been developed without empirical validation; that is, the scales have not been demonstrated to be undimensional and might instead lump disparate measures (the proverbial apples and oranges) together. Many scales measure "democracy," but fail to distinguish between procedural democracy (observance of political rights) and substantive democracy (representativeness). Consequently, higher scores on democracy scales have unsurprisingly been found to correlate with higher scores on scales of civil and political rights. Nevertheless, in *Improving Human Rights* (1994), I found high intercorrelations between data from six different sources. Other studies that compare alternative datasets have yielded comparable results.

HUMAN RIGHTS CLASSIFICATIONS

According to the Vienna Conference on Human Rights of 1993, "All human rights are universal, indivisible, interdependent and interrelated." Alternatively, several scholars have proposed analytically distinct categories of human rights (Table 1.2).

Yet both claims may be incorrect and simplistic, lacking empirical foundation. Human rights may be interrelated empirically in at least five ways (Table 8.2).

Unidimensionality. If a good record on civil and political rights predicts to a good record on social, economic, and cultural rights, then human rights would constitute a unidimensional phenomenon, consistent with the consensus reached at the Vienna Conference. Improvement on any one right may set in place the momentum for better observance of other human rights.

Multidimensionality. When progress on civil-political rights has no effect on socioeconomic rights, there may be two or possibly more empirical dimensions. If so, efforts to improve human rights must identify separate problem areas.

Hierarchy. The granting of some rights may unlock others; the attainment of some rights might have to wait until other rights are respected. In 1989, after the world community witnessed on television a massacre of dissidents near Tiananmen Square, the government in Beijing began to defend itself with the argument that the right of survival – the feeding of more than one billion persons – is more important than and prior to political rights. Although China's argument might be traced to the Jacobin desire to give priority to the welfare of the people over political freedoms, the country's dissidents appeared to agree with the contrary view that more political rights would open the door for opportunities to achieve greater prosperity, and current Premier Wen Jiabao (1942–), now places the ongoing development of a legal system as the last obstacle to democratic reform. In other words, if X leads to Y, then policymakers should pay most attention to improving X, whereupon Y will follow.

Inverse. Alternatively, an improvement in some rights might entail a decline in others. According to Samuel Huntington (1927–), the attempt to increase democracy can retard economic development, as the masses may demand a more equitable distribution of the benefits of increased prosperity, thereby disrupting the imperatives of capital accumulation by shrewd entrepreneurs. Political instability fomented by frustrated equalitarians, in short, might slow economic progress.

Curvilinearity. Human rights might improve under certain conditions up to an asymptote, then fluctuate randomly or decline while at intermediate levels until a second threshold is reached, whereupon improvements might further decline or improve in a linear manner again. In one study, for example, democracy was found to vary with socioeconomic development up to a threshold, but thereafter the two variables were unrelated.[3]

TABLE 8.2 HYPOTHETICAL EMPIRICAL DIMENSIONS

Type of dimensionality	Empirical implication
Unidimensionality	All rights cluster together.
Multidimensionlity	Two or more types of rights are empirically separate.
Hierarchy	One right is basic, others are derivative.
Inverse	As some rights are better observed, others decline.
Curvilinearity	Attainment of rights fluctuates up and down over time.

One practical implication of the alternative dimensional possibilities is that instead of holding all countries to the same high standards, policymakers might better "aim ameliorative efforts at specific types of noncompliance, and recognize clusters which may be too intractable to justify attention at this time [thereby] enabl[ing] the efficient application of limited resources," as David Banks (1956–) has argued. It is therefore important to determine which dimensionality assumption is correct so that potentially more effective strategies for advancing human rights can be devised.

EMPIRICAL DIMENSIONS

Are human rights unidimensional or are there empirically distinct types of human rights? One way to determine the number of empirical dimensions is to use a technique known as factor analysis. Simply stated, the procedure is to start with correlations between pairs of variables and then find out whether any such relationships hold when all other variables are held constant. What are then derived are one or more clusters of variables that are highly interrelated; if there are two or more uncorrelated clusters, then there are empirically distinct dimensions.

The largest test of empirical dimensionality, which has been corroborated by smaller-scale studies, can be found in my *Improving Human Rights* (1994). Using fifty qualitative scales of civil and political rights from Humana's ratings and ninety-one quantitative measures from mostly UN sources for the years 1982 and 1986, the principal finding is that civil and political rights are empirically distinct from economic and social attainments. In addition, there was no evidence of either inverse relationships or curvilinearity between types of human rights. Civil and political rights neither precede nor follow increases in economic and social rights. The two sets of rights appear to develop independently.

Cluster analysis, which assumes a hierarchical relationship, finds a distinct pattern with regard to civil and political rights: human rights are first granted to males in the mainstream ethnic group, then to minorities; after the rights of minorities are respected, women's rights are attained. After women's rights come gay rights. The statistical pattern is indeed corroborated by the historical development of human rights described in Chapters 3 and 4. The cluster analysis for economic and social attainments reveals a supercluster identifying quality of life in general, first joined by worker's rights, then minority rights, and finally women's rights.

CORRELATIONAL EVIDENCE

While some scholars have made specific predictions that may be checked through correlational analysis, others prefer to engage in case studies. Both statistical and case study analyses are valid methods for studying empirical phenomena; indeed, case studies are needed to validate statistical research.

More than 100 bivariate statistical efforts (involving correlations between predictor variable and levels of human rights observance)[4] agree that the countries most likely to respect human rights have a well-educated and homogenous population with a prosperous, stable, urbanized society in which there is relative income equality, considerable media development, and competitive multiparty systems. In addition, there is a consensus among empirical scholars that economic and social rights are better observed within affluent, stable democracies.

Bivariate correlational studies, however, are inherently shallow. Using multivariate techniques, including cluster analysis, factor analysis, and multiple regression, both comparatively and longitudinally, the principal findings regarding civil and political rights are that higher *levels of observance* are found in countries with the following characteristics: (1) The parliament has many parties, the largest party has a slim plurality, and the military budget is small. (2) Absence of forced labor is related to a prosperous, urban economy, with high media development and substantial education, health, and welfare budgets.

Variables associated with *improvements* in civil and political rights over time are as follows: (1) Countries with lower taxes and lower voter turnout improve the most. (2) Gender equality improves most rapidly within ethnolinguistically homogeneous, prosperous, domestically stable, urban countries that have a high degree of media development, income equality, and substantial education, health, and welfare budgets, though the same countries tend to have high deathrates from cancer, heart disease, and suicide.

There are two major findings regarding economic and social rights attainments: (1) Economic and social conditions improve most in ethnolinguisitically homogeneous, non-Muslim prosperous, urban countries with relative income equality and high media development and substantial education, health, and welfare budgets. (2) Workers' rights are most respected by civilian governments where parliaments have many parties, including leftist parties, and the largest party has a slim plurality.

Perhaps the most important finding is that there are separate patterns regarding **mainstream** and **nonmainstream** groups (minorities, women, gays, and lesbians). Human rights improve in stages, beginning with mainstream groups. After a dominant ethnic group enjoys human rights, military regimes are the main barriers to the extension of human rights to nonmainstream groups. When the military steps down, rights are granted first to minorities, next to women, and finally to gays and lesbians.

EMPIRICAL THEORIES

What accounts for the degree of observance of and progress in human rights? Mere statistical analyses mean very little until findings can be placed into a theoretical framework so that a coherent explanation can be formulated. Accordingly, several empirical theories currently compete as alternative explanations for the fact that some countries have better human rights records than others (Table 8.3).

The metaphilosophical justifications for human rights identified in Chapter 2 are primarily ethical theories. However, democratic theories and Marxism are predictive theories; that is, they make predictions about which variables explain levels of human rights attainment. Some opponents of human rights, as delineated in Chapter 2, are based on ethical or ideological postulates, but other opponents believe that the steady

TABLE 8.3   EMPIRICAL THEORIES OF HUMAN RIGHTS

Theory	Prediction
Liberal democratic theory	Political rights precede all other rights.
Social democratic theory	Social rights precede all other rights.
Stages-of-growth theory	Some rights must come before others.
Marxism	Economic elites block rights of workers.
Power elite theory	Elites block rights of nonelites.
Group conflict theory	Mainstream groups block rights of nonmainstream groups.
Mobilization theory	Rights are granted only after political struggles.
Mass society theory	Governments block rights to avoid turmoil.
Frustration-aggression theory	Human rights decline when economies collapse.
Freudianism	As industrialization increases, the population becomes "savage," so governments block rights.
Functionalism	Governments comply with human rights norms because of favorable experiences.
Social darwinism	Governments survive by being ready for war, so human rights are necessarily secondary.

advance in human rights is infeasible, so their predictions can be put to the test with empirical data. Finally, some social science theories, as specified within various chapters of my *Polity and Society: Philosophical Underpinnings of Social Science Paradigms* (1992), can also be tested with empirical data. Below, the various predictive theories are evaluated in terms of the empirical results.

Liberal democratic theory. Such theorists as Robert Dahl (1915–) and Max Weber (1864–1920) stress the need for free elections, the free flow of information, a competitive economy, contending political parties, and a neutral bureaucracy as preconditions of a social order that will bring human rights for all. Since empirical evidence demonstrates that support for human rights is greater in countries with competitive multiparty systems, there is strong support for liberal democratic theory.

Social democratic theory. The social democratic theories of Gerhard Lenski (1924–) and Gunnar Myrdal (1898–1987), reflecting especially on the experience of Scandinavian political systems, argue that human rights are best observed when the rich in a democracy favor social welfare reforms for the less wealthy. Liberal democratic theory does not insist upon the components of the welfare state, whereas social democrats conceive of social welfare programs as essential in providing human rights to the people. The empirical evidence demonstrates that higher education, health, and welfare budgets correlate with greater attainments of human rights in general, particularly with workers' rights and women's rights.

Stages-of-growth theory. Some theorists stress the need for economic growth as a precondition to human rights. Walt Rostow (1916–2003) applies the same logic to economic development, and Kenneth Organski (1923–2006) finds a parallel in political development. They appear to argue that the trickle-down of capital accumulated as a country shifts from an agricultural to an industrial to a post-industrial society will bring ever-increasing democracy, human rights, and prosperity. However, Samuel Huntington has provided evidence that instability results when political rights are granted before a developing country secures solid progress in improving living standards. He cautions that the hard decisions required to transform economies often require political authoritarian rule and are hindered by premature democracy. If human rights develop in stages, we would expect to find that after countries achieve greater economic attainments, they will gradually improve civil and political rights performance. Although bivariate students supports stages-of-growth theory, multivariate analyses demonstrate that economic development goes hand in hand with improvements in civil and political rights. Since the two elements move along parallel tracks, what provokes both processes to develop in the first place? Stages-of-growth theory, in other words, does not identify what inexorability factor specifically prompts movement from one stage to another, though Milton Friedman (1912–2007) suggests that the benefits of world trade in building up state resources can redound to the benefit of improvements in human rights.

Marxism. For Marxists, economic elites trample on human rights to preserve their economic hegemony, which ultimately rests on exploitation at home or abroad. Marxists believe that the bourgeoisie's imperative of capital accumulation is why economic elites under capitalism do not want nonelites to enjoy basic human rights, whereas worker's democracies promote equal treatment. Workers, in turn, must struggle to wrest power from the bourgeoisie. Multivariate evidence supports the prediction that countries with greater income equality have more respect for human rights in general; moreover, higher welfare budgets predict to more respect for workers' rights. In short, the Marxist prediction that social equality comes before legal equality has been turned on its side; both civil-political and economic-social rights improve as a country becomes more prosperous and income distribution is more equal. Marxism fails to predict that elites in wealthier capitalist countries decreasingly exploit workers.

Turning to a theory developed by opponents of human rights, **relativism** argues that the Western-oriented human rights conception of individualism does not fit the circumstances or outlook of non-Western peoples and hence cannot be advanced by applying foreign pressure. Relativists argue that socially constructed cultural norms determine the propensity to respect some human rights. The statistical evidence from several studies indeed finds that the percentage of Christians in a country is a much better predictor to support for civil and political rights than the percentage of Muslims. However, Turkey respects human rights more fully than other Muslim countries, and the United States lags behind other countries with large Christian populations, so there is variability with the two religious traditions. Relativism, therefore, is an inadequate explanation for variability in human rights attainments.

Power elite theory. Burkean elitism and social darwinism, which argue that humans are born unequal and therefore should not expect to be treated equally, have a counterpart in the social science approach known as power elite theory. According to power elite theory, those on top seek to maintain power by setting up barriers to equal rights for nonelites. One version believes that there is something akin to an "iron law of oligarchy"; exponents are Roberto Michels (1876–1936), Gaetano Mosca (1858–1941), and Vilfredo Pareto (1948–1923). A contemporary power elite theorist, notably Noam Chomsky (1928–), argues that the rhetoric of "national security" serves as a rationale for restricting human rights. The Cold War, according to Chomsky and others, was waged by ruling elites in both the Soviet Union and the United States to justify internal and external disinterest in democratization. Social constructionists, similarly, argue that elites maintain their dominance by controlling the verbal discourse, using such arguments as "national security" to dissuade nonelites from demanding their rights. One type of power elite is the military in a country, but corporations can seek plutocratic control as well. Charles Lindblom (1917–) believes that rulers carefully weigh costs and benefits of repression; by extension, rulers are predicted to respect human rights in order to maintain their grip on power without the costly expenditures required to maintain military rule or police states. Quantitative research, as reported above, supports power elite theory insofar as military juntas stay in power by refusing to grant equal rights to civilians. However, the history of human rights is that military and civilian elites do indeed step down from power and grant rights, though they often retake power when displeased with democratic rule, so the pessimism of power elite theory is somewhat exaggerated.

Group conflict theory. When elite groups grant rights, they do so to mainstream groups. Group conflict theory generalizes the Marxist notion of the class struggle and power elite theory's belief that an inner circle will cling onto power into a more generic approach to the study of human rights. Some theorists, notably Pierre Van Den Berghe (1933–), believe that certain ethnic groups in heterogeneous societies seek to advance their own kind and thus aim to restrict the rights of others. His conception of *Herrenvolk* democracy, based in part on his analysis of South Africa, is that mainstream groups allow civil and political rights among themselves while denying them to nonmainstream groups. According to group conflict theory, human rights fare better in homogeneous than in heterogeneous societies, as the latter will tend to have more internal conflict. Just as Japanese on the West Coast of the United States were relocated to internment camps during World War II, a current version of group conflict theory is advanced by leaders who restrict human rights to Arab-appearing individuals in the name of fighting terrorist groups. Statistical findings about greater human rights in homogeneous societies support group conflict theory as an explanation for why mainstream groups sometimes achieve their rights, yet nonmainstream groups do not. Nevertheless, group conflict theory does not explain why nonmainstream groups have advanced, especially during the twentieth century.

HISTORIC EVENT 8.1 JAPANESE ARE RELOCATED TO INTERNMENT CAMPS (1942–1945)

On December 7, 1941, Japanese airplanes bombed the naval base at Pearl Harbor, Hawai'i, and soon submarines surfaced and shelled locations on the West Coast of the United States. Fearing that residents of Japanese ancestry might cooperate with an invasion force, the U.S. Army requested President Franklin Roosevelt (1882–1945) to take drastic measures. After a nighttime curfew was imposed on Japanese residents on the West Coast, an order came in 1942 for all persons of Japanese ancestry on the West Coast, 62 percent of whom were American citizens, to report to temporary locations. Although 11,000 were allowed to move to other parts of the United States, some 110,000 were sent to War Relocation Camps in the interior, where most remained until 1945; however, some Japanese males were able to leave the camps if they volunteered to serve in the U.S. Army. Those of Japanese ancestry living in other parts of the United States, including Hawai'i, were not affected by the internment order unless specific evidence warranted their detention. In 1944, the Supreme Court ruled in *Korematsu v United States* (323US214) that the relocation was lawful because national security trumped Bill of Rights protections. Some American residents of Austrian, German, and Italian ancestry were also detained until the war ended in 1945. Some 23,000 Japanese on the West Coast of Canada were also relocated, and Perú sent about 2,000 persons of Japanese ancestry to the relocation camps in Texas. After the war, some compensation was provided to those who had been detained.

Mobilization theory. Historically, elites and dominant ethnic groups have granted human rights. An explanation for the transformation is offered by the social science approach known as mobilization theory. Such observers as Stokely Carmichael (1941–1998), later known as Kwame Ture, and Charles Tilly (1929–) believe that no rights are granted without a struggle, so well-organized groups can alone advance their own cause. Indeed, mobilization theory views politics in terms of the pressure group model of Arthur Bentley (1870–1957) in which the victor in a political contest is the strongest within a parallelogram of forces. If mobilization theory is correct, human rights will be highest in countries with a vigorous mass-based civil society, including minority movements, trade unions, and women's organizations that can work to develop a human rights culture. Of course, mobilization efforts might invite repression, which in turn may boomerang, so there is a possible curvilinear relationship, according to Eduard Ziegenhagen (1935–). The empirical evidence is indeed supportive, but for workers' rights more than for rights in general. Mobilization theory clearly supplies the explanation for why movement occurs from one stage of human rights development to the next but fails to account for what prompts mobilization campaigns themselves.

Mass society theory. Human rights transformations have occurred in some countries, but not in others, so mobilization theory fails. Since mass-based "people power" struggles are well understood by elites, the social science theory of mass society has arisen to explain why some elites are able to maintain power for long periods of time without granting human rights. There are two variants of mass society theory, which links the absence of civil society with denials of human rights. Samuel Huntington notes that no political system can cope with a massive social dislocation accompanying extremely rapid economic growth as the population moves from the countryside to the towns. If human rights are granted too quickly, according to mass society theory, the result will be political turmoil, so certain governments will back-burner human rights as their countries develop economically. A second form of mass society theory, as explicated by William Kornhauser (1925–2004), stresses that totalitarian rule, by depriving citizens of the freedom to form a civil society, serves to build up pressures that cannot be expressed politically but are instead evident in decreasing quality of life, such as rampant alcoholism. Although the evidence is that economic development can coincide with human rights progress, no scholar has yet correlated rates of economic development to test the rapid development variant. The second version is contrary to empirical evidence regarding women's rights, which were relatively well respected in former Communist countries.

Frustration-aggression theory. For Sigmund Freud (1856–1939) and his followers, notably Herbert Marcuse (1898–1979), the industrial revolution requires individuals to repress their spontaneity in order to have the discipline to perform repetitive tasks in factories and offices. Such repression supposedly creates a longing to express savagery, whether in the form of genocide or lesser violations of human rights. Some non-Freudians believe that socioeconomic deprivation and discrimination constitute frustrations that can lead the masses to engage in violent protest, thereby inviting government repression and escalating violence and repression. For Robert Lifton (1926–) and Ted Gurr (1936–), economic downswings and similar reversals precede human rights restrictions. However, higher levels of economic development and prosperity predict to better human rights records. Since economic improvement has been the rule over the last several decades in most of the world, empirical evidence is unavailable for anything more than temporary downswings.

Functionalism. Sociologists often assume that individuals behave in accordance with past conditioning, that is, a socialization process. Governments are more likely to observe human rights when elites and citizens are conditioned by their experience over time to appreciate the moral or pragmatic value of compliance. Frustration-aggression theory, particularly Freudianism, are pessimistic about human rights because they focus on negative socialization. The most prominent form of positive socialization theory is known as functionalism. David Mitrany (1888–1975) predicts that governmental participation in international cooperative activities in relatively nonpolitical technical matters inevitably spills over into sensitive political issues, such as human rights. Cooperative activities, in turn, involve discussion among experts and government officials, some of whom persuade others of the virtues of human rights. Ernst Haas (1924–2003), indeed, provided considerable support for what he called neofunctionalism in his analyses of decisionmaking in intergovernmental institutions. Correlational research thus far reveals that countries adopting human rights treaties are much more likely to implement them in their domestic law than otherwise.

Social darwinism. Based on the premise that a world without a neutral international police force is so inherently dangerous that governments must maximize their power and influence in order to avoid loss of territorial control by losing wars, social darwinism assigns a very low priority to human rights. The theory of *realpolitik* of Hans Morgenthau (1904–1980), sometimes referred to as "realism," is a social darwinistic theory in which concern for human rights is viewed as a distraction from the need of every state to defend its sovereignty by being prepared militarily. Empirical data demonstrate that military rule is indeed the form of government least likely to grant human rights, but few countries are so governed, and mobilization theory appears to explain why military rule has been be toppled.

Thus far, the data tentatively support several empirical theories, notably democratic theories, mobilization theory, and functionalism. However, critical tests of alternative explanations are needed to determine which theory is most applicable.

POLICY IMPLICATIONS OF EMPIRICAL RESEARCH

Several scholars have sought to determine whether foreign aid has served to encourage better human rights or instead has been used by recipient nations to suppress their people. However, the findings are by no means definitive.

The correlational and multivariate findings presented above demonstrate that human rights advance as a country develops economically, builds a communication infrastructure, and has competitive political parties. Accordingly, economic aid might appropriately be articulated toward economic and media development, whereas aid to political parties is usually covert and can easily boomerang when exposed. In view of the centrality of economic development in promoting human rights, one implication of the empirical findings presented above is that withholding economic aid might retard the advance of human rights. Although humanitarian aims justify pressuring notorious violators of human rights to release political prisoners, stop police torture of suspects, and the like, the data do not support blanket sanctions against regimes that take vigorous measures to promote economic development. Case studies indeed demonstrate the superiority of positive incentives (carrots) over negative sanctions (sticks).[5]

A successful strategy for less developed countries with ethnolinguistic heterogeneity, which tend to be under military rule, is to develop economic pluralism before human rights can advance on solid ground. Foreign aid, accordingly, should assist finance an information infrastructure, support increased educational opportunities so that a more literate population will emerge, and insist on a privatization of the economy that promotes economic pluralism.

Another implication of empirical research thus far is that the development of a legal system can provide many checks on the possibility of arbitrary actions by those in authority within a political system where there is a reasonable amount of consensus. The task of promoting constitutional rule ultimately falls upon leaders of loyal opposition parties to insist on multiparty elections with secret ballots. Although a loyal opposition is more likely in countries that have economic pluralism, current developments in China suggest that factions within a ruling elite may play a similar role.

Democracy cannot be implanted in a country by having bayonets or economic sanctions imposed from outside. A demand for "free and fair elections" as a condition of aid will not produce an increase in human rights unless the economic and social interests represented in a multiparty parliament are diverse but moderate. Too often, economically poor countries hold elections, but afterward parliamentarians represent their own personal interests. Such governments tend to be corrupt or gridlocked, thereby provoking military coups. One conception of democracy is of a form of government in which the legislature serves as an arena where lawmakers design compromises on behalf of pluralistic societal interests.

Foreign aid to the poorest countries should seldom be conditioned on progress in the rights of minorities, women, and workers, according to the empirical analyses reviewed herein. Since regimes are likely to provide basic human rights to the mainstream before nonmainstream groups, aid donors should apply pressure on recipient countries to establish an umbrella of general guarantees, notably a Bill of Rights, before trying to put special groups under the same umbrella. Since minority rights and workers' rights improve as economic aspects of liberal democracy emerge, the appropriate strategy is to provide aid for power grids, printing presses, telephone lines, elementary and secondary textbooks, and professionalism in broadcasting, thus expanding pluralism. When democratic states have sufficient economic prosperity to extend rights to nonmainstream groups, conditional aid will no longer be needed. When progress in minority rights and women's rights is assured, gays and lesbians will be accorded treatment that is more decent.

Historically, trade union rights came first, leading to the establishment of welfare states. The efforts of such leaders as Martin Luther King, Jr., (1929–1968) paved the way for advances in the rights of women and, much later, gays and lesbians. The evidence suggests that minorities and trade unionists should pursue separate but simultaneous struggles for their rights, whereas women, gays, and lesbians will derive benefit by forming coalitions that work for the success of both struggles while continuing to stress their own agendas.

CONCLUSION

Civil and political rights neither precede nor follow increases in economic and social rights. Instead, the two sets of rights are distinct and develop independently. The correlation between civil-political and social-economic rights is spurious. When the military pretends to be socially indispensable, civil and political rights are restricted. The end of autocratic rule, which tends to weaken as an information infrastructure expands, is essential before human rights can make substantial improvements. Human rights are complementary, not zerosum, so improvements in one area do not entail a risk of lesser attainments elsewhere.

Civil and political rights, in turn, appear to be granted sequentially and thus form a hierarchy. Mainstream groups, that is, males of the dominant ethnic group, are likely to gain increased rights as arbitrary state power collapses. Later, other forms of civil and political rights emerged, such as freedom of the press and the right to vote. While mainstream groups are securing basic rights, nonmainstream groups tend to be ignored, In due course, as the government abandons military and police methods for dealing with minorities, the status of minorities improves. As a government develops a welfare state, women's rights improve.[6] After minorities and women enjoy victories in their struggle for equal civil and political rights, gays and lesbians begin to enjoy success in achieving equal rights.

A domino effect appears to place the theory of liberal democracy as a precondition for the advancement of human rights. But liberal democracy alone can remain stagnant, without advances, until groups are mobilized to demand their own rights. Evidently liberal democratic theory explains the political climate for dominoes to stand on their own, while mobilization theory accounts for the process of extending rights. But such a scenario needs to be tested more rigorously in the years ahead.

Since the denial of basic human rights is a desperate strategy for maintaining power, advocates of human rights should urge more economic aid so that the infrastructure for a free flow of ideas and economic largesse for better social conditions can be established. Advocacy organizations that focus on particular abuses of the moment should be congratulated for successful efforts to free prisoners of conscience and similar short-term measures, but for the long run establishing the preconditions for a liberal and later a social democracy can best advance human rights. Current research findings and conclusions are, of course, tentative. They should be cross-checked through case studies, just as alternative theories should be put to critical tests.

Some of the empirically-based recommendations await policy decisions by individual governments. Others require concerted action in international and regional forums. Accordingly, Chapters 9–13 focus on all three levels.

DISCUSSION TOPIC 8.1 SHOULD FOREIGN AID GO TO COUNTRIES WITH POOR HUMAN RIGHTS RECORDS?

The Millennium Challenge Account of the United States screens recipients of foreign aid in accordance with human rights and other criteria. Countries with poor human rights records, in other words, are denied the very aid that might help to increase their human rights attainments. Is that the correct approach? What is the correct approach?

CHAPTER 9

United Nations Charter-based organizations

In an ideal world, all human rights violations by individuals will be handled by their own governments. When human rights are violated by an errant state, other states may need to act in order to handle a serious situation. Chapters 9–13 document the considerable extent to which members of the world community are now mobilized to act when victims of human rights seek redress from countries and international organizations beyond their borders.

There are four means by which pressure can be brought to bear on states that fail to observe human rights standards: (1) diplomatic and verbal efforts, (2) legal action, (3) economic and humanitarian action, and (4) military means. In all four cases, the action can be **proactive** or **punitive**. The proactive approach is known as the "carrot," whereas the punitive approach is called the "stick."

Because intergovernmental organizations act only when their members agree on a policy toward a human rights problem, proactive efforts are more common. One reason for the caution is that too much punitive action against a particular member country may frighten other members into believing that some day they might suffer from the wrath of others.

Several types of global organizations are relevant to human rights, constituting a form of political globalization that has become possible in an age of economic globalization. Most global international organizations either are a part of the United Nations or have close relations with the UN. The most prominent are the *Charter-based organs*, that is, bodies specified in the UN Charter (Table 9.1).

The Trusteeship Council, General Assembly, Security Council, the Secretariat, and many bodies subsidiary to the Economic and Social Council (ECOSOC) prefer

TABLE 9.1   **UNITED NATIONS CHARTER-BASED ORGANS FOCUSING ON HUMAN RIGHTS**

Organs	Acronym	Formed	Headquarters
Trusteeship Council	UNTC	1945	New York
General Assembly	UNGASS	1945	New York
• High Commissioner for Refugees	UNHCR	1949	Geneva
Security Council	UNSC	1945	New York
Secretariat		1945	
• Secretary-General	UNSG	1945	New York
• Office of the High Commissioner for Human Rights	OHCHR	1944	Geneva
• Human Rights Council	UNHRC	1946	Geneva
Economic and Social Council	ECOSOC	1945	New York
• Commission on the Status of Women	CSW	1946	Vienna
• Commission for Social Development	CsocD	1946	New York
• Commission on Crime Prevention and Criminal Justice		1992	Vienna
• Permanent Forum on Indigenous Issues	UNPFII	2000	New York
Specialized agencies			
• International Labor Organization	ILO	1919	Geneva
• UN Educational, Scientific, and Cultural Organization	UNESCO	1945	Paris
• Food and Agriculture Organization of the United Nations	FAO	1945	Rome
• United Nations Children's Fund	UNICEF	1946	New York
• World Health Organization	WHO	1948	Geneva
• World Food Program	WFP	1961	Rome
• UN Development Program	UNDP	1964	New York
• UN Conference on Trade and Development	UNCTAD	1966	Geneva
• UN Development Fund for Women	UNIFEM	1976	New York
• International Fund for Agricultural Development	IFAD	1977	Rome
• World Bank Group: International Bank for Reconstruction and Development	IBRD	1944	Washington
International Development Association	IDA	1960	Washington
• International Monetary Fund	IMF	1944	Washington
• International Atomic Energy Agency	IAEA	1957	Vienna
International Court of Justice	ICJ	1946	The Hague

proactive diplomatic and verbal efforts. Proactive legal pressure is the sole function of the International Court of Justice. Proactive economic and humanitarian approaches pervade ECOSOC and the Specialized Agencies. Both the General Assembly and the Security Council can authorize punitive economic and military sanctions. The discussion below focuses on each institution separately.

TRUSTEESHIP COUNCIL (UNTC)

Under the settlement after World War II, the League of Nations **mandates** were to be converted into **trusteeships**. Former colonies of Italy and Japan as well as the latter's mandate in the Pacific also became Trusteeships. The UN Charter gave explicit instructions for the Trusteeship Council to require reports from countries serving as trustees about measures taken to move the territories toward independence. South Africa, which had the League Mandate over former German South West Africa, was the only mandate power that refused to transfer jurisdiction to the Trusteeship Council.

While the Cold War dominated the General Assembly and the Security Council during the late 1940s and 1950s, the Trusteeship Council was in the forefront of human rights progress. Annual reports on progress toward self-government were carefully monitored, and individuals could submit oral petitions or written complaints. In 1994, Palau was the last territory under the trusteeship system to be granted independence. Accordingly, the Council suspended operations and has not met since then.

However, recent actions by the General Assembly have created what may be called **quasi-trusteeships**. When asked to handle the administration of Cambodia, East Timor (Timor-Leste), Kosovo, Liberia, and Namibia after periods of turmoil, the UN responded in a manner that nearly constituted a trusteeship arrangement.

GENERAL ASSEMBLY (UNGASS)

Colonies not under the jurisdiction of the Trusteeship Council have been monitored by the General Assembly's Fourth Committee, specifically by the Subcommittee on Non-Self-Governing Territories. The first serious involvement of the General Assembly in human rights came in the 1960s as new African states joined the UN, eager to end *apartheid* in South Africa, racism in the British colony of Southern Rhodesia, and independence for the remaining colonies.

In 1961, the General Assembly replaced the Subcommittee on Non-Self-Governing Territories with the Special Committee on the Situation with Regard to the Implementation of the Declaration on the Granting of Independence to Colonial Countries and Peoples (known as the *Special Committee on Decolonization*) to press metropolitan countries to grant independence or self-government to all remaining colonies. Most African countries did indeed achieve independence in the 1960s, and the last region to emerge from colonial status was the South Pacific, where island states became independent during the 1970s. The remaining non-self-governing territories are still being monitored.[1]

Racism has been another major concern of the General Assembly, which exerted pressure not only on Rhodesia and South Africa but also adopted resolutions condemning Israel. Tel Aviv was considered by many states to be operating a racist government after the Six-Day War of 1967 because Israel began a military occupation of homelands of the Arab-speaking population of Palestine. The United States opposed

General Assembly resolutions on the subject, most vehemently the resolutions of 1975–1991, stating that "Zionism is a form of racism and racial discrimination," and Washington vetoed Security Council resolutions from 1973–1997 calling for an end to the Israeli occupation. At Israel's insistence, the resolutions were dropped in 1998 so that negotiations could begin with the Palestine Liberation Organization to replace the occupation with a Palestinian state, though negotiations stopped in early 2001.

The General Assembly accredits delegations to represent member countries, but not always in accordance with human rights principles. During the 1980s, the Cambodian seat was held by the delegation of Democratic Kampuchea, which represented the murderous Khmer Rouge regime that had been ousted by Vietnam by 1979; the successor Cambodian government, considered by some countries to be a puppet regime of Vietnam, was not accredited until the UN provided a peace settlement in 1992. Similarly, in 1999, UNGASS refused to accredit the Taliban government as the representative of Afghanistan in view of many human rights violations, notably restrictions on the movements of females.

Delegates to the UN General Assembly generally are ambassadors. In recent years, the UN General Assembly chamber has been the venue for *World Summits*, that is, meetings of heads of state and government. The World Summit of 2000, which included 147 heads of state and government, adopted the Millennium Declaration to set measurable goals to be attained in seven key areas: (1) peace, security and disarmament; (2) development and poverty eradication; (3) protecting the environment; (4) protecting the vulnerable; (5) meeting the special needs of Africa; (6) strengthening the United Nations; and (7) human rights, democracy, and good governance. Under the latter heading, the following goals were declared:

- To respect fully and uphold the Universal Declaration of Human Rights.
- To strive for the full protection and promotion in all our countries of civil, political, economic, social and cultural rights for all.
- To strengthen the capacity of all our countries to implement the principles and practices of democracy and respect for human rights, including minority rights.
- To combat all forms of violence against women and to implement the Convention on the Elimination of All Forms of Discrimination Against Women.
- To take measures to ensure respect for and protection of the human rights of migrants, migrant workers and their families, to eliminate the increasing acts of racism and xenophobia in many societies and to promote greater harmony and tolerance in all societies.
- To work collectively for more inclusive political processes, allowing genuine participation by all citizens in all our countries.
- To ensure the freedom of the media to perform their essential role and the right of the public to have access to information.

In the 2004–2005 session, the General Assembly passed 312 resolutions, of which sixty-one were related to human rights, or about 20 percent. Clearly, human rights concerns remain a matter of considerable priority.

HIGH COMMISSIONER FOR REFUGEES (UNHCR)

A quintessential UN human rights component is the relief given to refugees. After World War II, the General Assembly set up the United Nations Relief and Rehabilitation Administration from 1943–1946 and the International Refugee Organization from 1947–1952, each of which handled millions of displaced persons; the latter body took over the functions of the refugee organization that operated under the League of Nations. Then in 1949, the General Assembly established UNHCR in view of the continuing presence of 1.2 million displaced persons, some of whom had not been resettled after World War II and others who fled countries occupied or controlled by the Soviet Union. The Geneva-based agency, based on the founding Statute and the Convention Relating to the Status of Refugees, both adopted in 1951, originally had a three-year mandate to resettle the refugees. After three years, the problem remained, and the life of UNHCR was extended for five-year intervals until 1993, when the agency was given permanent status. Thus far, the agency has helped an estimated 50 million people to restart their lives. Today, operations in some one hundred and sixteen countries help some 17 million persons.

The term **refugee** covers those who flee their homeland to seek sanctuary in a second country. UNHCR recognizes the right to seek asylum and to find safe refuge, with the option to return home voluntarily, integrate locally, or to resettle in a third country. A basic principle is that no person should be resettled in a country where there is a reasonable possibility of persecution. However, some governments have not ratified the 1951 Convention on the Status of Refugees, so UNHCR operates in an ambiguous context.

Although UNHCR's mandate does not apply to **internally displaced persons (IDPs)**, High Commissioner for Refugees Sadako Ogata (1927–) improvised during her tenure from 1991–2000 by providing relief to some of the estimated 20–25 million persons who have left their homes but not their countries to obtain greater security from civil wars, natural disasters, or political instability. Currently, UNHCR assists approximately 4.4 million IDPs.

The agency can only offer effective legal protection if a person's basic needs of food, medical care, sanitation, shelter, and water are also met, so the humanitarian task can be considerable, requiring the assistance of other UN agencies[2] and the cooperation of more than five hundred nongovernmental organizations. The annual budget has been as high as $1 billion. Although most countries are unwilling to accept refugees on anything more than a temporary basis, refugee camps can become nearly permanent. Sometimes, UNHCR must give food and supplies to warlords or they will not reach the refugees, so the work can be very frustrating.

UNHCR has also been called upon to assist countries after civil wars or major conflicts have ended, when large numbers of persons seek resettlement but resources are not immediately at hand. Since the refugees who return to their homelands usually lack the wherewithal to start anew, UNHCR provides "quick impact projects." After the Afghan War of 2001, the High Commissioner began to handle problems relating to two million refugees, the largest repatriation effort in three decades.

HISTORIC EVENT 9.1 THE AFGHAN WAR (2001–)

On September 20, 2001, President George W. Bush (1946–) issued an ultimatum to the government of Afghanistan, which he believed was culpable in the 9/11/2001 attacks on the United States by dint of harboring members of Al-Qaida, whom he believed were responsible for the attacks. Bush's principal demands were to close all terrorist training camps and to hand over every terrorist to "appropriate authorities." Afghanistan, ruled by a group known as the Taliban, reportedly offered to hand over Osama Bin Laden (1957–), the leader of Al-Qaida, for trial, but Bush deemed the response insufficient. On October 7, a coalition of North Atlantic Treaty Organization (NATO) countries led by the United States began to bomb in Afghanistan. On the ground, American troops supported an Afghanistan insurgent group, known as the Northern Alliance, which entered the capital of Kabul on November 13. A new Afghan government was installed, and the UN Security Council voted in December to authorize a security force, provided by NATO, to defend the new government. However, former government forces retreated to enclaves in Pakistan from which they have continued to fight, with an upsurge in attacks from 2006.

SECURITY COUNCIL (UNSC)

Although the United Nations has been very effective in **standard setting** (establishing norms and principles), there has always been difficulty in setting up institutions and procedures for enforcement. There are two types of **enforcement** actions.

Vertical enforcement involves military action. When war is imminent, breaks out, or a fragile peace emerges, the Security Council has authorized member states to send peacekeeping troops, which has occurred forty-three times thus far. Reports on the general human rights situation have been part of recent assignments, and specific investigations have been authorized in several cases. Electoral assistance has also been provided by UNSC peacekeeping organs. As of early 2007, there were some 100,000 UN peacekeepers operating in eighteen countries; only the United States stations more military personnel abroad.

Horizontal enforcement is the pressure by nations in the form of protests, threats of economic sanctions, and the actual imposition of economic sanctions. For example, in 1985 the UNSC issued a condemnation of Israel's bombing of the headquarters of the Palestine Liberation Organization in Tunisia, which killed seventy-five persons, in retaliation for the PLO's role in death of three Israelis on Cyprus. The Security Council has authorized nonmilitary sanctions eighteen times, mostly for threats to peace during the 1990s. Among economic sanctions imposed for human rights violations, those against Rhodesia, and South Africa have been judged to be successful by many observers because they were almost universally applied. Although the Security Council has a *Sanctions Committee* to monitor sanctions, coordination is difficult because export businesses can easily engage in sanction busting, whether through a long chain of import-export firms or through rewards to poor countries that serve as trade intermediaries.

HISTORIC EVENT 9.2 THE BOSNIAN CIVIL WAR (1992–1995)

In 1991, Yugoslavia's provinces of Croatia and Slovenia declared independence, and other provinces appeared interested in following suit. The UN Security Council, to head off a bloody civil war, authorized an arms embargo of all Yugoslavia. Meanwhile, the parliament of Bosnia and Herzegovina (usually known as Bosnia), which had roughly equal numbers of Croats, Muslims (Bosniaks), and Serbs, voted in 1991 to secede from Yugoslavia, and a referendum in 1992 backed independence. However, Serbs walked out of parliament and boycotted the election. Serbian members of the Yugoslav army soon put on uniforms of Republika Srpska, and took up arms against newly independent Bosnia, with financial and logistical support from Serbian-dominated Yugoslavia, in order to control as much territory as possible inside Bosnia. In 1992, the UN Protection Force, which had been assigned to keep Yugoslav troops from attacking Croatia, had its mandate extended to Bosnia; the mission was to secure the airport of Sarajevo, Bosnia's capital, so that relief supplies could reach the embattled population. In 1993, when the Srpskan army occupied about 70 percent of Bosnia, the Security Council declared several towns to be "safe havens" that Srpskan troops were forbidden to annex and authorized a "no-fly" zone, enforced by airplanes of the North Atlantic Treaty Organization (NATO), to ban Yugoslav military airplanes from entering Bosnian airspace. Subsequently, four Yugoslav aircraft were shot down, and Srpska positions were shelled. In 1994, a truce between Bosniaks and Croats, which had been fighting from time to time, was brokered in Washington. In 1995, in defiance of the UN and NATO, Srpskan troops engaged in "ethnic cleansing" of Bosniaks in Srebernica, one of the "safe havens"; some 8,000 males were slaughtered, and 12,000 women and children were expelled. After the UN Security Council authorized NATO to threaten military retribution on Belgrade, the United States brokered a peace agreement at Dayton, Ohio, between Bosnia and Yugoslavia later in 1995. The Dayton Accords established a federal structure in which the Federation of Bosnia and Herzegovina occupies about an equal amount of territory with Republika Srpska, and a NATO force was assigned to monitor the ceasefire. In all, at least 100,000 deaths had occurred, and 1.8 millions had been displaced as Srpskans forced Bosniaks out of their homes, and other ethnic groups did likewise.

Both horizontal and vertical UN sanctions came to the fore in the 1990s, as the Yugoslav government in Belgrade conducted what was characterized as "ethnic cleansing" in several former republics (Table 9.2). In 1991, the Security Council voted for an arms embargo of Yugoslavia, which was strengthened in 1992 as a complete economic boycott, as well as a prohibition on participation in cultural and sport events. When the Bosnian Serbs gave the name Republic Srpska to the territory that they were forming inside Bosnia and appeared to be operating independently of Serbia, the Security Council imposed a boycott on Srpska while lifting from Serbia all but the arms embargo. In 1994, as authorized by the Security Council, airplanes under the command of the North Atlantic Treaty Organization enforced a "no-fly" zone over Bosnia by shooting down Yugoslav military aircraft and bombing Srpska-held positions. After the Dayton Accords brought peace to Bosnia in 1995, the Security Council rescinded all sanctions.

In 1998, the resurgence of Serbian ethnic cleansing in Kosovo prompted a reimposition of sanctions against Serbia. However, the operations prompted China and Russia to consider that Western powers were using the UN for their own purposes, so they threatened to veto any proposed UN military force against Serbia. As a result, NATO forces went into Kosovo, though such action was clearly contrary to international law because the UN Charter confers on the Security Council the sole power in the world to authorize the use of force in order to settle an interstate dispute. In 1999, after Belgrade finally surrendered to NATO forces, the Security Council authorized the UN Interim Administration Mission in Kosovo with a European Union reconstruction team, NATO peacekeepers, and Organization for Security and Cooperation in Europe election workers.

In 1999, after the bombings of two American embassies in Africa, the Security Council established what is known as the *Al-Qaida and Taliban Sanctions Committee* to monitor implementation of sanctions against the Taliban regime for its support of the terrorist group that is often spelled "Al-Qaeda." Strengthened after 9/11/2001, the measures include an air embargo, freezing assets, stopping the sale or transfer of arms, and prohibiting members of Al-Qaida or the Taliban from entering the borders of any UN member. In 2001, a separate *Counter-Terrorism Committee* was established to monitor implementation of a resolution that asks countries to "criminalize assistance for terrorist activities, deny financial support and safe haven to terrorists and share information about groups planning terrorist attacks."

TABLE 9.2 **UNITED NATIONS SANCTIONS IMPOSED ON THE FORMER YUGOSLAVIA**

Year	Organ	Action
1991	Security Council	Resolution calling for an arms boycott of Yugoslavia
1992	General Assembly	Refusal to seat the Yugoslav delegation
1992	Security Council	Resolution calling for an economic, sporting, and travel boycott
1993	Security Council	Resolution calling for a continued arms boycott
1994	Security Council	Resolution calling for an economic boycott of Srpska, lifting the sporting and travel boycott of Serbia
1995	Security Council	Resolution lifting all sanctions
1998	Security Council	Resolution reimposing an arms boycott of Serbia-Montenegro
2001	Security Council	Resolution lifting all sanctions

The Security Council, through its *Human Rights Committee*, continues to take note of human rights problems around the world. In 2004, the body condemned human rights violations taking place in Darfur and called upon the government of Sudan to disarm the Janjaweed militias involved in violence against the population. In 2006, UNSC adopted sanctions on four Sudanese, accusing them of war crimes and of violating the peace agreement in Darfur; they consist of a travel ban and a freeze on their assets outside Sudan. The sanctions were the first penalties for the massacres and displacement of largely non-Arab tribes in Darfur by Arabic-speaking militias.

HISTORIC EVENT 9.3 THE DARFUR CONFLICT (2002–)

The western part of Sudan, known as Darfur, is inhabited by poor African Muslims. In 2001, they suffered some attacks by government forces. In 2002, a group of Darfurians attacked a government outpost, revealing themselves as the Darfur Liberation Front in 2003. Further antigovernment attacks followed in 2003. Because Sudanese government troops were already trying to cope with rebellions in the south, a decision was made in Khartoum, the capital, to supply arms to an Arab-speaking militia known as the Janjaweed in order to pacify Darfur. The Janjaweed, however, went beyond counterattacks on the rebels and began to burn many villages, rape women, and shoot unarmed men, producing an outmigration from Darfur as well as counterattacks by rival rebel groups. Thus far, at least 300,000 have died, and 2.5 millions have sought refuge inside neighboring Chad on the verge of starvation. UN humanitarian aid to the region has been sent, the largest relief effort in the world. In 2004, when the UN Security Council asked Sudan to disarm the Janjaweed in thirty days, Khartoum refused, Instead, the Arab League and the European Union brokered a peace agreement between Sudan and one of the rebel groups, and the African Union sent a ceasefire monitoring unit of 7,300 persons. In 2005, the European Union and the North Atlantic Treaty Organization provided logistical support to the African force. Nevertheless, Janjaweed attacks continued, even killing twenty members of the African Union peace observation unit, leading some to charge that Khartoum was backing a genocidal campaign to rid the region of Africans so that Arabic-speaking Sudanese could resettle there. A peace agreement was reached in 2006, but not all rebel factions signed on, and the Janjaweed continued attacks, including targeting aid workers. Although the UN Security Council authorized a larger force to succeed the African Union unit later in 2006, Sudan refused to allow the UN to do so until 2007.

Of the seventy-one UNSC resolutions passed in 2005, all but five dealt with human rights (93 percent). The percentage is much higher than for the General Assembly.

SECRETARY-GENERAL (UNSG)

The Secretary-General of the United Nations has become the world's secular pope. In recent years, the UNSG has undertaken personal visits on behalf of human rights and articulated pleas for action to respond to human rights violations. The Secretary-General is the chief executive officer of the Secretariat, which has offices around the world but is headquartered in New York.

While in office from 1997–2006, Secretary-General Kofi Annan (1938–) urged all UN agencies to "mainstream" human rights concerns, that is, to make human rights a part of their mandates. He made bold pronouncements to condemn human rights abuses around the world, including for example Israel's treatment of Palestinians. In 2001, he brought together the Afghan factions opposing the Taliban to agree to an election for a new Afghanistan. In 2004, he condemned the Anglo-American intervention to topple the regime of Saddam Hussein as contrary to international law. In 2005, he began to call attention to the inadequate measures in place to deal with genocide in Darfur, Sudan.

Natural disasters necessarily affect the quality of life in an adverse manner, and most are handled domestically. In 1991, the General Assembly created the position of Emergency Relief Coordinator, subsequently designated as the *Under-Secretary General for Humanitarian Affairs*, to coordinate assistance to victims of the most severe natural disasters. In 1998, because of the difficulty of coordinating so many agencies, the *Office for the Coordination of Humanitarian Affairs* was established. In recent years, agency personnel have been dispatched within twenty-four hours of a major natural disaster. They draw on the Central Emergency Revolving Fund so that the personnel will arrive on the scene with needed equipment and supplies, rather than merely engaging in needs assessment, and stay on the scene to assist in reconstruction after an emergency has ended. In 2006, the *Undersecretary General for Humanitarian Affairs* coordinated aid to twenty-five crisis sites, fed 97 million persons (including 550,000 tons of food to Darfur refugees), and inoculated 30 million children against measles on a budget of $4 billion.

The Secretary-General is also responsible for administering the *Voluntary Fund for Victims of Torture*, which the General Assembly created in 1982 to assist victims of torture and their relatives. In 1997, $3 million was disbursed from the Fund million. In 1987, the Secretary-General set up the *Voluntary Fund for Technical Cooperation in the Field of Human Rights*, managed by a Board of Trustees, which was created in 1993. The Fund is now administered by the UN High Commissioner for Human Rights.

The Department of Political Affairs, headed by the Under-Secretary General for Political Affairs, has an *Electoral Assistance Division*, which has provided aid for elections to ninety-five countries. The first effort, in Cambodia during 1992, carried out the terms of a peace settlement.

HISTORIC EVENT 9.4 TALIBAN RULE IN AFGHANISTAN (1996–2001)

In 1978, a coup established a pro-Soviet government in Afghanistan. In 1979, after the United States financed an anti-government force, the Soviet Union intervened to protect the Afghan government militarily, but they were unable to subdue Afghan resistance forces and departed in 1989. When the Soviet Union withdrew, the government gradually lost control in the provinces until a religious-oriented military force known as the Taliban gained control of Kabul, the capital, and controlled most of the country by 1996. While in power, the Taliban imposed harsh rule. Women, who had to wear *burkas* (full-body coverings), were forbidden to attend schools and could only leave their homes with male escorts. Communists were killed. Thieves had their hands amputated. However, opium production ceased. The Taliban also provided safe haven to terrorist leader Osama Bin Laden, who set up terrorist training camps where anti-Western Muslims learned bomb making and guerrilla fighting. In 2001, the United States ousted the Taliban with the aid of forces from North Atlantic Treaty Organization and an alliance of dissidents from the north of Afghanistan.

These are two special bodies under the UNSG:

- *Office of the High Commissioner for Human Rights* (OHCHR). In 1993, the UN convened the World Conference on Human Rights in Vienna. Due to conflict between Western and Third World countries, the only major structural recommendation was to set up a new position, the *Office of the High Commissioner for Human Rights* (OHCHR), so that a single person could play a more visible and active role to stop human rights violations within the Secretariat. Later that year, the General Assembly obliged. The first High Commissioner was selected in 1994. Since then, OHCHR has assumed ten functions: (1) secretariat assistance for several treaty-based human rights organs, (2) consciousness raising events, (3) studies, (4) field operations, (5) training courses, (6) good offices to negotiate release of prisoners and similar actions, (7) conflict prevention, (8) crisis response, (9) administration of the Special Committee to Investigate Israeli Practices Affecting the Human Rights of the Palestinian People and Other Arabs of the Occupied Territories, which was set up in 1968, and (10) complaint processing at the Quick Response Desk. In 2004, the High Commissioner's office received over nine hundred urgent appeals and five hundred and seventy petitions in which persons or groups in need sought protection from one hundred and nineteen governments.

- *UN Human Rights Council* (UNHRC). Initially established in 1946 with the Economic and Social Council (ECOSOC) as the fifty-three-member Commission on Human Rights, the General Assembly voted in 2006 to retitle the body, whose forty-seven members are elected annually by majority vote, and to locate the Council within OHCHR. Also in 1946, ECOSOC set up the Subcommission on Prevention of Discrimination and Protection of Minorities (from 1999, renamed the Subcommission on the Promotion and Protection of Human Rights) as UNHRC's principal subordinate body.

The first assignment of the Commission was to draft the Universal Declaration of Human Rights was completed in 1948. The second task, placing the Declaration on a treaty basis, was not completed until 1967 because of differences in approach between Cold War antagonists.

Over the years, the organ has acquired seven functions: (1) review of annual country reports, (2) studies, (3) advisory services, (4) on-site investigations, (5) establishment of working groups, (6) drafting resolutions, and (7) response to petitions. Concerning the latter, in 1967 ECOSOC adopted *Resolution 1236*, which established the principle that violations of human rights could be examined in the form of a study and/or could be debated in public. *Resolution 1503*, adopted in 1970, enunciates a criterion to identify violations of states – "a consistent pattern of gross and reliably attested violations of human rights and fundamental freedoms exists." As many as 25,000 such petitions have been received in recent years. UNHRC has several possible responses to a petition: nonaction, confidential consideration, a critical statement, or public condemnation. At least forty countries represented on UNHRC have been condemned in the post-Cold War era compared with ten before 1991. Today, individual petitions are now deemphasized in favor of studies, advisory services, expert visits, and on-site investigations, as noted next.

ECOSOC created a sensation in 2001 by failing to elect a delegate from the United States to serve on UNHRC. According to the delegates who voted, the exclusion was in response to the American opposition to such innovations as the treaty banning landmines, the International Criminal Court, and the Kyoto Protocol on global warming. In response, Congress froze a portion of the annual American assessments to the UN.

Over the years, countries elected to the UNHRC were often the very countries committing serious human rights abuses. Previously, countries deferred to the wishes of various regions, which rotated countries without regard to their human rights records, but in 2006 about fifty of the organization's one hundred and seventy seven members pledged to vote in the future against membership for countries with unacceptable human rights records. As a result, Libya, Sudan, Syria, Vietnam, and Zimbabwe did not even apply, though they formerly served on the Commission. The United States also decided not to seek a seat on the first Council, a possible admission that Washington's record might not garner majority support. China, Cuba, Russia, and Saudi Arabia, which have often been criticized for human rights issues, were nevertheless accorded seats.

The Office of the High Commissioner for Human Rights has been assuming functions that formerly burdened the Secretary-General. The result is increasing continuity and effectiveness in achieving human rights objectives, although controversy is inevitable when governments resist improvement.

ECONOMIC AND SOCIAL COUNCIL (ECOSOC)

ECOSOC has nine functional commissions, supervises five regional commissions, and has several other suborgans. Several subsidiary bodies directly relate to human rights:

- *Commission on the Status of Women* (CSW). In 1946, ECOSOC set up the Commission on the Status of Women as another functional commission. The Commission's administrative functions are performed by the Secretariat's *Division for the Advancement of Women*, not the UN High Commissioner for Human Rights.

   CSW has drafted many important **declarations** over the years. The most notable is the Declaration on the Elimination of Discrimination Against Women (1967), which led to Convention on the Elimination of All Forms of Discrimination Against Women. In 2005, the UN Conference on the Status of Women adopted many resolutions while defeating two anti-abortion resolutions authored by the United States.

   From the 1980s, the Commission has handled **complaints** about patterns of "reliably attested injustice and discriminatory practices against women." The complaints are utilized as windows into possible areas of global focus. The complaints, which tend to be authored by nongovernmental organizations on behalf of classes of aggrieved women, can prompt the formation of Working Groups, which may recommend action by ECOSOC.

   Each country is asked to draw up **action plans** for meeting targets. In 2000, several goals were established, one of which was to eliminate gender disparity in primary and secondary education by 2005. In 2003, the Commission focused on the role of women in the media and violence against women.

   Because a separate, treaty-based organization coordinates progress in implementing provisions of the Convention on the Elimination of All Forms of Discrimination Against Women, CSW's focus is more general. The treaty is discussed in Chapter 10.

- *Commission for Social Development* (CSocD). A third ECOSOC functional commission, the Commission for Social Development was formed in 1946. CSocD reviews social components of economic development plans and action programs of other agencies. Currently, the focus is on the opportunities for the disabled, elderly, families, and youth.

- *Commission on Crime Prevention and Criminal Justice.* In 1992, ECOSOC consolidated various units to deal with the issues of crime and justice over the years into the Commission on Crime Prevention and Criminal Justice. One of the four principal mandates is to facilitate improvements in the efficiency and fairness of criminal justice administration systems. A major concern thus far has been on standards of humane treatment of prisoners.

- *UN Permanent Forum on Indigenous Issues* (UNPFII). Some three hundred and seventy million indigenous peoples live in seventy countries but lack representation in the General Assembly and are threatened by activities that are carried out in the name of "development." In 1986, ECOSOC's Subcommission on the Promotion and Protection of Human Rights established the Working Group on Indigenous Populations, which began to prepare a declaration on indigenous peoples' rights that is still under discussion even though the statement would not be binding on sovereign states. In 2002, ECOSOC set up UNPFII as a body to meet annually in New York with a mandate to provide advice on issues affecting indigenous peoples. UNPFII sponsors conferences and workshops and provides a fellowship program for indigenous peoples.

SPECIALIZED AGENCIES OF THE UNITED NATIONS

The United Nations has nearly 100 organs called Specialized Agencies, which act semi-autonomously of other UN bodies. They report to the General Assembly through ECOSOC. Some of the more prominent organizations are described below.

- *International Labor Organization* (ILO). Formed in the aftermath of World War I, ILO was accepted as a Specialized Agency of the UN in 1946. The current Constitution, as adopted in 1944, states that the main purpose of the organization is to promote "social justice" by securing "humane conditions of labor." The main organs have a tripartite representation (one from business, one from labor, and two from government), so the tone of the organization is more communitarian than adversarial. Work is divided into four major sectors: (1) employment (human resource development), (2) social dialog (to build tripartite consensus), (3) social protection (improvement in conditions of work regarding health and safety, as well as unemployment insurance), and (4) workers' rights (formulating fair labor standards).

  ILO uses three procedures to check on implementation of its various treaties and recommendations – country reports, compliance monitoring, and complaint processing. In 1994, with more than 6,000 ratifications to monitor, ILO decided to require **reports** from member countries on fundamental and priority conventions biennially, whereas reports on compliance with other treaties are to be submitted every five years (formerly every four years) unless a treaty has become obsolescent. A report form for every convention, ratified and unratified, asks for an identification of the appropriate domestic laws, implementing structures, measures taken toward removing obstacles to compliance, legal opinions rendered, inspector's reports, and lists of employers and trade unions notified about provisions and their comments.

  Regarding **compliance monitoring**, the twenty members of the Committee of Experts on the Application of Conventions and Recommendations has met annually from 1927 to examine progress reports from governments. If the Committee finds a compliance problem, a comment goes to all three representatives from a country; the comment may either be an informal **direct request** or a formal **observation**. In 2002, for instance, there were 1,214 direct requests and six hundred and ninety six observations. Direct requests note discrepancies and ask for clarification; if the matter is handled satisfactorily, no written record is kept. If there is a longstanding or serious problem of non-compliance, an observation is published, and the problem is included in the annual report of the Committee, which may request a statement from an errant government on any problem and subsequently hold a public hearing on the matter. Hearings are extremely polite and nonaccusatory, focusing on difficulties of implementation. If a problem is resolved, another observation will be published. In the years 1964–2004, some 2,429 cases were resolved, of which fifty-three were in 2004 alone. From 1990, Myanmar has been repeatedly cited for violations of the Forced Labor Convention of 1930 and the Freedom of Association and Protection of the Right to Organize Convention of 1948. No other country has so consistently defied the ILO.

From 1926, the ILO has also engaged in **complaint processing**. There are four categories of complaints: (1) In an *Article 24 complaint*, a workers' or employers' organization can make a representation about a government that fails to abide by an ILO-sponsored treaty. (2) An *Article 26 complaint* may be filed by governments, ILO delegates, or ILO governing bodies; in response, ILO sets up a formal Commission of Inquiry, which solicits written comments from both parties, conducts hearings, does on-site investigations, and makes reports. (3) From 1950, *special freedom of association complaints* may be filed by workers' or employers' organizations, ILO bodies, the state concerned, or ECOSOC. In 1951, ILO set up the Committee on Freedom of Association (CFA) to handle complaints, which by 2003 numbered 2,325. In 2003, there were 110 before CFA, of which 31 were reviewed after comments were requested from governments. (4) From 1974, a panel of ILO experts can conduct *special surveys on employment discrimination* at the request of any state, employer, or worker organization. One subject is selected each year.

ILO's scope is highly intrusive into the way governments treat people. In 1964, the ILO adopted the Declaration Against Apartheid in South Africa; Pretoria then withdrew from the organization, effective 1966.[3] In 1981, the ILO adopted an updated Declaration of Apartheid, which involved technical assistance to liberation movements through a voluntary fund. ILO actions serve to strengthen the struggles of emergent unions by exerting political and moral pressure in favor of their demands against the government, notably standards on overtime and shift work. In 1986, ILO called for the release of trade union leaders imprisoned during the 1986 state of emergency in South Africa. Post-*apartheid* South Africa rejoined in 1994.

HISTORIC EVENT 9.5 SOLIDARNOŚĆ'S LEADER IS ELECTED PRESIDENT OF POLAND (1990)

In 1980, a strike broke out at the Lenin shipyards in Gdansk to protest poor working conditions. Lech Walęsa (1943–), who had been arrested in 1970 for leading a strike where eighty workers were killed by the government, assumed leadership of the work stoppage. Soon, his example persuaded workers throughout the country to go on a general strike, and the government decided to compromise by allowing the strikers to form a joint committee. Solidarność (Solidarity) was then formed as the committee gained legal recognition, with Wałęsa voted to chair the new body. In 1981, however, the government refused to negotiate with the union and instead declared martial law, imprisoned Wałęsa, and attempted to crush the union. Pressure, in the form of economic sanctions and papal disapproval, continued on the Polish government to grant workers the right to strike. While under house arrest in 1983, Wałęsa was awarded the Nobel Peace Prize. After his release from house arrest in 1987, he organized a strike in 1988 to gain formal recognition for the union. Negotiations during 1989 then led to an agreement to hold free elections in Poland. Wałęsa was elected president of Poland in 1990, but left office in 1995 when he lost reelection. Today, the union plays a relatively minor role in Polish politics.

From 1977–1980, the United States withdrew from ILO because of unhappiness that the organization was critical of Washington, which has only ratified 14 of the 185 treaties and two of the core eight conventions. In particular, the World Confederation of Free Trade Unions filed a complaint against Washington regarding trade union restrictions in Puerto Rico that was referred to the ILO. In 1979, after the ILO issued a statement criticizing the labor records of Czechoslovakia, Poland, and the Soviet Union and was about to exonerate the United States regarding the complaint involving Puerto Rico, the United States decided to rejoin, believing that the organization had become more evenhanded. Subsequently, the ILO played a role in the emancipation of Poland from Communism by supporting the legitimacy of the Polish trade union Solidarność.

ILO's human rights procedures have been a model that other human rights bodies in the UN system have tried to copy. But only ILO has the tripartite system of representation that enables employers, governments, and workers to work out problems collegially.

- *United Nations Educational, Scientific, and Cultural Organization* (UNESCO). Among the agencies established at Geneva during the era of the League of Nations was the International Committee of Intellectual Co-operation, which operated from 1922 and cooperated with the International Institute of Intellectual Co-operation (IIIC) at Paris from 1925. A separate International Bureau of Education (IBE) also began at Geneva in 1925. In 1942, European governments confronting Nazi Germany and its allies met in the United Kingdom for the Conference of Allied Ministers of Education, which in turn recommended UNESCO's establishment. When UNESCO's Constitution was ratified in 1946, IIIC ceased operation. IBE continued until being absorbed by UNESCO in 1969.

The Preamble to UNESCO's Constitution of 1945 begins with the resounding phrase "since wars begin in the minds of men, it is in the minds of men that the defenses of peace must be constructed," and declares that

the great and terrible war which has now ended was a war made possible by the denial of the democratic principles of the dignity, equality and mutual respect of men, and by the propagation, in their place, through ignorance and prejudice, of the doctrine of the inequality of men and races . . .

and goes on to say

That the wide diffusion of culture, and the education of humanity for justice and liberty and peace are indispensable to the dignity of man and constitute a sacred duty . . .

UN members are for the most part also members of UNESCO. However, Spain did not join until 1953, and the Soviet Union stayed out until 1954. In 1956, South Africa withdrew because of the organization's opposition to *apartheid*. In 1984, the United States withdrew, followed in 1985 by the departure of Britain and Singapore; all three right-wing governments objected to the proposed New International Information Order. South Africa resumed membership in 1994, Britain in 1997, and the United States in 2003.

There are two major functions: (1) to facilitate intellectual cooperation in the fields of education, science, and culture, both through conferences and by providing an information clearinghouse, and (2) to arrange technical assistance financing, mostly consisting of seed money for research and training to assist in developing the human resource infrastructure in the fields of culture and education. Funds for scientific endeavors are also handled by other UN agencies.

Human rights are found in all five of UNESCO's major thematic areas: (1) The communication and information theme is concerned with freedom of expression, freedom of the press, gender issues, and indigenous peoples. (2) The culture theme has a program on cultural diversity. (3) Within the education theme, the focus is on the right to education, diversity issues in education, as well as human rights education. (4) In the science theme, a major objective is to develop more female scientists. (5) The social and human sciences theme specifically focuses on human rights as well as on democracy, discrimination, gender equality, racism, and xenophobia. One project is the annual World Press Freedom Prize. In 2004, Raúl Rivero (1945–), who had been arrested the previous year in Cuba along with seventy-four other dissidents, won the World Press Freedom Prize in 2004. He was then released along with several others.

UNESCO has sponsored several agreements in the form of declarations, recommendations, and treaties. The treaty most concerned with human rights is the *Convention Against Discrimination in Education*, which was followed by a *Protocol* that set up a Conciliation and Good Offices Commission to handle disputes under the Convention. Among the various UNESCO-sponsored declarations are the Declaration on Race and Racial Prejudice (1978), the Universal Declaration on the Human Genome and Human Rights (1997), the Universal Declaration on Cultural Diversity (2001), and the International Declaration on Human Genetic Data (2003). The latter advocates keeping genetic data private.

Each member country is asked to submit **reports** on implementation of agreements on the following subjects: (1) adult, technical, and vocational education; (2) discrimination in education; (3) illicit import, export, and transfer of ownership of cultural property; (4) peace education; and (5) on the status of teachers. The Executive Board's Committee on Conventions and Recommendations monitors the reports.

The Committee on Conventions and Recommendations handles three **complaint procedures** to deal with violations of rights of artists, journalists, researchers, students, teachers, and writers in several areas – the right to education, the right to share in scientific advancement, the right to participate in cultural life, the right to information, and similar rights: (1) When an *individual communication* goes to UNESCO, the organization will ask the government charged with the alleged violation to comment. The government's case is next argued before the Committee, which usually meets in private biannually. From 1978, the Committee has considered five hundred and twenty-nine communications. (2) Individual communications may serve to expose a *pattern of complaints*. Based on the distinction between individual cases, where confidentiality is often critical, and questions, which are broader in scope, the Committee can go public to protest systematic violations. (3) In 1978, UNESCO developed a *third-party complaint* procedure, whereby human rights advocates, usually nongovernmental organizations, can complain on behalf of individuals or groups. To date, 437 such complaints have been received.

Generally, UNESCO does not go public with individual complaints, preferring to promote dialog between the complainants and the governments, and then recommending measures that might be taken to redress the situation. Thus far, some 330 out of 966 communications and complaints have been settled by the Committee, a success rate of about 30 percent.

- *Food and Agriculture Organization of the United Nations* (FAO). In 1941, President Franklin Roosevelt (1882–1945) articulated the concept of four freedoms, namely, freedom of speech and expression, freedom to worship, freedom from fear, and freedom from want. The fourth freedom was understood to mean freedom from disease and hunger. FAO was originally established in 1945 to provide technical assistance in the field of agriculture. The principle of the right to adequate food was stated in the Universal Declaration of Human Rights of 1948. Currently, FAO's main Millennium Development Goal, based in part on the statistic that 800 million people suffer from malnutrition, is to halve world hunger by 2015.

  The World Food Summit of 1996 mandated the UN High Commissioner for Human Rights to better define rights related to food and to propose ways to implement and realize them. With the advent of genetically-modified food crops in recent years, FAO has established several committees dealing with ethics in food and agriculture to promote dialog. Guidelines have not yet emerged.

- *UN Children's Fund* (UNICEF). In 1946, when many refugees were orphaned children who were confronted with disease and famine without the benefit of family resources, the UN International Children's Emergency Fund was established to assist in China and Europe. In 1950, the scope became worldwide. In 1953, the General Assembly made UNICEF a permanent organ of the UN, dropping the words "International" and "Emergency" but retaining the UNICEF acronym. By 2002, UNICEF had field offices in 157 countries with a budget of $1.3 billion annually.

  UNICEF's Mission Statement asserts that the primary focus of the organization is the "protection of children's rights, to help meet their basic needs and to expand their opportunities to reach their full potential." Although the organization continues to respond to natural and wartime emergencies, from 1995–2005, when Carol Bellamy (1942–) served as UNICEF Executive Director, the emphasis shifted from child survival to children's rights. The UN Convention on the Rights of the Child of 1989 began to provide a more detailed guide for UNICEF. UNICEF also assists the Committee on the Rights of the Child (CRC), which is discussed in Chapter 10.

During Bellamy's reign, priorities also shifted to the most disadvantaged children in the poorest countries, developing the "community capacity development" paradigm in which community empowerment and sustainable development were central elements. However, Ann Veneman (1949–) pledged to return the work of the organization to child survival when she succeeded Bellamy in 2005.

- *World Health Organization* (WHO). In 1948, the World Health Organization became a Specialized Agency, absorbing both the functions of the Rome-based International Office of Public Health (IOPH), which previously promoted sanitation and later studied epidemics, and the Geneva-based League of Nations Health Organization (LNHO). The Preamble to the WHO Constitution, as adopted in 1946, states that "The enjoyment of the highest attainable standard of human health is one of the basic human rights of every human being."

  The Director-General and nine Assistant Directors-General administer the organization. One unit under the Assistant Director-General for Sustainable Development and Health Environments is the Department of Ethics, Trade, Human Rights, and Law, which primarily assists health ministries in national governments to achieve greater awareness of human rights issues. WHO projects stress the equal treatment of females and minority populations as well as the appropriate treatment of the mentally disabled. In 1977, WHO set a goal of "health for all" by the year 2000, urging each country to develop "health of the nation" plans. WHO assumes credit for the global eradication of smallpox.

  Reports focusing on human rights have been prepared over the years, including the subject of torture. Operationally, the largest effort in recent years has been to cope with the spread of HIV-AIDS by providing programs of prevention and treatment, including efforts to reduce the cost of medicines. In the delivery of health care, WHO's focus has shifted from health ministries in the earlier years to the recent stress on developing networks of governmental and nongovernmental groups in local communities.

- *World Food Program* (WFP). FAO works alongside the World Food Program, which was set up in 1961 so that FAO could continue as a technical organization, leaving WFP to handle food aid. During 2004, WFP reached 113 million people in eighty countries. FAO's Director-General, with the approval of the UN Secretary-General, appoints WPF's Executive Director. Unfortunately, the food trade regime of the World Trade Organization has been accused of nullifying WPF's food aid regime by encouraging Third World countries to sell cash crops to rich countries while their own people starve.

- *UN Development Program* (UNDP). From 1966, UNDP has sought to alleviate social, economic, and cultural problems in Third World countries by marshalling resources for technical assistance from such UN Specialized Agencies as the UN Industrial Development Organization (UNIDO).[4] UNDP not only coordinates aid provided by other UN agencies but also serves as a clearinghouse for aid from non-UN sources to ensure that there will be no duplication of effort or funding.

One of the most famous UNDP efforts occurred in Somalia during 1992–1995, when the agency provided food for a starving population after law and order broke down. Currently, there are UNDP Country Representatives in one hundred and sixty-six countries. UNDP issues an annual *Human Development Report*, which facilitates comparisons over time as well as across countries. UNDP's proposed budget for 2004–2005 totaled approximately $575 million.

In 1997, UNDP launched a focus on poverty reduction. Among the five Millennium Development goals, democratic governance is at the top of UNDP's list. Accordingly, in 2002 the UNDP Democratic Governance Center opened at Oslo.

- *UN Conference for Trade and Development* (UNCTAD). In 1964, a conference was held to respond to the desire of developing countries for an organization specifically designed to analyze macroeconomic reasons why Third World countries were not advancing. The body, which became permanent that year, has served three functions: (1) providing an intergovernmental forum to build consensus between poor and rich countries, (2) data collection, policy analysis, and research, and (3) technical assistance for states to participate in such trade conferences as those sponsored by the World Trade Organization.

  The first development theme stressed by UNCTAD, import substitution, did not bridge the gap. In the 1970s, UNCTAD endorsed the call for a new international economic order (NEIO), but that idea was not accepted by the First World. In the 1980s, export promotion became the model for development. The current focus is on "sustainable development."

- *UN Development Fund for Women* (UNIFEM). In 1976, the General Assembly created UNIFEM to assist in improving the living standards of women in developing countries. In 2003, the agency operated with a budget of $34 million to focus on four priorities: (1) reducing feminized poverty, (2) ending violence against women, (3) stopping the spread of HIV among women and girls, and (4) obtaining gender equality in democratic governance. In recent years, there has been a shift in focus from a welfare model to a human rights model, not only in UNIFEM but also in UNDP.

- *International Fund for Agricultural Development* (IFAD). Established in 1977 as a Specialized Agency, IFAD provides low-interest loans and grants to assist developing countries in decreasing rural poverty, the primary structural cause of limited food production. In 2003, IFAD awarded ninety-nine grants and loans amounting to about $366 million.

- *World Bank Group and the International Monetary Fund.* There are five institutions in the World Bank Group. Two are called "the World Bank," namely, the *International Bank for Reconstruction and Development* (IBRD) and the *International Development Association* (IDA). IBRD, formed in 1944 primarily to aid European postwar reconstruction, now provides some $20 billion in infrastructure loans each year to developing countries. IDA was set up in 1960 to provide low interest, long-term loans to developing countries. Although the first IBRD loan to a developing country was to Chile for $2.5 million in 1948, IDA's establishment recognized that some developing countries were unable to afford loans at commercial rates, as the economic payoff might not emerge for many years. IDA annual lending amounts to about $2 billion.

The remaining three members of the *World Bank Group* assist private sector investment. They are the *International Finance Corporation* (IFC), set up in 1956; the *International Center for Settlement of Investment Disputes* (ICSID), established in 1966; and the *Multilateral Investment Guarantee Association* (MIGA) 1988.

In 1944, the *International Monetary Fund* (IMF) was also created. Although separate from the World Bank Group, IMF is still part of the UN system. IMF provides capital for countries that experience such a shortfall in foreign exchange (U.S. dollars) that they cannot pay debts owed to other countries.

IMF and World Bank Group legal experts have argued through the years that their actions are exempt from human rights treaties. Indeed, The World Bank's Articles of Agreement clearly state that "only economic considerations shall be relevant" in all Bank decisions, so human rights concerns have not been prominent. World Bank loans to developing countries often yielded more benefits to First World construction and consulting firms that to recipient countries, which remained in poverty and were unable to pay even the interest on the loans. IMF would then intervene to enable countries to pay back the loans, but the conditions applied by IMF involved cuts in government programs that increased poverty. During 1992, for example, the IMF required Mali to lift price controls and to end food subsidies during a famine, whereupon hoarders held back food, deaths from starvation increased, and what has been called an "IMF riot" toppled the government.

Accordingly, from the mid-1990s the World Bank began to stress poverty reduction as a primary focus for the poorest countries and to place a "good governance" condition on all loan recipients. **Poverty reduction**, which was initially defined in terms of per capita income, is now understood to apply to social exclusion and disenfranchisement, that is, the extent to which citizens are fragile or vulnerable. By **good governance**, the Bank means loan implementation effectiveness, as determined by the following criteria:

- voice and accountability (civil liberties and political stability);
- government effectiveness (quality of policy making and public service delivery);
- lack of regulatory burden;
- rule of law (notably, protection of property rights);
- independence of the judiciary;
- control of corruption.

From the 1990s, the World Bank has also developed "women in development" initiatives based on data demonstrating that females are often excluded from development projects. However, among some one hundred and twenty ongoing World Bank projects in 2005, a gender focus existed in only eight projects, education in eighteen projects, poverty reduction in fifteen projects, and two dealt with justice and law; the remaining seventy-seven projects had a strictly economic focus. Grants are also given for human rights institution building. In 2004, for example, the Bank gave a grant to the University of Chile Law School to provide scholarships for students interested in women's rights.

Complaints about human rights issues prompted the Bank in 1994 to establish the *Inspection Panel*, which consists of three independent experts. The Panel hears requests for inspectors from individuals who claim to have been adversely affected by Bank projects; a human rights violation can be one basis for a complaint. By mid-2005, the panel had heard thirty-six cases and made recommendations that prompted the Bank to make changes.

The Bank has also intervened on behalf of human rights defenders who have been attacked or jailed by recipient governments. In the case of the Chad-Cameroon Petroleum Development and Pipeline Project, the Panel responded to a request from someone who had been tortured because of his opposition to the project. In 2005, the Panel began to act on a complaint from the NGO Forum on Cambodia related to human rights abuses in connection with the Forest Concession Management and Control Pilot Project.

In 1999, when the United Nations sought to bring peace to East Timor, Indonesia expressed adamant opposition to peacekeepers. The IMF then surprised many observers by threatening to withhold aid to Jakarta, which soon capitulated, and the UN Mission in East Timor began work.

In 2005, the summit of industrial nations known as the G-8,[5] urged the World Bank to waive some $30 billion in loans to the eight poorest countries in the world. The loans were not being paid back, and the $100 million daily interest accumulating on the loans was crushing the ability of the countries to rise from poverty. Later in the year, the World Bank Group indeed agreed to excuse debts by many poorer countries.

The World Bank Group and IMF, in short, have recently been attempting to overcome a past in which human rights issues were neglected. Despite the ban on "political affairs" in the bank's Articles of Agreement, lending activities have increasingly focused on the empowerment of women, HIV/AIDS prevention, the need to consult communities in order to avoid launching controversial projects, as well as judicial reform to ensure the rule of law. The lending agencies still have far to go, according to Joseph Stiglitz (1943–), who resigned as IMF's chief economist in 2000 to protest the continuing blinders over the harm that international financial institutions have wrought for far too long.

INTERNATIONAL COURT OF JUSTICE (ICJ)

The first world court, the Permanent Court of Arbitration (PCA), as established at The Hague in 1899, still handles disputes. However, the Permanent Court of International Justice (PCIJ), which went into existence in 1921, was superseded in 1946, by the International Court of Justice.

PCIJ, which sits in The Hague, is composed of fifteen judges elected for nine-year terms by the General Assembly and Security Council from a list of persons nominated by each country that belongs to the PCA. The legal principles applied by the Court are found in treaties, international custom, precedent, legal theories propounded by widely accepted academic authorities, and *ex aequo et bono* (general principles of justice and fairness). About twenty treaties confer specific jurisdiction on the ICJ.

The court accepts **contentious cases** and is supposed to reject political questions. When India shot down a military aircraft inside Pakistan in 1999, the court ruled that the case was not justiciable but instead should be resolved by the UN Security Council.

The court makes three types of decisions – binding rulings, advisory opinions, and dispute resolutions. **Binding rulings** apply when all parties to a dispute agree in advance to accept the jurisdiction of the court in a matter that is identified as a "contentious case between states." **Advisory opinions** are issued to clarify a legal issue. Three UN treaties provide for ICJ mediation and other **dispute resolution** options.[6]

If threatened action is deemed "urgent" because irreparable harm might be done to individuals, a party may request **provisional measures** to stop the action, and the Court will promptly authorize interim protection in response. Both parties are asked to submit formal statements. If one party does not respond, the Court may proceed anyway if the statement of facts from the other party is judged to be accurate. Among the dozen cases in which provisional measures have been authorized, the first involved an order to release diplomats who were held hostage in the American Embassy in Tehran.

Of the 104 **contentious cases** before the Court, human rights issues have been involved in one-third of the cases, mostly dealing with the treatment of nationals of one country who live in another country. After a decision is issued in a contentious case, the Security Council may undertake enforcement measures if the rulings are not implemented.

A frequent source of international legal claims relates to how a government of one country treats citizens of another country who are inside the latter's borders. In four cases involving Colombia and Peru in 1949 and 1950, for example, an unsuccessful coup leader sought refuge at Colombia's embassy in Lima. Although the Court ruled that he was not entitled to asylum and safe conduct out of the country, Colombia was not required to surrender him to Peruvian authorities to stand trial for treason.

The rights of a foreigner inside another country have been litigated on the basis of customary international law and trade treaties. A case involving French nationals was amicably resolved in 1949, but a 1950 case involving Americans in French-occupied Morocco was decided on narrow grounds by interpreting treaties as far back as 1836.

The treatment of American airplanes that mistakenly landed in Czechoslovakia and Hungary was the subject of six cases in 1954–1955. The airplanes were seized on the grounds that the United States had frozen assets of both countries, but the crews were released, so the ICJ ruled that the case was outside the jurisdiction of the court. In 1958, ICJ found no legal grounds for intervening in a case in which the Netherlands objected to Sweden's decision to allow a Swedish guardian to bring up a child born of a Dutch father whose Swedish mother had died.

Self-determination has been an issue in at least one case. After Indonesia militarily annexed Portugal's colony of East Timor in 1975, Australia signed a treaty with Indonesia regarding the use of the continental shelf of East Timor. Since Indonesia did not accept ICJ's jurisdiction, Portugal filed suit against Australia in 1991. Rejecting the case on the ground that the proper party to the dispute was Indonesia, the Court nevertheless affirmed that the East Timorese retained the right of self-determination.

The Vienna Convention on Consular Relations of 1963 was supposed to ensure consular protection for citizens abroad, but the American federal system of government, in which there are some 25,000 independent police departments around the country, often complicates compliance. Few local jurisdictions are conversant with international legal requirements, and the Eleventh Amendment to the U.S. Constitution limits Washington's power to sue state governments in court. In 1998, Paraguay filed a case against the United States when a Paraguayan national was on death row in Virginia. From his arrest to his sentencing, he was not afforded the right to have his embassy provide legal counsel, contrary to the Optional Protocol to the Vienna Convention. As a result, he was deprived of a competent defense attorney, funds to pay the attorney, and the power to have visas issued for exonerating witnesses. Although the ICJ ordered provisional measures so that the death sentence would not be carried out, pending completion of deliberations, the execution occurred anyway, whereupon Paraguay withdrew the case from ICJ's docket as moot.

In a similar case involving two Germans in Arizona, the ICJ in 2001 issued its first ever binding provisional measure, and Washington promised not to repeat the violation, but the executions occurred. An identical situation emerged in 2004, involving fifty-one Mexican nationals on death row in ten states, including Arizona, but the promise was not kept. The Court ruling authorized reparations to Mexico and recommended a reconsideration of the sentences. In 2005, the United States withdrew from the Vienna Convention's Optional Protocol, which empowers ICJ to rule on consular representation disputes.

Military action without UN Security Council authorization can be considered to be a crime against peace. In regard to the hostile activity by the United States toward Nicaragua in 1983–1984, the ICJ ordered provisional measures, namely, for the United States to stop all military and paramilitary activities against Nicaragua. In ratifying the ICJ Charter, the Senate attached a reservation that excludes any prosecutions based on the UN Charter or any other multilateral treaty, so the ruling was based on *jus cogens* and the trade treaty between the two countries. Nicaragua also sued Costa Rica and Honduras for serving as staging areas for the American-backed rebels who sought to overthrow the regime in Managua, but in 1990 both cases were withdrawn in the context of a peace settlement.

Five cases relate to the former Yugoslavia. Bosnia filed the first case in 1993, the first time a sovereign state ever sued another state for genocide. The first response was for the Court to order provisional measures, requiring Belgrade to stop supporting genocidal actions. In 1999, Croatia filed a charge of genocide against Yugoslavia for the years 1991–1995, but Belgrade never responded, so the case is in limbo. Nevertheless, in 1999 Belgrade filed suit against NATO countries for attacking

Serbia. In response, ICJ rejected Belgrade's request for provisional measures and declared the complaint inadmissible against two NATO countries, Spain and the United States, because they had filed reservations to the Convention on the Prevention and Punishment of the Crime of Genocide. Other NATO countries were judged to be valid parties, but the case was dismissed because Serbia was not a member of the United Nations when Belgrade filed the case. In 2007, the court ruled that they could find no direct link between Serbia and the slaughter of some 8,000 Bosniaks in Srebrenica during 1995, thus rejecting the applicability of the **vicarious liability** principle; however, Serbia was found culpable in not acting to prevent the slaughter, which was identified as "genocide." The court assessed no damages for the offense. Bosnia had sued for reparations in the wholesale campaign to kill Bosniaks that had been financed by Serbia, but the court narrowed the scope of the complaint to the Srebrenica Massacre, a disappointment to Bosnia, insisting that evidence of culpability had to be incontrovertible rather than beyond a reasonable doubt.

Six recent cases involve the Democratic Republic of the Congo (Kinshasa), which objected to "acts of armed aggression" from three African countries. Although negotiations settled the cases with Burundi and Rwanda, the case with Uganda was different. Ugandan authorities shot down a civilian Congo Airlines airplane in 1998, resulting in forty deaths, seized a hydroelectric power plant, and allegedly mistreated Congolese prisoners. Although the UN Security Council ordered Uganda to refrain from further aggression in 2000, and Kampala complied, the Congo successfully requested the Court to issue provisional measures that duplicated the Security Council's order. In 2001, however, Uganda filed counterclaims with ICJ, alleging that Congo conducted aggression against Uganda. In 2002, Congo filed a new case against Rwanda for armed aggression as well as assassinations, degrading treatment of prisoners, looting, and rapes, but provisional measures were not approved. Hearings on all claims were held in 2005, and a decision is pending.

Developments in the Congo (Kinshasa) were followed closely in Belgium and France, particularly documents reporting torture by the Ministry of Interior. Arrest warrants and witness summons were issued to Congolese officials in both countries, which have laws that confer jurisdiction in domestic courts to human rights offenses committed abroad based on the principle of **universal jurisdiction**. Accordingly, Congo filed suit in the ICJ during 2000 in an effort to quash the legal action in Belgium, citing the principle of **immunity of prosecution** of government officials. Although ICJ did not immediately order Belgium to rescind the arrest warrant as a provisional measure in 2000, the final ruling in 2002 ordered Brussels to do so. The Congo filed a similar case involving France in 2002, and once again provisional measures were rejected. The Court instead awaited full statements from both parties before rendering a judgment. The outcome is pending.

There have been twenty-five **advisory opinions**, mostly submitted by the General Assembly. Advisory opinions enable the court to act proactively rather than punitively.

In 1966, the General Assembly terminated South Africa's League of Nations Mandate over South West Africa, and the Security Council in 1970 ordered Pretoria to withdraw from the territory, declaring that any further occupation was illegal. The South African government instead continued to administer the territory and even began to impose *apartheid* restrictions. In 1971, an advisory opinion not only stated that South Africa's control was illegal but also approved the imposition of appropriate sanctions on South Africa to force compliance. In 1988, South Africa finally agreed to depart, and Namibia became independent in 1990 after a brief period under UN administration.

During 2006, former Secretary of State Madeleine Albright (1937–) began to seek plaintiffs from among about 14,500 detainees in Iraq in order to sue President George W. Bush at the ICJ for the torture meted out to prisoners at the Abu Ghraib prison. Thus, a court that is not supposed to handle political questions can indeed become involved in high politics.

COURT CASE 9.1 *CONSTRUCTION OF A WALL IN THE OCCUPIED PALESTINIAN TERRITORY* (2004)

In 2003, the General Assembly asked ICJ to comment on the legality of the "security fence" constructed by Israel that intrudes into some of the territories that are likely to become part of a separate Palestinian state. Since the Palestinians do not live in a sovereign state, they could not bring the case to the court. In *Legal Consequences of the Construction of a Wall in the Occupied Palestinian Territory*, ICJ issued an advisory opinion, citing several human rights treaties in ruling that the wall violated international law, since the annexation of territory deprived Palestinians of the right of self-determination. The court also criticized Israel for depriving the Palestinians of specific water wells. The Court asked Israel to stop building the wall, to dismantle the wall, to pay reparations for damages caused by the construction, to prosecute those involved, and called upon the General Assembly and Security Council to take actions to implement the decision. Although Israel sought to justify the fence with the claim that every state has an inherent right of self-defense, the Court pointed out that Israel remains responsible to maintain order in the Occupied Territories as an occupying power without jeopardizing the rights of Palestinians. In addition, the Court called attention to Israel's defiance of previous General Assembly resolutions and asked all states to stop any aid to Israel that might assist in continuing to build the wall. Subsequently, the General Assembly voted to support the ICJ Advisory Opinion, but Israel has refused to comply.

ICJ's decisions are not always accepted. Ideally, two countries will submit a dispute in good faith, hoping that the court will clarify the legal issues so that the matter can be resolved. The court's rulings indeed add to the body of international law, but a country's political priorities may trump legal rulings.

Several other international courts have been established with the assistance of the UN. They are reviewed in the following chapter.

CONCLUSION

The delineation of UN agencies in the present chapter is not exhaustive. Kofi Annan's mandate for all UN agencies to focus on human rights in their operations has resulted in many changes throughout the UN. The International Civil Aviation Organization (ICAO), for example, decided in 2006 to raise the retirement age for airplane pilots from sixty to sixty-five.

The United Nations began as a forum to deal with international problems through diplomacy but has increasingly become an operational organization. Today, some 70 percent of the UN budget is spent on field operations, particularly in humanitarian relief and peacekeeping. Whereas interstate wars have declined since the end of the Cold War, serious human rights abuses inside countries have stimulated action in recent years. In a very real sense, the UN has come of age in regard to human rights, though proactively more than punitively.

The UN has often been ineffective, responding too late or not at all to human rights problems, because the organization acts only when member governments give authorization. The UN is not a world government, since states determine for themselves whether to abide by resolutions adopted by majority vote. The UN's effectiveness depends mostly upon the will of its members. Although some latitude is given to various UN agencies and leaders for raising concerns within the world community, governments have the final say on action taken in response.

DISCUSSION TOPIC 9.1 WHAT IF THERE WERE NO UNITED NATIONS?

There is no more blatant example of United Nations ineffectiveness than the withdrawal of UN peacekeepers from Rwanda in 1994, whereupon genocide proceeded unabated. Many officials in the United States have criticized the UN for following an agenda at odds with American policy, and indeed Washington has sometimes held up its payment of assessments to the UN in protest, thereby limiting the scope of UN operations. Although few seriously propose abolishing the United Nations, there should be considered answers to the various critics by pointing out wherein the UN is indispensable.

CHAPTER 10

Other treaty-based global international organizations

The United Nations has been intimately involved in drafting treaties devoted to human rights issues that have resulted in seven monitoring bodies, for which the UN provides secretariat functions. In addition, the UN has assisted in establishing several war crimes tribunals. Interpol and the World Trade Organization (WTO), outside the UN framework, are also reviewed below.

UN-sponsored treaty-based organs reviewed below attempt proactive diplomatic and verbal efforts to influence states to abide by human rights. The war crimes tribunals and Interpol are punitive. WTO has launched efforts at proactive diplomacy in the very recent past.

TREATY-BASED ORGANS SPONSORED BY THE UNITED NATIONS RELATING TO HUMAN RIGHTS

Human rights bodies have been established in the text of seven treaties sponsored by the UN (Table 10.1). Except for the Committee on the Elimination of Discrimination Against Women (CEDAW), which meets in New York, the rest have regular sessions in Geneva. Members of the various Committees, which serve as monitoring bodies for the treaties, are nominated by their governments, but tend to be technical experts who represent their expertise more than the priorities of their countries of origin.

The primary method used by the committees to advance human rights is by requiring **initial reports** from newly ratifying countries on measures taken to increase

TABLE 10.1 TREATY-BASED ORGANS SPONSORED BY THE UNITED NATIONS FOCUSING ON HUMAN RIGHTS

Adopted	Treaty	States ratifying	In force	Monitoring body	Committee acronym
1965	International Convention on the Elimination of All Forms of Racial Discrimination*	170	1969	Committee on the Elimination of All Forms of Racial Discrimination	CERD
1966	International Covenant on Civil and Political Rights*	154	1976	Human Rights Committee	HRC
1966	• Optional Protocol 1	105	1976		
1989	• Optional Protocol 2	54	1991		
1966	International Covenant on Economic, Social and Cultural Rights	151	1976	Committee on Economic, Social and Cultural Rights	CESCR
1979	Convention on the Elimination of All Forms of Discrimination Against Women	180	1981	Committee on the Elimination of Discrimination Against Women	CEDAW
1999	• Optional Protocol	71	2000		
1984	International Convention Against Torture and Other Cruel, Inhuman or Degrading Treatment or Punishment*	139	1987	Committee Against Torture	CAT
2002	• Optional Protocol	10			
1989	United Nations Convention on the Rights of the Child	192	1990	Committee on the Rights of the Child	CRC
2000	• Optional Protocol 1*	98	2002		
2000	• Optional Protocol 2*	95	2002		
1990	International Convention on the Protection of the Rights of All Migrant Workers and Members of Their Families	30	2003	Committee on the Protection of the Rights of All Migrant Workers and Members of their Families	CMW

*Ratified by the United States.

the level of voluntary compliance, followed by **periodic reports**. The committees then undertake a review of the reports, make recommendations in the form of **concluding observations**, and can engage in **follow-up monitoring** by evaluating responses to the recommendations. The reports, in turn, are supposed to be submitted annually to ECOSOC, though many countries fail to do so.

The agenda for annual plenary meetings of the committees usually consists of **discussions** on problems identified in several reports, often leading to **general comments** or **general recommendations** on thematic topics. Sometimes, a committee will make statements about problems in countries that have failed to ratify the respective treaty.

Most treaty-based committees also handle **petitions** against ratifying countries. There are three types of petitions: (1) **individual communications** (used by four committees), (2) **state-to-state complaints** (not yet used), and (3) **inquiries** (used by two committees). Procedures vary, though individuals are expected to exhaust remedies in their own countries before a complaint will be ruled admissible unless domestic procedures are unreasonably prolonged.

- *Committee on the Elimination of All Forms of Racial Discrimination* (CERD). In accordance with the International Convention on the Elimination of All Forms of Racial Discrimination, CERD employs three monitoring procedures: (1) reporting, (2) individual complaints, and (3) discussions at plenary meetings.

  The principal impact of CERD's review of country **reports**, which are required biennially, has been for the states to adopt legal innovations, such as constitutional provisions, laws, and enforcement agencies dealing with racial discrimination, often in response to CERD's **concluding observations** on the country reports. Because a large number of countries have been unwilling to submit reports at two-year intervals, CERD has launched **investigations** to fill the gap.

  According to the CERD Convention, **individual complaints** from non-self-governing territories are referred to CERD. From 1982, CERD has been able to handle petitions filed by individuals or groups, but only against countries that explicitly accept Article 14 of the Convention. The Committee allows states only three months to respond to the petitions; the identity of petitioners is kept confidential until a judgment is rendered. By 2004, some thirty-five cases were registered, of which six were ruled to violate the Convention, nine were deemed non-violations, thirteen were inadmissible, and the rest were still under consideration.

  The Committee also holds **discussions** on various topics. Interpretations of provisions of the treaty, known as **general recommendations**, are published in the context of reports on thematic issues or its methods of work. Among the twenty-nine issued thus far, CERD issued a general recommendation on problems of discrimination against the Roma (gypsy) people in 2000.

  In 1993, CERD adopted two implementation mechanisms. The **early-warning procedure** consists of suggesting confidence-building measures so that an ongoing problem will not escalate out of control. Criteria for determining when to employ the early-warning procedure are quite broad, including (1) a failure of a country to pass laws banning racial discrimination; (2) inadequate enforcement machinery;

(3) escalating racial hatred and violence, especially when officeholders are appealing to racial intolerance; (4) statistical evidence of a large gap between socioeconomic attainments of racial groups; and (5) a significant exodus of refugees due to discriminatory acts. The **urgent procedure** is invoked when there is a serious, massive, or persistent pattern of racial discrimination. CERD then acts to stop or lower the scope of human rights violations.

Early-warning and urgent procedures have been used in response to problems in more than twenty states thus far. In 2004, for example, CERD supported the recommendation of the UN Security Council (UNSC) to send a protection force to Darfur, and in 2005, CERD recommended an enlargement of the peace-keeping force. Also in 2005 CERD objected to a New Zealand law that failed to give adequate consideration to the wishes to the indigenous Maori people.

• *Human Rights Committee* (HRC). Under the authority of the International Covenant on Civil and Political Rights, ratifying countries are required to submit **compliance reports** every four years to HRC, which then makes comments in the form of **concluding observations**.

The First Optional Protocol to the Covenant gives the Committee competence to examine *individual communications* about countries ratifying the Protocol. Specific victims (not groups), or third parties on their behalf, can lodge complaints if they are under the jurisdiction of the country that is charged with violations of rights stated in the Covenant, but they must first exhaust national complaint procedures. Six months after allowing a country to respond to a complaint, the Committee can investigate, formulate its own views, and make a recommendation in the form of a remedy.

An offending country is required to make **reports** on corrective measures. From 1977–2004, there were 20,865 individual communications, of which 1,337 were registered as official complaints. Some 27 percent were deemed inadmissible, 14 percent were discontinued or withdrawn, 25 percent were still under consideration, but 34 percent were processed to a conclusion. Among the latter, violations were reported in 27 percent of the cases. In 1993, for example, the Committee ruled that the 1977 law making French the official language in Quebéc violated the linguistic rights of English-language speakers by requiring all outdoor signs to be in French.

Remedies may include payment of compensation, repeal or amendment of legislation, or release of a detained person. In 1993, Québec agreed to revise the law to permit other languages on public signs (though half the size of the French words). Next, the Committee organized a follow-up investigation to ensure that the remedy was adopted. Of the hundred and twenty-five follow-ups from 1990 to mid-1997, 30 percent were judged satisfactory. If a state refuses to accept the proposed remedy, a Conciliation Commission of five persons will be established to reach a settlement.

In 1990, for example, a communication came from a Zambian robber sentenced to death after eight years of legal proceedings because the country had a law imposing that penalty when a firearm is used in a crime. However, the felon fired the gun without causing any injury. The Committee ruled that the mandatory death penalty may be imposed only for the most serious crimes, that the judge erred by not informing the jury that the use of the firearm had not resulted in death or injury, that a speedy trial had been denied, and recommended a reduction in his sentence.

If a complaint is considered urgent, with irreparable harm possible to the victim, the committee will ask a state to adopt **interim measures**. In 2004, the case of a Uzbek officer, under sentence of death, was under consideration by the Committee. Accordingly, the Committee requested the interim measure of withholding execution. In 2005, however, the officer was executed, whereupon the Committee requested an explanation from the government in a letter that noted several similar situations in Uzbek's past.

Thematic reports have been issued in the form of **general comments**, which often cover procedural matters. In 1999, a substantive general comment was issued on freedom of movement.

HRC also monitors compliance with the Second Optional Protocol, which commits ratifying countries to abolish the death penalty. The United States is repeatedly criticized for excessive use of the death penalty.

- *Committee on Economic, Social and Cultural Rights* (CESCR). Based on the International Covenant on Economic, Social and Cultural Rights, **compliance reports** are required at five-year intervals. CESCR then reviews the reports and makes **concluding observations**. A proposed Optional Protocol to the Covenant that would enable complaint processing has not been adopted.

  The Committee has devoted considerable attention to thematic discussions and has made **general comments**, consisting of extended statements interpreting various economic, social, and culture rights. Sixteen topics have been covered so far, and three more are now under consideration, namely, gender equality, the right to work, and intellectual property rights.

- *Committee on the Elimination of Discrimination Against Women* (CEDAW). Due to efforts by the ECOSOC Committee on the Status of Women (CSW), the Convention on the Elimination of All Forms of Discrimination Against Women was adopted. CSW deals with more generic issues, whereas CEDAW focuses specifically on compliance issues. However, male dominance customs are so entrenched that more reservations are attached to the Convention than to any other UN-sponsored treaty.

  CEDAW requires **country reports** at four-year intervals, and often **follow-up reports** are requested. In addition, CEDAW receives **agency reports** from UN Specialized Agencies regarding the status of women. Some reports have stimulated **general recommendations**, but most have been notoriously overdue or absent. Thus far, there have been twenty-five general recommendations, addressing such topics as disabled women, equality in family relations, female circumcision, and violence against women. The Convention also gives the Committee the power to request an **exceptional report** when there is a pressing conflict involving women, such as rapes taking place during "ethnic cleansing" in the Bosnian Civil War.

DISCUSSION TOPIC 10.1 SHOULD FEMALE CIRCUMCISION BE BANNED WORLDWIDE?

In certain parts of Africa and the Middle East, unmarried women are in danger of being raped, and men will only marry women who are virgins. The practice of using artificial means to cut and sew protections to female anatomy has arisen as a result. However, female circumcision can lead to medical and psychological problems. Sometimes, uncircumcised females move to countries where the practice is illegal, but their parents insist, so they are sent to their homeland to be circumcised. Should female circumcision be banned internationally or should the world respect the practice as a cultural right?

CEDAW's Optional Protocol establishes procedures for **individual communications**, although gender-based complaints may also be filed with HRC. The Protocol creates an **inquiry** procedure whenever there is reliable information about widespread abuses in a particular country, though no complaints. In both cases, CEDAW refers the matter to the state for comment; names of complainants are kept confidential. An inquiry may result in a **site visit** to a country. Within six months, the state charged with discrimination is expected to report on corrective measures proposed or taken to remedy any problems that have been identified. CEDAW also has a **follow-up procedure** to ensure that proposed remedies have been implemented.

In 2005, CEDAW issued a report on an inquiry requested by two non-governmental organizations, Equality Now and Casa Amiga, about reported disappearances and uninvestigated murders of females working in factories at Ciudad Juárez, México. CEDAW's report, after a site visit and an exchange of information with the government in México City, led to several general recommendations, which in turn prompted the government to agree to allocate more resources in order to ensure better treatment of the workers, though implementation has lagged behind promises.

- *Committee Against Torture* (CAT). Parties to the International Convention Against Torture and Other Cruel, Inhuman or Degrading Treatment or Punishment must submit **reports** to the Committee every four years. The Committee examines each report and addresses its concerns and recommendations to the State party in the form of **concluding observations**.

For example, the Committee discussed the periodic report of Finland in 2005, reviewing such issues as preventive detention, prison conditions, deportation procedures, violence against women, asylum procedures, and treatment of mental patients, thus casting a wide net over practices where methods of torture might be employed.

In 2006, CAT commented on the report of the United States, which had been due in 2001 but was instead received in 2005, with several criticisms about torture meted out by American personnel at facilities in Abu Ghraib, Iraq, and

Guantánamo, Cuba. CAT recommended that "psychological torture" should be defined as any kind of mental suffering, secret detention facilities should be disclosed, imprisonment at Guantánamo should end, and those engaging in torture should be prosecuted according to American law.

The Committee has made only one **general comment**. The purpose was to clarify procedures for handling complaints.

CAT can act on **individual communications, interstate complaints**, or **inquiries**, provided that a state has not opted out of the Article 22 complaint procedure. Up to May 2004, CAT received two hundred and fifty-nine communications regarding at least nineteen countries. Violations were judged in twenty-nine cases, seventy-three resulted in statements of views on the subject without citing violations, fifty-nine were discontinued, forty-six were inadmissible, and the rest were pending. In 2005, CAT made an inquiry about several issues in Uganda, including reports of prison abuse and mob violence against alleged perpetrators of crimes.

Countries that ratify the Optional Protocol pledge to allow CAT's Subcommittee on Prevention to inspect detention centers. Lithuania, accordingly, was visited during 2004.

- *Committee on the Rights of the Child* (CRC). The UN Convention on the Rights of the Child, which established CRC, states a wide range of basic human rights of the child: (1) civil, political, economic, and social rights, (2) rights against separation from parents, and (3) immunity from dangers to which children are particularly vulnerable. The First Optional Protocol pledges states to end the practice of using children as armed combatants. The Second Optional Protocol commits states to end child pornography, child prostitution, and the sale of children.

  CRC reviews initial and periodic **reports** at five-year intervals, including additional reports based on the two Optional Protocols. During 2005, for example, the Committee reviewed a report from Costa Rica that covered such issues as adoption, child abuse, child labor, child poverty, and child prostitution.

  The Committee cannot consider individual complaints, although they may be raised before other committees, such as HRC. The Committee has made six **general comments**; education and health have been the main considerations. Thus far, CRC has made seven **recommendations**; although most are procedural in nature, there are substantive recommendations on children without parental care and juvenile justice.

  The Convention has been ratified by every country in the world except for Somalia, which lacks a procedure for ratification, and the United States. Congress has failed to ratify the treaty in part because various states execute children under sixteen and sometimes give life sentences to children, contrary to the Convention. According to Human Rights Watch, more than 2,000 children are now serving life sentences in the United States, including one aged thirteen. In some states, life sentences can be imposed on children as young as ten years old. Nevertheless, the Senate has ratified both Optional Protocols.

- *Committee on the Protection of the Rights of All Migrant Workers and Members of their Families* (CMW). The main aim of the International Convention on the Protection of the Rights of All Migrant Workers and Members of Their Families is to prevent the exploitation of more than 150 million migrants around the world who seek work and safety for their families. CMW, which first met in 2004, reviewed initial **reports** from countries ratifying the Convention; periodic reports are due every five years. CMW makes recommendations in the form of **concluding observations** on the reports.

The Committee will consider individual communications from those who claim that their rights under the Convention have been violated. CMW is empowered to publish interpretations of the content of human rights provisions, known as *general comments*. Neither the Convention nor CWM deals with the problems of undocumented migrant workers.

INTERNATIONAL TRIBUNALS ESTABLISHED BY THE SECURITY COUNCIL

In the former Yugoslavia and in Rwanda during the 1990s presented a challenge for the world community. Because the International Court of Justice (ICJ) was not set up to prosecute individuals, the UN Security Council decided to set up two special courts.

In early 2004, UNSC asked both ICTY and ICTR to wind up investigations by the end of the year, trials by 2008, and appeals by 2010. ICTY and ICTR have primary jurisdiction, but they can cede cases to domestic courts.

- *International Criminal Tribunal for the Prosecution of Persons Responsible for Serious Violations of International Humanitarian Law Committed in the Territory of the Former Yugoslavia Since 1991* (ICTY). Massive violations of human rights law associated with "ethnic cleansing" during the wars in the former Yugoslavia led the Security Council to try conciliation in 1991, condemnation in 1992, and then adoption of a Statute in 1993 to serve as terms of reference for a tribunal to punish violators for war crimes.

COURT CASE 10.1 THE TRIAL OF DUŠKO TADIĆ (1997)

Duško Tadić (1955–), a Bosnian Serb, was an official in charge of the Omarska Detention Camp, where some 7,000 Bosniak and Croat prisoners were beaten, mutilated, raped, tortured, and murdered amid inhumane conditions during the Bosnian War (1992–1995). In 1994, German police arrested him in Munich and turned him over to the International Criminal Tribunal for the Former Yugoslavia, which charged him with twelve counts of crimes against humanity, twelve counts of grave breaches of the Geneva Conventions, and ten counts of violations of the customs of war. He pleaded not guilty, was tried in 1977, found guilty of thirteen of the charges, and sentenced to twenty years in prison. When he appealed his case, the tribunal found him guilty of additional crimes. Currently, he is serving his sentence in Germany.

ICTY's first indictment was issued in 1995 against Duško Tadić (1955–), who was found guilty in 1997 and sentenced to a twenty-year prison term. He was one of twenty-one Serbs indicated in early 1995.

The most famous cases involve Srpskan leaders of the war in Bosnia, Radovan Karadžić (1945–) and Ratko Mladić (1942–), were indicted in 1995 for their role in the Srebrenica massacre that year. Both remain at large along with eight others who have been indicted. In 2001, Slobodan Milošović (1941–2006) was indicted for numerous offenses. Serbian authorities surrendered him to ICTY that year, and the trial continued until he died in his cell at The Hague. The World Court's ruling in 2007 that Serbia did not commit wholesale genocide against Bosnia in effect posthumously acquitted Milošović for responsibility in genocidal deaths estimated at 300,000.

Charges have also been pressed against several Albanian Kosovars. After the indictment of Kosovo Prime Minister Ramush Haradinaj (1968–), for his massacre of Serbs and even fellow Kosovars in Kosovo during 1998–1999, he surrendered to ICTY in 2004. He was placed on trial with two of his subordinates in 2007.

As of early 2007, fifty-three persons have been found guilty and are serving sentences from three years to life. Five have been found not guilty; one has committed suicide. Some appeals have caused a reduction in the years of the sentences. In 2005, the Court indicted four Croatian journalists for contempt of court after they published testimony of two protected witnesses in an ongoing trial, contrary to the rules of the Court.

ICTY has been developing important legal principles in the developing field of international criminal law. For example, to find a commander guilty of crimes committed by subordinates, a prosecutor must demonstrate not only **vicarious liability** but also **subjective awareness** or **aiding and abetting**. The tribunal has also identified rape as a new war crime. The decision to make rape a crime reflected a widespread practice during the Bosnian Civil War.

ICTY has forced those in the former Yugoslavia to rethink the past. The Tribunal has aided in reconciliation by enabling victims to ease their suffering by coming forward to share their stories and by disqualifying from political life those who committed heinous acts.

- *International Criminal Tribunal for Rwanda* (ICTR). In spring 1994, approximately 800,000 persons died in a civil war involving Hutus and Tutsis. Later in 1994, the Security Council drafted a statute for a tribunal to hear cases involving accusations of genocide inside Rwanda as well as actions violating international law committed by Rwandans outside the country.

  In 1998, ICTR handed down the first ever verdict by an international court on the crime of genocide, as well as the first sentence for that crime. Jean-Paul Akayesu (1953–), former mayor of Taba, was convicted and given a life sentence for participating in indiscriminate beatings, murders, and sexual violence on Tutsis who fled to his town for sanctuary.

  The most celebrated case involves former prime minister Jean Kambanda (1955–), who later pled guilty to genocide, conspiracy to commit genocide, direct

COURT CASE 10.2 THE TRIAL OF JEAN KAMBANDA (1998)

Ethnically a Hutu, Jean Kambanda (1955–) became President of Rwanda in 1994 after the assassination of President Juvénal Habyarimana, who assigned blame for the death to the Tutsi insurgency. On the radio, Kambanda incited Hutus to retaliate massively; in one statement, he said, "Genocide is justified in fighting the enemy." After 100 days in office, he fled the country. In 1997, he was arrested in Nairobi, Kenya, and transferred to the International Criminal Tribunal for Rwanda. To gain a lesser sentence, he confessed that the army had planned the assassination and the genocide in advance but that he was powerless to stop the army, which had forced him to act as president. The court, nevertheless, found Kambanda guilty of genocide, conspiracy to commit genocide, direct and public incitement to commit genocide, complicity in genocide, as well as two counts of crimes against humanity (for extermination and mass murder). His appeal of the life sentence was rejected in 2000. He is now imprisoned in Mali.

and public incitement to commit genocide, complicity in genocide, crimes against humanity (murder), and crimes against humanity (extermination), for which he was sentenced to life imprisonment. He is the first head of state to be convicted of the crime of genocide by an international court, which clearly rejected the state immunity doctrine that has often been invoked by governments to shield leaders from prosecution.

Although an estimated one million persons were perpetrators of the massacres, as of 2006 only twenty-eight cases had been tried and found guilty by ICTR, of which eight are still on appeal. Three have been acquitted, twenty-three cases are in progress, seventeen await trial, and eight accused persons are still at large. Most sentences are for life imprisonment, though one is for six years and another for fifteen years. In the latter case, the Reverend Arthanase Seromba (1963–), a Catholic priest, was convicted of ordering Hutu militiamen to lock and then bulldoze his church, where 2,000 Tutsis were taking shelter from the militia; those who were not crushed to death were either hacked to death or shot dead. Although the Rwandan government initially arrested at least 120,000 persons to be tried in traditional courts for lesser offenses, they have released at least 68,000 due to prison overcrowding.

INTERNATIONALIZED NATIONAL COURTS

In a few cases, technical assistance by the United Nations has assisted individual countries to conduct their own proceedings. Three have been established thus far.[1]

In 1999, during the UN plebiscite of Timor-Leste (East Timor), Indonesian troops slaughtered two thousand persons and burned homes, rendering 250,000 homeless. The United Nations Transitional Administration in East Timor created the *Serious*

Crimes Investigation Unit in 2000 to investigate and to prosecute cases. Accordingly, several East Timorese involved have been tried in the capital, Dili. Indonesia, which has refused to hand over anyone for trial, has conducted sixteen trials in Jakarta, convicting only one person out of one hundred named by an Indonesia inquiry commission. Because UN officials have considered the Indonesian trials to be shams, in 2005 Secretary-General Annan asked a special panel to investigate why more trials have not taken place, but the Security Council due to Indonesian objections has not endorsed the report, which recommends an international tribunal similar to ICTR and ICTY. Instead, a joint truth commission was established between Indonesia and East Timor in 2005.

Following a ten-year civil war, the *Special Court for Sierra Leone* was established in 2002 through an agreement by the UN and the Sierra Leone government to pursue "serious violations of international humanitarian law and Sierra Leone law." The UN Secretary-General appointed the Chief Prosecutor and seven of the eleven judges. Thus far, twelve persons have been indicted for crimes against humanity and war crimes; ten are being tried for rape and other forms of sexual violence. The first three convictions occurred in 2007.

One of those indicted is Charles Taylor (1948–), the former dictator of Liberia who brought war into Sierra Leone and is charged with forced recruitment of child soldiers, sexual slavery, and torture. Although he was granted asylum in Nigeria during 2003, Congress put a $2 million bounty on his head, and the International Criminal Police Agency (Interpol) placed him on its Most Wanted list and issued a "red notice" on him, suggesting that countries had the right to arrest him for "crimes against humanity [and] grave breaches of the 1949 Geneva Convention." In 2006, Nigeria withdrew his asylum status. He was then released but quickly captured and was transferred to Sierra Leone for trial on seventeen counts of war crimes and crimes against humanity. Later in the year, the UN Security Council authorized his removal to the International Criminal Court in The Hague, where his trial is pending.

In 2003, Cambodia and the UN concluded negotiations to set up the *Special Tribunal for Cambodia* to try those implicated in the wanton loss of about 1 million persons from disease, exhaustion, and starvation as well as the liquidation of the educated population and Vietnamese residents during the era of the Khmer Rouge (1975–1979). The agreement, ratified by Cambodia's legislature in 2004, authorized trials with seventeen Cambodian and ten UN-appointed judges. Trials began in 2007.

In 2005, Lebanese Prime Minister Rafik Hariri (1944–2005) was assassinated. Suspects were rounded up, and a UN report alleged involvement by the Syrian government as well as by the Syrian-backed Muslim group Hezbollah. The multi-ethnic country was poised on the edge of possible civil war when a majority in parliament voted in 2006 to establish an international tribunal to try the suspects. So angered were Hezbollah officials that they sponsored people power demonstrations to bring down the government. The lesson is that internationalized tribunals may serve to irreparably break a political consensus among competing factions.

INTERNATIONAL CRIMINAL COURT (ICC)

Both ICTR and ICTY have demonstrated that trials of those guilty of unspeakable acts are preferable to pretending that nothing happened worthy of attention. Clearly, the existence of the two simultaneous war crimes tribunals, engaging in some duplication of effort by the judges involved, suggested the need for a more permanent body. Accordingly, the Rome Statute for the International Criminal Court was adopted in 1998. After workshops around the world, jointly sponsored by Amnesty International Human Rights Watch, ratifications increased, and the Statute went into force in 2002.

The Statute elaborates and updates the three crimes identified at the Nuremberg War Crimes Trials. A special feature of ICC is a *Victims Trust Fund*, managed by a Board of Directors, for victims of crimes against humanity, either individually or collectively. Recalling the Conference on Jewish Material Claims Against Germany of 1951, the Statute authorizes the right of victims to compensation, rehabilitation, and restitution. However, Israel has not supported the ICC; one reason is that population transfers of Israelis into the Occupied Territories appear to be a violation of the Fourth Geneva Convention, which Tel Aviv has not ratified.

Cases, called **situations**, may be referred not only by the Security Council, by individual states, or by the ICC Prosecutor regarding charges of genocide, war crimes, or crimes against humanity taking place after July 1, 2002. Only the most serious crimes, therefore, are under the Court's jurisdiction. In both ICTR and ICTY, accused persons are subject to the **primacy principle**; that is, the two tribunals have exclusive jurisdiction and can overrule domestic courts. In contrast, ICC primarily operates on the basis of the **complementarity principle**; that is, to be charged with violations, a government must both ratify the ICC Statute and be unable or unwilling to handle cases. However, the UN Security Council can refer cases of nonratifying countries to ICC, and the Prosecutor can also initiate cases. In 2005, UNSC referred the Darfur conflict to ICC, though Sudan never ratified the ICC Statute.

To avoid having the ICC handle cases by default, many states have adopted legislation and established procedures to handle crimes under the Court's jurisdiction. An example is Britain's International Criminal Court Act, under which nearly a dozen British soldiers accused of torturing prisoners in Iraq were investigated in London during 2005.

By September 2005, ICC's Prosecutor had received more than 1,500 **communications**, as complaints are called, from more than one hundred countries and thus had to prioritize. The most numerous sources of complaints were from nongovernmental organizations in France, Germany, and the United States. Not all complaints have been made public.

Not all communications will result in prosecutions for the following reasons: (1) Acts committed before the starting date of July 1, 2002, are inadmissible. (2) Countries that ratify the Statute are exempt from ICC jurisdiction during their first seven years of membership. (3) Countries that do not ratify are exempt from prosecution. (4) The UN Security Council can stop an ICC prosecution for one year, thus allowing a political approach to resolve a problem. (5) A pretrial three-judge panel screens recommendations from the ICC prosecutor to place individuals on trial.

(6) When alleged war criminals are tried in their own countries, ICC is prohibited from playing a role. (7) In practice, accepted complaints are about "clearly excessive" cases in terms of casualties.

ICC's Prosecutor first acted on situations referred by the governments of the Democratic Republic of the Congo (Kinshasa) and Uganda, states that were experiencing or concluding civil wars. The Ituri region of the Congo, where 4 million died and others suffered sexual violence or torture from 1998–2002, initially caught the eye of the Prosecutor, who in 2003 asked the government for permission to start ICC's first investigation. The Congo government in Kinshasa agreed, and the investigation began during 2004.

In 2003, Uganda's president asked ICC to take up the case of the Lord's Resistance Army (LRA), which from 1986 was conducting a civil war in the north that involved 100,000 deaths, kidnapping of some 20,000 children, amputations of limbs of adversaries, rape, and forced cannibalism, resulting in some 1.6 million refugees. In 2005, ICC issued its first arrest warrants – for five members of the Lord's Resistance Army. Although Kampala had issued a partial amnesty with the conclusion of a ceasefire, Joseph Kony (1962–), who was one of the five indicted by ICC in 2005, is still at large. Kony refuses to surrender himself to the ICC and has even threatened to resume the civil war if ICC will not rescind the indictment.

From 2003–2006, some 200,000 Darfurians died and 2 million were driven out of their homes in the western part of Sudan by the Janjaweed, a militia believed to be supported by some in the Khartoum government. In 2004, the Security Council dispatched an International Commission of Inquiry to Darfur. The Commission's report in 2005 recommended that the ICC prosecute at least fifty-one persons for acting with "genocidal intent" but absolved the Khartoum government of collusion with the Janjaweed. The government of Sudan then attempted to negotiate a political settlement rather than submitting those accused to ICC's jurisdiction. After Washington's preference for another special court, similar to ICTR and ICTY, was strongly rejected, the American delegate abstained from an 11–0 Security Council vote to refer the cases to the ICC. In response, Sudan put two members of its armed forces on trial for the torture and killing of a Darfurian; they were found guilty at the end of 2005. Although the Sudan has not agreed to ICC jurisdiction, in 2007 the court issued arrest warrants for a Sudanese cabinet official and a Janjaweed leader for war crimes against humanity in Darfur, but they have not been arrested so as not to jeopardise a peace agreement.

In 2006, the first prisoner arrived at an ICC detention cell – Thomas Lubanga Dyilo (1982–) of the Democratic Republic of the Congo. He was charged with forced recruitment of some 30,000 child soldiers, which accounted for about 30 percent of all those in his militia. However, peace negotiations between the Uganda government and the Army ended when the indictments were issued.

The United States has refused to join ICC, preferring to have the Court as a subsidiary organ of the Security Council, where Washington or the other permanent members might veto case referrals. Although President Bill Clinton (1946–) signed the treaty in 2000, he did not submit the treaty to the Senate for ratification out of concern that American armed forces operating overseas might be prosecuted by the ICC even if the United States had not ratified. His successor, President George W.

Bush (1946–), "un-signed" the treaty and has been carrying out a campaign to undermine the Court out of fear that Americans might be indicted as a politically-motivated form of mischief to embarrass the country. However, the ICC Statute provides that individuals can only be prosecuted when a ratifying country is unable to provide a fair trial to an accused person or lacks the political will to do so. Since the United States has not ratified, the principal objection seems disingenuous. For example, allegations of mistreatment of prisoners by American military personnel in Guantánamo and Iraq have been investigated by the U.S. government, so no referrals to the ICC are likely.

In 2002, Congress passed the American Service-Members' Protection Act, which (1) prohibits the United States from cooperating with the ICC, (2) requires the president to insist that American soldiers will not participate in international peacekeeping operations unless exempted from ICC jurisdiction, (3) permits the termination of American military assistance to any country ratifying the ICC treaty, and (4) authorizes the use of military force to liberate any American or citizen of a country allied with the United States from detention by ICC at The Hague. The Dutch government has strongly protested the latter provision, which some critics refer to as the Netherlands Invasion Act. Based on the 2002 law, fifty-one countries thus far report that the United States has threatened to terminate military aid because they have not signed similar agreements, though the president has issued waivers to allow aid to some twenty-two countries that refuse to deny themselves the possibility of referring an American citizen to ICC. Washington also has signed bilateral agreements with nearly one hundred countries, providing that they will not extradite American citizens to the ICC for prosecution.

Pressure from the United States is clearly behind Security Council resolutions that ask ICC to refrain from investigating and prosecuting persons involved in UN peacekeeping operations from nonratifying states. The United States has threatened to withhold funds from peacekeeping operations, fearing that Americans who participate might be arrested for an ICC trial. Meanwhile, the European Union has been urging the seventy-eight countries that receive aid in accordance with the Cotonou Agreement to join ICC, thereby subjecting many poor countries to cross-pressures.

In 2007, ICJ surprised ICC and many observers by clearing Serbia of the crime of genocide against Bosnia. Nevertheless, the advent of international criminal courts means that the past culture of impunity is being replaced by a culture of accountability in regard to crimes against humanity, genocide, and war crimes. Although President Bush's opposition to the International Criminal Court is appears to be a retrograde development, the jury is still out on whether international criminal prosecutions are serving to deter gross human rights violations.

The legal principle of universal jurisdiction has clearly put many human rights violators on the defensive. However, there are some skeptics of the legal approach: (1) Some argue that courts can become so clogged with cases that justice will be delayed and thus the deterrent function will be lost. (2) Having an international court serve up justice instead of a Third World country may have the effect of delaying the judicial development of the latter to advance human rights in their countries. (3) Legal action can be responsible for increased violations of human rights. In 2005, for example, after protesters in Uzbekistan were massacred in Andijon, several Uzbeks residing in Russia, including a Russian citizen, criticized the action on the Internet. Within a month, fourteen Uzbeks were arrested by authorities north of Moscow for possible extradition to Uzbekistan, which has also been alleged to have abducted critics of the regime in recent years when Russia failed to extradite them. (4) Most defendants are far down on the chain of command; the major perpetrators who command human rights violations are seldom brought to justice. (5) The final objection is that the judicial approach is inherently a retail matter. Wholesale economic pressures, in contrast, are more likely to be effective when violations are ongoing.

Despite the five problems in applying the principle of universal jurisdiction to try human rights criminals, the fact remains that justice requires action, not inaction. If violators of human rights can no longer live a life of impunity but will ultimately be tried and punished for their misdeeds, the overall effect can be to deter future human rights violations.

DISCUSSION TOPIC 10.2 IS THE WORLD COURT OBSOLETE?

Only states can sue other states before the International Court of Justice, though states often sue on behalf of individuals and corporations in their countries. Implementation of ICJ decisions is voluntary. However, the defendants before various international criminal courts are individuals, who are held in custody after their arrest. Should the World Court be abolished or revised to guarantee justice?

INTERNATIONAL CRIMINAL POLICE ORGANIZATION (INTERPOL)

Founded in 1923, Interpol tracks down violators of international law and criminals who escape from jurisdictions where they face criminal charges. Originally called the International Criminal Police Commission, with a headquarters in Vienna, the organization was hijacked by the Nazi government in 1942, whereupon other countries withdrew. In 1946, the organization began a rebuilding process, head-quartered temporarily in Paris, until the adoption of a new constitution in 1956, which re-titled the organization. The permanent secretariat moved to Lyon, France, in 1989.

Interpol's constitution stipulates that "mutual assistance between all criminal police authorities [are to be] within the limits of the laws existing in the different countries and in the spirit of the 'Universal Declaration of Human Rights'." The constitution also forbids "activities of a political, military, religious or racial character."

Currently, police organizations cooperate with one another within the Interpol framework to bring criminals to domestic and international courts. The priority areas of cooperation are fugitives, public safety and terrorism, drugs and organized crime, trafficking in human beings, and financial as well as high-tech crime. When international arrest warrants are referred to Interpol, the organization places the named individuals on a watch list around the world. For example, Interpol is on the lookout for CIA agents sought by Germany, Italy, and Spain who are accused of kidnapping suspected terrorists after 9/11/2001.

WORLD TRADE ORGANIZATION (WTO)

In the belief that high tariffs, which worsened the Great Depression, may have been a factor in the onset of World War II, the General Agreement on Tariffs and Trade (GATT) was signed in 1947 and went into effect in 1948. GATT then became the premier international forum to encourage free trade by regulating and reducing tariffs. Several rounds of negotiation for tariff reduction culminated in the Uruguay Round (1986–1994), which drafted the text for a broader organization. The Agreement Establishing the World Trade Organization was signed in 1994, and in 1995 WTO superseded GATT, thereby becoming the chief institutional agency promoting economic globalization.

WTO satisfies the needs of export-oriented businesses to gain access to a worldwide market. However, an exclusive focus on trade issues meant that countries with sound environmental and humane labor standards suffered a competitive disadvantage. When disputes arose about health issues, labor conditions, and pollution, WTO's dispute resolution tribunal initially ruled that such concerns were irrelevant. Accordingly, an unusually large protest greeted WTO's third Ministerial Meeting at Seattle in 1999.

WTO adherents, however, point out that human rights concerns are discussed informally during WTO meetings. Since the global trade regime requires governmental transparency, the rule of law, and a middle class associated with increased entrepreneurs in developing countries, WTO rhetoric asserts that democratization is an inevitable consequence of free trade. According to WTO, environmental, health, and labor issues are to be included in future trade agreements. Indeed, in 2006, after the European Union filed the first environmental complaint with WTO about Brazil's ban on importing used tires, Brazil countered that non-retreadable used tires lying around a country pose a health danger to its citizens.

Human rights concerns have been used to screen some of the newest members. China's admission into WTO during 2001 was conditioned on the establishment of a "rule of law"; the subtext was for the first time a respect for human rights. Cambodia's admission in 2003 occurred only after Phnom Penh addressed several concerns, including the establishment of a judicial system where individuals and corporations could obtain a fair hearing. The right of minorities to participate in the economy was a screening criterion for Macedonia (2003), Nepal (2004), and Saudi Arabia (2005).

WTO members can use the procedure of **non-application** to punish WTO applicants for their human rights practices, as El Salvador, Perú, and the United States have done. In the latter case, Washington denies trade privileges to countries that sponsor international terrorism.

Members can apply **waivers** to WTO obligations in cases where trade may exacerbate human rights abuses. Because of the exchange of diamonds for guns to fight civil wars in the Congo (Kinshasa), Liberia, and Sierra Leone, fifty WTO members in 2003 adopted the Kimberley Waiver, which permitted countries to prohibit the import of what are known as "blood diamonds" from all three countries. The European Union's trade preferences with its former colonies under the Cotonou Agreement also operate as a waiver. In addition WTO has granted a waiver of obligations to ensure that nations can provide affordable medicines for their citizens under the public health exception. Although there are public morals and public order exceptions in the WTO founding agreement, no country has thus far used either provision.

HISTORIC EVENT 10.1 AN INTERNATIONAL CONFERENCE ADOPTS THE KIMBERLEY PROCESS (2002)

In the 1990s, a black market trade in uncut diamonds from African countries brought guns to rebels in Angola, Congo (Kinshasa), Ivory Coast, Liberia, and Sierra Leone, where they chopped off hands, raped women, and forced children to fight in their armies. In 2000, following a conference of diamond-producing states in Kimberley, South Africa, the UN General Assembly called for a certification scheme so that purchases of rough diamonds would no longer finance the various civil wars. Accordingly, a conference at Ottawa in 2002 established the Kimberley Process Certification Scheme whereby all diamonds sold worldwide must be certified to be not a part of the illicit "blood diamond" trade. Currently, 99.8 percent of all diamonds are now estimated to be covered by the scheme, which is managed by the World Diamond Council, representing the industry, in cooperation with forty-four countries and the European Union. The Congo, accordingly, was expelled from the process in 2004 because of uncertainties that its certification was valid. Some skeptics, however, believe that the scheme is far from foolproof.

Nevertheless, WTO often condones delays in compliance with internationally established human rights standards, thereby constituting a denial of those standards. WTO still has a long road to hoe.

CONCLUSION

One might easily be lost amid the large number of UN-related bodies monitoring human rights. The structure has been criticized not only for being unwieldy but also for duplicating efforts because some officials see the organs as competitive, not complementary. Whereas the Charter-based organs tend to have delegates representing governments, nonpolitical experts are assigned to the treaty-based organs set up with UN assistance. Governmental representatives may be more defensive about their own country's human rights performance, but they are in a better position to urge corrective measures than experts outside the political structure. On the other hand, experts tend to be objective about wrongdoing, and the weight of their findings can have an impact on policies, practices, and procedures, especially by democratic governments that seek to improve human rights standards in order to be reelected.

Although intergovernmental institutions have increasingly demonstrated a willingness to act on behalf of human rights, a consensus may take a while within a forum of more than one hundred countries. Countries where human rights concerns are considered to be of high priority may become impatient in relying on international institutions. Accordingly, the next three chapters deal with efforts outside global organizations.

CHAPTER 11

American approaches to international human rights

The United Nations and other international organizations can act on behalf of international human rights only when there is a wide consensus, so there is a lot of unfinished business in the struggle to promote human rights. What action can one country that respects human rights do about violations taking place in other countries?

International law permits a government to respond to abuses inflicted on its own citizens abroad through retorsions and reprisals. What happens in one country that offends a sense of morality in other countries, but responses by other states, individually or collectively, may be absent. Geopolitics and domestic politics often trump concerns over human rights.

Nevertheless, the United States has often seen its role as promoting democracy and human rights on a worldwide basis. Similar to intergovernmental organizations, the United States has used the same four tools of statecraft (diplomatic, legal, economic/ humanitarian, military) to have an impact on human rights abuses abroad. The vast economic and military power of the United States, which can be quickly mobilized, often leads to more punitive action than is the case in regard to intergovernmental organizations, but American diplomatic and legal efforts have a long and venerable history.

DIPLOMATIC AND VERBAL ACTIONS

One example of an American proactive verbal approach occurs when the president makes a congratulatory public statement to the winner of a democratic election in another country. Punitive statements may include formal or informal diplomatic protests, public statements of condemnation, publication of negative reports, declarations that a diplomat is *persona non grata*, and cancellations of cultural events, diplomatic meetings, or scientific visits.

Verbal protests can backfire. In 2003, a resolution decrying the "genocide" of Armenians in Turkey during 1915–1917 was placed on the agenda of the U.S. House of Representatives. In response, Ankara threatened to close air bases to American aircraft and to cancel contracts for American weapons. Despite overwhelming support for the resolution, the proposal was removed from the agenda. Turkey, the third largest recipient of American military aid, buys 80 percent of its weapons from the United States, so profits turned out to be more important than propriety.

A common form of proactive human rights action is to grant diplomatic **asylum** to those who have left a country or fear to return home because they fear persecution. Settlers of Massachusetts found religious freedom in the 1600s, Jews escaped ethnic discrimination in the 1930s by leaving Nazi Germany for America and elsewhere; and the United States accepted those fleeing Communist countries during the Cold War. In 1999, a West Hollywood man was granted asylum when he demonstrated that a return to China might result in severe punishment because he was openly gay, though by 2007 the climate in China appears to have changed considerably.

Contrariwise, a country may **deport** human rights violators. In 1978, Congress adopted the *Holtzman Amendment* to the Immigration and Naturalization Act, providing that anyone who had "persecuted any person on the basis of race, religion, national origin, or political opinion" should be denied entry to the United States and deported if already admitted. The Office of Special Investigations (OSI) at the U.S. Department of Justice was then set up to locate accused Nazi war criminals living in the United States and abroad. In 1983, OSI assisted in finding Klaus Barbie (1913–1991), who had been allowed by the U.S. Army to leave Europe at the end of World War II. Known as the "Butcher of Lyon" for his role in rounding up Jews for execution during the war, he was tracked down in Bolivia, which turned him over for $1 billion in cash and weapons to France, where he was tried and convicted.

In 2006, Gonzalo Guevara (1963–), who had applied for asylum in the United States, was seized in Los Angeles for eventual deportation because he was a member of the death squad that killed six Jesuit priests in El Salvador during 1989 even though he had been granted amnesty by the El Salvador government in 1993. He is one of several persons who have been tracked down by the Federal Bureau of Investigation, which established a unit in 2003 to locate notorious human rights violators living in the United States.

Asylum policy and immigration policy, however, can be counterproductive from a human rights standpoint, since those who flee from persecution are no longer on the scene to struggle against the errant country. Although decisions to grant asylum and to permit immigrants fall within a complex and worthy area of domestic and international law, the pressure on offending countries is minimal.

Diplomacy, a form of verbal pressure, can take at least two forms – quiet diplomacy and public diplomacy. **Quiet diplomacy**, sometimes known as **constructive engagement**, consists of regular bilateral diplomatic conversations in which complaints are brought up without informing the press. Through quiet diplomacy, the

United States has asked for specific persons to be released from the prisons of another country, but without producing any marked changes in overall human rights performance. The effectiveness of quiet diplomacy, however, is seldom supported by tangible results. America's "constructive engagement" with *apartheid* South Africa during the 1980s, for example, achieved nothing substantial.

Public diplomacy uses publicity to project a country's foreign policy abroad. Highly publicized **diplomatic meetings** may serve to pressure countries to make positive responses, though lower-level diplomats can rarely make concessions on the spot. The form of public diplomacy known as the **summit conference** brings together government heads or foreign ministers who can directly make compromises on important issues, with journalists in the wings eager to report progress. A **public statement** may also address a human rights policy. In 2005, for example, Secretary of State Condoleezza Rice (1954–) mentioned the word "democracy" thirty-seven times during a speech in Egypt, where she encouraged the government to hold free elections. As a result, the banned Muslim Brotherhood took to the streets, garnered 20 percent of the vote, and the government engaged in mass arrests of opposition demonstrators. In 2007, Rice spoke in Egypt without a single mention of the word "democracy." Washington did not fully anticipate the crackdown resulting from her earlier démarche.

Punitive diplomacy can range from a temporary **recall** of an ambassador, to an **expulsion** of a diplomat, to a **boycott** in order to show displeasure of a country's policies. One example is a suspension of diplomatic relations; the United States has had no direct diplomatic relations with Iran since personnel at the American embassy in Tehran were held hostage from 1979–1981. Perhaps the most famous **cultural boycott** occurred when the United States protested the Soviet invasion of Afghanistan in 1979 by refusing to send athletic teams to compete in the Moscow Olympics of 1980. President Jimmy Carter (1924–) was particularly annoyed when the invasion took place soon after he received personal assurances from Soviet leader Leonid Brezhnev (1906–1982) that Soviet troops massed on the Afghan border were not part of an invasion force.

Publication of human rights assessments in the U.S. State Department's annual *Country Reports on Human Rights Practices* (1975–) can exert diplomatic pressure by identifying unacceptable abuses, though reports of allies may be less critical. Many countries are quite sensitive to what the *Country Reports* say; counterelites may gain supporters as a result. However, a backlash is also possible. In 2005, Uzbekistan responded to human rights criticisms by rescinding approval for airplanes from the United States (and other members of the North Atlantic Treaty Organization) to land and to use the country's airspace.

Coercive diplomacy, which may seem an oxymoron, occurs when a state attempts to pressure another state by threatening to impose economic or military sanctions. To be effective, the threats must be clear and severe; otherwise, they may stiffen the resolve of a government to continue to violate human rights. For example, American coercive diplomacy was applied to the former Yugoslavia in the late 1990s in order to stop Serbian forces from massacring the majority Albanian population in Kosovo, then a province within Yugoslavia. When Belgrade ignored the threats, an intense bombing campaign on Serbia ensued in 1999.

LEGAL ACTION

Based on the principle of **universal jurisdiction**, lawsuits filed in one country can bring violators of human rights to justice for acts committed abroad. The universal jurisdiction principle justified prosecution of Nazis in the Nuremberg Trials, which took place in American-occupied Germany. The prosecution of persons accused of crimes with universal jurisdiction committed abroad can also take place in American courts. The principle of **extraterritorial jurisdiction**, as established in *Reid v Covert* during 1957, is that the Bill of Rights applies to U.S. citizens accused of crimes at American military bases abroad (354US1).

Four bases can establish the principle of universal jurisdiction to justify extraterritorial jurisdiction under American law: (1) Some offenses are prohibited under the **constitution**. (2) **Treaties** can authorize prosecution of certain crimes committed in one country by American courts. (3) **International custom**, that is, long-standing practices respected by many states, establishes standards under international law that may not be contained in a specific law or treaty. In some countries, notably Germany, international custom may even prevail over legislative enactments. *Legislative acts* may also establish the competence of American courts to try perpetrators of human rights violations committed abroad. (4) In regard to the first source, the American constitution calls upon Congress to define international crimes, notably piracy. In 1804, the Supreme Court ruled in *Murray v The Charming Betsy* (6US64) that American laws "ought never to be construed to violate the law of nations . . ." Nevertheless, in *Reid v Covert* (1957) the court ruled (354US1) that the constitution takes precedence over treaty obligations. In the latter case, a civilian defendant working for the U.S. military was court-martialed for murder based on a treaty with Britain regarding the legal status of American troops in Britain. However, the court ruled that the constitution requires American citizens to be tried in civilian courts.

Treaties, the second source of extraterritorial jurisdiction, are declared by the constitution to be the "supreme law of the land" when ratified by two-thirds of the Senate. Treaties may prevail over acts of Congress, executive orders, laws of the states, and even previous court decisions, provided that the treaties are both self-executing and "last in me." A **self-executing treaty** must specify implementation procedures. The **last-in-time** standard means that a later treaty supersedes earlier domestic legislation. However, few treaties ratified by the Senate are considered self-executing, and the United States has ratified very few human rights treaties.[1]

International custom, the third basis for prosecuting human rights cases, has been cited as a back-door approach to advance human rights. Judges presented with lawsuits often find authority for their decision in common international practices.

COURT CASE 11.1 *THE PAQUETE HABANA* (1900)

On March 25,1898, a small fishing boat licensed under Spanish law named the *Paquete Habana* left Havana for twenty-five days of fishing with a crew of three

Cubans. En route back to Havana, the Spanish–American war broke out. The vessel was seized by the American gunboat *Castine* as a prize of war, towed to Key West, Florida, and sold for $490. A second vessel was similarly captured and sold for $800. After the owners sued to recover their lost assets, the Supreme Court (175US677) ruled that proceeds of the sales should be restored to the owners and crew of both ships.

The earliest example of the use of international custom in deciding a case is *The Paquete Habana* (1900). The Supreme Court ruled that international custom dating from 1403 exempted civilian vessels from becoming prizes of war and went on to say that "the federal judiciary has the authority to invalidate executive action that runs counter to customary international law." When the United States was an international underdog, courts stressed international law to establish a legal framework with an equal playing field for all governments. As international topdog, however, the Supreme Court has increasingly cited international law as just one among several reasons for rulings. Today, some Supreme Court justices strongly object to any invocation of international law, arguing that provisions in treaties are subordinate to state and national legislation.

Legislative measures are the fourth basis for claiming extraterritorial jurisdiction. Two dozen laws have been used in American courts for the purpose (Table 11.1).

Implementing the Constitutional mandate to define crimes against the laws of nations, in 1789 Congress passed a comprehensive Judiciary Act in part to provide a legal basis not only for trying pirates in American courts but also to deal with the press-ganging of American sailors by the British navy. One provision, now known as the *Alien Tort Claims Act* (ATCA), gives Federal courts "original jurisdiction of any civil action by an alien for a tort . . . committed in violation of the law of nations or a treaty of the United States." The term "tort" refers to a deliberate act that causes injury to a person, including torture and death; ordinarily, torts involve civil suits between private individuals where monetary damages are sought from an aggrieved person. Specifically, ATCA act permits aliens to file suit in Federal courts for torts that either violate customary international law for which there is a universal jurisdiction or for violations of a treaty ratified by the United States.[2]

Perhaps the earliest ATCA case came in *Bolchos v Darrel* (1795), when a French privateer brought a District Court suit (3FCas810No.1,607) in South Carolina to settle a dispute over the rightful ownership of slaves seized in a British ship on the high seas. In 1820, the Supreme Court allowed the prosecution of a pirate on the grounds that piracy on the high seas was an international crime in *U.S. v Smith* (18US53).

Thus, private persons have sued private persons, utilizing ATCA. However, what if private persons seek to sue government officials for wrongful actions? According to the **act-of-state doctrine**, which the Supreme Court has traced to 1674,[3] a private person cannot sue a government executive for an official act. Thus, in *Underhill v Hernández*, the Supreme Court (168US250) ruled in 1897 that an American citizen could not sue General José Manuel Hernández, (1853–1921), the head of the

TABLE 11.1 SOME AMERICAN LAWS RELATING TO HUMAN RIGHTS VIOLATIONS ABROAD

Name	Passed	Issue addressed
Alien Tort Claims Act	1789	Civil damages to compensate victims of personal injury or property damage committed outside the United States
Neutrality Act	1794	American residents cannot take part militarily in a foreign war
Foreign Sovereign Immunities Act	1976	Legal grounds for suing a foreign state are defined as adverse commercial operations
Immigration and Naturalization Act amendment	1978	Persecutors (on the basis of race, religion, national origin, or political opinion) ineligible to be in the USA
Genocide Convention Implementation Act	1988	Criminalizes those who commit or incite genocide
Anti-Terrorism Act	1990	Permits victims of terrorism to sue those aiding the attacks
Torture Victim Protection Act	1991	Civil damages from a torturer
Religious Freedom Restoration Act	1993	Bans undue burdens on the exercise of religion by U.S. government actions
Protect Act[a]	1993	Criminalizes underage sex tourism by American residents abroad
Foreign Relations Authorization Act amendment	1994	Enables a victim of torture to sue the torturer
Anti-Terrorism Act and Effective Death Penalty Act	1996	Authorizes civil damages from foreign states complicit in injury due to torture, extrajudicial execution, aircraft hijacking, and hostage taking
War Crimes Act	1996	Criminalizes Geneva Convention war crimes
Expanded War Crimes Act	1997	Criminalize uses of landmines (but only when the United States ratifies the landmine treaty)
Civil Liability for State Sponsors of Terrorism Act (Flatow Amendment)	1997	Authorizes civil damages against personal acts of officials, employees, agents of terrorist states
Foreign Affairs Reform and Restructuring Act[b]	1998	Bans extradition to countries that practice torture

Act	Year	Description
Iraq Liberation Act	1998	Funds to groups opposing Saddam Hussein
Nazi War Crimes and Japanese Imperial Government Records Disclosure Act	1998	Authorizes an investigation of hidden assets
Armenian Genocide Victims Insurance Act	2000	Authorized a lawsuit in a California court on behalf of Armenian genocide survivors
Military Extraterritorial Jurisdiction Act	2000	Authorizes trials in the USA of defense contractors committing felonies outside the USA
Victims of Trafficking and Violence Protection Act	2000	Authorizes freezing foreign state assets to compensate victims of terrorism
USA Patriot Act[c]	2001	Criminalizes terrorism
Terrorism Risk Insurance Act	2002	Authorizes freezing private assets of terrorists to compensate victims
Japanese Imperial Army Disclosure Act	2004	Authorizes an investigation of hidden assets
Detainee Treatment Act	2005	Criminalizes torturing of detainees
Military Commissions Act	2006	Establishes procedures to try Guantánamo detainees

[a]The full title is Prosecutorial Remedies and Other Tools to End the Exploitation of Children Today Act.
[b]The full title is United States Policy with Respect to the Involuntary Return of Persons in Danger of Subjection to Torture, which is a provision in the Foreign Affairs Reform and Restructuring Act.
[c]The full name is the Uniting and Strengthening America by Providing Appropriate Tools Required to Intercept and Obstruct Terrorism Act.

Venezuelan government, for refusing to grant him an exit visa until he finished a construction contract. The reason for the denial of the suit was that Hernández's action was an "act of the government."

There are several exceptions to the act-of-state doctrine. In 1947, an Appeals Court found an exception in *Bernstein v Van Heyghen Frères Société Anonyme*, a case involving a person whose property was confiscated by the Nazi government because he was Jewish. The Court ruled (163F2d246) that the act-of-state doctrine does not preclude litigation against a sovereign state when the U.S. Department of State unambiguously certifies to a court that prosecution of a case can go forward without complicating the inherent ability of the executive branch to conduct foreign relations.

In 1976, Congress passed the *Foreign Sovereign Immunities Act*, which advanced the doctrine of **sovereign immunity**, namely, that most acts by foreign governments are immune from prosecution by private persons in the United States, as a successor to the act-of-state doctrine. However, the immunity is not absolute. The law allowed two exceptions: (1) insufficient compensation of the property of an American that is nationalized by a foreign government and (2) commercial operations by a foreign state with direct effects or operations in the United States.[4] *Bernstein*, of course, is a third exception to the sovereign immunity doctrine, namely (3), sovereign states may be sued if the U.S. Department of State does not object.

Subsequently, courts established three more exceptions to the sovereign immunity doctrine. In *Filártiga v Peña-Irala* (1980), an Appeals Court (630F2d876) decided (4) that an act can be prosecuted if a foreign government official violates a law of his own government. In the same ruling, the Court stated (5) that there is no immunity for a crime with universal jurisdiction, since "the torturer has become like the pirate and slave trader before him . . . an enemy of all mankind." In *Siderman de Blake v Argentina* (1992), an Appeals Court (965F2d 699) stated another exception, (6) that when a foreign government initiates a lawsuit against a private individual in an American court, the state has thereby waived sovereign immunity.

The Alien Tort Claims Act of 1789 was largely forgotten for most of the nineteenth and twentieth centuries. In 1961, ATCA was cited in *Abdul-Rahman Omar Adra v Clift* (195FSupp857), a child custody case that attracted little attention. However, from the 1970s various nongovernmental organizations have identified as many as 7,000 human rights violators and their victims living in the United States, including Orlando Bosch Ávila (1926–), who was pardoned in 1990 by President George H. W. Bush (1924–) despite his role in the bombing of a Cuban airplane during 1976.

COURT CASE 11.2 *FILÁRTIGA V PEÑA-IRALA* (1984)

In 1979, Amnesty International USA (AIU) learned that Américo Norberto Peña-Irala, a former Paraguayan Police Inspector General, was living in Brooklyn, New York. Two Paraguayans, Dr. Joel and Dolly Filártiga, then informed the U.S. Immigration and Naturalization Service and AIU that Joelito, their seventeen-year-old son and brother, respectively, had been tortured to death by that official in 1976. Accordingly,

INS arrested Peña-Irala, who had overstayed his tourist visa, with the intention of deporting him. Meanwhile, AIU telephoned the Center for Constitutional Rights in New York to suggest that Peña-Irala should be put on trial before being deported. In 1980, that case first came to trial as *Filártiga v Peña-Irala*, based principally on the Alien Tort Claims Act (ACTA), though also citing the UN Charter, the Universal Declaration of Human Rights, the UN Declaration Against Torture, and the American Declaration of the Rights and Duties of Man. Since the United States had not then ratified the Convention Against Torture and Other Cruel, Inhuman or Degrading Treatment or Punishment, the plaintiff's claim was that torture violates customary international law, citing the constitutions of fifty-five countries, including Paraguay and the United States. A District Court originally dismissed the complaint in 1979, believing that ATCA did not give the court jurisdiction, but in 1980 an Appeals Court reversed that judgment, so the case was remanded to the District Court. In 1984, the court ruled in favor of the plaintiffs. The defendant did not appear in court, having already been deported, so a default guilty judgment was entered. Punitive damages of slightly more than $5 million were awarded to each plaintiff, though the amounts were never collected.

The first major case involving ATCA was *Filártiga v Peña-Irala*. Private parties were allowed to pursue the case despite the sovereign immunity doctrine because in 1980 the Appeals Court (630F2d876) argued that since torture was a violation of Paraguay's constitution, Peña-Irala was liable in the United States because he had violated his own country's constitution.

The *Filártiga* case has spawned more than forty efforts to utilize ATCA in American courts. However, in *Argentina v Amerada Hess Shipping Corporation* (1989), the doctrine of sovereign immunity was again invoked to trump ATCA. The effect was to deny $11.9 million in damages for Argentina's bombing of a neutral American oil tanker under Liberian registration during the Anglo-Argentine War of 1982, when Argentina took military action to annex the British-controlled Falkland Islands, which Buenos Aires insisted on naming Las Malvinas.

In 1991, to clear up any confusion regarding *Filártiga* and similar cases, Congress passed the *Torture Victim Protection Act* (TVPA) as an amendment to the Foreign Sovereign Immunities Act. The law covers acts involving "severe pain or suffering" to obtain information from a person in custody, including threats to do so or to kill that person, and permits a lawsuit against a torturer who resides in or is traveling in the United States by a victim of that torture, provided that the torture occurred in the previous ten years and legal remedies in the other country have been exhausted. In 1994, the United States ratified the International Convention Against Torture and Other Cruel, Inhuman or Degrading Treatment or Punishment. That same year, Congress expanded TVPA provisions to implement the treaty in a section of the Foreign Relations Authorization Act. Similar legislation now exists to implement treaties on hijacking, hostages, sabotage, and terrorism.

Filártiga found a noncitizen to be liable under ATCA, but in 1992 a foreign government was for the first time ruled to violate ATCA by an Appeals Court in *Siderman de Blake v Argentina*. In *Saudi Arabia v Nelson* (1993), however, the Supreme Court (507US349) denied Scott Nelson, an American citizen, a remedy for being subjected to torture, a forced confession, and inhumane prison treatment (starvation) while he was detained by Saudi Arabian police for allegedly using a fake diploma to get a job. Although his mistreatment was a form of retaliation for his repeated complaints about defective oxygen and nitrous oxide lines as fire hazards and endangered patients at King Faisal Specialist Hospital in Riyadh, the doctrine of sovereign immunity was the basis for the dismissal of the case.

COURT CASE 11.3 *SIDERMAN DE BLAKE V ARGENTINA* (1992)

José Siderman de Blake was arrested and tortured in 1976 during a coup in Argentina. Subsequently, his property was seized. In 1982, after fleeing to the United States, Siderman filed suit against Argentina for torture and illegal expropriation, whereupon Argentina countersued to obtain more of his property, thereby waiving immunity from prosecution. Ten years later, Siderman won his case. Argentina then decided to compensate him out of court, a settlement that could be as high as $6 million: specific details were not released by either party. A significant aspect of the case is that the Appeals Court recognized state torture as a crime with universal jurisdiction.

Several famous cases have been litigated under ATCA and TVPA. In 1995, Radovan Karadžić (1945–), the political leader of the Serbian faction during the Bosnian Civil War (1992–1995), was assessed $745 million in *Kadić v Karadžić* (70F3d232) for having **command responsibility** in the torture of fifteen Bosnian women, though they not have collected the amount. In 2004, Álvaro Rafael Saravía was found guilty of assassinating Archbishop Óscar Romero (1917–1980) of El Salvador in *Doe v Saravía* (348FSupp2d1112).

Most ATCA cases begin as damage suits in Federal trial courts; appeal courts often clarify the scope of applicability of the law. However, since court decisions impact foreign relations, which is the usual prerogative of the president, court action might complicate cooperation with otherwise friendly countries on other issues. When the Supreme Court issued an ATCA-related opinion in 2004, a brief filed on behalf of President George W. Bush (1946–) argued for a minimalist interpretation of ATCA so that the court's ruling would not jeopardize good relations with other countries.

COURT CASE 11.4 *ÁLVAREZ-MACHAÍN V UNITED STATES* (2004)

In 1990, a federal grand jury indicted a Mexican physician, Dr. Humberto Álvarez-Machaín, for his alleged role in the torture and death of a Drug Enforcement Agency (DEA) official during 1985. After the Mexican government refused to assist in arresting the physician pursuant to a warrant, the DEA's Deputy Director hired José Francisco Sosa (1947–), a Mexican police officer, and five bounty hunters to kidnap him in Guadalajara and to bring him to California the following day for trial. México then objected to the abduction, which circumvented normal extradition procedures. Although the Supreme Court (504US655) ruled in *U.S. v Álvarez-Machaín* that his trial could go forward despite his arbitrary arrest, the trial court exonerated him in 1992, as the jurors accepted his explanation that he was merely present as a medical officer during the DEA agent's ordeal. Accordingly, in 1993 Álvarez-Machaín sued Sosa, five DEA agents, and the five bounty hunters under ATCA and TVPA in District Court (331F3d610), where he won $25,000 in damages due to the emotional distress suffered during his arrest and detention. Sosa then appealed the case, lost in the Appeals Court (266F3d1045 and 331F3d641) during 2003, and went to the Supreme Court, hoping to be exonerated on the basis of the **headquarters doctrine**, namely, that he was not liable for what his boss ordered him to do. In 2004, the Supreme Court rejected the headquarters doctrine defense, but nevertheless ruled in *Sosa v Álvarez-Machaín* that DEA's action in México to detain him for a single day did not constitute an offense actionable against the United States under ATCA, the Federal Tort Claims Act of 1946, or the extradition treaty with México. Sosa, thus, did not have to pay damages.

In response to Bush's effort to minimize ATCA's scope, the Supreme Court (124SCt2739) noted in *Sosa v Álvarez-Machaín* that ATCA was intended to apply to "violations of the law of nations," that is, offenses in common law, including international custom. Specifically, the court cited claims regarding commercial trade (such as prize captures) as well as "violation of safe conducts, infringement of the rights of ambassadors, and piracy" as offenses then recognized under international law. Hence, the ruling took note of a very limited scope of ATCA as of 1789, left uncertain which future claims brought under ATCA would be upheld in American courts, but approvingly cited the *Filártiga* case and thus did not accept a minimalist interpretation of ATCA.

Two ATCA-related cases were filed against Secretary of Defense Donald Rumsfeld (1932–) before he left office at the end of 2006. *Ali v Rumsfeld*, a class-action case on behalf of several persons who contended that Rumsfeld was responsible for their torture while under American confinement in Afghanistan and Iraq, was rejected under the sovereign immunity doctrine. *Kar v Rumsfeld*, a lawsuit regarding the arbitrary detention and later torture of an American filmmaker by the U.S. military while visiting Iraq, is one of about two dozen that are now pending in American courts for actions taking place in more than twenty countries.

Union Oil of California (Unocal) was the first major corporation to be involved in an ATCA-related case. The lawsuit, *Doe v Unocal* was filed in 1996 by the Washington-based International Labor Rights Fund on behalf of fifteen young females from Myanmar (formerly Burma), then living as refugees in Thailand, who claimed that they were enslaved by the Myanmar government to haul heavy loads, cut through thick jungle, and to grow food in connection with construction of a $1.2 billion natural gas pipeline. The women alleged that several forced laborers were killed by soldiers guarding the pipeline, and two said that they were raped. In 2002, an Appeals Court ruled in *Doe v Unocal* (395F3d140) that ATCA allowed foreigners to sue an American corporation in an American court for **vicarious liability**, that is, for not stopping human rights violations on the part of a subcontractor (the government of Myanmar). In 2005, Unocal settled out of court; the monetary award has not been made public.

The Unocal case may potentially have a large impact elsewhere in the private sector, as many pending cases based on ATCA and TVPA are against corporations. In 2002, Gap and forty-eight other clothing manufacturers settled cases involving sweatshops in Saipan, Northern Marianas. Some ATCA cases have served to discourage corporations from locating plants in companies with poor human rights records and to adopt codes of corporate conduct. More than 100 corporations have been sued for their vicarious liability in doing business with the *apartheid* government of South Africa, though a District Court (346FSupp2d538) dismissed one such case (*Brown v Amdahl*) in 2004. Currently, ATCA and TVPA are causes of action in some twenty pending cases allege human rights violations outside the United States. Among the defendants are Chrysler, Del Monte, ExxonMobil, Nestlé, Occidental, Pfizer, and Shell Oil.

COURT CASE 11.5 *UNITED STATES V PADILLA* (2007)

In 2002, upon his return from an overseas trip, José Padilla (1970–), an American citizen, was arrested at O'Hare Airport in Chicago on the basis of a warrant issued in New York to hold him as a material witness in connection with the attacks on the World Trade Center in 2001. However, rather than extraditing him to New York, President Bush issued an executive order to transfer him to a military brig in South Carolina as an "enemy combatant," where he was to be held indefinitely without access to an attorney or any prospect of a trial on specific charges. A court ruling in 2003, *Padilla v Rumsfeld* (352F3d695), ordered Padilla's release, a decision that was appealed to the Supreme Court. In 2004, the Supreme Court (542US426) ruled in *Rumsfeld v Padilla* that the case was improperly filed because the case was filed in New York instead of South Carolina, the state where Padilla was being held under military authority. After refiling the case, Padilla again won his release in a District Court in 2005, but an Appeals Court (423F3d386) instead ruled that his detention was legal, so the case went to the Supreme Court, which was expected to rule on the case later in 2005. Just before the ruling was to be issued, however, the U.S. government dropped war crimes charges against him and instead filed criminal charges based on the Neutrality Act of 1794, namely, conspiracy to "murder, kidnap and maim people overseas [in Bosnia and Chechnya]." In 2006, he was transferred from a military brig to a civilian jail in Miami. The defense moved for dismissal on the grounds that his abuse while in detention (solitary and shackled confinement, sensory deprivation, mind-altering drugs) rendered him incompetent to stand trial, but he was found guilty by a jury in Miami.

Several statutes other than ATCA and TVPA have been invoked in recent court decisions to bring alleged international human rights violators to justice. The *Neutrality Act* of 1794, which prohibits American residents from participating militarily in foreign wars, was passed when Alexander Hamilton (1755–1804) proposed that the United States to intervene on the side of Britain while Thomas Jefferson (1743–1826) sought the support of the government to aid France in the continental war fought by Napoléon Bonaparte (1769–1821). In 2006, José Padilla (1970–) was convicted of violating the 1794 act.

The *Anti-Terrorism Act* of 1990 enables victims of terrorist attacks to seek compensation from any persons who engage in or provide aid to the attackers. Accordingly, victims and survivors of the attacks on September 11, 2001, have filed a $1 trillion lawsuit in *Burnett v Al-Baraka* against various parties in Saudi Arabia, Sudan, and elsewhere, accusing them of financing Al-Qaida and Afghanistan's former Taliban regime. *Linde v Arab Bank* (384FSupp2d571), filed in 2004, alleges that Arab Bank, based in Amman, Jordan, publicly advertised a fundraising appeal to support those who have been committing terrorist acts inside Israel. Defendants in *Linde* include some 700 persons in eleven countries. Both cases will be difficult to pursue because crucial evidence may be based on confidential information that Washington may prefer not to disclose.

The *Religious Freedom Restoration Act* of 1993 prohibits the government from unreasonably interfering with the practice of religion, such as the use of a narcotic substance in a religious ritual. Based on the law, three former inmates under American custody at Guantánamo filed suit in 2006 to collect $10 million in damages for harassment of their Muslim religious practices, tossing the Koran into a toilet bucket, and confiscation of their religious beads in *Rasul v Rumsfeld*.

In 1993, revulsion against the practice of sex tourism in Southeast Asia with minors led Congress to pass the *Protect Act*. In 2003, after the law was amended to provide stiffer penalties, the U.S. Immigration and Customs Enforcement Agency formed Operation Predator, which by the end of 2005 had resulted in the arrest of more than 6,200 men. Complaints lodged with American embassies in Cambodia, Costa Rica, the Philippines, Vietnam, and elsewhere have resulted in the identification of child pornography in luggage searches at airports in the United States, such that pictures of victims can be matched with minors abroad. In one such case, a violator was sentenced to seventeen years in prison and fined about $16,000 in order to provide medical, occupational, and psychological therapy to his Philippine victims in their early teens. In 2004, the American government provided $1 million to International Justice Mission to conduct an investigation of human trafficking in Cambodia and other countries, and End Child Prostitution in Asian Tourism asked American travel agencies to adopt the Code of Conduct to Protect Children from Sexual Exploitation in Travel and Tourism, similar to what exists in Europe.

In 1995, the World Jewish Congress announced important discoveries about Swiss bank accounts and other assets of victims of Nazi persecution from 1933–1945. Swiss banks were then sued in 1996 for $20 billion for not distributing funds in dormant accounts to Holocaust survivors and their heirs and otherwise collaborating with the Nazis by holding deposits from Hitler's government. In response, the American and Swiss governments launched investigations into looted assets. In early 1997, a security guard at a Swiss bank reported the shredding of relevant documents. Two weeks later, the City of New York openly considered a boycott of Swiss banks in retaliation. In 1998, a settlement of $1.25 billion was reached between two banks, UBS AG and Credit Suisse, and lawyers representing Holocaust victims and the World Jewish Congress, resulting in the formation of the Claims Resolution Tribunal to handle individual cases. To date, more than 32,000 claims have been filed, although the Tribunal has reported that the banks destroyed records of nearly 7,000,000 accounts that had been opened in Swiss banks from 1933–1945.

Accordingly, in 1998 Congress passed the *Nazi War Crimes and Japanese Imperial Government Records Disclosure Act*, which mandated the disclosure of information that would facilitate survivors and their heirs to identify themselves in order to recover assets lost in World War II. Since only Jewish victims were initially to receive awards, two class action lawsuits on behalf of non-Jewish victims of the Nazis were filed in 2000 against the Swiss National Bank and Vatican Bank, both of which were accused of laundering dental gold, gold coins, wedding rings, and other gold looted from non-Jewish Belarusan, Russian, Ukrainian, and Yugoslavian concentration camp and war victims. Disabled people, homosexuals, Jehovah's Witnesses, and Roma gypsies also have also been recognized to have valid claims against the Nazis. As a result, many classes of victims of Nazi persecution were included in the $1.25 billion judgment announced during 2000 in the ruling of *In re Holocaust Victim Assets Litigation* (105FSupp2d139). In 1998, Germany signed an agreement with the United States to return all stolen art to their rightful owners.

COURT CASE 11.6 *AUSTRIA V ALTMANN* (2004)

In 1938, after Germany annexed Austria, many Jews were persecuted. One survivor of that era, Mrs. Maria Altmann (1916–), left Austria after the war, eventually settled in Los Angeles, and became an American citizen. In 1948, her family attempted to recover her family's personal property from Austria, including six paintings by Gustav Klimt hanging in the Austrian Gallery in Vienna that had been owned and willed to her by her former uncle. In 1998, two other paintings on loan from Austria in New York's Museum of Modern Art were identified as property confiscated by the Nazis. In response, the Austria Gallery began to search for the rightful owners of its art work, but Mrs. Altman's claim was denied. In 2000, she sued to recover them on the basis of the expropriation exception to the Foreign Sovereign Immunities Act. After winning in a lower court, Austria appealed, claiming that she had no standing to sue, since Austria was a sovereign state. However, the Supreme Court held in *Austria v Altmann* (541US677) that the law could be used to sue Austria because the property had been nationalized. Meanwhile, Austria established an arbitration procedure, so she decided instead to submit her claim to compulsory arbitration in order to avoid expensive court costs. In early 2006, an Austrian arbitration court ordered the government to return to her five of the six paintings, valued at $150 million, so they were quickly transferred for an exhibition at the Los Angeles County Museum of Art. The sixth, which the family of the woman in the portrait also claims to own, remains in the Austria Gallery.

In 2000, a California law authorized Armenian survivors of Turkish rule in 1915–1923, when approximately 1.5 million perished largely due to forced relocation from Turkey, to sue in order to recover unpaid payments of $7 million on some 2,300 life insurance policies issued from 1875–1915. As a result, in 1999 *Marootian v New York Life Insurance Company* (CV99–10273Cas(MCx);2001USDistLexis22274) was filed. Five years later, the New York company decided to settle out of court, offering survivors $11 million and $3 million for Armenian civic organizations. Efforts of the California legislature on behalf of victims of Japanese and Nazi slave labor, however, were dismissed during 2003 in *American Ins. Assn. v. Garamendi* (539US396) on the ground that the federal government preempts state authority in matters affecting foreign affairs.

Several cases have been pursued against Japan's conduct during World War II in American courts, notably the practice of forcing women to have sex with Japanese soldiers, only to find their cases rejected on the basis that the Japanese Peace Treaty of 1951 settled all such claims. For example, in 2003 a lawsuit filed on behalf of former sex slaves was rejected in *Joo v Japan* (332F3d649). Although some members of Congress sought to reinterpret the peace treaty through new legislation, a presidential veto was threatened on the grounds that new litigation against Japan might adversely affect cooperation with Tokyo on matters of terrorism, so the proposed law did not pass.

In 1996, Congress passed the *War Crimes Act* and the *Anti-Terrorism and Effective Death Penalty Act*. The former provides that any violation of the Geneva Conventions constitutes a felony. The latter permits plaintiffs to receive "money damages . . . against a foreign state for personal injury or death that was caused by an act of torture, extrajudicial killing, aircraft sabotage [or] hostage taking." Accordingly, thirty-seven family members filed *Acree v Iraq* on behalf of seventeen former Americans held as prisoners of war who were tortured in Iraq after the Gulf War of 1991. When then-President Saddam Hussein (1937–2006) failed to appear for the defense, the District Court in 2003 (271FSupp2d179) awarded the plaintiffs $959 million in damages. The court also rejected the Bush administration's refusal to disburse the settlement funds on the grounds that the successor Iraq regime should not be forced to pay for the wrongs committed under Saddam Hussein.

In 1997, Congress amended the Foreign Sovereign Immunities Act in passing the *Flatlow Amendment*, named after an American who was killed in an Iran-financed terrorist attack during 1995 in the Gaza Strip, then occupied by Israel. The amendment limits a possible defendant to personal acts by "an official, employee, or agent of a foreign state designated as a state sponsor of terrorism," but the government itself cannot be held liable. Plaintiffs then prevailed in two cases during 1997 – in *Alejandre v Cuba* (996FSupp1239), involving two civilian airplanes shot down by Cuba in international waters during 1996, and in *Flatlow v Iran* (999FSupp1). However, Cuban and Iranian assets, which had been confiscated due to prior legislation, were not disbursed by the American government, which claimed that the court action hampered diplomacy by the executive branch.

One loophole of American law was closed in 2000 by the *Military Extraterritorial Jurisdiction Act*. Previously, serious crimes committed abroad by civilians working under contracts for the American military could only be prosecuted abroad. Under the new law, they could be tried in American courts. In 2007, a civilian interrogator for the Central Intelligence Agency (CIA) in Afghanistan, David Passaro (1966–), was the first person convicted under the law; his offense was to beat a prisoner who subsequently died.

In 2000, Congress passed the *Victims of Trafficking and Violence Protection Act*, which provides that when Congress designates a country as a terrorist state, the assets can be frozen and paid out to victims of terrorist violence. Subsequently, Cuba, Iran, North Korea, Sudan, and Syria were identified as terrorist states. In early 2001, some $410 million was paid out in default judgments, including $97 million from Cuban assets paid to relatives of the heirs to those shot down in an airplane by the Cuban Air Force during 1996, and $22 million from Iranian assets to the Flatlow family. Later in 2001, assets from Afghanistan were frozen, though the procedure for determining which organizations are "terrorist" was ruled unconstitutionally vague during 2006 in *Humanitarian Law Project v Gonzales* (380FSupp2d1134).

After some 3,000 persons died in attacks on September 11, 2001, President Bush implemented several significant changes in the American approach to human rights in response to two Congressional laws passed later that year – the *Authorization for the Use of Military Force Act* and the *USA Patriot Act*. The *Terrorism Risk Insurance Act* of 2002 also extends the law to permit seizure of assets of terrorist–related groups.

Whereas previously terrorism was regarded in terms of the **criminal law** model, Bush framed the American struggle against terrorism as a **military** effort justified by **natural law** – as a fight to preserve civilization against modern-day barbarians. What has become known as the Bush Doctrine is a claim that terrorist threats in an age of rapid communication and potential mass destruction require new measures, indeed a new paradigm beyond the framework of the Geneva Conventions and international criminal law. However, the methods are similar to those used by Britain after World War II in dealing with the Communist insurgency in Malaya as well as Jewish terrorists in

Palestine. Several hundred suspected terrorists were rounded up in Afghanistan during 2001, and many were shipped to Guantánamo Naval Base, where their status remained to be determined. American citizen John Walker Lindh (1981–), who was in the Taliban army at the time of his capture, was returned to the United States, not Guantánamo, because he was an American citizen, protected by *Reid v Covert*. He pleaded guilty to treason in 2002 and was sentenced to twenty years in prison; his confession to other crimes was extracted through torture and therefore ruled inadmissible in court.

One argument used by Bush administration officials is that terrorist groups are not protected by the Geneva Conventions because they have not ratified the Conventions. However, the Geneva Conventions apply to actions of the United States, which has ratified by Conventions, and litigation to challenge the new approach has largely been successful (Table 11.2). As commander in chief, the Bush Doctrine claims that the president has inherent powers to act by executive orders without regard to international treaties or domestic laws in order to defend the country, but the Supreme Court declared that the president does not have a "blank check" to pursue terrorism in *Hamdi v Rumsfeld* (547US507) and in *Hamdan v Rumsfeld* (126SCt2749), cases decided in 2004 and 2006, respectively. Referring to a Red Cross report in 2005 that 80 percent of those captured in Afghanistan or Iraq have been wrongfully detained, critics have referred to the "new paradigm" as a justification for government terrorism.

Since the primary purpose of government is to provide order and stability, human rights necessarily are secondary concerns, though not matters of unconcern. Congress gave President Bush additional tools to fight terrorism after 2001 but reduced that authority after photographs of Iraqis under American custody in Abu Ghraib Prison, Baghdad, revealed in 2004 that unusual methods had been used, including having a vicious dog bark at a chained prisoner. Reports of extremely stressful methods of interrogation were also acknowledged by the government to have taken place in the detention facility at Guantánamo Naval Base, Cuba.

Congress' response was to pass the *Detainee Treatment Act* in 2005, requiring that interrogation techniques should be limited to those allowed by the Uniform Code of Military Justice, which includes Geneva Convention protections. The belief that evidence obtained by torture is meaningless was vindicated in 2007, when preposterously fanciful confessions of two detainees were made public by American prosecutors. In signing the 2005 act into law, nevertheless, Bush issued a statement that he would not abide by the law if he felt that "protecting the American people from terrorist attacks" was a higher priority.

In 2004, a military tribunal established by a presidential order proceeded to charge several detainees at Guantánamo, including Australian citizen David Hicks (1975–), with conspiracy to commit acts of terrorism, attempted murder, and aiding the enemy. *Hamdan* not only declared that the court was unconstitutional, because the Constitution only authorizes Congress to establish courts, but also noted that the military courts violated Article 3 of all four Geneva Conventions. A violator of a Geneva Convention provision is, of course, a war criminal, so the Supreme Court was not only implicating Defense Secretary Rumsfeld, who set up the court, but also President Bush, who authorized the court on November 13, 2001 by executive order.

TABLE 11.2 THE BUSH DOCTRINE AND COURT CHALLENGES

Elements of the Bush Doctrine

Elements of the Bush Doctrine	Challenges
Suspected terrorists are "enemy combatants," unprotected by the Geneva Conventions.	Rejected in 2004 by the Supreme Court in *Hamdi v Rumsfeld* (547US507) and in 2006 by *Hamdan v Rumsfeld* (126SCt2749).
Extraordinary renditions of ghost detainees (Terrorist suspects may be abducted, then flown to secret prisons, and their identities may be kept confidential.)	Ended in 2006 after the UN General Assembly adopted the International Convention for the Protection of All Persons from Enforced Disappearance, which bans the practice of extraordinary renditions and ghost detainees.
Indefinite detention (Terrorist suspects may be held until the "war on terror" ends.)	Rejected in 2004 by the Supreme Court in *Rasul v Bush* (541US466).
Terrorist suspects lack the right of legal representation.	Rejected in 2004 by the Supreme Court in *Hamdi v Rumsfeld*.
Terrorist suspects may be tried in secret.	Rejected in 2006 by the Supreme Court in *Hamdan v Rumsfeld*.
Guilt by association (An acquaintance of a suspected terrorist may be deported.)	Rejected in 2005 in *Elmaghraby v Ashcroft* (2005USDistLEXIS21434EDNY).
Aliens can be deported without a hearing for minor offenses.	Rejected in 2007 by the Supreme Court in *López v Gonzales* (US05-547).
E-mailing a website of a suspected "terrorist group" gives support to the group.	Rejected in 2004 by an Idaho jury that acquitted an Arab graduate student.
NGOs may be designated "terrorist groups" without administrative challenge.	Rejected in 2006 by *Humanitarian Law Project v Dept. of the Treasury* (CV05-8047ABC).
Assets of "terrorist groups" may be confiscated without administrative challenge.	Rejected in 2006 by *Humanitarian Law Project v Rumsfeld* (380FSupp2d1134).
Military commissions may use coerced testimony or hearsay in trying "illegal enemy combatants" and may censure testimony.	Accepted in 2007 by the Supreme Court in *Al Odah v United States* and *Boumediene v Bush*.
Terrorism suspects lawfully in the United States may be denied the right of *habeas corpus*.	Rejected in 2007 by an Appeals Court (06-7424) in *Al-Marri v Wright*.
Terrorist suspects may be tortured as "imperative security detainees" to obtain information about future plots but cannot be released if they allege torture.	Cases pending (*Kar v Gonzales*).
Allegations of torture as the reason for a confession are inadmissible in court under the state secrets doctrine.	Not yet challenged.
Government officials may authorize assassinations of suspected terrorist leaders.	Not yet challenged.

Congress then adopted the *Military Commissions Act* of 2006, with new procedural rules that apply neither to criminals nor to prisoners of war. Each detainee at Guantánamo is first screened by a Combatant Status Review Tribunal to be determined as an "alien unlawful enemy combatant" and then put on trial by a Military Commission, where the following procedures apply: (1) Coerced and hearsay testimony is allowed. (2) The prosecution may use classified testimony that the defendant will be unable to review or challenge. (3) There are no appeals from the commissions to other federal courts. (4) Suspected terrorists have no right of *habeas corpus*. In addition, (5) interrogators of the Central Intelligence Agency and their subcontractors can use severe interrogation methods, and (6) provisions of the War Crimes Act that formerly criminalized anyone from violating the Geneva Conventions have been repealed. However, a determination that someone has an "unlawful" status before a trial on the charges is, for many observers, Kafkaesque. Charging them on the basis of a "war on terror" poses the legal difficulty that the laws of warfare recognize that combatants can lawfully attack their enemies within the limits of the four Geneva Conventions.

Hicks, the first person processed by a military commission, pleaded guilty in 2007 to a different charge – providing material support to Al-Qaida, a designated terrorist organization, though the arbitrary procedure for branding organizations as terrorist had been declared unconstitutional during 2006 in *Humanitarian Law Project v Dept. of the Treasury*. In a plea bargain, the Australian agreed never to allege that he was tortured despite claims that he made in Afghanistan after his capture. He then was released and returned to Australia to serve a sentence of less than the year beyond his nearly five years of confinement. Thus, after detainees are designated as enemy combatants by the Combatant Status Review Tribunal, they can be released only after pleading guilty; if they maintain their innocence, they may be held indefinitely – until the end of the "war on terror." As of 2007, some 80 of 385 detainees are expected to be tried by the Military Commission procedure. Accordingly, Britain, France, and Germany have successfully persuaded Washington to release their nationals from Guantánamo, though in some cases former prisoners have later filed lawsuits against the United States, alleging wrongful detention.

The decriminalization of Geneva Convention violations in the 2006 law is particularly significant. The long tradition of using American courts to try individuals for violations of international human rights committed abroad appears to have been compromised. However, judicial and legislative checks on the executive branch have clearly weakened some elements of the Bush Doctrine. Meanwhile, according to the principal UN investigator on torture, several countries now point to America's lowering of standards as a justification for their own harsh methods of interrogation.

Violations of human rights are contrary to law, so the judicial approach is entirely appropriate; as the legal framework grows, the deterrent effect is strengthened. However, remedies for the misconduct of individuals rarely are effective vis-à-vis governments that have poor human rights records. Economic measures, such as foreign assistance and foreign trade have a more systemic effect.

ECONOMIC MEASURES: FOREIGN ASSISTANCE

Foreign aid can be a **proactive** approach to improve the attainment of economic and social rights. In 1947, the United States adopted the Marshall Plan to foster European postwar economic reconstruction, though no such program was extended to Asia. Subsequently, the United States maintained aid programs with Third World countries. Whereas the UN's Millennium Development goals encourages developed countries to devote 0.7 per cent of gross national income to foreign aid, American contributions, including both public and private, are the lowest among industrialized countries at about 0.2 per cent.

HISTORIC EVENT 11.1 THE MARSHALL PLAN (1947–1951)

When World War II ended, Europe's economic infrastructure had been severely damaged, and there was a lack of financial reserves for reconstruction. Due to serious food shortages and unemployment, Communist Parties in France, Italy, and Western Germany gained strength. In 1947, Secretary of State George C. Marshall (1880–1959) gave a commencement address at Harvard University in which he called upon European countries to meet together to design an economic recovery plan for the United States to fund. British and French leaders then met to discuss the terms of a plan. Moscow was interested, too, but the British and French insisted that any aid program had to be preceded by an economic assessment of the economic needs of each country, a condition that the closed economy of the Soviet Union could not accept. Next, sixteen Western European countries attended a conference in Paris; Spain, which was neutral during the war, was not invited. The result was the European Recovery Plan, which the press named the Marshall Plan. After providing emergency aid to Greece and Turkey in 1947, Congress in 1948 authorized the first $5 billion out of an eventual $12 billion to be provided to the Organization for European Economic Cooperation as the main recipient coordinating agency. European countries were to contribute matching funds. Most aid was used to purchase American goods, and 2 percent of the total was spent to advertise American products so that European consumers would be encouraged to buy them. As a result of the Marshall Plan, Western European industrial production increased by 35 percent. On gaining control of Congress in 1951, the Republican majority voted to discontinue the program as a "giveaway" that they could no longer support.

From 1961, the U.S. Agency for International Development (USAID) has been the primary foreign assistance agency, with field offices in more than one hundred countries. Currently, USAID administers the Millennium Challenge, in which human rights criteria are employed to screen potential aid recipients. USAID provides extensive humanitarian assistance, not only to international organizations but also bilaterally to the victims of natural disasters. Aid to victims of the Acquired Immune

Deficiency Syndrome (AIDS) was a factor in reducing the incidence of new cases in the latter part of the twentieth century; AIDS cases, however, have increased since the Bush administration banned the distribution of condoms.

In 1983, the National Endowment for Democracy (NED) was established to provide funds for the support of pro-democratic groups in other countries. Although the organization is a nongovernmental organization outside the American government, most funding comes from Congress. NED, thus, is proactive, providing technical assistance, supplies, and equipment to political groups, civic organizations, labor unions, and the media; the group also engages in election monitoring.

In 1984, after NED supported a candidate for office in Panamá, Congress stipulated that its funds could not be used to support officeseekers. Nevertheless, in 1990 NED used funds on behalf of candidates in Haiti and Nicaragua. In 2004, Venezuela's President Hugo Chávez (1954–) charged NED with providing about $1 million to an organization seeking to have him recalled from office. His government charged the leaders of the group with treason and conspiracy for receipt of NED funds, and those who signed the recall petition complained of harassment. In short, NED's meddling stirred up a hornets' nest.

In 1998, a Human Rights and Democracy Fund was established, not only to address human rights and democratization emergencies but also to support such activities as election monitoring and parliamentary development. Congress authorized $48 million in 2005, including $4 million to stop sweatshops.

Bilateral humanitarian aid for victims of natural disasters has been rushed to various countries over the years, including food, medicines and other necessities. In 2000, Congress amended the *Victims of Crime Act* of 1984 to authorize foreign aid for individual victims of terrorist acts outside the United States, and in 2003 the *International Disability and Victims of Warfare and Civil Strife Assistance Act* was passed in a similar vein.

Shady economic transactions with suspect businesses can be deterred through **public disclosure**. In 2001, for example, human rights groups persuaded the Securities and Exchange Commission to increase disclosure requirements, both for companies doing business in the United States and for those disallowed from doing business. The main purpose was to identify PetroChina as a corporation that was raising capital in order to operate in the Sudan, a country with nefarious human rights practices; the effect was that PetroChina went to Europe to raise money instead.

In 2002, a provision in the *Foreign Relations Authorization Act* required annual reports to Congress on actions taken by the executive branch to encourage respect for human rights. The *North Korean Human Rights Act* of 2004 authorized $136 million for humanitarian assistance, aid for North Korean refugees, and for nongovernmental organizations to promote human rights.

People in need are often misgoverned. More than two dozen laws authorize punitive **aid sanctions** either by prescreening recipients or by terminating aid (Table 11.3). Aid sanctions can also include negative votes on loans proposed to errant countries in multilateral institutions, such as the World Bank. However, unilateral aid sanctions are unlikely to be effective; often, Congress' purpose is to congratulate itself for acting morally when a president fails to take leadership in forging a multilateral sanction regime.

During the Cold War, little aid went from Western to Communist countries or to Communist-leaning countries. The *Mutual Security Act* of 1951, which authorized military assistance, had a provision that aid could be terminated if the UN General Assembly or Security Council determined that a country was guilty of an unacceptable threat or breach of the peace; North Korea was an immediate target; the prohibition continues to the present.

In 1960, the United States banned aid to Cuba, which had become aligned with the Soviet Union. The *Foreign Assistance Act* of 1961 was explicitly used to ban aid to Communist countries. In *The Hard Way to Peace* (1962), sociologist Amitai Etzioni (1929–) was among the earliest to propose that foreign aid should be reserved to democracies or to countries that are in the process of democratizing, though his suggestion fell on deaf ears at the time. Then in 1971, without specifying the reason, Congress cut off aid to Greece. Congress was clearly reacting to a military coup that toppled a democracy.

In 1973, the Committee on Foreign Affairs of the House of Representatives for the first time held hearings on the linkage between human rights and foreign aid, which continued to be denied to Greece up to 1974. What the members learned was so disappointing that legislative proposals to make **aid conditional** on human rights improvement were formulated, so Congress suggested that President Richard Nixon (1913–1994) deny economic and military aid to countries with political prisoners in the *Foreign Assistance Act* of 1973. After Nixon ignored the suggestion, the 1974 version of the law broadened to suggest that security assistance (military and police) be denied to countries that had political prisoners, practiced torture in interrogation or punishment, and otherwise had a systematic pattern of gross violations of human rights. Both were "sense of Congress" resolutions with no binding effect, but aid to Chile stopped in 1974 after a military coup led by Augusto Pinochet (1915–2006) ousted democratically elected President Salvador Allende (1908–1973).

The *Food for Peace Act* of 1954 originally provided a way to pay American farmers for food surpluses, which could be sent abroad to countries in need, even though the food was not always consumed for reasons of culture or spoilage en route. Later, the law was incorporated each year into the Foreign Assistance Act as the *International Development and Food Assistance Act* of 1975. In 1975, the *Harkin Amendment* to the act prohibited sending food aid to gross violators of human rights unless the food benefited those in need; if Congress objected to a country's food distribution system, the president had to submit a report within thirty days providing evidence that the food indeed went to the needy. Without such a report, the aid would have to stop. The first exclusion was imposed on Uganda because of the human rights violations of Idi Amin (1924–2003). Kampala's eligibility was restored in 1979 when he was forced out of office.

In 1976, the *Humphrey-Cranston Amendment* to the annual Foreign Assistance Act authorized the termination of economic aid to countries that massively violated human rights. In the same year, Congress overrode a veto by President Gerald Ford (1913–2006) and thereby institutionalized a human rights policy into the annual *International Security Assistance and Arms Export Control Act*. In 1977, while aid was terminated to Argentina and Zaïre (today, the Democratic Republic of the Congo), Brazil, El Salvador, Guatemala, and Uruguay refused military aid because of unfavorable State Department human rights reports in order to avoid the embarrassment of an announcement of aid cessation.

Nevertheless, there was much ambiguity in aid conditionality because of concern over the strength of Communist elements in a country. The law allowed aid to some human rights violators in three situations: (1) direct aid to benefit the needy, (2) extraordinary security needs, and (3) significant improvements in human rights. Indonesia was exempted because of a fear of the rise of Communist Vietnam without a counterweight in Southeast Asia. Iran was allowed aid under the repressive Shah Reza Pahlavi (1919–1980) because of its oil and its strategic position bordering on the Soviet Union. The United States usually ignored human rights problems in Liberia because of the country's huge Firestone Rubber investments and the fact that Liberia is the only country in Africa that grants landing and refueling privileges to American military aircraft. The Philippines received aid under President Ferdinand Marcos (1917–1989) because of the presence of U.S. bases and the presumed need to fight Communist guerrillas, who in turn capitalized on Marcos's numerous human rights violations to gain support. South Korea received aid under repressive regimes due to the possibility of an attack from North Korea.

In 1977, the *International Financial Assistance Act* mandated the application of human rights criteria to applicants for loans from the World Bank and other multilateral financial institutions. To the familiar prohibition to countries with widespread human rights abuses there was a new criterion: no loans were to be approved to countries that provide refuge to those who engage in aircraft hijacking; the obvious target was Uganda, which offered safe haven to Palestinians who hijacked a commercial airplane in 1976.

Under the broader restrictions of the *International Security and Development Cooperation Act* of 1980, Uganda and Zimbabwe were placed on a **watch list**. The list grew in 1981 to include Chile, El Salvador, and Nicaragua, and in 1985 expanded to Ethiopia, Liberia, Mozambique, the Philippines, South Africa, Sudan, and Tunisia.

In 1980, several foreign aid laws were amended to add the following type of human rights violation: "causing the disappearance of persons by the abduction and clandestine detention of those persons, and other flagrant denial of the right to life, liberty, or the security of person . . ." Congress also began to limit military aid and arms sales to specific states, usually for just one year, or to place countries on a watch list. Targeted over the years were Angola, Argentina, Bolivia, Brazil, Chile, El Salvador, Ethiopia, Guatemala, Haiti, Liberia, Mauritania, Morocco, Mozambique, Nicaragua, Paraguay, South Africa, South Korea, Tunisia, Uganda, Uruguay, and Zimbabwe.

In 1981, Ronald Reagan (1911–2004), on becoming president, announced that foreign aid would focus more on stopping international terrorism. One of his campaigns was against the Soviet Union as an "evil empire," another was to stop left-wing movements in Central America by supporting the El Salvador government's crackdown on insurgents as well as the Contras seeking to topple the democratically elected government of Nicaragua from a base in Honduras. However, the El Salvador government and the Contras committed many human rights abuses themselves.

From 1982–1985, the *Boland Amendment* to the Defense Appropriation Act prohibited the use of covert aid to the Contras. In 1983, Congress adopted the *Specter*

Amendment to the International Security and Development Cooperation Act, which required the president to certify progress in human rights conditions within El Salvador on a semiannual basis. The subtext of the amendment was to insist on the prosecution of the murderers of four American church workers in 1980 as a condition for the release of authorized American aid. The authorities in San Salvador then found scapegoats, and aid resumed. Later in 1983, Congress threatened to cut off all military aid because of evidence that death squads were operating with impunity. El Salvador then reassigned death squad leaders to postings outside the country, death squad activity was greatly reduced, and aid flowed again.

The *International Financial Institutions Act* of 1983, in superseding the International Financial Assistance Act of 1977, dropped the word "consistent" from the wording of the original act, which prohibited contributions to multilateral aid programs to countries that exhibit "a consistent pattern of gross violations of international recognized human rights." Dropping the word "consistent" had been interpreted by Reagan's subordinates as an escape clause to permit aid to El Salvador.

Under the annual Foreign Assistance Act, South Africa and Syria were denied aid in 1983. *Apartheid* was the reason for the former. Syria's military force in Lebanon was considered to be an unwelcome army of occupation.

In 1989, Congress passed the *International Narcotics Control Act* with four human rights requirements aimed primarily at cocaine-producing Colombia, where the military and police operated death squads. Aid was to be denied to any country that (1) was not a democracy, (2) where the military and police were engaged in a pattern of gross human rights violations, (3) the civilian exercised no control over the military, and (4) there was no improvement in human rights.

The *Support for the East European Democracy Act* of 1989 and the *Freedom Support Act* of 1992 were designed to assist former states of the Soviet Union to build democracies and market economies; the latter act superseded the former, adding the former Soviet republics of Central Asia (Kazakhstan, Kyrgyzstan, Tajikistan, Turkmenistan, Uzbekistan). However, any country that had a "consistent pattern of human rights violations" was considered ineligible for the assistance under the law unless there was evidence of "significant progress toward establishing democracy and respecting human rights." Azerbaijan, in particular, was denied aid because of systematic repression of its Armenian minority. A second aid precondition was the removal of Russian troops from Estonia, Latvia, and Lithuania.

The *Leahy Amendment* to the Foreign Operations Appropriation Act of 1997 banned security aid and training to any country with an army or police force that engaged in gross human rights. The aim was to stop aid to Colombia until the government rooted out death squads from security forces.

In 1998, Congress passed the *International Religious Freedom Act*, which called upon presidents to invoke aid sanctions against countries that engage in or tolerate violations of religious freedom, such as restrictions on assembly, accompanied by flagrant denials of the rights to life, liberty, or the security of persons, including torture. In 2004, China, Eritrea, Indonesia, Iran, Laos, Myanmar, North Korea, Pakistan, Saudi Arabia, Sri Lanka, Sudan, and Vietnam were designated by the Secretary of State as countries of particular concern.

Also in 1998, the *Iraq Liberation Act* officially endorsed regime change, citing human rights abuses, but prohibited the use of force to accomplish that goal. Instead, funds were distributed to seven groups opposing rule by Saddam Hussein.

In 2000, Congress passed the *Victims of Trafficking and Violence Protection Act* to focus on human trafficking, specifically "to protect children from exploitation, abuse, or forced conscription into military or paramilitary services." The statute, which is part of the larger Trafficking Victims Protection Act, quantifies the problem as affecting 700,000 (mostly girls) per year, of which 50,000 enter the United States to perform labor involuntarily, including sex slaves. Each year the president must make a determination based on evidence collected by the State Department regarding compliance with international treaties banning human trafficking; nonhumanitarian aid is banned to any country that condones or tolerates human trafficking. In 2005, President Bush imposed full sanctions on Cuba, Myanmar, and North Korea for failure to comply. Although Ecuador, Kuwait, and Saudi Arabia were also cited, they were allowed to receive specific aid aimed at promoting democratic reform, whereas Cambodia and Venezuela were restricted to democracy-building and humanitarian aid. Bolivia, Jamaica, Qatar, Sudan, Togo, and the United Arab Emirates were congratulated for taking positive steps toward compliance but remained on the watch list.

Aid conditionality can also be contrary to human rights goals. Although the International Criminal Court (ICC) in The Hague has been celebrated as a landmark event in the history of international human rights by many countries, the United States government has opposed the body. One form of opposition is embodied in the *American Service-Members' Protection Act* of 2001, which authorizes the president to cut off foreign aid to needy countries for their support of the ICC.

In 2001, Congress passed the *Zimbabwe Democracy and Economic Recovery Act* to oppose any loans or debt cancellations to the country, where an undemocratic government was dispossessing Europeans who owned and farmed agricultural land, thereby producing serious food shortages. Among the sanctions were travel restrictions and the seizure of the assets of President Robert Mugabe (1924–) and others responsible for the breakdown of law and order in the country. Some $26 million was appropriated to assist those losing their lands and to support opponents of the regime.

The *Sudan Peace Act* of 2002 not only condemned the Khartoum government for engaging in genocide in the civil war with the Christian south but also for allowing a slave trade to flourish. Some $100 million was authorized to supply food to the beleaguered Africans in the south. The *North Korean Human Rights Act* of 2004 provided that aid to North Korea must be contingent on human rights improvements. Specifically, were Pyongyang to make substantial progress in addressing human rights issues, nonhumanitarian aid would flow to meet the country's energy needs and food aid could increase, provided that there was more transparency in regard to those receiving the food. In response, North Korea turned down additional aid, considering the law to be evidence of a "hostile" policy.

Because much foreign aid tends to involve contracts from governments to private sector agencies in order to provide direct services to individuals, such as disease inoculations, the sanctions reviewed above tend to be more symbolic than punitive.

Food aid, for instance, tends to respond more to agricultural surpluses in the United States than to hunger in the world. One estimate is that at least 60 percent of foreign aid never leaves the country. American foreign aid amounts were steadily cut over the years, especially after the end of the Cold War, though they increased after the terrorist attacks on September 11, 2001. For example, American ties with the Indonesian military, severed in 1999 following the brutal action of the latter in East Timor, were restored in 2005 so that Washington could strengthen Jakarta's anti-terrorism capabilities.

ECONOMIC MEASURES: TRADE

Foreign aid is supposed to be a temporary measure that will enable a poorer country to develop into a self-sustaining economy. If aid is successful, a country can rely on the internal market as well as derive income from foreign trade. Aid can then stop. Whereas aid sanctions tend to be microeconomic, trade-related measures imposed on an entire country or an economic sector of that country can have a macroeconomic effect.

Proactive trade policies can be applied to promote Third World economic development by extending **foreign credit**; providing **loans, loan guarantees, insurance**; granting **licenses**; and making government **purchases** of goods from other countries. In addition, treaties can extend **most-favored-nation** (MFN) status to trade partners, that is, apply uniform tariffs to goods imported from other countries (or the lowest tariff in case there are different tariff schedules) in exchange for having other countries import goods on the same basis. World Trade Organization members apply MFN, now known as **normal trade relations** (NTR), to one another. From 1994, presidents have given annual waivers to most countries formerly considered ineligible for MFN. Currently, the United States has normal trade relations with all countries but Afghanistan, Cuba, Georgia, Kyrgyzstan, Laos, North Korea, Russia, and Serbia. Although they have not technically lost MFN/NTR status, various sanctions are now imposed on Iran, Myanmar, Syria, the Sudan, and Zimbabwe.

In response to the call for a New International Economic Order, the United States authorized a **generalized system of preferences** (GSP) scheme, with very low tariffs for certain goods imported from the Third World. Currently, the United States has designated some 4,650 products from 144 beneficiary countries and territories as duty-free.

Punitive trade measures, known as **sanctions**, can limit or cancel all the various trade benefits. For example, one country might either raise a tax (a tariff) on imported goods made by child labor or establish a quota (a nontariff barrier) on the estimated number of products estimated to be manufactured by child labor.

The most severe trade sanction is an **embargo** with a particular country, that is, a ban on imports and exports; a **boycott** is only a refusal to import. Businesses are unlikely to participate in boycotts or embargoes if they will lose money; instead, they may engage in "sanction busting." Countries less interested in human rights might sell the same goods to the errant country, thereby nullifying the boycott. For example, when the United States suspended grain sales to the Soviet Union in the 1980s to protest the Soviet invasion of Afghanistan, Argentina sold grain to fill the gap. Unless a restriction applies to military or strategic goods, where one country has a monopoly on a particular technology or spare parts, an economic boycott is unlikely to be effective.

Corporations that fail to adopt a code of conduct also risk **citizen boycotts**. While South Africa still maintained *apartheid*, many private organizations urged a boycott of Shell Oil Company, the only supplier of petroleum to the country. Citizen boycotts have been organized over the years, often by trade unions. Currently, boycotts are organized against Coca-Cola and Nestlé, two corporations involved in lawsuits over human rights violations.

Yet another way to end economic contact with a country is to engage in **divestment**, that is, for businesses to liquidate all investments from an offending state, though presumably a seller must find a buyer to liquidate an asset, and the effect may be to sell at a loss. One by one, many universities divested their endowment portfolio of companies doing business in South Africa during the 1980s, and the same is taking place in regard to the recalcitrant government of Myanmar today.

Washington has authorized trade sanctions from the early years of the republic (Table 11.4). In 1795, Congress passed the *National Emergencies Act* to authorize the president to take action to protect the national interest. The law, which does not specify the use of economic sanctions or identify human rights issues, provides a procedure to single out a particular country as a gross violator of human rights.

The impressments of sailors by British ships led to passage of the *Nonimportation Act* of 1806 (as amended by the *Embargo Act* of 1807 and the *Nonintercourse Act* of 1809). The legislation provided a pretext for Britain to launch the War of 1812.

Later in the century, human rights were for the first time a consideration in regard to international trade. Goods produced by prison labor were banned by the *Trade Act* of 1890.

Much current legislation dealing with trade sanctions is modeled on the *Trading With the Enemy Act* of 1917, which was applied to Germany and its allies in World Wars I and II and later to the Soviet Union and its allies in the Cold War. In 1963, for example, Cuba was designated as an enemy state under the Trading With the Enemy Act. The Cuban trade embargo continues to the present, although the UN General Assembly voted to condemn the blockage in 2005 by 182–4.

In 1935, Congress amended the *Neutrality Act* (in response to Italy's invasion of Abyssinia) to prohibit American citizens from selling arms to belligerents in international wars. An amendment in 1936 (due to the Spanish Civil War) bans providing credits and loans to belligerents in civil wars, and a 1939 amendment outlaws such war materials as oil and steel. In recent years, the law has been invoked to investigate American residents who may support terrorist groups, including expatriates in Southern California who favor the overthrow of the current governments in Cambodia and Vietnam and José Padilla, who was convicted of aiding terrorists in Bosnia and Chechnya.

Perhaps the earliest explicit use of economic sanctions as a response to human rights violations occurred in 1967, when President Lyndon Johnson (1908–1973) issued Executive Order 11322, authorizing a boycott of Rhodesia. His action served to implement a United Nations resolution.

TABLE 11.3 SOME AMERICAN LAWS ALLOWING AID SANCTIONS ON COUNTRIES VIOLATING HUMAN RIGHTS

Title of Statute	Passed
Mutual Security Act	1951
Foreign Assistance Act[a]	1961
International Development and Food Assistance Act	1973
International Security Assistance and Arms Export Control Act	1975
Harkin Amendment	1975
Humphrey-Cranston Amendment	1976
International Financial Assistance Act	1977
International Security Assistance Act	1978
International Security and Development Cooperation Act	1980
Boland Amendment[a]	1982
Specter Amendment	1983
International Financial Institutions Act[a]	1983
International Narcotics Control Act	1989
Support for the East European Democracy (SEED) Act	1989
Freedom Support Act[b]	1992
Leahy Amendment[a]	1997
International Religious Freedom Act	1998
Iraq Liberation Act	1998
Victims of Trafficking and Victims Protection Act	2000
American Service-Members' Protection Act	2001
USA Patriot Act[c]	2001
Zimbabwe Democracy and Economic Recovery Act	2001
Sudan Peace Act	2002
Belarus Democracy Act	2003
North Korean Human Rights Act	2004

[a]Sanctions were authorized in later versions of the law.
[b]The full title is Freedom for Russia and Emerging Eurasian Democracies and Open Markets Support Act.
[c]The full title is provided in Table 11.1.

In 1974, Congress made a stern statement in the annual Trade Act by including the *Jackson–Vanik Amendment*, cosponsored by Senator Henry Jackson (1912–1983) and Representative Charles Vanik (1913–), which provided that MFN status could be denied to a country with a non-market economy, especially one that either restricts emigration rights or fails to cooperate in identifying soldiers missing in action. The principal target was the Soviet Union, which was forbidding Jews from emigrating; in addition, Cambodia, Laos, North Korea, and Vietnam were encouraged to cooperate in searching for American MIAs. When Poland was placed under martial law in 1982, Washington withdrew MFN from Warsaw in protest. Other than Communist countries, MFN status over the years was denied to Afghanistan and

TABLE 11.4 SOME AMERICAN LAWS ALLOWING TRADE SANCTIONS ON COUNTRIES VIOLATING HUMAN RIGHTS

Title of statute	Passed	Human rights violation
Nonimportation Act	1806	Impressments of sailors
Embargo Act	1807	Impressments of sailors
Nonintercourse Act	1809	Impressments of sailors
Trade Act	1890	Prison labor
Trading With the Enemy Act	1917	Human rights and terrorism
Neutrality Act[a]	1935	War assistance
Trade Act (Jackson-Vanik Amendment)	1974	Human rights
International Security Assistance and Arms Export Control Act	1975	Human rights
Export Administration Amendments Act	1977	Terrorism
International Emergency Economic Powers Act	1977	Human rights and terrorism
Comprehensive Anti-Apartheid Act	1986	*Apartheid*
Cuban Democracy Act	1992	Lack of civil and political rights
Cuban Liberty and Democratic Solidarity Act (Helms-Burton Act)	1996	Lack of civil and political rights
Iran and Libya Sanctions Act (D'Amato Act)	1996	Terrorism
Cohen-Feinstein Amendment	1996	Political repression in Burma
International Religious Freedom Act	1998	Religious persecution
African Growth and Opportunity Act	2000	Human rights
United States — Caribbean Basin Trade Partnership Act	2000	Human rights
Trade Sanctions Reform and Export Enhancement Act	2000	Political repression and terrorism
Zimbabwe Democracy and Economic Recovery Act	2001	Political repression
Terrorism Risk Insurance Act	2002	Terrorism
Burmese Freedom and Democracy Act	2003	Political repression
Syria Accountability and Lebanese Sovereignty Restoration Act	2003	Undermining democracy
Clean Diamond Trade Act	2003	Human rights

[a]Amended later.

Serbia. In 1984, violation of workers' rights became another criterion for denying MFN status. Sanctions still apply to Russia today.

The *International Security Assistance and Arms Export Control Act* of 1975 not only authorized aid cutoffs but also trade embargoes. Military weapons would not be sold to countries with unacceptable human rights records.

The National Emergencies Act and the Trading With the Enemy Act were superseded in 1977 by the *International Emergency Economic Powers Act*, which in recent years has been interpreted to apply to human rights and terrorism issues. As further amended by the *Trade Sanctions Reform and Export Enhancement Act* of 2000, the president was authorized to designate a country as constituting a "national emergency," whereupon the Treasury Department's Office of Foreign Assets Control is able to **freeze assets** or to establish **trade embargoes** through a variety of means.

Over the years, Congressional legislation has identified particular countries or specific issues for economic sanctions but has preferred more limited sanctions over total embargoes. For example, when the Iranian government refused to assist in releasing diplomats who were held hostage at the American embassy in Tehran in 1980, Washington responded by freezing all Iranian assets in the United States. The assets are still frozen today.

When President Ronald Reagan (1911–2004) took office, terrorism was added to the list of serious human rights violations. In 1981, Iran was placed on the list of states supporting international terrorism, thus invoking sanctions that prohibited aid, loans, and weapons sales to Tehran. In 1987, the boycott was extended to imports of any goods or services from Iran. In 1997, President Bill Clinton (1946–) imposed comprehensive sanctions on Iran, prohibiting all commercial and financial transactions with Tehran, though in 2000 exceptions were allowed for imports of carpets, caviar, dried fruits, and nuts.

In 1986, after twenty-five states and 164 local governments adopted **selective purchasing** laws to stop business with corporations operating in South Africa, Congress enacted over the veto of President Reagan the *Comprehensive Anti-Apartheid Act*, the subtext of which was a rejection of the policy of constructive engagement. The law stated that United States government should employ diplomatic, economic, political, and other means to encourage the South African government to end *apartheid*, to establish democracy, and to respect human rights. Among the sanctions were prohibitions on licenses, loans, as well as trade (imports of armaments, coal, gold coins, petroleum, sugar, textiles, uranium, and any trade involving agencies enforcing *apartheid*). South African Airlines, for example, was not allowed to fly to the United States. The 1986 law also adopted the Sullivan principles, as discussed in Chapter 6.

The International Emergency Economic Powers Act was applied in 1988 following the Libyan-sponsored terrorist attack on Pan American flight 103. In response, the United States froze Libyan assets, and banned all trade and financial dealings with Libya. Then in 1992, Libya was added to the list of terrorist states, resulting in a ban on exports of petroleum, military, or aviation equipment to Libya, commercial flights to or from Libya, and restrictions on Libyan financial activities.

In 1989, following the brutal crackdown on demonstrators near Beijing's Tiananmen Square, many Anglo-European countries, including the United States, began a boycott of Chinese goods. Meanwhile, as China developed a market economy in the 1980s, Beijing had been seeking MFN status. In 1990, nevertheless, President George H.W. Bush granted China a waiver to the MFN prohibition, and a majority in Congress did not vote down the waiver. Bush, of course, hoped that China would not oppose the Gulf War of 1991, but interests supporting MFN for China inside the United States included the National Association of Wheat Growers, some one hundred trade associations and companies in the Business Coalition for U.S.-China Trade as well as the law firm of Jones, Day, Reavis and Pogue, which was paid by China to lobby for its interests. Congressional efforts to impose sanctions in response to human rights issues were twice vetoed by President Bush. However, when Chinese goods produced by forced laborers were disallowed by customs authorities in accordance with the Slavery Convention of 1926, the result was a backlash from Beijing. China was less cooperative in diplomacy with the United States whenever trade sanction threats were issued and more cooperative when threats were not a part of the recent diplomatic environment.

In 1992, the *Cuban Democracy Act* restricted arms sales to any country trading with Cuba. In short, the United States established a **secondary boycott**.

In 1995, President Clinton announced his intention to impose punitive tariffs on more than $1 billion of Chinese goods, the largest trade sanction in American history, because of piracy of American films, music, and software; within three weeks Beijing caved in to forestall the imposition of tariffs. On the same date when China agreed to combat piracy, Clinton announced in an apparent *quid pro quo* that he would separate American trade policy toward China from human rights concerns. Later in the same year, the United States lobbied to have the UN Commission on Human Rights stop issuing condemnations of Beijing's human rights record. The lobbying produced a 21–20 vote favorable to China.

The year 1996 was a banner year for passage of legislation that authorizes economic boycotts. The *Cuban Liberty and Democratic Solidarity Act*, cosponsored by Senator Jesse Helms, Jr., (1921) and Representative Dan Burton (1938–) and sometimes called the Libertad Act, prohibits trade with any company doing business with Cuba; European firms were the principal targets. Although restrictions on trade with Cuba began in opposition to Communist rule, human rights issues were stressed after the end of the Cold War.

The second 1996 law, the *Iran and Libya Sanctions Act*, authorized sanctions against non-American companies that provided new investments over $40 million for the development of petroleum resources in Iran or Libya and violated a UN trade boycott of Libya in arms, certain oil equipment, and civil aviation services. Sanctions consisted of a denial of Export-Import Bank assistance, trade licenses, bank loans or credits, government contracts, and some or all imports from the violating company. The act, which was to expire in five years, was renewed in 2001, but now applies only to Iran. When Libya's policies changed dramatically in 2004, sanctions were lifted.

HISTORIC EVENT 11.2   THE RESULTS OF BURMA'S ELECTION ARE IGNORED (1990)

In 1962, a military coup ended democratic rule in Burma. In 1988, the streets of the capital, Rangoon, were filled with protesters, including Aung San Suu Kyi (1945–), the daughter of Aung San (1915–1947), who negotiated Burma's independence from Britain in 1947. With the country on the verge of civil war, another military coup was launched to squelch the protests. However, the new military leaders agreed to hold free elections in 1990. Overwhelmingly, Aung San Suu Kyi's political party (the National League for Democracy) won, but the military leaders refused to respect the results of the election. Aung San Suu Kyi was first placed under house arrest in 1990 and has been released and rearrested several times since. The military government, which changed the name of the country to Myanmar in 1989, arrested many other members of the opposition and has steadfastly refused to hold elections even since.

The third 1996 law focused on Myanmar. The Massachusetts legislature banned contractors with the state government that did business with Myanmar in a law that was modeled on similar legislation at the state and local level in the 1980s regarding South Africa that implemented UN resolutions. Three months later, Congress adopted the *Cohen-Feinstein Amendment*, which authorized the president to have the power to prohibit new private investment in Myanmar as long as the government continued to engage in large-scale political repression or to hold Aung San Suu Kyi under house arrest. In 1998, the Massachusetts law and similar laws in various cities were declared unconstitutional in *National Foreign Trade Council v Baker* (26FSupp2d287) for interfering with executive prerogatives to be the exclusive branch involved in making foreign policy, a ruling affirmed by the Supreme Court during 1999 in *Crosby v National Foreign Trade Council* (530US363). The court also cited the Cohen-Feinstein Amendment as a basis for declaring that national laws preempt state laws in matters of foreign affairs. In any case, the effect was that Apple Computer, Eastman Kodak, Philips Electronics, and Hewlett-Packard were among the companies that withdrew their businesses from Myanmar.

By executive order, President Clinton imposed economic sanctions on the Sudan in 1997 for supporting international terrorism, destabilizing neighboring governments, and committing human rights violations, including slavery and the denial of religious freedom. Subsequently, five state legislatures followed suit, threatening to end investments by state pension funds in companies that do business in the Sudan.

In 1998, the *International Religious Freedom Act* authorized trade embargoes on countries that persecuted religious minorities. Further details are noted above.

In 2000, two initiatives for trade cooperation were adopted – the *African Growth and Opportunity Act* and the *United States–Caribbean Basin Trade Partnership Act*. Provisions in both laws restrict cooperation with countries determined to be violating human rights. In 2001, sanctions on Zimbabwe for undermining democratic processes were authorized under the *Zimbabwe Democracy and Economic Recovery Act*.

In reaction to the September 11 attack, the *Terrorism Risk Insurance Act* of 2002 permits seizure of bank and portfolio accounts of international terrorists. However, the law was struck down by a federal court when assets of a domestic organization were arbitrarily seized in *Humanitarian Law Project v Gonzales* (380FSupp2d1134) because the criterion for designating an organization as "terrorist" was vague, as noted in Chapter 7.

HISTORIC EVENT 11.3 LIBERIA'S SECOND CIVIL WAR (1999–2004)

After a civil war from 1989–1996, Charles Taylor's rebel forces, trained in Libya, overthrew the Liberian government, and he won an election in 1997 to become president. Taylor, however, employed brutal methods. A second civil war arose in 1999, when the Liberians United for Reconciliation and Democracy force entered Liberia from the north, with support from the government of neighboring Guinea, to depose Taylor. Several competing ethnic groups then began to struggle to control the natural resources of the country. In 2003, a second rebel group, the Movement for Democracy in Liberia, moved into the country from the south. Soon, the capital, Monrovia, was besieged and bombarded. After the rebels and the government reached a peace agreement, Nigerian troops of the Economic Community of West African States entered as peacekeepers, Taylor resigned and was granted asylum in Nigeria. His vice president, Moses Blah (1947–), then continued to struggle against the rebels until 2003, when peacekeeping troops authorized by the UN Security Council replaced the Nigerian troops and installed a transitional government. Taylor loyalists were finally subdued in 2004, and elections were held in 2005. The victor, Ellen Johnson-Sirleaf (1938–), took office as president in 2006. Taylor, meanwhile, was charged by a war crimes tribunal in Sierra Leone in 2003 with the crime of supporting rebels in that country whose tactics included mutilations, rape, forcing children to serve as soldiers, and committing other atrocities. In 2006, Taylor was released and then arrested in Nigeria, and handed over to the Sierra Leone court, which then obtained permission from the International Criminal Court to use its facilities in The Hague for his trial, which was scheduled to begin in 2008. In all, at least 150,000 Liberians died in the civil war, and two-thirds of the population was displaced, either internally or by seeking asylum abroad.

The year 2003 brought another wave of economic sanctions. Further repression in Myanmar led to the passage of the *Burmese Freedom and Democracy Act*, which requires comprehensive economic sanctions. Under the *Syria Accountability and Lebanese Sovereignty Restoration Act*, Damascus was cited for undermining the stability of Iraq and Lebanon; in the latter case. The law specifically objected to the presence of Syrian troops in Lebanon.

In 2003, Congress also adopted the *Clean Diamond Trade Act* to implement provisions of a multilateral agreement to stop serious human rights violations in Liberia and Sierra Leone, in which paramilitary rebels had been using uncut diamonds to purchase military armaments. The law prohibited the importation of rough diamonds from either country, whereupon the illicit trade shifted from diamonds to logs and timber. The same law put a $2 million bounty on the capture of Charles Taylor (1948–), Liberia's president, who left the country and was granted asylum in Nigeria, although the Liberian civil war continued with forces still loyal to him. In 2004, accordingly, sanctions were imposed on Taylor loyalists.

Thus, some economic sanctions are comprehensive; others are more limited in scope. Although the President can declare a "national emergency" and impose economic sanctions, the declaration is a fictional claim in most instances, since the United States is not at war except for the "war on drugs" and the "war on terrorism." Comprehensive American trade sanctions now apply to Cuba, Iran, Myanmar, North Korea, the Sudan, Syria, Zimbabwe, the Cali Cartel of Colombia and various identified drug kingpins, as well as against certain terrorist groups, notably Al-Qaida. More specific trade sanctions apply today to China (military sales) and Serbia (blocked assets). Nevertheless, the extent of economic restrictions is a mere drop in the bucket compared to all the international transactions of the United States.

Many skeptics, pointing for example to the survival of the Cuban government under Castro, argue that economic sanctions do not work. Nevertheless, multilateral sanctions imposed on South Africa played an important role in ending *apartheid* in South Africa. Sanctions reportedly convinced Serbia to turn over President Slobodan Milošević to The Hague in 2001 for trial at the international court on war crimes in the former Yugoslavia. Sanctions on Libya may have led the country to surrender two terrorists to a Scottish Court in 1999 and to abandon a nuclear weapons program in 2004.

Nevertheless, economic sanctions work slowly, and many corporations get around sanctions by using third parties. Countries subject to asset freezes will often relocate their assets to Swiss bank accounts in advance of the decision to impose sanctions. Because many observers are understandably impatient whenever millions of lives are in imminent jeopardy, the tendency for sanctions to fail to bring about the desired behavior will provoke some countries to contemplate military action.

DISCUSSION TOPIC 11.1 CAN NONMILITARY SANCTIONS EVER BE EFFECTIVE?

Reviewing examples of diplomatic, legal, and economic sanctions, when are they most and least likely to be effective? What kinds of nonmilitary sanctions should be used – and how? Why not threaten or employ military sanctions first?

MILITARY ACTION

Individual countries can use four types of military action in response to human rights problems. The principal proactive methods are (1) to participate in international **peacekeeping forces** that have human rights components and (2) to enforce **no-fly zones** that serve to prevent a country from attacking its own people. The punitive methods are (3) the **threat of force** and (4) the **use of force**, even in self-defense. Both punitive methods may violate the UN Charter, which declares that the United Nations has the exclusive right to authorize the use of force in order to settle interstate disputes, although military reprisals are an exception.

The United States has indeed supplied peacekeeping forces for the United Nations on several occasions. In 2005, American troops began to provide logistical support through the North Atlantic Treaty Organization to the African Union peacekeeping force in Darfur.

No-fly zones were established over Iraq between the two Gulf Wars from 1991–2003 and Bosnia in 1994 to deter further ethnic massacres. Although the United States continued to monitor the two UN-authorized no-fly zones over the northern and southern parts of Iraq to deter genocidal aerial massacres against Kurds and Shiites, respectively, Washington turned down a proposal from Saudi Arabian intelligence to establish a third zone over central Iraq. On several occasions, the Baghdad regime bombed insurgent groups that were acting to overthrow the Iraqi government.

American coercive diplomacy has sometimes **threatened the use of force**, though only occasionally in regard to human rights issues. In 1854, for example, Greytown declared itself independent of Nicaragua and destroyed American-owned property. An American official went to negotiate but was roughed up by a member of a crowd. A U.S. warship then went, demanding redress for the damage and an apology for the injuries to the diplomat. When there was no reply to a twenty-four hour warning, the town was bombarded. In 1979, after American diplomats were held hostage in Tehran during 1979 contrary to international law, Washington mounted a rescue attempt as a reprisal in 1980, albeit unsuccessfully. Terrorist attacks occasioned military counterattacks against Libya (for bombing a Pan American airplane) during 1988 and against locations reputed to be Al-Qaida training camps in Afghanistan (for bombing American embassies in Kenya and Tanzania) during 1998.

From 1950–1953, the United States and several other countries were authorized by the UN Security Council to defend South Korea from North Korean military aggression, a situation in which the right of self-determination was at issue. The United States has cited the principle of self-determination in **supplying military personnel** several times, from the defense of Egypt from an Anglo-French-Israeli attack during 1956 to Iraq's attack on Kuwait in 1991. However, critics of American foreign policy point out that anti-Communist justifications were used to topple democratic governments in Guatemala (1953), Iran (1953), the Dominican Republic (1965), Panamá (1989), and elsewhere. In 2001, a multilateral force headed by the United States invaded Afghanistan to drive out the ruling party, the Taliban, for its role in harboring personnel and training camps of Al-Qaida, which claimed credit for the attacks on the Pentagon and the World Trade Center on September 11, 2001. Afghan women then shed their *burkas* and were free to vote in subsequent elections.

The Authorization for Use of Military Force Against Iraq resolution of 2002 gave President Bush the authority "to use all necessary and appropriate force . . . to prevent any future acts of international terrorism against the United States . . ." In a secret document, as disclosed by journalist Bob Woodward (1943–), the American objectives were as follows: (1) eliminate Iraq's weapons of mass destruction, (2) prevent Iraq from threatening the Middle East and beyond, (3) maintain Iraq's territorial integrity, (4) cut links between the Iraq government and international terrorism, (5) deter Iran and Syria from aiding Iraq, (6) minimize disruption in oil markets, and (7) change from tyrannical rule to pluralistic democratic governance. In 2003, an Anglo-American coalition attacked and toppled Saddam Hussein from power.

After military intervention, there can be **military occupation**, the terms of which are governed by the Fourth Geneva Convention. Such multilateral military occupations as those of Austria, Germany, and Japan after World War II, can boast more success in promoting human rights than the American and Russian occupations of the two parts of Korea after World War II. The victorious armies in Afghanistan quickly installed a new government in Afghanistan during 2001, whereupon the UN Security Council authorized an International Security Assistance Force, including

American troops, to provide stability for the new government. However, the American victory in Iraq during 2003 did not install a new government. After the UN authorized an Anglo-American occupation authority, insurgents mounted a challenge to the occupation even before a new government was elected. Neither occupation forces nor the new Iraqi government have been able to stop violence that some observers have characterized as a civil war between a variety of Sunni and Shiite sectarian groups. The outcome in Iraq remains uncertain.

CONCLUSION

As the world's sole superpower in the twenty-first century, the United States role in regard to international human rights is ambivalent. The long tradition of proactive support for human rights clashes with the power to impose punitive measures, and disagreements on appropriate measures fill the political discourse today. American leaders rely on coercive diplomacy now more than in the past. The strong legal tradition provides victims of human rights abuse with an opportunity to have their day in court. Although American foreign aid is greater than any other country in the world in dollar terms, the ratio of aid to national income is 0.2 percent, far below the UN Millennium goal of 0.7 percent. Congress has passed a maze of aid and trade sanctions over the years, often when the geopolitical ambitions of the president ignore human rights issues. Finally, because the UN authorizes military action in regard to human rights primarily in peacekeeping, a frustrated Washington sometimes embarks on unauthorized military action in order to defend the right of self-determination. Criticisms of the United States, nevertheless, abound because a refusal of the UN to back American military adventures deprives them of legitimacy in the eyes of many countries in the world.

DISCUSSION TOPIC 11.2 DOES WASHINGTON HAVE AN EXEMPLARY RECORD IN PROMOTING HUMAN RIGHTS?

International human rights were in the forefront of concern when the United States constitution was written, as the focus was on state-sponsored terrorism in North Africa. A Bill of Rights was written as the first series of amendments to the constitution. Subsequently, the United States played a constructive role in the development of the original Geneva Convention, the Hague Conferences, the League of Nations, and the United Nations. Since the United States became a superpower, some observers believe that Washington has preferred geopolitics to exercising moral leadership. Do you agree? What are the plusses and minuses of American foreign policy in regard to human rights?

CHAPTER 12

European approaches to international human rights

Although European countries employ the four basic tools of diplomatic, judicial, economic, and military methods to cope with human rights problems around the world, a comparison of the human rights policies of individual countries is beyond the scope of the present volume. Nevertheless, several significant developments deserve mention.

Diplomatically, the primary achievement after World War II was the dismantling of the colonial empires of Belgium, Britain, France, and Portugal. The professional diplomacy of European countries deserves considerable praise. For example France's sponsorship of an international conference during 1991 enabled Cambodia to transition from civil war to UN-administered elections.

In 1931, London launched the British Commonwealth of Nations as a diplomatic framework including governments of most former colonies, dropping the word "British" in 1949. The organization also has welcomed countries that were never British colonies, such as Mozambique, but has suspended countries from membership when democratic or human rights have been violated (Fiji, Nigeria, Pakistan, Rhodesia, South Africa and Zimbabwe). In 1991, the forum issued the Harare Declaration, committing the organization to the goals of democracy and good government.

The diplomatic approach to human rights took an unusual turn in 2001, when as Israeli's ambassador-designate to Denmark, Carmi Gillon (1950–), was quoted on Copenhagen television as supporting the use of "moderate physical pressure" on terrorists. There was such indignation over his remark, interpreted as an endorsement of torture, that Danish authorities threatened to arrest him if he ever entered the country. Tel Aviv then withdrew his appointment.

The **legal** approach has also been used by countries that have passed laws claiming universal jurisdiction over serious human rights violations committed elsewhere, and criminal justice systems have been appropriately galvanized. Hundreds of cases have been filed in European courts, since individuals and nongovernmental organizations have standing to file complaints and do not have to await the action of state prosecutors to initiate court action.

Suits filed by former Nazi slave laborers in Eastern Europe were settled after the fall of the Berlin Wall, when the German government offered nearly $5 billion in compensation, half for property (from artwork to jewelry) that was seized during the war. Claims filed by the victims after World War II were not processed earlier because the West German government had no relations with formerly Communist governments.

The most famous case emerged in 1998, when Spanish Judge Baltasar Garzón (1955–) issued an arrest warrant that was served on Senator-for-Life Augusto Pinochet (1915–2006) in Britain for crimes committed against Spanish nationals in Chile while he was head of state from 1973–1989, ironically for violating a treaty that his government had ratified. Pinochet, who was receiving medical treatment at the time of his arrest, claimed immunity from prosecution as the head of a sovereign state. In 1999, however, the House of Lords issued a ruling that he had no such immunity as a former head of state, based on the International Convention Against Torture and Other Cruel, Inhuman or Degrading Treatment or Punishment, which requires each state party to take effective measures to prevent and punish acts of torture. The United Kingdom then had three choices: (1) Put Pinochet on trial in Britain if British citizens had been tortured in Chile. (2) Extradite him to Spain, as requested. (3) Extradite him to Chile, provided that the Santiago government wanted to try him. The Chilean government then intervened. London sent Pinochet to Santiago for trial upon conclusion of his medical treatment, but he died before his trial.

The Pinochet arrest, the first ever to involve a former head of state for human rights offenses, stimulated hundreds of similar lawsuits throughout Europe. One of the most notable cases is also from in Spain. In 1999, after issuing Pinochet's arrest warrant, Judge Garzón indicted ninety-nine military offers, including retired naval officer Ricardo Miguel Cavallo (1946–), also known as Serpico, on behalf of Spanish victims of torture in the junta's "dirty war." Because the military stepped down in 1983 on condition that they would be accorded immunity from prosecution for their offenses, Cavallo and the others could not be tried in Buenos Aires. In 2000, Mexican authorities seized Cavallo, who in 2003 was extradited to Spain, where he was put on trial in 2005.

In 2001, a French judge also issued warrants for the arrest of Cavallo and other former Chilean officials; charged with responsibility for the disappearance of French citizens during the Pinochet era, they have never been tried in court. In connection with the case, the judge summoned former Secretary of State Henry Kissinger (1923–), then staying at a Paris hotel, for questioning regarding the American role in the killing of Chilean opposition leaders in 1973, a role acknowledged in 2003 by Secretary of State Colin Powell (1937–). Kissinger quickly left town and also declined an invitation in 2002 by Judge Garzón, who sought specifics about the Chilean coup. (In 2005, an American court dismissed *Schneider v Kissinger* (412F3d190), which sued the former Secretary of State for his alleged role in the Chilean coup during 1973.)

In 2003, thirty-four alleged Al-Qaida operatives were indicted in Spain for terrorist acts, including three charged as accomplices of the World Trade Center bombings of 9/11/2001 that killed several persons of Spanish nationality. When the trial ended in 2005, one defendant was convicted of conspiracy to commit murder on 9/11 and for heading a terrorist group, nineteen were convicted of belonging to and collaborating with a terrorist group, and one was found not guilty. The prosecutor then told the press that the trial proved that the legal approach to combat terrorism is preferable to "wars and detention camps," obviously contrasting Spain's counter-terrorism methods with those of the United States. In a similar case in Germany, a 9/11 conspirator was found guilty, but on appeal the ruling was overturned because the trial was deemed unfair because the United States would not release crucial testimony on the pretext that such information would reveal ongoing investigative methods.

Belgium for a while surpassed Spain in implementing the universal jurisdiction principle. Among complaints against leading officials in seventeen countries, some were filed by persons characterized by critics as "opportunists" who were using the vagueness of the law to make political capital, and few cases led to indictments. A ruling on state immunity ultimately prohibited prosecutions of sitting foreign officials. Among the cases quashed thereby is one filed in 2001 by ten Cubans against Fidel Castro (1926–), claiming that he committed crimes against humanity against them, notably false imprisonment and torture. The suit also charged that some 100,000 Cubans have been tortured over the past four decades.

Brussels, nevertheless, indicted several United States officials for war crimes relating to the Iraq War of 2003. The Belgians first referred the case against the commanding general, Tommy R. Franks (1945–), to the U.S. Department of Justice, implicitly claiming that Belgium had jurisdiction in the first place. Belgian actions against the United States so infuriated President Bush that Washington threatened to move the headquarters of the North Atlantic Treaty Organization (NATO) from Brussels. In response to the threat, the Belgian government revised the law to apply only when Belgian citizens are victims of human rights abuse, and cases against most defendants were dismissed in the Belgian Supreme Court. Only cases involving Chad, Congo (Kinshasa), and Guatemala survived the revision of the law. In 2005, Sénégal turned over former President Hissène Habré (1942–) of Chad to Belgium after his indictment.

In 2004, charges were filed in Germany against Secretary of Defense Rumsfeld, former Central Intelligence Agency Director George Tenet (1953–), and other officials regarding four former Iraqi prisoners who were tortured at Abu Ghraib Prison (twenty hours of questioning per day, sleep deprivation, blasting music), as documented by the U.S. military. The German court in early 2006 refused to investigate the case, arguing the principle of the **exhaustion of local remedies**, in other words, that the matter should first be handled by a competent tribunal in the home country. (Rumsfeld had been scheduled to attend a conference in Germany, so he persuaded the Berlin government to drop the case so that he could travel with impunity.) But the New York-based Center for Constitutional Rights refiled the case later in 2006.

Arrest warrants were issued in Spain during 2005 for three American soldiers who were alleged to have killed a Spanish journalist during a shelling of a hotel in Iraq. The soldiers claimed that they were responding to someone who was firing upon them from the hotel.

In 2005, Italy began to issue arrest warrants for CIA agents and military personnel who in 2003 abducted Islamic cleric Abu Omar (1963–), an Italian citizen who had been granted asylum, from a street in Milan and flew him first to Germany and then to his native Egypt, where he was imprisoned and allegedly beaten, with electric shocks applied to his genitals. In 2004, he was released but rearrested soon after; he was finally released in 2007. In all, Italy issued five arrest warrants for Italian officials and twenty-five for CIA agents. Born with the name Hassan Mustafa Osama Nasr, Abu Omar is perhaps the first known "ghost detainee." The United States, which has refused to extradite the CIA agents, reportedly offered Abu Omar $2 million "to say that he had not been kidnapped and to say that he had come [to Egypt] of his own free will," but he refused.

In a similar case, Khaled Al-Masri (1963–), a German citizen of Lebanese origin, testified in a Spanish court in 2006 that he was vacationing in Macedonia during 2003 when at least a dozen CIA agents allegedly beat, blindfolded, and drugged him in a hotel room for three weeks, attempting to make him confess membership in Al-Qaida. When he refused, an airplane took off from Spain, picked him up in Macedonia, then went to Iraq, and later to Afghanistan, where he claims that he was tortured in an American-run prison for five more months. Afterward, he was flown to Albania and dropped on an abandoned road in a remote mountain area. The identities of the CIA agents emerged from photocopies of their passports retained by the Spanish hotel where they stayed, so they were indicted in Germany, which has warned the United States that the CIA agents involved in Al-Masri's mistreatment will be arrested if they return to Germany. (Al-Masri's case in an American court was dismissed based on the **state secrets doctrine**, that is, because testimony might reveal national security secrets.)

In 2006, French judge Jean-Louis Bruguière indicted ten Rwandans, including President Paul Kagame (1957–), for complicity in the Rwandan genocide of 1994. Although Kagame is immune from prosecution while in office, names of the remaining nine were forwarded to the International Criminal Tribunal for Rwanda. In response, Rwanda severed diplomatic relations with France.

Four paramilitary Serbs of the Scorpions, responsible in 1995 for killing six unarmed Bosniaks at Srberenica, Bosnia, were convicted in a Serbian court during 2007. The key evidence was a videotape of the slaughter that surfaced in 2005.

In 2007, Britain's highest court, the House of Lords, ruled that the British government was liable for the death of Baha Moussa (1987–2003) from torture while under detention by British troops in Basra, Iraq. The ruling was based on Britain's Human Rights Act of 1998, the European Convention for the Protection of Human Rights, and the Geneva Conventions. Although one British soldier had pleaded guilty to the offense at a court-martial, the Law Lords noted that others involved in breaking Moussa's nose and seventeen ribs had not been properly brought to justice.

In sum, cases involving extraterritorial jurisdiction for human rights violations have made a lot of publicity. They have served notice that perpetrators of future violations may not escape prosecution.

Turning to **economic** approaches to human rights, European countries have been in the forefront in providing development and disaster assistance, both bilaterally and through intergovernmental organizations. Many adopted generalized system of preferences (GSP) schemes to reduce tariffs on goods from the Third World, particularly from their former colonies.

Based on a 1948 treaty between West Germany and Israel and subsequent German legislation, the Bonn government paid more than $50 billion dollars to Nazi victims. However, insurance claims remained upaid in 1998, when the International Commission on Holocaust Era Insurance Claims was formed. Among more than twenty insurance companies involved, the largest are Germany's Allianz and Italy's Assicurazioni Generali. A major problem has been that documents containing names of those entitled to claims have not been fully disclosed; some are held in sealed archives. However, by 2007, the Italian firm agreed to pay out $135 million to cover 5,500 claims, fewer than 5 per cent of the more than $2 billion of policies sold to Jews.

In 1972, Norway became the first country to cite a lack of "social justice" rights as a reason to cut off foreign aid when Oslo pulled out its aid mission from Uganda because dictator Idi Amin (1925–2003) expelled at least 40,000 third-generation Indians and Pakistanis and systematically murdered 300,000 members of rival tribes. In 1973, the Netherlands adopted both human rights and social justice as criteria for aid conditionality and then dropped Uganda in 1974. Other countries followed in due course. In 1989, following the brutal crackdown on demonstrators near Beijing's Tiananmen Square, many European countries boycotted Chinese goods, but the boycott ended in time.

In 2001, Austria established a $210 million fund to compensate Holocaust survivors; after receiving 19,300 applicants, first payments began in 2006. In 2002, Belgian banks, insurance companies, and the government also agreed to pay $111 million to compensate the country's Jews for property abandoned, lost, and plundered during the Nazi occupation.

The use of **military** methods by individual European countries to stop human rights abuses abroad has been rare. European countries prefer to send their military forces as UN peacekeepers. France, nevertheless, has sent military contingents to protect French citizens in former French colonies on more than a dozen occasions from the 1960s. On one occasion, France acted to maintain the principle of self-determination by dispatching a military force to Chad in 1983 to prevent Libyan forces from overthrowing the government. French troops currently are stationed in Chad and the Central African Republic to assist the governments from external and internal threats, respectively.

After centuries of international conflict, the devastation of World War II and the horrors of the Holocaust persuaded many Europeans to place human rights as a top priority, domestically and internationally. Initially, the priority in the West was to deter an attack from the East, but Eastern Europeans so reviled the Soviet Union that they provided no secure launching pad. During the Cold War, Western European countries developed several important multilateral institutions, which secured the peace proactively and then expanded East after the fall of the Berlin Wall. Although individual countries have made important contributions, what is most distinctive is that Europe has developed an impressive set of regional institutions.

COUNCIL OF EUROPE (COE)

In September 1946, fourteen months after stepping down as Britain's wartime prime minister, Winston Churchill (1874–1965) gave a speech at the University of Zurich calling for "a United States of Europe" that would be as free and peaceful as multiethnic Switzerland. Three years later, ten Western European countries founded the Council of Europe by adopting the Statute of the Council of Europe, sometimes known as the Treaty of London, which was ratified within only three months. The purpose of the organization, as proclaimed in the Statute, is "to achieve a greater unity between its members for the purpose of safeguarding and realizing the ideals and principles which are their common heritage and facilitating their economic and social progress."

Subsequently, membership has increased more than fourfold, especially since the end of the Cold War. The principal membership requirement is that a state must have a genuine democracy that is committed to the rule of law and human rights; members must adopt the European Convention for the Protection of Human Rights and Fundamental Freedoms of 1950 but do not have to ratify the European Social Charter of 1961. Spain, for example, was considered ineligible for membership while governed by fascist Francisco Franco (1892–1975). Observer status has been granted to Canada, the Holy See, Israel, Japan, México, and the United States. Undemocratic Belarus is the only sizeable European country besides the Holy See that is not a member.

Legislatures of member countries send delegates to the Parliamentary Assembly of the Council of Europe (PACE), which can suspend countries for gross violations of human rights. From 1967–1974, Greece was suspended while under military rule. In 1981–1985, Turkey was suspended because of torture of prisoners. In 1997, Belarus's guest status was suspended for persecuting opposition leaders, and the suspension continues, in part because the country maintains the death penalty. In 2000–2001, PACE suspended the voting rights of Russia due to the crackdown in Chechnya and appointed a special committee to investigate whether Russian officials should be tried for war crimes. In 2003, PACE passed a resolution providing that a country could be stripped of voting rights if the delegation from a country contained no women. In 2004, Ireland and Malta were cited, pending the appointment of a woman to their delegations. In 2004, PACE threatened to suspend Ukraine over proposed extraconstitutional changes, but the issue was resolved when voters elected a new government in 2005.

From 1999, PACE elects a *Commissioner for Human Rights*, who is charged with four tasks: (1) promoting human rights awareness, (2) facilitating national human rights bodies, (3) identifying gaps in human rights law and practice, and (4) promoting the full enjoyment of human rights in member countries. The *Human Rights Co-operation and Awareness Division* within the Secretariat's *Directorate General of Human Rights* handles the functions of documentation, information compilation and dissemination, organizing meetings, research, training, and coordinating work with other international organizations, including the European Union.

The impetus for the European Convention for the Protection of Human Rights and Fundamental Freedoms was threefold: (1) a response to the atrocities of World

War II, (2) support for European integration aiming to prevent another general European war, and (3) an effort to show the human rights superiority of Western Europe over Soviet-controlled Eastern Europe. However, unlike the Universal Declaration of Human Rights adopted by the United Nations in 1948, the European Convention initially had no reference to self-determination or the protection of minority peoples, and there is a reference to responsibilities as well as rights. Thirteen Protocols have been adopted, dealing with such issues as the right to education and property; free elections and freedom of movement; prohibitions of the death penalty and discrimination; and various criminal justice procedures, including compensation for wrongful conviction.

Over time, COE has received an increasing number of complaints. **Intrastate complaints**, which are more numerous, involve individuals, groups, or nongovernmental organizations claiming denials of their rights by the states in which they reside. **Interstate complaints** are by one state against another.

Among the thirteen interstate complaints, five countries complained about Turkey's use of torture, to which there was a resolution involving a friendly settlement procedure in 1985. One interstate complaint involved torture allegations in Greece, and another was over British interrogation techniques in Northern Ireland. Most cases have been decided in favor of complainants, though rulings are not binding.

The initial procedure was for the Commission to hand over complaints to the Committee of Ministers, which could either make an **award** based on the principle of **just satisfaction** to the victim or refer the case to COE's *European Court of Human Rights* (ECHR) if the defendant state accepted the Court's jurisdiction. After the Court made a ruling, the Committee would monitor implementation of the decision.

Up to the mid-1990s, the Committee of Ministers handled more complaints than the Court. As COE membership increased dramatically after the end of the Cold War, the number of applications to the Commission rose exponentially – from 404 in 1981 to 4,750 in 1997, while cases annually submitted to ECHR rose from 7 to 119 over the same years. Since not all cases are decided during the year when they are filed, the Commission's backlog in 1997 was over 12,000.

Accordingly, a decision was made, effective 1998, to have ECHR handle all complaints and to become a fulltime body. The Committee of Ministers, through the *Steering Committee for Human Rights*, then restricted itself to its original powers of supervising implementation of the Court's decisions and making specific recommendations to member states. COE's Secretary General may also direct questions about implementation to an errant state.

Plaintiffs now must file an **application** alleging a violation of one of COE's treaties. Many applications are inadmissible for technical reasons or because there is no treaty basis for their complaint. After an application is ruled **admissible**, negotiations may ensue for a **friendly settlement** or ultimately there may be a **hearing** in court.

ECHR, the world's longest standing human rights tribunal, was set up in 1959. Unlike the Commission and the Council, ECHR can make legally binding decisions. If a plaintiff prevails, there are two possible outcomes. In the most common outcome, **individual measure**, the victim is compensated by the defendant. The Court has ordered more than forty governments thus far to provide financial restitution to injured parties. Alternatively, a **general measure** asks governments to change their laws or administrative procedures, though the affected state may take its time to comply. From 1982, ECHR has also issued **advisory opinions**.

From 1998, the Court has received an increasing number of complaints, particularly from individuals in Russia. For the years 1999–2004, ECHR gave judgments in 4,026 cases; in 2,960 a violation was found; there were 172 cases with no violations, 819 friendly settlements, and the remaining cases were handled procedurally. In 2004, the Grand Chamber processed twenty-two cases and issued one advisory opinion, while the four Chambers finalized work on 21,036 cases, of which 92 percent were ruled inadmissible. As of January 1, 2005, about 50,000 applications awaited action by ECHR.

Due to ECHR, several state practices have changed. Austria revised its criminal code and amount of payments for legal aid attorneys. Belgium gave rights to illegitimate children and dropped its vagrancy law. Britain changed laws dealing with freedom of information, privacy, prison rules, mental health, and compensation for wrongful arrest. France had to guarantee privacy of telephone calls after two cases about illegal wiretapping. Germany modified pre-trial detention procedures and had to provide interpreters free of charge. In Ireland, civil legal aid was instituted. Italy was ordered to revise regulations governing detention on remand and to shorten the length of criminal proceedings. In the Netherlands, the law on detention of mental patients was modified. Switzerland amended its military penal code and regulations governing reformatories. In 2005, the Court ordered Turkey to retry Abdullah Ocalan (1948–), the alleged leader of Kurdish dissidents, because he did not receive a fair trial, and the Court overturned a British law that banned all convicted prison inmates from voting.

Some governments have taken years rather than days to implement the decisions. Aside from ostracizing a government by suspending membership or voting rights, the COE can withhold technical assistance to member countries, a sanction that would particularly harm less prosperous countries.

In some cases, countries brought before ECHR have refused to accept jurisdiction, claiming that emergency conditions precluded the extension of full human rights. An example of the latter is *Brogan v United Kingdom*, a 1988 case in which the police without judicial action detained a Northern Ireland resident, and the Court accepted Britain's explanation. Nevertheless, ECHR decisions have had a worldwide impact, since they are cited by national courts in countries inside and outside Europe. Indeed, the European Court of Human Rights has been considered by some scholars as a world human rights court.

Other human rights bodies exist under the Council of Europe framework, as established by separate treaties. Many of the earliest, consistent with the Statute's emphasis on "economic and social progress," were in the field of social rights (Table 12.1). The broadest treaty relating to social rights is the European Social Charter, which contains several new rights, including protection against poverty and social exclusion, right to housing, right to protection in cases of harassment or termination of employment, and rights of workers with family responsibilities. The revised Charter established the *Committee of Social Rights*. A Protocol to the Social Charter empowers the Committee to receive complaints, and indeed some twenty-nine complaints were received by mid-2005. The COE Committee of Ministers and

TABLE 12.1   COE HUMAN RIGHTS TREATIES DEALING WITH SOCIAL RIGHTS

Adopted	Title	In force
1953	European Interim Agreement on Social Security Schemes Relating to Old Age, Invalidity and Survivors	1954
1953	European Interim Agreement on Social Security Other than Schemes for Old Age, Invalidity and Survivors	1954
1953	European Convention on Social and Medical Assistance Agreement on the Exchange of War Cripples Between Member Countries of the Council of Europe with a View to Medical Treatment	1954
1955	European Social Charter	1956
1962	Agreement Between the Member States of the Council of Europe on the Issue to Military and Civilian War-Disabled of an International Book of Vouchers for the Repair of Prosthetic and Orthopaedic Appliances	1963
1964	European Code of Social Security	1968
1972	European Convention on Social Security	1977
1974	European Convention on the Social Protection of Farmers	1977
1996	European Social Charter (Revised)	1999
1996	• Protocol	1998

PACE, both of which also have jurisdiction to act on complaints concerning economic and social issues, defer to the Committee of Social Rights. In 1998, the *European Committee for Social Cohesion* was set up to monitor implementation of the treaties governing social rights, especially the European Code of Social Security.

In the field of criminal justice, the treatment of convicts has drawn a lot of attention (Table 12.2). Although Article 3 of the European Convention for the Protection of Human Rights bans the use of torture, specific machinery was thought necessary to ensure compliance. Accordingly, the European Convention for the Prevention of Torture and Inhuman or Degrading Treatment or Punishment was adopted. The treaty created the *Committee for the Prevention of Torture and Inhuman or Degrading Treatment or Punishment*, which is composed of independent experts who have the power to make scheduled and unscheduled checks on prisons, police cells, psychiatric hospitals, and compounds for asylum seekers, except for places already visited by the Red Cross. Prisoners can be interviewed in private. Reports to the governments after site visits are confidential unless, as is usually the case, the country agrees to make them public. In 1992, by a provision requiring a two-thirds vote, the Committee released a report about torture of prisoners after three unsuccessful visits to Turkey's Anti-Terrorism Department. The delegation sent to investigate prisons in Belgium during March 2005 was the hundredth and ninety-sixth site visit.

Although the European Convention for the Protection of Human Rights does not refer to the right of self-determination or the protection of minority peoples, the issue could not be ignored (Table 12.3). The European Cultural Convention of 1954 encourages countries to foster learning about one another's culture and history.

Owing to the fact that hundreds of thousands of persons were refugees and stateless in Europe due to World War II and its aftermath, several early treaties dealt with nationality questions. The European Convention on Establishment granted rights of citizens of COE member countries to live and work in other COE member countries, and the Convention on the Reduction of Cases of Multiple Nationality and Military Obligations in Cases of Multiple Nationality drew up rules to enable individuals to avoid multiple governmental obligations.

TABLE 12.2 COE HUMAN RIGHTS TREATIES DEALING WITH CRIMINAL JUSTICE

Adopted	Title	In force
1957	European Convention on Extradition	1960
1964	European Convention on the Supervision of Conditionally Sentenced or Conditionally Released Offenders	1975
1970	European Convention on the International Validity of Criminal Judgments	1974
1974	European Convention on the Non-Applicability of Statutory Limitation to Crimes Against Humanity and War Crimes	2003
1977	European Agreement on the Transmission of Applications for Legal Aid	1977
1983	Convention on the Transfer of Sentenced Persons	1985
1983	European Convention on the Compensation of Victims of Violent Crimes	1988
1987	European Convention for the Prevention of Torture and Inhuman or Degrading Treatment or Punishment	1989
1998	Europol Convention	1998

TABLE 12.3 COE HUMAN RIGHTS TREATIES DEALING WITH DIVERSITY

Adopted	Title	In force
1954	European Cultural Convention	1955
1955	European Convention on Establishment	1965
1957	European Agreement on Regulations Governing the Movement of Persons Between Member States of the Council of Europe	1958
1959	European Agreement on the Abolition of Visas for Refugees	1960
1963	Convention on the Reduction of Cases of Multiple Nationality and Military Obligations in Cases of Multiple Nationality	1968
1977	European Convention on the Legal Status of Migrant Workers	1983
1980	European Agreement on Transfer of Responsibility for Refugees	1980
1992	European Charter for Regional or Minority Languages	1998
1995	Framework Convention for the Protection of National Minorities	1998
1997	European Convention on Nationality	2000
2001	Convention on Cybercrime	2004

The European Charter for Regional or Minority Languages provides an extensive list of protections against language discrimination. Member countries are required to submit reports on the status of language minorities to the COE Secretary General for analysis by a committee of experts.

The First Summit Conference of 1993 spawned the *European Commission Against Racism and Intolerance*, with a somewhat vague mandate that has focused in recent years on anti-Semitism, prejudice against Roma (gypsies) and Muslims, and the status of such aliens as migrants, refugees, and asylum seekers. In 2000, the Commission adopted Protocol 11 to the European Convention for the Protection of Human Rights and Fundamental Freedoms, which prohibits discrimination "on any ground such as sex, race, color, language, religion, political or other opinion, national or social origin, association with a national minority, property, birth or other status."

In 1994, the Framework Convention for the Protection of National Minorities was adopted. Site visits are conducted by an *Advisory Committee* of independent experts. The convention requires states to make reports on the status of minorities; thus far, all but one ratifying country has done so. Because of the desire to criminalize the explosion of "hate speech" over the Internet, the Council of Europe adopted the Convention on Cybercrime in 2001.

No specific treaty on gender equality has emerged thus far, though in 1979 the Committee of Ministers established the Committee for Equality Between Women and Men, which was superseded in 1988 by the *Committee of Ministers on Equality of Women and Men*. In 1997, the *Steering Committee for Equality Between Women and Men*, to which each country appoints an expert, embarked on a program of gender mainstreaming, preventing and combating violence against women, and stopping the trafficking in women. Within the Secretariat, the *Division of Equality Between Women and Men* coordinates meetings and other activities.

Children's rights have also concerned the Council of Europe (Table 12.4). The Convention on the Exercise of Children's Rights established a *Standing Committee*, consisting of one expert from each ratifying country, to monitor implementation of provisions that ensure legal representation for minors.

TABLE 12.4 COE HUMAN RIGHTS TREATIES DEALING WITH CHILDREN

Adopted	Title	In force
1967	European Convention on the Adoption of Children	1968
1969	European Agreement on Au Pair Placement	1971
1970	European Convention on the Repatriation of Minors	
1975	European Convention on the Legal Status of Children Born out of Wedlock	1978
1980	European Convention on Recognition and Enforcement of Decisions Concerning Custody of Children and on Restoration of Custody of Children	1983
1996	European Convention on the Exercise of Children's Rights	2000
2003	Convention on Contact Concerning Children	

TABLE 12.5 COE HUMAN RIGHTS TREATIES DEALING WITH LOCAL GOVERNMENT

Adopted	Title	In force
1980	European Outline Convention on Transfrontier Co-operation Between Territorial Communities or Authorities	1981
1985	European Charter of Local Self-Government	1988
1992	Convention on the Participation of Foreigners in Public Life at Local Level	1997

COE members must be democracies. However, the term "democracy" is vague, and democratic processes can be thick or thin, especially at the subnational level. In 1997, the Committee of Ministers established the *Steering Committee on Local and Regional Democracy* to assist in implementing provisions of three treaties on the subject (Table 12.5).

Regarding freedom of the press, the *Steering Committee on the Media and New Communication Services* (originally the Steering Committee on the Mass Media) was formed in 1981. The Steering Committee has several functions besides human rights, but monitors the contribution of the media to the promotion of tolerance, the fight against hate speech, the right to media privacy, and the right of freedom of expression.

In 1989, PACE set up the *North–South Center* to provide technical assistance outside Europe. Located in Lisbon, the Center focuses most of its attention on Africa and the Middle East with conferences and seminars on global education, issues relating to migration, and on problems of youth.

The *European Commission for Democracy Through Law* was set up by the Council of Europe in 1990 to advise states that are no longer under the influence of the Soviet Union to develop a new legal system. Because of its location, the body is known as the Venice Commission.

Under the aegis of the Council of Europe, some 200 treaties have been adopted, mostly aimed at harmonizing national laws. Several relating to human rights have not been discussed above, but are in force today (Table 12.6).

COE activities in the field of human rights may appear rather formalistic if summarized only in terms of committees, complaints, statistics, treaties, and the like.

TABLE 12.6 OTHER HUMAN RIGHTS TREATIES OF THE COUNCIL OF EUROPE

Adopted	Title	In force
1976	European Convention on the International Effects of Deprivation of the Right to Drive a Motor Vehicle	1983
1978	Convention on the Control of the Acquisition and Possession of Firearms by Individuals	1982
1981	Convention for the Protection of Individuals with Regard to Automatic Processing of Personal Data	1985
1997	Convention on Human Rights and Biomedicine	1999

In fact, a multitude of activities involving technical assistance to member countries serve to increase compliance with human rights standards, including conferences, country visits, task forces, and workshops. Technical experts predominate in the various working groups, where they soften the views of their countries to achieve consensus. Nevertheless, the organization has not been reluctant to identify violations of human rights, including criticisms of Russia's actions in Chechnya that are viewed in some quarters as war crimes.

Although COE has been criticized for expanding membership to countries with many human rights deficiencies, the reason for a low bar to new members is the experience that countries are more likely to improve inside the organization than outside. Indeed, ten of the most recent countries are currently being monitored very closely.

EUROPEAN UNION (EU)

The Council of Europe is mostly an **intergovernmental organization**, serving at the pleasure of its member countries, though decisions of the COE's European Court of Human Rights are supposed to bind governments. The European Union, however, is a **supranational organization**, empowered to make binding laws affecting individuals and governments. EU economic sanctions, which can affect both member and nonmember countries, are not to be taken lightly.

The impetus for EU came from three sources. One was an agreement in 1944, formalized by 1948, to form *Benelux*, a customs union among Belgium, Luxembourg, and the Netherlands. The second development was the formation of the Organization for European Economic Cooperation (OEEC) to distribute Marshall Plan aid.[1] The most dramatic event was a speech by French Foreign Minister Robert Schuman (1886–1963) on May 9, 1950 (now celebrated as Europe Day), in which he proposed economic integration of the coal and steel industry, which was largely concentrated in the Saarland, a German province along the River Rhine that was under French postwar occupation until 1957.

In 1951, France, Germany, Italy, and the Benelux countries formed the *European Commission for Steel and Coal* (ECSC). In 1957, the six set up the *European Economic Community* (EEC) and the *European Atomic Energy Agency* (Euratom). In 1960, seven EEC nonmembers organized the Geneva-based *European Free Trade Association* (EFTA), though over the years, most countries left EFTA.[2] In 1958, the Benelux Economic Union Treaty was signed, forming the *Benelux Economic Union*.

In 1986, ECSC, EEC, and Euratom were merged into the *European Community* (EC) by the Single European Act, the Preamble of which referred for the first time to promoting democracy and fundamental rights. The text also established four internal market freedoms (free movement of goods, services, people and capital).

In 1992, when ECSC was about to expire, the three EC organizations and the Benelux Economic Union were consolidated into the *European Union* (EU) by the Treaty on European Union, known as the Maastricht Treaty, which went into force in 1993. The treaty has provisions encouraging cooperation in regard to the following matters of concern to human rights: (1) employment, (2) labor law and working conditions, (3) occupational safety and hygiene, (4) social security, (5) the right of collective bargaining, (6) the right to work, and (7) the right to travel.

The Maastricht Treaty was revised in 1997 by the Treaty of Amsterdam, which identified the founding principles of the European Union as (1) liberty, (2) democracy, (3) human rights, (4) fundamental freedoms, and (5) the rule of law. From 1999, when the Amsterdam Treaty went into effect, the EU human rights mandate was broadened to ban discrimination based on sex, race, color, ethnic or social origin, genetic features, language, religion, political beliefs or any other opinion, membership of a national minority, property, birth legitimacy, disability, age, sexual orientation, and nationality. In addition, EU citizens have a right of residence throughout member countries, and any citizen can vote and run for office. Appended to the Amsterdam Treaty is the Charter of the Fundamental Social Rights of Workers, known as the Social Charter, as well as the Schengen Agreement and Convention. The latter treaty, not yet ratified by Britain and Ireland, guarantees free movement of persons across borders and other rights regarding asylum and immigration.

The Maastricht Treaty permits the EU to respond to persistent and serious human rights violations by its members through two procedures. **Preventive procedures** are various forms of technical assistance – education and cooperation, and information. **Sanctions** can involve suspension of economic privileges or of EU membership itself.

During negotiations for the Maastricht treaty, EU members agreed to establish the *European Law Enforcement Organization* (Europol). In 1998, the Europol Convention was drafted and ratified. The headquarters, known as the European Police Office, are in The Hague. Europol works closely with law enforcement agencies throughout Europe as well as with Interpol, which defers to Europol in making arrests inside EU countries. In 2005, when Italy issued arrest warrants for Central Intelligence Agency suspects in the abduction of an Egyptian cleric from Milan to Egypt, Europol was authorized to make the arrests.

Several important developments occurred in 2000. The EU published its first *Annual Report on Human Rights*, identified Millennium Development goals including promotion of democracy and human rights, and the *European Parliament* (Europarl) consolidated previous human rights treaties into a single Charter of Fundamental Rights of the European Union for inclusion as Part II of the proposed EU constitution, which has not been ratified.

Several COE countries remain outside EU – Albania; Norway; Switzerland; such diminutive states as Andorra; four westernmost countries of the former Soviet Union (Belarus, Moldova, Russia, and Ukraine); and four republics of the former Yugoslavia (Bosnia-Herzegovina, Croatia, Macedonia, Montenegro, and Serbia). After the Soviet Union collapsed, several countries applied to join, so in 1993 the EU adopted the following criteria for membership: (1) stable institutions, (2) a functioning democracy, (3) rule of law, (4) respect for human rights, (5) respect for and protection of minorities, (6) a functioning market economy, (7) and the *acquis*, that is, both the ability to assume membership obligations and an adherence to the aims of the economic, monetary, and political union. Some time was required for Eastern European countries to reestablish capitalist economies and to incorporate human rights in their legal frameworks. Then in 2004, ten new countries joined. Bulgaria and Romania joined in 2007, bringing the total to twenty-seven.

Serbia's desire to join EU prompted Belgrade to turn over additional persons charged with war crimes to the International Criminal Tribunal for the Former Yugoslavia in 2005, whereupon the membership application of Serbia-Montenegro was formally opened. In 2006, the application was suspended because Belgrade had not arrested the Serbians who led the Bosnia War, namely, Radovan Karadžić (1945–) and Ratko Mladić (1943–). Montenegro, independent in 2006, has applied for membership.

The poorer European countries are so desperate to gain the economic advantages of membership that they generally take actions to meet the stiff preconditions. Turkey, which began negotiations for membership in 2005, has adopted dozens of amendments dealing with women's rights to meet the required conditions. However, Ankara must resolve several more problems – allowing the Kurdish minority to educate and broadcast in their native language, ending torture in the criminal justice system, and opening diplomatic relations with Cyprus, an EU member, where a Turkish minority claims to have a separate sovereign status that has only been recognized by Ankara from 1974. Although France wants Turkey to acknowledge guilt for a genocide against Armenians from 1915–1923 as a condition of membership, that condition is not among the official preconditions. Nevertheless, Prime Minister Recep Tayyip Erdogan (1954–) called for an impartial study of the matter in 2005. Although some EU countries are skeptical that Turkey will ever be admitted, Ankara's efforts to qualify for membership clearly are applauded by Europeans who want human rights to advance as far as possible around the world as well as by Kurds inside the country who are enjoying greater freedoms.

Countries that are deemed to persistently violate human rights in a serious manner may have their voting rights or **membership suspended**. Such action requires a two-thirds vote of the European Parliament, followed by a unanimous European Council decision (excluding the country concerned). During 2000, after the neo-Nazi party of Jörg Haider (1950–) joined the ruling coalition in the Austrian parliament, the remaining fourteen EU members voted to impose sanctions against Austria, consisting of a freeze on bilateral relations with Vienna. One concern was that his Freedom Party, which garnered 27 percent of the vote, would encourage other neo-Nazi groups to run for office elsewhere throughout Europe.

EU's organizational structure contains many layers. The headquarters in Brussels is known as the *European Commission*. In 1980, Europarl established a Human Rights Working Group, which was renamed over the years until 2004, when Europarl established the *Committee on Civil Liberties, Justice and Home Affairs* to handle problems inside the Union. Within the Secretariat, the official that deals with human rights issues is the *Commissioner for External Relations*.

From 1988, Europarl has awarded the **Sakharov Prize for Freedom of Thought** to an individual or group that has advanced human rights anywhere in the world. In 2005, Ladies in White won for their efforts to free some seventy-five dissidents in Cuba who were imprisoned in 2003. Later in 2005, Cuba freed fifteen of the dissidents for medical reasons.

In 1989, after the massacre near Tiananmen Square, EU imposed an **arms embargo** on China. In 2000, the organization condemned Russian military action in Chechnya, where up to 100,000 civilians have lost their lives, though no embargo was ordered.

In 2003, the EU ordered a **diplomatic freeze** with Cuba for imposing severe sentences on the seventy-five dissidents noted above and then lifted the freeze when some of the dissidents were released in 2005. In 2005, the EU was divided on imposing sanctions on the Sudan regarding the Darfur genocide, preferring to refer the matter to the International Criminal Court despite opposition from Washington. Currently, leaders of Belarus, Myanmar, and Zimbabwe are not allowed to travel to EU countries because of their poor human rights records.

Revelations about the role of European countries in extraordinary renditions by the CIA prompted Europarl to initiate **investigations**. In 2006, an investigator reported allegations that fourteen COE member countries allowed secret prisons or airfields for secret flights to other countries where suspected terrorists were tortured, and in 2007 Poland and Romania were cited as providing secret prisons.

Subsidiary bodies with greatest relevance to human rights are the *Economic and Social Committee*, consisting of interest groups that give advice on EU activities and proposals, and the *European Ombudsman*, to which citizens can complain about problems with any EU institution. The latter institution, created by the Maastricht Treaty, received 3,726 complaints in 2004, of which 176 involved charges of discrimination. The Ombudsman, which processes complaints in accordance with the Code of Good Administrative Behavior adopted by Europarl in 2001, can pursue a complaint on its own initiative. Possible responses are a **friendly settlement**, **transfer** of the complaint to another competent body, a **finding of mal-administration**, a **critical remark**, or a **recommendation** to another body, including Europarl.

The *Court of Justice of the European Union* ensures compliance with EU regulations. To gain respect for impartiality and professionalism, the Court established human rights principles in its proceedings, namely, the rights to a fair trial, an appeal, privacy, free association and expression, property, and professional secrecy. From 1969, the Court often referred to human rights issues in its rulings regarding commercial litigants but without the power to do so against governments. Later, the Court began to rule that fundamental rights must be respected not only by EC institutions but also by member governments in implementing EC law. In 1977, Europarl, the European Commission, and the EC Council of Ministers signed a joint declaration vowing to respect fundamental rights, as defined by the Court of Justice.

In 2004, the Court handled twelve cases in the area of "freedom, security, and justice." In three cases, the Commission charged France, Greece, and Luxembourg with failure to adopt the latest EU directives regarding procedures to follow before expelling third country nationals. Otherwise, human rights complaints in Europe go to the COE's European Court of Human Rights.

Any EU citizen may file a **petition** with Europarl's *Committee on Petitions*, which may include human rights complaints. During 2003–2004, some 1,313 petitions were filed; German citizens filed the largest number. If a violation is found, Europarl may ask the EU Commission to bring action against the offending state.

EU policy on **foreign aid** is premised on a *proactive* rather than a *punitive* approach to human rights, reasoning that negative measures do not address the root causes of human rights abuses but instead punish peoples for inadequacies of governments. EU policy is that poverty reduction, the main objective of its overseas development policy, is only possible in a democracy, and the aid is generally distributed at the local level rather than to a bureaucracy for redistribution. In addition to aid for economic development projects, much aid is provided with the specific aim of promoting democracy through institution-building, such as the funding of an election or legal training.

In 1991, the European Community adopted the Resolution on Human Rights, Democracy, and Development, which provides equal stress on civil-political and economic-social rights. From 1992, all EC agreements on trade or cooperation with third countries must contain a clause stipulating that human rights are an essential element in the relations between the parties. More than 120 such agreements have been negotiated, including the Cotonou Agreement of 2000, the latest trade and aid pact that links the Union with seventy-eight developing countries in Africa, the Caribbean and Pacific (the ACP group). The 1991 resolution provides for **reduction** in or **suspension** of aid programs or trade concessions to any country that fails to respect human rights in two circumstances: "grave and persistent" human rights violations or "serious interruption of democratic processes."

The first country sanctioned by the EU was Uganda in 1977 due to the excesses of Idi Amin (1923–2003); several others have been sanctioned over the years, including Haiti, Malawi, Myanmar (Burma), Serbia, Sudan, Zaire, and Zimbabwe. Besides the Cotonou Agreement, similar provisions apply to countries that are applying for EU membership, to the former countries of the Soviet Union, and to recipients in the Middle East. An exception is allowed for emergency humanitarian assistance, where natural disasters or oppressive governments produce large-scale human suffering.

The European Union can also **freeze assets** and impose **trade restrictions** on errant countries. Currently, EU's blacklist, which is imposed by individual states, includes Bosnia, China, the Democratic Republic of the Congo (formerly Zaïre), Croatia, Iraq, Ivory Coast, Liberia, Sierra Leone, Serbia, Somalia, Sudan, Zimbabwe, and specific terrorist groups. The most common restriction is an embargo on arms sales.

In 1994, the European Parliament created the European Initiative for Democracy and Human Rights to launch aid programs for nonmember countries. From 1999, the Initiative is administered by the *Human Rights and Democracy Committee*. Priority areas are as follows: (1) strengthening democracy, good governance, and the rule of law; (2) cooperating with civil society to promote political pluralism, a free media, and a sound justice system; (3) abolishing the death penalty; (4) combating repression and torture (through better police training and creating criminal courts); (5) fighting racism and discrimination; (6) gender equality; and (7) the protection of children. An early activity was election monitoring in South Africa during 1994. In 2005, the Initiative supplied observers for elections in Afghanistan, Burundi, and Palestine's Gaza and the West Bank. Other current projects include setting up rehabilitation centers for victims of torture and supporting women's organizations in North Africa.

In 1997, the *Council of Ministers* set up the European Monitoring Center for Racism and Xenophobia in Vienna to collect information on racism, xenophobia,

Islamphobia, and anti-Semitism on an annual basis. In 2002, the focus was clarified as the areas of employment, education, legislation, and racist violence and crimes, including ethnic disparities in education, attitude surveys, and statistics on hate crimes. In 2003, the Council upgraded the Center to become the *Fundamental Rights Agency*.

Another area of progress concerns migrant workers, asylum seekers, and refugees. Rights have been defined for some 5 million non-EU migrant workers, including the right of family members to join them.

When Yugoslavia began to disintegrate in the 1990s through secession by several states, the EU played an unprecedented role in several respects. EU officials tried to mediate and sent monitors to Kosovo in 1998, but Belgrade was not initially interested in compromise. In 1999, the EU voted economic sanctions against the country. After the wars in Bosnia and Kosovo ended, the UN Interim Administration in Kosovo included an EU unit to provide economic recovery. When the conflict between Serbs and Kosovars (ethnic Albanians) heated up in Kosovo during 2001, the EU again attempted to mediate. Logistical cooperation between EU and the North Atlantic Treaty Organization (NATO) was launched in Darfur at the request of the African Union during 2005.

Large numbers of refugees fled from conflicts in the former Yugoslavia. In response, several EU innovations emerged in 1999. Uniform procedures were adopted for applicants for political asylum, known as the Common European Asylum System. A *European Refugee Fund*, set up in 2002, supports the reception, integration and voluntary repatriation of refugees, and for up to three years provides displaced persons residency, work permits, living accommodations, access to social and medical services, and schooling for their children.

Europarl provided the leadership for the Stability Pact for South-Eastern Europe of 1999, which provides for projects to achieve free trade agreements, the free movement of people across the region, eradication of corruption and organized crime, and the creation of conditions for the voluntary return of refugees. The Pact is administered outside the Union and involves several EU nonmembers, including some outside Europe, as well as more than ten international organizations.

The European Union was formed for economic reasons but has increasingly been concerned with human rights. Despite considerable rhetoric about human rights, the EU's most stringent concern for human rights shows up primarily as **aid conditionality**. In 1990, the EU banned arms exports to Myanmar, and in 1997 the EU withdrew its trade privileges under the organization's generalized system of preferences (GSP), citing the widespread use of forced labor. In 1999, however, EU filed a complaint against the United States with the World Trade Organization because of a Massachusetts state law banning business with companies operating in politically repressive Myanmar; the case was dropped in 2000, when the Massachusetts law was ruled unconstitutional in *Crosby v National Foreign Trade Council* (530US363).

EU economic sanctions are far more effective than COE or ECHR rulings in dealing with errant governments. If the EU's new constitution is adopted, with a single Foreign Minister and other cabinet-level positions, a Defense Minister may be one of the new positions, poised to use a military force to act in cases of humanitarian need, but acting independently of NATO and the United States.

ORGANIZATION FOR SECURITY AND COOPERATION IN EUROPE (OSCE)

The Conference on Security and Cooperation in Europe was formed in 1975 as a bargain between the Western and Soviet blocs. The West recognized Soviet hegemony in Eastern Europe, while the Soviets allowed human rights monitoring. Over time, reports on human rights abuses inside the Iron Curtain chipped away at the legitimacy of Communist regimes. In 1989, the Berlin Wall was breached, so the organization sought a new role. The transitions from communism to capitalism in Eastern Europe provided unique opportunities. Accordingly, CSCE members met in 1990 to sign the Charter of Paris for a New Europe, which codified guiding principles governing the "human dimension," and refocused the human security basket as (1) promoting tolerance, (2) strengthening democratic processes, and (3) combating racism, xenophobia, and discrimination.

In July 1992, Yugoslavia's membership was suspended for its support of ethnic cleansing in Bosnia. A fact-finding mission was dispatched in September, and in December a report condemned Yugoslavia. Belgrade finally regained membership in 2000.

In 1995, CSCE was re-titled the Organization for Security and Cooperation in Europe. By 2007, membership had increased to fifty-six, with eleven partner states. Members now include those who have joined COE plus Belarus, the Holy See, Central Asian states (Kazakhstan, Kyrgyzstan, Tajikistan, Turkmenistan, Uzbekistan), and North American states (Canada and the United States). The partner states are Afghanistan, Algeria, Egypt, Israel, Japan, Jordan, Mongolia, Morocco, South Korea, Thailand, and Tunisia.

CSCE and OSCE have distinguished themselves from COE and EU by following a process approach in which conferences are held on specific topics, discussion is wide-ranging, a consensus is sought on particular goals and plans of action, and a document is issued. *Action plans* involve reports, site visits, workshops, and similar vehicles. The Helsinki Final Act, the founding instrument, is thus supplemented by many documents that state binding commitments, norms, principles, and standards; together, the documentary basis is known as *acquis* OSCE. The organization has grown by accretion rather than by a systematic design and is result-oriented rather than legalistic.

OSCE is highly decentralized. The International Secretariat of the *Parliamentary Assembly* is in Copenhagen. The *Permanent Council*, composed of senior embassy officials, meets in Vienna. In 1991, CSCE set up a *Secretariat* in Prague, but in 1994 the Secretariat moved to Vienna, leaving a small public information office in Prague. Within the Vienna office, there are several units; the only one directly relating to human rights is the *Senior Gender Adviser*, who operates a program on gender mainstreaming.

In 1989, CSCE decided to launch the *Human Dimension Mechanism*, the initial element of which was a formal complaint process. The complaint process, known as the *Vienna Mechanism*, enables one member government to complain about another, triggering an investigation and, in the event that a problem is uncovered, an effort to conciliate. During the first year of operation, the Mechanism attracted about one hundred complaints, dealing with such matters as the imprisonment of Václav Havel

(1936–) in Czechoslovakia and Turkey's treatment of its Kurdish minority. In 1991, a second function was added, known as the *Moscow Mechanism*, in which *ad hoc* missions of independent experts assist in resolving a specific problem. The latter has been used to investigate atrocities and attacks on unarmed civilians in Croatia and Bosnia-Herzegovina, Estonian legislation in regard to human rights, Moldova's legislation and implementation of minorities' rights and interethnic relations, human rights violations in Yugoslavia (in which the latter refused to cooperate), and the attempted assassination of Turkmenistan President Saparmurat Niyazov (1940–2006) in 2002.

In 1990, the *Council of Ministers for Foreign Affairs* was created. The Council's Chairperson-in-Office is OSCE's top executive, assisted by *Special Representatives* in such areas as (1) trafficking in human beings; (2) racism, xenophobia and discrimination, including intolerance and discrimination against Christians and members of other religions; (3) anti-Semitism; and (4) intolerance and discrimination against Muslims.

In 1991, the Office for Free Elections was established to administer the Human Dimension Mechanism. In 1997, the structure became the *Office for Democratic Institutions and Human Rights*, charged primarily with the function of providing technical assistance and monitoring member and partner states. The Office, located in Warsaw, handles three tasks: (1) In the field of democratization, there are workshops to strengthen the rule of law, promote leadership skills for females, and combat violence against women. (2) In regard to election monitoring, the Office dispatches observers to elections; OSCE was on the scene in the Ukraine during 2005 to condemn election fraud in the first election and then returned to certify that the rescheduled election was free and fair. (3) The human rights function includes monitoring trials, visiting prisons, and holding workshops on nondiscrimination and tolerance.

In 1992, the first annual Parliamentary Assembly met; the aim is to involve national parliaments in OSCE activities. There are three General Committees, one of which is the *Democracy, Human Rights and Humanitarian Questions Committee*.

The *High Commissioner on National Minorities* was established in 1992 at The Hague to promote ethnic dialog and to recommend prompt action to deescalate tensions that might lead to large-scale violence against minorities. The following month, missions were dispatched to Kosovo, Sanjak, and Vojvodina, though Belgrade did not cooperate. The High Commissioner has actively sought to defuse tensions within many of the newest members. In a mission to Latvia in 2005, problems of the Russian minority were reviewed, thereby pacifying Moscow's anger over frequent OSCE criticisms regarding such matters as Russian troops in Georgia and Moldova and the suppression of the democratic process in Chechnya. In the latter case, Russia first asked OSCE officials to monitor elections and later asked them to leave when their report was unfavorable.

OSCE ultimately was given responsibility for negotiating the implementation of provisions of the Dayton Peace Agreement of 1995 regarding Bosnia, including military disengagement, holding elections, and monitoring human rights compliance. The latter task, which continues to the present, provides a model of how a regional organization can serve to improve human rights after peace is negotiated among parties to a war that had genocidal aspects. When Kosovo flared up in 1998, OSCE dispatched observers, but they pulled out in 1999 due to Serbian obstruction. War then ensued. After the war stopped, OSCE returned to organize elections in Kosovo.

The *Representative on Freedom of the Media*, created in 1997, has an office in Vienna. The main task is to monitor press restrictions and to intervene on behalf of news media and journalists who are under threat.

During 2005, there were OSCE field offices in sixteen countries. The first field office opened in Skopje during 1992, to ensure that the ongoing conflict in Yugoslavia would not spill over into Macedonia. Later, in 1992, an OSCE office was set up in Georgia to play a peacekeeping role; the office has remained to provide assistance in matters of human rights. From 1997, when a pyramid scheme impoverished many Albanians, OSCE established an office in Tirana to assist the country's democratization process.

OSCE, thus, is now involved in conflict prevention, post-conflict rehabilitation, and democracy building. The organization plays an important role in the diplomatic and political aspects of the human dimension of security, leaving military functions to the North Atlantic Treaty Organization and other bodies. Nearly three-quarters of the OSCE budget is spend on field operations, especially in the Balkans and in the independent states that were formerly part of the Soviet Union.

NORTH ATLANTIC TREATY ORGANIZATION (NATO)

One basic human right is the right to personal security. In 1948, to deter a possible invasion of Western Europe by the Soviet Union that might unleash a nuclear holocaust, five countries (Belgium, France, Luxembourg, the Netherlands and the United Kingdom) signed a defense agreement at Brussels, the Treaty of Economic, Social and Cultural Collaboration and Collective Self-Defense, forming the Brussels Treaty Organization (BTO).

In 1949, ten countries of Western Europe (BTO countries plus Denmark, Iceland, Italy, Norway, and Portugal), Canada, and the United States signed the Treaty of Washington to form the North Atlantic Treaty Organization as a collective security agreement. The preamble to the treaty states that NATO is "founded on the principles of democracy, individual liberty and the rule of law." BTO military responsibilities were then transferred to NATO.[3] A Summit in 1999 adopted the Strategic Concept, which acknowledged "new risks to Euro-Atlantic peace and stability, including [1] oppression, [2] ethnic conflict, [3] economic distress, [4] the collapse of political order, and [5] the proliferation of weapons of mass destruction."

From 1952–1982, four more Western European countries joined (Greece, Spain, Turkey, and West Germany). To develop liaison with Eastern European countries, the 1991 Summit set up the North Atlantic Cooperation Council, which in 1997 became the *Euro-Atlantic Partnership Council* (EAPC) through which ten Eastern European countries have joined NATO, while twenty-three other countries are in earlier stages of cooperation, including Russia and countries of the Caucasus and Central Asia.[4] In 1994, NATO began the Mediterranean Dialogue with Algeria, Egypt, Israel, Jordan, Mauritania, Morocco, and Tunisia.

Originally, the *Executive Secretariat* was in Paris, but in 1966 the headquarters moved to Brussels after French President Charles de Gaulle (1890–1970) expressed displeasure of America's intervention into the civil war in Vietnam. The *Secretary-General* handles the administrative affairs of the headquarters. The Secretariat's *Office of Information and Press* has occasionally been assigned to handle human rights activities. NATO also has offices in Sarajevo, Skopje, and Tirana.

In 1997, the NATO-Russia Permanent Joint Council was set up as a consultative body to mitigate tensions associated with NATO's expansion; however, Russia withdrew temporarily in 1999, while NATO bombed Serbia. In 2002, the body was renamed the NATO-Russia Council, with a broader scope, including the possibility of joint action. One activity emerging from closer relations with Russia occurred later that year, when NATO's Office of Information and Press sponsored a conference in Moscow on the human rights responsibilities of the military in armed domestic conflicts.

The first significant human rights role for NATO was in regard to Bosnia. In 1995, the UN Security Council authorized NATO air strikes to stop genocide and to force the Bosnian Serbs to negotiate a peace agreement. The resulting Dayton Peace Agreement set up the multinational peacekeeping Implementation Force (IFOR) under NATO command, with a grant of authority from the UN. The General Framework Agreement establishing IFOR had a human rights clause. In 1996, the Security Council authorized NATO to operate the Stabilization Force (SFOR) as IFOR's successor. In 1998, when the UN mandate expired, NATO operated SFOR, primarily for civilian reconstruction. One of SFOR's assignments was to cooperate with International Criminal Tribunal for the Former Yugoslavia in arresting the two top Bosnian Serb leaders. NATO, which has been criticized for not arresting Radovan Karadžić and Ratko Mladić, still supports a small contingent in Bosnia, though in 2004 SFOR responsibility was passed on to the European Union under the acronym EUFOR.

HISTORIC EVENT 12.1 THE KOSOVO WAR (1999)

In 1389, in the Battle of Kosovo, Serbia fought to prevent the armies of the Ottoman Empire from bringing Islam into Europe. Serbia lost and was an Ottoman province until 1815. After World War I, Kosovo and Serbia became part of the same country, first known as the Kingdom of Serbs, Croats, and Slovenes, and after 1929 as Yugoslavia. Serbia, the dominant republic in Yugoslavia, split Kosovo administratively into several counties. Ethnic Albanians (Kosovars), who comprised a majority within Kosovo, protested to the League of Nations in 1921 that they were denied self-determination, but the League rejected their complaint. After World War II, as the Kosovar population increased to about 80 percent of Kosovo, efforts to achieve more autonomy within Yugoslavia were also frustrated. Street protests led to Serbian repression and in 1990 to the cancellation of what little autonomy that Kosovo enjoyed within Yugoslavia. Protesters then declared Kosovo an independent country, but no other country recognized the declaration. In 1995, the Kosovo Liberation Army (KLA) was formed, and its attacks on Serbian police led to the intervention of the Serbian army. As violence escalated, in 1999, NATO airplanes bombed Serbia, which then agreed to an armistice, under which representatives of the Organization for Security and Cooperation in Europe sent observers to monitor the truce. When the KLA broke the ceasefire in 1999, Serbian troops went into Kosovo with the apparent intention of killing as many Kosovars as possible or so it seemed when forty-five Kosovars were massacred in Račak. As a result, the European Union imposed economic sanctions on Serbia. When Belgrade rejected terms of a proposed peace agreement, which would give the North Atlantic Treaty Organization unlimited access within Kosovo as well as Serbia, NATO forces bombed Serb military targets in Kosovo and ultimately civilian and military targets in Serbia. After seventy-eight days, Serbia sued for peace. The United Nations then took over the civilian admini-stration of Kosovo and authorized a NATO-led force of 50,000 troops from thirty-nine countries to maintain order. The UN considered the recognition of Kosovo as an independent country during 2007.

A similar pattern was repeated in regard to Kosovo. In 1998, EAPC began to provide humanitarian relief to ethnic Kosovar refugees fleeing from Kosovo into Albania and Macedonia. After a military exercise in Albania, NATO bombed Serbia. In response, Serbia stopped harassing Kosovars, so NATO ceased military operations. But in 1999 Serbia resumed ethnic cleansing in Kosovo, whereupon NATO launched Operation Allied Force, which engaged in an eleven-week bombing of Serbia to stop genocide against Albanians in Kosovo. After the war ended, the UN Security Council author-ized NATO troops to organize the peacekeeping force, the Kosovo Force (KFOR). In 2001, NATO began operating missions in Albania and Macedonia to prevent a Kosovar insurgent group from using the border areas for staging operations to unleash raids into Kosovo. The EU replaced NATO's mission in 2003.

NATO's bombing of Serbia in 1999 hit more than five hundred civilians and many civilian targets, prompting an outcry in some quarters that NATO was violating human rights while invoking the principle of humanitarian intervention. UN Secretary-General Kofi Annan (1938–) expressed reservations over NATO's military operation without Security Council authorization. The following year, Human Rights Watch submitted a complaint on behalf of some of the civilian victims of the NATO bombing to the International Criminal Tribunal for the Former Yugoslavia, which ruled in 2001 that the case, *Banković v Belgium et al.*, was not within its mandate.

In 2003, NATO took over command of the International Security Assistance Force in Afghanistan, which had been established by the United Nations in 2001 after the Afghan War. The aim is to provide a secure environment conducive to free and fair elections, the spread of the rule of law, and the reconstruction of the country. In 2004, NATO provided security for the election in Afghanistan, and in 2005 the force began to fight a Taliban-led insurgency in the south.

In 2004, NATO adopted a policy to combat the trafficking in human beings. Naval vessels patrolling the Mediterranean under the NATO flag are among the ways in which the policy is implemented. NATO has also conducted workshops on human rights in recent years.

For a decade, NATO has exercised the capability to enforce human rights obligations through military action. However, NATO's human rights enforcement has been selective. In 2003, some NATO members, notably France and Germany, blocked possible military action in Iraq because they perceived that insufficient evidence backed Washington's claim that the regime headed by President Saddam Hussein (1937–2006) was hiding weapons of mass destruction. After the war, NATO forces arrived to equip and to train the Iraq security forces.

EU and NATO have cooperated with independent missions in Bosnia since 2004 and in Darfur from 2005. The Darfur operation, which involves airlifting African Union peacekeeping forces, is NATO's first effort in Africa. In 2005, NATO also provided humanitarian relief to the victims of a severe earthquake in Pakistan, the first NATO operation in Asia.

Any controversy over NATO's role underscores the fact that the four European regional organizations reviewed above have complementary responsibilities. COE has a promotional and judicial role. The EU can apply economic sanctions to egregious cases but hopes one day to be able to refer less serious matters to COE's judicial process. OSCE is particularly adept at diplomatic and political negotiations as well as monitoring elections. NATO's military capabilities are both in the areas of enforcement and logistics. Overlapping organizational interests can serve to ensure that a human rights problem will receive condign attention. Nevertheless, relations between COE and OSCE have not always been friendly, and France has begun to persuade other European governments that an EU military force might be desirable as an alternative to NATO.

DISCUSSION TOPIC 12.1 WHICH FOREIGN POLICY DOES NATO PRIMARILY SERVE?

Among human rights problems around the world, NATO has only operated as an effective instrument on a few occasions. Identify human rights concerns that have galvanized NATO. Do NATO's actions show a pattern in which American foreign policy is in reality the top priority?

NORDIC COUNCIL

In 1952, the parliamentarians of Denmark, Iceland, Norway, and Sweden decided to meet together on a regular basis in an organization known as the Nordic Council. Finland joined in 1956, and the autonomous regions of Åland, the Faroe Islands, and Greenland are now separately represented; the Sami minority (Laplanders living in the northernmost countries) has Observer status. The organization was formalized by the Treaty of Cooperation Between Denmark, Finland, Iceland, Norway, and Sweden in 1962. The Presidium, formed from members of the Plenary Assembly in 1996, is the governing body. Among the committees, the *Citizens' and Consumer Rights Committee* deals with civil and political rights and the *Welfare Committee* focuses on social rights.

The organization sought to achieve some political integration in a manner that anticipated the European Union. In 1955, a citizen of one country working in another country was eligible for the same social and welfare benefits while in the latter country. The same applies to political rights: a citizen of one country residing in another can vote or run for office in the country of residence. In 1995, the organization adopted a comprehensive Nordic Model of gender equality and mainstreaming that has inspired feminists around the world. The exemplary Nordic Model also applies to labor relations and welfare systems.

COUNCIL OF THE BALTIC SEA STATES (CBSS)

Modeled in part on the Nordic Council, the Baltic Council was set up by a Terms of Reference agreement in 1992 among the ten countries bordering on the Baltic Sea. Iceland joined in 1995.[5]

Two among the six CBSS "subjects for cooperation" in its Terms of Reference are "assistance to new democratic institutions" and "humanitarian matters and health." In 1999, the *Baltic High Commissioner for Democratic Institutions, Human Rights and Ethnic Minorities* drew praise from UN Secretary-General Annan for achieving progress on improving the status of Russian minorities in Estonia, Latvia, and Lithuania. At the Summit in 2000, the basic principles referenced were "democracy, rule of law, [and] human rights." The Council's *Working Group on Democratic Institutions* sponsors expert conferences on a wide range of issues, most recently freedom of the press, trafficking in minors and women, civil society, and women's rights. In March 2002, the Children's Unit, which services the *Working Group for Cooperation on Children at Risk*, was integrated into the structure of the Secretariat.

At the 2005 meeting, Russia not only discussed possible compensation with Poland over the Katyń Massacre of some 20,000 Polish citizens in 1940 but also continued to criticize Estonia, Latvia, and Lithuania for mistreatment of their Russian minority populations.

HISTORIC EVENT 12.2 THE KATYŃ MASSACRE (1940)

In 1939, Nazi Germany attacked Poland and easily defeated the army. Fearing that Russia would be the next target, the Soviet Union negotiated a nonaggression pact with Germany under which Soviet troops occupied Eastern Poland and began to

continued

intern Polish officers while Germany did likewise. However, some 4,443 Polish officers were shot from behind by the Russian army and secretly stacked into mass graves in the Katyń forest in Western Russia. In 1941, the graves were discovered after Germany invaded Russia. Berlin then blamed the Soviets, but only in 1990 did the Soviet Union admit culpability after years of claiming that the Germans were responsible.

ARCTIC COUNCIL

In 1996, foreign ministers of the six European states bordering on the Arctic Ocean, Canada, and the United States formed the Arctic Council as a forum for cooperation between national governments and indigenous peoples. A unique feature is that six nongovernmental international organizations representing indigenous communities are Permanent Participants in the Arctic Council – the Aleuts, Athabaskans, Gwich'ins, Inuits, Samis, and the Russian Association of the Indigenous Peoples of the North. Although the Arctic Council's Secretariat is in Moscow, the *Arctic Council Indigenous Peoples' Secretariat* is in Copenhagen. The principal goal is sustainable development. Living conditions of the indigenous peoples are a central focus of the *Sustainable Development Working Group*, which has projects on children, education, health, and youth.

CONCLUSION

Europeans clearly prefer proactive methods in approaching human rights issues around the world. The labyrinthine array of institutions means that care must be exercised to avoid rivalry or least having different organizations duplicate one another's efforts. The comprehensive scope of European human rights programming attests to the ability of countries with similar cultural backgrounds to cooperate in depth. Other regions, as indicated in the following chapter, have not always been as successful.

CHAPTER 13

Third World approaches to international human rights

The present chapter delineates efforts to deal with human rights problems within the regions of Third World countries.[1] Regional intergovernmental organizations are more prominent than national efforts with a few notable exceptions.

THE AMERICAS

What is most noteworthy in the American hemisphere is a long tradition of regional cooperation, which began in 1826 when Simón Bolívar (1783–1830) convened the Congress of Panamá in 1826. After several more inter-American conferences, the Bogotá Conference of American States of 1948 produced the Charter of the Organization of American States (OAS) and adopted the American Declaration on the Rights and Duties of Man; signed several months before the Universal Declaration of Human Rights, they form the basis for most of the discussion in the present section.

Although **diplomacy** regarding human rights has largely taken place within the OAS forum, Costa Rican President Óscar Arias (1940–) deserves special mention. For negotiating the Esquipulas Accords of 1987 that brought peace to Central America, including an end to civil wars, increasingly free elections, and refugee assistance, he received the Nobel Peace Prize.

Regarding **economic** measures, the United States has provided an abundance of foreign aid. From 1959, Washington has maintained an economic boycott of Cuba that is decreasingly observed. Special mention should be made of the Canadian International Development Agency, which has special programs on human rights and for indigenous peoples.

▌ HISTORIC EVENT 13.1 OPERATION CONDOR (1975–1983)

During the Cold War, the United States was eager to stop the spread of Communist ideology. When Cuba decided to ally with the Soviet Union after 1959, Washington feared that the island would become a base for Communist insurgencies. Accordingly, the secret police of Argentina, Bolivia, Chile, Paraguay, and Uruguay, meeting in Chile during 1975, agreed to eliminate and persecute left-leaning politicians and their sympathizers in what was called Operation Condor; Brazil joined in 1976. The program included assassinations of leftist leaders when they visited France, Italy, Portugal, Spain, and the United States, where officials cooperated. Some South American operatives received training for the operation at the School for the Americas in the Panama Canal Zone, where a facility also assisted in coordinating communications for Operation Condor. Intelligence services of Colombia, Perú, and Venezuela also assisted in tracking down targets for assassination. The most famous assassination was of former Chilean Defense and Foreign Minister Orlando Letelier (1932–1976), who was carbombed during 1976 in Washington, D.C., an incident planned by various officials, including Luis Posada (1928–) and General Juan Manuel Guillermo Contreras Sepúlveda (1929–) of Chile's secret police. While Operation Condor proceeded as an international cooperative program, the South American countries domestically sought to arrest leftists, who in turn disappeared without a trace in what was known as "dirty wars." In some cases those arrested were tortured to obtain intelligence about the whereabouts of other opponents of the repressive regimes, and many were dropped into the ocean so that their bodies would never be found. Due to an outcry in Washington over Posada's role in the Letelier assassination, the United States is said to have ceased cooperation with Operation Condor, which officially ended in 1983 when Argentina's junta stepped down from power. Nevertheless, death squads continued to operate subsequently in other South American countries.

Argentina has taken the lead in the **legal** approach to human rights, seeking justice in regard to Operation Condor, the multicountry program to murder Latin American leftists. In 2001, some 200 indictments were issued, naming former Bolivian President Hugo Banzer (1926–); three Chileans, including former President Augusto Pinochet (1915–2006); former Paraguayan President Alfredo Stroessner (1912–2005) and three other Paraguayans; and six Uruguayans. Among those indicted, Manuel Contreras (1929–) was also indicted in France, Italy, and the United States for ordering assassinations in those countries; he was ultimately tried and convicted in his own country, Chile. In his defense, he submitted documents identifying Pinochet as specifically ordering human rights violations. In connection with the investigation, a request for a deposition from Henry Kissinger (1923–) was issued, but the former Secretary of State declined the invitation.

In 2006, Argentina charged Ali Akbar Hashemi Rafsanjami (1934–), former president of Iran, and eight associates for their alleged role in the bombing of a Jewish

Center in Buenos Aires during 1994, the worst terrorist attack in the country. Arrest warrants were issued for the Iranian government's role in financing the Hezbollah of Lebanon, which is accused to planting a bomb that killed eighty-five persons and injured more than 200 others. A similar blast at the Israeli embassy in Buenos Aires during 1992 is now under investigation. Argentine officials believe that the attacks may have been in retaliation for the country's refusal to provide nuclear materials and technology to Teheran. In contrast, Washington has refused to allow Venezuela to exercise extraterritorial jurisdiction over Luis Posada (1928–) for his alleged role in shooting down a Cuban airliner during 1976.

COURT CASE 13.1 *LUIS POSADA V UNITED STATES* (2007)

In 1976, Luis Posada was partly responsible for bombing a Cuban civilian airplane, and in 1977 he facilitated the bombing of hotels in Cuba, acts for which some observers earned him the designation as the top terrorist in the Western Hemisphere. Cuban born, he relocated to the United States in 1961, was recruited as a CIA operative, and was involved in Operation Condor. In 1968, the CIA dropped him because of his association with criminal elements, so he moved to Venezuela, where he became a citizen, though he was later imprisoned there on criminal charges, and he eventually escaped from prison. While in Panamá in 2000, he was convicted and imprisoned for plotting to kill Fidel Castro at a summit conference. Pardoned by the Panamanian president in 2005, he sneaked into the United States to seek asylum and was soon jailed as an illegal entrant, subject to deportation. When his whereabouts became known, the Venezuelan government requested his extradition to serve out his prison sentence, and Cuba sought him on charges of terrorism, though Havana decided to defer the case to Venezuela. Although Cuba and Venezuela sought to put him on trial for crimes that he has admitted publicly, a federal judge accepted the American government's prediction that he might be tortured upon arrival in Venezuela, whereupon Caracas attacked the United States for hypocrisy in the "war on terrorism" by not allowing him to be extradited and tried.

Military actions by the United States in the region have not always been appreciated by Latin American countries. Canada deserves special praise for the professionalization of its army to provide peacekeeping forces for the United Nations, though outside the Americas.

- *Organization of American States* (OAS). The OAS Charter states that member states are committed to "democratic institutions, [and] a system of individual liberty and social justice based on respect for the essential rights of man" and "all human beings, without distinction as to race, nationality, sex, creed or social condition, have the right to attain material well-being and spiritual growth under circumstances of liberty, dignity, equality of opportunity, and economic security." The American Declaration on the Rights and Duties of Man lists specific rights, including the rights to education, a family, and to protection of children, mothers, and personal reputation. Other agreements in the area of human rights have been adopted over the years (Table 13.1).

The American Convention on Human Rights was adopted in 1969. Some rights were granted that were not in the original European Convention for the Protection of Human Rights and Fundamental Freedoms – the right of reply, rights of children, the right to a name and a nationality, and the right of asylum.

All twenty-one independent states in the Western Hemisphere joined the OAS in 1948. Three years after the Cuban revolution of 1959, Havana was charged with subversion in the region and formally expelled, though six countries abstained in the vote. In 1992, the Protocol of Washington provided that a government which overthrows a democracy can be expelled from OAS. In 2001, the OAS adopted the Inter-American Democratic Charter, which broadened the focus on civil and political rights by defining essential elements of a "democracy."

The supreme organ is the annual General Assembly. A member state may request a Meeting of Consultation of Ministers of Foreign Affairs to consider urgent situations that threaten peace. A Secretary General heads the General Secretariat (the Pan-American Union up to 1970), which has several units. In

TABLE 13.1 HUMAN RIGHTS TREATIES OF THE ORGANIZATION OF AMERICAN STATES

Adopted	Title of the declaration or treaty	In force
1948	Charter of the Organization of American States*	1951
1967	• Protocol of Buenos Aires*	1970
1985	• Protocol of Cartagena de las Indias	1988
1992	• Protocol of Washington*	1997
1993	• Protocol of Managua*	1996
1954	Convention on Diplomatic Asylum	
1954	Convention on Territorial Asylum	
1969	American Convention on Human Rights	1978
1988	• Protocol of San Salvador	
1990	• Protocol to Abolish the Death Penalty	
1985	Inter-American Convention to Prevent and Punish Torture	1987
1994	Convention on the Prevention, Punishment and Eradication of Violence Against Women	1995
1994	Convention on Forced Disappearances of Persons	1996
1999	Convention on the Elimination of All Forms of Discrimination Against Persons with Disabilities	

*Ratified by the United States

1990, the *Unit for Promotion of Democracy* was established; the current mission to coordinate election supervision missions and to administer country programs to improve democratic institutions. In 1999, the *Justice Studies Center* of the Americas was located at Santiago, Chile, to assist countries in improving their criminal justice systems.

In 1959, OAS established the *Inter-American Commission on Human Rights*. In contrast with European human rights organs, which work with governments trying to improve and to harmonize practices, many governments in the Americas have been hostile to human rights, so progress was sporadic until more democracies emerged in the 1990s. The Commission performs several functions: (1) drafting declarations and treaties, (2) holding conferences and seminars to raise consciousness about the need to advance human rights, (3) monitoring situations, (4) publishing country and thematic reports, (5) responding to complaints, (6) making visits, and (7) issuing recommendations.

The Commission was first authorized to handle complaints in 1965. Today, nearly one thousand **petitions** are received each year. When ruled admissible as possible violations of the treaties ratified by the members, the petitions are considered **cases** and are first referred to the states for a response. Compared with other human rights bodies around the world, the Commission imposes few technical requirements for individual complaints, so the complaints can be used as pretexts for wide-ranging surveys of the entire country of the complainant. In response to a petition, the Commission may hold **hearings**, make **recommendations** to states, issue **precautionary measures** (for immediate action in urgent cases), undertake **friendly settlements**, or make a **decision on the merits**. In the latter case, the Commission may either publish a **report** or **refer** the matter to the jurisdiction of the Inter-American Court of Human Rights as **contentious cases** or for **advisory opinions**. When a complaint is about a dangerous situation, the Commission can ask the Court to issue **provisional measures** to states so that individuals can be placed out of harm's way before cases are tried. Since the Commission prefers informal settlements, they can be determined with great speed, but implementation may often drag on for years.

From 1997–2004, the Commission received 9,522 petitions. Among 1,021 complaints processed in 2004, the Commission issued a precautionary measure to Argentina for deaths in prison and ruled that Jamaica failed to provide legal aid, conducted an irregular trial, and violated the rights of detention of a person accused of a capital offense. In the latter case, the Commission asked for a retrial and for Jamaica to revise detention and trial procedures.

From 1961–2004, the Commission carried out eighty-seven **visits** *in loco* to investigate member states. Authorization for the visits, which involve observing the human rights situation in a country in response to petitions from member states, expanded in 1965 to involve investigation of complaints from individuals and in 1969 to nonmember states. In 2000, OAS representatives were present in Perú to monitor national elections.

In 1991, the OAS General Assembly adopted *Resolution 1080*, which requires the Secretary General to convene the Permanent Council and the Meeting of Consultation within ten days after a coup or other interruption of a legitimate, elected government. Resolution 1080 has been invoked several times: Haiti (1991, 2002), Peru (1992, 2000), Guatemala (1993), Paraguay (1996, 1999), and Venezuela (twice in 2002).

In addition, OAS **Secretary-General visits** to countries may be appropriate to advance human rights. In 2005, for example, the Secretary-General visited Nicaragua regarding the forthcoming general election, in which an opposition political party expressed concern about the fairness of the electoral process.

COURT CASE 13.2 THE TRIALS OF LORI BERENSON (1996 AND 2001)

In 1995, an American citizen, Lori Berenson (1970–), was arrested on a bus in Lima, Perú, amid a mass arrest of suspected terrorists for aiding an abortive attack on Perú's Congress by leftist rebels. In 1996, she was tried by a hooded military tribunal without the benefit of cross-examination under an anti-terrorism law decreed during a state of emergency. She was found guilty and sentenced to life imprisonment for "treason against the fatherland," a trial later condemned by the UN Commission on Human Rights. In 1998, she appealed her case to the Inter-American Commission on Human Rights. (Meanwhile, the Committee on Arbitrary Detentions of the UN High Commissioner for Human Rights visited her in prison in 1998 and condemned her detention as arbitrary and a violation of the International Covenant on Civil and Political Rights the following year.) In 1999, after the Inter-American Court of Human Rights ruled that four other detainees should be retried in civilian courts, Perú withdrew from the Court. In 2000, Perú's Supreme Military Justice Commission vacated Berenson's military trial and ordered a civilian court trial. When in 2001 she was again found guilty and sentenced to a twenty-year term, she appealed to the Commission, which in 2002 judged that she was denied due process, subjected to inhumane detention, and that Perú should bring its terrorism law up to international standards. When Perú refused to revise the terrorism law, the Commission referred her case to the Inter-American Court of Human Rights, which in 2004 inexplicably reversed the Commission's ruling. Berenson is still in prison.

Commission **recommendations** need not await complaints. In 2002, the Commission criticized Perú for lack of judicial due process in the celebrated trial of Lori Berenson, whereupon Perú withdrew from the Inter-American Court of Human Rights. In the following year, Trinidad and Tobago was informed that its use of the death penalty was inconsistent with the 1990 Protocol to Abolish the Death Penalty, whereupon the country withdrew from the Protocol. In 2002, when reports emerged of possible mistreatment of detainees at the Guantánamo Naval Base in Cuba, the Commission recommended that the United States hold hearings required by the Geneva Conventions to determine which persons were prisoners of war. Washington rejected the request, so American membership on the Commission was suspended in 2003.

OAS also has some specialized organs, a few of which date before World War II. In 1902, the Pan American Sanitary Bureau was established to fight the spread of disease from ships; the name changed in 1947 to Pan American Sanitary Organization and again in 1949 to the *Pan American Health Organization*. The *Inter-American Children's Institute*, founded in 1927, engages in research and social action on problems of minors and families, including trafficking, child labor, commercial sexual exploitation, international abduction, and war-affected children. The *Inter-American Commission of Women*, set up in 1928, the first international organization focusing on the civil, political, economic, social, and cultural rights of women, requires periodic reporting. The *Inter-American Indian Institute*, which dates from 1940, coordinates programs on the needs and rights of indigenous peoples.

The Inter-American Economic and Social Council, created in 1967 to advance social and economics rights, was replaced in 1983 by the *Inter-American Council for Integral Development*. The *Inter-American Cultural Council*, also set up in 1967, promotes cultural exchanges though the *Committee for Cultural Action*.

Examples of OAS's transformation are the ways in which Chile and Nicaragua were handled during two difficult decades. In 1973, the Executive Secretary of the Inter-American Commission on Human Rights went to Chile after General Augusto Pinochet (1915–2006) toppled President Salvador Allende (1906–1973); he then asked the Commission to conduct an on-site visit. The Commission's report of 1974 lambasted the new Chilean government for human rights violations based on a thorough inspection of courts, legislation, and prisons. In 1975, the Commission received complaints from almost one thousand persons regarding disappearances and torture. Annual reports on the situation in Chile kept up the pressure until the government agreed to hold elections in 1989.

As for Nicaragua, in 1979 the OAS General Assembly called for President Anastasio Somoza (1896–1956) to resign as President after the Commission cited human rights violations of the National Guard and mediation efforts failed. After Somoza stepped down, the Sandinista Party won elections. A Nicaraguan insurgent group then formed, with American assistance, inside the border of Honduras to launch a civil war, which ended in 1989 through the mediation of Óscar Arias. One provision of the ceasefire was to have OAS and UN agencies monitor the demobilization of the insurgents, an operation that lasted from 1990-1993, involving relocation and humanitarian assistance of some 120,000 displaced persons within demobilization areas. As a result, OAS was transformed into an operational organization, aiding refugees.

- *Inter-American Court of Human Rights* (IACHR). In 1907, the Central American Court of Justice (CACJ) was formed. Of the ten cases decided during the eleven years of the Court's existence, all five human rights cases were dismissed. In 1978, sixty years after CACJ suspended operations, the American Convention on Human Rights came into force, creating the Inter-American Court of Human Rights, a body independent of OAS. Of the twenty-six OAS members that have ratified thus far, only Dominica, Grenada, Jamaica, and the United States have not ratified the Optional Clause to the Convention and thus do not accept the jurisdiction of the Court. If a state has not accepted the Optional Clause of the Convention on Human Rights, the Court instead invokes the American Declaration of the Rights and Duties of Man of 1948 as the basis for decisions.

Cases may be filed with the Court either by the OAS Commission on Human Rights or by a ratifying government. Litigation must be about specific violations rather than general patterns, as the OAS Commission handles the latter type of question. The Court may award compensatory damages, including attorneys' costs and amounts for emotional harm, but not punitive damages. If a state fails to abide by a decision of the Court, the matter may be referred to the OAS General Assembly.

In 2004, the Court processed some fifty-nine cases, including thirty-four **provisional measures** (similar to the Commission's precautionary measures), three **friendly settlements**, and four **decisions on the merits**. In one case, a complaint decided on the merits, Belize was cited for allowing logging and oil drilling operations that jeopardized ancestral lands of the Mayan people. The Court ordered the government to delineate the ancestral lands more carefully, thus following the precedent in *Awas Tingni v Nicaragua* (2001), as noted in Chapter 6.

Thus far, the court has issued eighteen *advisory opinions*. In 2000, because the United States has not ratified the Optional Clause, the Court issued an advisory opinion that seventeen Mexicans on death row in Texas, who had not been afforded the opportunity to seek consular representation, were being denied due process.

- *South American Community of Nations* (SACN). In 2007, a merger was expected between two free-trade areas, the *Andean Community* (ANCOM) and the Common Market of the South known as *Mercado Común del Sur* (MERCOSUR). Nearly all South American countries would belong; the exceptions are Chile, French Guiana, and two members of the Caribbean Community (Guyana and Suriname). Both ANCOM and MERCOSUR have long been in the forefront of human rights advocacy.

  ANCOM's founding Cartagena Agreement of 1969 pledged members to "the principles of equality, justice, peace, solidarity, and democracy." In 1980, the Riobamba Code of Conduct was a pledge to observe human rights. In 2000, the Andean countries (Bolivia, Colombia, Ecuador, Perú, Venezuela) formalized the Presidential Declaration on the Andean Community Commitment to Democracy of 1998 into the Andean Community Commitment to Democracy as an Additional Protocol to the founding Cartagena Agreement of 1969 that would have the effect of suspending the benefits of membership to any country that might have a "disruption of the democratic order." In 2001, the Machu Picchu Declaration on Democracy, the Rights of Indigenous Peoples and the War Against Poverty provided further evidence of a strong human rights commitment. ANCOM also set up a Court of Justice in 1996 and the Andean Health Organization in 1998.

  In 1997, MERCOSUR (composed of Argentina, Brazil, Paraguay, and Uruguay) first demonstrated a concern for human rights during an attempted coup in Paraguay. Argentina, Brazil, and the United States so warned the military in

Asunción that they backed down and restored civilian rule. In 1997, MERCOCUR then amended the founding agreement of 1991 to have a clause requiring all members to be democracies. Both Bolivia and Chile, which have free trade agreements with MERCOSUR, have accepted what is known as the "democratic clause," which could be invoked to withdraw economic cooperation from a country that becomes undemocratic.

- *Caribbean Community* (CARICOM). In 1973, the Caribbean Community (CARICOM) superseded the Caribbean Free Trade Association, setting the goal of a common market among the countries, which then numbered fifteen. In 1997, the organization adopted the Charter for Civil Society, enunciating the following principles: "[1] fair and open democratic process; [2] the effective functioning of the parliamentary system; [3] morality in public affairs; [4] respect for fundamental civil, political, economic, social and cultural rights; [5] the rights of women and children; [6] respect for religious diversity; and [7] greater accountability and transparency in government."

  To promote the goals of the Charter, the *Council for Human and Social Development* was established in 1998. Priorities are on cultural preservation and women's rights.

- *Summit of the Americas*. In 1994, heads of hemispheric governments met with the aim of building a consensus on a wide range of issues, most notably the possibility of a Free Trade Area of the Americas (FTAA), which might merge ANCOM, the Caribbean Community (CARICOM), the Central American Common Market (CACM), MERCOSUR, and the North American Free Trade Area (NAFTA). Four subsequent Summits have been held, but most governments are skeptical, given the World Trade Organization's perceived bias toward developed countries.

Clearly, regional organizations in the Americas have been leaders in the quest to improve human rights. Instead of Europe's overlapping organizations, the Americas have the advantage of somewhat more coherence.

THE MIDDLE EAST

Most countries in the Middle East are united in opposition to the way in which Israel governs the West Bank of the River Jordan, where a Palestinian state might come into existence. Saudi Arabia has attempted **diplomacy** to resolve the issue. Very limited **legal** approaches to human rights are found principally inside regional organizations. Saudi Arabia, however, has **funded** Wahhabic educational institutions around the world, where in some cases the teachers preach death to infidels. The **military** approach to Palestinian self-determination failed when Israel defeated enemies in 1948, 1967, and 1973.

- *League of Arab States* (LAS). Founded in 1945, the League of Arab States (also known as the Arab League) has twenty-two members,[2] including the Palestine Liberation Organization (PLO), which was admitted in 1976. The original purpose was to pressure colonial powers to grant independence to Arab states and to prevent the establishment of the state of Israel. In 1949, the League agreed that citizenship should not be given throughout the Arab world to Palestinians forced out of their homelands, thus ensuring that there would be a refugee problem. Arab countries also began expelling Jewish residents, many of whom then resettled in Israel with bitter anti-Arab attitudes. In 1954, the League called for a comprehensive economic boycott of Israel that was extended in 1967 to a ban on films with pro-Israeli American actors.

In 1979, Egypt's membership was suspended because President Anwar Sadat (1918–1981) signed a peace treaty with Israel, whereupon the League's Secretariat moved from Cairo to Tunis. In 1989, the headquarters returned to Cairo. No punitive action was taken against Jordan, which signed a peace treaty with Israel in 1994.

The Charter of the Arab League provides the foundation for the organization. In the early years, the organization adopted the Cultural Treaty of the Arab League (1946). LAS has given support to Arabic language textbooks and to the preservation of artifacts.

Two committees of the LAS *Council* are relevant to human rights – the *Arab Women's Committee* and the *Human Rights Committee*. Council meetings regularly condemn Israel, ask for the immediate return of the Golan Heights to Syria, and back Palestinian rights in accordance with UN General Assembly resolutions. From time to time, heads of state and government convene in what is called the *Arab Summit*. In 2002, Israel would not give PLO President Yasser Arafat (1929–2004) permission to attend.

In 1968, the League decided to create the *Permanent Arab Commission on Human Rights*. Among the promotional activities of the Commission is the offer to assist Iraq in writing its new constitution. In 1972, an Arab League Educational, Scientific, and Cultural Organization was approved, but never implemented. A Women's Summit was held in 2001.

Over the years LAS has addressed cultural issues, economic goals, problems of migrant laborers, and has pledged to advance the role of women. LAS has attempted to mediate several regional conflicts, not always successfully. In 1989, the League drew up an agreement to end the civil war in Lebanon. In 2003, the League opposed the American intervention of Iraq. After Israel began construction of a security wall in 2003 to fence in the Palestinian Authority, the League submitted a legal statement to the International Court of Justice, which agreed with LAS' opposition.

In 1990, the League adopted the Cairo Declaration on Human Rights in Islam. In 1994, the Council adopted the Arab Charter on Human Rights, which recognizes the "right to a life of dignity based on freedom, justice and peace," and also rejects Zionism and racism as violations of human rights and threats to peace. In 2004, the Charter was slightly revised, after approval by the Permanent Arab Commission on Human Rights, but there has been no progress toward ratifications. In 2004, the Joint Defense and Economic Cooperation Treaty was amended to set up an *Economic and Social Council*. The Summit in 2005 proposed an Arab Parliament, a Court of Justice, an Arab Security Council, and an Arab Investment Bank.

In 2004, the League sent a fact-finding mission to Darfur. According to a press release from the Secretariat, the report found "gross human rights violations" committed by government forces and pro-government militias, whereupon the scheduled Summit meeting was postponed for two months because Sudan, an LAS member, objected to the statement. Soon, a new press release promised relief for the human suffering in Darfur, and Sudan not only welcomed that relief but also pledged to make peace with rebels in Darfur. The League, in short, engaged in quiet diplomacy in an effort to stop the imposition of threatened sanctions on Khartoum. The League then joined the European Union in negotiations to reach a settlement of the dispute in Darfur. Although neither the Summit nor the Council condemned Sudan's human rights violations, they urged member governments to improve their implementation of the concepts of democracy and human rights, notably the rights of children and women. Never before had the League adopted a measure that would involve significant changes in internal governance of a member country.

Also in 2004, the LAS Secretary-General called for a UN investigation of charges of inhuman prison conditions in Israel, contrary to the Geneva Conventions, after some 8,000 Palestinian prisoners began a hunger strike. After American abuse of prisoners in Iraq was exposed in 2005, Arab governments began to pay closer attention to their own prison conditions. In 2005, the League called upon the United States to apologize for abuses committed against the Koran in the Guantánamo detention center.

Although security issues have often trumped other issues, human rights are of increasing priority. Because consensus is sometimes difficult within the League, several subregional organizations are discussed next.

- *Cooperation Council for the Arab States.* In 1981, six Arabic-speaking countries bordering on the Persian Gulf, under the leadership of Saudi Arabia, formed an organization known for short as the Gulf Cooperation Council (GCC). The members are Bahrain, Kuwait, Oman, Qatar, Saudi Arabia, and the United Arab Emirates.

  GCC has been most active in pursuing economic development goals. The major human rights interest is over the treatment of Palestinians by Israel, though prison conditions have been a recent concern.

  Although the primary objective of the founding Charter is economic, cultural and educational goals are mentioned. The latter focus is on social care, social security, social aid and social development. To coordinate social rights projects, there are several bodies, most prominently the *Executive Bureau of the Ministers of Labor and Social Affairs Council,* a technical commission. Other coordination committees exist for problems of children and the handicapped; the aim is to draft model legislation for rehabilitation and employment of the handicapped, as well as to promote the quality of the services to children.

- *Arab Cooperation Council* (ACC). In 1989, riots broke out in Jordan from a population demanding political liberalization, whereupon Amman forged the Arab Cooperation Council with Egypt, Iraq, and Yemen. The organization collapsed after Iraq military forces attempted to annex Kuwait in 1990.

- *Union du Maghreb Árabe* (UMA).[3] One day after ACC was formed, five North African government heads formed the Arab Maghreb Union through a Declaration that includes a pledge "to work together with the international community for establishing a world order where justice, dignity, freedom and human rights prevail . . ." The members are Algeria, Libya, Mauritania, Morocco, and Tunisia. The organization has been hamstrung by the dispute between Algeria and Morocco over a territory that the former calls Western Sahara, the latter Moroccan Sahara.

Although regional intergovernmental organizations in the Middle East have a potential to address human rights issues, traditional views on such issues as the role of women continue to prevail. Progressive groups have instead formed nongovernmental organizations in the region.

ASIA AND THE PACIFIC

Indonesian **diplomacy** stands out in the region in efforts to negotiate an end to the Cambodian civil war during the 1980s, but was notably absent during Jakarta's military annexation of Portugal's former East Timor colony from 1975–1999. China and Korea have issued diplomatic denunciations whenever Japanese leaders or textbooks have glossed over human rights violations committed by Japan during World War II.

In 1990, after a Korean woman spoke out for the first time in public about the use of "comfort women" by Japanese soldiers during World War II as sex slaves, involving about ten encounters daily, the Japanese government immediately denied the accusation. However, a Japanese historian found incriminating documentation in government archives, prompting Tokyo to make an official apology in 1992. However, the government refused to provide direct compensation, instead establishing a private fund to compensate the women, though fewer than 30 percent of an estimated 50,000–200,000 survived the ordeal.

The **legal** approach has had mixed results in Japanese courts. At least fifty suits have been filed by Chinese, Korean, and Taiwanese workers who were forced to work for Japanese corporations during World War II. In 1989, eight Chinese workers conscripted by Kajima Corporation demanded compensation; after being offered $565,000 in 1995, they refused the amount and filed suit, and in 2000 the corporation agreed to pay $4.6 million. A similar suit, filed on behalf of forty Koreans forced to work for Mitsubishi Corporation, was successful in 1999. In 2001, a Japanese court ordered the government to compensate slave laborers for failing to pay them when they returned to China, Korea, and Taiwan after the war. In 2002, a mining firm was found guilty of importing Chinese as involuntary laborers during the war, and in 2004 both the government and a corporation were ordered to pay $75,000 to ten Chinese forced laborers and a surviving family of an eleventh wartime slave laborer. Encouraged by the settlement, some eighty-six Chinese went to Tokyo in 2006 to file suit on behalf of three hundred forced laborers and their survivors. In 2007, on the basis that China had renounced reparations in a joint statement with Japan in 1972, the High Court voided a lower court decision dealing with slave laborers and another involving sex slaves.

Claims by 180 Chinese that they were victims of a germ-warfare program were dismissed in 2005 by the Tokyo High Court on the basis of Japan's peace treaty with China of 1978. Some 270,000 were adversely affected by the program, according to a Chinese government estimate.

Tokyo has taken the lead in providing generous **economic** assistance throughout the world, including Asia and the Pacific. In accordance with the Japanese Peace Treaty of 1951, Japan paid reparations to the Philippines for damages caused in World War II, but China, Korea, and Taiwan were not parties to the treaty. However, Japanese foreign aid has been criticized for being too closely articulated to the needs of outsourced suppliers of components imported by Japanese businesses, notably through the intergovernmental Asian Productivity Organization.

Military approaches to human rights are regarded with suspicion in the region. Nevertheless, as a million or more deaths occurred in Cambodia after the Khmer Rouge seized power in 1975, Vietnam responded to attacks on its borders by launching a large-scale invasion, after efforts to find a peaceful settlement at the UN and elsewhere failed. Easily driving the Khmer Rouge out of the country, Hanoi justified the action as humanitarian intervention, but other countries objected and persuaded the world community to withhold diplomatic recognition from the new Cambodian government, which was protected for a decade by the Vietnamese army.

The Australian army has played a key role in cases of civil unrest the South Pacific. In 2004, Australia sent troops to Papua New Guinea, and as recently as 2006 Canberra sent deployments to East Timor and the Solomon Islands.

Among more than seventy-five regional intergovernmental organizations in Asia and the Pacific, civil and political rights issues have not been prominent. Technical bodies address social issues, such as education, but offer technical assistance without identifying gaps in human rights standards. Whereas the South Pacific has region-wide intergovernmental organizations, the vast Asian continent only has subregional bodies.

- *Organization of the Black Sea Economic Cooperation* (BSEC). In 1992, at the initiative of Turkey, eleven countries[4] bordering on or near the Black Sea formed an organization to promote economic cooperation as well as "human rights and fundamental freedoms, prosperity through economic liberty, social justice, and equal security." The primary human rights focus, enhancing the incomes of agricultural workers, is a matter for discussion in the *Working Group on Agriculture and Agro-Industry*. Human rights recommendations have been issued regarding displaced persons, refugees, and the social protection of pensioners.

- *Eurasian Economic Community* (EurAsEC). A successor to the attempted Commonwealth of Independent States, the Eurasian Economic Community was formed in 2000 among Belarus, Russia, and the former Soviet Central Asian republics (Kazakhstan, Kyrgystan, Tajikistan, Turkmenistan, and Uzbekistan). Apart from the goal of an eventual common market, the organization is committed to equal rights in education and health care.

- *Economic Cooperation Organization* (ECO). Established initially as Regional Cooperation for Development (RCD) from 1964–1979, ECO began in 1980. In

1992, membership expanded from Iran, Pakistan, and Turkey to include Afghanistan, Azerbaijan, and the five "Stan" countries of Central Asia. The basic document, the Treaty of Izmir of 1977, as amended in 1990 and 1992, provides one human rights goal – raising "the standard of living and quality of life." In addition, the declaration issued from the Istanbul Summit of 1992 called attention to a desire to enhance the "empowerment of women and their full participation in the economic development activities in the ECO region." Human development has been identified as a priority. One relevant project is the establishment in 2002 of a special fund to rebuild war-torn Afghanistan.

- *South Asian Association for Regional Cooperation* (SAARC). Consisting of the countries bordering India except for China (Bangladesh, Bhutan, Nepal, Pakistan, and Sri Lanka), plus the Maldive Islands. The founding Charter of 1985 establishes such goals as "social justice" and "promoting the welfare and improving the quality of life of the peoples of the region."

  Human rights issues emerged quite early, with a focus on women due in part to the fact that female prime ministers have headed governments in India, Pakistan, and Sri Lanka. One of the seven standing committees is entitled *Women, Youth, and Children*; another is the *Human Resource Development Committee*. In 1998, the SAARC *Human Resource Development Center* was set up at Islamabad to sponsor conferences and studies. The 1993 Summit adopted a declaration that places the goal of relieving poverty as a high priority. The Social Charter, adopted in 2004, establishes targets to be achieved in (1) alleviating poverty, (2) empowering women, (3) mobilizing youth, (4) developing human resources, (5) promoting health and nutrition, and (6) protecting children.

- *Association of South East Asian Nations* (ASEAN). In 1967, ASEAN superseded the former Association of South Asia (Malaysia, the Philippines, and Thailand) with five members (Indonesia, Malaysia, the Philippines, Singapore, Thailand). The Bangkok Declaration that launched ASEAN references the goals of "freedom, social justice, and economic well-being" and "respect for justice and the rule of law." The meaning of "social justice" was understood as the "elimination of poverty, hunger, disease and illiteracy."

  The next five countries to join, some of the world's worst violators of human rights, were Brunei, the three Indochinese countries (Cambodia, Laos, Vietnam), and Myanmar. Myanmar's admission in 1977 so rankled many European Union countries that they called off an ASEAN-Europe Meeting in 1998 and began to insist on the exclusion of Myanmar from any future meetings with ASEAN. In 1997, ASEAN was scheduled to admit Cambodia, but a coup in Phnom Penh prompted the organization to delay membership until 1999, when rival factions became reconciled.

  ASEAN's efforts to employ "constructive engagement" with Myanmar have produced almost no results. In 2003, Malaysian Prime Minister Mahathir bin Mohamad (1925–) even suggested Myanmar's expulsion from ASEAN if the military regime remained obstinate. The noninterference policy was also shattered in 1998, when Philippine President Joseph Estrada (1937–) openly criticized Malaysia for imprisoning Deputy Prime Minister Anwar Ibrahim (1947–), whose increasing popularity was a threat to Mahathir's continuation in power.

In 1998, the Plan of Action adopted at the ASEAN Summit focused on economic issues, including human resource development. But there was a section pledging that ASEAN would "promote and protect all human rights and fundamental freedoms of all peoples" and delineating such problems as the plight of children, the disabled, the elderly and women.

- *Shanghai Cooperation Organization* (SCO). In 1996, China's foreign ministry hosted a meeting with foreign ministers from Kazakhstan, Kyrgystan, Russia, and Tajikistan to enhance border security. Annual meetings thereafter were formalized by a Declaration at a meeting in Shanghai during mid-2001, when Uzbekistan joined, that identifies three "evil forces" – extremism, separatism, and terrorism. A Charter, signed in 2002, states the following aim: the "promotion of a new democratic, fair and rational political and economic international order." The declaration about extremism refers to radical Islamic elements that have been suppressed, at times brutally, in several member countries. In 2004, SCO established a *Regional Anti-Terrorism Structure* at Tashkent. Otherwise, SCO has no operational programming on human rights.

- *Pacific Community*. In 1947, Australia sponsored the formation of the South Pacific Commission, which then had as members Australia, Britain, France, the Netherlands, New Zealand and the United States. In 1997, after the admission of many independent countries in Micronesia, north of the equator, the organization was renamed Pacific Community. Today, twenty-two island states, some not yet sovereign, are members along with all the founding countries but the Netherlands.[5]

  Among the goals set forth in the founding Canberra Agreement is "to study, formulate and recommend measures for the development of, and where necessary the coordination of services affecting, the economic and social rights and welfare" of the peoples of the region. Among the services identified in the agreement are education, health, housing and social welfare. Although the subject of human rights is not formally discussed, the project work of the organization serves to alleviate economic and social inequality.

- *Pacific Islands Forum* (PIF). In 1971, Fiji hosted a conference of the leaders of five newly independent island states plus Australia and New Zealand; the result was the establishment of the South Pacific Forum. In 1999, the organization changed its name from South Pacific Forum in recognition of the presence of the North Pacific island states of Micronesia among the newest members. Today, all sixteen independent states in the region are members.[6]

  The Forum initially encouraged self-determination for the remaining territories. Accordingly, the Forum still exerts pressure on France to grant independence to French Polynesia and New Caledonia. New Caledonia attends as an Observer since France promises to grant independence to the territory, to be named Kanaky, by 2013 or 2018. The Forum also welcomed East Timor's participation while the country was spurned by ASEAN. A dissident group in West Papua, which Indonesia governs as the province of Irian Jaya, has petitioned the Forum for Observer status; the response in 2001 was to ask Indonesia to respect human rights in the province.

Whereas most discussions focus on economic development, the third Forum in 1973 mentioned the goal of promoting the "social and economic well-being" of the island peoples. Several subsequent declarations have supported human rights. The Vision Statement of 1995 pledged the Forum to work toward "improvement in the quality of people's lives, including human development, equality between women and men, and protection of children." The 2004 Forum declaration committed members to the "full observance of democratic values" and for the "defense and promotion of human rights." Since the region contains several indigenous peoples, including those in Australia and New Zealand, the Forum's policies are always mindful of cultural rights.

Most Pacific island countries have experienced stable, democratic rule. Fiji, however, has experienced three coups (1987, 2000, and 2006) in which a major issue has been how power should be shared between the native Fijians and descendents of the sugarcane workers who were recruited from India by colonial Britain. From 1999, there was a breakdown of law and order on the Solomon Islands, as longtime residents of the main island began to forcibly expel newcomers of another ethnic group from neighboring islands. In 2000, at the first meeting of Forum foreign ministers, the Biketawa Declaration was adopted in response to both the Fiji and Solomon Islands situations, giving unequivocal support to the principles of democracy and human rights. The Declaration adopted a process of conflict resolution for the region under which the Forum dispatched its first election monitoring team to the Solomons in 2001. Two years later, responding to urgent pleas from the Solomon Island government, ten Forum members sent the *Regional Assistance Mission* to the Solomon Islands, a peacekeeping force that assists law enforcement officers in rounding up lawbreakers and handling the burgeoning prison population.

Forum-sponsored conferences have addressed the need for cultural sensitivity and on the role of women in economic development. In 2005, the Regional Workshop on National Human Rights Mechanisms was held under the auspices of the Forum Secretariat. Comprehensive programs on education and health have been pursued over the years, but not specifically as efforts to meet human rights goals.

Within Asia and the Pacific, there has been no effort to establish intergovernmental organizations focusing on human rights. Nongovernmental organizations have developed instead. The Asia-Pacific Regional Forum of National Human Rights Commissions, which was convened for the first time by the UN High Commissioner for Human Rights in 1996, meets annually, sometimes with participation from over one hundred national organizations.

AFRICA

Black African countries attempted **diplomatic** efforts at the UN to pressure Rhodesia and South Africa to stop their racist policies, and ultimately they persuaded the world to invoke **economic** sanctions, which proved quite effective. Post-*apartheid* South Africa has assumed some leadership in diplomatic efforts to resolve various conflicts in the region, but Pretoria surprised many countries in 2007 by voting against mild UN Security Council condemnations of human rights problems in Myanmar and Zimbabwe.

Sierra Leone has most prominently attempted the **legal** approach to human rights through its *Special Court for Sierra Leone*. In 2006, Nigeria cooperated by terminating asylum granted to former Liberian President Charles Taylor (1948–) so that he could be tried before the court for his role in fomenting the civil war in Sierra Leone, though he was later transferred to the International Criminal Court in The Hague.

In 1978, after Idi Amin (1925–2003) waged war on Tanzania, the government in Dar-es-Salaam formed a coalition with Rwandan and Ugandan rebels and achieved a **military** victory over Uganda that could be claimed in part to have the objective of ending of massive violations of human rights. Currently, Nigeria is the main contributor to military enforcement of human rights norms in the region, with deployments entirely within the framework of regional organizations, which are discussed below.

- *African Union* (AU). The Organization of African Unity (OAU) was launched with the adoption of a Charter in 1963 that proclaimed the aims of (1) ending colonization and *apartheid*, (2) promoting solidarity among African states, (3) providing a forum for cooperation in development, and (4) ensuring the sovereignty and territorial integrity of independent states in Africa. Unlike other regional organizations, OAU began with human rights at the forefront. However, the organization was often known as the "dictator's club" that scrupulously avoided commenting on the internal affairs of member countries except for the white-dominated regimes of Southern Africa.

    In 1999, member states agreed on a new organization, known as the African Union (AU). Then in 2000 the annual Assembly adopted the Constitutive Act of the African Union, which provides for "non-indifference" (instead of "non-interference") regarding the internal affairs of member countries when human rights violations and security issues emerge, as well as respect for the following: "[1] democratic principles, [2] human rights, [3] the rule of law, . . . [4] good governance" and [5] "respect for the sanctity of human life."

    The secretariat in Addis Ababa, Ethiopia, known as the *Commission*, is headed by a Secretary-General and administers several Departments, including the following: *Human Resources; Social Affairs*; and *Women, Gender and Development*. Foreign ministers, who meet semiannually, form the *Executive Council*. Among their seven technical committees are the *Committee on Health, Labor and Social Affairs* and the *Committee on Education, Culture and Human Resources*.

    The *Economic, Social, and Cultural Council* sponsors studies on thematic issues, including human rights, while encouraging an African-wide civil society. Through OAU leadership, several human rights treaties have been adopted (Table 13.2).

    OAU's peacekeeping efforts in Chad during 1981–1982 provided a model that has been copied by other organizations in Africa. In 1993, OAU adopted the Mechanism for Conflict Prevention, Management and Resolution, which established the *Peace and Security Council*, a body that monitors threats to peace as well as human rights violations and can deploy an African Standby Force. In

TABLE 13.2 **HUMAN RIGHTS TREATIES PROMOTED BY THE AFRICAN UNION**

Adopted	Title	In force
1969	Convention Governing the Specific Aspects of Refugee Problems in Africa	1974
1976	Cultural Charter for Africa	1990
1977	Convention for the Elimination of Mercenaries in Africa	1985
1981	African Charter on Human and Peoples' Rights	1986
1998	• Protocol to the African Charter on Human and Peoples' Rights on the Establishment of an African Court on Human and Peoples' Rights	2004
2003	• Protocol to the African Charter on Human and Peoples' Rights on the Rights of Women in Africa	
1990	African Charter on the Rights and Welfare of the Child	1999
2002	Protocol Relating to the Establishment of the Peace and Security Council of the African Union	2003
2002	Memorandum of Understanding on the Conference on Security, Stability, Development and Cooperation in Africa	2002
2003	Memorandum of Understanding on the New Partnership for Africa's Development	2003

1998, OAU assisted in negotiating a ceasefire in the Democratic Republic of the Congo (Kinshasa).

In 2000, the *Conference on Security, Stability, Development and Cooperation in Africa* (CSSDCA) was adopted in principle at the OAU summit and then formalized by a Memorandum of Understanding in 2002. The Memorandum states commitments on the four goals contained in the title of the Conference and also contains deadlines for adopting various measures to advance democracy, human rights, and the rule of law, including such issues as refugee protection; principles of good governance; term limits for officeholders; dismantling political parties formed on the basis of ethnic, religious, or other divisions; and establishing independent electoral commissions. CSSDCA commitments and monitoring mechanisms are binding on and accepted by all AU member states. Monitoring is done by the CSSDCA unit within the AU Commission. CSSDCA visitation panels of eminent persons make biennial reviews, which are submitted to the Conference on Security, Stability, Development and Cooperation in Africa at AU summits.

At the OAU summit in 2001, members[7] adopted a program known as the *New Partnership for Africa's Development* (NEPAD), which has an explicit human rights focus. The primary aim is to end poverty in Africa by achieving the 7 percent growth rate set by the United Nations Millennium Development goals. NEPAD emphasizes the concept of **mutual accountability**, so that both Africans and those who trade with or give aid to Africa have responsibilities to promote "[1] peace, [2] security, [3] democracy, [4] good governance, [5] human rights and [6] sound economic management" as conditions for sustainable development.

In 2002, countries supporting NEPAD issued the Declaration on Democracy, Political, Economic and Corporate Governance, subsequently endorsed by a summit of African leaders, which sets out an action plan to support democratic institutions of government, good governance (including strengthening the civil service and judicial system), and human rights. Under human rights, the states pledge to develop civil society institutions; support the African Charter on Human and Peoples' Rights, the African Commission, and the African Court on Human and Peoples' Rights; and ensure "responsible free expression," including freedom of the press. The declaration also contains pledges on economic and corporate governance and socioeconomic development.

Implementation of NEPAD, which has had a coordinating office in Pretoria from 2003, is monitored by the *African Peer Review Mechanism* (APRM), a team of African "eminent persons." After making an APRM report, the team will first discuss problem areas with each government and, within six months, put the report on the agenda of the African Commission on Human Rights and the appropriate subregional body. If a government fails to rectify the problems, NEPAD can engage in "constructive dialogue" or even recommend sanctions. In early 2003, a Memorandum of Understanding on the APRM was adopted by the NEPAD heads of state implementation committee meeting and went into force within two months. States can opt out of APRM by not ratifying the Memorandum. In 2004, report questionnaires went out to the first four countries.

CSSDCA and NEPAD overlap. CSSDCA's requirements are more detailed and specific than those in NEPAD, which is a voluntary program. AU coordinates both processes.

In 2002, shortly after the first AU summit, the organization sent election observers to Togo. AU also held up Madagascar's membership application until verifying that legislative elections were in accordance with the wishes of the people.

In 2003, the Executive Council reviewed the security and human rights situations in several African countries – Angola, Burundi, Central African Republic, Comoros, Congo (Kinshasa), Ivory Coast, Liberia, Somalia, and the Sudan. AU's first peacekeeping force was sent to Burundi in 2003; the UN later took over the operation. In Somalia, AU provided a Military Observer Mission. In Sudan, there was an AU Verification and Monitoring Team. In 2004, AU assisted in and reviewed the work of the Sierra Leone Truth and Reconciliation Commission and sent observer missions to monitor Malawi's and South Africa's elections in 2004 as well as to Ethiopia and Guinea-Bissau in 2005.

HISTORIC EVENT 13.2 THE SUDANESE CIVIL WAR (1955–1972, 1983–2005)

Before World War II, Sudan was a British colony administratively separated into the Arabic-speaking Muslim north and the African animist and Christian south. When

continued

Britain promised independence to Sudan as a unitary state, effective 1956, those in the south were displeased that the arrangement did not grant them autonomy. Accordingly, a few army officers loyal to the south mutinied in 1955. After the mutiny was suppressed, small-scale insurgencies began. By 1971, the various anti-government groups merged into the Southern Sudan Liberation Movement, which negotiated a peace agreement in 1972 after 500,000 had lost their lives. However, the peace agreement was shattered in 1983, when the president of Sudan declared the country to be an Islamic state and imposed traditional *shari'ah* law, including amputation for theft and public flogging for possession of alcohol. Accordingly, the civil war resumed, but with more ferocity than before. Some 200,000 women and children in the south were enslaved following raids from the north, and the south was on the verge of starvation. Negotiations for a peace treaty, which began as early as 1993, finally bore fruit in 2005. Under the peace agreement, which is now monitored by a UN force, the south will enjoy regional autonomy until 2011, when a plebiscite will determine whether those in the south prefer independence. From 1983, the civil war the most lethal internal conflict of the twentieth century, as 1.9 million died and 4 millions were displaced.

In 2004, AU authorized peacekeeping brigades on the part of five subregions (ECOWAS, SADC, ECCAS, COMESA, and CEN-SAD), organizations that are discussed below. Accordingly, an African Mission on the Sudan (AMIS) was sent in 2004 to monitor the ceasefire in the north-south civil war, and in 2005 AMIS II authorized some 7,300 monitoring troops for the conflict in Darfur. In both cases, AU did not take sides but simply documented truce violations and sought to provide a layer of protection to the refugees and villagers. However in September 2005, the AU envoy to the Sudan condemned the government for painting Sudanese government military vehicles with AU colors and for violating the ceasefire. In 2005, when the African Union requested the UN to take over the operation, Sudan expressed a preference for AU troops over a UN or a North Atlantic Treaty Organization contingent out of fear that the latter could serve as an occupation force, even though UN forces were continuing to assist implementation of a peace agreement in Southern Sudan. The AU mandate was extended to 2007.

AU had a busy year in 2005. With civil war imminent in Togo, AU dispatched a Special Envoy to mediate between the parties in conflict. AU also brokered an agreement to disarm an armed group in the Congo (Kinshasa). Mauritania's membership was suspended in 2005, when army officers seized power, and AU called for the "restoration of constitutional order." Nevertheless, AU did not take up the case of Zimbabwe until 2005, after two years of serious human rights abuses, including replacing Caucasian agricultural landowners with locals without agricultural experience or training, thereby prompting thousands of starving Zimbabweans to flee to neighboring Botswana.

The African Union has close relations with other independent African organizations, including the African Commission on Human and Peoples' Rights, the

African Committee of Experts on the Rights and Welfare of the Child, and various subregional organizations. They are discussed below.

- *African Commission on Human and Peoples' Rights.* The African Charter on Human and Peoples' Rights was signed in 1981 within the OAU framework but is not mentioned in AU's founding agreement. Although the Universal Declaration of Human Rights cryptically says that "everyone has duties to the community" the African Charter is unique in enumerating specific duties, such as the harmonious development of the family and the duty of individuals not to discriminate against one another, thereby recognizing the fundamentally communitarian nature of African society.

  The Charter, which has been ratified by all AU countries, established the *African Commission on Human and Peoples' Rights*, which has six functions: (1) The education and information function is accomplished by promoting human rights awareness, such as by encouraging each country to set up human rights bodies. (2) The institutional cooperation function involves holding joint seminars with nongovernmental organizations; recent topics include refugees and contemporary forms of slavery. (3) Regarding the complaint resolution function, the Commission has received more than two hundred communications (complaints) from individuals, organizations, and member states, but tends to conciliate, lacking the authority to issue binding rulings. (4) The quasi-legislative function is to set standards for legal principles to be adopted by member countries and to interpret the Charter on Human and Peoples' Rights in specific terms. (5) The monitoring function is carried out by soliciting member states to submit periodic reports on measures taken to implement the Charter. (6) The research function is to assign thematic issues to rapporteurs to make studies; current subjects under review are prison conditions, extrajudicial executions, and women's rights.

  In Malawi, for example, the Commission ruled in 1995 that a new democratic government was responsible to undo the wrongs committed by the previous government, notably the release of those imprisoned for up to twelve years without charges or trial, others sentenced to life imprisonment in faulty trials, and many others subjected to inhumane prison conditions. In the same year, the Commission ruled that seven persons in Nigeria were being denied a fair trial. Decisions of the Commission are based on the African Charter on Human and Peoples' Rights.

  Although the Commission has had a reputation of being less effective than similar bodies in other regions, in 1998 the AU Assembly adopted a Protocol to the Charter, establishing the *African Court on Human and Peoples' Rights*. Cases and advisory opinions may be referred to the Court by AU member states, the Commission, or by other African intergovernmental organizations. The Court may refer cases to the Commission, attempt an amicable settlement, or give considerations on the merits. The Court's recommendation may include a request for compensation or reparations to those found to be victims of violations. AU's Secretary-General is empowered to check whether the recommendation is honored. The Court can invoke not only the Charter to provide a legal foundation but also can cite other human rights documents.

- *African Committee of Experts on the Rights and Welfare of the Child*. In 1999, when the African Charter on the Rights and Welfare of the Child went into force, states were required to submit triennial implementation reports to the African Committee of Experts on the Rights and Welfare of the Child. The Committee is technically a treaty-based organ separate from the African Union. Among the Committee's current priorities is the elimination of polio from Africa. Thirty-seven of the fifty-three African countries have ratified thus far.

- *East African Community* (EAC). In 1999, several antecedent organizations in the region were superseded by the Treaty for the Establishment of the East African Community, which has established programs in culture, health, human resource development, and social welfare. The primary goal of the members (Kenya, Uganda, Tanzania) is to develop a common market.

- *Economic Community of West African States* (ECOWAS). In 1975, ECOWAS was formed primarily for economic cooperation. In 1990, the fifteen members[8] agreed that ethnic conflicts inside West African countries were so endemic that an *ECOWAS Monitoring Group* (ECOMOG) was established as a peace enforcement organ that has intervened in Liberia (1990–1996, 2003) Sierra Leone (1997–1998, 1999), Guinea-Bissau (1998), and Guinea (2001). The interventions are controversial, however, because Nigeria has been the primary source of troops, and the interventions have tended to take sides.

  In 1991, member countries agreed on a declaration to uphold democracies in the region. ECOWAS sent election observers to Togo in 2002 and to Guinea-Bissau in 2005. ECOWAS also brokered a truce between rival factions in Togo in 2005.

  ECOWAS has sponsored several nongovernmental bodies – the Organization of Trade Unions of West Africa, the West African Youth Association, the West African Universities Association, the West African Women's Association – as well as the intergovernmental *West African Health Organization*. In 2005, the ECOWAS *Committee on Women and Child's Rights* called for stiffer restrictions against small arms producers.

- *Southern African Development Community* (SADC). In 1980, the Southern African Development Co-ordination Conference (SADCC) was formed in part to reduce economic dependence on *apartheid* South Africa and to promote democracy, human rights, and the rule of law. Originally, the organization sought the dismantling of the system of racial separation practiced by the Pretoria government. SADC, which superseded SADCC in 1997, now applies more broadly and has identified three major goals – (1) free trade, (2) regional infrastructure integration, and (3) good governance, the latter including human rights and democracy.

  SADC's thirteen member countries[9] are committed to the goal of economic integration. Several projects exist in the field of human resource development, including the establishment of labor, public health, and welfare standards. In 1997, the SADC Declaration on Gender and Development set a goal of at least 30 percent women in political and decision making structures by 2005. Accordingly, the *Secretariat* in Gaborone, Botswana, set up a *Department of*

Strategic Planning, Gender and Development and Policy Harmonization to promote gender mainstreaming in SADC programming.

In 1994, when post-*apartheid* South Africa joined SADCC, the organization agreed to establish a regional peacekeeping force. In 1995, the *Inter-State Defense and Security Committee* was established for that end.

In 1998, a SADC force was first deployed to quell unrest in Lesotho after violence erupted over a disputed election. SADC sought to negotiate an end to the conflict in the Congo (Kinshasa) in 1998 and the Central African Republic in 1999, respectively, though diplomacy proved difficult. Multinational peace-keeping exercises have been held.

Another activity has been to send *Forum Observer Missions* to monitor elections in Zambia (2001), Zimbabwe (2002), and South Africa (2004). Despite criticism from the head of the SADC *Parliamentary Forum* regarding undemocratic practices in Zimbabwe's 2002 election, delegates to the 2003 SADC conference applauded President Robert Mugabe (1924–) of Zimbabwe, whose regime has been boycotted economically by the European Union.

- *Economic Community of Central African States* (ECCAS). Although formed in 1983 as a successor to two earlier organizations, ECCAS was inactive from 1992–1999 due to the labyrinthine conflict involving eleven Central African states that produced nearly 3 million deaths. The organization seeks to improve economic and social development, leading to an eventual common market. In 1999, the eleven members[10] agreed to form the *Council for Peace and Security in Central Africa*, including an early-warning system and a multinational military force to handle conflicts in the region. The organization then participated in negotiations with SADC to end the war in the Democratic Republic of the Congo in 2000. After mediating an end to the coup in São Tomé and Príncipe in 2003, ECCAS set up a monitoring unit. The military force was first deployed in 2005 to implement the peace agreement in the Congo.

  In 2002, ECCAS launched the *Center for Human Rights and Democracy in Central Africa* at Yaoundé, Cameroon. In 2004, a declaration on gender equality was adopted by the ECCAS summit conference, and a meeting of agriculture ministers approved a program on food security.

- *Common Market for Eastern and Southern Africa* (COMESA). Set up in 1994 primarily to forge a free trade area and otherwise to promote cooperative economic development, the treaty establishing COMESA also stresses the need to include women in development planning, a goal reiterated in 2002 by a formal Declaration on the COMESA Gender Policy. In 2005, the twenty COMESA foreign ministers[11] agreed to set up an *African Standby Brigade*, which was available to be committed by the African Union to serve in Darfur.

  Community of Sahel-Saharan States (CEN-SAD). In 1998, the twenty-two member[12] organization was formed not only to promote economic integration but also to confer equal rights to citizens of one CEN-SAD country while living or working in another CEN-SAD country. One of the principal organs is the *Economic, Social and Cultural Council*. Conferences of health ministers met together in 1999 to forge important links. In 2002, CEN-SAD sent election observers to Togo along with the African Union and ECOWAS.

CONCLUSION

Third World regional intergovernmental organizations differ considerably in the scope of human rights activity, but the follow generalizations apply: (1) Some African organizations actively pressure countries to improve human rights by using military means. (2) Multi-purpose regional bodies are more effective than single-purpose organizations in regard to civil and political rights, while the opposite is the case for economic and social rights. (3) Quiet diplomacy is more common among regional organizations than in the klieg lights of UN deliberations. (4) Some regional human rights organizations have successfully prompted members to change their laws or to reverse their actions in order to conform to the higher standards. (5) Nevertheless, there is room for improvement in regional organizations, many of which need to go beyond mere verbal statements on the subject of human rights and establishing structures that lack operational functions.

DISCUSSION TOPIC 13.1 WHY ARE SOME REGIONAL ORGANIZATIONS MORE EFFECTIVE THAN OTHERS?

Euro-Atlantic organizations are clearly more effective in regard to human rights than regional organizations elsewhere. Why? Is the reason found in common culture, history, and language or due to the existence of a dominant country, economic resources, or the gravity of the human rights problems? Does the same analysis apply when comparing European organizations with the United Nations and other global organizations?

For many years, Some UN officials looked upon regional efforts as breakaway movements, somehow subversive to the world body. From the 1980s, however, the General Assembly began to encourage regions lacking human rights arrangements to set up regional bodies. Meanwhile, many countries looked upon the UN as too distant from their concerns, so they were already establishing regional bodies in which there would be sufficient cultural affinity that they could operate in a manner more in keeping with national traditions. Thus, regional organizations play an important role in regard to human rights.

CHAPTER 14

New dimensions and challenges

The volume thus far has focused on many dimensions of human rights, but not all. Similarly, as civil rights progress for ethnic and racial minorities occurred in the 1960s, the American Civil Liberties Union (ACLU) discovered that several types of persons had fallen through the cracks, excluded from enjoying the rights of free speech, free press, and the like. Such persons, who together constitute a numerical majority, were still hobbled by restrictions imposed by the dominant group in American society. Accordingly, ACLU began a series of publications under the title *The Rights of* _____ focusing on aliens, chronically and acutely ill persons, crime victims, the disabled, former offenders, gays and lesbians, hospital patients, military personnel, the poor, prisoners, refugees, single people, suspects, tribes and native peoples, women, and young people. A volume on the rights of adoptees is lacking, and other categories could doubtless be added. Currently, ACLU has discontinued the series, which is out of print. Although some issues on their list have been covered in the chapters above, others have not.

At least two issues are increasingly emerging as important aspects of international human rights – environmental rights and the rights of gays, lesbians, bisexuals, and the transgendered. In addition, the human responsibilities to animals, sometimes known as animal rights, have increasingly been asserted. Since the moral claims of today often become the rights of tomorrow, the chapter below explores all three topics and concludes after a discussion on the efficacy of the rights-based approach.

GAY RIGHTS

In 2003, Sandra Day O'Connor (1930–), then U.S. Supreme Court Justice, was asked what "the burning issue might be for the twenty-first century." Her response, which astonished many, was the effort to define the scope of gay rights, which she identified as "the first important civil rights struggle of the twenty-first century."

Sexual activity among persons of the same gender has taken place for millennia, sometimes unremarkably, as when prosperous Athenians sponsored the training of handsome young athletes for the original Olympic Games with an expectation that sexual favors might be exchanged. Although church records demonstrate that Christian religious leaders have sometimes blessed same-sex relationships,[1] those who engaged in such practices were persecuted during the Spanish Inquisition from 1478, though Leonardo da Vinci (1452–1519) and Michelangelo Buonarroti (1475–1564) are also remembered as men who enjoyed the company of younger men during the European Renaissance. Male concubines were a part of the royal courts in some Asian countries, a practice continued by some of the original peoples who left Asia to populate Polynesia. From ancient times, Hindu priests in India have performed same-sex rituals, and some do today.

Taboos on sexual activity have also existed, especially when supported by religious authorities. Indeed, Jewish and Christian scriptures condemned men who dressed as women to be available as prostitutes at the temples of fertility religions, where married men presumably could overcome sexual dysfunctions and return to their wives with renewed virility. The debatable belief that such prohibitions apply to contemporary gays and lesbians has been a major source of persecution of sexual minorities.

Masculinized Jeanne d'Arc (1412–1431) was accepted by the French army as a leader in battling the English, whereupon the English placed a handsome bounty on her head. In 1430, she was captured by a Frenchman, turned over to a priest who was in the pay of the English, and then condemned to death. There is some unsubstantiated speculation that Jeanne was in fact a man (Jean d'Arc) dressed as a woman rather than the reverse.

Transgendered persons have sometimes played nonsexual roles in society, notably the effeminate Bugi men who dressed as women so that order could be maintained among the women left ashore while Bugi fishermen and pirates were at sea in Southeast Asian waters. The *Kamasutra* classifies humans into three sexes and accepts attraction between persons of the same gender. In the performance of the plays of Shakespeare (1564–1616), men took the parts of women and then shed women's clothes to appear as men off stage.

In 1533, Henry VIII (1491–1547) promulgated the Buggery Law, which provided the death penalty for anal intercourse between two men or between a man and an animal. The term "bugger" was slang for what the English perceived as a practice among Bulgarians of demasculinizing men by raping them. Britain's thirteen colonies in North America adopted the same law, later known as the sodomy law, and Britain imposed its peculiar obsession in India and other colonies. Nevertheless, references to male prostitution and buggery as common phenomena are found in the writings of Michael Drayton (1563–1631) and Samuel Pepys (1633–1703).

The first work censored by the English government on grounds of "obscenity," *Sodom, or The Quintessence of Debauchery* (1684), by John Wilmot (1647–1680), dealt with sex between persons of the same gender. In 1698, Captain Edward Rigby was the first to be tried for sodomy; in his defense he claimed to be an eyewitness to same-sex lovemaking involving Peter the Great (1672–1725), and he evidently repeated a false rumor about the same conduct on the part of Louis XIV (1638–1715). Publicity about his trial throughout Europe encouraged police to engage in entrapment of men who frequented male brothels, parks, pubs, and similar meeting places.

Meanwhile, women had liaisons with one another over the ages with hardly a negative comment until unmarried women were identified as witches and burned at the stake. Sometimes underneath the fire were effeminate men, who were burned before the flames reached the so-called witches (thus, the origin of the term "faggot"). The witch-hunting craze swept through Europe and North America from 1450–1750, though rumors about sexual proclivities were only one reason for the practice.

The right to have sex with adults of the same gender was not a part of the early development of the concept of human rights. In 1862, however, Karl Heinrich Ulrichs (1825–1895), declaring that he was a Uranian, provided legal and moral support to a man arrested for having sex with another man in Germany and continued to argue for decriminalization of sexual behavior among consulting adults; his books, however, were confiscated and banned. In 1869, Austrian writer Károly-Mária Kertbeny (1824–1882) coined the term "homosexual." Ulrichs and Kertbeny, thus, opened discussion on the subject, as gay and lesbian subcultures became more visible in the cities that grew around the increasing numbers of factories of the industrial revolution.

The first use of the word "gay" to mean a male who enjoys the company of other males in a sociosexual sense emerged in 1889. In the Cleveland Street scandal, a male prostitute in a London brothel described himself as "gay" while testifying in court to defend himself against prosecution under an 1885 law banning prostitution and the procuring of sex by one male from another.

In 1891, Oscar Wilde (1854–1900) published *A Picture of Dorian Gray*, a novel that was condemned for its homoerotic theme. Although bisexual, shortly after his novel appeared, Wilde befriended twenty-two-year old Lord Alfred Douglas (1870–1945), and they became lovers. Alfred's father, John Sholto Douglas (1844–1900), soon demanded that his son must end his "intimacy" with Wilde and engaged in a campaign against Wilde for his "indecency." In 1895, Wilde sued Douglas for libel but dropped the charges when Douglas threatened to bring to court young male witnesses who were prepared to testify that they had sex with him. Next, Wilde was put on trial for sodomy by some of his former sex partners. Rather than fleeing England, as expected, Wilde decided to appear in court, where he was convicted. He then served two years in prison, became a social outcast, and the publicity generated negative attitudes toward what was thereby revealed as a secret community of males who had social and sexual relations with one another.

The quest to recognize the right of adults to have sex with consenting same-sex partners gained some momentum when John Addington Symonds (1840–1893) published *A Problem in Modern Ethics* (1891). In 1897, Magnus Hirshfeld (1868–1935) set up a foundation in Berlin to promote greater understanding of the human sexual condition and to decriminalize sexual practices involving consenting males.

The first large-scale gay rights activism occurred in Berlin between the world wars, and in 1924 the Society for Human Rights in Chicago became the earliest known gay rights organization in the United States. However, the German gay rights movement ended when Nazis persecuted gays and sent them to concentration camps along with Jews and others.

During World War II, sexual liaisons formed among some American soldiers, many of whom stayed in the larger cities, notably New York and San Francisco, before and after their discharge from the armed services in 1945. Those who were identifiably gays and lesbians increasingly appeared in public on their way to social occasions, such as "gay bars" and public parks, though gay pubs existed in England more than a half century earlier.

In 1948, Alfred Kinsey (1894–1956) published *Sexual Behavior in the Human Male*, one finding of which was that homosexual behavior was a more common practice than previously thought, with 10 percent of the population engaging in sex with members of the same sex at least once in their lives. Since gays were closeted and unwelcome in the larger society, they were often subjected to blackmail and thought to be easily forced to engage in treasonous activity. In 1953, President Dwight Eisenhower (1890–1969) issued Executive Order 10450 barring gay men and lesbians from all federal jobs, and many state and local governments and private corporations did so as well. The Federal Bureau of Investigation (FBI) began to compile information about activities of homosexuals so that they could be rejected if they applied for government employment.

The problems encountered by nonheterosexuals after World War II, thus, came to the fore at a time when the defeat of militarism and racism was inspiring democracies to advance human rights. Among the special concerns of gays are protection from violence and freedom from discrimination, issues in common with minorities and women. In addition, nonheterosexuals sought a right to privacy so that they might associate together in public and engage in private sexual activity without fear of prosecution for criminal offenses.

The silence of traditional international law on the subject of sexual lifestyles has meant that progress occurred within particular countries as a spillover from generic concerns about human rights. Gays and lesbians have challenged various unfriendly laws, although political authorities have not responded uniformly.

In 1954, Reading University Vice Chancellor Sir John Wolfenden (1906–1985), whose son was gay, was asked to chair an investigation of British laws on homosexuality after several prosecutions of gays received wide publicity. The resulting Wolfenden Report of 1957, which did not condone homosexuality, said that homosexuality was not a psychiatric illness and should be decriminalized. The first positive response occurred in 1962, when Illinois became the first state in the United States to decriminalize private sex between consenting adults, male or female. Britain followed suit in 1967. In 1973, the American Psychiatric Association removed homosexuality from its list of diseases.

On July 4, 1965, some forty gays and lesbians held a demonstration in front of the Liberty Bell at Independence Hall in Philadelphia, and soon the demonstrations expanded to New York and Washington, DC. In 1967, some 200 gays demonstrated on Sunset Boulevard in the Silverlake district of Los Angeles to protest police raids that occurred at two gay bars on New Year's Eve. And the following year the Reverend Troy Perry (1940–) put an ad in a gay newspaper in Los Angeles, asking Christian gays to meet at his residence. He soon founded the Universal Fellowship of Metropolitan Community Churches, a denomination that now flourishes in twenty-three countries around the world and consecrates holy unions between gay and lesbian partners.

The Stonewall Riot of 1969, however, did more to launch the gay rights movement than any other event. In 1970, some 5,000 gays and lesbians participated in a Gay Pride march in New York, a practice that soon spread throughout the country and the world.

Various progressive cities then began to outlaw discrimination based on sexual orientation, and in 1975 the U.S. Civil Service Commission rescinded the prohibition on employing homosexuals in most government jobs. In 1982, Wisconsin became the first state to pass a law banning employment discrimination based on sexual orientation. In 1998, Executive Order 13087 banned discrimination in most federal government jobs, but not for military service.

HISTORIC EVENT 14.1 THE STONEWALL RIOT (1969)

After World War II, police throughout the United States were accustomed to disrupting gay bars by entering in the phony pretext of checking the identification of patrons so that they could fine the owners for serving alcohol to minors or knowingly serving liquor to gays. Although police often entered public restrooms to entrap gays by exposing their genitals and arresting men who showed some interest, in 1966 the New York City police chief adopted a policy against entrapment as well as against bar shutdowns on the basis of the clientele. On June 28, 1969, the police unexpectedly raided a Greenwich Village gay bar, Stonewall Inn, which was frequented by nonwhite drag queens. Usually, gays left quietly while such raids were conducted, but on that night the patrons objected, attacked police, and soon outnumbered them. Several gays were severely beaten. Demonstrations during two subsequent nights attracted "gay power" signs on the nearby buildings, and an activist gay liberation movement had been launched.

In 1965, the U.S. Supreme Court identified a right to privacy in *Griswold v Connecticut* (381US479), declaring unconstitutional a state law prohibiting birth control devices, including condoms. However, in 1986 the court in *Bowers v Hardwick* (478US186) did not extend privacy rights to strike down sodomy laws; the case involved two men found in bed together during a police raid. Justice O'Connor ruled with the majority that Georgia had a right to enforce its sodomy law. However, in 1990 immigration authorities began to grant asylum applications to gays who could demonstrate that they faced persecution on returning to their home countries, and in 1996 the same ruling was extended to persons with HIV or AIDS.

Then in 2003, O'Connor concurred with the majority to reverse *Bowers* in *Lawrence v Texas* (539US558). The effect of *Lawrence* was to declare all sodomy laws in the United States to be unconstitutional infringements on the right to privacy. A similar ruling had already been issued during 2001 by the European Court of Human Rights.

Meanwhile, efforts began in 1921 to adopt a constitutional amendment that would provide equal treatment for women and men on the same basis as the Fourteenth Amendment to the American Constitution, which guarantees racial equality before the law. After the proposed federal amendment was adopted by Congress in 1972, known as the Equal Rights Amendment, several states voted to incorporate such an amendment into their own constitutions. However, the amendment was not adopted into the national constitution because of a failure to be ratified by the required three-quarters of the states by the deadline in 1982.

The full significance of the state equal rights amendments for gays and lesbians was not recognized until 1990, when six persons went to the Department of Health in Honolulu to apply for marriage licenses. After being turned down because their three applications listed names of persons of the same gender, *Baehr v Lewin* was filed, and the Hawai'i Supreme Court in 1993 ruled that the Equal Rights Amendment prohibited the state from denying marriage licenses on the basis of gender (74Haw645;852 P2d 44) and remanded the case to the lower court for a remedy. However, the ruling sparked controversy, and in 1996 voters in the Aloha State adopted a constitutional amendment to prohibit same-sex marriage.

Similar challenges were then mounted in other states. In 1999, Vermont's Supreme Court ruled in *Baker v State* (744 A2d864) that same-sex couples could not be denied the same rights as opposite-sex couples, leaving the resolution of the issue to the state legislature, which then established civil unions in 2000. In 2003, the Massachusetts Supreme Court ruled in *Goodrich v Massachusetts* (798NE2d941) that the state must issue certificates of marriage to same-sex couples.

Whereas some countries have provided more rights to gays and lesbians in recent years, the same countries were merely dismantling barriers that they earlier erected in the first place. Not all countries have used government to regulate morals, preferring to allow society to do so instead. In any case, a survey of countries that currently criminalize sexual conduct demonstrates that there is a lot of sexual freedom today. European Union countries lead among countries that provide a variety of nondiscrimination protections to gays, lesbians, and bisexuals (Table 14.1).

Governmental recognition of civil unions, domestic partnerships, or common-law partners of the same sex first emerged in 1982 within the Québec Province of Canada but did not spread to other Canadian provinces until the early 1990s. Meanwhile, Denmark took the lead in Europe, establishing a domestic partner registry in 1989, followed by Norway in 1993, Sweden in 1994, and then Iceland in 1996; in all cases, active gay/lesbian organizations pressured their parliaments. The first domestic partnership law (called the Reciprocal Beneficiaries Act) in the United States was adopted during 1997 in Hawai'i as a ploy by the state legislature seeking to avoid a ruling by its Supreme Court to legalize gay marriage, although the reciprocal beneficiaries concept envisaged a family unit in traditional Asian terms as consisting of a single elderly grandparent living with a single grandson or granddaughter, as the last

TABLE 14.1 GAY, LESBIAN, AND BISEXUAL RIGHTS AROUND THE WORLD

Issue	Countries Providing Protections or Provisions
Noncriminalization of sexual conduct between consenting adults of the same sex	Albania, Andorra, Argentina, Armenia, Aruba, Austria, Azerbaijan, Bahamas, Belarus, Belgium, Bolivia, Bosnia, Brazil, Bulgaria, Burkina Faso, Cambodia, Canada, Cape Verde, Central African Republic, Chad, Chile, China, Colombia, Comoros, Congo (Brazzaville and Kinshasa), Costa Rica, Croatia, Cyprus, Czech Republic, Denmark, Dominican Republic, Ecuador, Egypt, El Salvador, Estonia, Finland, France, Gabon, Georgia, Germany, Greece, Guatemala, Guinea-Bissau, Haiti, Honduras, Hong Kong, Hungary, Iceland, Indonesia, Iraq, Ireland, Israel, Italy, Japan, Jordan, Kazakhstan, Kosovo, Kyrgyzstan, Latvia, Liechtenstein, Lithuania, Luxembourg, Macau, Macedonia, Madagascar, Mali, Malta, México, Moldova, Monaco, Montenegro, Netherlands, New Zealand, Niger, Norway, Panamá, Paraguay, Perú, Philippines, Poland, Portugal, Romania, Russia, Rwanda, San Marino, São Tomé and Príncipe, Serbia, Slovakia, Slovenia, South Africa, South Korea, Spain, Suriname, Sweden, Switzerland, Taiwan, Tajikistan, Thailand, Turkey, Ukraine, United Kingdom, Uruguay, Vanuatu, Venezuela, Vietnam
Antidiscrimination laws protecting gays, lesbians, and bisexuals	Andorra, Argentina, Australia, Belgium, Bosnia, Brazil (2 cities), Bulgaria, Canada, Denmark, Ecuador, Estonia, Fiji, Finland, France, Germany, Greece, Honduras, Hungary, Iceland, Ireland, Israel, Kosovo, Latvia, Liechtenstein, Luxembourg, Malta, México, Netherlands, New Zealand, Norway, Poland, Portugal, Romania, Slovakia, Slovenia, South Africa, Spain, Sweden, Switzerland, United Kingdom, United States (20 states)
Civil unions/domestic partnerships recognized	Andorra, Argentina (2 states), Australia, Austria,[a] Belgium, Brazil (1 state), Canada, Croatia,[a] Cuba, Czech Republic, Denmark, Finland, France, Germany, Hungary,[a] Iceland, Israel, Italy (2 states), Luxembourg, México (2 states), New Zealand, Norway, Poland, Portugal,[a] South Africa, Spain (4 states), Sweden, Switzerland, United Kingdom, United States (10 states, 1 city), Uruguay
Gay and lesbian marriage laws	Belgium, Canada, Netherlands, Portugal, Slovenia, South Africa, Spain, United States (1 state)
Hate crime laws/court decisions protecting sexual minorities	Austria, Croatia, France, Ireland, Liechtenstein, Luxembourg, México (1 state), Netherlands, Norway, Spain, United States (4 states), Uruguay

Source: www.actwin.com/eatonohio/gay/world.htm; other news sources.
[a]Common-law recognition.

child in the family is expected to provide filial care and is not supposed to marry if an elderly widow or widower would otherwise be left to live alone.

The first country to provide for gay marriage was the Netherlands in 2001, followed in 2003 by Belgium, and then in 2005 by Canada and Spain. The Massachusetts Supreme Court authorized gay marriage in 2003. The California State Legislature passed a gay marriage bill in 2005, but the law was vetoed by the governor. Former President Jimmy Carter has argued that governments should leave marriages to churches and instead grant civil unions to any couples who otherwise meet normal age requirements.

More recently, gay rights issues have been recognized under international law. In *Dudgeon v United Kingdom* (1981), *Norris v Ireland* (1991), and *Modinos v Cyprus* (1993), the European Court of Human Rights found that the right to privacy was violated by the criminalization of sexual acts between consenting adults.

In 1994, the European Parliament asked the Commission of the European Community to recommend member states to stop "barring of lesbians and homosexual couples from marriage or from an equivalent legal framework . . . [and] any restriction on the right of lesbians and homosexuals to be parents or to adopt or foster children." The European Union also has made respect for sexual orientation rights a requirement for states that seek membership in the European Union.

In 1997, the former COE European Commission for the Protection of Human Rights struck down the unequal age of consent for homosexual and heterosexual acts in the United Kingdom in *Sutherland v UK*; a similar ruling came from the European Court of Human Rights in *L and V v Austria* (2003). However, in 1997 the COE European Court of Human Rights ruled in *X, Y and Z v UK* that a transgendered male partnered with a female for eighteen years did not constitute a "family." In 2000, the European Court of Human Rights ruled in *Lustig-Prean and Beckett v UK* and *Smith v UK* that the European Convention on Human Rights prohibited Britain from banning a gay person from enlisting the country's military service.

COURT CASE 14.1 *X, Y AND Z V UNITED KINGDOM* (1997)

The European Court of Human Rights has made one landmark ruling regarding the rights of transsexuals and transgendered persons. At issue was whether a birth certificate of a child born from artificial insemination of the mother could show the mother's partner, a female-to-male transsexual, as the father of the child. Under British law, X and Y could not marry because X was not regarded as a male. The Court held that X (a female-to-male transsexual), Y (a woman with whom X had enjoyed a permanent and stable relationship for eighteen years), and Z (a child born to Y as a result of artificial insemination by a donor) were not legally a "family" under the European Convention for the Protection of Human Rights and Fundamental Freedoms.

The Human Rights Committee, which handles complaints filed on the basis of the International Covenant on Civil and Political Rights, ruled in *Toonen v Australia* (1994), that the nondiscrimination and privacy rights provisions in the Covenant apply to sexual orientation, thereby decriminalizing the sodomy law of the State of Tasmania. In *Young v Australia* (2000) the Committee ruled that Australia could not deny a government pension to the deceased spouse of a same-sex civil union. Four other treaty-based UN bodies (CAT, CEDAW, CRC, CESCR) have interpreted their treaties to embody the protection of sexual minorities. Brazil and the European Union have sponsored a resolution, Sexual Orientation and Human Rights, at meetings of the former UN Commission on Human Rights, but strong opposition has come from Muslim states.

However, various states in the United States have been alarmed that partners of gay marriages in one state might move to other states, forcing the latter to recognize their legal status. Accordingly, Congress in 1996 passed the Defense of Marriage Act to authorize such nonreciprocity, and forty states have passed laws explicitly banning gay marriages. Eleven states also prohibit recognition of civil unions granted between persons of the same gender in other states.

In several press conferences, President George W. Bush (1946–) has argued against recognition of gay marriage on the basis of cultural relativism, that is, because of a Christian tradition in the United States. However, China and some other Asian countries have asserted that human rights priorities of the West are inapplicable to its Confucian culture. If Washington now claims that some human rights are culture-bound, then other countries may feel free to do so. China, for example, might file suit in the International Court of Justice (ICJ), asking the court to issue an "order of provisional measure" that would prohibit the United States from criticizing its human rights record under the principle of **estoppel**, a doctrine affirmed in *Thailand v Cambodia* (1962), in which ICJ settled a border dispute. Were such an order issued, Asian, Muslim, and other states could withdraw from human rights treaties, arguing that human rights requirements are no longer universal, contrary to the International Covenant on Civil and Political Rights. Soon, four centuries in the development of international law on human rights would fall into quicksand. The advance of gay rights, in short, is a critical question today.

DISCUSSION TOPIC 14.1 SHOULD GAYS AND LESBIANS BE ALLOWED TO MARRY?

Traditional expectations are that two partners of opposite sexes (a man and a woman) who are deeply in love will seek recognition as a married couple and will then form a household and start a family. However, same-sex couples have lived together for centuries under many circumstances. If loving same-sex couples share expenses, eat together, engage in social activities together, share a bedroom, and are allowed to adopt children or have children from a previous opposite-sex marriage, should they be allowed legal recognition by means of a governmentally-issued certificate of marriage? Or should they instead be recognized as partners in a civil union? Alternatively, should the government now certify civil unions to all couples of marriage age, leaving religious ceremonies for faith communities to perform and to record, as in most human history?

ANIMAL RIGHTS

Although concern for the rights of animals might be considered irrelevant in a book on human rights, in fact the term "animal rights" refers to human conduct vis-à-vis animals and thus regulates how humans behave in situations where the consequences of their actions usually cannot be challenged by the victims. Animal rights have been largely ignored historically because humans probably would not have assumed dominion on the planet without first winning a contest for supremacy. During snowbound winters in prehistoric times, there were no vegetables to harvest but plenty of animals to kill and eat. But today humans have no such logistical problems in obtaining food, so the custom of eating animals may be anachronistic. Similarly, cotton and synthetic fabrics have replaced the need for animal skins as the basis for clothing. There are other reasons to link human rights with animal rights, as noted below.

Humprhey Primatt (1736–1779) wrote the first coherent statement on the need to respect animal rights in his *Dissertation on the Duty of Mercy and the Sin of Cruelty to Brute Animals* (1776), which was published in Edinburgh, Scotland. In 1796, John Lawrence published *The Rights of Beasts*. And in 1824, Anglican priest Arthur Broome (1779–1837) formed the Society for the Prevention of Cruelty to Animals (SPCA). In *The Rights of Man* (1792), Thomas Paine (1737–1809) also raised animal rights issues. Henry Salt's *Animals' Rights* (1905) was the next major treatise on the subject.

More analytically, theologian Andrew Linzey (1952–) helps to explain the case for animal rights by suggesting three practices that are touchstones for determining views toward animal rights:

- *Battery hen production.* About 9 billion hens currently lay eggs in the United States in small cages, five confined to a cage of wire mesh the size of a sheet of 9 by 11 inch looseleaf notebook paper, eating a diet of dry mash along with antibiotics to prevent disease. They stay encaged for about one year, whereupon they go to the slaughterhouse, are hung upside down, pre-stunned with an electric shock, have their throats cut electronically, and are then put into scalding water to make their feathers fall off. Male chicks live only three days; afterward, they are gassed, suffocated or fed through chopping machines.
- *Deer hunting with hounds.* In England each year, from April to October, deer of both sexes, including pregnant females, have been chased by hounds for three to four hours to weaken and exhaust them. Although the hounds sometimes catch them, and they are occasionally shot by hunters in the fields, most are caught in the riverbeds and shot dead.
- *Animal experimentation.* There is a creature called the "oncomouse," which is patented in Europe and the United States. The animal is a normal mouse that is genetically altered to develop cancer. In Europe, the patent extends to all non-human mammals, so the oncopig, oncochicken, and oncosheep are also possible. After experimentation on oncomice, medical science next conducts experiments on primates, that is, chimps and monkeys. Universities and medical labs currently have committees to determine whether animal experimentations (or experiments upon humans) are legally and scientifically justifiable, but oncomice pass the test

every time. The Animal Protection Institute estimates that 27 million animals are used in education, research, and testing each year and feels that "replacement techniques" could reduce the number to 2.7 million.

The question to consider is whether any of the three practices might violate animal rights. Linzey offers several theories, some already considered in Chapter 2, to place the debate in perspective (Table 14.2).

Humanocentrism. Animals have no moral status, and humans have no obligations to animals, according to such thinkers as Aristotle (384–322 BCE), Thomas Aquinas (1227–1274), and Réné Descartes (1596–1650). Aquinas has a twofold justification: (1) Animals are intended for man's use according to biblical and natural law, and (2) animals are not rational beings and thus lack a soul. In the mid-nineteenth century, for example, Pope Pius IX (1792–1878) cited humanocentrist doctrine by forbidding the opening of an animal protection office in Rome. Cruelty to animals is wrong, according to humanocentrism, not because animal rights are infringed but because cruelty makes humans into beasts, and thus the habit of cruelty will inevitably carry over to humans. There is nothing in humanocentrism to stop hen battery production or deer hunting. Although oncomice might be considered to alter the order of creation, experimentation is justified because for the benefit of humans.

Contractualism. A second theory argues that rights are conferred only on those who enter into contracts. Since animals cannot make contracts, the argument goes, they have no rights. Social contract theorists, from Thomas Hobbes (1588–1679) to John Locke (1632–1704) to Jean-Jacques Rousseau (1712–1778) to contemporary John Rawls (1921–2002), thus, have no place for animal rights in their conceptions of rights. Once again, humans determine the moral rules of the game and load the dice against animals, just as males have been thinking up various justifications to denying rights to females, the poor, and down the list of groups that have not enjoyed their full rights because they were not writing the rules. Under contractualism, battery production, deer hunting, and animal experimentation will continue regardless of how much animals suffer.

Humanitarianism. Broome and Primatt believed that humans should prevent unnecessary cruelty and promote kindness while exercising benevolence or

TABLE 14.2 **ANIMAL RIGHTS THEORIES AND ANIMAL RIGHTS TREATMENT IN PRACTICE**

Theory	*Major Exponents*	*Battery Hen Production*	*Deer Hunting*	*Experi- mentation*
Humanocentrism	Aquinas, Aristotle, Descartes	Allowed	Allowed	Allowed
Contractualism	Hobbes, Locke, Rawls, Rousseau	Allowed	Allowed	Allowed
Humanitarianism	Bentham, Broome, Primatt	Disallowed	Disallowed	Allowed
Utilitarianism	Bentham, Singer	Disallowed	Disallowed	Allowed
Rights theory	Regan	Disallowed	Disallowed	Disallowed
Generosity theory	Linzey	Disallowed	Disallowed	Disallowed
Vegetarianism	Buddha, Montaigne, Plato	Disallowed	Disallowed	Disallowed

philanthropy toward others. They specifically ground their views on the Christian faith and equate cruelty with atheism and heresy. However, humanitarianism opposes unnecessary cruelty only. Humanitarianism would stop deer hunting, mitigate the suffering of hens, stop the slaughter of male chicks, but animal experimentation would continue.

Utilitarianism. According to animal rights advocate Peter Singer (1946–), any being that has feeling or consciousness is entitled to equal rights, so he draws the line at mollusks (clams, oysters, and the like). However, rights are considered from a utilitarian perspective, such that more suffering on the part of a few animals is justified if thousands will experience less suffering as a result. Jeremy Bentham (1748–1832), indeed, was an advocate of extending rights to animals. Utilitarianism would stop deer hunting and possibly hen battery production, but experimentation on animals would continue.

Rights theory. Tom Regan (1938–) and others rely on three premises: (1) Animals are ends in themselves and should not be regarded as means to human ends. (2) All animals have inherent value and therefore have rights. (3) Animals have equal rights with humans. One variant is theological, arguing that God created animals separately from humans for their own sake. Hen battery production, deer hunting, and animal experimentation are wrong because animals have not consented. However, rights theory is a theory of what should not be done to animals, providing no imperative to do something positive for animals.

Generosity theory. Animals should not only be respected, according to Linzey, but they should also be given greater consideration. The weak, according to Linzey's Christian view, should have moral priority. Humans should not only have dominion over nature, but also should care for the creatures of God; the higher creatures should sacrifice for the lower, not the reverse. Generosity theory stresses affirmative action for animals, just as parents give special care to dependent infants: because they are innocent and so easily abused, they should be protected. The biblical Noah, perhaps, was the earliest practitioner of generosity theory.

Vegetarianism. In Buddhism and Hinduism, animals, even cockroaches, are considered sacred. Some vegetarians drink milk but do not eat cows and other animals; others, known as **vegans**, are fully vegetarian. Even the killing of insects is unacceptable. Why? According to the theory of reincarnation, all creatures are equal, and the insect that someone might kill could have been their great grandparent. Of course, some vegetarians may choose to avoid meat for health reasons rather than any concern for the rights of animals. Plato (427–347 BCE) and Michel de Montaigne (1533–1592) are among the various philosophers who are claimed to have been exponents of vegetarianism. More practically, vegans argue that the abolition of meat consumption would do more to reduce carbon emissions than widespread use of hybrid motor vehicles.

Currently, animals rights advocates have several agendas. Some seek to abolish the exploitation of animals for human clothing, consumption, as well as for entertainment. Britain's Act to Prevent the Cruel and Improper Treatment of Cattle of 1822, the first law adopted by a country on the subject, was generalized by the Protection of Animals Act of 1911. Several countries now have legislation about animal cruelty and endangered species. However, international law on animal rights has mainly been interested in protecting species from extinction, such as dolphins, porpoises, and whales.

Stephen Coleridge (1854–1936), longtime president of the British National Anti-Vivisection Society, proposed an *Animals' Charter* to the League of Nations, which was further developed into *An Animals' Bill of Rights* by Geoffrey Hodson (1886–1983), president of the Council of Combined Animal Welfare Organizations of New Zealand. André Géraud (1882–1974) produced *A Declaration of Animal Rights* in 1924, which in turn led Florence Barkers to draft the *International Animals Charter* (1926). No generic animal rights treaty, however, has been adopted to date.

Fish are the subjects of the earliest recorded treaties that deal with animals. A treaty between France and Great Britain in 1867 was the first, followed by similar agreements concerning fishing in the Rhine River and in the North Sea. However, all three agreements deal with the rights of commercial exploitation more than the rights of fish, so they are not relevant to the present discussion.

The next treaties sought to limit the hunting of species with commercial value (Table 14.3). After agreements between Britain and the United States on fur seals in the late nineteenth century, there was a more general agreement on birds.

In 1913, the Swiss government convened the International Conference on Nature Protection, which agreed to establish a Consultative Committee for the International Protection of Nature as an information clearinghouse. However, World War I frustrated that goal.

TABLE 14.3 **ANIMAL CONSERVATION TREATIES**

Adopted	Treaty	In force
1891	Agreement Between the Government of the United States . . . and the Government of Her Britannic Majesty for a Modus Vivendi in Relation to Fur Seal Fisheries in the Bering Sea	1891
1892	Convention Between the Government of the United States of America and the Government of Her Britannic Majesty for the Renewal of the Existing Modus Vivendi in the Bering Sea	1892
1902	Convention for the Protection of Birds Useful to Agriculture	1902
1911	Convention Between the United States of America, the United Kingdom of Great Britain and Northern Ireland, and Russia, for the Preservation and Protection of Fur Seals	1911
1931	International Convention for the Regulation of Whaling	1935
1933	Convention on Preservation of Fauna and Flora in Their Natural State	1936
1940	Convention on Nature Protection and Wild Life Preservation in the Western Hemisphere	1942
1950	International Convention for the Protection of Birds	1963
1957	Interim Convention on Conservation of North Pacific Fur Seals	1957
1959	Antarctic Treaty	
1964	• Agreed Measures for the Conservation of Antarctic Flora and Fauna	1964
1972	• Convention for the Conservation of Antarctic Seals	1978
1976	• Convention on the Conservation of Antarctic Marine Living Resources	1982

TABLE 14.3 (CONTINUED)

Adopted	Treaty	In force
1968	African Convention on the Conservation of Nature and Natural Resources	1969
1969	Convention for the Conservation and Management of the Vicuña	1969
1970	Benelux Convention Concerning Hunting and the Protection of Birds	1972
1971	Convention on Wetlands of International Importance Especially as Waterfowl Habitat	1975
1973	Agreement on the Conservation of Polar Bears	1976
1973	Convention for International Trade in Endangered Species of Wild Fauna and Flora	1975
1976	Convention on Conservation of Nature in the South Pacific	1990
1978	Treaty for Amazonian Cooperation	1980
1979	Convention for the Conservation and Management of the Vicuña	1983
1979	Convention on the Conservation of Migratory Species of Wild Animals (CMS)	1983
1979	Convention on the Conservation of European Wildlife and Natural Habitats	1982
1980	International Convention on the Conservation of Antarctic Marine Living Resources	1981
1982	Convention on Biological Diversity	1993
1982	Benelux Convention on Nature Conservation and Landscape Protection	1983
1985	ASEAN Agreement on the Conservation of Nature and Natural Resources	1985
1985	Protocol Concerning Protected Areas and Wild Fauna and Flora in . . . Eastern Africa . . .	
1987	Agreement on the Action Plan for the . . . Common Zambezi River System	1987
1990	Agreement on the Conservation of Seals in the Wadden Sea	1991
1991	Agreement on the Conservation of Populations of European Bats	1994
1991	Convention Concerning the Protection of the Alps	1998
1992	Convention on Biological Diversity	1993
1992	Convention for the . . . Biodiversity and . . . Wilderness Areas in Central America	1994
1992	Convention Concerning the Conservation of the Biodiversity and the Protection of Priority Forestry Areas of Central America	
1992	Agreement on the Conservation of Small Cetaceans of the Baltic and North Seas	1994
1993	Agreement Establishing the South Pacific Regional Environment Program	1995
1994	Lusaka Agreement on Cooperative Enforcement Operations Directed at Illegal Trade in Wild Flora and Fauna	1996
1995	Agreement on the Conservation of African-Eurasian Migratory Waterbirds	1999
1996	Agreement on the Conservation of Cetaceans of the Black Sea, Mediterranean Sea and Contiguous Atlantic Area	2001
2001	Agreement on the Conservation of Albatrosses and Petrels	2004

The *International Convention for the Regulation of Whaling* of 1931, which was adopted to limit whale hunting, has been renewed on several occasions. For example, approximately 250,000 blue whales existed before they were commercially harvested in the nineteenth century; today, there are only 1,000. In 1982, the International Whaling Commission adopted a moratorium, effective 1986, on commercial whaling to enable whales to regain their numbers after more than a century of slaughtering them, though leaving a loophole for "scientific whaling," that is, killing of unlimited numbers of whales for scientific research. Although Iceland and Japan then engaged in "scientific whaling," Norway rejected the moratorium. Originally, the Convention had an exception for indigenous peoples, but the treaty was amended to abolish the aboriginal exception in 1977, two years after Greenpeace's effort to prevent a Soviet ship from catching whales. Some 2,000 whales are still slaughtered each year.

HISTORIC EVENT 14.2   GREENPEACE STOPS A SOVIET WHALING SHIP (1975)

In 1975, with a Soviet fishing fleet of thirteen ships reportedly harvesting whales in the North Pacific, the nongovernmental organization Greenpeace chartered the *Phyllis Cormack* at Vancouver and sailed toward the whale hunters. Upon arrival in the area, Greenpeace saw one of the Soviet vessels in pursuit of a whale and proceeded to place Zodiac inflatables between the harpoon ship and the whale. The image of a harpoon being fired over the Greenpeace crew, which was caught on a videocamera, was later broadcast on television, thereby dramatizing the lengths to which whalers are often prepared to go. Subsequently, Greenpeace established itself as a major activist nongovernmental organization and has continued to pursue Japanese whaling ships.

In 2006, after intense lobbying by Japan to allow secret ballots, the vote to rescind the ban was 33–32, but the Commission can only rescind the moratorium with an affirmative vote by 75 percent of the seventy members of the Commission. Subsequently, Iceland resumed commercial whaling for the first time in twenty years. There has been similar difficulty in efforts to limit the hunting of fur seals and vicuña; both agreements have expired.

The goal of saving species from extinction prompted two later treaties. The *Convention on Preservation of Fauna and Flora in Their Natural State* of 1933 focused on Africa, and the *Convention on Nature Protection and Wild Life Preservation in the Western Hemisphere* of 1940. Among other regional treaties adopted over the years, the *Convention for the Prohibition of Fishing with Long Driftnets in the South Pacific* of 1989 responded to an outcry over fishnets of two hundred miles in length that trapped and killed dolphins, porpoises, and turtles.

Meanwhile, generic statements on animal rights emerged in several quarters. In 1953, retired Presbyterian minister W.J. Piggott published an *Appeal for the*

International Animals' Charter, and in 1954 he presented his appeal as a revised *International Animals' Charter* to a World Congress of Animal Welfare Societies in London. From 1953 to 1956, more preliminary charters were drawn up by the World Federation for Animal Protection Associations. In 1972, Georges Heuses submitted a *Universal Declaration of Animal Rights* to UNESCO; the following year, the declaration was adopted in France by the National Council for the Protection of Animals.

The UN Environmental Program (UNEP), formed in 1972, has forged several agreements. The Whaling Convention served as the model for the adoption in 1973 of the *Convention for International Trade in Endangered Species of Wild Fauna and Flora* (CITES), for which UNEP provides secretariat services. CITES classifies animals into three categories: (1) those threatened with extinction, (2) those possibly threatened with extinction, and (3) those overexploited. Appendices to CITES list specific animal and plant species. International trade in all three categories is regulated by import and export licenses. Currently under debate within the CITES framework is a ban on caviar, since sturgeon appears increasingly to be an endangered species.

In 1979, UNEP efforts resulted in the adoption of the *Convention on the Conservation of Migratory Species of Wild Animals* (CMS), which operates in a manner similar to CITES. The focus is on efforts to conserve subspecies of such animals as antelopes, bats, cranes, deer, and turtles. Under the CMS framework, agreements on specific species for particular geographic subregions have been adopted for Antarctic marine animals, Wadden Sea seals, European bats, Euroafrican waterbirds, European-Mediteranean dolphins, porpoises, and albatrosses.

Conservation may be beneficial to humans who view animals as commercially profitable objects. However, in recent years the Council of Europe has adopted agreements that focus on human maltreatment of animals (Table 14.4). A treaty dealing with transportation of animals has provisions on the space, ventilation and hygiene, transportation means, food and water, loading and unloading of animals, and veterinary assistance for the international transport of animals. Farm animals are protected against maltreatment in their care, feeding, housing, machinery used with them, and slaughtering, which are in turn subject to COE inspection. A recent Protocol to the treaty updates coverage to reflect newer methods, especially bio-technology. COE's treaty on experimentation urges countries to conduct animal experimentation only when absolutely necessary and establishes conditions that must be met in those cases; in particular, animal suffering is prohibited.

In the 1957 Treaty of Rome, which launched the European Economic Community, one provision stated that animal welfare was a goal, but no specific right was stipulated. The Single European Act of 1986 opened the door for further action, and the European Union has adopted regulations similar to those of the Council of Europe by adopting directives. Based on evidence that zoo animals are maltreated, a Council Directive in 1999 established a licensing and inspection system. The EU's Amsterdam Treaty of 1997 has a *Protocol on Animal Welfare* which declares that the "agricultural, transport, internal market and research policies . . . shall pay full regard to the welfare requirements of animals."

In 1969, the International Fund for Animal Welfare (IFAW) began by taking action to stop a hunt for white-coat harp seals on the eastern coast of Canada. Current priorities of the Fund are to stop foxhunting, the trade in ivory tusks, and whale-hunting. People for the Ethical Treatment of Animals (PETA), founded in 1980, has lobbied for the human treatment of animals on factory farms, in laboratories, in the clothing trade, and in the entertainment industry, although some PETA funds have gone to the militant Animal Liberation Front (ALF), which has been accused of being a terrorist organization. The Animal Protection Institute recommends several ways to reduce cruelty in animal experimentation, such as computer simulation and in-vitro techniques.

TABLE 14.4 ANIMAL PROTECTION TREATIES

Adopted	Treaty	Protection	In force
1968	European Convention for the Protection of Animals During International Transport	Mishandling	1971
1979	• Additional Protocol to the European Convention for the Protection of Animals During International Transport		1989
1976	European Convention for the Protection of Animals Kept for Farming Purposes	Against suffering in animal husbandry	1978
1992	• Protocol of Amendment to the European Convention for the Protection of Animals Kept for Farming Purposes	Updated to include biotechnology	
1979	European Convention for the Protection of Animals for Slaughter	Humane slaughtering	1982
1986	European Convention for the Protection of Vertebrate Animals Used for Experimental and Other Scientific Purposes	Humane experimental methods	1991
1987	European Convention for the Protection of Pet Animals	Ban on extinct animals as pets; humane treatment of pets	1992
1989	Convention for the Prohibition of Fishing with Long Driftnets in the South Pacific	Ban on driftnets that kill innocent fish, turtles, etc.	1989
1990	• Protocol I	Procedural	1990
1990	• Protocol II	Procedural	1990
1997	Treaty of Amsterdam	Humane treatment in agriculture, experi-mentation, transport	1999
1997	• Protocol on Animal Welfare		1999
1998	Convention on the Protection of Environment Through Criminal Law	Criminalizes harm to animals	
1999	Protocol on Wildlife Conservation and Law Enforcement of the Southern African Development Community	Ban on poaching	2003

Efforts to adopt a more general international animal rights agreement have continued. In 1977, the International League of Animal Rights and Affiliated National Leagues, during the International Meeting on Animal Rights in London, adopted a *Universal Declaration of Animal Rights*, which was presented in 1978 in the main hall of the UNESCO House in Paris.

In 1988, the Committee for the Convention for the Protection of Animals, a coalition of two animal rights organizations, proposed an International Convention for the Protection of Animals to consolidate all existing animal rights concerns into one document, including transportation of animals, methods of taking wildlife, care of exhibited wildlife, and protection from cruel treatment. But the proposal languishes, too sweeping for consideration by countries more protective of their sovereignty than of their animals. The Earth Summit at Río de Janeiro in 1992 adopted the *Convention on Biological Diversity*, which further promotes conservation of near-extinct species.

The latest innovation came in 2003 at the Manila Conference on Animal Welfare. Delegates agreed that captive animals should be guaranteed the basic Five Freedoms and Three R's:

- freedom from hunger, thirst and malnutrition;
- freedom from fear and distress;
- freedom from physical and thermal discomfort;
- freedom from pain, injury and disease;
- freedom to express normal patterns of behavior;
- reduction in numbers of animals;
- refinement of experimental methods;
- replacement of animals with non-animal techniques.

In addition to the Animal Protection Institute, the Committee for the Convention for the Protection of Animals, and SPCA, several animal rights organizations are active today. The Humane Society, originally founded in Holland during 1767 to rescue shipwrecked sailors, spawned organizations in other countries and eventually evolved into an organization to protect animals.

Animal research is responsible for the development of medicines and vaccines that have saved millions of human lives from deformities, pain, and premature death. For that reason, Congress defined "animal" in the Animal Welfare Act of 1966 to exclude birds, mice, and rats, which together account for 90 percent of all laboratory animals; "warm-blooded animals," such farm animals and pets, are protected by the law.

In 1991, the United States decided to ban the import of tuna caught by driftnets, some of which were ten miles in length, because they tended to capture and kill dolphins, an endangered species. México, however, then complained that the import restriction was contrary to rules under the General Agreement of Tariffs and Trade (GATT). In 1993, when Norway resumed whalehunting, the United States threatened a boycott of all Norwegian products. In response to both complaints, the GATT panel in Geneva ruled that import bans were unacceptable nontariff barriers to trade. Although GATT had no way to enforce the ruling, Washington backed down on the Norwegian ban but continued to ban Mexican tuna. In 1995, when the World Trade Organization (WTO) went into effect to supersede GATT, México complained again. WTO then ruled that the United States must either rescind its ban, compensate México, or the rest of the world would retaliate by imposing restrictions on American imports. Washington's response was to place a "dolphin safe" warning label on imported tuna, prompting México to file another complaint with WTO in 2003 on the basis that the label served as an NTB. Washington then dropped the use of the warning label.

In 2002, meanwhile, WTO agreed to begin negotiations on an agreement that would take animal protection considerations into account. Although a draft text was completed in 2005, the matter is still being debated within WTO.

In recent years, the Humane Society and PETA have met some success in lobbying for better treatment of the animals in the United States. In 2000, McDonald's Corporation became the first company to ask egg producers to comply with guidelines for the humane treatment of hens – providing at least 72 square inches per hen, adequate food and water, and a ban on trimming beaks. In the same year, McDonald's decided to purchase meat only from suppliers that guarantee minimum humane treatment of livestock. Burger King soon followed.

In 2000, Chipotle Mexican Grill, which operates some 500 restaurants in the United States, advertised that its pork is humanely raised, and some upscale restaurants now do likewise. In 2006, Whole Foods Market, a grocery chain of one hundred and eighty-three stores in Britain, Canada, and the United States, decided to label beef, chicken, and pork with the label "animal compassionate" to indicate that they have been raised in a humane manner before slaughter. Smaller grocery retailers now use "cage free," "certified humane," "free farm," and "free range" labels. Although the cost of the newly labeled produce is higher, affluent consumers not only do not mind but also claim that the food tastes better.

Because the DNAs of humans and simians are similar, some animal rights exponents argue that apes are entitled to the right to life, freedom from torture, and many other rights. During 2007, an Austrian court was asked to name a human as the legal guardian of two chimpanzees, in effect giving them the status of legal persons. The issue involved two chimps being held by the government that might potentially sell them outside Austria to countries that allow animal torture. The court, however, denied the petition.

DISCUSSION TOPIC 14.2 WHAT ARE THE LIMITS TO ANIMAL RIGHTS?

Which theory about the human treatment of animals is most optimal? Do theories of animal rights suggest deeper theories about human rights than have been discussed thus far in this volume?

In summary, the focus on animal rights gets to the roots of the issue of rights. Is not the campaign to advance human rights in reality an effort to protect those who are weak, powerless, and capable of being abused? If humans have rights because of the need to protect against abuse, so may animals. However, since animals cannot assert their rights, any discussion about animal rights is really about human responsibilities. One reason for inclusion of the topic in a book about human rights is to emphasize that rights cannot protect anyone without a corresponding sense of obligations. The same argument applies to the next topic, the environment, where a failure to take human responsibilities seriously may have the consequence of jeopardizing all life.

ENVIRONMENTAL RIGHTS

Humans have long believed that they have a right to exploit their environment in order to survive. At the same time, urban civilizations have sought to keep their cities and roads free from garbage and their water supplies free from contamination. With wide acceptance of the principle of economic self-interest and the advent of the industrial revolution, however, urban filth became a byproduct of economic growth, a phenomenon known as the **tragedy of the commons** because individuals benefit from discarding small quantities of what they do not need without realizing the consequences of their collective behavior. Efforts to set aside pristine environments into national parks in the late nineteenth century were among the first to recognize the value of the natural environment, which can be regarded as the common heritage of all humans, but today the effort to save the wilderness has been lost by most accounts.

After World War II, London and Los Angeles became particularly notable for a mixture of fog and smoke known as smog. During 1952, such a thick layer of smog began to collect over London that by December hospitals were overcrowded with patients suffering from respiratory problems. An estimated 12,000 died up to the end of February 1953 due to complications from what became known as "killer smog," while Angelenos suffered eye and respiratory discomfort.

In 1959, as I drove east from smoggy Los Angeles to attend Yale University, I noticed a strange pigmentation in a body of water flowing through downtown Cleveland into Lake Erie; the bright orange color was an example of eerie industrial pollution. In 1962, biologist Rachel Carson (1907–1964) published *Silent Spring*. Her argument, that nature was dying because of DDT and other pesticides, stunned the world; indeed the *New York Times* referred to her book as a twentieth-century version of the Rights of Man. Later that year, London's killer smog claimed another one hundred and six lives.

In 1969, John McConnell (1915–) proposed an Earth Day at the 1969 National UNESCO Conference in San Francisco. Shortly thereafter, his proposal was accepted by San Francisco City and County, which proclaimed the first Earth Day. In the same year, Congress voted to establish the Environmental Protection Agency. The concept of a worldwide Earth Day quickly gained support, and the March equinox is now marked each year by the tolling of the United Nations Peace Bell. McConnell went on to form the Earth Society Foundation in 1976, and has issued such documents as *Earth Rights* (1974), *Earth Charter* (1979), and an *Earth Magna Carta* (1995).

Today, the global warming from environmental pollution is likely to cause such catastrophic climate changes that the health of the planet may be in jeopardy. Although many environmental concerns may be categorized as human health issues, planetary health has become a major concern for the first time in recent years. Meanwhile, many industrial producers are reluctant to spend additional amounts in order to stop profitable practices that destroy natural resources, and politicians derive more campaign financing from industry than from environmentalists.

In short, the political will to cope with pressing environmental issues is stymied by alternative perspectives regarding the environment. At least four coexist today:

- **Econocentrism.** Economic growth should be maximized with no concern for environmental consequences except when there are direct adverse economic consequences. For less affluent countries, the right to development trumps environmental concerns.
- **Utilitarianism.** There should be a balance so that the costs of minimizing pollution will not be so excessive that jobs and economies will be jeopardized. Under the label **sustainable development**, intergovernmental banks appear to tilt toward industry rather providing a compromise that would save the environment from disaster.
- **Anthropocentrism.** The health and survival of humans prevails over all other values, including animal survival. Although the onset of disaster from global warming is impossible to predict, anthropocentrics insist on immediate action.
- **Ecocentrism.** Environmental damage should be prevented, stopped, and reversed so that the planet can return to as pristine a condition as possible.

In part because of a lack of consensus on the appropriate strategy, the concept of environmental rights has only gained substance through incremental treaties and court actions that deal with two basic issues – **damage** and **prevention**. Agreements to prevent environmental damage, whether ongoing or anticipated, have been difficult to gain adoption. Although there are many environmental concerns, the discussion below primarily focuses on the pollution of air, land, water, and the planet itself.

The earliest efforts to deal with environmental issues on an international basis occurred in Europe and North America (Table 14.5). Although the Final Act of the Congress of Vienna of 1815 set up the Central Commission for the Navigation of the Rhine and in 1856 the Treaty of Paris established the European Commission of the Danube, both commissions dealt with disputes concerning the principle of free navigation. A half-century of Rhenish cooperation led to the *Convention Between the Riverine States of the Rhine Respecting Regulations Governing the Transport of Corrosive and Poisonous Substances* of 1900, the first treaty dealing with pollution.

Friendly relations between Canada and the United States facilitated the further development of international environmental law. In 1909, the *Treaty Between the United States and Great Britain Relating to Boundary Waters Between the United States and Canada* provided that water "shall not be polluted on either side to the injury of health or property on the other." An International Joint Commission was established in case of future disputes.

TABLE 14.5 **EARLY INTERNATIONAL ENVIRONMENTAL AGREEMENTS**

Date	Agreement
1900	Convention Between the Riverine States of the Rhine Respecting Regulations Governing the Transport of Corrosive and Poisonous Substances
1909	Treaty Between the United States and Great Britain Relating to Boundary Waters Between the United States and Canada
1921	Convention Concerning the Use of White Lead in Painting
1931	Convention for Settlement of Difficulties Arising from Operation of Smelter at Trail

After World War I, the newly established International Labor Organization recognized the health risks of paints containing lead. As a result, the *Convention Concerning the Use of White Lead in Painting* emerged in 1921.

Before 1931, there was no international legal precedent to resolve a dispute between Canada and the United States regarding air pollution in the Trail Smelter Arbitration cases. Accordingly, new principles had to be developed. The joint commission established in the 1909 treaty was then constituted as an arbitration tribunal, which ruled that pollution moving from one country to another was a form of criminal **trespass**, and the consequence of pollution was determined to be a **nuisance** subject to compensation. In other words, the "polluter pays" principle was enunciated.

COURT CASE 14.2 THE TRAIL SMELTER ARBITRATION CASES (1931, 1938, 1941)

In 1928, the United States' complained that sulfur dioxide emissions from the Canadian copper smelting industry in Trail, British Columbia, were causing environmental damage through rain falling in the Columbia River Valley of the State of Washington, but Canada refused to compensate the United States. The two countries, however, referred the matter to the U.S.-Canadian International Joint Commission for arbitration. In 1931, the commission ruled that the United States should be compensated $350,000 and sulfur dioxide emissions should be reduced. The same year, the two countries adopted the *Convention for Settlement of Difficulties Arising from Operation of Smelter at Trail*. When pollution continued, an arbitral tribunal was set up, issuing opinions in 1938 and 1941 for additional compensation. In all, Canada paid to the United States approximately $420,000 so that the American government could compensate farmers whose crops were adversely affected.

After World War II, international agreements about oceans and waterways gradually shifted focus from matters of navigation to larger issues, particularly pollution. The use of large oil tankers from the Middle East to Europe, the Americas, and Asia prompted concern about the possibility of oil spilling into the ocean. Accordingly, in 1954, the

International Convention for the Prevention of Pollution of the Sea by Oil (OILPOL) was adopted. However, ship operators made little effort to comply.

Many major international treaties on the environment deal with water pollution (Table 14.6).[3] The Intergovernmental Maritime Consultative Organization (IMCO), which began operation on a treaty basis in 1958, originally had a primary mandate over navigation in international waters. By 1969, IMCO shifted focus to pollution with the adoption of the *Convention Relating to Intervention on the High Seas in Cases of Oil Pollution Casualties*, which empowered ships to act in case of actual or possible oil spillage. The 1969 treaty was then amended in 1983 to cover substances other than oil. Since OILPOL had little effect, IMCO sponsored the *International Convention for the Prevent of Pollution from Ships* (MARPOL) in 1973, but once again there was resistance, and the treaty was not ratified. However, after several serious oil spills, two Protocols were adopted, incorporating the terms of the treaty. The later Protocol was ratified in 1983; annexes dealing with garbage and sewage followed in 1988 and 2003, respectively.

In 1982, the *United Nations Convention on the Law of the Sea* was adopted, providing for the International Seabed Authority to coordinate implementation and the International Tribunal for the Law of the Sea (ITLOS) to handle disputes regarding protection of the marine environment as the "common heritage of mankind" and other matters through arbitration. In 1994, when the Convention received sufficient ratifications to go into force, the International Seabed Authority was established at Kingston, Jamaica, and ITLOS at Hamburg.

Although most cases filed with ITLOS have involved the seizure of fishing vessels of one country in the territorial waters of another country, the case of *Ireland v United Kingdom* (2001) involves British transportation of radioactive materials in the Irish Sea to a nuclear power plant in England. After Britain suspended shipments of radioactive materials in response to Ireland's request for *provisional measures* from ITLOS, the tribunal ruled that the two countries should establish cooperative arrangements to ensure that no mishaps would occur in the future. In 2003, Malaysia filed a case against Singapore regarding the latter's plans to reclaim land that might adversely affect Malaysia's navigation, coastal deposition, and deteriorating ecohydraulic and water quality conditions; however, ITLOS dismissed the case.

In 1982, IMCO became the International Maritime Organization (IMO). IMCO and IMO have fathered more treaties relating to pollution than any other organization. Agreements dealing with pollution in the air and on land have been sponsored by other organizations.

HISTORIC EVENT 14.3 THE CHERNOBYL ACCIDENT (1986)

In 1986, at a government nuclear power plant in the Soviet Union that disregarded numerous safety procedures, a chain reaction in the reactor went out of control. Explosions and a fireball blew off the reactor's heavy steel and concrete lid. More than two dozen persons died instantly, 135,000 were evacuated from a twenty-mile radius, and estimates of deaths due to radiation-associated cancer range as high as 200,000.

TABLE 14.6 **MAJOR CONTEMPORARY AGREEMENTS DEALING WITH WATER POLLUTION**

Adopted	Agreement	In force
1954	International Convention for the Prevention of Pollution of the Sea by Oil	1958
1963	Treaty Banning Nuclear Weapon Tests in the Atmosphere, in Outer Space and Under Water	1963
1969	Convention Relating to Intervention on the High Seas in Cases of Oil Pollution Casualties	1957
1969	• Protocol Relating to Intervention on the High Seas in Cases of Marine Pollution by Substances Other than Oil	1983
1969	International Convention on Civil Liability for Oil Pollution Damage	1975
1971	International Convention on the Establishment of an International Fund for Compensation for Oil Pollution Damage	1978
1972	International Convention for the Prevention of Marine Pollution by Dumping of Wastes and Other Matter	1975
1973	International Convention for the Prevention of Pollution from Ships	
1978	• Protocol of 1978 Relating to the International Convention for the Prevention of Pollution from Ships	1983
1997	• Protocol of 1997 to Amend the International Convention for the Prevention of Pollution from Ships, 1973, as Modified by the Protocol of 1978, Relating Thereto	
1982	United Nations Convention on the Law of the Sea	1994
1990	International Convention on Oil Pollution Preparedness, Response and Cooperation	1995
1992	Convention on Biological Diversity	1993
2000	• Cartagena Protocol on Biosafety	2003
1997	Convention on the Law of the Non-Navigational Uses of International Watercourses	

In the 1950s, while the Cold War frightened the world by the prospect of mutual annihilation, nuclear weapons testing in Nevada and Siberia began without full knowledge of the adverse consequences. However, so much radioactive rain from Siberia landed in the Pacific Northwest and in Northern California in 1957 that agricultural crops were deemed unfit for human and animal consumption, and an outcry for a ban on atmospheric tests became strident. Ever since, the dangers of nuclear pollution have been well recognized in international treaties (Table 14.7), particularly after the disaster at Chernobyl.

The environment was considered more generically in 1970, when President Richard Nixon (1913–1994) signed the National Environmental Policy Act, the first national effort to deal comprehensively with environmental concerns. In 1972, the year when the United States banned DDT, Nixon urged the UN to act on a proposal by former President Lyndon Johnson (1908–1973) in 1965 for a World Heritage Trust to protect the environment in special areas around the world.

TABLE 14.7 TREATIES DEALING WITH NUCLEAR ACCIDENTS AND POLLUTION

Adopted	Agreement	In force
1960	Convention on Third Party Liability in the Field of Nuclear Energy	1968
1963	• Convention Supplementary to the Paris Convention on Third Party Liability in the Field of Nuclear Energy	1977
1988	• Joint Protocol Relating to the Application of the Vienna Convention and the Paris Convention	1992
1997	• Protocol to Amend the Vienna Convention	2003
1997	• Convention on Supplementary Compensation for Nuclear Damage	
1963	Vienna Convention on Civil Liability for Nuclear Damage	1977
1963	Treaty Banning Nuclear Weapon Tests in the Atmosphere, in Outer Space and Under Water	1963
1971	Treaty on the Prohibition of the Emplacement of Nuclear Weapons and Other Weapons of Mass Destruction on the Sea Bed and the Ocean Floor and in the Subsoil Thereof	
1971	Convention Relating to Civil Liability in the Field of Maritime Carriage of Nuclear Material	1975
1979	Convention on the Physical Protection of Nuclear Material	
1985	South Pacific Nuclear Free Zone Treaty	
1986	Convention on Early Notification of a Nuclear Accident	
1986	Convention on Assistance in the Case of a Nuclear Accident or Radiological Emergency	
1988	Joint Protocol Relating to the Application of the Vienna Convention and the Paris Convention	
1994	Convention on Nuclear Safety	

In response, UNESCO in 1972 adopted the *Convention Concerning the Protection of the World Cultural and Natural Heritage*, which established the World Heritage Committee to identify World Heritage Sites around the world. Currently, there are six hundred and forty-four cultural, one hundred and sixty-two natural, and twenty-four mixed cultural/natural World Heritage Sites in one hundred and thirty-eight countries. Three examples of natural World Heritage Sites are Kew Gardens in London, the Galápagos Islands, and the rice terraces of Bauaue, Philippines. In 1998, the Heritage Committee asked Australia to stop uranium mining near Kakadu Park, which was listed as a World Heritage site, or the site would be listed as "in danger."

Also in 1972, a major international effort to deal with global environmental issues came when the United Nations sponsored the Conference on the Human Environment at Stockholm. One key provision of the *Stockholm Declaration on the Human Environment* stated, "Man has a fundamental right to freedom, equality and adequate conditions of life, in an environment of a quality that permits a life of dignity and well-being . . ." The principles of nuisance and trespass from the Trail Smelter case were recognized in the Declaration. The concept of sustainable development was also endorsed at the conference as a compromise, namely, that the goal of substantially increasing living standards of the impoverished was to occur in an environmentally sustainable manner. The United Nations Environmental Program was established in the same year.

Subsequently, UNEP and other organizations have sponsored international environmental agreements that have expanded from retail to wholesale approaches. Among the larger foci have been global pollution, conservation of ecosystems, comprehensive river-basin regimes, and enforcement inside national borders. UNEP also has encouraged regional environmental agreements. For some environmentalists, however, UNEP's action-oriented eclipsed a desire for a more generic statement of environmental rights.

Implicit in the Stockholm Declaration, nevertheless, is that there is a **right to water** for human consumption. Target 10 of the Millennium goals mandates the "reductions by half [of] the proportion of people without sustainable access to safe drinking water and basic sanitation" by 2015, a tall order indeed, since 1.1 billions lack adequate water and 2.6 billions go without basic sanitation. The right to water is addressed in several treaties (the Fourth Geneva Convention and the Additional Protocols, the Convention on the Elimination of All Forms of Discrimination Against Women, and the UN Convention on the Rights of the Child). The *Convention on the Law of the Non-Navigational Uses of International Watercourses*, which was adopted in 1997, however, competes with efforts of transnational corporations to buy up sources of fresh water, which are more limited than the supply of chemicals to pollute the water. Recently, several countries have included the right to water in their constitutions: Uganda (1995), the Gambia, South Africa, and Zambia (1996); Ethiopia (1998) and Uruguay (2004).

One of the most significant agreements was the *Convention on Long-Range Transboundary Air Pollution* of 1979, an effort of the UN Economic Commission for Europe. Eight subsequent Protocols have identified deadlines for reducing various airborne chemicals by specific percentages, including nitrogen, sulfur, and toxic organic pesticides.

TABLE 14.8 **MAJOR CONTEMPORARY AGREEMENTS DEALING WITH AIR AND LAND POLLUTION**

Adopted	Agreement	In force
1971	Convention Concerning Protection against Hazards of Poisoning Arising from Benzene	
1977	Convention Concerning the Protection of Workers Against Occupational Hazards in the Working Environment due to Air Pollution, Noise and Vibration	
1979	Convention on Long-Range Transboundary Air Pollution	1983
1984	• Protocol on Long-Term Financing of the Cooperative Program for Monitoring and Evaluation of the Long-Range Transmission of Air Pollutants in Europe	1988
1985	• Protocol to the 1979 Convention on Long-Range Transboundary Air Pollution on the Reduction of Sulfur Emissions or Their Transboundary Fluxes by at Least 30 Per Cent	1987

1988	Protocol . . . Concerning the Control of Emissions of Nitrogen Oxides or Their Transboundary Fluxes*	1991
1991	• Protocol . . . Concerning the Control of Emissions of Volatile Organic Compounds or their Transboundary Fluxes	1997
1994	• Protocol . . . on Further Reduction of Sulfur Emissions	1998
1998	• Protocol . . . on Heavy Metals	2003
1998	• Protocol . . . on Persistent Organic Pollutants	2005
1999	• Protocol to Abate Acidification, Eutrophication and Ground-level Ozone	
1985	Vienna Convention for the Protection of the Ozone Layer	1988
1987	• Montréal Protocol on Substances that Deplete the Ozone Layer	1989
1990	• London Amendment to the Montréal Protocol on Substances that Deplete the Ozone Layer	
1992	• Copenhagen Amendment to the Montréal Protocol on Substances that Deplete the Ozone Layer	
1989	Convention on the Control of Transboundary Movements of Hazardous Wastes and Their Disposal	1992
1989	Convention on Civil Liability for Damage Caused During Carriage of Dangerous Goods by Road, Rail and Inland Navigation Vessels	1991
1991	Convention on the Ban of the Import into Africa and the Control of Transboundary Movement and Management of Hazardous Wastes Within Africa	
1991	Convention on Environmental Impact Assessment in a Transboundary Context	
1993	• Protocol on Strategic Environmental Assessment	
1991	Convention Concerning the Protection of the Alps	1998
1992	United Nations Framework Convention on Climate Change	1994
1997	• Kyoto Protocol on Climate Change	2005
1993	North American Agreement on Environmental Cooperation	1995
1995	Convention to Ban the Importation into Forum Island Countries of Hazardous and Radio Active Waste and to Control the Transboundary Movement of Hazardous Waste Within the South Pacific Region	2001
1998	Rotterdam Convention on the Prior Informed Consent Procedure for Certain Hazardous Chemicals and Pesticides in International Trade	2004
2001	Stockholm Convention on Persistent Organic Pollutants	2004

* "to the 1979 Convention on Long-Range Transboundary Air Pollution"

Efforts to reduce air pollution continued in the 1980s (Table 14.8), particularly after the leaking of chemicals from a plant in Bhopal, India, during 1984. In 1985, when a hole in the ozone layer of the Antarctic was first discovered, the *Vienna Convention for the Protection of the Ozone Layer* was adopted as a framework agreement while provisions of the *Montréal Protocol on Substances that Deplete the Ozone Layer* were developed. The Protocol then banned most known causes of ozone depletion, especially chloroflurocarbons, setting a compliance deadline of 2000. The two agreements, sponsored by UNEP, were the first efforts to control global pollutants. The ozone layer is expected to be repaired by 2025 as a result.

HISTORIC EVENT 14.4 THE BHOPAL INDUSTRIAL ACCIDENT (1984)

In 1984, the world's worst industrial accident occurred when forty tons of chemicals leaked from the Union Carbide pesticide plant in Bhopal, India, immediately resulting in some 7,000 deaths and 200,000 injuries. Two years later, an Indian court attempted to summon the head of the company for questioning, but he refused to appear, and he remains a fugitive who has eluded Interpol. Efforts to have Washington extradite him have failed. An investigation concluded in 1987 that Union Carbide was liable because alarm and safety systems had been scaled back to reduce costs. In 1989, the Indian government accepted a civil settlement of $470 million, though the government still has not disbursed $390 million to the victims. However, the company abandoned the plant without cleaning up the toxic chemicals, so the poisons remain to haunt the people, and one person per day dies from the exposure. In all, some 600,000 persons have been affected to date. In 1992, the head of Union Carbide and several Indian operators of the plant were charged *in absentia* with manslaughter in an Indian court. In 1999, Union Carbide was sued under the Alien Tort Claims Act in the United States, a case now on appeal. In 2001, Dow Chemical Company bought Union Carbide, which thereby hoped thereby to escape liability, but in 2005 the Indian court added Dow to the lawsuit and again asked the U.S. government to serve the former Union Carbide head with a subpoena. Charges brought against Dow in an American court to effect a cleanup were dismissed in 2003 because the Indian court was already handling the case.

In 1986, the *Single European Act* empowered the European Community to act on environmental and natural-resources issues. The European Union's *Amsterdam Treaty* of 1997 specifically states that environmental protection should be on the basis of the polluter pay principle. The EU's activities in regard to environmental pollution mostly involve strict implementation of international agreements. In 2001, the EU adopted the Clean Air for Europe Program as a coordinated effort involving scientific information, legislative proposals, and cost-effective methods for compliance.

A nongovernmental initiative, Rainforest Alliance (RA), was founded in 1987 to stem the wanton felling of trees and damaging of ecosystems by promoting sustainable agriculture and forestry. Headquartered in New York, in 1989 RA founded SmartWood, a forestry product certification system. In 1994, RA joined with similar groups in five countries to form the Sustainable Agricultural Network (SAN), which has certified more than 460,000 acres of bananas, citrus products, cocoa, coffee, cut flowers, ferns, pineapples, and timber as ecologically sound. Currently, SAN involves organizations in ten Central and South American countries; RA provides SAN's secretariat in New York. Most certification criteria focus on conservation (ecosystem, water, wildlife) and agricultural management (crop, soil, and waste management), but community development and fair labor standards for workers are also involved, thereby overlapping with Fair Trade standards, as described in Chapter 6. RA certification deals primarily with ecological and scientific elements; the Fair Trade movement focuses on uplifting farmers from poverty.

RA's first success came in 1994, when a Chiquita Banana plantation received the initial RA certification. In the next decade, Dole Corporation spent $20 million to gain RA certification for all its banana plantations. RA also promotes ecotourism.

In 1992, meanwhile, the United Nations Conference on Environment and Development, known popularly as the Earth Summit, was held in Rio de Janeiro. The resulting *Río Declaration on Environment and Development* avoided the use of the word "right." Of the twenty-seven Principles, the first instead states, "Human beings are at the center of concerns for sustainable development. They are entitled to a healthy and productive life in harmony with nature."

The Río conference resulted in several agreements. Perhaps the most ambitious was *Agenda 21*, a 900-page action plan for protecting global resources, which urged accountability for all new development projects, including environmental impact statements. The *Convention on Biological Diversity* not only focuses on the need to preserve biological species before they become extinct but also deals with the regulation of biotechnology, as the fear is that genetically altered organisms will cannibalize existing species, resulting in a loss of species. The *Cartagena Protocol* establishes procedures for countries to follow when they import modified organisms. A nonbinding *Statement of Principles for Global Consensus on the Management, Conservation and Sustainable Development of All Types of Forests* was adopted instead of a treaty to limit logging in rainforests because developing countries feared that their forests would be internationalized.

Perhaps the most important agreement at Río, the *United Nations Framework Convention on Climate Change*, contains a pledge to decrease greenhouse gases, with specific Protocols expected to follow. The best known is the *Kyoto Protocol on Climate Change*, which came into force in 2005. The agreement requires three dozen industrial countries to reduce greenhouse-gas emissions at least 5 percent below the 1990 level by 2008–2012. A clever feature is the Clean Development Mechanism by which developed countries can made reductions by supporting energy projects in developing countries that produce electricity through alternatives that reduce carbon dioxide emissions, such as hydropower projects. A developed country can trade one ton of CO_2 produced in excess of the 1990 level for a project in a developing country that will save an equivalent amount of carbon dioxide. Although some 150 countries have ratified the Kyoto Protocol, the coalburning United States has refused to do so, and developing countries are not required to implement provisions until 2012. Nevertheless, some 500 American cities and nearly 300 colleges and universities have adopted "green power" as the sole basis for their utilities; Oakland, California, is among the largest. In 2003, the European Union adopted the Greenhouse Gas Emission Trade Scheme to meet the Kyoto targets by 2012. Since Kyoto's application to developing countries expires in 2012, and the EU scheme is behind its goal, the G-8 Summit in 2007 agreed in principle to negotiate a new agreement that might halve CO_2 emissions by 2050.

But climate change has already had an adverse effect on the South Pacific island nation of Tuvalu. In 2002 the first of 11,000 citizens began an evacuation from their nine coral atolls to New Zealand, since the country is gradually becoming inundated as the ocean floor rises.

DISCUSSION TOPIC 14.3 HOW CAN COUNTRIES BE PERSUADED TO STOP GLOBAL WARMING?

Developed countries are responsible for a large percentage of greenhouse gas emissions today, and the developing countries of China and India are catching up. Meanwhile, less developed countries seek prosperity, and may not seek to bear the high cost of environmental measures to stop pollution. The Kyoto Protocol was supposed to provide a way for compromise, but leaders in the United States have objected to the considerable cost of reducing CO_2 and other sources of pollution. What is the best way to stop global warming? An alternative to the Kyoto agreement?

Since methane from animal excrement in open pits accounts for about 7 percent of the CO_2 in the atmosphere, an Irish firm with UN funding installed a biomass project in Villegrán, México, during 2005. One of thousands of projects consistent with the Kyoto Protocol, the biomass facility not only produces electric power but also eliminates the stench from pig excrement that formerly bothered local residents.

In 1993, the European Union established the European Environmental Agency, with a secretariat at Copenhagen, to facilitate data collection so that over two hundred environmental protection directives, mostly regarding air and water pollution and waste disposal, can be enforced. The agency also has suggested new environmental standards.

A meeting of Experts on Human Rights and the Environment at the United Nations in 1994 produced a *Draft Declaration of Principles on Human Rights and the Environment*, stating that everyone has "the right to a secure, healthy and ecologically sound environment." Once again, there was a reluctance to state environmental issues in terms of rights, and the statement was never issued. That same year, President Bill Clinton (1946–) coined a new term, **environmental justice**, within Executive Order 12898, entitled *Federal Actions to Address Environmental Justice in Minority Populations and Low-Income Populations*, which recognizes that environmental problems are often dumped into communities with the least political power.

The European Court of Human Rights decided its first case on environmental pollution in 1994. In *López Ostra v Spain*, the plaintiff complained that for three years a licensed waste-treatment plant emitted polluting fumes, pestilential and irritant smells, and repetitive noise that prompted the family to move because of adverse health to a family member. The Court ruled that Spain had violated the European Convention for the Protection of Human Rights because, apart from health considerations, the plant adversely affected the family's "private and family life." A similar ruling emerged in *Guerra et al. v Italy* (1998).

In addition to the Bhopal case, corporations alleged to have committed offenses against the environment with adverse effects on the local populations have been sued in American courts under the Alien Tort Claims Act, though most cases have been dismissed. *Doe v Unocal* (395F3d932) resulted in an out-of-court settlement to the plaintiffs, though for their personal suffering, not for the environmental effects of building a gas pipeline. American courts have consistently argued that there is no clear basis for asserting environmental rights under international law. Currently, the World Trade Organization is debating whether to adopt an agreement that will take environmental concerns into account.

The Millennium Declaration, issued by the United Nations in 2000, provided eight major goals to be achieved by 2010. One of the goals, sustainable development, mandates the reversal of the loss of environmental resources without sacrificing economic development.

In 2002, at the World Summit on Sustainable Development, a *Plan of Action* was adopted that only took note of "the possible relationship between environment and human rights, including the right to development." The statement went on to endorse "good governance" (public participation and government responsiveness) as central to the task of development alongside the need for a clean and healthy environment.

Evidence of global warning, however, suggests a doomsday scenario in which much of the earth will be flooded, and the rest will turn into desert, making planet earth largely uninhabitable. A major need is to find a way to stop the continual increase in temperature before a tipping point is reached. The urgency of acting to save civilization provides solemn responsibilities to the human race.

PROBLEMS OF THE RIGHTS-BASED APPROACH

The incremental problem-oriented approach to international human rights presented in the present volume stands in contrast with the more philosophical rights-based approach. Although many treaties can identify specific problems and establish institutional mechanisms for dealing with each problem, some make more generic statements that allow some latitude for interpretation. Accordingly, some scholars argue that a rights-based discourse is not capable of advancing the goals sought by the human rights project. They have at least five important arguments.

- One point is that the major threat to liberty and freedom is not from government but instead in the private sector. For example, prejudiced people massively continue to discriminate socially despite laws to the contrary; they simply do not accept rights for anyone but themselves. Corporations often respect profits more than rights, and thereby marginalize workers, even entire countries, in the world economy. Because the human rights project focuses on what governments should or should not do, the major arena in which violations occur is often ignored.

- The concept of state sovereignty protects governments from accountability for violating human rights. A "sovereign" state is immune from pressure from another country under international law. Appealing to tyrants with a rights-based discourse is thus futile. Military action seems alone appropriate to enforce regime change, yet there is insufficient will throughout the world to turn every state that seriously violates human rights into a UN trusteeship.

- Another argument is that rights-based discourse is vague and indeterminate. A politician who engages in malicious name calling of another politician can be sued in Britain but not in the United States, so the identification of rights is ultimately arbitrary and inconsistent. Since rights-based thinking does not provide a uniform guide concerning what are the basic or derivative rights, those who want to promote human rights must step outside rights-based discourse to determine what is or is not acceptable.
- Freedom is granted by struggles rather than appeals to the concept of "rights." Power does not yield unless confronted by mobilizations of the oppressed, as in the case of the civil rights movement in the United States. Most progress has been through the political process rather than through litigation based on rights.
- Finally, the "Asian values" thesis accuses the right-based discourse of a fundamental contradiction. The Western conception of human rights wants the individual protected from government, but government turns out to be the primary instrument of protection. Instead, the Asian values approach wants government to have the discretion to protect society from unbridled individualism.

There are answers to all five objections:

- Governments are major violators of rights but can also protect human rights, so a rights-based discourse keeps the pressure on governments to limit abuses in the private and public sectors. In the United States, the Equal Employment Opportunity Commission, whose members are appointed by Congress and the president, is independent of all three branches of government; the Commission's jurisdiction covers both private and public employment discrimination.
- Military action occasionally has been used to stop massive human rights violations, though on a priority basis. The principle of humanitarian intervention in international law has been applied to several cases.
- Lack of uniformity in recognizing human rights violations serves as a challenge for world leaders to urge improvements. The people in various countries can humble governments to increase their respect for human rights by pointing to other countries. Amnesty International, the United Nations Development Program, and other organizations publish annual reports that compare most countries in the world on a set of human rights parameters. The European Union and the United States base foreign aid allocations in part on human rights records.
- Human rights movements, including the American civil rights struggle of the 1960s, led to legislative reforms, but implementation of the new legal norms must rely ultimately on voluntary compliance, which is easier to achieve when justified in moral terms by legal principles. Court action, now imbedded in the global human rights culture, is needed only for those who are recalcitrant violators.
- In answer to the "Asian values" approach, the human rights approach points out that government protection of society from dysfunctional individualism leaves government as the arbiter of what is dangerous to society. If governments do their job properly, they must utilize a theory of rights to determine when individuals act dangerously; if governments fail to protect society, then they are either

incompetent or tyrannical, so the people need to reserve the right to overthrow rulers whose injustices can only be identified by a right-based critique.

Meanwhile, the concern over international terrorism in the twenty-first century has provoked a willingness on the part of nervous populations to sacrifice some civil rights in order to gain greater security. As a result, debate has ensued about how to achieve a proper balance between liberty and security. As long as such debates about international human rights continue, nevertheless, the struggle to make humans accountable for decent treatment will endure. In other words, unless the debate is silenced, the pendulum will swing back to greater respect toward human rights.

DISCUSSION TOPIC 14.4 HOW MANY FREEDOMS SHOULD BE JETTISONED TO GET SECURITY FROM TERRORISM?

Surveillance and intelligence-gathering operations are being conducted today to prevent terrorist attacks. To what extent is the right to privacy in jeopardy? How easily can efforts to monitor peaceful organizations, the Internet, and telephone traffic be abused? Is the proper approach to combating terrorism a matter for routine police work or for military officials with a larger agenda?

CONCLUSION

Many cynics pooh-pooh the influence of human rights in the world today. The present volume clearly refutes their skepticism by identifying significant advances in recent years.

For example, the present volume demonstrates that human rights debates are raging within time-honored religious traditions (Chapter 2). Historical social movements that brought about major human rights advances are even stronger today (Chapter 3). Nongovernmental organizations are now the most relentless source of challenge to violators of civil and political rights as well as a vital resource that actively works to overcome deprivations of economic, social, and cultural rights (Chapter 4). Ruthless dictators have been forced to step down by people power movements and now truth commissions have enabled countries to go beyond a dark past (Chapter 5). Hundreds of businesses have adopted codes of conduct, pledging to accept no products made by child labor, prison labor, or under substandard working conditions, while the fair trade movement has brought similar benefits to small-scale farmers in Third World countries (Chapter 6). The law of warfare has expanded to include crimes against humanity, a development that has promoted the world community to treat systematic human rights violations in one country as problems of global concern (Chapter 7). Empirical research has identified a pragmatic, step-by-step strategy for improving human rights, stressing carrots rather than sticks (Chapter 8). The framework for multilateral action has borne fruit in countless situations, both inside and outside the United Nations (Chapters 9–10). Individual countries and regional organizations have used diplomatic, legal, economic, and military means to stop human rights abuses in ways unimagined in previous periods of world history (Chapters 11–13). There has even been some development of rights for sexual minorities, animal rights, and environmental rights (Chapter 14). Many other examples of human rights progress have been identified in the present volume, which has amply demonstrated that intellectual debates about whether to pursue human rights issues have been upstaged by direct action from the streets, the courts, the legislatures, the executives, and even the armies around the world.

As Victor Hugo (1802–1885) once said, "Nothing can stop an idea whose time has come." Although the path has been stony, the upward trend over the centuries suggests that the future is even brighter. On the world stage, the subject of human rights has gone beyond the era of debate and promise to the era of accountability and action.

GLOSSARY

acquis	obligations of membership
act-of-state doctrine	immunity of a government official from prosecution for official acts
admissibility	a complaint that falls within a court's jurisdiction
advisory opinion	a nonbinding court ruling to provide guidance
amnesty	a waiver of culpability for a crime
anthropocentrism	the view that the health and survival of humans prevails over animal and ecological survival
anticipatory self-defense	the use of force by a government which expects that another government is about to attack
apartheid	racial segregation (in South Africa)
application	a formal complaint to an international body
arbitration	quasi–judicial settlement by an independent third party
assimilationism	a policy requiring minority peoples to conform to the customs and language of the mainstream group
award	a settlement for a plaintiff who prevails
bill of attainder	a law convicting a person of a crime without a trial
binding ruling	court decision that parties agree in advance to accept
boycott	refusal to import from or deal with a country or company
buffer stock	a commodity stockpiled for emergencies
burka	full body covering for females
cartel	a group of businesses or governments who fix prices above the cost of production
Caux Principles	corporate codes of conduct based on human dignity and the common good
Ceres Principles	environmentally sound corporate practices
chivalry principle	in case of war, no harming of civilians
civil liberties	freedom from unwarranted governmental regulation, as stated in a Bill of Rights
civil rights	claims of protection from discrimination
civil society	the set of social and political organisations outside government control in which people participate freely
claim-rights	obligations of individuals toward others
code of conduct	a set of just operating principles for corporations
command responsibility	culpability of superior officers for war crimes violations by subordinates

communitarian globalization	the process of forging common world norms
communitarianism	the view that individual rights should be limited to achieve social order
compensatory financing	loan terms adjusted to the likely long-term return on the investment
concessional rate	an interest rate on a loan below the world market rate for a longer term than average
constitutional rights	freedoms stated in the basic law of a country
constructive engagement	unpublicized diplomatic efforts of one country to urge another country to change a policy
contentious case	a formal complaint against a party
contractualism	the view that rights only exist when agreed in legal documents by all affected parties
corporate imperialism	the practice of giant corporations controlling the politics of Third World countries to permit unsafe working conditions and exploitation of workers
correlation	a statistical association between variables
crimes against humanity	inhumane acts committed against a civilian population, or persecutions on political, racial, or religious grounds
crimes against peace	planning, preparation, initiation or waging of a war of aggression, or a war in violation of international treaties, agreements or assurances, or participation in a common plan or conspiracy for the accomplishment of any of the foregoing
criminal law	statutes that define offenses against governments
cultural rights	claims to observe a group's longstanding customs, language, and/or religion
curvilinearity	a statistical relationship in which two variables are positively related to an asymptote and then are inversely related
democide	acts committed by a government with intent to massively kill members of its own population
democracy	rule by the people
democratic rights	claims to have government decisions made by the people
deportation	expulsion of a foreigner from a country
deregulation, economic	reduction in governmental economic restrictions
derogation, right of	the claim of a government to be able to ignore legal obligations during an emergency
developmentalism	the view that economic and social rights are superior and prior to civil and political right
diplomacy	interactions between countries through ambassadors and other officials
diplomacy, coercive	use of threats of force to gain concessions from other countries
diplomacy, public	publicized interactions between countries conducted by ambassadors and other officials
diplomacy, quiet	unpublicized interactions between countries conducted by ambassadors and other officials
direct trade	trade from primary producer to retail company without intervention from import-export companies
discrimination principle	in case of war, avoidance of civilian targets
displaced person	an imperiled individual fleeing from a home residence

divestment	selling off stocks of companies that condone unpalatable practices
DNA	the molecule containing genetic instructions used in the development and functioning of all living organisms (deoxyribonucleic acid)
early-warning procedure	confidence-building measures so that an ongoing problem will not escalate out of control
ecocentrism	the view that the environment should be maintained in a pristine state
econocentrism	the view that economic growth should be maximized, avoiding only adverse economic consequences to the environment
economic liberalization	a policy of encouraging privatization, deregulation, free trade, and export promotion
economic rights	claims to engage in remunerative activity
elitism	the view that those born superior should rule
emancipation	lifting legal restrictions on a person or group so that they can enjoy rights accorded to the mainstream
embargo	ban on exports and imports
environmental justice	the practice of not polluting in poor neighborhoods
environmental sustainability	production without adverse impacts on ecosystems or humans
equality of states	the legal view that all governments are equal under international law
estoppel	a legal doctrine that bans a litigant from denying a fact that has already been established
ethnic cleansing	establishing ethnic purity in a territory by expulsions, murders, and rapes of persons of all but one ethnic group
ethnocide	denial of a people's right to enjoy, develop, and transmit its own culture
ex aequo et bono	general principles of justice and fairness
ex post facto law	a statute that criminalizes something in the past
exceptional report	a compliance report requested before the due date
exhaustion of local remedies	the principle that world courts do not try cases until national courts have first had a chance to do so
export promotion	an economic policy of encouraging local industries to compete internationally
extraordinary rendition	the secret practice of capturing and transporting a suspected criminal to a prison for interrogation
extraterritorial jurisdiction	a country's claim to have the authority to try persons who commit offenses abroad
fair labor	workers with freedom of association, safe working conditions, and a living wage
fair price	an economic charge reasonably close to the cost of production
fair trade	purchases restricted to small-scale farmers who provide humane working conditions
First World	industrial democracies
Fourth World	indigenous peoples
free–market environmentalism	allowing corporations to establish environmental regulations instead of the government
free trade	international commerce without barriers
Freudianism	the view that human behavior is conditioned by base instincts

friendly settlement	mutual agreement by complainer and complainant
frozen assets	a government order to a financial institution to disallow transactions by an account
frustration-aggression theory	the view that violence occurs in response to trauma
functionalism	the view that cooperative human behavior results from a conditioning based on past positive experiences
gay rights	claims of persons who prefer relations with same-sex friends to enjoy the benefits accruing to those who bond with members of the opposite sex
gender equity	equal pay for women as well as female involvement in community decisionmaking
general measure	a settlement when a state found in violation of an international treaty changes its laws to conform to the treaty
generalized system of preferences	tariff reductions granted by rich countries to poor countries
generosity theory	the view that the strong should protect the rights of the weak
genocide	systematic acts committed with intent to destroy, in whole or in part, a national, ethnical, racial or religious group
ghost detainee	a person captured for an offense and held in a secret prison without disclosing the person's identity
globalism	the view that a single world economy, polity, and society should be promoted
globalization	the process of forging a single world economy, polity, and society
good governance	a government that operates accountably, democratically, effectively, by the rule of law with only essential economic regulations, and without corruption
group conflict theory	the view that politics can be explained by a struggle among competing, usually ethnic, groups
group rights	claims of subordinate subcultures to enjoy the same privileges as the mainstream group
habeas corpus, writ of	the right of a detained individual to appear in court in order to learn charges for the detention
headquarters doctrine	a legal claim that subordinates are not culpable for following orders
Herrenfolk democracy	rule of and by the people of the dominant group, while others are denied political rights
hierarchical relationship	an empirical pattern in which the attainment of some conditions serve as preconditions to attaining other conditions
horizontal enforcement	pressure by governments in the form of protests, threats, and economic sanctions to secure compliance with international norms
human rights	the claim of individuals to enjoy a minimally restrictive yet optimal quality of life with liberty, equal justice before law, and an opportunity to fulfill basic cultural, economic, and social needs
human rights commission	a body set up to receive complaints about human rights violations and to investigate the complaints
human rights infrastructure	a situation in which legal norms establish the parameters of human rights, governmental institutions monitor, publicize, implement, and enforce

	human rights standards, and nongovernmental groups pressure governments to advance the cause of human rights.
human trafficking	transporting persons to conditions of slavery
humanitarian intervention	action of one government on the territory of another country to rescue seriously imperiled individuals
humanitarianism	the view that humans are obligated to promote kindness toward others
humanity principle	in case of war, treating civilians and prisoners with respect
humanocentrism	the view that humans have no obligations toward animals except to avoid cruelty
illiberal democracy	a polity with civil rights but not political rights
imminent jeopardy	severe use of force anticipated without delay
immunities	exemptions from legal requirements
import substitution	an economic policy of erecting trade barriers so that a country can develop local industries and keep out foreign competition
indemnity	a sum recovered by the victor from a war aggressor
individual measure	a settlement that a wrongdoer provides to a victim
informational globalization	increasing dissemination of information around the world
interim measure	temporary action or inaction to avoid irreparable harm while a dispute is under consideration
intergovernmental organization	an institution whose members are governments
internally displaced person	an imperiled individual who has fled a home residence to live elsewhere inside the homeland
international	involving or transcending two or more individual states in the world
international custom	practices conventionally observed by states in relation to other states
international law	legal requirements applied primarily to states
international law, hard	international law that is enforced by a penalty
international law, soft	international law that lacks a penalty
internationalized court	a domestic tribunal set up in cooperation with and staffed in part by judges from another country or international organization
inverse relationship	a statistical relationship in which an increase in one variable correlates with a decrease in another variable or vice versa
irredentism	advocacy of changing the sovereignty of one territory to a country where the people of that territory are claimed to belong
jus ad bellum	an international law principle that war can be waged legitimately in defense, to recover losses, to stop a gross injustice, and in last resort
jus cogens	an international law principle that certain state practices cannot be derogated
jus in bello	an international law principle that legitimate means of warfare include discrimination, humanity, and proportionality
just authority	a government or international body legitimately empowered to take action
just cause	a legitimate pretext for righting a wrong through war
just intervention	legitimate military action by one government in the territory of another country to stop severe human rights violations

just peace	after war ends, actions of the victor to maintain order, repair economic damages, prosecute human rights violations, and transfer sovereignty to the country being occupied
just satisfaction	a condign settlement for a prevailing complainant
just war	an armed conflict launched for honorable reasons and conducted in an honorable manner
justice, restorative	the outcome of a proceeding that heals a conflict between a lawbreaker and a victim
justice, retributive	the outcome of a proceeding that penalizes a lawbreaker
justice, transitional	the outcome of a proceeding that enables a current government to go beyond a previous era with a minimum probability of backsliding to that era
last resort	an international law principle that war can only be legitimately launched after peaceful methods for resolving a serious conflict have failed
last-in-time principle	the legal custom of interpreting later agreements to supersede earlier agreements
legal rights	freedoms from government misconduct, as established in law
letter of marque and reprisal	a written authorization by a government for person outside government to use force to respond to an unfriendly act abroad
liberal democracy	a form of government in which the majority rules, provided that minority rights are respected
libertarianism	opposition to unwarranted government restrictions
liberties	actions exempt from unwarranted government regulation
MacBride Principles	rules used in Northern Ireland to ensure nondiscrimination
mainstream group	a country's dominant ethnolinguistic or religious group
mandate	a territory that the League of Nations entrusted to a government to promote self-government
market economy	commercial transactions where prices are determined by supply and demand, not by governments
mass society	a social system lacking a civil society, that is, political groups independent of government control
mercenary	civilians of a country who are paid to play a military role in a war abroad without joining the armed forces of any government
military necessity	a legal justification for using force in response to aggression
military occupation	rule imposed by a victor on a defeated country
minority rights	the claim of population subgroups to be treated the same as members of the mainstream
minority treaty	an international agreement to protect a nonmainstream group inside a country
mixed arbitral tribunal	an arbitration court that settles disputes involving judges from at least two countries
mobilization, political	the process of raising consciousness of likeminded individuals to redress grievances
mobilization of shame	a campaign to use public opinion in order to embarrass those engaging in misconduct
moral rights	claims of just treatment based on ethical principles

Moscow Mechanism	the use of independent experts to resolve human rights complaints, using on-site visits
most-favored-nation principle	according the same trade conditions to one country that are granted to the country that enjoys the most favorable conditions
multidimensionality	a statistical relationship in which interrelated variables form separate empirical clusters
natural law	self-evident principles justified by God or by nature
natural rights	freedoms that governments must respect that existed before humans established governments
negative liberty	limits on adverse human behavior
negative rights	claims to prohibitions on government action
neutrality	a government's impartiality toward a foreign war
New International Economic Order	a proposed restructuring of the world economy to benefit poor countries
no-fly zone	airspace that a country is prohibited from using
noblesse oblige	benevolent, honorable behavior of the nobility toward those of lower rank
non-application procedure	refusal to act on a formal request
nongovernmental organization	a group composed of persons outside government
noninterference principle	the international law view that a government has no jurisdiction over how another government treats its own people inside its homeland
normal trade relations	commerce between states without special restrictions
notification principle	an international requirement for a government to make a public statement before using force abroad
nuisance	a legal term describing something annoying to individuals
ozone	a form of oxygen (O_3) that absorbs ultraviolet rays so that they cannot reach the earth's surface
pacta sunt servanda	the practice of following legal precedent
peacekeeping	monitoring a peace agreement
people power	the use of mass demonstrations to force governments to make a change
persona non grata	an unwelcome diplomat
petition	a citizen's request to have a government redress a grievance
plebiscite	an election by residents of a territory to choose which state under which they prefer to be governed
political rights	claims to participate in politics without restrictions
population exchange	a practice of allowing minorities in two or more countries to move in order to live in an ethnic homeland abroad
positive liberty	power to act autonomously
positive rights	claims to have government improve the well-being of the people
positivism	a theory of knowledge that rejects metaphysics
positivism, legal	the view that rights and obligations only exist when stated by governments in law
power elite	economic leaders who command political power
powers	legal capabilities
precautionary measure	immediate action in an urgent situation

preclusion	action taken when there is no alternative response
preemptive war	armed aggression by one government to stop imminent, severe aggression by another
preventive procedure	technical assistance provided so that a country can improve human rights observance
primacy principle	exclusive jurisdiction of a court over certain offenses
prisoner of war	a soldier captured and detained by an enemy army during combat
privateer	a private shipowner authorized by a government to harass and seize enemy ships
privatization	selling government corporations to private hands
privilege	a power reserved to those who qualify
prize of war	tangible property, such as an enemy ship, that is seized in time of armed interstate conflict
proactive action	measures taken to encourage positive behavior
procedural rights	claims that government must follow standard practices and processes
pro forma trial	a judicial proceeding that observes forms of a trial though guilt has already been determined
program rights	obligations of governments to meet certain goals over time, such as extending schooling to all
proportionality	condign response of one state to actions of another state
protocol, optional	a supplementary agreement to a treaty
provisional measure	action ordered by a court before a ruling to forestall irreparable harm
punitive action	retaliatory measure
quasi-trusteeship	a territory that the UN administers temporarily until a new government is legitimized by an election
quid pro quo	a condition that must be met by one party to gain a favor from another party
rationalism	the philosophy that bases principles on reason, not experience
realism	the view that powerful states will dominate weak states
realpolitik	actions by powerful states to maintain dominance over weak states
rebus sic stantibus	a doctrine that a fundamental change in the assumptions of a legal agreement serves to void the agreement
refugee	an imperiled person who flees the homeland to seek sanctuary in a second country
relativism	the view that universal moral absolutes do not exist
reprisal	reaction short of war by one government in response to an unfriendly act by another government
reprisal, private	reaction short of war by an individual that has been authorized by a government to respond to an unfriendly act by another government
reprisal, self-defense	limited military action by one government in response to force by another government
reservation, treaty	statement made by a government that expresses exceptions or interpretations of provisions of a treaty being ratified
retorsion	a peaceful but negative response by one government to an unfriendly act by another government
right to life	a claim to enjoy subsistence (food, clothing, shelter)

right to peace	a claim to have conflicts resolved nonviolently
right to water	a claim that governments must provide clean water to all
rights theory	the view that all should be treated as free and equal
sanction	a penalty imposed on a state for disapproved conduct
scepticism	a philosophy that distrusts all claims to knowledge
Second World	nonmarket socialist countries
security rights	claims to freedom from violations of the human person
self-determination	ability of peoples to govern themselves
self-executing treaty	an international agreement containing implementation procedures
shari'ah	Islamic law
show trial	a highly publicized trial aimed at frightening the public into compliance
social constructionism	the view that elites determine truth, not science
social contract	the primordial agreement between individuals and governments to secure a stable social order
social darwinism	the view that only superior humans are worthy of survival in the process of biological evolution
social democracy	a form of government in which the majority rules, minority rights are respected, and government protects those suffering economic misfortunes
social market capitalism	a nonsocialist welfare state
social rights	claims on governments to provide well-being to those living in its borders
sovereignty	unlimited power of governments within the borders of their countries
stages of growth	a series of distinct thresholds for progress
state secrets doctrine	the principle that courts cannot review evidence in which national security secrets might be revealed
standard setting	specification of the norms and principles of various rights
state immunity doctrine	the international law practice of exempting top government officials from prosecution for official acts
state sovereign immunity	exemption of a government from prosecution for official acts
statism	the view that the only legitimate units of international politics are national states
structural violence	deprivation by the rich of food and shelter to the poor
subjective awareness	a legal principle that a superior who aids and abets a subordinate's war crimes is also culpable
substantive rights	claims on governments to respect freedoms
suffragette	the name applied to women who organized to seek the right to vote through dramatic civil action in the late nineteenth and early twentieth centuries
Sullivan Principles	fair labor practices designed to end *apartheid*
summit conference	a formal meeting involving heads of governments
supranational organization	an international body that can require government members to change national laws and practices under penalty of sanctions
sustainable development	economic growth that observes environmentally sound practices and enables future generations to satisfy basic human needs
technical assistance	use of experts to train in using new technology
terrorism	the use of violence and threats to make political statements

third-party complaint	an allegation that one country or person is violating the rights of another but brought by neither party
Third World	developing countries
traditionalism	respect for customs of the past
tragedy of the commons	minor, uncoordinated individual acts that produce a collective wrong
treaty	a legal agreement that goes into effect when ratified by legislatures of governments
trespass	an unlawful entry on lands owned by another
trusteeship	a territory that the UN entrusted to a government in order to promote self-government in the territory
truth commission	a body that gathers evidence to establish facts about culpability but does not prosecute
unidimensionality	a statistical relationship in which variables are so highly interrelated that there are no subclusters
universal jurisdiction	legal competence claimed by states to prosecute criminals regardless of where the crime took place
urgent procedure	measure taken to stop a serious, massive, or persistent pattern of misconduct
utilitarianism	a belief that what is good is what gives pleasure and avoids pain to the greatest number of persons
vegan	a person who consumes no animal products
vegetarianism	the view that humans should not consume animals
vertical enforcement	use of military action to enforce norms on states
vicarious liability	culpability of a superior for not stopping war crimes violations known to be committed by subordinates
Vienna Mechanism	procedure in which one government member of the OSCE can complain about another
visit in *loco*	on-site visit
waiver	exception
war	a state of armed hostility between sovereign nations or governments
war crimes	violations of the laws or customs of armed state aggression
yellow dog contract	an employment contract in which management prohibits workers from joining a union

REFERENCES AND FURTHER READING

CHAPTER 1

Anonymous (2003) *How Should Human Rights Be Defined?* San Diego: Greenhaven Press.

Beitz, Charles (2003) "What Human Rights Means," *Daedalus*, 132(1): 36–46.

Berlin, Isaiah (1958) *Two Concepts of Liberty*. Oxford, UK: Clarendon Press.

Boli-Bennett, John (1981) "Human Rights or State Expansion? Cross-National Definitions of Constitutional Rights, 1870–1970." In *Global Human Rights: Public Policies, Comparative Measures, and NGO Strategies*, eds. Ved P. Nanda. James R. Scarritt. and George W. Shepherd, Jr., Chap. 11. Boulder, CO: Westview.

Brown, Seyom (2000) *Human Rights in World Politics*. New York: Longman.

Claude, Richard Pierre, and Burns H. Weston, eds. (1989) *Human Rights in the World Community: Issues and Action*. Philadelphia: University of Pennsylvania Press.

Colburn, Theo, Dianne Dumanoski and John Peterson Myers (1996) *Our Stolen Future. Our Stolen Future: Are We Threatening our Fertility, Intelligence, and Survival?: A Scientific Detective Story*. New York: Dutton.

Condé, H. Victor (2004) *A Handbook of International Human Rights Terminology*. 2nd ed. Lincoln, NB: University of Nebraska Press.

Constant, Benjamin (1814) *Political Writings*. Cambridge, UK: Cambridge University Press, 1988.

Cranston, Maurice (1983) "Are There Any Human Rights?," *Daedalus*, 112 (Fall): 1–17.

Donnelly, Jack (1989) *Universal Human Rights in Theory and Practice*. Ithaca, NY: Cornell University Press.

Donnelly, Jack (1998) *International Human Rights*. 2nd ed. Boulder, CO: Westview.

Donnelly, Jack and Rhoda E. Howard (1988) "Assessing National Human Rights Performance: A Theoretical Framework," *Human Rights Quarterly*, 10 (May): 214–48.

Dworkin, Ronald (1978) *Taking Rights Seriously*. London: Duckworth.

Egendorf, Laura K. ed., (2003) *Human Rights: Opposing Viewpoints*. San Diego: Greenhaven Press.

Finnis, John (1980) *Natural Law and Natural Rights*. Oxford, UK: Clarendon.

Fleiner, Thomas (1999) *What Are Human Rights?* Sydney: Federation Press.

Forsythe, David P. (1991) *The Internationalization of Human Rights*. Lexington, MA: Lexington Books.

Forsythe, David P. (2006) *Human Rights in International Relations*. 2nd ed. Cambridge, UK: Cambridge University Press.

Freeman, Michael (2002) *Human Rights: An Interdisciplinary Approach*. Cambridge, MA: Polity.

Galtung, Johan (1994) *Human Rights in Another Key*. Cambridge, MA: Polity Press.

Gewirth, Alan (1978) *Reason and Morality*. Chicago: Chicago University Press.

Gewirth, Alan (1982) *Human Rights: Essays on Justification and Applications*. Chicago: University of Chicago Press.

Gibson, John (1996) *Dictionary of International Human Rights Law*. Lanham, MD: Scarecrow Press.

Haas, Michael (1994) *Improving Human Rights*. Westport, CT: Praeger.

Hanski, Raija, and Markku Suksi, eds. (1999) *An Introduction to the International Protection of Human Rights: A Textbook*. 2nd ed. Turku, Finland: Åbo Akademi University.

Harvard Human Rights Journal (1988–).

Hohfeld, Wesley N. (1919) *Fundamental Legal Conceptions as Applied in Judicial Reasoning*. Burlington, VT: Ashgate, 2001.

Human Rights Quarterly (1979–)

Human Rights Law Journal (1980–).

Human Rights Law Review (2001–)

Jones, Peter (1994) *Rights*. Basingstoke, UK: Macmillan.

Journal of Human Rights (2002–)

Langley, Winston, comp. (1999) *Encyclopedia of Human Rights Issues Since 1945*. Westport, CT: Greenwood Press.

Lawson, Edward, comp. (1996) *Encyclopedia of Human Rights*. 2nd ed. Washington, DC: Taylor and Francis.

Mackie, J. L. (1977) *Ethics: Inventing Right and Wrong*. Harmondsworth, UK: Penguin.

Marshall, Thomas H. (1964) *Class, Citizenship, and Social Development*. Garden City, NY: Doubleday.

Morris, Lydia (2005) *Rights: Sociological Perspectives*. New York: Routledge.

Muskie, Edmund S. (1980) "The Foreign Policy of Human Rights," *Department of State Bulletin*, 80 (December): 7–9.

Nickel, James (1987) *Making Sense of Human Rights: Philosophical Reflections on the Universal Declaration of Human Rights*. Berkeley: University of California Press.

Nowak, Manfred, and Theresa Swinehart, eds. (1989) *Human Rights in Developing Countries: 1989 Yearbook*. Arlington, VA: Engel.

O'Byrne, Darren J. (2003) *Human Rights: An Introduction*. New York: Longman.

Robertson, A. H., and J. G. Merrils (1996) *Human Rights in the World: An Introduction to the Study of the International Protection of Human Rights*. 4th ed. New York: St. Martin's Press.

Robertson, David (2004) *A Dictionary of Human Rights*. 2nd ed. London: Europa Publications.

Schwelb, Egon (1964) *Human Rights and the International Community*. Chicago: Quadrangle Books.

Shue, Henry (1980) *Basic Rights: Subsistence, Affluence, and U.S. Foreign Policy*. Princeton, NJ: Princeton University Press.

Shute, Stephen, and Susan Hurley, eds. (1993) *On Human Rights: The Oxford Amnesty Lectures*. New York: Basic Books.

Smith, Rhona K. M. (2005) *Textbook on International Human Rights*. 2d ed. Oxford, UK: Oxford University Press.

Sreenivasan, Gopal (2005) "A Hybrid Theory of Claim-Rights," *Oxford Journal of Legal Studies*, 25(2): 257–274.

Steiner, Henry J., and Philip Alston, eds. (1996) *International Human Rights in Context: Law, Politics, Morals: Text and Materials*. 1st ed. New York: Oxford University Press.

Steiner, Henry J., and Philip Alston, eds. (2000) *International Human Rights in Context: Law, Politics, Morals: Text and Materials*. 2nd ed. New York: Oxford University Press.

United Nations Development Program (1992) *Human Development Report*. New York: Oxford University Press.

Van Ness, Peter, ed. (1999) *Debating Human Rights: Critical Essays from the United States and Asia*. New York: Routledge.

Vance, Cyrus R. (1977) "Law Day Address on Human Rights Policy." In *Human Rights and American Foreign Policy*, eds. Donald P. Kommers and Gilburt D. Loescher, pp. 309–15. Notre Dame, IN: University of Notre Dame Press.

Vasak, Karl, ed. (1982) *The International Dimensions of Human Rights*. Westport, CT: Greenwood.

Vincent, R. J. (1986) *Human Rights and International Relations*. Cambridge UK : Cambridge University Press.

Waldron, Jeremy, ed. (1984) *Theories of Rights*. Oxford, UK: Oxford University Press.

Zakaria, Fareed (1997) "The Rise of Illiberal Democracy," *Foreign Affairs*, 76(6): 22–43.

CHAPTER 2

Ahmad, Ilyas (1965) *Sovereignty, Islamic and Modern: Conception of Sovereignty in Islam*. Karachi: The Allied Book Corporation.

Al-Sadr, Muhammad B. (1980) *Islam and Schools of Economics*. Karachi: Islamic Seminary Pakistan.

An-Na'im, Abdullah Ahmed (1990) *Toward an Islamic Reformation: Civil Liberties, Human Rights, and International Law*. Syracuse, NY: Syracuse University Press.

Arberry, A. J. (1995) *Aspects of Islamic Civilization as Depicted in the Original Texts*. Westport, CT: Greenwood Press.

Armstrong, Karen (2006) *The Great Transformation: The Beginning of Our Religious Traditions*. New York: Knopf.

Aslan, Reza (2005) *No God But God: The Origins, Evolution, and Future of Islam*. New York: Random House.

Bauer, Joann R. and Bell, Daniel A., eds. (1999) *The East Asian Challenge for Human Rights*. Cambridge: Cambridge University Press.

Berdal, Aral (2004) "The Idea of Human Rights as Perceived in the Ottoman Empire," *Human Rights Quarterly*, 26 (May): 454–82.

Berger, Peter and Luckmann, Thomas (1967) *The Social Construction of Reality: A Treatise in the Sociology of Knowledge*. New York: Anchor.

Berryman, Phillip (1987) *Liberation Theology: Essential Facts about the Revolutionary Movement in Latin America – and Beyond*. Philadelphia: Temple University Press.

Bigongiari, Dino ed. (1953) *The Political Ideas of St. Thomas Aquinas*. New York: Hafner.

Bloom, Irene, J. Paul, Martin, and Wayne L. Proudfoot, eds. (1996) *Religious Diversity and Human Rights*. New York: Columbia University Press.

Boswell, John (1994) *Same–Sex Unions in Premodern Europe*. New York: Villard.

Bryce, James (1961) *The Holy Roman Empire*. New York: Schocken.

Buchanan, Allan (2004) *Justice, Legitimacy, and Self-Determination: Moral Foundations for International Law*. New York: Oxford University Press.

Bull, Hedley, Benedict Kingsbury, and Adam Roberts, eds. (1992) *Hugo Grotius and International Relations*. New York: Oxford University Press.

Burston, W. H. (1973) *James Mill on Philosophy and Education*. London: Athlone Press.

Calvar, Georg (1999) *Kant and the Theory and Practice of International Right*. Cambridge UK : Cambridge University Press.

Cohler, Anne (1988) *Montesquieu's Comparative Politics and the Spirit of American Constitutionalism*. Lawrence, KS: University Press of Kansas.

Cohn, Haim H. (1989) *Human Rights in the Bible and Talmud*. Tel-Aviv: MOD Books.

Cox, Richard H. (1982) *Locke on War and Peace*. Washington, DC: University Press of America.

Crowe, Ian, ed. (2004) *An Imaginative Whig: Reassessing the Life and Thought of Edmund Burke*. Columbia, MO: University of Missouri Press.

Dalai Lama (1975) *The Buddhism of Tibet and the Key to the Middle Way*. New York: Harper and Row.

Darwin, Charles (1871) *The Descent of Man*. Amherst, NY: Prometheus Books, 1998.

Davidson, Herbert A. (2005) *Moses Mainmonides: The Man and His Works*. New York: Oxford University Press.

de Bary, William T. (1998) *Asian Values and Human Rights: A Confucian Communitarian Perspective*. Cambridge, MA: Harvard University Press.

Donnelly, Jack (1989) *Universal Human Rights in Theory and Practice*. Ithaca, NY: Cornell University Press.

Durr, Clifford (1981) *Jesus as a Free Speech Victim: Trial by Terror 2000 Years Ago*. New York: Basic Pamphlets.

El Guindi, F. (1995) "Hijab." In *The Oxford Encyclopedia of the Modern Islamic World*, ed. John L. Espisito, 2: 108–111. New York: Oxford University Press.

Etzioni, Amitai (1995) *Rights and the Common Good: The Communitarian Perspective*. New York: St. Martin's Press.

Falk, Richard A. (1981) *Human Rights and State Sovereignty*. New York: Holmes and Meier.

Falk, Richard A. (2001) *Religion and Humane Global Governance*. New York: Palgrave Macmillan.

Ferrara, Alessandro (2003) "Two Notions for Humanity and the Judgment Argument for Human Rights," *Political Theory*, 31(3): 392–420.

Finnis, John (1980) *Natural Law and Natural Rights*. New York: Oxford University Press.

Fonte, John (2004) "Democracy's Trojan House," *Institute of Public Affairs Review*, 56 (December): 3–6.

Foucault, Michel (1977) *Discipline and Punish: The Birth of the Prison*. New York: Pantheon Books.

Franklin, Julian H. (1963) *Jean Bodin and the Sixteenth-Century Revolution in the Methodology of Law and History*. New York: Columbia University Press.

Freeman, Michael D. A. (2004) "The Problem of Secularism in Human Rights Theory," *Human Rights Quarterly*, 26 (May): 375–400.

Freud, Sigmund (1930) *Civilization and Its Discontents*. London: Hogarth Press.

Fukuyama, Francis (2001) "Natural Rights and Human History," *The National Interest*, 64 (Summer): 19–30.

Fukuyama, Francis (2002) *The End of History and the Last Man*. New York: Free Press.

Galtung, Johan (1992) *The Way Is the Goal: Gandhi Today*. Ahmenabad, India: Gujarat Vidyapith.

Galtung, Johan (1993) *Buddhism: A Quest for Unity and Peace*. Ratmalana, Sri Lanka: Sarvodaya.

Galtung, Johan, and Anders Wirak (1976) *Human Needs, Human Rights, and the Theory of Development*. Oslo: University of Oslo Press.

Gandhi, Mahatma (1948) *The Gospel of Selfless Action*. Ahmedabad, India: Navajivan Publishing House.

George, Robert P. (2001) *In Defense of Natural Law*. New York: Oxford University Press.

Goldie, Mark (1999) *The Reception of Locke's Politics*. Brookfield, VT: Pickering and Chatto.

Goodell, Edward (1994) *The Noble Philosopher: Condorcet and the Enlightenment*. Buffalo, NY: Prometheus Books.

Goodman, Lenn E. (1998) *Judaism, Human Rights, and Human Values*. New York: Oxford University Press.

Gopnik, Adam (2005) "Voltaire's Garden: The Philosopher as a Campaigner for Human Rights," *The New Yorker*, 81(March 7): 74.

Habermas, Jürgen (2005) *Time of Transitions*. Oxford, UK: Blackwell Publishing.

Hastrup, Kirsten, ed. (2001) *Legal Cultures and Human Rights: The Challenge of Diversity*. The Hague: Kluwer Law International.

Hayden, Patrick (2001) *The Philosophy of Human Rights*. St. Paul, MN: Paragon House.

Hendricks, Obery M. (2006) *The Politics of Jesus: Rediscovering the True Revolutionary Nature of the Teachings of Jesus and How They Have Been Corrupted*. New York: Doubleday.

Hindu Human Rights Group (2001) *Charter on Hindu International Human Rights*. (www.hinduhumanrights.org)

Hoffmann, Stanley, and David Fidler, eds. (1991) *Rousseau on International Relations*. New York: Oxford University Press.

Hofstadter, Richard (1944) *Social Darwinism in American Thought*. Boston: Beacon.

Huntington, Samuel P. (1968) *Political Order in Changing Societies*. New Haven, CT: Yale University Press.

Huntington, Samuel P. (1996) *The Clash of Civilizations and the Remaking of World Order*. New York: Simon and Schuster.

Ishay, Micheline R., ed., (1997) *The Human Rights Reader: Major Political Essays, Speeches, and Documents from the Bible to the Present*. New York: Routledge.

Jacobsen, Michael, and Ole Brunn, eds. (2000) *Human Rights and Asian Values: Contesting National Identities and Cultural Representations in Asia*. Richmond, VA: Curzon.

Jaspers, Karl (1953) *The Origin and Goal of History*. New York: Routledge.

Kendall, Willmoore (1941) *John Locke and the Doctrine of Majority-Rule*. Urbana, IL: University of Illinois Press.

Kolakowski, Leszek (2006) *Main Currents of Marxism*. 3 vols. New York: Norton.

Kraynak, Robert P. (2001) *Christian Faith and Modern Democracy: God and Politics in the Fallen World*. Notre Dame, IN: University of Notre Dame Press.

Kuran, Timur (2004) *Islam and Mammon: Critical Perspectives on the Economic Agenda of Islamism*. Princeton, NJ: Princeton University Press.

Langlois, Anthony J. (2001) *The Politics of Justice and Human Rights: Southeast Asia and Universalist Theory*. New York: Cambridge University Press.

Lee Kuan Yew (2000) "America's New Agenda." In *From Third World to First: The Singapore Story, 1965–2000*, chap. 30. Singapore: Straits Times Press.

Levinson, David, ed. (2003) *The Wilson Chronology of Human Rights: A Record of the Human Striving for Freedom from Ancient Times to the Present*. Bronx, NY: Wilson.

Long, Douglas G. (1977) *Bentham on Liberty: Bentham's Idea of Liberty in Relations to His Utilitarianism*. Toronto: University of Toronto Press.

Lyons, Gene (1994) *Rights, Welfare, and Mill's Moral Theory*. New York: Oxford University Press.

McDonough, Sheila (1984) *Muslim Ethics and Modernity: A Comparative Study of the Ethical Thought of Sayyid Ahmad Khan and Mawlana Mawdudi*. Waterloo, Ont.: Wilfred Laurier University Press.

MacIntyre, Alasdair (1981) *After Virtue: A Study in Moral Theory*. Notre Dame, IN: University of Notre Dame Press.

Madison, James, Alexander Hamilton, and John Jay (1787–1789) *The Federalist Papers*. New York: Pocket Books, 2004.

Marcuse, Herbert (1941) *Reason and Revolution: Hegel and the Rise of Social Theory*. New York: Oxford University Press.

Martin, Wayne M. (1997) *Idealism and Objectivity: Understanding Fichte's Jena Project*. Stanford, CA: Stanford University Press.

Mayer, Ann E. (1991) *Islam and Human Rights: Tradition and Politics*. Boulder, CO: Westview.

Morgan, Robert J. (1988) *James Madison on the Constitution and the Bill of Rights*. New York: Greenwood Press.

Morgenthau, Hans J. (1948) *Politics Among Nations: The Struggle for Power and Peace*. 1st ed. New York: Knopf.

Moussalli, Ahmad S. (2001) *The Islamic Quest for Democracy, Pluralism, and Human Rights*. Gainesville: University Press of Florida.

Mutua, Makau (2002) *Human Rights: A Political and Cultural Critique*. Philadelphia: University of Pennsylvania Press.

Nardin, Terry and David R. Mapel, eds. (1992) *Traditions of International Ethics*. New York: Cambridge University Press.

Nye, Joseph S., Jr. (2004) *Soft Power: The Means to Success in World Politics*. New York: Public Affairs.

Orfield, G., and C. Lee (2006) *Racial Transformation and the Changing Nature of Segregation*. Cambridge, MA: The Civil Rights Project, Harvard University.

Paine, Thomas (1792) *The Rights of Man*. London: Symonds.

Perera, L. P. N. (1991) *Buddhism and Human Rights: A Buddhist Commentary on the Universal Declaration of Human Rights*. Colombo, Sri Lanka: Karunaratne and Sons.

Rasmussen, Douglas, and J. Den Uyl (1991) *Liberty and Nature: An Aristotelian Defense of Liberal Order*. La Salle, IL: Open Court.

Rawls, John (1971) *A Theory of Justice*. Cambridge, MA: Harvard University Press.

Renteln, Alison D. (1990) *International Human Rights: Universalism Versus Relativism*. London: Sage.

Rouner, Leroy S., ed. (1988) *Human Rights and the World's Religions*. Notre Dame, IN: University of Notre Dame Press.

Rumble, Wilfred E. (1985) *The Thought of John Austin: Jurisprudence, Colonial Reform, and the British Constitution*. London: Athlone Press.

Searle, John (1995) *The Construction of Social Reality*. New York: Free Press.

Sen, Amartya (1997) "Human Rights and Asian Values: What Lee Kuan Yew and Le Peng Don't Understand About Asia," *The New Republic*, 217 (July 14): 33–40.

Sen, Amatya (2004) "Elements of a Theory of Human Rights," *Philosophy and Public Affairs*, 27 (Fall): 315–356.

Sharma, Arvind (2004) *Hinduism and Human Rights: A Conceptual Approach*. New York: Oxford University Press.

Sheldon, Garrett W. (1991) *The Political Philosophy of Thomas Jefferson*. Baltimore, MD: Johns Hopkins University Press 1991.

Shestack, Jerome J. (1998) "The Philosophic Foundations of Human Rights," *Human Rights Quarterly*, 20(2): 201–234.

Smith, Steven (1989) *Hegel's Critique of Liberalism: Rights in Context*. Chicago: University of Chicago Press.

Spencer, Herbert (1864) *Social Statics*. New York: Appleton.

Strawson, John (1997) "A Western Question to the Middle East: 'Is There a Human Rights Discourse in Islam?'," *Arab Studies Quarterly*, 19 (Winter): 31–58.

Sumner, William Graham (1883) *What Social Classes Owe to Each Other*. New York: Harper.

Swidler, Arlene, ed. (1982) *Human Rights in Religious Traditions*. New York: Pilgrims Press.

Tuck, Richard (1979) *Natural Rights Theories*. Cambridge UK : Cambridge University Press.

Tuck, Richard (1989) *Hobbes*. New York: Oxford University Press.

Waldron, Jeremy, ed. (1987) *"Nonsense upon Stilts": Bentham, Burke and Marx on the Rights of Man*. London: Methuen.

Waltz, Susan (2004) "Universal Human Rights: The Contribution of Muslim States," *Human Rights Quarterly*, 26 (November): 799–844.

Waltzer, Michael (1994) *Thick and Thin: Moral Argument at Home and Abroad*. Notre Dame, IN: University of Notre Dame Press.

Watkins, Frederick M., ed. (1953) *Jean-Jacques Rousseau: Political Writings: Containing The Social Contract, Considerations on the Government of Poland, and Part I of the Constitutional Project for Corsica*. New York: Nelson.

Wedgwood, C. V. (1938) *The Thirty Years War*. London: Cape.

Wernick, Andrew (2001) *Auguste Comte and the Religion of Humanity: The Post-Theistic Program of French Social Theory*. Cambridge UK : University of Cambridge Press.

Wood, Neal (1991) *Cicero's Social and Political Thought*. Berkeley: University of California Press.

Woods, Jeanne M. (2003) "Rights as Slogans: A Theory of Human Rights Based on African Humanism," *Black Law Journal*, 17(1): 52–66.

Yogi, Maharishi M. (1963) *The Science of Being and Art of Living*. New York: Allied Publishers.

▌CHAPTER 3

Amar, Akhil R. (2005) *America's Constitution: A Biography*. New York: Random House.

Barone, Michel (2007) *Our First Revolution: The Remarkable British Upheaval that Inspired America's Founding Fathers*. New York: Crown.

Best, Geoffrey (1999) "Peace Conferences and the Century of Total War: The 1899 Hague Conference and What Came After," *International Affairs*, 55(3): 619–34.

Carlyle, Thomas (1839) *Chartism*. New York: Lovell, 1885.

Clarkson, Thomas (1787) *A Summary View of the Slave Trade and of the Probable Consequences of Its Abolition*. London: Phillips

Coplin, William D., and Martin J. Rochester (1972) "The Permanent Court of International Justice, The International Court of Justice, The League of Nations, and the United Nations: A Comparative Empirical Survey," *American Political Science Review*, 66(2): 529–50.

Dunant, Henri (1862) *A Memory of Solferino*. Washington, DC: American National Red Cross, 1939.

Eubanks, Rodney (1971) "International Arbitration in the Political Sphere," *Arbitration Journal*, 26(3): 129–146.

Fairbanks, Charles H., Jr. (1982) "The British Campaign Against the Slave Trade: An Example of Successful Human Rights Policy." In *Human Rights and American Foreign Policy*, ed. Fred E. Baumann, pp. 87–135. Gambier, OH: Public Affairs Conference Center, Kenyon College.

Falk, Richard A. (1981) *Human Rights and State Sovereignty*. Teaneck, NJ: Holmes and Meier.

Ferrell, Robert H. (1952) *Peace in Their Time: The Origins of the Kellogg-Briand Pact*. Hamden, CT: Archon.

Foner, Philip (1975) *History of the Labor Movement in the United States*. New York: International Publishers.

Goldenberg, David M. (2006) *The Curse of Ham: Race and Slavery in Early Judaism, Christianity, and Islam*. Princeton, NJ: Princeton University Press.

Haas, Michael (1992) *Polity and Society: Philosophical Underpinnings of Social Science Paradigms*. Westport, CT: Praeger.

Halpern, Rick, and Enrico Dal Lago, eds. (2002) *Slavery and Emancipation*. Malden, MA: Blackwell.

Herzl, Theodor (1896) *A Jewish State: An Attempt at a Modern Solution of the Jewish Question*. 3rd ed. New York, Federation of American Zionists, 1917.

Heyrick, Elizabeth (1825) *Immediate, not Gradual Abolition, or, An Inquiry into the Shortest, Safest, and Most Effectual Means of Getting Rid of West Indian Slavery*. New York: Seaman.

Hochschild, Adam (2005) *Bury the Chains: Prophets and Rebels in the Fight to Free an Empire's Slaves*. Boston: Houghton Mifflin.

Hudson, Manley O. (1944) *International Tribunals, Past and Future*. Washington, DC: Carnegie Endowment for International Peace and Brookings Institution.

Ishay, Micheline R. (2004) *The History of Human Rights: From Ancient Times to the Globalization Era*. Berkeley: University of California Press.

Jennings, Judi (1997) *The Business of Abolishing the British Slave Trade, 1783–1807*. Portland, OR: Frank Cass.

Lauren, Paul Gordon (2003) *The Evolution of International Human Rights: Visions Seen*. Philadelphia: University of Pennsylvania Press.

Lenin, Valdimir I. (1914) "The War and Russian Social-Democracy." In J. Fineberg, ed., *Selected Works*, 5:123–30. New York: International Publishers, 1935.

Leo XIII (1891) *Rerum Novarum, Encyclical Letter of Pope Leo XIII on the Condition of Labor*. New York: Paulist Press, 1940.

Levinson, David, ed. (2003) *The Wilson Chronology of Human Rights: A Record of the Human Striving for Freedom from Ancient Times to the Present 2003*. New York: H. W. Wilson.

MacMunn, George Fletcher (1938) *Slavery Through the Ages*. London: Nicholson and Watson.

Mair, Lucy Philip (1928) *The Protection of Minorities: The Working and Scope of the Minorities Treaties Under the League of Nations*. London: Christophers.

Mair, Lucy Philip (1929) *Human Welfare and the League*. 5th ed. London: League of Nations Union.

Margalith, Aaron Morris (1930) *The International Mandates: A Historical, Descriptive, and Analytical Study of the Theory and Principles of the Mandates System*. Baltimore, MD: Johns Hopkins Press.

Marx, Karl, and Friedrich Engels (1848) *Manifesto of the Communist Party*. Moscow: Foreign Languages Publishing House, 1948.

Meyer, Carl Ludwig Wilhelm (1923) *Memorandum on the Origin, Status, and Achievements of the Hague Tribunal and of the Permanent Court of International Justice*. Washington, DC: Library of Congress.

Miller, David Hunter (1928) *The Peace Pact of Paris: A Study of the Briand-Kellogg Treaty*. New York: Putnam's Sons.

Northedge, F. S. (1986) *The League of Nations: Its Life and Times 1920–1946*. Leicester, UK: Leicester University Press.

Owen, Robert (1831) *A New View of Society*. New York: Woodstock Books, 1991.

Schindler, Dietrich, and Jiří Toman, comp. (2004) *The Laws of Armed Conflicts: A Collection of Conventions, Resolutions, and Other Documents*. Boston: Martinus Nihjoff.

Scott, James Brown (1909) *The Hague Peace Conferences of 1899 and 1907*. Baltimore, MD: Johns Hopkins Press.

Scott, S. P., ed. (1932) *The Civil Law, Including the Twelve Tables, the Institutes of Gaius, the Rules of Ulpian, the Opinions of Paulus, the Enactments of Justinian, and the Constitutions of Leo*. Cincinnati, OH: Central Trust Company.

Sen, Amartya (2005) *The Argumentative Indian: Writings on Indian History, Culture and Identity*. New York: Farrar, Straus and Giroux.

Sewell, Samuel (1700) *The Selling of Joseph: A Memorial*. Amherst, MA: University of Massachusetts Press, 1969.

Sharp, Granville (1774) *A Declaration of the People's Natural Right to a Share in the Legislature; Which Is the Fundamental Principle of the British Constitution of State*. New York: Da Capo Press, 1971.

Stowe, Harriet Beecher (1852) *Uncle Tom's Cabin*. West Berlin, NJ: Townsend Press, 2005.

Szabo, Imre (1982) "Historical Foundations of Human Rights and Subsequent Developments." In *The International Dimensions of Human Rights*, eds. Karal Vasak and Philip Alston, 1: 11–42. Westport, CT: Greenwood.

Walters, Francis P. (1952) *A History of the League of Nations*. New York: Oxford University Press.

Wambaugh, S. (1933) *Plebiscites Since the World War*. Washington, DC: Carnegie Endowment for International Peace.

Wesley, John (1744) *Thoughts Upon Slavery*. London: Hawes.

Wollstonecraft, Mary (1792) *A Vindication of the Rights of Woman, With Strictures on Political and Moral Subjects*. New York: Vale, 1845.

CHAPTER 4

Albert, Peter J., and Ronald Hoffman (1990) *We Shall Overcome: Martin Luther King, Jr., and the Black Freedom Struggle*. New York: Pantheon Books.

Alfredsson, Gudmundur, and Asbjørn Eide, eds. (1999) *The University Declaration of Human Rights: A Common Standard of Achievement*. Boston: Nijhoff.

Alston, Philip, ed. (2005) *Non-State Actors and Human Rights*. New York: Oxford University Press.

Bereffi, Gary, Ronnie García-Johnson, and Erika Sasser (2001) "The NGO-Industrial Complex," *Foreign Policy*, 125 (July/August): 556–565.

Brysk, Alison, ed. (2002) *Globalization and Human Rights*. Berkeley: University of California Press.

Burgenthal, Thomas, Dinah Shelton, and David P. Stewart (2002) *International Human Rights in a Nutshell*. 3rd ed. St. Paul, MN: West Group.

Carter, Jimmy (1995) *Keeping Faith: Memoirs of a President*. Fayetteville: University of Arkansas Press.

Chayes, Abraham, and Antonia Chandler Chayes (1995) *The New Sovereignty: Compliance with International Regulatory Agreements*. Cambridge, MA: Harvard University Press.

Coicaud, Jean-Marc, Michael W. Doyle, and Anne-Marie Gardner, eds. (2003) *The Globalization of Human Rights*. New York: United Nations University Press.

Drinan, Robert F. (2001) *The Mobilization of Shame: A World View of Human Rights*. New Haven, CT: Yale University Press.

Falk, Richard A. (1995) *On Human Governance: Toward a New Global Politics*. University Park: Pennsylvania State University Press.

Falk, Richard A. (1999) *Predatory Globalization: A Critique*. Malden, MA: Polity Press.

Glendon, Mary Ann (2001) *A World Made New: Eleanor Roosevelt and the Universal Declaration of Human Rights*. New York: Random House.

Gray, Robert C., and Stanley I. Michalak, Jr., eds. (1984) *American Foreign Policy Since Détente*. New York: Harper and Row.

Harris, Whitney R. (1999) *Tyranny on Trial: The Trial of the Major German War Criminals at the End of World War II at Nuremberg, Germany, 1945–1946*. Dallas, TX: Southern Methodist University Press.

Jacobs, Steven L., ed. (1992) *Raphael Lemkin's Thoughts on Nazi Genocide: Not Guilty?* Lewiston, ME: Mellen Press.

Kaufman, Burton I. (1993) *The Presidency of James Earl Carter, Jr.* Lawrence: University of Kansas Press.

Keck, Margaret E., and Kathryn Sikkink (1998) *Activists Beyond Borders: Advocacy Networks in International Politics*. Ithaca, NY: Cornell University Press.

Keenan, Joseph B., and Brendan Francis Brown (1950) *Crimes Against International Law*. Washington, DC: Public Affairs Press.

Khagram, Sanjeev, James V. Riker, and Kathryn Sikkink, eds. (2002) *Restructuring World Politics: Transnational Social Movements, Networks, and Norms*. Minneapolis: University of Minnesota Press.

Korey, William (1998) *NGOs and the Universal Declaration of Human Rights: A Curious Grapevine*. New York: Palgrave Macmillan.

Kuper, Leo (1981) *South Africa: Human Rights and Genocide*. Bloomington: Indiana University Press.

Lauren, Paul Gordon (1998) *The Evolution of International Human Rights*. Philadelphia: University of Pennsylvania Press.

Lincoln, C. Eric, ed. (1970) *Martin Luther King, Jr.: A Profile*. New York: Hill and Wang.

Lipstadt, Deborah (1993) *Denying the Holocaust: The Growing Assault on Truth and Memory*. New York: Plume.

Mayall, James, and Gene M. Lyons (2003) *International Human Rights in the 21st Century: Protecting the Rights of Groups*. Lanham, MD: Rowman and Littlefield.

Minear, Richard H. (1971) *Victors' Justice: The Tokyo War Crimes Trial*. Princeton, NJ: Princeton University Press.

Moorehead, Caroline (1999) *Dunant's Dream: War, Switzerland, and the History of the Red Cross*. New York: Carroll and Graf.

Morsink, Johannes (1999) *The Universal Declaration of Human Rights: Origins, Drafting, and Intent*. Philadelphia: University of Pennsylvania Press.

Neier, Aryeh (2003) *Taking Liberties: Four Decades in the Struggle for Rights*. New York: Public Affairs Press.

O'Donovan, Katherine, and Gerry R. Rubin, eds. (2002) *Human Rights and Legal History*. New York: Oxford University Press.

Parker, Peter, and Joyce Mokhesi-Parker (1998) *In the Shadow of Sharpeville: Apartheid and Criminal Justice*. New York: New York University Press.

Power, Jonathan (2001) *Like Water on Stone: The Story of Amnesty International*. Boston: Northeastern University Press.

Risse, Thomas, Stephen C. Ropp, and Kathryn Sikkink, eds. (1999) *The Power of Human Rights: International Norms and Domestic Change*. New York: Cambridge University Press, 1999.

Roosevelt, Eleanor (1992) *The Autobiography of Eleanor Roosevelt*. New York: Da Capo Press.

Rummel, R. J. (1994) *Death by Government*. New Brunswick, NJ: Transaction Publishers.

Smith, Jackie, and Ron Pagnucco (1998) "Globalizing Human Rights: The Work of Transnational Human Rights NGOs in the 1990s," *Human Rights Quarterly*, 20(2): 378–412.

Stannard, David (1992) *American Holocaust*. New York: Oxford University Press.

Storey, Robert G. (1968) *The Final Judgment? Pearl Harbor to Nuremberg*. San Antonio, TX: Naylor.

Taylor, Telford (1992) *Anatomy of the Nuremberg Trials: A Personal Memoir*. Boston: Back Bay Books.

Thomas, Daniel C. (2005) "Human Rights Ideas, the Demise of Communism, and the End of the Cold War," *Journal of Cold War Studies*, 7 (Spring): 110–141.

Tomuschat, Christian, and Jean Marc Thouvenin, eds. (2006) *The Fundamental Rules of the International Legal Order: Jus Cogens and Obligations Erga Omnes*. Boston: Nijhoff.

Tsutsui, Kiyoteru, and Christine Min Wotipka (2004) "Global Civil Society and the International Human Rights Movement: Citizen Participation in Human Rights International Nongovernmental Organizations," *Social Forces*, 83(2): 587–620.

Urquhart, Brian (1989) *Decolonization and World Peace*. Austin: University of Texas Press.

Urquhart, Brian (2000) "Mrs. Roosevelt's Revolution," *New York Review of Books*, 46(7): 32–4.

Van Tuijl, Peter (1999) "NGOs and Human Rights: Sources of Justice and Democracy," *Journal of International Affairs*, 53(2): 493–512.

Weeranantry, C. G. (2004) *Universalizing International Law*. New York: Nijhoff.

CHAPTER 5

Bair, Johann (2006) *The International Covenant on Civil and Political Rights and Its (First) Optional Protocol: A Short Commentary Based on Views, General Comments, and Concluding Observations by the Human Rights Committee*. New York: Lang.

Bales, Kevin (1999) *Disposable People: New Slavery in the Global Economy*. Berkeley: University of California Press.

Blum, William (1998) *Killing Hope: U. S. Military and CIA Interventions Since World War II*. Buffalo, NY: Black Rose Books.

Brahm, Eric (2004) *Truth Commissions*. (www2.beyondintractability.org/m/truth_commissions.jsp).

Brahm, Eric (2007) "Uncovering the Truth: Examining Truth Commission Success and Impact," *International Studies Perspectives*, 8(1): 16–25.

Braithwaite, John (2002) *Law Versus Justice: From Adversarialism to Communitarianism*. New York: Oxford University Press.

Bronkhorst, Daan (1995) *Truth and Reconciliation: Obstacles and Opportunities for Human Rights*. Amsterdam: Amnesty International Dutch Section.

Brysk, Alison, and Gershon Shafir, eds. (2004) *People out of Place: Globalization, Human Rights, and the Citizenship Gap*. New York: Routledge.

Carlson, Scott N., and Gregory Gisvold (2003) *Practical Guide to the International Covenant on Civil and Political Rights*. Ardsley, NY: Transnational Publishers.

Conte, Alex, Scott Davidson, and Richard Burchill (2004) *Defining Civil and Political Rights: The Jurisprudence of the United Nations Human Rights Committee*. Burlington, VT: Ashgate.

Franck, Thomas M. (2001) "Are Human Rights Universal?," *Foreign Affairs*, 80(1): 191–204.

Goldsmith, Jack L., and Eric A. Posner (2005) *The Limits of International Law*. New York: Oxford University Press.

Gordenker, Leon (1987) *Refugees in International Politics*. New York: Columbia University Press.

Hayner, Priscilla B. (1994) "Fifteen Truth Commissions – 1974 to 1994: A Comparative Study," *Human Rights Quarterly*, 16(4): 597–655.

Hayner, Priscilla B. (2001) *Unspeakable Truths: Facing the Challenge of Truth Commissions*. New York: Routledge.

Kausikan, Bilahari (1997) "Asian Versus 'Universal' Human Rights," *The Responsive Community*, 7(3): 9–21.

Leach, Susan Llewelyn (2004) "Slavery Is Not Dead, Just Less Recognizable," *Christian Science Monitor*, September 1.

Meijer, Martha, ed. (2001) *Dealing with Human Rights: Asian and Western Views on the Value of Human Rights*. Bloomfield, CT: Kumarian Press.

Moravcsik, Andrew (2000) "The Origins of Human Rights Regimes," *International Organization*, 54 (Spring): 217–52.

Mungazi, Dickson A. (1989) *The Struggle for Social Change in Southern Africa: Visions of Liberty*. New York: Crane Russak.

Neier, Aryeh (1997) "Asia's Unacceptable Double Standard," *The Responsive Community*, 7(3): 22–30.

Nowak, Manfred (1993) *U.N. Covenant on Civil and Political Rights: CCPR Commentary*. Arlington, VA: Engel.

Plender, Richard (1988) *International Migration Law*. 2nd ed. Boston: Nijhoff.

Theofilopoulou, Anna (2006) *The United Nations and Western Sahara: A Never-Ending Affair*. Washington, DC: U.S. Institute of Peace, Special Report 166.

CHAPTER 6

Addo, Michael K., ed. (1999) *Human Rights Standards and the Responsibility of Transnational Corporations*. Boston: Kluwer.

Anaya, S. James, and Claudio Grossman (2002) "The Case of *Awas Tingni v Nicaragua*: A New Step in the International Law of Indigenous Peoples," *Arizona Journal of International and Comparative Law*, 19(1): 1–15.

Appiah, Kwame Anthony (2006) "Whose Culture Is It?," *New York Review of Books*, 53 (February 9): 38–42.

Bales, Kevin (1999) *Disposable People: New Slavery in the Global Economy*. Berkeley: University of California Press.

Bhagwati, Jagdish N., ed. (1977) *The New International Economic Order: The North South Debate*. Cambridge, MA: MIT Press.

Brecher, Jeremy, John Brown Childs, and Jill Cutler, eds. (1993) *Global Visions: Beyond the New World Order*. Boston: South End Press.

Brecher, Jeremy, Tim Costello, and Brendan Smith (2000) *Globalization from Below: The Power of Solidarity*. Boston: South End Press.

Cobo, José Martínez (1986) *The Study of the Problem of Discrimination Against Indigenous Populations*. UN Document E/CN.4/Sub.2/1986/7. New York: United Nations.

Cowan, Jane K., Marie-Bénédicte Dembour, and Richard A. Wilson, eds. (2001) *Culture and Rights: Anthropological Perspectives*. New York: Cambridge University Press.

Darrow, Mac, and Amparo Tomás (2005) "Power, Capture, and Conflict: A Call for Human Rights Accountability in Development Cooperation," *Human Rights Quarterly*, 27(2): 461–540.

Dorgan, Byron L. (2006) *Take This Job and Ship It: How Corporate Greed and Brain-Dead Politics Are Selling out America*. New York: St. Martin's Press.

Easterly, William (2006) *The White Man's Burden: Why the West's Efforts to Aid the Rest Have Done So Much Ill and So Little Good*. New York: Penguin.

Eide, Asbjørn, Catarina Krause, and Allan Rosas, eds. (2001) *Economic, Social, and Cultural Rights: A Textbook*. 2nd ed. Boston: Nijhoff.

Elliott, Kimberly Ann, and Richard B. Freeman (2003) *Can Labor Standards Improve Under Globalization?* Washington, DC: Institute for International Economics.

Felice, William F. (2003) *The Global New Deal: Economic and Social Human Rights in World Politics*. Lanham, MD: Rowman and Littlefield.

Freeman, Marsha A. (1999) "International Institutions and Gendered Justice," *Journal of International Affairs*, 53 (Spring): 513–532.

Friedman, Tom (2006) *The World Is Flat: A Brief History of the Twenty-First Century*. New York: Farrar, Strauss and Giroux.

Galtung, Johan (1964) "A Structural Theory of Aggression," *Journal of Peace Research*, 1(2): 95–119.

Ganji, Manouchehr (1975) *The Realization of Economic, Social and Cultural Rights: Problems, Policies, Progress*. New York: United Nations.

Hodgson, Dorothy L. (2002) "Introduction: Comparative Perspectives on the Indigenous Rights Movement in Africa and the Americas," *American Anthropologist*, 104(4): 1037–51.

Howard, Bradley Red (2003) *Indigenous Peoples and the State: The Struggle for Native Rights.* DeKalb: Northern Illinois University Press.

Hunt, Paul (1996) *Reclaiming Social Rights: International and Comparative Perspectives.* Brookfield, VT: Dartmouth.

International Labour Office (1991) *Still So Far to Go: Child Labour in the World Today.* Geneva: ILO.

Lâm, Maivân (2004) "Remembering the Country of Their Birth: Indigenous Peoples and Territoriality," *Journal of International Affairs*, 57(2): 129–52.

Leach, Susan Llewelyn (2004) "Slavery Is Not Dead, Just Less Recognizable," *Christian Science Monitor*, September 1.

Leary, Virginia (1994) "The Right to Health in International Human Rights Law," *Health and Human Rights*, 1(1): 24–56.

Levine, Ruth (2004) *Millions Saved: Proven Successes in Global Health.* Washington, DC: Center for Global Development.

Merryman, John Henry (1986) "Two Ways of Thinking About Cultural Property," *American Journal of International Law*, 80 (October): 831–53.

Moghadam, Valentine M. (2005) *Globalizing Women: Transnational Feminist Networks.* Baltimore, MD: The Johns Hopkins University Press.

Muehlebach, Andrea (2001) "'Making Place' at the United Nations: Indigenous Cultural Politics at the U.N. Working Group on Indigenous Populations," *Cultural Anthropology*, 16(3): 415–50.

Murphy, Craig (1984) *Emergence of the NIEO Ideology.* Boulder, CO: Westview.

Niezen, Ronald (2003) *The Origins of Indigenism: Human Rights and the Politics of Identity.* Berkeley: University of California Press.

Pogge, Thomas (2002) *World Poverty and Human Rights: Cosmopolitan Responsibilities and Reforms.* Malden, MA: Polity.

Robinson, Mary (2004) "Advancing Economic, Social and Cultural Rights: The Way Forward," *Human Rights Quarterly*, 26(4): 866–72.

Rodrick, Dani (1999) *The New Global Economy and the Developing Countries.* Washington, DC: Overseas Development Council.

Roht-Arviaza, Naomi (1999) "Institutions of International Justice," *Journal of International Affairs*, 52 (Spring): 473–91.

Rothstein, Robert L. (1979) *Global Bargaining: UNCTAD and the Quest for a New International Economic Order.* Princeton, NJ: Princeton University Press.

Sachs, Jeffrey D. (2006) *The End of Poverty: Economic Possibilities for Our Time.* New York: Penguin.

Scheppele, Lim Lane (2004) "A Realpolitik Defense of Social Rights," *Texas Law Review*, 82(4): 727–68.

Sen, Amartya (1981) *Poverty and Famines: An Essay on Entitlement and Deprivation.* New York: Oxford University Press.

Sen, Amartya (2001) *Development as Freedom.* New York: Oxford University Press.

Spar, Debora L. (1988) "The Spotlight and the Bottom Line," *Foreign Affairs*, 77(2): 7–12.

Springer, Jane (1997) *Listen to Us: The World's Working Children.* Toronto: Groundwood.

Wilmer, Franke (1993) *The Indigenous Voice in World Politics.* London: Sage.

Winston, Morton (2002) "NGO Strategies for Promoting Corporate Social Responsibility," *Ethics and International Affairs*, 16(1): 71–88.

Yamin, Alicia Ely (2005) "The Right to Health Under International Law and Its Relevance to the United States," *American Journal of Public Health*, 95(7): 1156–61.

CHAPTER 7

Bassiouni, M. Cherif (2003) *Introduction to International Criminal Law.* Ardsley, NY: Transnational Publishers.

Bonner, Raymond (2007) "The CIA's Secret Torture," *New York Review of Books*, 54(1): 28–31.

Boyd, K. Lee (2004) "Universal Jurisdiction and Structural Reasonableness," *Texas International Law Journal*, 90 (Fall): 1–58.

Chang, Iris (1997) *The Rape of Nanking: The Forgotten Holocaust of World War II*. New York: Penguin.

Charles, J. Daryl (2005) *Between Pacifism and Jihad: Just War and Christian Tradition*. Downers Grove, IL: InterVarsity Press.

Chatterjee, Deen, and Don E. Scheid, eds. (2003) *Ethics and Foreign Intervention*. Cambridge, UK: Cambridge University Press.

Chomsky, Noam (2006) *Failed States: The Abuse of Power and the Assault on Democracy*. London: Hamish Hamilton.

Cohen, David B., and John W. Wells, eds. (2004) *American National Security and Civil Liberties in an Era of Terrorism*. New York: Palgrave Macmillan.

Cohen, Esther R. (1985) *Human Rights in the Israeli-Occupied Territories, 1967–1982*. Manchester, UK: Manchester University Press.

Cole, David (2006) "Why the Court Said No," *New York Review of Books*, 53 (August 10): 41–3.

Edsall, Robert M. (2006) *Rescuing Da Vinci: Recovering Europe's Art from Hitler and the Nazis*. Dallas, TX: Laurel.

European Parliament (2006) *Draft Report on the Alleged Use of European Countries by the CIA for the Transportation and Illegal Detention of Prisoners* (www.europarl.europa.eu/comparl/tempcom/tdip/default_en.pdf).

Falk, Richard A. (1986) "Forty Years After the Nuremberg and Tokyo Tribunals: The Impact of the War Crimes Trials on International and National Law," *Proceedings, Eightieth Annual Meeting, The American Society of International Law*, pp. 65–7.

Falk, Richard A., Gabriel Kolko, and Robert Jay Lifton, eds. (1971) *Crimes of War: A Legal, Political-Documentary, and Psychological Inquiry into the Responsibility of Leaders, Citizens, and Soldiers for Criminal Acts in Wars*. New York: Random House.

Fein, Helen (1993) *Genocide: A Sociological Perspective*. London: Sage.

Ferrell, Robert H. (1952) *Peace in Their Time: The Origins of the Kellogg-Briand Pact*. Hamden, CT: Archon Books, 1968.

Glueck, Sheldon (1944) *War Criminals, Their Prosecution and Punishment*. New York: Knopf.

Greenberg, Karen J., and Joshua L. Dratel, eds. (2005) *The Torture Papers: The Road to Abu Ghraib*. New York: Cambridge University Press.

Grotius, Hugo (1609) *The Freedom of the Seas, or, The Right Which Belongs to the Dutch to Take Part in the East Indian Trade*. Union, NJ: Lawbook Exchange, 2001.

Grotius, Hugo (1625) *De Jure Belli ac Pacis*. The Hague: Nijhoff, 1948.

Harris, Robert, and Jeremy Paxman (2002) *A Higher Form of Killing: The Secret History of Chemical and Biological Warfare*. New York: Random House.

Holzgrefe, J. L., and Robert O. Keohane, eds. (2003) *Humanitarian Intervention: Ethical, Legal, and Political Dilemmas*. New York: Cambridge University Press.

International Commission on Intervention and State Sovereignty (2001) *The Responsibility to Protect*. Ottawa: International Development Research Centre.

Keene, Edward (2002) *Beyond the Anarchical Society: Grotius, Colonialism and Order in World Politics*. New York: Cambridge University Press.

Kelly, Michael J. (2003) "Time Warp to 1945 – Resurrection of the Reprisal and Anticipatory Self-Defense Doctrines in International Law," *Journal of Transnational Law and Policy*, 13(1): 1–39.

Kennedy, David (2004) *The Dark Sides of Virtue: Reassessing International Humanitarianism*. Princeton, NJ: Princeton University Press.

Klintworth, Gary (1989) *Vietnam's Intervention in Cambodia in International Law*. Canberra: Australian Government Publishing Service.

Kuper, Leo (1981) *Genocide: Its Political Use in the Twentieth Century*. New Haven, CT: Yale University Press.

Lang, Anthony F., Jr., ed. (2003) *Just Intervention*. Washington, DC: Georgetown University Press.

Lelyveld, Joseph (2007) "No Exit," *New York Review of Books*, 54 (February 15): 12–17.

Margulies, Joseph (2006) *Guantánamo and the Abuse of Presidential Power*. New York: Simon and Schuster.

Marrus, Michael R. (1997) *The Nuremberg War Crimes Trial 1945–46: A Documentary History*. Boston: Bedford Books.

Meron, Theodore (2000) "The Humanization of International Humanitarian Law," *American Journal of International Law*, 94(April): 239–78.

Miles, Steven H. (2006) *Oath Betrayed: Torture, Medical Complicity, and the War on Terror*. New York: Random House.

Moore, John Bassett (1906) *A Digest of International Law*. Washington, DC: Government Printing Office.

Morris, Benny (1999) *Righteous Victims: A History of the Zionist-Arab Conflict, 1881–1999*. New York: Knopf.

Murphy, Sean D. (1996) *Humanitarian Intervention: The United Nations in an Evolving World Order*. Philadelphia: University of Pennsylvania Press.

Neff, Stephen C. (2005) *War and the Law of Nations: A General History*. New York: Cambridge University Press.

Neier, Aryeh (1998) *War Crimes: Brutality, Genocide, Terror, and the Struggle for Justice*. New York: Times Books.

Nicholas, Lynn H. (1994) *The Rape of Europa: The Fate of Europe's Treasures in the Third Reich and the Second World War*. New York: Knopf.

O'Hanlon, Michael E. (2003) *Expanding Global Military Capacity for Humanitarian Intervention*. Washington, DC: Brookings Institution.

Oppenheim, Lassa (1991) *International Law: A Treatise*. 9th ed. New York: Longmans, Green.

Prunier, Gérard (1995) *The Rwanda Crisis: History of a Genocide*. New York: Columbia University Press.

Prunier, Gérard (2005) *Darfur: The Ambiguous Genocide*. Ithaca, NY: Cornell University Press.

Ramsbotham, Oliver, and Tom Woodson (1996) *Humanitarian Intervention in Contemporary Conflict: A Reconceptualization*. Cambridge, MA: Polity Press.

Ratner, Steven R., and Jason S. Abrams (2001) *Accountability for Human Rights Atrocities in International Law: Beyond the Nuremberg Legacy*. 2nd ed. New York: Oxford University Press.

Rees, Laurence (2002) *Horror in the East: Japan and the Atrocities of World War II*. Cambridge, MA: Da Capo Press.

Rieff, David (2005) *At the Point of a Gun: Democratic Dreams and Armed Intervention*. New York: Simon and Schuster.

Robertson, Geoffrey (1999) *Crimes Against Humanity: The Struggle for Global Justice*. London: Allen Lane.

Rogers, A. V. P. (2004) "Humanitarian Intervention and International Law," *Harvard Journal of Law and Public Policy*, 27 (Summer): 725–36.

Roht-Arriaza, Naomi, ed. (1995) *Impunity and Human Rights in International Law and Practice*. New York: Oxford University Press.

Rupérez, Javiet (2005) "The Role of the United Nations in the Fight Against Terrorism: A Provisional Balance," *Perceptions*, 10 (Summer): 41–8.

Schindler, Dietrich, and Jiří Toman, eds. (2004) *The Laws of Armed Conflicts: A Collection of Conventions, Resolutions, and Other Documents*. Boston: Nihjoff.

Segev, Tom (1973) *The Seventh Million: The Israelis and the Holocaust*. New York: Hill and Wang.

Simons, Lewis M. (2006) "Genocide and the Science of Proof," *National Geographic*, 209(1): 28–35.

Singer, Peter W. (2005) *Children at War*. New York: Pantheon.

Terry, Fiona (2002) *Condemned to Repeat? The Paradox of Humanitarian Action*. Ithaca, NY: Cornell University Press.

Turner, Bryan S. (2006) *Vulnerability and Human Rights*. University Park: Pennsylvania State University Press.

Vreeland, Hamilton, Jr. (1917) *Hugo Grotius: The Father of the Modern Science of International Law*. Little, CO: Rothman, 1986.

Walzer, Michael (2000) *Just and Unjust Wars: A Moral Argument with Historical Illustrations*. 3rd ed. New York: Basic Books.

Weiss, Thomas G., and Cindy Collins (2000) *Humanitarian Challenges and Intervention*. 2nd ed. Boulder, CO: Westview.

Wells, H. G. (1919) *The Idea of the League of Nations*. Boston: Atlantic Monthly Press.

Wheeler, Nicholas J. (2001) *Saving Strangers: Humanitarian Intervention in International Society*. New York: Oxford University Press.

Williams, Robert E., Jr., and Dan Caldwell (2006) "*Jus Post Bellum*: Just War Theory and the Principles of Just Peace," *International Studies Perspectives*, 7(4): 309–20.

Wypijewski, Joann (2006) "Conduct Unbecoming," *Mother Jones,* January/February: 24, 26–27.

Yoo, John (2005) The *Powers of War and Peace: The Constitution and Foreign Affairs After 9/11*. Chicago: University of Chicago Press.

CHAPTER 8

Abouharb, M. Rodwan, and David L. Cingranelli (2006) "The Human Rights Effects of World Bank Structural Adjustment, 1981–2000," *International Studies Quarterly*, 50 (June): 233–62.

Abrams, Burton A., and Kenneth A. Lewis (1993) "Human Rights and the Distribution of U.S. Foreign Aid," *Public Choice*, 77(4): 815–21.

Adelman, Irma and Cynthia Taft Morris (1967) *Society, Politics, and Economic Development: A Quantitative Approach*. Baltimore, MD: Johns Hopkins University Press.

Adeola, Francis O. (1996) "Military Expenditures, Health, and Education: Bedfellows or Antagonists in Third World Development?" *Armed Forces and Society*, 22(3): 441–67.

Alesina, Alberto, and David Dollar (2000) "Who Gives Foreign Aid to Whom and Why?" *Journal of Economic Growth*, 5(1): 33–63.

Alston, Philip (2000) "Using Indicators for Human Rights Accountability." In UN Development Program, *Human Development Report*, chap. 5. New York: Oxford University Press.

Amnesty International (1962–) *Report*. London: Amnesty International, annual.

Apodaca, Clair (2001) "Global Economic Patterns and Personal Integrity Rights after the Cold War," *International Studies Quarterly*, 45(4): 587–602.

Apodaca, Clair and Michael Stohl (1999) "United States Human Rights Policy and Foreign Assistance," *International Studies Quarterly*, 43(1): 185–98.

Arat, Zehra F. (1991) *Democracy and Human Rights in Developing Countries*. Boulder, CO: Lynne Rienner.

Banks, Arthur S. (1971) *Cross-Polity Time-Series Data*. Cambridge, MA: MIT Press.

Banks, Arthur S. (1979) *Cross-National Time Series Data Archive*. Binghamton: Center for Social Analysis, State University of New York.

Banks, Arthur S., and Robert B. Textor, comp. (1963) *A Cross-Polity Survey*. Cambridge, MA: MIT Press.

Banks, David L. (1985) "Patterns of Oppression: A Statistical Analysis of Human Rights," *American Statistical Association, Proceedings of the Social Statistics Section*, 62: 154–62.

Banks, David L. (1986) "The Analysis of Human Rights Data Over Time," *Human Rights Quarterly*, 8 (December): 654–80.

Banks, David L. (1992) "New Patterns of Oppression: An Updated Analysis of Human Rights Data." In *Human Rights and Statistics: Getting the Record Straight*, eds. Thomas B. Jabine and Richard P. Claude, chap. 14. Philadelphia: University of Pennsylvania Press.

Barsh, Russel L. (1993) "Measuring Human Rights: Problems of Methodology and Purpose," *Human Rights Quarterly*, 15 (February): 87–121.

Bentley, Arthur F. (1908) *Process of Government: A Study of Social Pressures*. New Brunswick, NJ: Transaction Books.

Blanton, Shannon Lindsey (1994) "Impact of Human Rights on U.S. Foreign Assistance to Latin America," *International Interactions*, 19(4): 339–58.

Blasi, Gerald J., and David Louis Cingranelli (1996) "Do Constitutions and Institutions Protect Human Rights?" In *Human Rights and Developing Countries*, ed. David Louis Cingranelli, pp. 223–37. Greenwich, CT: JAI Press.

Blondel, Jean (1969) *An Introduction of Comparative Government*. New York: Praeger.

Boli-Bennett, John (1981) "Human Rights or State Expansion? Cross-National Definitions of Constitutional Rights, 1870–1970." In *Global Human Rights: Public Policies, Comparative Measures, and NGO Strategies*, eds. Ved P. Nanda, James R. Scarritt, and George W. Shepherd, Jr., chap. 11. Boulder, CO: Westview.

Bollen, Kenneth A. (1979) "Political Democracy and the Timing of Development," *American Sociological Review*, 44 (August): 572–87.

Bollen, Kenneth A. (1980) "Issues in the Comparative Measurement of Political Democracy," *American Sociological Review*, 45 (June): 370–90.

Bollen, Kenneth A. (1983) "World System Position, Dependency, and Democracy: The Cross-National Evidence," *American Sociological Review*, 45 (June): 468–79.

Bollen, Kenneth A. (1986) "Political Rights and Political Liberties in Nations: An Evaluation of Human Rights Measures, 1950 to 1984," *Human Rights Quarterly*, 8 (December): 567–91.

Bollen, Kenneth A. (1992) "Political Rights and Political Liberties in Nations: An Evaluation of Human Rights Measures, 1950 to 1984." In *Human Rights and Statistics: Getting the Record Straight*, Thomas B. Jabine and Richard P. Claude, eds., chap. 7. Philadelphia: University of Pennsylvania Press.

Bollen, Kenneth A. (1993) "Liberal Democracy: Validity and Method Factors in Cross-National Measures," *American Journal of Political Science*, 37(4): 1207–30.

Bollen, Kenneth A., and Burke D. Grandjean (1981) "The Dimension(s) of Democracy: Further Issues in the Measurement and Effects of Political Democracy," *American Sociological Review*, 46 (October): 651–9.

Bollen, Kenneth, and Robert W. Jackman (1989) "Democracy, Stability, and Dichotomies," *American Sociological Review*, 54 (August): 612–20.

Booysen, Frederik (2002) "An Overview and Evaluation of Composite Indices of Development," *Social Indicators Research*, 59(2): 115–51.

Boswell, Terry, and William J. Dixon (1990) "Dependency and Rebellion: A Cross-National Analysis," *American Sociological Review*, 55 (August): 540–59.

Bueno de Mesquita, Bruce, Alastair Smith, Randolph M. Siverson, and James D. Morrow (2003) *The Logic of Political Survival*. Cambridge, MA: MIT Press.

Bueno de Mesquita, Bruce, Feryal Marie Cherif, George W. Downs, and Alastair Smith (2005) "Thinking Inside the Box: A Closer Look at Democracy and Human Rights," *International Studies Quarterly*, 49 (September): 439–57.

Byers, Michael (2006) *War Law: Understanding International Law and Armed Conflict*. New York: Grove Press.

Cain, Michael, Richard P. Claude, and Thomas B. Jabine (1992) "A Guide to Human Rights Data Sources." In *Human Rights and Statistics: Getting the Record Straight*, eds. Thomas B. Jabine and Richard P. Claude, chap. 15. Philadelphia: University of Pennsylvania Press.

Carey, Sabine, and Steven C. Poe, eds. (2004) *Understanding Human Rights Violations: New Systematic Studies*. Burlington, VT: Ashgate.

Carleton, David, and Michael Stohl (1985) "The Foreign Policy of Human Rights: Rhetoric and Reality from Jimmy Carter to Ronald Reagan," *Human Rights Quarterly*, 7 (May): 205–29.

Carleton, David, and Michael Stohl (1987) "The Role of Human Rights in U.S. Foreign Assistance Policy: A Critique and Reappraisal," *American Journal of Political Science*, 31(4): 1002–18.

Carmichael, Stokely (later, Kwame Ture), and Charles V. Hamilton (1967) *Black Power*. New York: Random House.

Charny, Israel W. (1982) *How Can We Commit the Unthinkable? Genocide, the Human Cancer*. Boulder, CO: Westview.

Chayes, Abram, and Antonia Handler Chayes (1993) "On Compliance," *International Organization*, 47(2): 175–205.

Chomsky, Noam (1991) *Deterring Democracy*. New York: Hill and Wang.

Cingranelli, David L., and Thomas E. Pasquarello (1985) "Human Rights Practices and the Distribution of U.S. Foreign Aid to Latin American Countries," *American Journal of Political Science*, 29 (August): 539–63.

Cingranelli, David L., and Kevin N. Wright (1988) "Correlates of Due Process." In *Human Rights: Theory and Measurement*, ed. David L. Cingranelli, chap. 9. New York: St. Martin's Press.

Cingranelli, David L., and David I. Richards (1999a) "Measuring the Level, Pattern, and Sequence of Government Respect for Physical Integrity Rights," *International Studies Quarterly*, 43(2): 407–17.

Cingranelli, David L., and David I. Richards (1999b) "Respect for Human Rights After the End of the Cold War," *Journal of Peace Research*, 36(5): 511–34.

Cohn, Norman (1967) *Warrant for Genocide: The Myth of Jewish World-Conspiracy and the Protocols of the Elders of Zion*. New York: Harper and Row.

Cohn, Norman (1970) *The Pursuit of the Millennium: Revolutionary Millenarians and Mystical Anarchists of the Middle Ages*. New York: Oxford University Press.

Cohn, Norman (1977) *Europe's Inner Demons: An Enquiry Inspired by the Great Witch-Hunt*. New York: Meridian.

Cole, Wade M. (2005) "Sovereignty Relinquished? Explaining Commitment to the International Human Rights Covenants, 1966–1999," *American Sociological Review*, 70(3): 472–95.

Conway, Henderson (1982) "Military Regimes and Rights in Developing Countries," *Human Rights Quarterly*, 4(1): 110–23.

Crotty, Patricia McGee, and Harold Jacobs (1996) "Women's Rights: Legislating Equality." In *Human Rights and Developing Countries*, ed. David Louis Cingranelli, pp. 31–42. Greenwich, CT: JAI Press.

Cutright, Phillips (1963) "National Political Development: Its Measurement and Social Correlates," *American Sociological Review*, 28 (April): 253–64.

Cutright, Phillips (1965) "Political Structure, Economic Development, and National Social Security Programs," *American Journal of Sociology*, 70 (March): 537–50.

Cutright, Phillips (1967a) "Inequality: A Cross-National Analysis," *American Sociological Review*, 32 (August): 562–78.

Cutright, Phillips (1967b) "Income Redistribution: A Cross-National Analysis," *Social Forces*, 46 (December): 180–90.

Cutright, Phillips, and James A. Wiley (1969) "Modernization and Political Representation, 1927–1966," *Studies in Comparative International Development*, 5(2): 23–44.

Dahl, Robert A. (1971) *Polyarchy: Participation and Opposition.* New Haven, CT: Yale University Press.

Davenport, Christian (1988) "Liberalizing Event or Lethal Episode? An Empirical Assessment of How National Elections Affect the Suppression of Political and Civil Liberties, *Social Science Quarterly*, 79(2): 321–40.

Davenport, Christian (1995) "Multi-Dimensional Threat Perception and State Repression," *American Journal of Political Science*, 39(3): 685–713.

Davenport, Christian (1996) "Constitutional Promises and Repressive Reality," *Journal of Politics*, 58(3): 627–54.

Derian, Patricia (1979) "Human Rights in American Foreign Policy," *Notre Dame Lawyer*, 55 (December): 264–80.

Dixon, William J. (1984) "Trade Concentration, Economic Growth, and the Provision of Basic Human Needs," *Social Science Quarterly*, 65 (September): 761–74.

Donnelly, Jack (1989) *Universal Human Rights in Theory and Practice.* Ithaca, NY: Cornell University Press.

Donnelly, Jack, and Rhoda E. Howard (1988) "Assessing National Human Rights Performance: A Theoretical Framework," *Human Rights Quarterly*, 10 (May): 214–48.

Duff, Ernest A., and John F. McCamant (1976) *Violence and Repression in Latin America.* New York: Free Press.

Duvall, Raymond D., and Michael Stohl (1988) "Governance by Terror." In *The Politics of Terrorism*, ed. Michael Stohl, chap. 7. New York: Dekker.

Feierabend, Ivo K., and Rosalind L. Feierabend (1971) "The Relationship of Systemic Frustration, Political Coercion, International Tension and Political Instability: A Cross-National Analysis." In *Macro-Quantitative Analysis: Conflict, Development, and Democratization*, eds. John V. Gillespie and Betty A. Nesvold, chap. 19. Beverly Hills, CA: Sage.

Fein, Helen (1993) *Genocide: A Sociological Perspective.* Newbury Park, CA: Sage.

Feng, Yi (2001) "Political Freedom, Political Instability, and Policy Uncertainty: A Study of Political Institutions and Private Investment in Developing Countries," *International Studies Quarterly*, 45(2): 271–94.

Fitzgibbon, Russell H. (1956) "A Statistical Evaluation of Latin American Democracy," *Western Political Quarterly*, 9 (September): 607–19.

Fitzgibbon, Russell H., and Kenneth F. Johnson (1961) "Measurement of Latin American Political Change," *American Political Science Review*, 55 (September): 515–26.

Flanigan, William, and Edwin Fogelman (1971) "Patterns of Democratic Development: An Historical Comparative Analysis." In *Macro-Quantitative Analysis: Conflict, Development, and Democratization*, eds. John V. Gillespie and Betty A. Nesvold, chap. 21. Beverly Hill, CA: Sage.

Foweraker, Joe, and Todd Landman (1997) *Citizenship Rights and Social Movements: A Comparative and Statistical Analysis.* New York: Oxford University Press.

Foweraker, Joe, and Todd Landman (1999) "Individual Rights and Social Movements: A Comparative and Statistical Inquiry," *British Journal of Political Science*, 29(2): 291–322.

Frakt, Phyllis, M. (1977) "Democracy, Political Activity, Economic Development, and Governmental Responsiveness: The Case of Labor Policy," *Comparative Political Studies*, 10 (July): 177–212.

Franck, Thomas M. (1995) *Fairness in International Law and Institutions.* New York: Oxford University Press.

Frank, André Gunder (1967) *Capitalism and Development in Latin America: Historical Studies of Chile and Brazil.* New York: Monthly Review Press.

Franklin, James (1997) "IMF Conditionality, Threat Perception and Political Repression," *Comparative Political Studies*, 30(5): 576–606.

Freedom House (1978–) *Freedom in the World: Political Rights and Civil Liberties*. Lanham, MD: Freedom House, annual.

Freud, Sigmund (1930) *Civilization and Its Discontents*. London: Hogarth.

Frey, R. Scott, and Ali Al-Roumi (1999) Political Democracy and the Physical Quality of Life: The Cross-National Evidence," *Social Indicators Research*, 47(1): 73–97.

Friedman, Milton (1988) "A Statistical Note on the Gastil Survey of Freedom." In *Freedom in the World*, ed. Raymond D. Gastil, pp. 183–7. Lanham, MD: Freedom House.

Gartner, Scott Sigmund, and Patrick M. Regan (1996) "Threat and Repression," *Journal of Peace Research*, 33(3): 273–87.

Gastil, Raymond D. (1973) "Comparative Survey of Freedom," *Freedom at Issue*, 14:4.

Gibney, Mark, and Matthew Dalton (1996) "The Political Terror Scale," in *Human Rights and Developing Countries*, ed. David Louis Cingranelli, pp. 73–84. Greenwich, CT: JAI Press.

Goldstein, Robert J. (1986) "The Limitations of Using Quantitative Data in Studying Human Rights Abuses," *Human Rights Quarterly*, 8 (November): 607–27.

Green, Maria (2001) "What We Talk About When We Talk About Indicators: Current Approaches to Human Rights Measurement," *Human Rights Quarterly*, 23(4): 1062–97.

Gupta, Dipak K., Albert J. Jongman, and Alex P. Schmid (1994) "Creating a Composite Index for Assessing Country Performance in the Field of Human Rights: Proposal for a New Methodology," *Human Rights Quarterly* 16(1): 131–62.

Gurr, Ted Robert (1966) *New Error-Compensated Measures for Comparing Nations: Some Correlates of Civil Violence*. Princeton, NJ: Center of International Studies, Princeton University.

Gurr, Ted Robert (1970) *Why Men Rebel*. Princeton, NJ: Princeton University Press.

Gurr, Ted Robert (1986) "The Political Origins of State Violence and Terror: A Theoretical Analysis." In *Government Violence and Repression: An Agenda for Research*, eds. Michael Stohl and George A. Lopez, pp. 45–71. Westport, CT: Greenwood.

Gurr, Ted Robert (1988) "War, Revolution, and the Growth of the Coercive State," *Comparative Political Studies*, 21 (April): 45–65.

Gurr, Ted Robert (1993) *Minorities at Risk: A Global View of Ethnopolitical Conflicts*. Washington, DC: U.S. Institute of Peace.

Gurr, Ted Robert, and Erika B. K. Gurr (1983) "Group Discrimination and Potential Separatism in 1960 and 1975." In *World Handbook of Political and Social Indicators*, 3rd ed., eds. Charles L. Taylor and David Jodice, 1: 50–7, 66–75. New Haven, CT: Yale University Press.

Haas, Ernst B. (1958) *The Uniting of Europe: Political, Social, and Economic Forces, 1950–1957*. Stanford, CA: Stanford University Press.

Haas, Ernst B. (1964) *Beyond the Nation State: Functionalism and International Organization*. Stanford, CA: Stanford University Press.

Haas, Ernst B. (1970) *Human Rights and International Action*. Stanford, CA: Stanford University Press.

Haas, Ernst B. (1990) *When Knowledge is Power: Three Models of Change in International Organizations*. Berkeley: University of California Press.

Haas, Michael (1992) *Polity and Society: Philosophical Underpinnings of Social Science Paradigms*. Westport, CT: Praeger.

Haas, Michael (1994) *Improving Human Rights*. Westport, CT: Praeger.

Haas, Michael (1996) "Empirical Dimensions of Human Rights." In *Human Rights and Developing Countries*, ed. D. L. Cingranelli, pp. 43–73. Greenwich, CT: JAI Press.

Haas, Michael (2007) "From Human Rights Numbercrunching to Human Rights Theory," Paper Archive of the International Studies Association annual convention website.

Hadenius, Axel (1992) *Democracy and Development*. New York: Cambridge University Press.

Hafner-Burton, Emilie M. (2005a) "Right or Robust? The Sensitive Nature of Repression to Globalization," *Journal of Peace Research*, 42(6): 679–98.

Hafner-Burton, Emilie M. (2005b) "Trading Human Rights: How Preferential Trade Agreements Influence Government Repression," *International Organization*, 59(30): 593–629.

Hafner-Burton, Emilie M., and Kiyoteru Tsutsui, K. (2005) "Human Rights in a Globalizing World: The Paradox of Empty Promises," *American Journal of Sociology*, 110 (March): 1373–412.

Harff, Barbara (1986) "Genocide as State Terrorism." In *Government Violence and Repression: An Agenda for Research*, eds. Michaell Stohl and George Lopez, chap. 6. Westport, CT: Greenwood.

Harff, Barbara and Ted Robert Gurr, (1988) "Toward an Empirical Theory of Genocides and Politicides: Identification and Measurement of Cases Since 1945," *International Studies Quarterly*, 32(3): 359–71.

Harvey, David (2005) *A Brief History of Neoliberalism*. New York: Oxford University Press.

Hathaway, Oona (2002) "Do Treaties Make a Difference? Human Rights Treaties and the Problem of Compliance," *Yale Law Journal*, 111(8): 1935–2042.

Henderson, Conway W. (1982) "Military Regimes and Rights in Developing Countries," *Human Rights Quarterly*, 4(1): 110–23.

Henderson, Conway W. (1991) "Conditions Affecting the Use of Political Repression," *Journal of Conflict Resolution*, 35(1): 120–42.

Henderson, Conway W. (1993) "Population Pressures and Political Repression," *Social Science Quarterly*, 74(2): 322–37.

Hertel, Shareen (2006) "Why Bother? Measuring Economic Rights: The Research Agenda," *International Studies Perspectives*, 7(August): 215–30.

Hewitt, Christopher (1977) "The Effect of Political Democracy and Social Democracy on Equality in Industrial Societies," *American Sociological Review*, 42 (June): 450–64.

Hibbs, Douglas A., Jr. (1973) *Mass Political Violence: A Cross-National Causal Analysis*. New York: Wiley.

Hicks, Alexander (1988) "Social Democracy, Corporatism and Economic Growth," *Journal of Politics*, 50(August): 677–704.

Hoffenbert, Richard I., and David Louis Cingranelli (1996) "Democratic Institutions and Respect for Human Rights." In *Human Rights and Developing Countries*, ed. David Louis Cingranelli, pp. 145–59. Greenwich, CT: JAI Press.

Hofrenning, Daniel J. B. (1990) "Human Rights and Foreign Aid: A Comparison of the Reagan and Carter Administrations," *American Politics Quarterly*, 18(4): 514–26.

Horowitz, Irving Louis (1976) *Genocide: State Power and Mass Murder*. New Brunswick, NJ: Transaction. (The third edition in 1980 was retitled *Taking Lives*.)

Howard, Rhoda E. (1990) "Monitoring Human Rights: Problems of Consistency," *Ethics and International Affairs*, 4: 33–51.

Human Rights First (2003) *Holding the Line: A Critique of the Department of State's Annual Reports (for 2002) on Human Rights Practices*. (www.humanrightsfirst.org/pubs/descriptions/holdingtheline.pdf).

Humana, Charles (1983) *World Human Rights Guide*. 1st ed. New York: Pica Press.

Humana, Charles (1987) *World Human Rights Guide*. 2nd ed. New York: Pan Books.

Humana, Charles (1992) *World Human Rights Guide*. 3rd ed. New York: Oxford University Press.

Huntington, Samuel P. (1968) *Political Order in Changing Societies*. New Haven, CT: Yale University Press.

Innes, Judith E. (1992) "Human Rights Reporting as a Policy Tool: An Examination of the State Department Country Reports." In *Human Rights and Statistics: Getting the Record Straight*, eds. Thomas B. Jabine and Richard P. Claude, chap. 9. Philadelphia: University of Pennsylvania Press.

International Association for Official Statistics (2000) Conference on Statistics, Development and Human Rights, Montreaux (www.iaos2000.admin.ch).

Jackman, Robert W. (1975) *Politics and Social Equality: A Comparative Analysis*. New York: Wiley.

Johnson, M. Glen (1988) "Human Rights in Divergent Conceptual Settings: How Do Ideas Influence Policy Choices?" In *Human Rights: Theory and Measurement*, ed. David L. Cingranelli, chap. 2. New York: St. Martin's Press.

Keith, Linda Camp (2002) "Constitutional Provisions for Individual Human Rights (1977–1996): Are They More than Mere 'Window Dressing'?" *Political Research Quarterly*, 55(1): 111–43.

Keith, Linda Camp, and Steven C. Poe (2000) "The United States, the IMF, and Human Rights: A Policy-Relevant Approach." In *The United States and Human Rights: Looking Inward and Outward*, ed. David P. Forsythe, pp. 273–99. Lincoln: University of Nebraska Press.

Kerr, Clark, John T. Dunlop, Frederick H. Harbison, and Charles A. Myers (1964) *Industrialism and the Industrial State*. New York: Oxford University Press.

Koh, Harold Hongju (1997) "Why Do Nations Obey International Law?," *Yale Law Journal*, 106(8): 2599–659.

Kolakowski, Leszek (1983) "Marxism and Human Rights," *Daedalus*, 112 (Fall): 81–92.

Kornhauser, William (1959) *The Politics of Mass Society*. Glencoe, IL: Free Press.

Kuper, Leo (1981) *Genocide: Its Political Use in the Twentieth Century*. New Haven, CT: Yale University Press.

Lai, Brian (2003) "Examining the Goals of US Foreign Assistance in the Post-Cold War Period, 1991–96," *Journal of Peace Research*, 40(1): 103–28.

Landman, Todd (2005) *Protecting Human Rights: A Comparative Study*. Washington, DC: Georgetown University Press.

Lawyers Committee for Human Rights (2003) *Holding the Line: A Critique of the U.S. Department of State's Annual Reports on Human Rights Practices for 2002*. New York: Lawyer's Committee for Human Rights.

Lawyers Committee for International Human Rights (1982) *A Critique of the Department of State's Country Reports on Human Rights Practices for 1981*. New York: Lawyers Committee for International Human Rights.

Lebovic, James H. (1988) "National Interests and US Foreign Aid: The Carter and Reagan Years," *Journal of Peace Research*, 25(2): 115–33.

Lee Hsien Long (1987) *When the Press Misinforms*. Singapore: Information Division, Ministry of Commerce and Industry.

Lenin, Vladimir I. (1917) *Imperialism: The Highest Stage of Capitalism*. Peking: People's Publishing House, 1964.

Lenski, Gerhard (1966) *Power and Privilege: A Theory of Social Stratification*. New York: McGraw-Hill.

Lerner, Daniel (1958) *The Passing of Traditional Society: Modernizing the Middle East*. New York: Free Press.

Lifton, Robert J. (1986) *The Nazi Doctors: Medical Killing and the Psychology of Genocide*. New York: Basic Books.

Lindblom, Charles E. (1977) *Politics and Markets: The World's Political Economic Systems*. New York: Basic Books.

Lipset, Seymour M. (1959) "Some Social Requisites of Democracy: Economic Development and Political Legitimacy," *American Political Science Review*, 53 (March): 69–105.

Lizhi, Fang (1990) "The Chinese Amnesia," *New York Review of Books*, 37 (October 27): 30–1.

Locke, John (1688) *Second Treatise of Government*. Cambridge, UK: Cambridge University Press, 1967.

London, Bruce, and Bruce A. Williams (1988) "Multinational Corporate Penetration, Protest, and Basic Needs Provision in Non-Core Nations: A Cross-National Analysis," *Social Forces*, 66(3): 747–73.

Lopez, George A., and Michael Stohl (1992) "Problems of Concept and Measurement in the Study of Human Rights." In *Human Rights and Statistics: Getting the Record Straight*, eds. Thomas B. Jabine and Richard P. Claude, chap. 8. Philadelphia: University of Pennsylvania Press.

Lowenstein, Ralph L. (1967) *Measuring World Press Freedom as a Political Indicator*. Columbia, MO: Ph.D. dissertation, University of Missouri.

McCamant, John F. (1981) "A Critique of Present Measures of 'Human Rights Development' and an Alternative." In *Global Human Rights: Public Policies, Comparative Measures, and NGO Strategies*, eds. Ved P. Nanda, James R. Scarritt, and George W. Shepherd, Jr., chap. 9. Boulder, CO: Westview.

McCann, James A., and Mark Gibney (1996) "An Overview of Political Terror in the Developing World, 1980–1991." In *Human Rights and Developing Countries*, ed. David Louis Cingranelli, pp. 15–27. Greenwich, CT: JAI Press.

McCormick, James, and Neal Mitchell (1997) "Human Rights Violations, Umbrella Concepts, and Empirical Analysis," *World Politics*, 49(4): 510–25.

McCrone, Donald J., and Cnudde, Charles F. (1967) "Toward a Communications Theory of Democratic Political Development," *American Political Science Review*, 61(March): 72–9.

McKinley, R.D., and R. Little (1979) "The US AID Relationship: A Test of the Recipient Need and Donor Interest Models," *Political Studies*, 27(2): 236–50.

McNitt, Andrew D. (1988) "Some Thoughts on the Systematic Measurement of the Abuse of Human Rights." In *Human Rights: Theory and Measurement*, ed. David L. Cingranelli, chap. 8. New York: St. Martin's Press.

Marcuse, Herbert (1955) *Eros and Civilization: A Philosophical Inquiry into Freud*. Boston: Beacon.

Marshall, Monty, and Keith Jaggers (2000) *Polity IV: Political Regime Characteristics and Transitions, 1800–1999*. College Park, MD: Integrate Network for Societal Conflict. (The data are updated from time to time.)

381

Marx, Karl, and Friedrich Engels (1848) *Manifesto of the Communist Party*. Reprinted in *The Marx-Engels Reader*, ed. Robert C. Tucker, pp. 331–62. New York: Norton.

Mazian, Florence (1990) *Why Genocide? The Armenian and Jewish Experiences in Perspective*. Ames: Iowa State University Press.

Meernik, James, Eric L. Krueger, and Steven C. Poe (1998) "Testing Models of U.S. Foreign Policy: Foreign Aid During and After the Cold War," *Journal of Politics*, 60(1): 63–85.

Meyer, William H. (1996) "Human Rights and MNCs: Theory Versus Quantitative Analysis," *Human Rights Quarterly*, 18(2): 368–97.

Michels, Roberto (1915) *Political Parties*. New York: Collier.

Mills, C. Wright (1956) *The Power Elite*. New York: Oxford University Press.

Mitchell, Christopher, Michael Stohl, David Carleton and George A. Lopez (1986) "State Terrorism: Issues of Concept and Measurement." In *Government Violence and Repression: An Agenda for Research*, eds. Michael Stohl and George A. Lopez, chap. 1. Westport, CT: Greenwood.

Mitchell, Neil J., and James M. McCormick (1988) "Economic and Political Explanations of Human Rights Violations," *World Politics*, 40(4): 476–98.

Mitrany, David (1943) *A Working Peace System: An Argument for the Functional Development of International Organization*. New York: Oxford University Press.

Moaddel, Mansoor (1994) "Political Conflict in the World Economy: A Cross-National Analysis of Modernization and World-System Theories," *American Sociological Review*, 59 (April): 276–303.

Moon, Bruce E., and William J. Dixon (1985) "Politics, the State, and Basic Human Needs: A Cross-National Study," *American Journal of Political Science*, 29(4): 661–94.

Moravcsik, Andrew (2000) "The Origin of Human Rights Regimes: Democratic Delegation in Postwar Europe," *International Organization*, 54(4): 217–52.

Morgenthau, Hans J. (1979) *Human Rights and Foreign Policy*. New York: Council on Foreign Relations.

Morris, Morris David (1979) *Measuring Conditions of the World's Poor: The Physical Quality of Life Index*. New York: Pergamon.

Morris, Morris David (1996) "World's Poor are Better off Despite Misleading Economic Measures," *Austin American Statesman*, August 22: A15.

Mosca, Gaetano (1896) *The Ruling Class*. New York: McGraw-Hill, 1939.

Muller, Edward N. (1988) "Democracy, Economic Development, and Income Inequality," *American Sociological Review*, 53 (February): 50–68.

Myrdal, Gunnar (1957) *Economic Theory and Under-Developed Regions*. London: Duckworth.

Nesvold, Betty A. (1969) "Scalogram Analysis of Political Violence," *Comparative Political Studies*, 2(July): 172–94.

Neubauer, Deane E. (1967) "Some Conditions of Democracy," *American Political Science Review*, 41 (December): 1002–9.

Neumayer, Eric (2003a) "Do Human Rights Matter in Bilateral Aid Allocation? A Quantitative Analysis of 21 Donor Countries," *Social Science Quarterly*, 84(3): 650–66.

Neumayer, Eric (2003b) "Is Respect for Human Rights Rewarded? An Analysis of Total Bilateral and Multilateral Aid Flows," *Human Rights Quarterly*, 25(2): 510–27.

Neumayer, Eric (2005) "Do International Human Rights Treaties Improve Respect for Human Rights?," *Journal of Conflict Resolution*, 49(6): 925–53.

Nincic, Miroslaw (2006) "The Logic of Positive Engagement: Dealing with Renegade Regimes," *International Studies Perspectives*, 7(4): 321–41.

Nixon, Raymond B. (1960) "Factors Related to Freedom in National Press Systems," *Journalism Quarterly*, 37 (Winter): 13–28.

Nixon, Raymond B. (1965) "Freedom in the World's Press: A Fresh Appraisal with New Data," *Journalism Quarterly*, 42 (Winter): 3–5,118–19.

Nye, Joseph S., Jr. (2004) *Soft Power: The Means to Success in World Politics*. New York: Public Affairs Press.

Ogwang, Tomson (1997) "The Choice of Principal Variables for Computing the Physical Quality of Life Index," *Journal of Economic and Social Measurement*," 23(3): 213–22.

Organski, A. F. K. (1965) *The Stages of Political Development*. New York: Knopf.

Pareto, Vilfredo (1916) *The Mind and Society*. New York: Harcourt, Brace, 1935.

Park, Han S. (1987) "Correlates of Human Rights," *Human Rights Quarterly*, 9(3): 405–13.

Pasquarello, Thomas E. (1986) "Human Rights and US Bilateral Aid Allocations to Africa." In *Human Rights: Theory and Measurement*, ed. David L. Cingranelli, chap. 14. New York: St. Martin's Press.

Payaslian, Simon (1996) "Human Rights and U.S. Bilateral Assistance to Developing Countries: The Bush Administration, 1989–1990." In *Human Rights and Developing Countries*, ed. David Louis Cingranelli, pp. 163–81. Greenwich, CT: JAI Press.

Poe, Steven C. (1991a) "Human Rights and the Allocation of US Military Assistance," *Journal of Peace Research*, 28(2): 205–16.

Poe, Steven C. (1991b) "U. S. Economic Aid Allocation: The Quest for Cumulation," *International Interactions*, 16(4): 295–316.

Poe, Steven C. (1992) "Human Rights and the Allocation of US Military Aid Allocation Under Ronald Reagan and Jimmy Carter," *American Journal of Political Science*, 36(1): 146–67.

Poe, Steven C. and James Meernik (1995) "U.S. Military Aid in the 1980s: A Global Analysis," *Journal of Peace Research*, 32(4): 399–411.

Poe, Steven C., and Rangsima Sirirangsi (1992) "Human Rights and US Economic Aid to Africa," *International Interactions*, 18(4): 309–22.

Poe, Steven C., and Rangsima Sirirangsi (1994) "Human Rights and US Economic Aid During the Reagan Years," *Social Science Quarterly*, 75(3): 494–509.

Poe, Steven C., and Neal Tate (1994) "Repression of Human Rights to Personal Integrity in the 1980s: A Global Analysis," *American Political Science Review*, 88(4): 476–98.

Poe, Steven C., Deirdre Wendel-Blunt, and Karl Ho (1997) "Global Patterns in the Achievement of Women's Human Rights to Equality," *Human Rights Quarterly*, 19(4): 813–35.

Poe, Steven C., Neal Tate, and Linda Camp Keith (1999) "Repression of the Human Right to Personal Integrity Revisited: A Global Cross-National Study Covering the Years 1976–1993," *International Studies Quarterly*, 43(2): 291–313.

Poe, Steven C., Suzanne Pilatovsky, Brian Miller, and Ayo Ogundele (1994) "Human Rights and US Foreign Aid Revisited: The Latin American Region," *Human Rights Quarterly*, 16(3): 539–58.

Poe, Steven C., Sabine C. Carey, and Tanya C. Vazquez (2001) "How Are These Pictures Different? A Quantitative Comparison of the U.S. State Department and Amnesty International Human Rights Reports, 1976–1995," *Human Rights Quarterly*, 23(3): 650–77.

Population Crisis Committee (1987) *The International Human Suffering Index*. Washington, DC: Population Crisis Committee.

Population Crisis Committee (1992) *The International Human Suffering Index*. Washington, DC: Population Crisis Committee.

Pourgerami, Abbas (1992) "Authoritarian Versus Nonauathoritarian Approaches to Economic Development: Update and Additional Evidence," *Public Choice*, 74(3): 365–77.

Pritchard, Kathleen (1988) "Comparative Human Rights: Promise and Practice." In *Human Rights: Theory and Measurement*, ed. David L. Cingranelli, chap. 8. New York: St. Martin's Press.

Pritchard, Kathleen (1989) "Human Rights and Development." In *Human Rights and Development: International Views*, ed. David P. Forsythe, chap. 19. New York: St. Martin's Press.

Raworth, Kate (2001) "Measuring Human Rights," *Ethics and International Affairs*, 15(1): 111–32.

Regan, Patrick M. (1995) "U.S. Economic Aid and Political Repression," *Political Research Quarterly*, 48(3): 613–28.

Richards, David L. (1999) "Perilous Proxy: Human Rights and the Presence of National Elections," *Social Science Quarterly*, 80(4): 648–65.

Richards, David L., Ronald D. Gelleny, and David H. Sacko (2001) "Money with a Mean Streak? Foreign Economic Penetration and Government Respect for Human Rights in Developing Countries." *International Studies Quarterly*, 45(2): 219–39.

Rosh, Robert M. (1986) "Militarization, Human Rights and Basic Needs in the Third World." *Human Rights: Theory and Measurement*, ed. David L. Cingranelli, chap. 11. New York: St. Martin's Press.

Rubin, Barnett R., and Paula R. Newberg (1980) "Statistical Analysis for Implementing Human Rights Policy." In *The Politics of Human Rights*, ed. Paula R. Newberg, pp. 268–84. New York: New York University Press.

Rubison, Richard (1976) "The World-Economy and the Distribution of Income Within States: A Cross-National Study," *American Sociological Review*, 41 (August): 639–59.

Ruggie, John Gerard, ed. (1993) *Multilateralism Matters: The Theory and Praxis of an Institutional Form*. New York: Columbia University Press.

Rummel, R. J. (1972) *The Dimensions of Nations*. Beverly Hills: Sage.

Rummel, R. J. (1983) "Libertarianism and International Violence," *Journal of Conflict Resolution*, 27(1): 27–71.

Russett, Bruce N., Hayward R. Alker, Jr., Karl W. Deutsch, and Harold D. Lasswell (1964) *World Handbook of Political and Social Indicators*. 1st ed. New Haven, CT: Yale University Press.

Rustow, Dankwart A. (1967) *World of Nations: Problems of Political Modernization*. Washington, DC: Brookings.

Samuelson, Douglas A., and Herbert F. Spirer (1992) "Use of Incomplete and Distorted Data in Inference About Human Rights Violations." In *Human Rights and Statistics: Getting the Record Straight*, eds. Thomas B. Jabine and Richard P. Claude, chap. 3. Philadelphia: University of Pennsylvania Press.

Schoultz, Lars (1981a) "U.S. Foreign Policy and Human Rights Violations in Latin America," *Comparative Politics*, 13(January): 149–70.

Schoultz, Lars (1981b) "U.S. Policy Toward Human Rights in Latin America: A Comparative Analysis of Two Administrations." In *Global Human Rights: Public Policies, Comparative Measures, and NGO Strategies*, eds. Ved P. Nanda, James R. Scarritt, and George Shepherd, Jr., chap. 6. Boulder, CO: Westview.

Scoble, Harry M. and Laurie S. Wiseberg (1981) "Problems of Comparative Research on Human Rights," in Ved P. Nanda, James R. Scarritt, and George W. Shepherd, Jr., eds., *Global Human Rights: Public Policies, Comparative Measures, and NGO Strategies*, pp. 147–71. Boulder, CO: Westview.

Simmons, Beth A. (forthcoming) *International Human Rights: Law, Politics and Accountability*.

Singer, J. David (1961) "The Level of Analysis Problem in International Relations," *World Politics*, 14(1): 77–92.

Sivard, Ruth Leger (1975–) *World Military and Social Expenditures*. Washington, DC: World Priorities, annual.

Smith, Adam (1776) *An Inquiry into the Nature and Causes of the Wealth of Nations*. New York: Modern Library, 1937.

Smith, Arthur K., Jr. (1969) "Socio-Economic Development and Political Democracy: A Causal Analysis," *American Journal of Political Science*, 13(February): 95–125.

Spalding, Nancy L. (1988) "Democracy and Human Rights in the Third World." In *Human Rights: Theory and Measurement*, ed. David L. Cingranelli, chap. 10. New York: St. Martin's Press.

Spalding, Nancy L. (1996) "Structural Adjustment Policies and Economic Human rights in Africa." In *Human Rights and Developing Countries*, ed. David Louis Cingranelli, pp. 193–210. Greenwich, CT: JAI Press.

Spirer, Herbert F. (1990) "Violations of Human rights – How Many? The Statistical Problems of Measuring Such Infractions Are Tough, But Statistical Science Is Equal to It," *American Journal of Economics and Sociology*, 49(2): 199–210.

Stack, Steven (1978) "International Political Organization and the World Economy of Income Inequality," *American Sociological Review*, 43 (April): 271–2.

Staub, Ervin (1989) *The Roots of Evil: The Psychological and Cultural Origins of Genocide and Other Forms of Group Violence*. Cambridge, UK: Cambridge University Press.

Stohl, Michael (1986) "The Superpowers and International Terrorism." In *Government Violence and Repression*, eds. Michael Stohl and George A. Lopez, chap. 8. New York: Greenwood.

Stohl, Michael, David Carleton, and Steven E. Johnson (1984) "Human Rights and U.S. Foreign Assistance from Nixon to Carter," *Journal of Peace Research*, 21(3): 215–26.

Stohl, Michael, David Carleton, George A. Lopez, and Stephen Samuels (1986) "State Violations of Human Rights: Issues and Problems of Measurement," *Human Rights Quarterly*, 8 (November): 592–606.

Strouse, James C., and Richard P. Claude, eds. (1976) *Comparative Human Rights*. Baltimore, MD: Johns Hopkins University Press.

Svensson, Jakob (1999) "Aid, Growth and Democracy," *Economics and Politics*, 11(3): 275–97.

Taylor, Charles Lewis, and Michael C. Hudson (1972) *World Handbook of Political and Social Indicators*, 2nd ed. New Haven, CT: Yale University Press.

Taylor, Charles Lewis, and David A. Jodice, eds. (1983) *World Handbook of Political and Social Indicators*. 3rd ed. New Haven, CT: Yale University Press.

Tilly, Charles (1978) *From Mobilization to Revolution*. Reading, MA: Addison-Wesley.

Timberlake, Michael, and Kirk R. Williams (1984) "Dependence, Political Exclusion, and Government Repression: Some Cross-National Evidence, " *American Sociological Review*, 49(1): 141–6.

Tomaševski, Katarina (1992) "A Critique of the UNDP Political Freedom Index 1991." In Bård-Anders Andreassen and Theresa Swinehart, eds., *Human Rights in Developing Countries Yearbook 1991*, pp. 3–24. Oslo: Scandinavian University Press.

Tomaševski, Katarina (1997) *Between Sanctions and Elections: Aid Donors and Their Human Rights Performance*. Washington, DC: Pinter.

Travis, Rick (1995) "U. S. Security Assistance Policy and Democracy: A Look at the 1980s," *Journal of Developing Areas*, 29(4): 541–62.

Trumbull, William N. and Howard J. Wall (1994) "Estimating Aid-Allocation Criteria with Panel Data," *Economic Journal*, 104 (July): 876–82.

Tsutsui, Kiyoteru, and Christine Min Wotipka (2004) "Global Civil Society and the International Human Rights Movement: Citizen Participation in Human Rights International Nongovernmental Organizations," *Social Forces*, 83(2): 587–620.

United Nations Development Program (1990–) *Human Development Report*. New York: Oxford University Press, annual.

United Nations Statistical Office (1948–) *Statistical Yearbook*. New York: United Nations, annual.

United States, Department of Health and Human Services (1958–) *Social Security Programs Throughout the World*. Washington, DC: Social Security Administration Research Report series, biennial.

United States, Department of State (1975–) *Country Reports on Human Rights Practices*. Washington, DC: Government Printing Office, annual.

United States, Department of State (1999–) *Annual Report to Congress on International Religious Freedom*. Washington, DC: Government Printing Office, annual.

Valverde, Gilbert A. (1999) "Democracy, Human Rights, and Development Assistance for Education: The USAID and World Bank in Latin America and the Caribbean," *Economic Development and Cultural Change*, 47(2): 401–18.

Van Den Berghe, Pierre L. (1981) *The Ethnic Phenomenon*. New York: Elsevier.

Vanhanen, Tatu (2000) "A New Dataset for Measuring Democracy, 1810–1998," *Journal of Peace Research*, 37(2): 251–65.

Vorhies, Frank, and Fred Glahe (1988) "Liberty and Social Progress: A Geographical Examination." In *Freedom in the World*, pp. 189–201. Lanham, MD: Freedom House.

Walker, Scott, and Steven C. Poe (2002) "Does Cultural Diversity Affect Countries' Respect for Human Rights?," *Human Rights Quarterly*, 24(1): 237–63.

Watchirs, Helen (2002) "Review of Methodologies Measuring Human Rights Implementation," *Journal of Law, Medicine and Ethics*, 30(4): 716–34.

Weber, Max (1913) *The Theory of Social and Economic Organization*. Glencoe, IL: Free Press.

Weber, Max (1918) *Economy and Society: An Outline of Interpretive Sociology*. Berkeley: University of California Press, 1979.

Weede, Erich (1980) "Beyond Misspecification in Sociological Analyses of Income Inequality," *American Sociological Review*, 45 (June): 497–501.

Weiner, Myron (1987) "Empirical Democratic Theory." In *Competitive Elections in Developing Countries*, eds. Myron Weiner and Ergun Ozbudun, chap. 1. Durham, NC: Duke University Press.

Weisberg, Laurie S., and Harry M. Scoble (1981) "Problems of Comparative Research on Human Rights." In *Global Human Rights: Public Policies, Comparative Measures, and NGO Strategies*, eds. Ved P. Nanda, James R. Scarritt, and George Shepherd, Jr., chap. 10. Boulder, CO: Westview.

Wolpin, Miles (1986) "State Terrorism and Repression in the Third World: Parameters and Prospects." In *Government Violence and Repression*, eds. Michael Stohl and George A. Lopez, chap. 5. New York: Greenwood.

Zanger, Sabine C. (2000) "A Global Analysis of the Effect of Regime Change on Life Integrity Violations, 1977–1993," *Journal of Peace Research*, 37(2): 213–33.

Ziegenhagen, Eduard A. (1986) *The Regulation of Political Conflict*. New York: Praeger.

Ziegler, Harmon (1988) "The Interrelationships of Freedom, Equality, and Development." In *Freedom in the World*, pp. 203–28. Lanham, MD: Freedom House.

Zvobgo, Eddison J. M. (1979) "A Third World View." In *Human Rights and American Foreign Policy*, eds. Donald P. Kommers and Gilburt D. Loescher, chap. 5. Notre Dame, IN: University of Notre Dame Press.

CHAPTER 9

Abouharb, M. Rodwan, and David L. Cingranelli (2006) "The Human Rights Effects of World Bank Structural Adjustment, 1981–2000," *International Studies Quarterly*, 50 (June): 233–62.

Alexander, Michael (1999) "Refugee Status Determination Conducted by UNHCR," *International Journal of Refugee Law*, 11(April): 251–88.

Alfredsson, Gudmundur, and Rolf Ring, eds. (2000) *The Inspection Panel of the World Bank: A Different Complaints Procedure*. Leiden, Netherlands: Brill.

Arnove, Anthony, ed. (2002) *Iraq Under Siege: The Deadly Impact of Sanctions and War*. 2nd ed. Boston: South End Press.

Bain, William (2003) *Between Anarchy and Society: Trusteeship and the Obligations of Power*. New York: Oxford University Press.

Beitz, Charles (2003) "What Human Rights Means," *Daedalus*, 132(1): 36–46.

Bellamy, Carol, ed. (2004) *The State of the World's Children 2005: Childhood Under Threat*. United Nations: UNICEF.

Bellamy, Carol (2005) *Mental Health, Human Rights and Legislation*. United Nations: UNICEF.

Blustein, Paul (2001) *The Chastening: Inside the Crisis That Rocked the Global Financial System and Humbled the IMF*. New York: Public Affairs Press.

Bond, Patrick (2004) "Should the World Bank and the IMF Be 'Fixed' or "Nixed'? Reformist Posturing and Popular Resistance," *Capitalism, Nature, Socialism*, 15(June): 85–105.

Brysk, Alison, and Gershon Shafir, eds. (2004) *People out of Place: Globalization, Human Rights, and the Citizenship Gap*. New York: Routledge.

Buergenthal, Thomas, and Judith V. Torney (1976) *International Human Rights and International Education*. New York: U.S. National Commission for UNESCO.

Caplan, Richard (2005) *International Governance of War-Torn Territories: Rule and Reconstruction*. New York: Oxford University Press.

Clark, Dana L. (2002) "The World Bank and Human Rights," *Harvard Human Rights Journal*, 15 (Spring): 205–26.

Cohen, Roberta, and Francis M. Deep (1998) "Exodus Within Borders: The Uprooted Who Left Home," *Foreign Affairs*, 77(4): 12–16.

Colclough, Christopher (2005) "Rights, Goals and Targets: How Do Those for Education Add Up?," *Journal of International Development*, 27(1): 101–111.

Cortright, David, and George Lopez (2000) *The Sanctions Decade: Assessing UN Strategies in the 1990s*. Boulder, CO: Lynne Rienner.

Dallaire, Roméo (2004) *Shake Hands with the Devil: The Failure of Humanity in Rwanda*. New York: Carroll and Graf.

Daniel, Donald C. F., and Bradd C. Hayes, eds. (1995) *Beyond Traditional Peacekeeping*. New York: St. Martin's Press.

Dennis, Michael J. (2003) "Human Rights in 2002: The Annual Sessions of the UN Commission on Human Rights and the Economic and Social Council," *American Journal of International Law*, 97 (April): 364–86.

Darrow, Mac (2003) *Between Light and Shadow: The World Bank, the International Monetary Fund and International Human Rights Law*. Portland, OR: Hart-Oxford.

Flood, Patrick James (1998) *The Effectiveness of UN Human Rights Institutions*. Westport, CT: Praeger.

Green, Nick (2004) "Stonewalling Justice," *Harvard International Review*, 26 (Summer): 34–7.

Haas, Ernst B. (1964) *Beyond the Nation State: Functionalism and International Organization*. Stanford, CA: Stanford University Press.

Haas, Ernst B. (1970) *Human Rights and International Action: The Case of Freedom of Association*. Stanford, CA: Stanford University Press.

Haas, Peter (1992) "Epistemic Communities and International Policy Coordination," *International Organization*, 45(1): 1–35.

Horta, Korinna (2002) "Rhetoric and Reality: Human Rights and the World Bank," *Harvard Human Rights Journal*, 15 (Spring): 227–44.

Hüfner, Klaus (1998) *How to File Complaints on Human Rights Violations: A Manual for Individuals and NGOs*. Bonn: UNESCO National Commission for Germany.

Ignatieff, Michael (2003) *Empire Lite: Nation-Building in Bosnia, Kosovo and Afghanistan*. London: Vintage.

International Labour Organization (2005) *Rules of the Game: A Brief Introduction to International Labour Standards*. Geneva: International Labour Office.

Joyner, Christopher C. (1999) "The United Nations and Democracy," *Global Governance*, 5 (July–September): 333–57.

Kaufman, Daniel, Aart Kraay, and Pablo Zoido-Lobaton (1999) *Governance Matters*. Washington, DC: World Bank, Policy Research Working Paper 2196 (October).

Levovic, James H., and Eric Voeten (2006) "The Politics of Shame: The Condemnation of Country Human Rights Practices in the UNCHR," *International Studies Quarterly*, 56(4): 861–88.

Marquette, Heather (2001) "Corruption, Democracy and the World Bank," *Crime, Law and Social Change*, 36(4): 395–407.

Mattioli, Maria C., and V.K. Sapovadia (2004) "Laws of Labor," *Harvard International Review*, 26 (Summer): 60–4.

Oestreich, Joel E. (2004) "The Human Rights Responsibilities of the World Bank," *Global Social Policy*, 4(1): 55–76.

Ogata, Sadako N. (2005) *The Turbulent Decade: Confronting the Refugee Crises of the 1990s*. New York: Norton.

Ogata, Sakako N., and Barbara John (1996) *The Right of Asylum Must Be Strongly Upheld*. Berlin: Free University of Berlin.

Payer, Cheryl (1974) *The Debt Trap: The IMF and the Third World*. Harmondsworth, UK: Penguin Books.

Payer, Cheryl (1982) *The World Bank: A Critical Analysis*. New York: Monthly Review Press.

Perkins, John (2004) *Confessions of an Economic Hit Man*. San Francisco, CA: Berrett-Koehler Publishers.

Ramcharan, Bertrand G. (2002) *The United Nations High Commissioner for Human Rights: The Challenges of International Protection*. New York: Nijhoff.

Roberts, Alisdair (2004) "A Partial Revolution: The Diplomatic Ethos and Transparency in Intergovernmental Organizations," *Public Administrative Review*, 64 (July/August): 410–14.

Shawcross, William (2001) *Deliver Us from Evil: Peacekeepers, Warlords, and a World of Endless Conflict*. New York: Simon and Schuster.

Shelton, Dinah (2005) *Remedies in International Human Rights Law*. 2nd ed. New York: Oxford University Press.

Skogly, Sigrun (2000) *The Human Rights Obligations of the World Bank and the IMF*. London: Cavendish.

Stiglitz, Joseph E. (2002) *Globalization and Its Discontents*. New York: Norton.

Szasz, Paul C. (2002) "The Security Council Starts Legislating," *American Journal of International Law*, 96 (October): 901–5.

Tolley, Howard, Jr. (1987) *The U.N. Commission on Human Rights*. Boulder, CO: Westview.

Tomaševski, Katarina (1997) *Between Sanctions and Elections: Aid Donors and Their Human Rights Performance*. Washington, DC: Pinter.

van Genugten, Willem J. M., and Gerard A. de Groot, eds. (1999) *United Nations Sanctions: Effectiveness and Effects, Especially in the Field of Human Rights: A Multi-Disciplinary Approach*. Antwerp: Intersentia.

Wallensteen, Peter, and Carina Staibano (2005) *International Sanctions: Between Words and Wars in the Global System*. New York: Cass.

Weissbrodt, David, and Rose Farley (1994) "The UNESCO Human Rights Procedure: An Evaluation," *Human Rights Quarterly*, 14(2): 391–414.

Wilde, Ralph (2001) "From Danzig to East Timor and Beyond: The Role of International Territorial Administration," *European Journal of International Law*, 95 (July): 583–606.

Williams, Sope (2002) "The International Human Rights Obligations of the World Bank and the International Monetary Fund," *Journal of Financial Regulation and Compliance*, 10(2): 195–99.

Winslow, Anne, ed. (1995) *Women, Politics, and the United Nations*. Westport, CT: Greenwood.

World Bank (2003) *Accountability at the World Bank: The Inspection Panel 10 Years On*. Washington, DC: World Bank.

Zhang, Ruosi (2004) "Food Security: Food Trade Regime and Food Aid Regime," *Journal of International Economic Law*, 7(3): 565–84.

Zinn, Howard (2003) *A People's History of the United States*. New York: HarperCollins.

CHAPTER 10

Attanasio, John B. (1995–1996) "Rapporteur's Overview and Conclusion: of Sovereignty, Globalization, and Courts," *New York University Journal of International Law and Politics*, 28(1): 1–33.

Bass, Gary J. (2000) *Stay the Hand of Vengeance: The Politics of War Crimes Tribunals*. Princeton, NJ. Princeton University Press.

Bayefsky, Anne F., ed. (2000) *The UN Human Rights Treaty System in the 21st Century*. Boston: Kluwer Law International.

Bedjaoui, Mohammed (1995–1996) "The Reception by National Courts of Decisions of International Tribunals," *New York University Journal of International Law and Politics*, 28(1): 45–64.

Butler, Israel de Jesús (2004) "A Comparative Analysis of Individual Petitions in Regional and Global Human Rights Protection Mechanisms," *University of Queensland Law Journal*, 23(1): 22–53.

Charnovitz, Steve (1994) "The World Trade Organization and Social Issues," *Journal of World Trade*, 28(5): 17–33.

Doughtery, Beth (2004) "Victims' Justice, Victors' Justice: Iraq's Flawed Tribunal," *Middle East Policy*, 11(2): 61–74.

Evatt, Elizabeth (2002) "Finding a Voice for Women's Rights: The Early Years of CEDAW," *George Washington International Law Review*, 34(3): 515–53.

Gow, James (2003) *The Serbian Project and Its Adversaries: A Strategy of War Crimes*. London: Hurst.

Heyns, Christof, and Frans Viljoen, eds. (2002) *The Impact of the United Nations Human Rights Treaties at the Domestic Level*. Boston: Kluwer Law International.

Keith, Linda Camp (1999) "The United Nations International Covenant on Civil and Political Rights: Does It Make a Difference in Human Rights Behavior?," *Journal of Peace Research*, 36(1): 95–118.

Kirsche, Philippe (2004) "The Role and Functions of the International Criminal Court," *World Affairs Journal*, 16(1): 111–18.

López-Hurtado, Carlos (2002) "Social Labelling and WTO Law," *Journal of International Economic Law*, 5(3): 719–46.

Petersmann, Ernst-Ulrich (2003) "Human Rights and the Law of the World Trade Organization," *Journal of World Trade*, 37(2): 241–81.

Rodley, Nigel S. (2003) United Nations Human Rights Treaty Bodies and Special Procedures of the Commission on Human Rights: Complimentarily or Competition?" *Human Rights Quarterly*, 25(4): 882–908.

Roth, Kenneth (1998) "The Court the U.S. Doesn't Want," *New York Review of Books*, 45(18): 45–47.

Sands, Philippe, ed. (2003) *Pluralizing International Criminal Justice from Nuremberg to The Hague: The Future of International Criminal Justice*. Cambridge, UK: Cambridge University Press.

Simmons, Beth A. (forthcoming) *International Human Rights: Law, Politics and Accountability*.

Sivakumaran, Sandesh (2004) "The Rights of Migrant Workers One Year On: Transformation or Consolidation?" *Georgetown Journal of International Law*, 36 (Fall): 113–53.

Slaughter, Anne-Marie (2000) "Judicial Globalization," *Virginia Journal of International Law*, 40(4): 1103–24.

Zoglin, Katie (2005) "The Future of War Crimes Prosecution in the Former Yugoslavia: Accountability or Junk Justice?" *Human Rights Quarterly*, 25(1): 41–77.

CHAPTER 11

Anker, Deborah E. (1999) *The Law of Asylum in the United States*. 3rd ed. Boston, MA: Refugee Law Center.

Apodaca, Clair (2006) *Understanding U.S. Human Rights Policy: A Paradoxical Legacy*. New York: Routledge.

Askari, Hossein G. (2003) *Case Studies of U.S. Economic Sanctions: The Chinese, Cuban, and Iranian Experience*. Westport, CT: Praeger.

Barkan, Elazar (2000) *The Guilt of Nations: Restitution and Negotiating Historical Injustices*. New York: Norton.

Bazyler, Michael J. (2003) *Holocaust Justice: The Battle for Restitution in America's Courts*. New York: New York University Press.

Bluhm, William (2002) Rogue State: *A Guide to the World's Only Superpower*. London: Zed Books.

Burgermann, Susan (2004) "First Do No Harm: U.S. Foreign Policy and Respect for Human Rights in El Salvador and Guatemala." In *Implementing U.S. Human Rights Policy*, ed. Debra Liang-Fenton, pp. 267–98. Washington, DC: U.S. Institute of Peace Press.

Chatterjee, Deen K., and Don E. Scheid, eds. (2003) *Ethics and Foreign Intervention*. Cambridge, UK: Cambridge University Press.

Chung, Ellen Y. (2002) "A Double-Edged Sword: Reconciling the United States' International Obligations Under the Convention Against Torture," *Emory Law Journal*, 51 (Winter): 355–78.

Danner, Mark (2004) *Torture and Truth: America, Abu Ghraib, and the War on Terror*. New York: New York Review Books.

de Grazia, Victoria (2006) *Irresistible Empire: America's Advance Through Twentieth-Century Europe*. Cambridge, MA: Belknap.

Diven, Polly (2006) "A Coincidence of Interests: The Hyperpluralism of U.S. Food Aid Policy," *Foreign Policy Analysis*, 2(2006): 307–24.

Dobson, Alan P. (2002) *US Economic Statecraft for Survival, 1933–1991: Of Sanctions, Embargoes, and Economic Warfare*. New York: Routledge.

Drury, A. Cooper, and Yitan Li (2006) "U.S. Economic Sanction Threats Against China: Failing to Leverage Better Human Rights," *Foreign Policy Analysis*, 2(October): 307–24.

EarthRights International (2004) *In Our Court: ATCA, Sosa, and the Triumph of Human Rights*. Washington, DC: EarthRights International.

Eizenstat, Stuart E. (2003) *Imperfect Justice: Looted Assets, Slave Labor, and the Unfinished Business of World War II*. New York: Public Affairs.

Fry, Earl H. (1998) *The Expanding Role of State and Local Governments in U.S. Foreign Affairs*. New York: Council on Foreign Relations.

George, Alexander L., David K. Hall, and William E. Simons (1971) *The Limits of Coercive Diplomacy: Laos, Cuba, Vietnam*. Boston: Little, Brown.

Guay, Terrence (2000) "Local Government and Global Politics: The Implications of Massachusetts' 'Burma Law'," *Political Science Quarterly*, 113 (Fall): 353–76.

Hawkins, Darren (2003) "Universal Jurisdiction for Human Rights: From Legal Principle to Limited Reality," *Global Governance*, 9(3): 347–65.

Hertzke, Allen D. (2000) "Defending the Faiths," *The National Interest*, 61 (Fall): 74–81.

Hiebert, Murray (2004) "Red Light for Sex Tourists," *Far Eastern Economic Review*, 24 (April 22): 18–19.

Hufbauer, Gary C., Jeffrey J. Schott, and Kimberly A. Elliott (1990) *Economic Sanctions Reconsidered: History and Current Policy*. 3rd ed. Washington, DC: Institute for International Economics.

Ignatieff, Michael (2004) *The Lesser Evil: Political Ethics in an Age of Terror*. Princeton, NJ: Princeton University Press.

Klare, Michael T., Cynthia Arnson, Delia Miller, and Daniel Volman (1981) *Supplying Repression: U.S. Support for Authoritarian Regimes Abroad*. Washington, DC: Institute for Policy Studies.

Lelyveld, Joseph (2007) "No Exit," *New York Review of Books*, 54(February 15): 12–17.

Levi, Werner (1974) "International Statecraft." In *International Systems*, ed. Michael Haas, chap. 6. San Francisco: Chandler.

Murphy, Sean D. (1999) "U.S. Involvement in Claims by Victims of the German Holocaust or Their Heirs," *American Journal of International Law*, 93 (October): 883–92.

O'Connor, Sandra Day (1995–1996) "Federalism of Free Nations," *New York University Journal of International Law and Politics*, 28(1): 35–43.

Power, Samantha (2002) *A Problem from Hell: America in the Age of Genocide*. New York: Basic Books.

Roth, Kenneth (2004) "The Fight Against Terrorism: The Bush Administration's Dangerous Neglect of Human Rights." In Thomas G Weiss, Margaret E Crahan and John Goering, eds., *Wars on Terrorism and Iraq: Human Rights, Unilateralism and US Foreign Policy*, pp. 113–31. London: Routledge.

Slaughter, Anne Marie, and David Bosco (2000) "Plaintiff's Diplomacy," *Foreign Affairs*, 79(5): 102–16.

Steinhardt, Ralph G., and Anthony D'Amato, eds. (1999) *The Alien Tort Claims Act: An Analytical Anthology*. Ardsley, NY: Transnational Publishers.

Stephens, Beth (2002) "*Translating Filartiga:* A Comparative and International Law Analysis of Domestic Remedies For International Human Rights Violations," *Yale Journal of International Law*, 27(1): 1–57.

Tarnoff, Curt, and Larry Nowels (2005) *Foreign Aid: An Introductory Overview of US Programs and Policy*. Washington, DC: Congressional Research Service.

Tomaševski, Katarina (1997) *Between Sanctions and Elections: Aid Donors and Their Human Rights Performance*. Washington, DC: Pinter.

Townley, Stephen (2006) "*Kilburn v Libya*: Cause for Alarm?," *Yale Law Journal*, 115(5): 1177–85.

United States, Nazi War Criminal Records Interagency Working Group (1999) *Implementation of the Nazi War Crimes Disclosure Act: An Interim Report to Congress*. Washington, DC: The National Archives.

Vázquez, Carlos Manuel (1995) "The Four Doctrines of Self-Executing Treaties," *American Journal of International Law*, 89(4): 695.

White, Richard Alan (2004) *Breaking Silence: The Case That Changed the Face of Human Rights*. Washington, DC: Georgetown University Press.

Woodward, Bob (2004) *Plan of Attack*. New York: Simon and Schuster.

▌ CHAPTER 12

Alston, Philip, ed. (1999) *The EU and Human Rights*. New York: Oxford University Press.

Archer, Clive, and Stephen Maxwell, eds. (1980) *The Nordic Model: Studies in Public Policy Innovation*. Farnborough, UK: Gower.

Azimov, Anvar (2005) "OSCE at the Crossroads," *International Affairs* (Moscow), 51(2): 57–66.

Christiansen T., and E. Kirchner, eds. (2000) *Committee Governance in the European Union*. Manchester, UK: Manchester University Press.

Christou, Theodorea A., and Juan Pablo Raymond, eds. (2005) *European Court of Human Rights: Remedies and Execution of Judgments*. London: British Institute of International and Comparative Law.

Clauwaert, Stefan, ed. (1998) *Fundamental Social Rights in the European Union: Comparative Tables and Documents*. Brussels: European Trade Union Institute.

Coombes, David L. (1979) *The Future of the European Parliament*. London: Policy Studies Institute.

Costa, Jean-Paul (2003) "The European Court of Human Rights and Its Recent Case Law," *Texas International Law Journal*, 38(3): 455–67.

Crawford, Oliver (1970) *Done This Day: The European Idea in Action*. London: Hart-Davis.

Donkerly, Craig G. (2004) "Considering Security Amidst Strategic Change: The OSCE Experience," *Middle East Policy*, 11(Fall): 131–38.

Ellert, Robert B. (1963) *NATO "Fair Trial" Safeguards: Precursor to an International Bill of Procedural Rights*. The Hague: Nijhoff.

European Movement (1949) *European Movement and the Council of Europe*. With forewords by Winston S. Churchill and Paul-Henri Spaak. New York: Hutchinson.

European Union, Council (2000–) *Annual Report on Human Rights*. Luxembourg: Office for Official Publications of the European Communities.

Gilbert, Geoff (1996) "The Council of Europe and Minority Rights," *Human Rights Quarterly*, 18(February): 160–89.

Gilbert, Geoff (2002) "The Burgeoning Minority Rights Jurisprudence of the European Court of Human Rights," *Human Rights Quarterly*, 24(3): 736–80.

Haas, Ernst B. (1958) *The Uniting of Europe: Political, Social, and Economic Forces, 1950–1957*. Foreword by Desmond Dinan; new introduction by Ernst B. Haas. Notre Dame, IN: University of Notre Dame Press, 2004.

Haas, Ernst B. (1960) *Consensus Formation in the Council of Europe*. Berkeley: University of California Press.

Harris, Seth R. (2000) "Asian Human Rights: Forming a Regional Covenant," *Asian-Pacific Law and Policy Journal*, 1 (June): 1–22.

Heyns, Christof (2002) *Human Rights Law in Africa*, volume 4. Amsterdam: Brill.

Hopmann, P. Terrence (2003) "Managing Conflict in Post-Cold war Eurasia: The Rise of the OSCE in Europe's Security 'Architecture'," *International Politics*, 40(1): 75–100.

Johnstone, Ian (2003) "The Rule of the UN Secretary-General: The Power of Persuasion Based on Law," *Global Governance*, 9 (October–December): 441–58.

Jordan, Pamela A. (2003) "Does Membership Have Its Privileges? Entrance into the Council of Europe and Compliance with Human Rights Norms," *Human Rights Quarterly*, 25 (August): 660–91.

Katsumata, Hiro (2004) "Why Is ASEAN Diplomacy Changing from 'Non-Interference' to 'Open and Frank Discussions'?" *Asian Survey* 44(2): 237–54.

Kechichian, Joseph A. (1994) *Security Efforts in the Arab World: A Brief Examination of Four Regional Organizations*. Santa Monica, CA: Rand Corporation.

Knaus, Gerald, and Marcus Cox (2005) "The 'Helsinki Movement' in Southeastern Europe," *Journal of Democracy*, 16 (January): 39–53.

Knodt, Michèle, and Sebastiaan Princen, eds. (2003) *Understand the European Union's External Relations*. London: Routledge.

Mahncke, Dieter, *et al.* (2004) *Defining Transatlantic Security Relations: The Challenge of Change*. Manchester, UK: Manchester University Press.

Maksoud, Clovis (1995) "Diminished Sovereignty, Enhanced Sovereignty: United Nations-Arab League Relations at 50," *Middle East Journal*, 49 (Autumn): 582–94.

Manby, Bronwen (2004) "The African Union, NEPAD, and Human Rights: The Missing Agenda," *Human Rights Quarterly*, 26 (November): 983–1027.

Melby, Kari, ed. (2000) *The Nordic Model of Marriage and the Welfare State*. Copenhagen: Nordic Council.

Mohan, Giles, Bob Milward, and Alfred B. Zack-Williams, eds. (2000) *Structural Adjustment: Theory, Practice and Impacts*. New York: Routledge.

Moir, Lindsay (2003) "Law and the Inter-American Human Rights System," *Human Rights Quarterly*, 25(1): 182–212.

Nicoladis, Kalypso (2004) "'We the Peoples of Europe . . .'," *Foreign Affairs*, 83 (November–December): 97–110.

O'Flaherty, Michael (2004) "Sierra Leone's Peace Process: The Role of the Human Rights Community," *Human Rights Quarterly*, 26 (February): 29–62.

Organization for Security and Cooperation in Europe (1998) *Combating Torture and Other Cruel, Inhuman or Degrading Treatment or Punishment: The Role of the OSCE*. Warsaw: Organization for Security and Cooperation in Europe, Office for Democratic Institutions and Human Rights.

Packer, Corrine A. A., and Donald Rukare (2002) "The New African Union and Its Constitutive Act," *American Journal of International Law*, 46(2): 365–79.

Pastor, Robert (1987) *Condemned to Repetition: The United States and Nicaragua*. Princeton, NJ: Princeton University Press.

Patel, Preeti, and Paolo Tripodi (2001) "The Challenge of Peacekeeping in Africa," *Contemporary Review*, 279 (March): 144–50.

Peers, Steve, and Angela Ward, eds. (2004) *The European Union Charter of Fundamental Rights*. Portland, OR: Hart.

Petersmann, Ernst-Ulrich (2002) "Time for a United Nations 'Global Compact' for Integrating Human Rights into the Law of Worldwide Organizations: Lessons from European Integration," *European Journal of International Law*, 13(3): 621–50.

Reid, T. R. (2004) *The United States of Europe: The New Superpower and the End of American Supremacy*. New York: Penguin.

Ress, Georg (2005) "The Effect of Decisions and Judgments of the European Court of Human Rights in the Domestic Legal Order," *Texas International Law Journal*, 40(3): 359–82.

Robertson, A. H. (1961) *The Council of Europe: Its Structure, Functions and Achievements*. With a foreword by Guy Mollet. 2nd ed. New York: Praeger.

Schubert, Carlos Buhigas, and Hans Martens (2005) *The Nordic Model: Recipe for Success?* Brussels: European Policy Center.

Tang, James T. H., ed. (1995) *Human Rights and International Relations in the Asia-Pacific Region*. New York: St. Martin's Press.

Tennberg, Monica (1998) *The Arctic Council: A Study in Governmentality*. Rovaniemi, Finland: University of Lapland Press.

Tomaševski, Katarina (1997) *Between Sanctions and Elections: Aid Donors and Their Human Rights Performance*. Washington, DC: Pinter.

Westlake, Martin (1999) *The Council of the European Union*. London: Catermill.

Williams, Andrew J. (2004) *EU Human Rights Policies: A Study in Irony*. New York: Oxford University Press.

CHAPTER 13

Adebajo, Adakeye (2002) *Building Peace in West Africa: Liberia, Sierra Leone, and Guinea-Bissau*. Boulder, CO: Lynne Rienner.

Bach, Daniel, ed. (1999) *Regionalization in Africa: Integration and Disintegration*. Bloomington: Indiana University Press.

Davidson, Scott (1997) *The Inter-American Human Rights System*. Brookfield, VT: Ashgate.

Doebbler, Curtis Francis (2002) "Reading the African Charter on Human and Peoples' Rights," *Texas International Law Journal*, 37(1): 227–30.

Domínguez, Francisco, and Marcos Guedes de Oliveira, eds. (2004) *Mercosur: Between Integration and Democracy*. New York: Oxford University Press.

Flint, Jule, and Alex de Waal (2005) *Darfur: A Short History of a Long War*. London: Zed Books.

Haas, Michael (1989a) *The Asian Way to Peace: A Story of Regional Cooperation*. New York: Praeger.

Haas, Michael (1989b) *The Pacific Way: Regional Cooperation in the South Pacific*. New York: Praeger.

Ryan, Curtis R. (1998) "Jordan and the Rise and Fall of the Arab Cooperation Council," *Middle East Journal*, 52 (Summer): 386–401.

Salafi, Ali (1989) *The League of Arab States: Role and Objectives*. Washington, DC: Arab Information Center.

Zachariah, George (2004) "Regional Framework for State Reconstruction in the Democratic Republic of the Congo," *Journal of International Affairs*, 58(Fall): 215–36.

CHAPTER 14

The Advocate (2006) "Death by Sodomy," September 12: 25.

Baldwin, Belinda (2006) "L.A., 1/1/67: The Black Cat Riots," *Gay and Lesbian Review*, 13(2): 28–30.

Berg, Charles, and Clifford Allen (1958) *The Problem of Homosexuality*. New York: Citadel Press.

Boswell, John (1994) *Same-Sex Unions in Premodern Europe*. New York: Villard.

Boyle, Alan E., and David Freestone (1999) *International Law and Sustainable Development: Past Achievements and Future Challenges*. New York: Oxford University Press.

Broome, Arthur (1824) *Prospectus of the SPCA*. Volume 2. London: SPCA Records.

Carson, Rachel (1962) *Silent Spring*. Boston: Houghton Mifflin.

Cruikshank, Margaret (1992) *The Gay and Lesbian Liberation Movement*. New York: Routledge.

Dombrowsky, Daniel A. (1984) *The Philosophy of Vegetarianism*. Amherst: University of Massachusetts Press.

Engel, Stephen M. (2001) *The Unfinished Revolution: Social Movement Theory and the Gay and Lesbian Movement.* New York: Cambridge University Press.

Evans, Tony (1998) *Human Rights Fifty Years On: A Reappraisal.* Manchester, UK: Manchester University Press.

Falk, Richard A. (1974) "Ecocide, Genocide, and the Nuremberg Tradition of Individual Responsibility." In *Philosophy, Morality, and International Affairs*, eds. Virginia Held, Sidney Morgenbesser and Thomas Nagel, pp. 123–37. New York: Oxford University Press.

Falk, Richard A. (1984) "Environmental Disruption by Military Means and International Law." In *Environmental Warfare: A Technical, Legal, and Policy Appraisal*, ed. Arthur H. Westing, pp. 33–51. Philadelphia: Taylor and Francis.

Fields, A. Belden (2003) *Rethinking Human Rights for the New Millennium.* New York: Palgrave Macmillan.

Francione, Gary L. (2000) *Introduction to Animal Rights: Your Child or the Dog?* Philadelphia: Temple University Press.

Godlovitch, Stanley, Roslind Godlovitch, and John Harris, eds. (1971) *Animals, Men and Morals: An Enquiry into the Maltreatment of Non-Humans.* New York: Taplinger.

Hayward, Tim (2005) *Constitutional Environmental Rights.* Oxford, UK: Oxford University Press.

Hegarty, Angela, and Siobhan Leonard, eds. (1999) *Human Rights: An Agenda for the 21st Century.* London: Cavendish.

Helminiak, Daniel A. (1994) *What the Bible Really Says About Homosexuality.* San Francisco, CA: Alamo Square Press.

Hill, Barry E., Steve Wolfson, and Nicholas Targ (2004) "Human Rights and the Environment: A Synopsis and Some Predictions," *Georgetown International Environmental Law Review*, 16(3): 359–404.

Ignatieff, Michael (1999) Human Rights: The Midlife Crisis," *New York Review of Books*, 46(9): 58–62.

Kausikan, Bilahari (1997) "Asian Versus 'Universal' Human Rights," *The Responsive Community*, 7(3): 9–21.

Kennedy, Sean (2006) "Jimmy Carter," *The Advocate*, January 17: 6.

Kibel, Paul S. (1999) *The Earth on Trial: Environmental Law on the International Stage.* New York: Routledge.

Kinsey, Alfred C., Wardell B. Pomeroy, and Clyde E. Martin (1948) *Sexual Behavior in the Human Male.* Philadelphia: Saunders.

Klare, Karl E. (1991) "Legal Theory and Democratic Reconstruction: Reflections on 1989," *University of British Columbia Law Review*, 25(1): 69–103.

Lau, Holning (2004) "Sexual Orientation: Testing the Universality of International Human Rights Law," *University of Chicago Law Review*, 71(4): 1689–720.

Laures, Robert Anthony, and Ronald Edward Zupko (1996) *Straws in the Wind: Medieval Urban Environmental Law: The Case of Northern Italy.* Boulder, CO: Westview.

Leahy, Michael, and Dan Cohn-Sherbok, eds. (1996) *The Liberation Debate: Rights at Issue.* New York: Routledge.

Levak, Brian P. (1995) *The Witch Hunt in Early Modern Europe.* 2nd ed. New York: Longman.

Linzey, Andrew (1976) *Animal Rights: A Christian Assessment.* London: SCM Press.

Linzey, Andrew (1996) "For Animal Rights." In *The Liberation Debate: Rights At Issue*, eds. Michael Leahy and Dan Cohn-Sherbok, chap. 13. New York: Routledge.

Lytle, Mark Hamilton (2007) *The Gentle Subversive: Rachel Carson, Silent Spring, and the Rise of the Environmental Movement.* New York: Oxford University Press.

McKibben, Bill (2006) *The End of Nature.* New York: Random House.

McNeill, J. R. (2000) *Something New Under the Sun: An Environmental History of the Twentieth-Century World.* New York: Norton.

Madders, Kevin J. (1981) "Trail Smelter Arbitration." In *Encyclopedia of Public International Law*, ed. Rudolf Bernhardt, pp. 276–80. New York: North-Holland Publishing Company.

Marotta, Toby (2006) "What Made Stonewall Different?," *Gay and Lesbian Review*, 13(2): 33–5.

Meijer, Martha, ed. (2001) *Dealing with Human Rights: Asian and Western Views on the Value of Human Rights.* Bloomfield, CT: Kumarian Press.

Merrett, Stephen (1997) *Introduction to the Economics of Water Resources: An International Perspective.* London: University College, London.

Meyer, Stephen M. (2007) *The End of the Wild.* Cambridge, MA: MIT Press.

Neier, Aryeh (1997) "Asia's Unacceptable Double Standard," *The Responsive Community*, 7(3): 22–30.

Paine, Thomas (1792) *The Rights of Man*. London: Symonds.

Price, Richard (1997) *The Genealogy of the Chemical Weapons Taboo*. Ithaca, NY: Cornell University Press.

Primatt, Humphrey (1776) *Dissertation on the Duty of Mercy and the Sin of Cruelty to Brute Animals*. Edinburgh: Constable.

Rawls, John (1972) *A Theory of Justice*. Oxford, UK: Oxford University Press.

Regan, Tom (1983) *The Case for Animal Rights*. Berkeley: University of California Press.

Renteln, Alison Dundes (1990) *International Human Rights: Universalism Versus Relativism*. London: Sage.

Ross, Susan Deller (1983) *Rights of Women: The Basic ACLU Guide to a Woman's Rights*. 3rd ed. New York: American Civil Liberties Union.

Ryder, Richard D. (1989) *Animal Liberation: Changing Attitudes Toward Specieism*. Oxford, UK: Blackwell.

Sands, Philippe, ed. (1994) *Greening International Law*. New York: New Press.

Singer, Peter (1975) *Animal Liberation*. Wellingborough, UK: Thorsons.

Stone, Christopher D. (1993) *The Gnat Is Older than Man: Global Environment and Human Agenda*. Princeton, NJ: Princeton University Press.

Stone, Richard (2002) "Counting the Cost of London's Killer Smog," *Science*, 298 (December 13): 2106–7.

Sunstein, Cass R. (1995) "Rights and Their Critics," *Notre Dame Law Review*, 70(4): 727–68.

Tahmindjis, Phillip, and Helmut Graupner, eds. (2005) *Sexuality and Human Rights: A Global Overview*. Binghamton, NY: Haworth Press.

Turner, Bryan S. (2006) *Vulnerability and Human Rights*. University Park: Pennsylvania State University Press.

Vanita, Ruth (2006) *Love's Rite: Same-Sex Marriage in India and the West*. New York: Palgrave Macmillan.

Weiss, Edith, ed. (1992) *Environmental Change and International Law: New Challenges and Dimensions*. Tokyo: United Nations University Press.

Wilmer, Franke (1993) *The Indigenous Voice in World Politics*. London: Sage.

Wolfenden, Sir John (1957) *Report of the Departmental Committee on Homosexual Offences and Prostitution*. London: Her Majesty's Stationery Office.

Yokota, Yozo (1999) "International Justice and the Global Environment," *Journal of International Affairs*, 52 (Spring): 583–98.

Young, Oran R., ed. (1999) *The Effectiveness of International Environmental Regimes: Causal Connections and Behavioral Mechanisms*. Cambridge, MA: MIT Press.

NOTES

CHAPTER 1

1   In the American terminology, "civil liberties" are the guarantees in the Bill of Rights, whereas "minority rights" are called "civil rights." Elsewhere, "civil rights" refer to the civil liberties in Bills of Rights.

CHAPTER 2

1   Ezekiel 16:49, Isaiah 1:10, and Jeremiah 23:14 explicitly identify the "sin of Sodom" as inhospitality, though many later authorities prefer to sexualize the story to refer exclusively to anal intercourse.
2   The historian J. Boswell, *Same-Sex Unions in Premodern Europe*, New York: Villard, 1994, has uncovered early church records of male–male unions blessed by Catholic priests. The topic of same-sex marriage is discussed in more detail within Chapter 14.
3   Aquinas was influenced by Al-Farabi and relied on the commentary of Aristotle by the Spanish-born Islamic philosophy scholar Ibn Rushd, also known as Averroës (1126–1198). However, when Europeans feared the advance of Muslim invaders into France and Spain, cooperation with the Islamic world stopped, and both were embroiled in issues of internal security and warfare. Accordingly, the opportunity for continued ecumenical human rights progress was missed.
4   Although laws requiring school segregation were struck down in 1954 by the Supreme Court ruling in *Brown v Board of Education* (347US483), statistical evidence demonstrates as much *de facto* segregation today as in 1954, according to G. Orfield and C. Lee, *Racial Transformation and the Changing Nature of Segregation*, Cambridge, MA: The Civil Rights Project, Harvard University, 2006. In 1981, federal financial assistance to assist desegregation was abolished. In *Missouri v Jenkins* (495US33), the Supreme Court allowed the Kansas City school district to stop expensive but ineffectual efforts at desegregation, a precedent that affects other school districts.

CHAPTER 3

1   The Second Amendment's statement about the right of citizens to "bear arms," that is, to own such weapons as pistols and rifles, is not generally recognized as a human right under international law.
2   At diplomatic conferences, the five countries authorized Austrian troops to go to Spain in 1820 and French troops to Italy in 1822 to stop democratic uprisings. However, Britain supported neither Austria's military intervention in Italy in 1821 nor France's intervention in Spain in 1823. France opted out from 1830. Nevertheless, the congress system did support the independence of Greece in 1830 and Belgium in 1831.
3   There was no organized effort to end serfdom, the practice of requiring peasants to work land owned by feudal lords. When feudalism ended, serfs were emancipated. England did so in the 1660s. Russia's emancipation of serfs was in 1861. The latest country to abolish serfdom was Bhutan in 1956.

4   Except for matters of race discrimination, the Fourteenth Amendment had very little civil rights applicability until a 1925 case, *Gitlow v New York* (268US652), in which the Supreme Court for the first time ruled that the Fourteenth Amendment required state governments to abide a provision in the Bill of Rights, specifically the First Amendment guarantee of freedom of speech. Subsequently, other provisions of the Bill of Rights were ruled in various court cases to apply to the states.

5   According to the Treaty of Versailles, the highly industrialized Saar was governed by the League of Nations for fifteen years, during which its coalfields were ceded to France. When a plebiscite was held in 1935, more than 90 percent of the population voted to accept German sovereignty, so the Jewish population applied for refugee status.

6   South Africa refused to allow the UN to take over monitoring its South West Africa mandate until 1988. Namibia, the former South West Africa, became independent after a UN-organized transition in 1990.

7   The Rhineland, a territory along the River Rhine between France and Germany, was occupied by Allied forces at the end of the war. Demilitarized under the terms of the Treaty of Versailles to provide a buffer between the two countries, the area was divided into three occupation zones. Forces were to be withdrawn at five-year intervals until 1935, but as a good-will gesture to the German government they left in 1930. In 1936, German troops bicycled and marched in to take control. By Monday, when British and French officials might have launched a response to the blatant violation of the treaty, the occupation was a *fait accompli*.

CHAPTER 4

1   Some observers also apply the term more broadly: to the 1.5 million Armenians killed by the Turks during 1915–1917; the 7 million who died from forced famines in the Soviet Union from 1932–1933; Japan's massacre of 300,000 Chinese in Nanking during 1937–1938; the 1.5 million Cambodians who died from disease, execution, exhaustion, and starvation from 1975–1978; the 1 million Tutsis slaughtered by the Hutus of Rwanda in 1994; and to the death of tens of millions Native Americans from disease and massacres during the expansion of the Europeans into the New World. Indeed, Hitler made reference to the Armenian and American exterminations as precedents for his own ethnic cleansing. However, several observers insist that there has been only one Holocaust, the Jewish Holocaust by the Nazis, whereas the rest are either **genocides** (intentional and systematic exterminations of entire ethnic, linguistic, or religious groups) or the more comprehensive **democides** (mass murders, including genocides, for any other reason).

2   Charges were initially brought against Admiral Karl Dönitz (1891–1980) for waging unrestricted submarine war in violation of the London Naval Agreement of 1930. However, when Fleet Admiral Chester Nimitz (1885–1966) admitted that he authorized similar offences, charges were dropped. Instead, Dönitz was convicted of waging aggressive war, that is, of committing a crime against peace, and of the war crime of sinking neutral ships without warning.

CHAPTER 5

1   In 2005, an estimated 2,100 executions occurred worldwide, of which China accounts for 1,700; some 90 per cent of all executed corpses in China supply transplanted organs, some of which are sold abroad. Although China banned the use of organs from executed corpses in 2006, enforcement is difficult since the practice is very lucrative.

2   See K. Bales, *Disposable People: New Slavery in the Global Economy*. Berkeley: University of California Press, 1999, and www.freetheslaves.net. The *Convention for the Suppression of the Traffic in Persons and of the Exploitation of the Prostitutions of Others of 1949* and the *Convention Against Transnational Organized Crime*, adopted in 2000, have provisions regarding the smuggling of persons for slave labor. Within the United States, an estimated 16,000 are trafficked each year, of which half are in debt bondage. In a case involving forty-eight welders from Thailand who were paid in other jobs below the minimum wage as debt slaves, the Equal Employment Opportunity Commission responded to a complaint from the Thai Community Development Center in Los Angeles (after the U.S. Department of Justice refused), resulting in settlements from $5,000 to $7,500 in cash, resettlement assistance, and the opportunity to apply for permanent residency in the United States.

3   The UN Office of the High Commissioner for Human Rights identifies seven treaties to be "core" international human rights instruments. In addition to the *International Covenant on Civil and Political Rights*, the *International Convention on the Elimination of All Forms of Racial Discrimination*, the *International Convention Against Torture and Other Cruel, Inhuman or Degrading Treatment or Punishment*, and the *International Convention on the Protection of the Rights of All Migrant Workers and Members of Their Families*; the rest are identified in Chapter 6 (Table 6.2).

4   The East Timor and Guatemala bodies are described below. Haiti's National Truth and Justice Commission investigated human rights abuses from 1991–1994, when the democratically elected government of Jean-Bertrand Aristide (1953–) was overthrown by a military coup that was reportedly financed by the CIA. Aristide was restored to power in 2001 but deposed by another military coup in 2004. The Truth and Reconciliation Commission of Sierra Leone, organized with assistance from the Office of the UN High Commissioner for Human Rights, investigated war crimes committed in a civil war from 1991–2002 in which there were some 75,000 deaths, 20,000 victims of mutilation, and 2 million displaced; an estimated 5,400 children were forced into combat, or were victims of forced labor or sexual slavery, and many women were raped.

5   In 2004, a truth and reconciliation commission was set up within Greensboro, North Carolina. Although remembered as the Southern city where some 400 students took turns sitting at a lunch counter until it was desegregated in 1960, the reason for the commission was a massacre in 1979, when members of the American Nazi Party and the Ku Klux Klan opened fire on a biracial "Death to the Klan" demonstration in which police were allowed to go off duty at a prearranged time before the shooting. When the carnage stopped, at least four were dead and ten were wounded. All-white juries acquitted six defendants, a widow won a civil damage suit, but the incident was quickly suppressed. Unlike official truth commissions, the impetus for nongovernmental efforts is usually not a shift in political power. The sponsors are private citizens operating without public funds seeking to discredit those who engaged in misdeeds outside the judicial system.

6   One of the campaign promises of Mexican President Vicente Fox (1942–) was to expose the "dirty war" against dissidents that was conducted by previous Mexican governments from the late 1960s to the early 1980s. However, a few days before Fox left office in 2006, a special prosecutor quietly posted on the Internet an 800-page report based on declassified documents about the "dirty war." In contrast, Congressional investigation committees in the United States compile reports after holding hearings, and independent prosecutors sometimes compile reports based on grand jury testimony.

CHAPTER 6

1   Among the current members of FLA are Adidas-Salomon, Asics, Eddie Bauer, GEAR for Sports, Gildan Activewear, Liz Claiborne, New Era Cap, Nordstrom, Nike, Outdoor Cap, Patagonia, Phillips-Van Heusen, Puma, Reebok, Top of the World, and Zephyr Graf-X.

CHAPTER 7

1   During World War II, some 140 American service personnel were convicted of war crimes against civilians (seventy-two for murder, fifty for rape, and eighteen for both murder and rape). During America's intervention in the Vietnamese Civil War, the most famous court martial convened to try soldiers for murdering innocent civilian Vietnamese involved Lieutenant William Calley, Jr., (1943–), who in 1971 received a life sentence for directing the massacre in 1968 of at least twenty-two persons at My Lai, although the conviction was overturned in 1974 by a civilian court, citing pretrial publicity prejudicial to a fair trial; in the same year, he was pardoned by President Richard Nixon (1913–1994) and paroled. Whereas at least thirty-six American soldiers were convicted and disciplined for human rights violations in Vietnam, eighteen American soldiers had been found guilty of human rights violations in Iraq by the end of 2006 out of sixty-four charged, including ten officers. Prosecutions of American soldiers for offenses committed in Iraq are ongoing.

2   When MacArthur proposed using nuclear weapons, he was relieved of his command by President Harry Truman (1884–1972).

3 The situations are as follows: the Anglo-French-Israeli invasion of Suez (1956), Hungary (1956), the Middle East (1958, 1967), Congo (1960), Afghanistan (1980), Palestine (1980, 1982), Namibia (1981), and Israeli actions in occupied East Jerusalem and the rest of the occupied Palestinian Territory (1982, 1997, 1998, 1999, 2000, 2001, 2002). In 2003, several countries during a General Assembly debate called upon the American-led invasion of Iraq to cease, but no vote was taken.

CHAPTER 8

1 Amnesty International's judgment is based on the following: (1) The United States is the largest exporter of military weapons. (2) Recipients of American military weapons, often through military aid, are countries that engage in gross human rights abuses (genocide, torture, etc.). (3) American allies in the Third World have engaged in serious human rights abuse over the years (Argentina, Colombia, Indonesia, Liberia, etc.) (4) More recently, the United States has refused to abide by the Geneva Conventions, instead engaging in such practices as indefinite detention and torture.
2 The following have been added over the years: disappearances (1980); economic and social circumstances (1981); extrajudicial killing (1982); right of citizens to change their government (1983); race, sex, religious, social discrimination (1986); status of labor (1986); excessive force in internal conflict (1989); rights of women, children, indigenous people, the disabled, and national, racial, and ethnic minorities (1993); refugees and asylum (1996); forced and bonded child labor (1997); religious freedom, access to political prisoners, genocide (1999); workers rights, trafficking in persons, corporate responsibility (2000).
3 See D. E. Neubauer, "Some Conditions of Democracy," *American Political Science Review*, 41(1967): 1002–9.
4 A tabulation of more than one hundred statistical studies can be found in M. Haas (2007).
5 R. E. Williams, Jr., and D. Caldwell, "*Jus Post Bellum*: Just War Theory and the Principles of Just Peace," *International Studies Perspectives*, 7(2006):309–20.
6 The original text of Civil Rights Act of 1964 had no provision regarding sex discrimination. Congressional opponents of the law prohibiting race discrimination decided to advance a "killer amendment" by voting to add sex discrimination to the provision on employment discrimination, hoping that proponents of the legislation would vote against. However, the bill passed anyway. The women's movement, which exerted no pressure to pass the amendment, was revived on learning that the law now unexpectedly covered sex discrimination.

CHAPTER 9

1 The Special Committee is still active and now focuses attention on American Samoa, Anguilla, Bermuda, British Virgin Islands, Cayman Islands, the Falkland or Malvinas Islands, Gibraltar, Guam, Montserrat, New Caledonia, Pitcairn, St. Helena, Tokelau, the Turks and Caicos Islands, United States Virgin Islands, and Western Sahara. In 2007, Puerto Rico asked the UN to monitor its status. The Territory of Hawai'i was on the agenda of the General Assembly's Committee on Non-Self-Governing Territories up to 1959, when voters chose to accept American statehood. Many Native Hawaiians, however, point out that the Kingdom of Hawai'i was annexed by the United States in 1898 without a plebiscite; President Grover Cleveland (1837–1908) stated that annexation was contrary to international law, and a return to the monarchy was the platform of the winning party in Hawai'i's first post-annexation election in 1900, the closest equivalent to a plebiscite.
2 The other UN agencies are the World Food Program (WFP), the UN Children's Fund (UNICEF), the World Health Organization (WHO), the UN Development Program (UNDP), the Office for the Coordination of Humanitarian Affairs (OCHA) and the Office of High Commissioner for Human Rights (OHCHR). Among nongovernmental organizations, the most prominent are the International Committee of the Red Cross, the International Federation of Red Cross and Red Crescent Societies, and the International Organization for Migration.
3 The Bantustan enclave of Lesotho also withdrew from 1971–1980 because a complaint was lodged over unfair treatment of a trade union.
4 Other UN Specialized Agencies include the International Civil Aviation Organization, International Maritime

Organization, International Telecommunications Union, UN Environmental Program, UN Population Fund, Universal Postal Union, World Intellectual Property Organization, and the World Meteorological Organization.

5 The eight are Britain, Canada, France, Germany, Italy, Japan, Russia, and the United States.

6 The treaties are as follows: *Convention Against Illicit Traffic in Narcotic Drugs and Psychotropic Substances, Single Convention on Narcotic Drugs*, and the *Convention on Psychotropic Substances*.

CHAPTER 10

1 The *Iraq Special Tribunal* was set up in 2004 by the provisional Iraqi National Congress to try Saddam Hussein (1937–2006) and twelve other members of the Ba'ath Party. Iran and Kuwait have sought in vain to bring Iraqi war crimes to the attention of the same court. In 2006, Saddam Hussein was found guilty and sentenced to death. Although Amnesty International and Human Rights Watch faulted the proceedings for failing to observe established international procedures, and human rights groups in Europe and elsewhere objected to the death penalty sentence, many international law experts believe that the verdict was appropriate.

CHAPTER 11

1 Federalism is one reason why the United States has failed to ratify international human rights treaties. Members of the Senate, the body that ratifies treaties, come from the fifty states. From the founding of the United States, each state has jealously guarded its own prerogatives from encroachment by the national government. For example, the constitutional right to free speech was applied at first only to actions of the national government; states were covered for the first time in 1925 after the Supreme Court ruling in *Gitlow v New York* (268US652). Thus, states often view obligations under international law as further encroachments on their authority, and Senators often attach reservations to the treaties, thereby watering down the obligations stated in the text. Some states permit the death penalty and thus their Senators will neither subscribe to the *Optional Protocol of the International Covenant on Civil and Political Rights* that bans the death penalty nor to the *Convention on the Rights of the Child* because of restrictions on abortion for minors in various states. An excellent example of the American reluctance to ratify human rights treaties is the *International Convention on the Prevention and Punishment of the Crime of Genocide*, which was adopted in 1948 and went into force without American ratification in 1951. From his first day in the Senate in 1957, Senator William Proxmire (1915–2005) of Wisconsin spoke to urge his colleagues to ratify the Genocide Convention of 1948. Indeed, he spoke on the subject every single day when the Senate was in session for twenty-nine years until 1986, when his colleagues finally gave in. As noted above, the Torture Convention was ratified in 1994 only after a flurry of domestic court cases on the subject. At the same time, the United States is not necessarily violating international law by not violating human rights treaties. Washington is simply staying outside much of the development in international human rights law.

2 In 1946, Congress passed the *Federal Tort Claims* Act to provide remedies to American citizens about misconduct by American government officials but specifically exempted claims of aliens from the scope of the law.

3 The Supreme Court (376US398) used the act-of-state doctrine to deny a legal remedy when property was nationalized by the Cuban government under Fidel Castro (1926–) in *Banco Nacional de Cuba v Sabbatino* (1964). Sabbatino Corporation, a company in Cuba mostly owned by American investors for wholesale sugar purchases, was in effect directed to petition the President of the United States or Congress to seek a diplomatic or political remedy rather than to seek a judgment in court. American courts, however, have held insurance companies liable for payments when foreign governments have nationalized properties without just compensation; the reason is that contractual obligations (as in an insurance policy) can never be nationalized.

4 The law was passed in part to reverse the *Sabbatino* ruling.

CHAPTER 12

1   When Marshall Plan aid ended by 1952, OEEC languished until 1961, when a new body, the Organization for Economic Co-operation and Development (OECD), was established with membership from the major industrial countries. There are now thirty members of OECD, including Australia, Canada, Japan, South Korea, and the United States. OECD produces many macroeconomic analyses and assists developing countries.

2   EFTA currently has four members – Iceland, Norway, Liechtenstein, and Switzerland. When EFTA began, members signed bilateral agreements with EU countries. In 1992, EFTA and EU sponsored the formation of the European Economic Area (EEA) so that EFTA members could enjoy the benefits of EU membership without joining the latter. EEA currently has twenty-eight members; Switzerland, a member of EFTA, opted out of EEA. The EEA mandate is for the free movement of goods, persons, services and capital. The EFTA Surveillance Authority and the EFTA Court parallel the work of the EU's European Commission and European Court of Justice and, respectively; they act in accordance with the *Agreement Between the EFTA States on the Establishment of a Surveillance Authority and a Court of Justice* of 1992. The only Court action relating to human rights was filed in 1994 and concerned the issue of legal aid; the Court dismissed the case for lack of jurisdiction. The founding *Convention Establishing the European Free Trade Association* of 1960 has no provision relating to human rights. The Annex to the Convention, adopted in 2001, provides for the free movement of persons from one member country to another, thereby generalizing an earlier Protocol between Lichtenstein and Switzerland on the subject.

3   However, in 1954 West Germany and Italy ratified the Brussels treaty, and the organization was renamed the Western European Union (WEU), with a headquarters in London. In 1960, WEU transferred its cultural and economic activities to the Council of Europe. In 1984, WEU was reactivated; some saw the organization as a possible military arm of the European Union, but the decision to do so was not finalized until 1991. In 1992, the WEU agreed in principle to form humanitarian, rescue, peacekeeping, and peacemaking missions, including combat forces in crisis management. In 1993, the headquarters moved to Brussels in preparation for eventual absorption into EU. In 1996, the Council of the European Union asked the WEU to assist EU's humanitarian operations involving displaced persons and refugees and displaced persons in the Great Lakes region in Africa. WEU–EU cooperation resulted in evacuation operations, supported African peacekeeping efforts, and mine clearance. In 1999, NATO as well as WEU Secretary-General Javier Solana (1942–) was named EU Secretary-General, thereby smoothing the way for the European Union to incorporate most of WEU's remaining military and nonmilitary functions in 2000. In 1955, legislators from NATO countries set up an independent organization outside NATO, known as the North Atlantic Assembly; the body, now called the NATO Parliamentary Assembly, has provided input to NATO and carried the policies adopted by NATO to national parliaments.

4   East and West Germany merged in 1990. The ten new Eastern European members are Bulgaria, the Czech Republic, Estonia, Hungary, Latvia, Lithuania, Poland, Romania, Slovakia, and Slovenia. The twenty-three countries, aside from Russia, are as follows: Albania, Austria, Belarus, Bosnia, Croatia, Macedonia, Moldova, Montenegro, Serbia, and Ukraine in Eastern Europe; Armenia, Azerbaijan, and Georgia in the Caucasus; the Central Asian states of Kazakhstan, Kyrgyzstan, Tajikistan, Turkmenistan, and Uzbekistan; as well as Finland, Ireland, Sweden, and Switzerland. Cyprus and Malta have also applied.

5   In addition to Iceland, member countries are Denmark, Estonia, Finland, Germany, Latvia, Lithuania, Norway, Poland, Sweden, and Russia. CBSS should not be confused with the separate Baltic Sea Parliamentary Conference, which began in 1991 as a more informal organization among members of parliament.

CHAPTER 13

1   Some First World countries are located within Third World regions, namely, Australia, Israel, Japan, New Zealand, Singapore, and South Korea.

2   The current members are Algeria, Bahrain, Comoros, Djibouti, Egypt, Iraq, Jordan, Kuwait, Lebanon, Libya, Mauritania, Morocco, Oman, Qatar, Saudi Arabia, Somalia, Sudan, Syria, Tunisia, United Arab Emirates, and Yemen.

3 The Arabic word "Maghreb" means "Western" and is used to refer to the geographic area of Northwest Africa.
4 The members are Albania, Armenia, Azerbaijan, Bulgaria, Georgia, Greece, Moldova, Romania, Russia, Turkey, and the Ukraine.
5 The island members are American Samoa, Cook Islands, Federated States of Micronesia, Fiji, French Polynesia, Guam, Kiribati, Marshall Islands, Nauru, New Caledonia, Niue, Northern Mariana Islands, Palau, Papua New Guinea, Pitcairn Islands, Samoa, Solomon Islands, Tokelau, Tonga, Tuvalu, Vanuatu, and Wallis and Futuna.
6 In addition to Australia and New Zealand, the members consist of the island states enumerated in Footnote 5 minus American Samoa, French Polynesia, Guam, New Caledonia, Pitcairn Islands, Tokelau, and Wallis and Futuna.
7 All African countries are members but Morocco.
8 The members currently are Benin, Burkina Faso, Cape Verde, Gambia, Ghana, Guinea, Guinea-Bissau, Ivory Coast, Liberia, Mali, Niger, Nigeria, Sénégal, Sierra Leone, and Togo.
9 Angola, Botswana, Congo (Kinshasa), Lesotho, Madagascar, Malawi, Mauritius, Mozambique, Namibia, South Africa, Swaziland, Tanzania, Zambia, and Zimbabwe.
10 Angola, Burundi, Cameroon, Central African Republic, Chad, Republic of the Congo (Brazzaville), Democratic Republic of the Congo, Equatorial Guinea, Gabon, Rwanda, and São Tomé and Príncipe. Rwanda suspended itself in 2001–2002.
11 Current members are Angola, Burundi, Comoros, Democratic Republic of the Congo, Djibouti, Egypt, Eritrea, Ethiopia, Kenya, Libya, Madagascar, Malawi, Mauritius, Rwanda, Seychelles, Sudan, Swaziland, Uganda, Zambia, and Zimbabwe. Lesotho, Mozambique, Namibia, and Somalia, and Tanzania signed the founding agreement but are not members. Egypt and Libya joined later.
12 Benin, Burkina Faso, Central African Republic, Chad, Djibouti, Egypt, Eritrea, Gambia, Guinea-Bissau, Ghana, Ivory Coast, Liberia, Libya, Mali, Morocco, Niger, Nigeria, Sénégal, Sierra Leone, Somalia, Sudan, Togo, and Tunisia.

CHAPTER 14

1 See J. Boswell, *Same-Sex Unions in Premodern Europe*, New York: Villard, 1994, for more details.
2 The argument is further developed in H. Lau, "Sexual Orientation: Testing the Universality of International Human Rights Law," *University of Chicago Law Review*, 71(2004):1689–1720.
3 In addition, several treaties deal with regional waterways, including the River Amazon, Baltic Sea, Caribbean Sea, Lake Constance, Mediterranean Sea, Persian Gulf, Red Sea, River Rhine and the South-East Pacific Ocean.

INDEX